Different Drummer

Different Drummer
The Life of Kenneth MacMillan

JANN PARRY

faber and faber

First published in 2009 by Faber and Faber Ltd
Bloomsbury House
74–77 Great Russell Street
London WC1B 3DA

Typeset by RefineCatch Limited, Bungay, Suffolk
Printed and bound in the UK by CPI Mackays, Chatham

A CIP record for this book
is available from the British Library

ISBN 978-0-571-24302-0

2 4 6 8 10 9 7 5 3 1

To Richard

Contents

Illustrations

Family photos used courtesy of Deborah MacMillan and Jean
Gardner

Acknowledgements

My thanks must go, above all, to Deborah MacMillan for entrusting me with the task of chronicling Kenneth's life. She has been incredibly patient over the years, giving generously of her time and making no reservations about what I chose to include or how I interpreted his character and his creations. She gave me access to his personal papers, including his draft memoir and his diaries, which she had never read. An inveterate hoarder, he had kept most of his correspondence (his own drafts as well as letters addressed to him), bills, invoices, scraps of paper with jottings for ballets on them and torn-out newspaper reviews of his work. They were in no particular order, apart from two cuttings books from the 1950s that had evidently been compiled for him. He claimed that he had few recollections of his childhood, though he did attempt, near the end of his life, to set down his first memories of Scotland and of growing up in Norfolk.

In piecing together his early years, I relied on the extraordinary diligence of Cecilia Ebbage, a Gorleston resident then in her eighties, who tracked down Great Yarmouth locals who had known Kenneth as a boy. She sifted their stories and helped me find and interview them. She guided me through Yarmouth's history and wartime records, lending me her books. Mrs Ebbage was instrumental in setting up a scholarship fund in MacMillan's name. Victor Stowers, Kenneth's school friend and fellow evacuee, was very helpful to me, including me in a Yarmouth evacuees' reunion in Retford. Kenneth's first ballet teacher, Joan Thomas, put me in touch with her 'girls' in Retford, and Wendy Roche told me about his subsequent ballet training with her mother, Phyllis Adams.

Among the many former dancers who shared their vivid memories with me, Greta Hamby, Gilbert Vernon and Michael Boulton offered thoughtful perceptions about Kenneth's formation as a dancer, a choreographer and as a man. Jeffrey Solomons told me, most entertainingly, about his friend's life and interests outside dance. Lynn Seymour was candid and helpful about her often difficult relationship with Kenneth as his muse, close friend, working partner and embattled associate. Ray Barra and Frank Frey provided insights into his time in Germany, in Stuttgart and Berlin. Georgina Parkinson told me her memories of Kenneth in London, Berlin and New York and Roy Round, her husband, provided photographs. Deborah MacMillan gave me an understanding of him as her husband, as well as a creative artist, and Charlotte MacMillan volunteered an acute account of him as her father.

Edward Thorpe's 1985 biography of *Kenneth MacMillan: The Man and the Ballets* guided my research, and he and his wife, Gillian Freeman, have been generous with their help. I would like to express my gratitude to Antonia Franceschi and Patsy Rodenberg for their encouragement, advice and expertise on matters theatrical.

My thanks are due to the following people who generously made their own research material available to me: Anya Dobler, for her MA dissertation, 'Success or Failure? Kenneth MacMillan in Berlin 1966–1969', University of Surrey, 2000; Cathy Gomez for her BA dissertation 'Kenneth MacMillan's choreography in relation to his culture and society', University of East London; Susan Crow, whose MA thesis, 'Kenneth MacMillan 1945–1955, Emergence of a Choreographer' (1987), in the University of Surrey's National Centre for Dance Studies provided valuable background material, and whose chairmanship of the *Revealing MacMillan* conference at the Royal Academy of Dance in 2002 was exemplary; Graham Hair for information about Mátyás Seiber and the *Invitation* scenarios and score in the British Library; Zoe Anderson, who alerted to me to details in the Royal Opera House Board minutes; Ismene Brown, for her clarification of the cultural politics of the Soviet Union; Brian Elias, for disclosing the extensive research he had undertaken before writing the score for *The Judas Tree*, MacMillan's last, Gnostic ballet.

The late Cormac Rigby gave me transcripts of his insightful Radio Three programmes about music and ballet, as well as some of his diary notes about what was going on in the ballet world. Peter Hollamby kindly provided copies of his diary entries about a crisis period for MacMillan in 1972. Derek Bailey handed over uncut transcripts of interviews he had conducted for his television documentary about MacMillan, *Out of Line*, as well as informing me of his collaboration with Kenneth on recordings of his ballets. I am profoundly grateful to Elaine Garwood for giving me so much of her time, providing lists of MacMillan's ballets with their casts from her programmes and presenting me with a complete collection of *Ballet Annuals*.

I would like to record my thanks to the following archivists: Francesca Franchi and her colleagues, especially Julia Creed, Cristina Franchi, Gabrielle St John-McAlister, and David Ogden at the Royal Opera House Collections; Sarah Woodcock, formerly at the Theatre Museum; Jane Pritchard and her colleagues at the Theatre Museum and for her help with the archives of Ballet Rambert (Rambert Dance Company) and English National Ballet; Rainer Woihsyk, former archivist of the Stuttgart Ballet; James Steward and Damian Eaton of Great Yarmouth Museums; the staff of the National Centre for Dance Studies at the University of Surrey, the Royal Academy of Dance and the Dance Collection at the New York Public Library for the Performing Arts.

Sheila Pitcairn assisted me with MacMillan's Scottish genealogy and gave me her book *A History of the 'fitpaths' and streets of Dunfermline, then and now*.

Suzanne Lahusen skilfully translated German press reviews and documents in the files MacMillan kept from his Deutsche Oper period in West Berlin. Anya Dobler helped with résumés of material in German that she had assembled for her dissertation.

I am indebted to the estates of Dame Ninette de Valois, John Osborne, Jerome Robbins and Dame Margot Fonteyn for permission to quote from their letters to Kenneth MacMillan. Every reasonable effort to trace copyright owners has been made. The publishers would be pleased to hear from those whom it has been impossible to trace, or who have been inadvertently omitted, and to whom the apologies of the author and publisher are extended.

I owe thanks to those who read drafts of the book and made invaluable comments and corrections, as well as providing moral support: Clement Crisp, Jeffrey Solomons, Nathalie Wheen, David Leonard, Sir Jeremy Isaacs, and Alastair Macaulay, whose eagle eye and reliable memory picked up errors and solecisms, and who challenged my descriptions and conclusions.

I would like to thank my agent, Georgina Capel, for her faith in the book, and my editor at Faber and Faber, Belinda Matthews, for her whole-hearted enthusiasm in taking it on. My thanks also to Elizabeth Tyerman for project-editing the book with such care and attention. Jill Burrows has ordered the text meticulously, providing sympathetic suggestions as well as adjustments.

My final, heartfelt gratitude must go to my husband, Richard Kershaw, for his love, encouragement, patience and unconditional support during the long gestation of this book.

Jann Parry

29 October 1992

Sirens screeched in Covent Garden, the streets and alleyways around the Royal Opera House resounding with their wails until the former market area seemed to be howling. Ambulances had rushed to respond to the Opera House's emergency call, while the first-night audience cocooned inside the old theatre remained unaware of the turmoil behind the scenes. A body had been found backstage, slumped in an unlit corridor. The off-duty member of the stage crew who found the unconscious man assumed he was a tramp who had somehow wandered in from the street and collapsed in the maze of artists' dressing-rooms. She informed the stage-door staff; overhearing her report, Anthony Dowell, the Artistic Director of the Royal Ballet, realised at once who it must be. Company staff had been searching with increasing concern for the choreographer of the three-act work that was nearing its conclusion on stage. He was inexplicably absent and the dancers were becoming aware, as they glanced into the wings, that something was terribly wrong. They could see ashen faces, running figures, frantic consultations. Meanwhile the audience was engrossed in the unfolding drama of *Mayerling*, Kenneth MacMillan's tragic ballet, remounted with a new star in the lead.

MacMillan had arrived at the theatre early in the evening of 29 October 1992, accompanied by his wife, Deborah. He wanted to reassure the dancers that he was confident they would justify his faith in them. In fact, he was tense and nervous himself, as always before a production of one of his ballets. *Mayerling* is a demanding work, requiring the dancer in the role of Crown Prince Rudolf of Austro-Hungary to remain on stage almost throughout the three acts. The former Bolshoi principal, Irek Mukhamedov, was taking the role for the first time; the Royal Ballet's young Italian ballerina, Viviana Durante, was making her debut as Rudolf's mistress, Mary Vetsera.

As MacMillan and Deborah took their usual house seats in the Grand Tier, the theatre's General Director, Jeremy Isaacs, leaned across the aisle and whispered, 'Good luck.' The curtain rose on the funeral with which the ballet begins and ends. Black-clad mourners shelter from the rain under glistening umbrellas as a coffin is lowered through a trapdoor at the rear of the stage. Only when the scene is reprised at the conclusion of the ballet does the audience appreciate that the burial is that of Mary Vetsera, killed by Rudolf in a suicide pact.

Overcome with anxiety during the first act, MacMillan left his seat, telling his wife he was suffering from a panic attack. He had been prone to such attacks for most of his life. He had learned to recognise the symptoms – breathlessness, palpitations, cold sweats – and to some extent, how to deal with them. He also knew that he had a damaged heart after a serious heart attack four years previously. But on this occasion, he ascribed his distress to nerves about the first-night performance of *Mayerling*, revived after a gap of six years.

Deborah tried to calm him down and offered to fetch him a cup of tea. They went together through the pass door leading from the front of house to the backstage area and the staff canteen. She brought him the tea while he sat on the stairs leading to the canteen, talking to staff and dancers passing by during the interval. When the warning bell rang for the start of the second act, he told Deborah to go back and watch the performance on his behalf, while he rested in the green room.

During the next interval, Deborah searched for her husband to let him know that all was going extremely well on stage. He was not in the green room and had not been seen in the canteen. She asked Anthony Dowell to have MacMillan urgently paged over the backstage Tannoy. Dowell joined in the search, while Deborah alerted other members of staff.

Desperately worried, she went back into the auditorium for the last act, standing behind the row of staff seats. Suddenly, St John Ambulance first-aiders, always present during performances, ran past her. She knew her worst fears had been realised. As the audience remained absorbed in the onstage drama, Dowell led her to the opera dressing-room corridor, where MacMillan was lying. His body was cold, the look on his face one of surprise. He had probably been dead for about an hour.

While Deborah cradled her husband's body in her arms in the dressing-room corridor, Jeremy Isaacs was fetched from his seat.

The ballet was coming to an end and decisions needed to be taken. The dancers would have to be told as they came offstage, with Mukhamedov and Durante among the last to know. The cast could hardly be expected to take their bows smiling as if nothing had happened. Isaacs was convinced that the audience should be made aware that a great choreographer's life and an era of the Royal Ballet's history had ended while they were watching a magnificent performance. He would break the news of MacMillan's death on stage soon after the curtain came down – even though no doctor had yet officially declared MacMillan dead.

At the conclusion of *Mayerling*, Rudolf takes Mary behind a screen and shoots her before turning his gun on himself. He crashes to the ground, bringing down the screen that has hidden Mary's body, lying on a bed. Her clandestine funeral is a sombre coda to this devastating scene of self-destruction.

In the audience we were still struggling to regain our composure as the heavy, red Opera House curtains reopened and Mukhamedov stood alone on stage to receive our applause. After such a shattering finale, applause is normally a cathartic release for spectators and performers alike. Mukhamedov looked stricken, his face and body drained. The sound of clapping swelled to let him know that he had conquered a challenging ballet, but he seemed unable to acknowledge the applause. The curtains closed to let the entire cast assemble for their communal bows – the usual convention.

By now, most of the company knew what had happened. The stage manager, Keith Gray, had broken the news to Mukhamedov shortly before he took the first curtain call on his own. He had had to face the audience deep in shock. Gray, as agreed with Isaacs, waited until the rest of the cast had swept forward and back in their initial curtain call before giving Isaacs the signal to go on stage and make the announcement to the audience. Isaacs stepped in front of the dancers and held up his hand for silence. The applause ceased as he said, 'It is with deep sadness, and in shock, that I have to tell you that the great master whose work we have seen performed here tonight, Kenneth MacMillan, has, during the performance, suffered a heart attack and died.' A woman's voice wailed in disbelief. Isaacs continued, 'I ask you to rise and bow your heads, and to leave the theatre in silence.'

The horseshoe-shaped auditorium was charged with emotion that had no outlet. Reactions to Isaacs's brief speech reverberated around the packed house of over two thousand people, arranged in tiers up to the domed ceiling. Apart from some strangled sobs, the unnatural hush in the theatre was broken only by shuffling feet as the audience filed out of the dimmed theatre – an eerie echo of the funeral scene we had just witnessed in the ballet. The curtains had closed on the cast, by now holding each other in distress. There was nowhere more fitting for them to grieve: they were part of the drama of MacMillan's death.

For a man of the theatre, it was an impressive way to go. Nobody present will ever forget the impact of learning of the choreographer's death – although each person remembers the details of the experience slightly differently. For those close to MacMillan, however, it was a private tragedy transformed into a public spectacle. For Deborah MacMillan, Isaacs had made an over-hasty decision to declare her husband dead before a crowd of strangers, who were to know of his death even before their teenage daughter, Charlotte. Deborah rushed home to tell her. Charlotte had to be told before the news broke on the radio. Deborah would otherwise have wished to remain with her husband's body, which she had to leave in the theatre.

MacMillan, a reclusive man who let his ballets speak for him, had sought privacy in his last moments, dreading the indignity of collapsing in public. Deborah believed that the announcement of his death should have waited until the following day, after which obituaries would appear. Friends, admirers, ballet-lovers and the rest of the world would have time to absorb the news of his death, and further tribute could be paid at his memorial service. This took place four months later in Westminster Abbey, where the achievements of national figures, from political leaders to great artists, are ceremonially honoured. Yet perhaps for Kenneth, the working-class boy whose fierce ambition had been to perform on the Covent Garden stage, and then to direct the famous ballet company based there, the Royal Opera House was indeed the right place to bow out.

I

The Making of a Dancer

1929–1952

I

To his public, Kenneth MacMillan was an enigmatic figure. His ballets would lay emotions bare, challenging and provoking audiences, but the man who created them remained a mystery. He would grant interviews when required to do so, but there were few profiles or long articles about him in the press. He'd agree to be recorded, occasionally, for radio or television – but he gave little away. He wasn't disobliging, just laconic. He would not, or could not, explain his ballets or reveal the sources of his inspiration. He was cagey about his early experiences, often misleading interviewers if he did talk about his youth.

For many years, he hid his face behind dark glasses and a moustache. The dancers with whom he worked were often unable to see his eyes during rehearsals. When he appeared on stage (without the glasses) to take a bow after the premiere of one of his ballets, he looked like an animal caught in the headlights. Although he sometimes wore a suit, or very occasionally a dinner-jacket for first-night curtain calls, he frequently appeared in ill-fitting trousers whose crotch hung down to his knees. It was hard to imagine he had once been an elegant classical dancer.

When he first came to attention as a talented choreographer in the 1950s, he was a tall, languid young man with a mop of dark hair and an ever-present cigarette. By the time of his international success with *Romeo and Juliet*, his first three-act ballet in 1965, his hair had gone prematurely grey. Shortly afterwards he left the Royal Ballet for three years to become Artistic Director of the (then) West Berlin Deutsche Oper Ballet company. Reports filtered out that he was having a hard time with the German opera-house system, in which ballet traditionally occupied second place. On his return to take over the directorship of the Royal Ballet in 1970, he was a changed man. His health was poor: he had collapsed in Germany as a result of stress and alcoholism, and although he appeared to have recovered fully from a stroke, he was psychologically fragile.

He kept his difficulties private, acquiring a reputation for remaining obdurately silent at Royal Ballet press conferences and at Board and committee meetings. Only his closest friends, and the woman who was to become his wife, knew the extent of the anxieties he suffered. The first Director of the Royal Ballet to have come from within its ranks, he was beset by managerial problems from the start. He had inherited a company riven with resentment at his appointment and at the changes inflicted on the way it was run. The nature of the Royal Opera House as an institution, and its relationship with its funding body, the Arts Council, had altered radically by the 1970s. Expectations of what ballet should be were also shifting, as Opera House audiences grew more conservative and contemporary dance broke new ground.

MacMillan came in for savage criticism, both as Director of the nation's leading classical ballet company and for his own creations. Reviewers in Britain and in America, when the Royal Ballet went on tour there, split into two camps, defenders and deplorers. Their reactions affected box-office takings and influenced management attitudes towards him, making him feel beleaguered, even paranoid. Yet he continued to choreograph extraordinary ballets, a number of which have won acceptance as modern masterpieces.

After he resigned as Artistic Director of the company in 1977, his work became darker, even more controversial. He pushed the boundaries of ballet further than anyone had dared, courting hostility from critics and audiences alike. He remained elusive, spending part of his time in the United States with American Ballet Theatre, as artistic associate and choreographer. Although he valued his four-year experience with ABT (while retaining his links with the Royal Ballet), he was scarcely known to the American public as a personality. The opposite of a self-promoter, reluctant to make use of the media, he was also ill-suited to socialising at fund-raising galas on tour across the States.

When he re-emerged on the London ballet scene at the end of the 1980s to create a long-awaited three-act ballet, *The Prince of the Pagodas*, few people outside the Royal Ballet knew how ill he had been after a serious heart attack. He had to pace himself carefully to complete the choreography, which starred an unknown youngster, Darcey Bussell, who was to become one of Britain's favourite ballerinas.

The *Pagodas* premiere coincided with his sixtieth birthday. Assumptions that he had mellowed were soon confounded by what turned out to be his last work, *The Judas Tree*. Brutal and uncompromising, it contained themes that had preoccupied him throughout his creative life: sexual provocation, betrayal, collusion in wrong-doing, crippling guilt and a longing for redemption. *The Judas Tree* initially confounded its audiences. MacMillan was more of a puzzle than ever, shielding himself in obligatory publicity photographs behind the huge upturned collar of a black overcoat.

After his death, obituaries and eulogies described his career but not the man himself. He had kept his secrets, confiding only in his wife and the psychiatrists and psychotherapists he consulted over the years. He let his ballets speak for him, preferring not to discuss them with his dancers or his closest friends, let alone with journalists. He dreaded and disliked writing, although towards the end of his life he started to draft an account of his early memories. He gave up, dissatisfied by his attempts to express himself in words. (His draft memoir informs the first part of this biography.)

Stories recounted by friends and former dancers who remember him as gregarious and funny as a young man are hard to reconcile with the reclusive figure seen at the theatre or heard on the radio, talking in a melancholy drawl. People who had known him during the lowest time of his life in Germany painted conflicting pictures of him, ranging from a fiercely creative artist to a lonely man sunk in abject misery.

Acquaintances who had lost touch with him over the years were surprised to learn that he had married, had had a daughter, and had been honoured with a knighthood.

His family knew a different side to him from the one he presented in public. Even they, however, found out more about him from his ballets than from his conversations at home. The diaries he kept during his last years are tantalisingly unrevealing about his inner life; they are aide-memoires, briefly noting events and his terse opinions about his own work and that of others. Researching his biography has required detective work in assembling the missing-pieces jigsaw of his boyhood and early career as a dancer. Once he started choreographing in his twenties, the ballets reveal how closely he identified with his central character – the damaged innocent, the vulnerable young person whose trust is betrayed. This person is marked from the start as a misfit, someone who longs to be like the others but who is destined to remain an outsider, ultimately alone.

In many of his ballets, the key figure is the heroine, traumatised by events over which she has no control; in his later works, however, the already damaged central character, often male, is culpable, bringing about his (or her) own destruction.

MacMillan created over seventy works in a variety of genres, and he was never consciously autobiographical. His overt source of inspiration might come from films or books; above all, it sprang from the music he chose and from the bodies and personalities of the dancers who interested him. What came out in the rehearsal studio often surprised him: he preferred not to analyse what he had done, even while acknowledging that his subconscious had been at work. Then, once his ballets entered the repertoire of a company, they took on a trajectory of their own as performers' interpretations of roles changed, though the choreography remained the same. The dramatic power of the roles – for women, Juliet, Manon, Mary Vetsera, the Chosen Maiden in his *Rite of Spring*; for men, Romeo, Des Grieux, Lescaut, Crown Prince Rudolf, the Foreman in *The Judas Tree* – continues to attract dancers from many different countries. Internationally famous guest artists have taken them on, while the MacMillan repertoire has been an important reason for dancers choosing to join the Royal Ballet.

The ballets have been performed widely since MacMillan's death in 1992, as companies have clamoured to stage them. Meanwhile, the man who created them has remained more elusive than ever. This biography sets out to examine his background and the origins of the themes that recur so obsessively in his work. It is an account of how the neuroses that tormented him fuelled his career as a creator. He was never to have an easy life: he achieved his ambition to be an artistic director at considerable cost to himself, and although he eventually found happiness as a husband and father, he always felt himself an outsider, marching to a different drum from his fellows.

The source of his sense of dislocation, of never belonging, lies in his childhood. Yet his handwritten memoir does not give the picture of a troubled boyhood: his deepest feelings remained buried. Although his perception of himself was of a lonely child, his schoolmates and early friends report that he was not an outcast, isolated in the playground or picked on by bullies. Indeed, he seems to have been a confident, outgoing youngster until his mother's death when he was twelve set him apart. Then, like the fictional Billy Elliot, a motherless miner's son, he found his own means of expression through dance, defying his working-class background to do so.

According to his draft memoir, and the recollections of his surviving relatives, he had been a much loved child, an afterthought when his mother was forty, following three surviving siblings. He was born on 11 December 1929, as the worldwide economic depression followed the Wall Street crash. 'I must have been an expensive baby to have been delivered in a nursing home,' he speculated. The earlier MacMillan children (one of whom died in infancy) had been born at home: Kenneth saw the light of day in the Davar Maternity Clinic in Dunfermline, the ancient royal capital of Scotland, birthplace of the philanthropist Andrew Carnegie and of Moira Shearer, the ballerina and film star.

The MacMillan family had established itself in Fife, across the Firth of Forth from Edinburgh. Kenneth's father, William, was one of six children born to David MacMillan, bricklayer and stonemason, and Jane McNeil. She had been a weaver in a damask linen factory at the time of their marriage in Dunfermline in 1892, when she was nineteen. They were recorded on their marriage certificate as living next door to each other in Golfdrum Street, an old part of the town, in north-west Dunfermline. David MacMillan's father, a tinsmith, was evidently illiterate, for he had signed David's birth certificate with an 'X'. Jane's father, Matthew McNeil, Kenneth's great-grandfather, is variously described on marriage and death certificates as a coal miner, a labourer and 'a hawker of earthenware' – a pedlar of jugs and pots, sold door to door.

David and Jane would appear to have been the first in their families to have done quite well for themselves, to judge from photographs of them, soberly dressed and surrounded by their large family. By the time that Kenneth was old enough to remember his paternal grandmother, she was a formidable Scottish matriarch in her sixties. David had earned enough as a builder to provide for all six children, although the youngest, Jean, William's baby sister, remembered that they celebrated birthdays with simply a dumpling for the birthday child: with luck, if she had been a good girl, there was a threepenny bit inside.

William had left home to earn his living as a coal miner shortly before the First World War broke out in 1914. He enlisted in the army, aged twenty-four, in May 1915, serving as a gunner with the

Highland Fifth Royal Garrison Artillery. A photograph of him in uniform, taken at the Dunfermline studio of D. Cummings Simpson, intrigued Kenneth, possibly because the resemblance between father and son was so marked. He wrote in his memoir:

Gunner MacMillan W stares stubbornly at Mr Simpson (or was it an assistant?). Behind him is a would-be elegant rococo screen edged with sham pre-Raphaelite stained glass. Father's feet firmly planted on a grubby tufted carpet show off his polished boots and puttees, but his fierce grip on the back of the chair beside him betrays his unease in this boudoir composition. A badly placed aspidistra and some cut flowers complete this ill-conceived picture. My father was not good humoured enough to find it funny.

In fact, the formally posed photograph was typical of those taken of soldiers at the time, many of them later serving as mementoes of men killed in action.

William MacMillan's Highland regiment was posted to East Anglia on its way to the battlefields of France. The soldiers, as part of their training, were required to guard the waterworks that served the coastal resort of Great Yarmouth. There William met and courted Edith Shreeve. Her family lived in a tied cottage belonging to the Ormesby Waterworks, the private company that managed the reservoir, built in 1855 to provide fresh water for Yarmouth. Her father, George William Shreeve, was employed as an engine minder, operating the water pumps – a step up from his previous job as an agricultural labourer. Her mother, Mary Anne (née Sales), was a local girl, born and married in the same rural parish as her husband: Rollesby, West Flegg, a short distance along the coast from Great Yarmouth.

Edith May Shreeve was the youngest of three children, with a ten-year gap between her and the eldest, Louise. Edith was 'in service', working as a kitchen maid in the nearby town of Sheringham, when she fell for her Scottish soldier. She was already twenty-eight when she married William MacMillan on 2 December 1916, though she took a year off her age on the wedding certificate. He was three years younger than she was and about to leave for France, with a strong likelihood of being killed. Edith was very probably pregnant by the time of her wedding, for her first child, Jean, was born just seven months later, on 3 July 1917. Family legend had it that the bungled delivery was in the cottage at Ormesby, and in using forceps, the local doctor had ripped off the baby's ear and punctured her eardrum. The ear was stitched back on, leaving a scar and permanent damage to Jean's hearing. Although her hearing had seemed passable as a youngster, she had to rely increasingly on guesswork and lip-reading as it deteriorated. She was completely deaf by the time she reached her twenties, and her voice became flat and gruff once she could no longer hear herself speak.

William, who had been mustard-gassed during the Battle of the Somme, was officially demobilised from the army in January 1919, two months after Armistice Day. He had been unfit for action since suffering the German gas attack, an experience that left him mentally and physically scarred. His lungs were permanently damaged and the skin on his face and neck, burnt by the mustard gas, would break out into sores. He had been sent back from the front to hospital in Scotland. Once discharged, he refused further medical treatment and would not apply for a disability pension. He wanted nothing more to do with the army and never spoke to his family about his wartime experiences. Later in life, he even discouraged his youngest son from joining the Scouts: 'the uniform' was the only reason he gave Kenneth.

Disillusioned by post-war conditions, William often talked of taking his family to the Soviet Union. He listened to broadcasts from Russia (in English) on the radio and believed that Soviet socialism had abolished poverty and unemployment. He was not, however, a member of the Communist Party and made no moves to emigrate to the USSR. Years later, his eldest son, George, would repeat the claim that 'someone in authority' had visited the family house to deliver a warning against listening to communist propaganda. William brought up both his sons to mistrust the 'authorities' who tried to exercise control over their lives.

Damaged though he was, William managed to find a job as a labourer at a gasworks near Dunfermline. He had sent for his wife and young daughter to join him in Scotland, where they lived with his parents before moving into a stone-clad terrace house in the village of Crossford, a mile and a half from Dunfermline. The house, on Main Street, was near the post office and the Pitfirane Arms Hotel. The next MacMillan children would be born there. Betty arrived in 1920; then came the first son, David, who died at six months in 1923. After the birth of another son, George (named after Edith's elder brother), two years later, there was a five-year gap before Kenneth, the last and dearest to his mother's heart. According to his Scottish aunt Jean, Kenneth was always called 'my pet' by Edith. 'She wouldn't let the wind blow on him,' said Jean, disapprovingly. 'Whatever he wanted, she gave in to him.'

Edith MacMillan, transplanted from her East Anglian setting, found her husband's Scots family daunting – especially her redoubtable mother-in-law. Kenneth recalled as a small boy tiptoeing quietly around his grandmother's house with his mother, both of them overawed by the way that Jane MacMillan doled out linen from a large wooden box like some Eastern empress. 'Presumably dispensing such largesse helped her manipulate her large family. She was a great fat lady who dominated her small husband and many children, including my father, who was always subdued in her presence.'

Soon after Kenneth was born, his father lost his job at the gasworks. A workmate had been injured in an industrial accident. William MacMillan testified at the compensation hearing that the accident had been caused by the gas company's negligence. The injured worker won his compensation; William was sacked.

In the Depression years of the 1930s this could have been a calamity. Resourceful, William turned to poultry farming, selling eggs and dressed chickens in Dunfermline market. He had kept hens in the garden at the back of the house to feed his family and supplement his earnings; now he leased extra land for two thousand free-range birds, rearing them from chicks in incubators. His eldest son George remembered the family sitting up late on Friday nights, plucking the feathers from forty to fifty chickens into tin baths, arms covered with Vaseline to prevent fleas running up them. Kenneth was too young to help with the plucking but remembered the pleasure of collecting eggs from under the warm breasts of the hens, and marvelled at his gentle mother's ability, 'without turning a hair', to wring the necks of chickens due to go to market.

On Saturday mornings, the family transported their produce by car, a bull-nose Morris Oxford, to Dunfermline, a grey-granite city dominated by its cathedral, built in the ruins of an eleventh-century Benedictine Abbey. The kings of Scotland are buried there, including Robert the Bruce. The Scotsman credited as the creator of modern Freemasonry, William Schaw (1550–1602), has a monument in the Abbey. Membership of a Freemasons' lodge is usually confidential, but William MacMillan left his membership card among his papers after his death. It is dated 1920, the year he returned to Dunfermline after the First World War.

While William and his older children sold eggs and chickens in Dunfermline marketplace, Edith would go to variety-show matinees, taking Kenneth with her, as soon as he was old enough to keep still. He usually sat on her lap, unwilling to lose physical contact with her until he had to. Dunfermline's main music-hall on Reform Street, grandly named the Opera House, held Highland-dancing classes on Saturday mornings, before the variety show. (The building was to be dismantled in the 1980s and reassembled in Sarasota, Florida, as part of the Asolo Centre for the Performing Arts.) Kenneth joined in the classes from the age of four. 'That was where it all started,' reckoned his brother George. 'Kenneth was always interested in dressing up and dancing, so Mother let him pursue it as he grew up.'

Scottish children routinely learn their country's dances from an early age. Such youthful training helped develop the co-ordination and elegantly arched feet that Kenneth was to display as a ballet dancer. He retained few memories, however, of his early dance classes or indeed of his first five years in Scotland. His visual flashbacks were disconcertingly bleak. Instead of the golden days of a happy childhood, he recalled an umbrella blowing inside out as he and his sisters struggled against the wind, crossing a hump-backed bridge. 'Like dreams, unimportant details persist and try to take on a significance, but only the quality of the bleached northern light remains to disturb me.' Another memory of bad weather was even more disturbing: 'Once when a great storm cracked over our village, Mother was so terrified that she hid with me in a cupboard under the stairs. Her fear of storms has stayed with me since.' It was an experience that later merged with wartime terrors, when he and his mother cowered together in fear of falling bombs, listening for explosions as the Luftwaffe attacked Britain.

He clearly recollected his first shock at being parted from his mother when he went to infant school in Dunfermline. He had enjoyed the bus ride with her and had no idea that he was going to be left behind in the classroom until he saw her leaving through a glass door. He was outraged when the teacher 'hauled me to the front of the class and called me a cry-baby'. He refused to attend school unless his mother accompanied him. She gave in, indulging her youngest child and washing her hands of George, a blond, head-strong boy who played truant from school, risking the strap from his father. George was frequently beaten by William, who never laid a hand on Kenneth, protected as he was by his mother. Kenneth later confided to a friend that his mother had breast-fed him until he was four. He told a psychotherapist that he and his mother were 'far too close': the therapist, Marianne Jacoby, concluded that he had never been weaned psychologically.

Kenneth was five when he left Scotland for East Anglia in 1935, realising when he was somewhat older that the family had done a 'moonlight flit', leaving unpaid bills behind. He, George and their mother went south by overnight train; William and the two teenaged girls travelled in the family car, their sole remaining possession apart from their clothes. Kenneth was told never to mention the circumstances in which the MacMillans had arrived in Great Yarmouth – the first of many secrets that were to haunt his youth.

He came to believe that his father had gone shamefully bankrupt, unable to keep up the lease on the failing chicken farm. George, however, in recounting the family's history, attributed the move from Scotland to their father's stubborn pride. When the limited lease on the farmland expired, William had been outbid for its renewal. He was offered the loan of some land elsewhere by a friend, possibly a fellow Freemason, but 'said he'd have no more of it and sold up, basically for pennies'. The family had been told by Edith's elder sister Louise that plenty of jobs were available in Yarmouth. William opted to take his chances down south – an unwise decision, as it turned out, for the economic Depression of the 1930s affected every part of Britain.

Great Yarmouth, then as now, was a popular seaside resort, with numerous piers straddling its pebble beaches. Once an important fishing port, especially for herring, and a naval base, it had become increasingly reliant on visitors in search of inexpensive family holidays. Hotels, boarding houses and hostels crowded along the sea front in the 1930s. They still do, although almost all have been redeveloped; mobile-home parks now cater for those who are on tighter budgets.

Before the extensive damage inflicted by World War II bombing, the town retained much of the street layout of its medieval past.

Yarmouth (the 'Great' incorporates once neighbouring villages) was originally a settlement on a sandbank at the mouth of the Yare estuary. As the town grew and prospered in the twelfth century, its expansion was restricted by the narrow space between the sea and the rivers Yare and Bure. A fortified wall, completed by the end of the fourteenth century, prevented it extending further for centuries to come. The cramped town Charles Dickens described in *David Copperfield* had scarcely changed in structure by the time the MacMillans moved there. The three main streets, running parallel to the coast and river, were still connected by narrow, cobbled alleys known as 'rows': the narrowest, 'Kittywitches', was only thirty inches wide. The upper floors of the houses in this area overhung the passageways; the inhabitants could reach out of their bedroom windows and touch each other's walls (or so Kenneth remembered).

The higgledy-piggledy Old Town, with its cobbled market at the centre, was where the MacMillans would end up living. The rows, whose housing was considered substandard and overdue for redevelopment in the 1930s, were largely destroyed by wartime bombing. The few buildings that remained were subsequently demolished, so that no complete row remains today. Yarmouth's historic past, including the streets and dwellings Dickens described so vividly, is no longer visible.

When the MacMillan family arrived in 1935, they stayed first with Louise, 'Aunt Louie', Tiptod, in her small house at Runham Vauxhall, near Great Yarmouth railway station, while William looked for work. He was reduced to taking whatever short-term jobs he could, as a labourer or a cook in hotels. The battered car from Scotland was soon sold, for just £5. The impoverished family of six outstayed its initial welcome with the Tiptods, 'straining sisterly affection to breaking point', Kenneth was told. They moved into two-room lodgings near by: the boys shared one bed, their sisters another in the same room. Their parents slept in the remaining room. Their landlady refused to acknowledge that the beds were infested with bugs: 'The old lady squirmed uncomfortably when Mother drew back the sheets and squeezed a bedbug between her thumbs. It occurred to me that it might have been my blood that made dark spots on the linen.'

They moved again, to the low-rent area near the market square where Kenneth was to stay with his family for the rest of his childhood. The terrace in which the MacMillans lived was made up of former fishermen's smoke-houses, in which kippers had been strung up to cure under the roof. Even in their own two-up, two-down rented house, there was little privacy. Aged six or so, Kenneth walked in on his parents making love: 'I wandered into their bedroom smoking a make-believe sugar cigarette, hoping to shock them. At first they did not hear me and I watched fascinated, knowing and not knowing what they were doing. They hardly paused in their love-making and told me to leave the room.'

Whether or not young Kenneth was psychologically disturbed by seeing his parents in the act of sex, he recorded the event in his memoir decades later with affection, pleased that his parents were still physically attracted to each other in spite of their straitened circumstances. He continued to share a bedroom with his brother George. The five-year age gap between the two boys meant they had little in common, especially since they went to different schools. Kenneth was sent first to Northgate Infants, then to Northgate Junior, while George went to Yarmouth's Hospital School, originally established in the seventeenth century to educate poor children from the town's workhouse. It retained a reputation as a 'rough' school, whose pupils would end their education at the age of fourteen.

The brothers squabbled in their shared room. One night, during a pillow fight, Kenneth was knocked off the bed and broke his collar-bone. His father had to carry him two miles to the nearest hospital. George was in trouble yet again. He was supposed to be old enough to know better, while Kenneth, his mother's pet, was the innocent victim.

He might also have been subjected to his brother's sexual experimentation. Although there is no mention of such taboo intimacy in Kenneth's draft memoir about his childhood, he told his wife that George had involved him in activities about which he felt ashamed and resentful. Such memories, recounted later in life, are impossible to verify. However, as Kenneth grew older, his animosity towards George became pronounced – unusually so, even for brothers who were very different in character and interests. The curdled sibling relationships in his ballet *My Brother, My Sisters* might owe something to Kenneth's uneasy feelings about his own brother, whatever did or did not take place between them as they grew up.

While they were still youngsters, the two boys were prepared to collaborate in earning whatever money they could on Saturday mornings. Their uncle had made them a handcart out of fruit boxes and perambulator wheels, which they used to ferry holiday-makers' luggage from the station to the hotels and boarding houses, waiting expectantly for a tip. A useful source of small change was the Garibaldi Hotel, a large multi-storey hostel (now a single-storey disco club), where working men from the East End of London were housed for their summer holidays. The men, a boisterous bunch, used to take part in the town's street carnival, jiggling collecting boxes for local charities. They were happy to lean out of their upstairs windows and throw coins to street-urchin Kenneth, who improvised a tap dance on one of the wide downstairs windowsills, while George whistled a tune and collected the pennies.

As a child, Kenneth had no inhibitions about performing in pub-lic. He had enjoyed his Scottish-dancing lessons in Dunfermline, and he soon discovered end-of-the-pier talent competitions in Yarmouth. Lots of children performed in them, as much for enter-tainment as in the hope of winning not very valuable prizes. Kenneth had learned to tap dance by joining up with two girls of about his age, Joan Tooley and Daphne Morley, who lived at the bottom of his street and who went to Saturday-morning dance classes at the Little Theatre. Joan Tooley believes that Kenneth's mother paid for his weekly tap classes, which cost one shilling – 'quite a lot in those days, but somehow our mums managed it'. Joan liked Kenneth's mother: 'She was always kind to us children. She was plump, with grey hair. His father was dark and a bit fierce, with a Scottish accent. We were frightened of him. I think he had a touch of Scottish temper. Once something upset him and he got hold of me and tore my dress.'

William MacMillan might not have approved of his younger son's activities, but he let Edith indulge him. She was proud of his dancing ability, especially when he started to come home with prizes. The Little Theatre classes were run by Miss Jean Boulton, a 'no-nonsense' teacher whose pupils regularly took part in competi-tions on Britannia Pier. She taught ballet as well as tap, so Kenneth must have been aware of ballet from quite early on. Unable to afford a costume for the talent competitions, he exploited his waiflike appearance by wearing short trousers with braces over his thin, shirtless shoulders. 'I must have got this idea from some film,' he said. 'Obviously, I was hoping for the sympathy of the audience.' Small and skinny, he won the end-of-the-pier competitions so regularly that 'Uncle' Neville Bishop, who organised them, bribed him not to compete. By then, Kenneth had accumulated enough prizes in the form of ashtrays and fish knives to keep the family over-stocked with fancy items.

The MacMillans lived in genteel poverty while William struggled to find and keep a job. In the summer-holiday season he worked as a cook in seaside hotels, as did Edith once Kenneth was old enough to look after himself. In winter, jobs were hard to come by. William, angry and despairing at his loss of dignity as the unemployed head of the family, turned to alcohol for comfort. 'I sensed that my mother colluded with him and turned a blind eye when he kept back his drinking money from his infrequent wage packets.' The two girls, Jean and Betty, contributed to the house-keeping when they found work as shop assistants or hotel maids; they probably helped pay for Kenneth's tap classes.

His clothes were bought on credit, under an arrangement known as 'buying on the club'. As he recorded in his memoir:

'Wear now and pay later' read the sign in the shop where my new Sunday suit was chosen. I accidentally ruined this new suit on its first outing when I fell into a ditch, catching minnows on my long walk home from Sunday School.

The suit had still to be paid for, to his mother's distress.

Mother shopped for food around the corner at the Co-op. The cashier sat in a glass booth high above the counters, receiving the shoppers' money from an overhead tramway system and despatching the change and receipt back along the same route. 'Can I pay you later?' I heard my mother shout at the cage. The cashier looked around anxiously and then nodded her agreement. The other shoppers stared at us. Mother had shamelessly asked for credit and was given it. I did not know what anguish it caused her, but I squirmed in disbelief, wrapped in my infantile snobbery.

He wondered whether the cashier had been one of Edith's clients at her fortune-telling sessions.

My mother was often asked to tea because she said she could foretell the future by reading the tea leaves. Mysterious and convincing, she spoke like an actress savouring the subtlety of her performance. 'I come from gypsy blood,' she told her listeners conspiratorially. I nearly fell off her lap in surprise. She never could substantiate this claim but the idea appealed to me. Her need to be admired by an audience surprised me but I was aware how much she enjoyed it. I realise now that it was from these moments that my love of theatre began.

He was already entranced by the cinema. As a small boy, he was a regular at the Saturday-morning children's shows at the Plaza cinema in the marketplace, featuring cowboy serials and 'Flash Gordon'. 'I would sit with one leg tucked under me – a surprisingly comfortable position – endeavouring to make out what the actors were saying through the cacophony of noise the forty or more excited children were making during the hour-long show.' As he grew older, he and his brother would go to the double feature in the evening, watching Judy Garland and Mickey Rooney films, Hollywood romances and musicals: young Kenneth was a keen fan of Fred Astaire's elegant tap dancing. The boys' Saturday-night treat was tripe and chips, soaked in vinegar and wrapped in newspaper packets, from one of the stalls opposite the cinema. 'In winter, when the greenish-yellow glow of the lamps in the marketplace tried to penetrate the coastal fogs and mists, it was cosy and inviting in the cinema.' It was his place of safety and escape; films would continue to feed his imagination as he grew up, becoming a prime source of his inspiration as a creator of ballets. When he was a child, there were no books at home. Films were his window into a world outside Great Yarmouth.

2

Kenneth was nine when Britain declared war against Germany in September 1939. By May 1940, when German troops occupied the Low Countries, across the North Sea from the East Coast of England, Britain prepared itself for invasion. The government decided to evacuate children from the coastal areas most at risk. The official notice, issued on 28 May 1940, warned parents: 'You are free to make up your own mind. BUT YOU MUST MAKE UP

YOUR MIND AT ONCE. It is your duty to do so for the sake of your children.' Registration forms agreeing to evacuation had to be returned to schools by 9 o'clock the next morning. It was a difficult decision for Kenneth's parents, especially Edith, to make. George, eager to leave school, wanted to stay in Yarmouth and start working; ten-year-old Kenneth was the one who would have to be sent away. He had never been parted from his mother before, and there was no knowing where he might be sent or what kind of people would look after him. Other local children, however, including most of those from his school, would be going. His parents signed the registration form and packed his bag in readiness. They waved goodbye to him at Great Yarmouth train station at the end of the week, a stifling hot Sunday, 2 June 1940. In a massive feat of organisation, 47,000 children from East Coast towns were put onto 97 trains and sent inland.

Kenneth and his Northgate Junior schoolmates were transported to the small Nottinghamshire town of Upper Broughton, not far from Melton Mowbray, and a long way from Yarmouth. They gathered in the village hall, luggage labels bearing their names and addresses hung about their necks, waiting to be selected by local families. Kenneth, an urban child, ended up on a farm, where the farmer's wife bathed him in a rainwater butt – or so he reported indignantly to his friends when he left Broughton after just a couple of weeks. He had written to his mother threatening suicide if she did not come and take him home at once. He was justified in being confident of his mother's love and of his power over her. Instead of telling him to stick it out in Broughton with his schoolmates, Edith fetched him back to Yarmouth – unwittingly exposing him to an onslaught of bombing raids as the Battle of Britain began.

The first German air raid on the town was on 11 July 1940. By August, a continuous stream of bombers and fighter planes flew overhead as the Luftwaffe attacked Royal Air Force bases near by. The Luftwaffe carried out more raids on Great Yarmouth than on any other East Coast town. Its wide harbour was an easy target for bombers aiming at the port and the naval and merchant ships moored there. (Two naval bases had been established in the harbour in 1940 to protect convoy routes and sweep sea-mines.) Kenneth remembered overhearing conversations at the start of the war between Yarmouth people, reassuring each other that their long, narrow town would be quickly overflown: 'It never occurred to them that the bombers would go in longways, which is what happened.' In addition to deliberate attacks on the port, German planes returning from inland raids on the Midlands jettisoned their remaining bombs on the town as they were chased out to sea.

On 31 October 1940, the family had a narrow escape when a bomb landed on a house close to theirs, in Swirle's Place by the market square. Kenneth was playing in the street; George was down by the river, fishing; their mother, who was in the back yard, took shelter in the outside privy; Jean, safe indoors, was unable to hear the full effect of the devastation because of her deafness and was unaware that her mother was banging on the door to be let back in. Their house, though not directly hit, was sufficiently damaged for the MacMillans to have to abandon it and move near by to 12 Stanley Terrace, which they rented for the rest of the war (and which Kenneth was eventually to buy for his sister Betty's family).

William MacMillan, by now forty-eight, had been required by the wartime Labour Exchange to return to Scotland, where he worked as a labourer in the King George V Docks in Glasgow. Jean and Betty were employed in Great Yarmouth as factory hands, often on night shifts, so they came home mainly to sleep by day. George was working as an apprentice carpenter in the building trade. Kenneth, after his unscheduled return from evacuation, stayed with his mother at home. At night, during air raids, he, George and their mother slept under their newly acquired Morrison shelter, a large steel contraption that could also be used as a table. 'I used to lie awake, nudging George and asking if the plane that in my imagination targeted our house was Ours or Theirs. Always he replied "one of ours" and to my irritation went back to sleep.' During the day, Kenneth attended lessons organised by an enterprising woman in the back room of an ice-cream parlour while he waited for a place at the Hospital School, where George had been. It was one of the few schools to remain open in Yarmouth during the early years of the war.

The family's latest house in the centre of the Old Town was in a very vulnerable area. The tightly packed streets contained factories as well as dwellings; the German bombers knew exactly where their industrial targets were, as their maps, captured later, revealed. On 1 February 1941, a stick of twelve high-explosive bombs dropped by a Dornier 17z demolished Grout's silk factory, which made bandages and parachutes, and Dyson's glassworks, both close to the marketplace and its surrounding houses.

Kenneth, out in the streets with other children, heard the Dornier flying dangerously close overhead and actually saw a bomb leave the aircraft. The plane flew so low that bombs ricocheted off the road into the upper storeys of buildings alongside. The panic-stricken boys managed to reach an air-raid shelter just in time. They were then led through the rubble outside and taken into an undamaged house to recover from shock. Grout's factory was ablaze, the streets were closed off and Kenneth was unable to return home for several hours, by which time his family was frantic with worry. News had spread that a boy injured or perhaps killed in the raid had been taken to hospital. George was sent to find out, fearing the worst. By the time he returned to find Kenneth safe at home in the kitchen, being fussed over, he 'wasn't best pleased' with his brother. Kenneth recalled 'getting my ears boxed by George for not going straight home and telling my mother I was OK'.

That night, as they listened to the wireless, George remembered hearing 'Lord Haw-Haw' (William Joyce) broadcasting Nazi propaganda, claiming that the compassionate German pilot of the Dornier bomber had waited until Yarmouth factory hands had clocked off at noon before releasing his bombs at 12.21 p.m.

Just four days later, a bomb fell through the roof of the Regal cinema, where Kenneth's mother Edith was in the audience watching the film *The Doctor Takes a Wife*, starring Loretta Young. The bomb did not explode and no one was hurt, but Kenneth knew how scared his mother must have been, having just had a similar experience himself. After these close shaves, Edith decided to move out of town with her two youngest children to her mother's cottage by the waterworks in Ormesby, further along the coast. The house was small and simple, with an outdoor privy, a pump in the yard for cold water and no electric light, but they would be safer there at night, when the air raids were at their worst. From Ormesby, they could see the sky over the port at Yarmouth lit up by fires caused by the bombs and hear the pounding of anti-aircraft guns. During 1941, Great Yarmouth experienced 167 air raids, which killed 109 people and destroyed much of the congested Old Town – although the MacMillans' terraced house remained standing.

Kenneth was very fond of his maternal grandmother, Mary Anne Shreeve, who entertained him by teaching him how to knit and crochet – skills he never lost. Edith needed her mother's help in looking after the boys because of her own ill-health. She was increasingly subject to seizures, seemingly brought about by high blood pressure and kidney disease. (There is no record of the diagnosis.) Her body had become bloated, probably through retention of fluid caused by her malfunctioning kidneys. She suffered epileptic fits, during which she made an alarming noise as her muscles convulsed before she fell unconscious. Sometimes she lost control of her bladder. These fits frightened and disturbed Kenneth. They were a family secret that had to be kept from his friends – a potential source of shame. He was acutely embarrassed on his mother's behalf by her seizures, dreading that she might make a spectacle of herself in public. He was also terrified that she might have a fit while they were alone together during an air raid and he would not know what to do. She had been his rock, his source of love and security; now she was vulnerable, unreliable, and he was helpless.

Kenneth's grandmother, by now in her eighties, could not be of much assistance when Edith was taken ill. One night, the brothers were woken by the sound of their mother having a particularly bad seizure. She frothed at the mouth, lost consciousness and would not come round. Knowing there was nothing their grandmother could do, George banged frantically on the wall of the bedroom to summon the next-door neighbour to fetch a doctor. There were no telephones in the cottages and the nearest public phone box was some distance away. The anxious boys could only sit and wait. By the time the doctor came, Edith was conscious again, her body flaccid and very sore. The doctor tried to reassure her frightened sons, saying, 'Don't worry, your mother will never die of a fit.'

3

In spite of his worries at home, and the almost nightly bombing of Yarmouth, Kenneth managed to do well at school. He had been found a place at the Hospital School in time to prepare for the

11-plus examination, which determined whether a pupil went to a grammar school (and possibly to university) or left school at fourteen, as George had done. No one on either side of Kenneth's family had gone on to further education: the men started their working lives as labourers, the women mostly went into service. Wartime conditions meant that Jean and Betty, Kenneth's older sisters, were trapped in factory work. Clever Kenneth, his parents hoped, would have a different future.

His promise was evident in a play he wrote when he was eleven, ringingly entitled *Right Shall Triumph!* The Hospital School teacher who set the assignment might not have conquered Kenneth's erratic spelling, but had evidently taught his pupils how to prepare a play script, developing the plot from scene to scene. The list of dramatis personae was headed by the hero: 'The Prince, K. MacMillan, disguised as a begger'; subsidiary characters included 'the Lord High Chanseller' and a 'peasent girl'. Special effects required by the young writer–producer encompassed thunder and lightning ('short sharp flashes with a torch') and rain ('rice on brown paper').

The carefully handwritten script concluded with Act IV celebrations in the palace ballroom, as the prince graciously invited his bride-to-be, the humble peasant girl, to dance with him. With hindsight, it was the childish forerunner of one of MacMillan's earliest ballets, *Laiderette*, which involved a low-born girl swept off her feet in an aristocrat's ballroom – though the ballet's ending would not be the statutory happy one.

Soon after writing the play in the summer of 1941, Kenneth passed the 11-plus examination with ease. He did well enough to be awarded one of twenty-four places at Great Yarmouth Grammar School, his schooling paid by a scholarship from the Borough Council's Education Committee. His proud mother filled in his entrance form, explaining that his father was absent on war work in Scotland. Her youngest child was launched on a route that would set him apart from the rest of his family. To her regret, he would all too soon be physically separated from them: the Grammar School had been evacuated to East Retford, in Nottinghamshire.

Retford, at the heart of the East Midlands, some twenty miles from industrial Sheffield, is an ancient market town surrounded by agricultural land. Situated at the junction of two railway lines, one linking London and York, the other serving the Midlands, it was an important rail centre. Many evacuees were sent there, from Leeds, Birmingham and the West Midlands, as well as from the East Coast. Several military camps were based nearby, swelling the population with soldiers and airmen. Thanks to Retford's position on the Great North Road, the A1, a constant flow of wartime traffic roared through the town, as convoys made their way to and from the southern coastal towns. The youngsters from Yarmouth (who included the girls from the High School, also evacuated to Retford in 1940) were still very much caught up in the war, though they were safer than they would be at home.

This time, Kenneth was well prepared to leave home and even looked forward to escaping from his restricted life at his grandmother's cottage, with the constant worry about his epileptic mother. He went by train with other Yarmouth pupils in the middle of August, ten days before term began. New arrivals reported first to the King Edward VI School, an imposing redbrick Victorian edifice housing the local grammar school, which now shared its premises with the transplanted Great Yarmouth boys. There the newcomers were allocated their billets, the homes of Retford families who were required to take in evacuee children for a weekly payment of 10s 6d a head.

Kenneth was initially placed on a temporary basis with the Greenham family. Betty, one of the daughters, remembers their new 'guest' staging a performance in their back garden. Kenneth borrowed her red jacket as his costume and tap-danced on the board that her brother used for his model railway set. The attendance fee was a sweet. Betty was impressed by his self-confidence. 'I was quite a little show-off,' Kenneth said of himself as a boy. His next billet was not nearly so congenial, as he informed an older schoolmate, Victor Stowers, with whom he linked up on the daily walk to school. Kenneth said he was lonely, so Vic asked his kindly foster-parents (as evacuees' paid hosts were known) if they would take Kenneth as well.

Bill and Annie Selby were a childless couple in their mid-forties, living in a short street of railway workers' houses. Everyone in the cul-de-sac knew each other well. They were all familiar with the 'knocker-up' from the railway company, who would come down Richard Street at four in the morning to summon engine drivers like Bill Selby to work at the goods yard. The three-bedroom houses, built in 1889 at the height of the railway boom, had long, narrow gardens overlooking fields and woods. A pig sty at the bottom of each garden was put to good use during the war: the pigs ate the household scraps and the householders ate the pigs.

Annie Selby was a jolly, warm-hearted woman, proud of her cooking. The two schoolboys sat down to four meals a day, though Kenneth remained thin as a rake. 'It must have been very strange for them [the Selbys] to have had their home and their lives invaded by two teenage boys, when they had never had any children of their own,' he marvelled later in a newspaper article about his childhood. But the Selbys were generous people, who opened their house at No. 7 to other youngsters living in the street, as the two girls who lived next door recalled with affection at a reunion of locals and evacuees sixty years later. They and Victor Stowers remembered the routine all the families in Richard Street followed. Bath night was once a week on Fridays, in a tin bath in front of the fire, followed by a change of underclothes; during the rest of week, especially after sports, the boys strip-washed. Monday was washday, clothes laundered in a copper container that had to be heated from the early hours of the morning until the water reached boiling point.

Vic had a bicycle, which he would ride on errands for the Selbys, such as fetching pails of maggots from the reeking Retford tannery for Bill to use as fishing bait in the River Idle. Kenneth's parents couldn't afford to buy him a bike, so he walked everywhere. Annie would take the two boys with her on regular twice-weekly visits to the cinema – usually the Majestic or the Roxy. Kenneth was already a film addict, and Victor soon became one. 'We were partly educated by Hollywood,' Stowers (who became a teacher) commented.

They had time to go to the cinema during the day because the Great Yarmouth boys had to fit their schedule of lessons in between those for the resident Retford pupils. Great Yarmouth Grammar School occupied the King Edward VI School building between 8.50 and 10.10 in the morning, then between 3 and 5 in the afternoon. Saturday-morning lessons were between 8.50 a.m. and 12.45 p.m. The rest of the day had to be filled with sports, lectures, debates, cadet parades, drama rehearsals, choir practice and other activities – otherwise it was thought the boys would get up to mischief in town. The evacuees profited from the extra attention their teachers, *in loco parentis*, felt obliged to give them. 'We probably became more middle-class,' said Graham Swann, one of Kenneth's schoolmates, who went on to become a scientist and pioneer of satellite communication. 'Dedicated teachers who were with us all the time saw the potential in us working-class lads and raised our aspirations. They filled our spare hours with music and plays and lectures. We were better off than we would have been at home.'

Many more opportunities for entertainment were available to them than in bomb-damaged Yarmouth. Thanks to the large number of servicemen and land girls in the area, all three cinemas remained in operation and there were frequent performances, professional and amateur, in the Town Hall, Corn Exchange and Little Theatre. As he grew older, Kenneth would take part in performances for 'Salute the Soldier' and 'Wings for Victory' weeks, organised to raise money for the war effort. Retford was proud of its patriotic enterprise, which included releasing schoolchildren from their lessons during harvest time to help local farmers collect the crops: 'We bent to the task until it was difficult to unbend, picking fifteen tons of potatoes a day,' reported the *GYGS Chronicle* in May 1942.

Retford did not entirely escape the German air raids. Townspeople could see the sky lit up by fires caused by bombs in Sheffield, and hear German planes overhead. A bomb was jettisoned by Grove Woods, not far from the Selbys' back garden, leaving a huge crater. Incendiary devices landed near the school playing fields, in a dramatic firework display. The schoolboys collected shrapnel as souvenirs: Kenneth hung on to his for years, until the handle dropped off the suitcase in which he kept the heavy metal fragments. Later in the war, on 4 February 1944, a Wellington bomber, 'one of ours', crashed into Whisker Hill Woods, killing the aircrew. The souvenir-hunting boys retrieved the crew's Horlicks tablets and added tracer bullets to their collections. Although Kenneth later remembered these near-encounters with death with horror, at the time they were exciting to boys who considered themselves indestructible.

Kenneth had been at the school for only two terms when personal tragedy struck. He returned home for the Easter holidays in April 1942 to learn that his mother had died. Victor Stowers remembered the school train arriving at the station in Yarmouth and Kenneth's father and sisters waiting with drawn faces to break the bad news.

Edith MacMillan had died the night before of a heart attack during a seizure – the doctor's reassuring prognosis had been wrong. While Kenneth was away at school, her health had deteriorated so badly that William MacMillan had been granted compassionate leave to return from his wartime job in Scotland in order to care for her. Kenneth, by now aged twelve, had not been told how ill she had become. On his arrival home, his father instructed him to kiss the corpse, which had been laid out in the front room of the Stanley Terrace house, and told him not to cry.

Kenneth's physical distaste at having to kiss his mother's cold, dead lips was mixed with guilt. Although he loved her, he had felt huge relief at being able to go away to school, free from his dread of her frightening fits. 'I used to wish she'd die,' he told his wife many years later, 'and then she did.' He reproached himself that, as a small, needy child, he had forced her to love him. He had clung to her physically, demanding to be breast fed, to sit on her lap, to be with her at home; and then he had been repelled by her disability as he grew more independent. (He invariably said in interviews that he was eleven rather than twelve when his mother died, so he must have thought of himself still very much a child, divided by loss from his older self.) In his distress, he was angry at his mother for deserting him just as he was making the first, temporary break from home; he was far from ready to leave her. 'At her funeral, I felt like a stranger,' he wrote. 'A darkness settled on me like a cloak.' Unable to express his welter of confused feelings and his terrible grief, he bottled up his emotions. He was to pay the price later in life, as a succession of psychiatrists would tell him.

After his mother's funeral, Kenneth went back to school in Retford for the start of the summer term. The long train journey was a period of limbo, cutting him off from home and the distress of his family. He had no time to mourn with them and he had to cope, on his own, with life at school. His father had told him not to cry, so he didn't. Vic Stowers, who shared a double bed with him for a while at the Selbys' before a separate room was made available, reported that Kenneth never cried himself to sleep. He was quiet and withdrawn, however, especially in the months that followed his mother's death. His teachers' comments in their end-of-term reports on his work and conduct made no mention of the loss he had suffered. He continued to do 'good, keen work' in English and history and was 'most promising' in art classes: 'He uses his imagination as well as his brush.'

The hardest period for him was the return home in the holidays. He spent much of his time alone with his father, as his sisters were working and his brother George had been sent by the Labour Exchange to work in the docks in Tilbury, the port serving London. Kenneth had never had a close relationship with his father, who had left the boy's upbringing to Edith. William didn't know what to make of his youngest son. Distraught after his wife's death, he was lost and lonely without her. He asked Kenneth to share his bed so that he would feel some kind of warmth and companionship at night. Kenneth was reluctant, but he, too, felt isolated and afraid. He lay silent and rigid with terror at the air raids alongside his father, who forbade him to give in to his fear.

Jean and Betty, who worked night shifts at the sugar-processing plant on the outskirts of Great Yarmouth, tried to come to his rescue by taking him with them to the factory. For Kenneth, it was an adventure that turned out to be a disappointment. 'The women had to lug heavy sacks of sugarbeet into piled-up mounds, on which they perched me, hoping that I would fall asleep. But I could still hear the bombs falling on the town. I disliked my father but I was conscience-stricken at leaving him, so I remained at home after that, still afraid but less full of remorse.'

Worst of all was the Christmas holiday at the end of the year Edith had died. William had been unable to find employment in Yarmouth. Redundant and aimless, he turned more and more to alcohol. The responsibility of caring for Kenneth, who turned thirteen in December, was almost too much for him. 'Every day he listened for rumours of a fresh coal supply, ready to rush to the depot to scoop up what he could to keep us warm. He shuffled around the town like a derailed train. It was impossible for him to get back on course.' Although Kenneth's sisters managed to organise a semblance of a family Christmas dinner, they both escaped to celebrate New Year's Eve with friends. William and Kenneth stayed bleakly at home, listening on the radio to the Hogmanay celebrations in Scotland. 'Our lack of communication was highlighted by the silence that followed. It was my father's winter and he froze me out. He pulled his hair into an odd little forelock as he sat on the fender in front of the now-empty grate.'

The hair-twisting detail is recorded in one of the drafts of Kenneth's memoir, but he had nothing more to say about his father's or his own grief. Most of his early adolescent years, apart from school holidays, were spent away from his family. Yet his painstaking account of his childhood concentrates on Yarmouth, largely ignoring his schooldays in Retford, where he lived with his 'foster-parents' and grew up with his peer group at school. The interests he developed were formed during term time, at what must have seemed a long distance from home. His relationships with his own family, however, were the crucial ones, which is no doubt why he focused his written descriptions on his father and Jean.

Jean, his favourite sister, mothered him as best she could. His affection for her was tinged with guilt, for he felt awkward about her deafness and the loud, gruff way she spoke. 'I thought she sounded like a man and hoped my embarrassment did not show. Inwardly, I suffered from the usual teenage self-consciousness. My flawless view of Jean was shattered by her inadvertent demonstration of imperfection.' He was painfully aware that she was damaged, as his mother had been by her fits, reinforcing his sense that he could not totally rely on the women who loved him most. He was torn between compassion for their weakness and fear of being somehow involved in their humiliation.

None the less, he greatly admired Jean and the stylish way she and Betty managed to dress, in spite of wartime clothes rationing. Jean was the prettier of the two, slender, with a cloud of dark hair. 'They went to "Irene", a hatshop in the King's Road near the town hall. They sported twin "Mrs Miniver" hats and Astrakhan-trimmed swagger coats when they paraded into town to have a cup of ersatz coffee at Green's cafeteria.' Movie-mad Kenneth thought that the headgear had come straight from Hollywood, for under each hat in the shop window a printed card announced 'The Rita Hayworth', 'The Betty Grable', 'The Lana Turner'. He was disillusioned when he discovered that Jean's 'Greer Garson' could be seen on other heads around the town.

Whenever they had a night off, smartly dressed Jean and Betty went to 'the pictures' or the local dance halls. Great Yarmouth was filled with servicemen out for a good time and there were plenty of local women ready to provide it. William MacMillan deplored these 'bloody pick-up joints' and tried to impose a curfew on his daughters.

He resented their independence – and the fact that they had jobs while he did not – and feared for their reputations. Without his wife to soften his overbearing nature, he behaved like a martinet with his adult children. Betty soon escaped his control by marrying an airman, Victor Harmer, but Jean was trapped, being called a whore by her alcohol-fuelled father when she returned home late.

Kenneth vividly recalled a night when Jean, eager to get out of the house, asked him to escort her to the Aquarium Ballroom; he was to be her dancing partner in order to disarm their father's suspicions. Prudish young Kenneth was appalled to find the staircase leading to the sleazy dance hall jammed with soldiers and sailors reeking of body odour, beer and Brylcreem. They sized up the girls as they entered and Jean was immediately swept away from Kenneth's side. Standing awkwardly against the wall, he was disconcerted to see Jean gazing dreamily into her partner's eyes. 'She was adept at pretending to hear the band (which was excruciating) when she had a strong enough partner to lead her. When it was my turn, I felt small and feeble as I foxtrotted her awkwardly around the room. I hated the men who ogled her.'

He was well aware what the dancing often led to. Youngsters roaming the streets around the dance halls would find used condoms floating in the town's emergency water tanks. Although Kenneth refused to believe that Jean could be capable of casual sex, he might have shared some of his father's turbulent feelings when William pursued her one night and dragged her screaming from the dance floor. William swore violently at her in front of the other revellers and continued cursing her on the way home. Then he threw her out of the house, shouting at her never to return. Kenneth, aghast, was strictly forbidden to go in search of her or to speak to her. Conflicting loyalties made him nervous about meeting her by chance after she rented a room not far from Stanley Terrace. When he did see her approaching on the far side of the street soon after she had been banished, he turned his head 'like a traitor' to avoid looking at her.

'She called to me and as I ran into her arms I was shocked that I had even feigned indifference. How could I so easily abandon her?' This acute experience of his – of anyone's – capacity for betrayal would appear in his ballets time and again. So would his understanding of a vulnerable individual, at the mercy of an uncaring society: Jean, his mother, his father, himself. It was a knowledge that would be hard won, scarring the barely adolescent boy he still was.

With hindsight, he believed he had sensed something incestuous in his father's obsessive concern for Jean, and his absolute refusal to countenance her having a sexual life of her own. Kenneth thought she had once tried to tell him about it while he was a youngster, implying that their father had 'broken the rules and could no longer hide his feelings for her', but she stopped when she saw Kenneth's baffled reaction. He wrote in his memoir that when he later raised the subject with her, long after their father's death, she turned away and did not answer. He interpreted her evident unease as shame and anger at the memories he had stirred up. He became convinced that their family was riven with abusive secrets that no one dared acknowledge.

William's very different attitude to his daughter Betty had puzzled young Kenneth, as he tried to make sense of adult morality. Betty's husband Victor had no sooner been posted to Singapore than she took up with the captain of a gunboat stationed in Yarmouth harbour. The sailor was made welcome in Stanley Terrace, even though it was obvious he was having an adulterous affair with Betty. William appeared to condone Betty's behaviour while punishing Jean harshly, making her the scapegoat of his confused feelings. Kenneth was caught up in the collusion over Betty's affair by being invited on board the gunship, where the captain gave him a pair of leather gloves of the kind seamen wore on their North Sea missions. He flaunted the gloves at school but knew that his silence, when Betty's husband Victor returned, had been bought.

Girls of his own age were still something of a mystery to Kenneth as he reached puberty. He consulted the agony columns of his sisters' magazines, hoping to gain an insight into the opposite sex and sex itself. Copies of *Health and Strength* magazine, with its unerotic nude photographs, were of little help either. 'I had a healthy curiosity about sex, but my fantasies were unfocused and narcissistic. The women that I saw on the cinema screen were beautiful, wayward and enigmatic, unlike my mother, sisters and the girls I knew. I remained relatively uninformed about female anatomy.'

His own anatomy was a source of bewilderment. He had been daunted by the size of the penis of a boy he met at the outdoor swimming pool adjoining Yarmouth marina. The pool was supposed to be reserved for members of the armed forces, but local children managed to sneak in. Bertie, a big stout youth, was soon surrounded by admiring small boys in the changing room. 'Quite at ease, he proudly accepted our compliments on his big dick. The masculine preoccupation with size made me feel inferior and I jealously wondered if with a little work I could make mine as big.'

Bertie's confident air of experience, however, turned out to be misleading. Kenneth befriended him, in the hope of acquiring information. ' "It's so embarrassing when I get an erection on the bus. What do you do with yours?" I enquired. He looked bemused and I suspected his knowledge of sex was as limited as my own.' Some years later, he heard that Bertie had got a job as a bus conductor in Yarmouth (misled, Kenneth conjectured wickedly, into expecting 'a life of priapic bliss').

Back at school in Retford, Kenneth described, graphically, to other boys in his class a naughty soft-porn picture he had seen in a book. It was an illustration of a small boy sitting on a chamber pot, alarmed by his erection. Two scantily dressed women were standing by, one with a big sword. The boy's hands were clasped in an entreaty not to cut off his penis. Kenneth's startled schoolmates assumed he must have access to 'adult' publications issued by the well-known publisher Macmillan, whose name resembled his. He apparently said nothing to disabuse them.

Writing about his early sexual memories, he blamed his poor marks and lack of concentration in maths lessons on his sexual daydreams. 'I was troubled by the frequently changing objects of my desire,' he wrote, noting that his girlfriends' names were Thelma, Sylvia and Hazel. He made no mention of boys. His fumbling experiments with girls never amounted to much because he lacked the courage to go further. He might have been intimidated by the headmaster's warning to the older boys at school assembly of the consequences of 'a moment of ecstatic passion'. The vivid turn of phrase was repeated to Kenneth by Vic Stowers, by then a prefect. He had been informed that a much admired boy at the school, who was in the football first eleven, had been expelled for getting a schoolgirl pregnant. They were both still under sixteen when the child was born. The scandal electrified the school. Over fifty years later, at an evacuees' reunion in Retford attended by the author, GYGS old boys recounted this story as one of their enduring memories.

4

Kenneth's urge to dance became stronger than ever after his mother's death. He had always enjoyed dancing, from his earliest Highland-dancing classes in Scotland to his end-of-the-pier performances in Yarmouth. Now, in his adolescence, he dreamed of being like Fred Astaire – fleet-footed, elegant, witty, able to transform an everyday world into something fantastical. Dancing would become his way of channelling and controlling his welter of inarticulate emotions – and it was something he knew he could do well. He would not have been able to formulate exactly what he was searching for, but he knew he needed guidance.

Thanks to a stroke of luck, he found the finest dance teacher in the area. Annie Selby's sister lived across the road in Richard Street and she had a granddaughter, Jean Bradley, who was determined to go on the stage. Jean's elder brother, Ron, also wanted to become a performer. They were both promising pupils of Miss Joan Thomas, the best-known dance teacher in the region. Miss Thomas taught in Retford three days a week, staying at the Bradleys' house from Thursday to Sunday. In return for her accommodation, she gave Jean free private lessons. Hanging over the Selbys' front garden fence, Kenneth used to watch Jean practising for her lessons. Jean also borrowed a room in which to practise at the local tax office, after hours. Kenneth, accompanied by a local boy whose mother worked at the office, would come and watch her, fascinated by her ability to do both ballet and acrobatics.

Joan Thomas, then in her early twenties, was an enthusiastic and enterprising teacher, performer and producer. She lived with her parents in the Admiral Rodney public house in Southwell, a village some way from Retford. Her former pupils remember her as 'rather well bred, not working-class, as a lot of us were'. She taught dancing in the back room of her parents' pub during the first half of the week. Then she came to Retford, where she rented a small industrial shed as a dance studio, offering classes in tap, musical comedy, acrobatics, ballroom and ballet. She had about a hundred pupils in all from the local catchment area: a core of regulars, almost all girls, and numbers of children and adults who came and went. 'Everybody knew me,' she said proudly in her eighties, when she was still involved, with her daughter, in running what become known as the Rodney Schools of Dancing.

Her most ambitious wartime project had been in May 1941, four months before Kenneth first arrived in Retford for the start of the school year. She had recruited ninety local children for her biggest ever pantomime, *The Shoe Woman* (based on the nursery rhyme of 'The Old Woman Who Lived in a Shoe'). 'Stupendous attraction!' announced her advertisement in the *Retford, Gainsborough and Worksop Times*. 'Nearly 500 gorgeous costumes, set in a number of beautiful scenes. Produced and presented by Joan G. Thomas, in the Town Hall. All dance classes cancelled owing to panto rehearsals.'

The five performances sold out and the production was reviewed at enthusiastic length in the *Retford, Gainsborough and Worksop Times*, in spite of wartime restrictions on newsprint. The balance sheet, however, revealed a loss of £10. Expenses – costumes, sets, the hire of the Town Hall and a local band – had accounted for the vast sum of £246 14s 5d. After that, Miss Thomas scaled down her productions.

She continued to enter her pupils for dancing competitions and examinations, ensuring that their successes were recorded in the local paper as well as the specialist national magazine, the *Dancing Times*. She was a hard taskmistress, insisting that her favoured pupils practise for at least an hour every day. 'You had to have an adult sign your honesty book that you had done your practice, and woe betide you if you hadn't,' said Jean Bradley. 'I practised every day except Christmas.' Jean had already passed her first 'major' ballet exam, the Royal Academy of Dancing Elementary examination, at the age of nine. When Ken, as she called him, asked her to teach him some steps, she suggested he joined Miss Thomas's classes.

Annie Selby said he shouldn't, as dancing wasn't right for boys, but Annie's sister stood up for Kenneth. Her grandson Ron danced, she said, so if Kenneth wanted to learn, nobody should stand in his way. He started with once-a-week tap lessons, brushing up his end-of-the-pier skills. He paid for his classes out of his pocket money. When Miss Thomas spotted him trying out pirouettes, copying the girls in her ballet classes, she promptly recruited him as a potential partner for the girls. Boys were prized because so few were prepared to endure the inevitable teasing at school. Although Kenneth later claimed that he was the only boy in Miss Thomas's school, there were others, as well as Ron Bradley. One of them, Roger Levick, remembers being impressed by Kenneth's passion for dancing: 'He was a very vital young fellow – always leaping about, trying things out.'

Kenneth could not afford ballet classes as well as tap, so Miss Thomas wrote to his father, saying that Kenneth's talent should be encouraged. William MacMillan, who had little idea what ballet was but mistrusted it as an occupation for the male sex, replied that he was not prepared to fund extra lessons and that, in any case, his son was destined to be a doctor or a lawyer. There was no point in wasting his time in dancing classes. Doreen Anthony (whose mother played the piano for the classes) remembers that Miss Thomas 'had quite a tussle with Ken's father . . . he obviously didn't realise how formidable she was. She would go to war for talent she wanted to nurture.' When William refused to pay up, Miss Thomas taught Kenneth for free, disregarding his father's objections.

She co-opted him into her musical-comedy classes, also called 'stage dancing', so that he could participate in her shows. She encouraged her pupils to make up dances for themselves as homework, and to co-operate in groups, setting things for each other in their favourite style – stage, ballet or tap. 'Ken definitely had a good brain,' Miss Thomas said. 'He picked up steps very quickly, and made lots of suggestions about what we should do. He wasn't a bundle of joy but he fitted in, specially when we all went off together to do shows and competitions.'

Kenneth had found the first of his substitute families. Although the elderly Selbys were good to him, they did not share his interests, any more than his own family did back in Yarmouth. Here, in Miss Thomas's classes, was a group of like-minded young people, all eager to please their teacher. Joan Thomas was vital and inspiring, full of self-confidence: her impressionable pupils believed she was the fount of all dance wisdom. Many of them, including Kenneth, probably had a crush on her. According to her former 'girls', she was a theatrical Miss Jean Brodie. She was adept at harnessing adolescents' ambitions, urging them to make the best of themselves, to be disciplined young professionals. 'She gave you pride in yourself, though she was careful about handing out praise: "If I said you were any good, you wouldn't work",' remembered Jean Bradley. Her elite pupils were distinguished by uniform clothing when they travelled to competitions. The girls wore siren suits: all-in-one outfits with elasticated waists and a hood, the wartime equivalent of modern tracksuits; the boys wore dark trousers, a white shirt and a red bow-tie. They were told that they represented Miss Thomas wherever they were, so they were not to be seen loitering in the streets or eating fish and chips out of newspapers. 'The other kids thought we were snooty because we didn't mingle outside our dance group,' says Doreen Anthony.

That was fine by Kenneth. He needed to keep his dance activities and his school life separate. He could be two different people, without having to explain himself. To be dance mad was normal in Miss Thomas's troupe, and anyone who didn't understand would be excluded. He had succumbed to the compulsive nature of dance training, with its clear code of rules and rewards. For a talented youngster, as he was, every new achievement was a source of pride. The physically demanding classes obliged him to shut out, temporarily at least, his anxious internal monologue: by concentrating entirely on what his limbs and feet were doing, he could think of nothing else. His naturally obsessive tendencies, instead of gnawing at him inwardly, would go into mastering a discipline. He did his hour's practice every day, holding on to the wooden fence at the end of the Selbys' back garden. Vic Stowers, sworn to secrecy, noticed that skinny Ken was developing strong leg muscles. The harder he practised, the more adept he became at accomplishing difficult exercises. His self-esteem rose and he was gratified by the respect shown by Miss Thomas's pupils and by their rivals on the dance circuit, as he began entering competitions.

His schoolteachers must have given him permission to perform in public with Miss Thomas's troupe. There is no mention of his dance activities in his end-of-term reports, however, until the final one. His teachers might have accepted that his out-of-school interests were his own affair; his father, reading his reports at home, did not need to be informed about his dancing. He kept very quiet among his schoolmates about his dance classes, fearing that he would be mocked. Learning ballet, in particular, would be regarded as unmanly – or so he thought, knowing his father's reaction. Ballet has always suffered from the assumption that male dancers must be effeminate, and schoolboys can be callously cruel. So Kenneth was secretive about his dancing, although his closest schoolfriends,

Ernie Fulcher and Percy Read, would sometimes come and watch him. They, like Vic, had promised not to tell.

Once school lessons were over, Kenneth hurried to join in Miss Thomas's rehearsals, which took place either in Ebsworth Hall, at the back of St Swithin's Church, or in her dance studio, a tin shed near the slaughterhouse. She had kitted out the stark space with borrowed mirrors, barres around the walls and a coke-burning stove with a big flue pipe. 'It was cold, but you soon got warm,' says Doreen Anthony. Miss Thomas and the pianist – Doreen's mother – huddled by the stove while the students worked up a sweat. Only live music was used for Miss Thomas's classes and performances, played either on the piano or by a hired band, such as the local factory's 'light orchestra'. 'She was just as tough on the players as she was on us performers,' said Mary Fawkes. 'We carried on rehearsing until we all got it right.'

They performed frequently. Retford, like other towns, organised 'Holiday at Home' weeks, encouraging local talent (not that Miss Thomas needed much encouraging) to put on shows for residents unable to travel to holiday resorts in wartime. For the regular fund-raising weeks in aid of the armed forces, Miss Thomas would hire the Town Hall and the Butter Market beneath it, which provided a dressing-room area for her numerous pupils. The audience sat on folding chairs lined up on the hall's wooden floor, which was otherwise used for ballroom dancing. Miss Thomas's troupe was always ready to take part in concerts in factory canteens and perform at fêtes and sports days.

Mary Fawkes's mother was largely responsible for the recital costumes, with the help of other mothers. Mr Fawkes kept a haberdashery shop, so his wife had access to sequins, feathers and elastic corset material – scarce commodities during clothes rationing. Outfits were made of parachute silk or black-out material, dotted with sequins. No flesh-coloured tights were available for the girls, who slapped wet-white lotion, mixed in a bucket, on their legs. Boys usually wore their basic dance uniform of dark trousers, white shirts and bow-ties. Kenneth initially performed in musical-comedy routines, singing and dancing to popular tunes such as 'Deep Purple' and 'Ain't Misbehavin'. Miss Thomas commented, however, that he wasn't a showbiz extrovert, craving attention and applause: 'He was lanky and lyrical – he danced with his soul. He did everything as well as possible,' she said, 'but for himself, not for other people.'

He must, however, have been seeking her approval. She was now the most powerful woman in his young life, and the most alluring. For most of the time he spent with her, engaged in a very physical artistic discipline, she was stripped down in practice clothes or wearing revealing stage costume when she performed with her troupe. For him, she represented ambition, pleasure, excitement, feminine sensuality; and paradoxically, being with her, whether in dance classes, rehearsals or exposed to the public's gaze in performances, was to be in a place of safety. He had no need to be fearful. He knew exactly what was required of him as a dancer, what was good and what needed improvement. On stage, dancing a well-rehearsed routine, he could be in control, no longer lost or lonely. Since Miss Thomas valued him, encouraging him far more than her girls because he was a talented boy, he knew she wouldn't abandon him.

Back in Yarmouth for the summer holidays, Kenneth continued to perform – tap dancing, not ballet. He needed to get out of the Stanley Terrace house and away from his morose father, so he joined the Empire Orpheans, an amateur concert-party troupe based at the Empire cinema. The group was run by Edward Bowles, the manager of the cinema, which included live shows. The fourteen or so members, mainly plump teenage girls, provided their own costumes: Kenneth wore his Retford bow-tie outfit; his tap shoes were cricket boots with metal taps added by the local shoemaker. The Empire Orpheans, accompanied by Mr Bowles on the piano, toured American and British air-force bases in Norfolk. (The Second Air Division of the US Army Air Force had fifteen bases in East Anglia.) One Empire Orphean show, *Forces' Delight*, augmented by guest artists, lasted two-and-a-half hours. 'My mind boggles today to think how awful we must have been,' Kenneth told Peter Crookston in *The Times* in 1991. 'The airmen were very kind. They would feed us well and give us chocolates.'

William MacMillan remained uncomfortable with his son's dancing activities, mistrusting the attraction of dressing up and greasepaint for a growing teenager. He had no way of keeping Kenneth entertained during the school holidays, leaving him to wait, silent and resentful, outside the pubs William frequented. Whenever George was at home, he was instructed to take Kenneth around with him and his mates, so that the boy would move in masculine, older company. This enforced arrangement suited neither brother. Kenneth recollected, in his memoir, being posted as look-out, bored and suspicious, while George tried to seduce local girls under the pier. When George MacMillan learned, late in his life, that Kenneth had used this experience as the germ of a ballet, *Triad*, he scoffed at his younger brother's account of what went on: 'Absolute nonsense. Kenneth had a vivid imagination. A gang of us used to play fox-and-hounds along the sea front. If we set out first, we'd hide while the ones who were hounds searched for us. Kenneth had to keep watch to see if they were coming. I wasn't up to anything with the girls – their brothers would have been with us.'

True or otherwise, Kenneth was disturbed by the sexual conquests George and his friends boasted about while he hung around, eavesdropping. Still inexperienced, he was surrounded by older girls in the Empire Orpheans who enjoyed the attentions of the servicemen for whom they performed. The girls in the troupe were his main opportunity for sexual discovery but his encounters with them led only to frustration:

Early experiments with Sylvia were clinical and passionless. A couple of terms later, pretending sophistication, I lay on top of Thelma in her Morrison shelter but I still did not know how to proceed. Clearly aroused, I kissed her frantically but lacked the courage to take the next step. Her silent reproach made me think I should have stuck with Sylvia instead. But she was soon impregnated by a sailor and forced to marry when she was sixteen.

Kenneth became practised at keeping his life in separate compartments: home had nothing to do with school; dancing was distinct from both. He could be one kind of performer when he was with the Empire Orpheans, another when he was with Miss Thomas's troupe in Retford. At school, he was adept at entertaining his fellow pupils by imitating their teachers – a mimic's gift he exploited all his life. He could take off women as well as men, enjoying the school's odd convention of addressing all lady teachers (pressed into teaching boys during the war years) as 'sir'. His fellow pupils' laughter made him feel popular and accepted; he was disguising his deep-rooted sense of isolation as a motherless boy.

His theatrical talents had been meanwhile been recognised by his schoolteachers. In his first year, he, Ernest Fulcher and Percy Read had persuaded their form mistress, Mrs Phyllis Pereira, to help them produce *A Christmas Carol*. Kenneth was Scrooge, wearing a dressing-gown, his thick dark hair powdered grey. Ernie Fulcher was Marley's Ghost and Percy Read was Bob Cratchit. The Christmas goose consisted of papier mâché covered in batter, 'cooked' with the help of a teacher, Rose Masters, who still remembered the enterprising production decades later. Candles, a precious wartime commodity, could be used only on the night of the performance itself, which took place in St Swithin's Church Hall, to an invited audience of 'foster-parents', who were obligingly appreciative.

Then, before his voice broke, Kenneth was cast in the leading role of Kate in the school production of *The Pirates of Penzance* in 1942, boldly playing against teachers such as John Benson Whitehead, the deputy head. Whitehead ran the school's dramatic society and produced the annual play (or operetta) in Retford Town Hall. Kenneth enjoyed singing as a boy soprano and would accompany Vic Stowers to all sorts of church services in order to join in the hymns. Neither boy was particularly religious, but there was precious little else to do on Sundays, especially in winter.

The whole school was required to learn Stanford's setting of the *Te Deum* by heart as a 'leaving present' for the headmistress of Great Yarmouth Girls' High School. Both schools, jointly evacuated to Retford, took over St Swithin's Church for their choral performance to mark the headmistress's retirement. The boys' headmaster, A. H. G. Palmer, was a keen musician who played the organ for the *Te Deum* and for Naylor's *Benedicite*, another substantial work sung by the school. Percy Read said both works, which were learned over a considerable length of time, were imprinted on his memory for ever after.

The headmaster, Mr Palmer, nicknamed 'Alfie', organised a fortnightly music-appreciation circle for senior boys at his house. They listened to records from his large collection and were taken to concerts in nearby towns. Kenneth was eligible to join the circle in his third year, when he was fourteen. Palmer would sometimes begin morning assembly by announcing a piece of music – the third movement of Tchaikovsky's Fourth Symphony, for example – and the whole school would stand and listen to the recording. Kenneth always received good marks for music, though he never learned to read a score. He would continue to absorb music by listening, as he had been taught to do at school.

He also profited from the dedication of an art master, Gilbert ('Sammy') Sayer, who noted Kenneth's 'remarkable aesthetic qualities' in his final school report. Kenneth and Percy Read were keen members of the art guild Sayer had established, rivalling each other to achieve the highest marks or have their work put on display. Sayer would often ask the two boys to suggest subjects and settings for sketching expeditions around Retford and its countryside. According to Read, he was a teacher of the old school, who insisted on a proper grounding in the 'disciplines' of art, rather than encouraging free expression: 'Sammy used to say, "Learn to look and not just see", and he set us exercises in composition, light and shade, perspective, proportion . . . I am amazed at how much we absorbed from him.'

Sayer instructed them in the principles and practice of stage design. The art master was responsible for the set of one of the school plays, Patrick Hastings's thriller *Escort*, performed in the Town Hall in December 1943. He showed the boys how to make a model stage, build a staircase and paint a lifelike portrait as part of the decor. Kenneth was later to try his hand at designing sets for ballets, years before he started choreographing his own work. Once fully fledged as a choreographer, he was confident about collaborating with professional designers and fine artists. Great Yarmouth Grammar School had given him a good grounding for his future career in the theatre.

5

The year that Kenneth turned fourteen, 1944, was to be a momentous one for him. By now in Miss Thomas's Senior Troupe, he was appearing frequently in her shows. He was beginning to be fancied by the girls he was required to partner. They found him good-looking, with his soulful eyes and crop of dark brown hair. 'Hazel Ledger had quite a crush on him,' remembers Doreen Anthony, who was still a junior girl and therefore not in his league. 'Hazel went all goo-ga over him – we used to tease them. But I think the girls were keener than he was, at that age.'

His preoccupation was not girls but ballet: 'I woke up one day at the age of fourteen to find that out of the blue everything had crystallised. I had to be a ballet dancer,' he told Peter Crookston in 1991. His revelation was partly the result of hours of reading in Retford's municipal library, as he told Glenys Roberts in 1985: 'There I found lots of books on Nijinsky and I was transported into a world which seemed so exotic to me, living at a time when death and destruction was an everyday occurrence.' Also in the library were copies of the *Dancing Times*, going strong since 1910. In its paper-rationed pages was an advertisement from the Sadler's Wells Ballet School in London, established by Ninette de Valois to supply dancers for her company – later to become the Royal Ballet. The wording was enticing: 'The entry of suitable male students under the age of seventeen will, owing to wartime conditions, be particularly welcome, and in such cases, the Sadler's Wells Ballet School is willing to provide free tuition.'

De Valois had kept her school and company running throughout most of the war, even when Sadler's Wells Theatre was requisitioned as a shelter for bombed-out Londoners. The company had to move out, but the school remained in a rehearsal studio at the top of the theatre. De Valois needed a constant supply of male students to replace dancers called up for military service. As well as the advertisement offering free tuition for boys, she appealed, through the *Dancing Times*, to teachers throughout the country to let her know of any promising male dancer: 'At sixteen he may be vital to the continuance of British Ballet; at seventeen it may be too late.'

Kenneth urged Miss Thomas to intensify his ballet training so that he would be eligible for a scholarship before he was too late. He had spotted his escape route from his home life into an exciting profession that was crying out for boys like him. Miss Thomas decreed that he should prepare himself with proper qualifications. She entered him for the Grade One examination in the Royal Academy of Dancing's ballet syllabus, which then encompassed five junior grades. It was a courageous undertaking for a fourteen-year-old, since the girls taking Grade One at the same time would have been very much younger. (Miss Thomas's infant prodigy, Rosemary

Burton, had passed Grade One at the age of four.) Kenneth was awarded the top ranking of Honours, with 90 marks out of 100. 'The examiner [Irene Hammond, a well-respected RAD figure] remarked upon the great promise he showed in ballet work,' reported the *Retford Times* on 26 May 1944 – no doubt prompted by Miss Thomas. She started teaching him the rudiments of the first major RAD examination, Elementary.

But first she entered him and her other best pupils in the All-England Dancing Competition at Northampton in June. An annual contest, even in wartime, it received a record national entry of two thousand competitors in 1944. Kenneth MacMillan gained honours in 'musical comedy with song' and came fourth in ballet, out of nearly sixty entries. Jean Bradley won the All-England Acrobatic Cup and later went on to star as a contortionist at the Blackpool Ice Drome. She married Paul Raymond, the 'erotic entrepreneur', and became choreographer for the strip shows in Raymond's Revue Bar in Soho from 1958 to 1972.

Miss Thomas's troupe appeared shortly afterwards in Retford Town Hall, reprising their prize-winning numbers in a 'musical revuette' entitled *Reaching for the Stars*. One of the numbers for Kenneth and the senior girls, to 'If I Had My Way', had been adapted from a solo he had devised for himself. Miss Thomas had been too busy to think up a dance for him, so he had invented his own. He had won £10 performing it in a competition, a considerable sum for a youngster. Many years on, Joan Thomas, still agile in her eighties, demonstrated to the author a hornpipe step she had been impressed enough to remember from his original dance. He had begun to choreograph, without fully understanding the meaning of the term.

Since Kenneth's ballet exam results and the *Reaching for the Stars* revue were reported in detail in the *Retford Times*, his dancing triumphs can hardly have remained a secret from his schoolmates. He claimed, in an interview with Nicholas Tomalin in 1965, 'When I won any little prizes and my name was in the local paper I used to swear blind it wasn't me.' He wouldn't have fooled them for long.

The boys' attitude to ballet was in any case changing, thanks to the initiative of the headmaster and the Retford Arts Committee on which he sat. They organised a lecture–demonstration in the school hall on 24 June, entitled 'Ballet How and Ballet Why'. Retford had just experienced its first-ever visit from a professional ballet company, organised by the Committee for the Encouragement of Music and the Arts (CEMA), the wartime forerunner of the Arts Council. Ballet Rambert had performed for two nights (and one matinee) in the Town Hall on 11 and 12 April, during the Easter holiday. The programme had comprised *Les Sylphides, Bar aux Folies Bergères, Death and the Maiden, Façade, Carnaval,* and the pas de trois from *Swan Lake.* GYGS boys who had remained in Retford during the Easter break had gained free access to the performances by arranging the chairs and helping unload the scenery. But ballet-mad Kenneth wasn't there. He had to return home to Great Yarmouth because his grandmother was seriously ill.

He was present, however, for the lecture–demonstration in June explaining the background to ballet. The speaker, Deryck Lynham, was one of the founders of the Ballet Guild in London, and author of several books on ballet. The demonstration was given by Molly Brierley, who had just danced the leading role in the Ballet Guild's latest production, *The Last Curtain.* However rudimentary the school hall may have been, the lecture–demonstration was given by people who knew what they were doing. Equally evidently, Kenneth's school had no firmly held prejudice against ballet.

He, however, was in a certain amount of trouble. He had received three detentions for unsatisfactory conduct in the spring term of 1944, and seven during the summer term. His school reports did not explain the reason for the detentions, but since the sudden increase in bad conduct marks coincided with his fixation on ballet, his Grade One exam and the number of performances he was doing, he was probably inattentive and late for school lessons. Although his father was angry with him when he came home for the summer holidays, William MacMillan was even more furious with the master who had administered a caning severe enough to leave weals on his son's bottom. William, who resented overbearing authority, wrote a letter of protest to the school on his son's behalf. Vic Stowers, who remembered being surprised and impressed that the letter had been sent, doubted that it would have had any effect.

By the next term, the school was back in Great Yarmouth. As far as the pupils were concerned, the return to their home town after the school's four-year stay in Retford came as a surprise. The decision had been taken by the governors of the boys' and girls' grammar schools after the youngsters had broken up for the summer holidays in July 1944. By then, the Allies had landed in France and were battling to advance. Since Britain was no longer under direct threat of attack from the Continent, Great Yarmouth was considered safe enough for its schools to reoccupy their original buildings. The beaches along the coast were being cleared of the landmines and barbed-wire barriers placed against invaders, although it would be years before the resort could return to normality.

Both head teachers wrote to the *Retford Times* to thank 'the loyal citizens of Retford for their kindness, generosity, patience and self-sacrifice over the past four years'. The paper's editor commented, 'The news has been received with mixed feelings by the townspeople . . . joy that the evacuees are at home, though they will be greatly missed.' The youngsters had left for the summer holidays without realising that they would not return: they had not been able to say goodbye to their 'foster-parents'. Vic Stowers kept in touch with the Selbys, returning to visit them as well as writing to them regularly; Kenneth did not, for which he later felt remiss: ' I was so hell-bent on a career in the theatre that I could not wait to get away,' he wrote in a letter to Stowers in 1991. 'I must have seemed so careless and unthinking.'

He was still only fourteen and incapable of seeing further than himself. As far as he was concerned, the Selbys were already in the past. He was totally absorbed in planning his future.

Kenneth's brother George had been posted abroad after joining the Royal Army Service Corps. Life at home was going to be bleak enough without being deprived of his all-important ballet lessons. Kenneth's priority was to find himself another ballet teacher before his father realised what he was up to. Fortunately, the best-qualified instructor in the area was easy to track down: Kenneth had only to ask his school teachers' advice. Conveniently for him, Miss Phyllis Adams (Mrs Roche) was related by marriage to two of his teachers: the deputy head, 'Jimmy' Whitehead, and the English teacher, Amy Roche – 'a real old battleaxe', according to Percy Read. Her sister-in-law, Phyllis,. was to prove the next mentor and mother figure that Kenneth craved. Miss Thomas in Retford had set him on the right route; Miss Adams was to be the key that opened his future career.

Born in Yarmouth, Phyllis Adams had won a scholarship to Flora Fairbairn's Mayfair School of Dancing in London, where she studied for five years in the 1920s. Her teachers included Anna Pruzina and Laurent Novikoff, who had danced with Anna Pavlova's company and Diaghilev's Ballets Russes. Phyllis performed in *A Midsummer Night's Dream* at the Old Vic and danced at the London Coliseum. Instead of pursuing a professional career as a dancer, she decided to return home to Yarmouth at the age of twenty-four and establish her own dancing school. She continued to use her maiden name of Adams even after she had married a merchant seaman, by whom she had four children. She brought them up on her own during the war years, while her husband was at sea with the merchant fleet.

In 1944, the Roche family was living in a white stucco villa, Appledore, along the cliffs at Gorleston, across the river from Yarmouth proper. Miss Adams's dancing school was closed during the war because most of her pupils had been evacuated, but she still gave classes when and where she could. Her securest form of income was from the ballroom-dancing lessons she gave to soldiers at the Conservative Club in Yarmouth.

Kenneth had to pluck up the courage to face Miss Adams, whom he feared might be as formidable as his teacher Amy Roche. He rode his bicycle to the cliffs at Gorleston two or three times after school, still wearing his blazer, and circled the streets, not daring to knock on the door of 4 Bernard Road, which still had an anti-aircraft barrage balloon tethered outside. When he finally tapped on the door, and a kindly woman opened it, he blurted out as fast as possible, 'I want to be a ballet dancer. I want to get a scholarship to the Sadler's Wells School.' 'Oh, do you really?' she said. 'In that case, you'd better come in.' Kenneth had found his next surrogate family.

Phyllis Adams's children, Merrill, Wendy, Martin and Andrea, were all younger than Kenneth. She had a sick mother to look after, so the family had forgone evacuation from Yarmouth. Miss Adams was unwilling to leave the house for long, so she would sometimes give private dancing tuition in the kitchen at the back of the villa. Wendy remembers a sailor coming for tap lessons while the children waited hungrily outside the kitchen door.

The warm kitchen was where Kenneth did his daily class, straight after school, hanging on to a dresser in lieu of a ballet barre. It was curious piece of Arts and Crafts oak furniture, part kitchen dresser, part bookcase, known to the family as 'Road and River', after the inscription carved along its front. Miss Adams, aware of her partly trained pupil's talent, was happy to teach Kenneth without charge. She found him a pair of green tights and some black ballet shoes; when they wore out, his sister Jean paid for another pair. Miss Adams praised Kenneth's instinctive grasp of technique: he had to be shown a step only once to understand how to do it.

She must have been dismissive about the quality of his former ballet teaching, for Kenneth was later to play down the role of Joan Thomas in his training, saying he owed everything to Phyllis Adams. Miss Thomas and her troupe receive no mention in his draft memoir, nor does the signet ring that her students clubbed together to buy him as a memento after he had left Retford. He might have embarrassed about their amateur entertainments now that he was preparing to become a proper ballet dancer. In any case, he had relegated his involvement with them to his Retford past, along with the Selbys, and switched his allegiance to Miss Adams.

She impressed upon Kenneth the artistry of the career he wished to pursue, telling him about the Russian ballet tradition in which she had been taught, as well as the English virtues of de Valois's Sadler's Wells company. She had a stack of back copies of the *Dancing Times*, piled up to the ceiling of her little office. Wendy used to watch Kenneth set out to cycle home, laden with *Dancing Times* magazines. 'He'd come back the next day for more and question Mother like mad about what he'd read. She suspected he sat up all night and devoured them. She'd never had a pupil so hungry to learn.'

Kenneth took to eating his meals with the Roche family. They grew their own vegetables in the garden, so wartime rationing was less of a problem than it might have been. Wendy, the middle daughter, looked on Kenneth as an elder brother because he was around so much. 'We used to play together, even though he was a lot older than I was. We'd play ball games and chase each other around the house and along the beach. He hadn't really had a family childhood, so he was catching up, in a way.'

Mary Miller, another of Miss Adams's pupils, although at a slightly later period than Kenneth, had much the same experience with the Roche family: 'For me, like him, it was a revelation that life could be fun – not just a question of survival during the war. We'd both had rather bleak times at home in Yarmouth.' Mary had been evacuated to Retford, along with the Great Yarmouth Girls' High School, at the same time as Kenneth. One of her many billets was near his at the Selbys, so she sometimes joined him on the walks to and from school. 'He was the first boy who didn't tease me, and he had lovely big, dark eyes.' She had to leave school at fourteen to look after her mother, but she managed eventually to follow Kenneth's path to Miss Adams's school and house when the ballet bug bit her. 'Phyllis Adams was a rather imposing lady, with a big bosom and beautifully arched feet in high-heeled shoes. Very fine ankles,' Mary recalled. 'She wouldn't let anyone get above themselves, but she had a great sense of humour. She was a natural mother figure, without being sentimental about it.'

According to Wendy, her mother was a firm but kindly teacher: 'She wasn't a shouter. She believed in bringing things out in her pupils.' Kenneth was sufficiently confident of his progress – and impatient for his future – to apply for an audition at the Sadler's Wells Ballet School by the end of 1944, less than six months after meeting Miss Adams. He wrote a letter in his father's name, without consulting him, to Miss Ninette de Valois, Principal of the school: 'Dear Madam, My son, who is nearly fifteen, wants to be a ballet dancer and many people think he is very talented.' William MacMillan must have been taken aback when a letter arrived inviting his son to an audition in London.

Ninette de Valois was not likely to have been taken in by the youthful handwriting. She would, however, have paid attention to the separate letter that Phyllis Adams had written to the Sadler's Wells Ballet School, recommending her hard-working pupil. An audition was arranged for Kenneth shortly before his fifteenth birthday in December 1944. His father must have agreed, however reluctantly, because Kenneth, accompanied by his sister Betty, set out on the earliest morning train from Yarmouth to London. They had to make their way to the Prince's Theatre (now the Shaftesbury) in Shaftesbury Avenue, where the Sadler's Wells Ballet had, temporarily, been in residence since September. The company carried on performing throughout the hostilities, apart from a brief hiatus after war was declared. When they were not on tour, their London seasons were usually at the New Theatre (which in 1973 became the Albery and since 2006 has been the Noël Coward Theatre); they had moved towards the end of 1944 into the more spacious Prince's Theatre, which had a larger stage.

Kenneth's ad hoc audition simply involved taking part in the company's daily ballet class. De Valois had little time to spare for try-outs of hopeful students for her school, so he just had to cope as best he could. Kenneth always remembered his acute embarrassment and anxiety when she barked at him for arriving after the class had started. (He had lost time searching for the rehearsal room in which the class was held.) He cannot have been unacceptably late, for the dancers were still at the barre. He was placed between two ballerinas, Margot Fonteyn and Beryl Grey, a nerve-racking position for an inexperienced fourteen-year-old: he would have recognised who they were from his avid reading of the *Dancing Times*. He copied whatever they did, trying to remember Miss Adams's instructions and corrections for his still raw technique. He had never seen professional dancers in action before, let alone ballerinas of the stature of Fonteyn, Grey and Moira Shearer. When he returned to Yarmouth, he confided to Wendy Roche that he was over-awed by 'all these girls who could bend backwards until their heads touched their bottoms'.

He had to wait until after Christmas to learn whether he had won the longed-for scholarship. Ninette de Valois wrote to 'Miss Roche' on 8 January 1945, provisionally accepting him for the Sadler's Wells Ballet School, if his parents (*sic*) agreed. The school, which had closed for three months at the height of the v1 'flying bomb' attacks in mid-1944, after a bomb had landed very near Sadler's Wells, had reopened, though London was still under threat. Miss Adams must have explained that Kenneth was eager to start full-time training, as he was a relatively late starter in ballet. In her letter, de Valois commented:

I was extremely impressed with the boy from every angle. He was well grown, well made, has a good presence and is obviously intelligent.

What he has managed to do in one year nine months is quite extraordinary. I think his parents would be very wrong to stop him taking it up. I have to go to France with the company for the next eight weeks and would suggest that we hold over the matter of his Scholarship, maintenance, etc., until the Summer Term, which would start somewhere about May.

I would most definitely like to take him on, but it is almost impossible for me to arrange, at such short notice, matters with his parents; also,

London is pretty 'lively' at the moment at nights. [Censorship forbade direct reference to v1 bombs and v2 rockets.] I do not feel he has anything to lose by waiting another eight weeks or so.

For your information the maintenance grant is given when the parents have submitted to some form of 'Means Test'. Actually, the tuition would be free anyway, so it is only a question of his board and lodging in London. You have my permission to show this letter to his parents, and I thank you for bringing to my notice such a talented youngster.

Yours sincerely,

NINETTE DE VALOIS

Kenneth had achieved his ambition and no one was going to hold him back. His father had to give way, even though he had wanted his youngest son to pursue a 'respectable' (and well-paid) profession. Jean and Betty would have added their pleas to those of Miss Adams to give Kenneth his chance. William MacMillan might even have been secretly proud that his 'well-made' son had been chosen for a scholarship to a training institute in London.

The two months' wait would have seemed interminable to Kenneth, as he went back to school for his last term. His final report in March 1945 was a good one: under 'personal qualities', he was commended for being 'a thoughtful and conscientious worker . . . a pleasant personality with a keen sense of loyalty'. An unnamed teacher had added the bald comment: 'Learns ballet and dancing.' This time, he had had only three detentions for unsatisfactory conduct. He had won prizes for Junior Art and Junior French Reading, which were announced at school assembly along with other boys' achievements – and then he was singled out as the winner of a scholarship to the Sadler's Wells Ballet School. 'I nearly died of embarrassment because I didn't realise he [the headmaster] was going to do anything like that,' Kenneth recalled later, in the television documentary *Out of Line*. Ernest Fulcher, who was standing next to Kenneth, says that a titter ran round the assembly hall, from the Shells (the lowest form) to the Upper Sixth. Kenneth took his schoolmates' reaction stoically at the time but was too mortified to show his face at the school ever again. He was convinced he was a figure of fun. Other former members of the school, however, claim that they were impressed by his achievement.

Aged fifteen years and three months, Kenneth had effectively finished his formal education, leaving grammar school without any qualifications. He had been given a solid early academic foundation: many of his schoolmates went on to university. But in spite of his consistently good end-of-term marks, especially in English, Kenneth was always to feel inhibited about expressing himself in writing. Later in life, he would prepare drafts of letters to sort out what he wanted to say in advance; he would ask writer friends, such as the critic Clement Crisp, to check and advise on articles and programme notes that were to appear under his name. When he tried to start writing his own memoirs towards the end of his life, he went over the same ground, time and again, anxious about committing himself to a final choice of words. He wrote in pencil, then in ballpoint, scratching out and repeating variations of the same phrases. Although he could sometimes become blocked when creating choreography, he never felt as uncertain of himself as he did when faced with a sheet of paper.

6

When Kenneth finally arrived in London in the spring of 1945, the v1 and v2 scare was over, though the war in Europe would not be declared at an end until VE Day on 8 May. Although the Sadler's Wells Ballet company did not return to its home theatre until July, performing in the meantime at the New Theatre, the students had come back the previous year. Kenneth joined their daily classes, which took place between 9 a.m. and 2 p.m. in the rehearsal studio at the top of the 1930s theatre. There was some attempt to continue their academic education in the late afternoons, though the youngsters paid little attention. 'We were all packed into the upstairs bar at Sadler's Wells and we sat at long tables. We used to scrawl all over the wooden tables and ignore the unfortunate teacher, Mr Greenwood,' Kenneth recalled. Not until well after the war was over could the school offer proper educational facilities.

Kenneth had been found a place to stay in Highgate, North London, in a house filled with other dance students. The large property in Hornsey Lane was owned by Michael Boulton's mother, who looked after her son's friends and fellow students. Michael had joined the Sadler's Wells Ballet School after leaving Summerhill, the co-educational school run along experimental lines by A. S. Neill. 'I was a wartime gamble by Ninette de Valois,' said Boulton. 'I was given a scholarship without ever having put on a pair of tights, whereas Kenneth already knew how to dance.'

Mrs Boulton was a great organiser: 'One of those women who managed to do things, even during the war,' her son said. 'We had a big garden at the back, with vegetables and hens to lay eggs for us all. There were around ten students in the house at any one time, boys and girls, lots of them in transit as they found other lodgings nearer Sadler's Wells.' De Valois, in her book *Come Dance with Me*, paid tribute to the parents who allowed their children to train at the school during wartime conditions in London. By the time Kenneth arrived and the worst was over, there were only ten boys, all on scholarships, out of some forty pupils. Their numbers were to be boosted, once the war was over, by young recruits from the Commonwealth: Canadians, Australians, New Zealanders and South Africans, who arrived in force. They came because their dance teachers, most of whom had trained in Britain, had impressed on them that Sadler's Wells – and London – was the Mecca of the ballet world. Many of the Commonwealth students, homesick and hungry in post-war austerity, passed through Mrs Boulton's house before finding lodgings together.

The main meeting place, outside the theatre itself, was a dingy little café near the Angel underground station. It was run by a Miss Coe, an ageless spinster who took the orders, and her mother, who prepared them. The Coes were willing to serve tea and toast all day long, as the youngsters gathered at the trestle tables after class and rehearsals. Between them all, they had little money to spend. Kenneth relied on postal orders from his family: his brother George contributed regularly from his army posting abroad, and his sisters sent what they could. Jean would sometimes supply him with the treat of a home-made cake, which was carefully shared out among his friends.

The choice of meals at the Coes' café was limited. Kenneth became one of the ringleaders in obliging Miss Coe to recite the menu (which they all knew by heart) so that they could hear her unchanging Cockney litany: 'Mutton toad, sausage toad, beef and two veg., or I'll do you a nice egg.' Kenneth would then request politely, while the others muffled their giggles, 'Miss Coe, I didn't quite get that – would you run through it again?' 'Toad' consisted of a cheap meat filling cased in batter, usually accompanied by cabbage. Miss Coe's mother sat behind the serving hatch all day, patting the cabbage helpings into shape. Kenneth perfected his imitation of her: long chin, hairnet, cabbage-patting. He was equally adept at mimicking her daughter's weary whine.

Quiet and shy at first, Kenneth had found his milieu. He had learned at school how to make people laugh, but he had protected himself against mockery by guarding his secrets – especially his passion for dancing. 'For the first time, I was with people I could talk to about the things I really felt,' he wrote in his memoir. The Coes' 'cayff' was a great place for gossip and heated discussion, mainly about ballet. The students assessed each other's progress and argued about the abilities of dancers in the Sadler's Wells company: 'Every performance was dissected in detail,' said Michael Boulton. The students were given tickets to three or four performances in the New Theatre every week. If the theatre was sold out, four students at a time were allowed to watch from the wings. Competition was fierce for places allocated on a first-come, first-served basis. Boulton went regularly, as did Kenneth, arriving early to be sure of a place.

The first ballet Kenneth ever saw was *Giselle* at the New Theatre in April 1945, with Beryl Grey and Alexis Rassine in the leading roles. In those days, *Giselle* was given as part of a double bill – preceded in this case by Frederick Ashton's comic *Façade*. *Façade* was entertaining, but *Giselle*, for Kenneth, was, at last, the real thing. It was the perfect introduction to ballet as powerful dance-theatre: it has a tragic story that gripped his imagination, and a poetic second act in which a female corps of ghostly Wilis haunt the night in long white tutus. They move in unison as if with a single will, their skirts flying as they leap and dart in fleet steps. Giselle, as ethereal as a nineteenth-century romantic-ballet lithograph, dances tirelessly to save her remorseful lover from death. 'It was as if I'd been watching ballet all my life,' Kenneth said. 'It wasn't surprising at all. It was exactly as I'd imagined it.' There on stage were the images he had seen only in photographs, as he pored for hours over copies of the *Dancing Times*. His teachers, Joan Thomas and Phyllis Adams, had described ballets to him, giving him mental pictures of what he was striving towards. Now, watching the company he hoped to join, he saw what his amateurish efforts were supposed to look like, danced by experienced artists on stage, with dramatic lighting and scenery. This was the theatrical magic he craved and in which he continued to believe, even as he and his fellow students analysed how it was done.

There were no male teachers at the Sadler's Wells Ballet School when Kenneth joined. Classical-ballet classes were given by Ninette de Valois and Ailne Phillips. Ursula Moreton taught mime and Ruth French was in charge of the Royal Academy of Dancing syllabus. Boys were taught alongside girls, without male role models. Given wartime conditions followed by post-war austerity, most of the young men lacked the necessary upper-body strength to lift their partners convincingly in pas-de-deux work.

The students had been fortunate, however, in benefiting from the teaching of Vera Volkova. She was a Russian exile who had trained with Agrippina Vaganova in Leningrad (now St Petersburg), before leaving for Shanghai, where she met her English husband. She came to London with him and set up her own ballet studio in West Street, near Leicester Square. Margot Fonteyn, Pamela May and other Sadler's Wells Ballet dancers would go to her West Street classes, braving de Valois's disapproval at what she perceived as their treachery. Then, bowing to the inevitable, de Valois co-opted Volkova in 1943 to give company class and to teach at the Sadler's Wells School.

Their relationship subsequently soured, and de Valois told Volkova to choose between Sadler's Wells and West Street. Volkova chose her own studio. Many dancers (and students) followed her there, defying de Valois's ban. West Street became a Mecca for visiting dancers during the post-war period until Volkova left Britain for good in 1950. She eventually ended up in Copenhagen, where she trained the Royal Danish Ballet and a succession of internationally famous dancers, who came to her for expert coaching.

Volkova, with her Russian background, was particularly good at developing strong jumpers – one of the reasons that Rudolf Nureyev was to seek her out in Copenhagen after he defected to the West in 1961. Thanks to her classes, Kenneth became a proficient leaper, learning to split his long legs in the air like a Russian. Still gangly as a student, he was very supple and had highly arched feet – so much so that he used to borrow a pair of pointe shoes after class from tall, long-footed Nancy McNaught, to demonstrate that he could do the same steps *en pointe* as the girls.

De Valois wanted her students to gain as much theatrical experience as possible while they were still in training. Before Kenneth arrived, she had drafted senior students into the Sadler's Wells Opera production of Smetana's *The Bartered Bride*. They went on tour with the Opera company during the war, performing dances arranged in 1943 by a Czech exile, Sasha Machov. When *The Bartered Bride* returned to Sadler's Wells Theatre at the end of 1945, de Valois intended that the latest batch of students would perform in it as well. Her plan was that once they graduated from the School, the chosen ones were to form the core of a new, junior company, based at the Wells. As the Sadler's Wells Opera Ballet, they would dance in opera productions and develop their own repertoire of ballets to take on tour. At Sadler's Wells Theatre, they would take the place of the senior troupe, which was about to become the resident ballet company at the Royal Opera House in Covent Garden.

The move had been planned even before the war ended. The Opera House was leased during the war years to Mecca Enterprises as a palais de danse. Seats in the auditorium had been boarded over to make a dance floor for amusement-starved Londoners and servicemen on leave. When the five-year lease ran out at the end of 1944, Mecca was out-manoeuvred in its plan to renew it by a consortium of opera-lovers, headed by the music publishers Boosey & Hawkes. The Covent Garden Trust was formed and the government persuaded to take over the building. The Royal Opera House, instead of being run by a commercial company, would be subsidised as a lyric theatre for ballet and opera by public funds, channelled through CEMA (which was to become the Arts Council in 1945). CEMA's chairman was the influential economist John Maynard Keynes, who was married to the Russian ballerina Lydia Lopokova.

Instead of assuming that opera would take pride of place, Keynes was predisposed to favour the interests of ballet. He knew that de Valois's company had grown out of Sadler's Wells Theatre and into the heart of the nation, thanks to its valiant wartime performances. Audiences, including servicemen in the armed forces, had become loyal followers of the dancers, who had toured the country in trying conditions. It was effectively Britain's national ballet company and it deserved to be housed at the centre of the capital, in Covent Garden. A national opera company could be established later from scratch: the Sadler's Wells Opera was considered too weak for such exposure. In a series of adroit moves, Keynes arranged for Sadler's Wells to be compensated for the loss of its ballet company with a transfer fee of £15,000 and a second troupe of dancers to serve its opera company and entertain its ballet fans.

De Valois, alarmed at the scale of the prospect before her, had hesitated over moving her hitherto small-scale company into the big league. But this was an offer she could not refuse and the deal was agreed by the end of 1945. The Sadler's Wells Ballet (which would retain its original name until it was granted a Royal Charter in 1956) started preparing its grand production for the reopening of the Royal Opera House. It would dance the full-length version of Petipa's *The Sleeping Beauty*, until then better known in Britain by its Diaghilev-era title of *The Sleeping Princess*. By the time of the opening gala on 20 February 1946, every dancer in the company would be involved, as well as numbers of students as extras: they were needed to fill out the stage picture, costumed as pages, peasants and courtiers.

Overawed, Kenneth and his classmates inspected the empty auditorium while the theatre was under construction. It adjoined the Covent Garden fruit and vegetable market, which was still very much in action. The cavernous stage seemed to them 'as large as an aircraft hangar', as Kenneth was to describe it later in his programme notes for *The Prince of the Pagodas*. They were longing to appear on it, but although many of the girls in the ballet school would be needed as pretty pages or junior nursemaids, boys such as Kenneth were still too green and gawky to be entrusted with such an important premiere. They could only stand and watch *The Sleeping Beauty* rehearsals, while they waited to find out if they would make their stage debuts at Sadler's Wells, dancing in the *Bartered Bride* opera production.

The opera revival's first night at the Wells was on 26 December 1945, two weeks after Kenneth's sixteenth birthday. Eager for his first chance to appear in a professional production, he and another youngster, Donald Britton, put their names down for an audition. More experienced students had already been accepted as members of the new Opera Ballet company but Kenneth and Donald were still trainees. They prepared themselves carefully for their try-out, having been told by a practical joker in the opera company that they would, of course, be expected to audition wearing full stage make-up. The boys arrived with garishly painted faces for what turned out to be a routine rehearsal in street clothes. The opera staff were not particularly concerned about the dancers' ballet skills, provided they knew what they were doing. These two did, so they both got their first jobs as clowns and peasants – the best Christmas present two stage-struck sixteen-year-olds could have wanted.

The principal focus of the students' excitement, however, was the main company's lavish new production for Covent Garden, with sets and costumes designed by Oliver Messel. *The Sleeping Beauty* was to symbolise the awakening of the Royal Opera House – and the nation – from wartime austerity to peace and eventual prosperity. The theatre's meagre resources had to be stretched to the limit. Scene-painters transformed war-issue canvas into a fairy-tale palace; wardrobe seamstresses concocted courtiers' robes out of rationed fabrics and old curtains. The numerous costumes, including the tutus that looked so light and gauzy, needed to be durable: the production was to run for seventy-eight consecutive performances in the opening season before being given a rest.

On the first night, 20 February 1946, there was no room in the wings for ballet students not required in the production. The gala was as splendid as post-war conditions permitted: apart from invited dignitaries, many in the audience were still wearing uniforms or utility clothing. More formal outfits had evidently just come out of storage, for there was a perceptible smell of mothballs. King George VI, Queen Elizabeth and the two young princesses, Elizabeth and Margaret, arrived to occupy the royal box to the right of the stage, where they were visible to most spectators. Lord Keynes, standing by to greet the Royal Family, was overcome by severe chest pains. He was taken to his box to rest, while Lydia Lopokova did the honours for him. Although he felt able to watch the ballet after the second interval without further distress, he did not have much longer to live. Several weeks later, following an arduous trip to the United States, he suffered a major heart attack. He died at home at Easter, while *The Sleeping Beauty* continued its run.

The gala has gone into Royal Ballet legend as a triumph, setting the seal of Establishment approval on de Valois's hitherto modest company. De Valois had developed the young Margot Fonteyn (by now aged twenty-six) into the company's prima ballerina, flanked by other excellent principal dancers, such as Beryl Grey, Pamela May and Moira Shearer, as well as the former Bolshoi soloist, Violetta Prokhorova. But apart from Australian Robert Helpmann, who partnered Fonteyn's Aurora on the opening night, most of the male contingent were rusty after serving in the armed forces. Many had been demobbed only at the end of 1945, giving them less than two months in which to transform themselves back into dancers.

The corps de ballet was unaccustomed to performing in such an imperial-scale production on such a large stage. Mary Clarke, describing the first performances in her history of the company, noted, 'Large groups of courtiers or fairies were not making their presence felt sufficiently, and although the performance was beautifully rehearsed and well executed, it did not have any great strength of impact.' None the less, for enthusiastic youngsters such as Kenneth and his fellow students, who had no basis for comparison, *The Sleeping Beauty* was the most magnificent production imaginable. They were able to be in the audience by the second night, impatient to be part of it. Kenneth saw every performance for three weeks before he was co-opted first as an extra, then as a dancer in the Act III mazurka.

Standing at the back of the stalls, night after night, he struck up a friendship with another avid student, John Cranko, recently arrived from South Africa. Cranko, at eighteen, two years older than Kenneth, was already determined to become a choreographer. He had tried his hand at ballets in Cape Town and had come to London as soon as he could to join the Sadler's Wells School and then the company. He and Kenneth first enthused over the production and then discussed it in depth. Cranko, more analytical than inexperienced Kenneth, who had only recently seen his first *Giselle*, led their discussions about *The Sleeping Beauty*'s structure and the challenges it posed for dancers. 'We, John Cranko and I, were immensely impressed with the choreography of the Petipa classic and I knew that I had not seen anything so magical in my young life,' Kenneth remembered in *Dance Gazette* (June 1990). Both future choreographers were thus imprinted, early on, with the steps and structure of

The Sleeping Beauty, 'as beautifully and formally laid out as the gardens of Versailles', according to Kenneth.

Both were soon appearing on stage in Oliver Messel's fairy-tale costumes, continuing their friendship as they graduated from walk-on roles into dancing ones, swelling out the corps de ballet. (Their first, shabby, communal dressing-room bore a sign marked 'Pages, Mice and Students'.) Cranko's main ambition was not to make his way through the ranks to soloist status: he was interested in learning more about how ballets worked. Kenneth, a much better dancer than Cranko, dreamed of taking on the roles he watched. In a few years' time, he would be dancing featured roles in the Act III divertissement of *The Sleeping Beauty*: Florestan in the pas de trois, and, briefly, the virtuoso Bluebird.

Kenneth was formally accepted into the junior company, initially called the Sadler's Wells Opera Ballet, in time for its first season of ballets, which opened at the Wells on 8 April 1946. His pride in his first full-time contract was undermined by the news that his father was seriously ill with broncho-pneumonia. A telegram to Sadler's Wells summoned him urgently to the Yarmouth hospital on 29 March. George, whose regiment had been posted to Mombasa in East Africa, was not granted compassionate leave, so Kenneth and his two sisters went to their father's deathbed without him.

Struggling to describe the scene in his notes for his memoir, Kenneth recalled trying to shut out his feelings, and his father's ranting voice, by concentrating on the drunken swearing of another patient on the ward. His father, meanwhile, was cursing Jean as a 'bloody whore'. Uncomprehending in her deafness, she asked what he had said. 'We pretended that he was delirious, which was a half-truth. My father asked me to kiss him, and I hesitated for a moment, taken aback by this sudden and simple request for affection.' William then declared that Kenneth was the only one of them who would come to any good. 'Betty looked at me in disbelief as he focused on the end of the bed and called out "Edith", as if he could see our mother. This supernatural experience seemed to calm him and he closed his eyes.'

A nurse came in and pronounced William MacMillan dead. Betty and Jean gave way to tears, while Kenneth sat like a stone.

I was overcome by loneliness, and later at the funeral, when George had returned, I felt like a stranger, unable to join the others in their grief or to offer any comfort. My mother's death had left me untrusting of love and I was unable to give my father the warmth he craved. It was an emotional paralysis that masked my real feelings for years to come.

Puzzled by his seeming indifference to the most dramatic personal events in his life, sixteen-year-old Kenneth returned to London immediately after his father's funeral. Parentless, he no longer had a home to which he felt he belonged. De Valois had been reluctant to let him go for more than a few days, since he was needed for the final rehearsals before the launch of the Sadler's Wells Opera Ballet. His souvenirs of his father were a clock in a wooden case, presented to 'Gunner MacMillan on the occasion of his wedding to Edith Shreeve', and a 'silk' dressing-gown. Kenneth had requested it as a present from his father, to wear in theatre dressing-rooms over his ballet clothes. William had sent the imitation-Noël-Coward dressing-gown (probably made of artificial silk) to Kenneth for his sixteenth birthday. Proud of his youngest son's success, William had swallowed his distaste for the unmanly ballet world: if Kenneth wanted a dressing-gown, he deserved one as good as any of his fellow performers.

William did not live to see Kenneth perform as a professional ballet dancer. George, who died in 2000, never attended any of his brother's ballets. He did not ask for an invitation to a performance, and Kenneth seems never to have extended one. He had elected to make his career in dance without the involvement of the male members of his family.

7

De Valois's plan for her junior company at Sadler's Wells was that it should dance an audience-friendly combination of existing ballets and specially created ones. Young dancers could cut their teeth on such well-tried favourites as *Les Sylphides* and Act II of *Casse-Noisette* (as the Nutcracker was then called); she and Ashton would give them those of their ballets no longer suited to the large Covent Garden stage, and the company would have its own resident chore-ographer, Andrée Howard.

Performances at first were to be just once a week on Monday nights, with occasional Saturday matinees. Ticket prices were kept low, in accordance with Lilian Baylis's policy of accessibility for her Sadler's Wells Theatre. The novice corps de ballet, aged between fifteen and seventeen, was reinforced with experienced soloists from the Covent Garden company. With time, the most talented of the juniors would graduate into the senior company. Choreographers who had learned their craft at Sadler's Wells could then make ballets for the Royal Opera House stage.

The Sadler's Wells Opera Ballet danced its first full evening of ballets on Monday, 8 April, ten days after the death of Kenneth's father. The programme opened with de Valois's *Promenade* from 1943, adapted for the new company. It was a slight and charming suite of dances, linked by a lepidopterist who concentrated on catching butterflies in a park while young people came and went about him. The Lepidopterist was Claude Newman, the company's ballet master. Kenneth, who was not entrusted with a role in *Promenade* on the opening night, was later cast in the pas de trois, with Peter Darrell and Diana Field.

The first mention of MacMillan's name in a printed programme is in the second ballet, as a Gentleman in Andrée Howard's *Assembly Ball*, created for the company. Set to Bizet's Symphony in C, the ballet had no story other than the interplay of guests at a society ball. Kenneth was one of four sophisticated gentlemen, along with Michael Hogan, Peter Darrell and Alan Baker. The triple bill ended with the 'Kingdom of the Sweets' divertissement from *Casse-Noisette*. The leading role of the Sugar Plum Fairy was taken by Margaret Dale, a guest from the Covent Garden company. Seven years later, she would choreograph a ballet with Kenneth MacMillan as the leading character.

The young company's debut was warmly received. 'There was such infectious vitality, the dancers were manifestly so eager and enthusiastic, that they persuaded us to ignore minor shortcomings and simply enjoy the occasion with them,' reported the *News Chronicle*. Kenneth, even though numbed by his father's death, could not help being caught up in the excitement. He was a professional dancer at last, earning all of £2 10s a week. His time was fully occupied with rehearsals for the growing repertoire. By July, when the company set out on its first regional tour, four more ballets had been added: Fokine's *Les Sylphides*, Ashton's *Façade*, de Valois's *The Gods Go A-Begging* and a new work, *Khadra*, by a member of the senior company, Celia Franca.

Kenneth by now had moved from Mrs Boulton's house in Highgate to lodgings in Myddleton Square, just behind Sadler's Wells Theatre. He shared a room with Michael Hogan, known to fellow dancers as Michel because his mother was French. According to Hogan, the place was so shabby that the lace curtains disintegrated if they were touched. 'The house was run by an old lady, a Jehovah's Witness, who was always trying to convert us.' Hogan had no objections to sharing a room because he came from a large family and was used to acting as big brother:

Kenneth was shy, hiding his nervousness. He didn't articulate his feelings. We talked endlessly but not about ourselves. We were both grammar-school products who had become totally obsessed with ballet, so we had quite a lot in common. We played records and discussed the ballets we'd seen and how the other dancers performed.

The discussions continued at Miss Coe's 'cayff', where the company, no longer students, still gathered for tea and toast after rehearsals. On pay-day Friday afternoons, they abandoned the cheap, dingy café for the brighter lights of the Lyons Corner House near the Angel underground station. After treating themselves to chocolate éclairs with synthetic cream for tea, they went to the local flea-pit cinema, keeping just enough money from their wage packets to pay for their lodgings.

The lease of the house in Myddleton Square was soon taken over by Paul Wilson, a former major in the Intelligence Service who became a photographer. He kept on the tenants, including an art student named Anthea, who had become a close friend of Kenneth. 'Not necessarily a girlfriend,' says Hogan. 'He needed someone outside the ballet world.' They used to go to art exhibitions and galleries together. Once the company started touring, however, Kenneth's constant companion became Greta Hamby, a dancer he had known since their time together at ballet school, when she was still only fourteen. A photograph from those days shows her smiling, sitting on his knee.

Greta, as a youngster, was small, fair and skinny, 'hungry for everything', she says. 'You have to bear in mind how young we all were. We were like a family of kids, all going round together. We'd go and watch horror movies, Cocteau films, *The Red Shoes* [released mid-1948] over and over – we couldn't get enough.' Josephine Gordon, one of their gang of dancer friends, remembers Kenneth saving Greta's life in the Lyons Corner House: 'She choked and went blue in the face. Ken pulled her arms up with a flourish – he seemed to know what to do.'

This action-man image sits oddly with one of Kenneth's nick-names of the time, Lily Loo. 'He was tall, gangly, gazelle-like, with these lovely dark eyes. He'd outgrown his strength,' says Jo Gordon. Hamby emphasises fondly what fun he was as a young man: 'He was very gentle, with a wicked sense of humour. His impersonations were quite lethally good. And he was used to going around with girls, because of his sisters and the kids at his dancing classes.'

As well as being ringleader at Miss Coe's café, he conducted seances in a Sadler's Wells dressing-room. There are echoes of his mother's theatrical tea-leaf readings in the way the dancers were required to put their fingers on an upturned glass as Kenneth summoned the spirit of Joseph Grimaldi, the Victorian clown who used to perform in the old Wells Theatre. 'Grimaldi' would prophesy via the movements of the glass who would get married and who would dance certain roles, until laughter or tears brought the session to an end. The seances became a craze within the company, played whenever time was heavy on their hands.

The teenage dancers treated the theatre like a playground. When they were required to perform in a long opera such as *Faust*, in which they were needed only for the *Walpurgisnacht* ballet, they would play hide-and-seek for the rest of the time through the theatre, hiding in skips and going onto the flat roof, forbidden territory at night. They would cut it fine for their entry, rushing on stage at the last minute, barging into the opera chorus and getting into trouble for singing along instead of dancing mutely. Outside rehearsal hours, they expended energy practising the ballet lifts they were learning and inventing new ones, using the smallest and lightest of the girls, like Hamby and Gordon, as gallant guinea-pigs.

'We were an odd generation because we hadn't really had time to grow up,' reflects Greta.

We were children of the war, and then we were pushed hard, physically, while we were still very young. De Valois used to tell us, 'You have to grow up three years for every one because you're professionals.' If a girl was missing from class because she had a bad period pain, Madam [the form of address by which she was known to members of her company] would say, 'Get her in here at once.'

No quarter was given. However immature and undisciplined the dancers might be in their private lives, they were expected to be perfectionists where work was concerned.

For the first time, Kenneth and other former students from the school were being instructed by expert male teachers. Their ballet master, Claude Newman, taught the boys' class; Keith Lester, a well-known professional dancer and choreographer, and Michael Somes, from the Covent Garden company, gave them pas-de-deux lessons. The home-grown contingent of male dancers was still pretty frail in technique and physique. The stronger men were mostly better-fed 'colonials' from the Commonwealth, as the post-war arrivals began to be taken into the Sadler's Wells Opera Ballet. It was soon nicknamed the Home and Colonial, after the London department stores of the time.

South African John Cranko, for example, got into the company simply because he could accomplish lifts the British youngsters could not. George Gerhardt, one of the few mature male dancers to join the company in its earliest days, announced that he was leaving as it was about to go on tour for the first time in July. Gerhardt, built like a tank, was the only man who could bring off the impressive lifts in Celia Franca's ballet *Khadra*. Cranko persuaded Peggy van Praagh, the junior company's ballet mistress, to let him audition by trying the difficult lifts. Still a student at the ballet school, he trained every night in his digs with weights and got the job – though he subsequently suffered a hernia.

Nearly nineteen, Cranko soon became a magnet around whom a coterie of dancers clustered. He had a charming, outgoing personality and a fund of stories about his life in South Africa, as well as about the racy social circles he was discovering in London. Allegiances were starting to shift as the youngsters found their feet and forged their new identities. Most of them, especially the teenage girls, were sexually inexperienced, still rather shocked by those who 'went all the way'. They were more interested in discovering themselves as performers, learning fast in the hot-house atmosphere of their early tours. Cranko, worldly, openly homosexual, was studying them as potential material for his choreography. The company was to be his laboratory.

The first provincial tour, for six weeks in July and August 1946, was to Exeter, Brighton, Bath, Cambridge and Cheltenham, ending with a season in Finsbury Park, North London. The Sadler's Wells Opera Ballet was intended to serve the smaller theatres in the regions, which had little or no other opportunity of seeing ballet, while the Covent Garden company visited the cities with large theatres. Peggy van Praagh, later to be the junior company's Assistant Director, was in sole charge of the troupe on tour. She had been a member of the Ballet Rambert and of Antony Tudor's London Ballet before joining de Valois's company during the war. Well accustomed to the rigours of touring, she dealt good-humouredly with her young charges' boisterous behaviour. The boys became so drunk during their first week on tour that they failed to turn up for morning class, learning their lesson the hard way as they struggled to make it through matinee performances.

The tour served as their summer holiday, especially in the pleasant seaside resort of Brighton. There they strolled along the pier and promenade and practised ballet lifts in their bathing suits on the beach. Photographs of the period show Kenneth laughing among his dancer friends, a peer group equivalent of the family album snaps of him as a boy on the seashore at Great Yarmouth. He and his fellow dancers had bonded into a close-knit clan, all of them young, mutually supportive and living in a near-fantasy theatrical world that had largely dislocated them from family life.

He no longer had much cause to return to his former home town. His sister Betty and her husband, Victor Harmer, had moved into 12 Stanley Terrace, where their two sons would grow up. Kenneth did not belong there any more. He had cut himself off from George, who was still with the army in Mombasa, by writing to tell him that he wanted to end their one-way correspondence. Hurt, George stopped writing. He had sent dutiful letters to all the family while he served abroad, enclosing money orders, some of which were passed on to Kenneth. If Kenneth snubbed his brother as abruptly and heartlessly as George recalled, it might have been because Kenneth was trying to obliterate their shared past. He believed, in any case, that his ballet career would have met with scorn from George and his fellow soldiers in an army barracks. He saw no point in exchanging letters containing information that could have been of little or no interest to either of them.

He did remain in regular contact with Jean, his favourite sister, who had married after their father's death. Her husband, Arthur Sparham, who was ten years younger than she was, had been a kitchen porter in a hotel where she had worked at the end of the war. They set up together as boarding-house keepers in Yarmouth. Kenneth was always welcome there if he did want to visit her and the town. Jean wrote regularly, and lovingly, to Kenneth throughout her life; he kept her letters, and evidently did reply, if not as often as she would have wished. He confided in Greta Hamby how concerned he was about Jean's deafness: he was always investigating better hearing-aids for her. He rarely talked about the rest of his family, however, even to Greta, and he expunged all trace of a Yarmouth accent from his voice. He was reinventing himself, adopting the distinctive light camp whine that successfully disguises so many dancers' origins, as well as signalling a group identity.

Back in London for the last leg of the tour in late August, the Opera Ballet performed in the little open-air theatre in Finsbury Park. 'If it rained, we used to count how many people turned up to see us,' remembers Greta Hamby. 'If there were fewer than in the company, we were allowed to abandon the performance and go off to see something else. Usually another ballet company.' During their tour, Peggy van Praagh had brought them briefly back to Covent Garden to catch the first-ever visit of the Ballet Theatre company from New York (later known as American Ballet Theatre). The young dancers were wildly excited by their first exposure to American ballet, in particular Jerome Robbins's *Fancy Free*. Created in 1944, it depicts in vivid vernacular dance the adventures of three sailors on shore leave in New York – the genesis of the movie musical *On the Town*. Robbins himself was one of the sailors in the 1946 London performances, along with Michael Kidd and John Kriza. British audiences had never seen men in a ballet company perform so exuberantly and so engagingly. Returning to their touring digs, the Opera Ballet boys danced their version of *Fancy Free* up and down the train corridors, leaping off the tables and seats in emulation of the sailors.

They had already been stimulated by chic, modern French ballet. The Ballets des Champs-Elysées had arrived at the Adelphi Theatre in London in April, just as the Sadler's Wells Opera Ballet launched its own season. Since the Wells company was performing only on

Monday nights, they had spare evenings to see their French contemporaries. The newly formed Ballets des Champs-Elysées, run by Boris Kochno, Diaghilev's former assistant, featured ballets by Roland Petit, still only twenty-one. Kenneth was particularly taken by his *Les Forains*, about a wistful group of strolling players. Its motley performers looked like weary Picasso acrobats as they went through their circus routines in Christian Bérard's stylishly minimalist set.

Petit returned regularly to London in the years to come, with the Ballets des Champs-Elysées, then with his own company, the Ballets de Paris. They were part of an influx of foreign companies, introducing new and old repertoires to ballet-hungry audiences. Ballets from the Diaghilev era and its aftermath were still doing the rounds, revived by, among others, Colonel de Basil's Ballets Russes and the Marquis de Cuevas's Grand Ballet de Monte Carlo. Kenneth was able to catch up fast with works he had only read about, performed by these visiting troupes as well as by British companies.

Post-war audiences were avidly curious, not yet ossified into wanting to see the same handful of 'classics' whose names they recognised in advance: *Swan Lake*, *The Sleeping Beauty*, *The Nutcracker*, *Giselle*. Choreographers were experimenting with all kinds of styles and subject matter. There was no consensus view, then, that ballet was a minor art form, dealing mainly with fairy stories. As Kenneth had found within months of seeing his first-ever ballet performance, ballet could encompass, murder, insanity, suicide and unbearable grief: it could also be comic, vulgar, witty and sophisticated.

The Opera Ballet's repertoire expanded rapidly as it settled in for its first full season at Sadler's Wells, from October 1946 to the following May. Among the new works it acquired were some gorily melodramatic ones, providing the dancers with opportunities to try out their acting abilities. Anthony Burke, who had recently joined the company as a choreographer as well as a dancer, came up with *The Vagabonds*, based on a Thomas Hardy poem, 'A Trampwoman's Tragedy'. Two gypsy men want the same girl. Her lover kills his rival and in the ballet is in turn ritually executed by the tribe. The girl goes mad with remorse and dies; the lovers are reunited in death. Kenneth, whose own ballets would often feature such sexual triangles, had a minor part as one of the gypsy band.

Kenneth had already appeared in a workshop ballet by Burke, *Masquerade*, which was later taken into the repertoire. Burke had made it for the Royal Academy of Dancing Production Club, which had been set up before the war to encourage the creation of new works. The Production Club flourished in the immediate post-war years, presenting matinees at the New Theatre and Sadler's Wells. Kenneth danced in a number of these workshop matinees.

Andrée Howard, the company's resident choreographer, had also taken on a nightmarish subject for her new ballet, *Mardi Gras*. She had been a successful choreographer and designer with the Ballet Rambert, but she had suffered a succession of nervous breakdowns after the war. She was given electric-shock treatment, which distressed her and impaired her confidence. By the time de Valois asked her to make ballets for the new touring company, Howard was prone to agonise over her creations. For *Mardi Gras*, in November 1946, she took as her theme a quotation from a Shakespeare sonnet that reflected her own inner turmoil: 'My grief lies onward and my joy behind'. A young girl is lost in a terrifying world of fantasy, surrounded by grotesque carnival figures and circus performers. Anne Heaton, still only sixteen, was the girl who eventually sees herself lying in her own coffin. Kenneth was one of the sinister revellers.

Mardi Gras came in for criticism as being too morbid for a young company, so Howard revived one of her earlier ballets, *La Fête étrange*, based on the chateau-party episode in the novel *Le Grand Meaulnes*. Delicate and wistful, the haunting work had been created for the small wartime London Ballet. Howard expanded its choreography and its designs, by Sophie Fedorovitch, for the Sadler's Wells stage. Greta Hamby, paired with Kenneth as party guests, remembers having a row with Kenneth because she claimed he wouldn't partner her properly. He was entrusted only with corps-de-ballet roles, mostly anonymous. One of the few ballets in which his flair for comedy could be exploited was Ashton's *Façade*, in which he was one of the clod-hopping Tyrolean mountaineers, along with Cranko and Peter Darrell.

By the time the company set out on its second tour in May 1947, it had a new name. Instead of the Sadler's Wells Opera Ballet, which implied it existed mainly to perform in operas, it would be known as the Sadler's Wells Theatre Ballet. The tour opened in Brighton, where Kenneth made his debut in his first featured role as a professional dancer: Florestan in Fokine's *Carnaval*. The role is a small but important one in a charming ballet from 1910 that is now rarely performed. It requires technically accomplished dancers who can also make a strong impression as *commedia dell'arte* characters. The leading roles went to Leo Kersley, alternating with David Poole as Pierrot; Donald Britton as Harlequin; and Anne Heaton as Columbine. The company was coached by the former Russian ballerina Tamara Karsavina, who had been Fokine's original Columbine – and the production was much praised.

Brighton also saw John Cranko's first ballet for the company. *Adieu* had originally been given as a party piece at the Vic–Wells New Year Ball, where de Valois had enjoyed it. Only five dancers were involved but the whole company was aware that Cranko was being tried out as a future choreographer, and his status rose accordingly. Kenneth, who knew that his friend was not highly regarded as a dancer, was impressed that John's ideas for ballets were being taken seriously by Peggy van Praagh and de Valois. Cranko's *Tritsch-Tratsch Polka*, which de Valois had seen on the same occasion as *Adieu*, was soon added to the repertoire, and Kenneth would have a role in the next one, *Children's Corner*. Cranko was on his way.

When the company returned to Sadler's Wells, tired after the twelve-week tour, they were coerced back into shape by Harijs Plucis, the burly Latvian ballet master of the Covent Garden company. Kenneth still had a lot to learn. 'For the first time, Plucis made me realise how, actually, men should move. He was appalling to us in class if we didn't jump at the speed he wanted us to – and we were mostly skinny little boys who were starved from the war,' he said in an interview with Susan Crow.

Greta Hamby confirmed that Kenneth 'wasn't filled out enough on top to be a good partner', but he was fast becoming an elegant dancer. He had certainly advanced sufficiently to catch the eye of Frederick Ashton who came to cast his new ballet that October. Peggy van Praagh had requested his *Valentine's Eve*, an early Ballet Rambert piece from 1935, but Ashton decided to create a fresh work for the company to the same music, Ravel's *Valses nobles et sentimentales* – the title of the new ballet.

He wanted it danced by five very young couples; Kenneth, one of the chosen men, was still only seventeen. In the original for

Rambert, a red velvet Valentine heart had been passed among the performers, as the principal girl tried to make up her mind whom to choose. The new version was more abstract, though the girl (Anne Heaton) still flirted with two rival suitors. The couples changed partners from waltz to waltz, silhouetted sometimes against curved screens that suggested an ante-room to a ballroom. Ashton demanded that his dancers yielded their bodies to the music rather than to each other, preserving an almost Edwardian decorum. The theatre director Peter Brook, writing as a critic in the *Observer*, commented that Sophie Fedorovitch's pink and claret designs 'evoke a mood, hot-house and Proustian, that catches the very essence of the waltz'.

Kenneth told Susan Crow he was intrigued by Ashton's collaborative approach in choreographing *Valses nobles*:

He'd ask me, 'What did you think of that?' which surprised me – that someone like him would ask a mere dancer what they thought. Actually, he must have sensed something in me that I didn't even know then: that I wanted to be a choreographer, because he used to bring me out of the corps de ballet and sit me down next to him and say, 'What do you think?'

Company members of the time – Maryon Lane, Nadia Nerina, Leo Kersley, Peter Darrell – remembered Kenneth constantly improvising and experimenting in rehearsals, which Ashton must have noticed. He gave Kenneth challenging steps, with frequent turns, twists and changes of direction.

His interest in Kenneth may also have been because Ashton was a promiscuous homosexual, to a degree that drove Michael Boulton's mother to warn de Valois that Ashton was a threat to the young dancers in her charge at her boarding house. At the time of *Valses nobles*, however, he was in love with an American dancer, Dick Beard. He wrote to Beard that *Valses nobles* was 'a ballet about us'. Ashton's biographer, Julie Kavanagh, points out that the ballet contains poses echoing those in Ashton's treasured collection of photographs of Beard by the *Life* magazine photographer Hans Wild: 'Behind every dreamy, photogenic attitude of the five boys lies the image of Beard . . . the narcissistic poses have the studied elegance and veiled erotic charge of fashion plates.'

Although Ashton the romantic might have been evoking the glamorous, absent Beard as he created the ballet, he was involved at the same time in a more down-to-earth affair with a young English dancer in the Covent Garden company, Brian Shaw. Shaw (whose family name was Earnshaw) was friendly with several dancers in the junior company, including Peter Darrell. While Shaw was still a ballet student, he had lodged with the Skinners, Peter's parents. Peter Skinner, on joining the junior company at the same time as Kenneth, had adopted the stage name of Darrell: Skinner was felt to be too reminiscent of the untheatrical shoe-store chain, Lilley & Skinner.

Darrell, the same age as Kenneth, was openly homosexual. His mother, Floss, assured one of her son's gay friends, 'Don't worry, I know all about Peter. I just let him get on with it.' The Skinners lived in West Drayton, near Heathrow Airport, above and behind the tobacconist's and newsagent's shop owned by Peter's father, Leonard. Kind and rather fey, Leonard would collect his son's friends after Saturday performances and drive them to West Drayton to stay. When the Skinners moved to Pulborough in Sussex, Leonard would meet the dancers on tour in Brighton and take them home for the weekend. Ashton and Shaw were often among the car's passengers, which included Kenneth as well as Cranko, Peter Wright and anyone else who wanted to get away from the theatre. Darrell would remark in later years that if his father's car had crashed with them all in it, Britain's choreographic talent would have been wiped out overnight.

Kenneth certainly moved in homosexual circles – it would have been hard not to in a ballet company at that period – without yet knowing what his sexual orientation might be. Discreet friends suggest that he experimented with men, which was far easier than with the inexperienced young women in the company, who would be terrified of pregnancy. Whatever he did he kept secret, for he was never seen with a 'pal' even among friends who were unabashedly camp. Gay theatricals had no inhibitions when they were among their own kind, but he did. If the objects of his teenage lust were indeed male, he was uncomfortable with the realisation, and he was embarrassed by the attentions of older men. He told Lynn Barber in 1982, 'I was terribly, terribly shy. I used to think, you know, that people of thirty were old, and to have a conversation with an older person was agony for me. I thought I was hideous looking because I had adolescent acne – I thought I was awful. And I was very puritanical, very shockable . . . I was so shy I wouldn't dare do anything, not even kiss'. He could not escape the internalised pressure he had known since childhood of his father's and older brother's hostility towards homosexuality. Kenneth knew that if he was attracted to men, he was confirming their conviction that all male ballet dancers were 'queer'.

His closest emotional relationships were, and always would be, with women. After his mother's death, the important women during his boyhood had been his sisters and his ballet teachers, Miss Thomas and Miss Adams. The powerful figures in both Sadler's Wells Ballet companies were women: Ninette de Valois and her assistant Ursula Moreton; Peggy van Praagh and her assistant Barbara Fewster. He had been used to the company of young female dancers during his adolescence, and got on well with the girls in the corps de ballet, who regarded him as Greta Hamby's boyfriend. 'They were inseparable – young and sweet like a couple of does,' remembers Leo Kersley. 'Yes, we were an "item" for a long time when we were young,' Hamby confirms. 'But we held hands, nothing more. In those days, we didn't have sex with each other. After we'd known each other for ages, he once said to me, "If we feel like this in a year's time, shall we get engaged?" But when the time came, it was rather too late for me.'

In the meantime, there was the attraction of the smart talk, bitchy gossip and intellectual stimulation of the gay world – whether or not sexual activity was involved. Those with ambitions to be choreographers talked endlessly about what could be done – what they would do – with ballet. They were educating themselves by going to art-house films and getting to know the work of the stylish artists who designed for the Ballets des Champs-Elysées. Darrell and Cranko, both well connected with London's gay scene, seemed immensely sophisticated to Kenneth. Darrell, raffish and good-looking, was taken up by the remnants of the Bloomsbury Group. He used to boast of being invited to Bunny Rogers's bohemian fancy-dress parties. (Rogers, a socialite from the 1920s onwards, was a friend of Ashton.)

Cranko had been introduced to the gay underground world of London soon after he arrived in Britain. According to a letter quoted by his biographer, John Percival, a friend from South Africa had taken Cranko to 'some queer pubs which are too fantastic and revolting to be true. Lewd songs are sung over the microphone . . .

Leicester Square on a Sunday night has to be seen to be believed, and half the police are queer too!' Homosexual acts were still illegal at the time, and were to remain so, even among consenting adults, until well after the Wolfenden Report was published in 1957, but a gay subculture flourished in post-war London. Notoriously louche bars and clubs were not difficult to find; more discreet establishments were well known through the gay grapevine. The politically inspired crackdown on homosexuals (which was to catch Cranko 'soliciting' in Leicester Square) was not brought ostentatiously into effect until a high-profile campaign in the late 1950s.

Cranko and Darrell, both ruthlessly promiscuous, were briefly lovers. Darrell was aware (as he later told a friend, Geoffrey Baskerville) that Kenneth had resented their closeness at the time, feeling unfairly excluded from 'the sexual timbre of their triangle'. Darrell had soon acquired the nickname Vida, after the character played by Ann Blyth in the Hollywood film *Mildred Pierce*. The story goes that as he and a group of friends came out of the cinema showing the film, one of them protested, 'Surely, nobody would steal their mother's lover' – and everyone turned and looked at Darrell.

Darrell and his coterie (sometimes including Kenneth) would entertain themselves by dressing up in drag for cabaret turns at parties or simply to pass the time in each others' digs. One weekend when Darrell's parents were not at home, he and the others raided Floss's wardrobe and went down to West Drayton station. There they flaunted themselves in Floss's clothes, waving at trainloads of soldiers going past. They took delight in shocking the respectable landladies of Jack Carter's flat by posing as catwalk mannequins during Sunday-afternoon tea parties. Whenever Carter, a freelance dancer and choreographer who was often 'between jobs', invited company members round to tea, he and his boyfriend, Norman MacDowell, would go to the United Dairies corner shop and distract the shopkeeper by asking for something off the top shelf while they filched cakes for their guests.

Carter played the piano for the afternoon's entertainment. He was 'Eileen Joyce', the celebrity concert pianist, while the boys swapped outfits with the girls, modelling their street clothes. They were delighted to overhear the two landladies tut-tutting about 'strange women' in the house. As one of the party, Ronald Emblen, remarked years later, with the wisdom of maturity, 'We used to get high just on tea and laughter. We were so poor that not a drop of alcohol passed our lips. Nobody would have predicted we'd turn into alcoholics as we grew older.'

Recollections of those who were young and skint in the immediate post-war period are rose-tinted with wonder at their innocence. No drink, no drugs, all the excitement of sexual experimentation, if they were lucky, without major heartbreaks. They were not yet burdened with responsibilities, and they had still to make their reputations – reputations that would later be imperilled if they were exposed as homosexuals. This was the happiest, least-troubled period of Kenneth's life. He was accepted as an insider among people who shared his obsession with dancing. They were all confident about their future in ballet, though at this stage Kenneth had not formulated his ambition to be a choreographer. Inevitably, as they grew older, their optimism soured. A remarkable number (including Kenneth, Cranko, Darrell and Carter) turned to alcohol to numb their anxiety and distress as their careers became more demanding and their emotional lives messier.

8

Kenneth's big chance to prove himself as a dancer came at the start of the Sadler's Wells Theatre Ballet's next tour in May of 1948. Ashton had so enjoyed the enthusiastic response of the young company to *Valses nobles* that he offered to revive his 1933 *Les Rendezvous* for them. This effervescent ballet had entered the repertoire at the end of 1947 and was a favourite on tour. Kenneth, initially, was only in its corps de ballet but he had such a retentive memory that he knew all the roles. Only a few dancers are blessed with a photographic memory that enables them to pick up all the steps in a ballet, whoever performs them: men or women, soloists or corps de ballet.

At the start of the tour in Brighton, the leading male dancer slipped during the finale of *Les Rendezvous* on the greasy Theatre Royal stage. The accident happened at successive performances to three different men. Kenneth, dancing in the corps, stepped in during each performance to replace first Leo Kersley, then Donald Britton, then Michael Boulton. By the next night, there were no uninjured principals left to perform the role. Kenneth took over as leading man in his own right, dancing choreography that had been created in 1933 for the Polish virtuoso Stanislas Idzikowski. His fellow dancers were impressed by his insouciance, as well as envying his ability. As Kersley remarked in 1992, 'Kenneth was lucky. He had no time to work up a state of nervous anticipation for weeks, but simply jumped on, into one of the most technically demanding roles in the repertoire.'

Shortly afterwards, on tour in Cheltenham, the leading lady in *Les Rendezvous*, Elaine Fifield, injured herself in mid-performance. As she finished her solo variation, with its spinning *grands jetés en tournant*, whirling faster and faster on the steeply raked stage, she crashed into one of the braces holding the scenery. She fell, winded, into the wings, and Kenneth promptly replaced her, dancing her numerous entrances and exits across the stage as well as his own. Since he remembered all her steps and could do them, most of the audience was unaware what had happened.

The surge of adrenalin, which would result in panic attacks and crippling stage fright later in his career, here helped him out. The young company was trained, in theory at least, to respond in a professional fashion to any theatrical setbacks. Kenneth was congratulated for his coolness and rewarded with more prominent roles. Peggy van Praagh, like de Valois, tended to categorise dancers according to physical types. Kenneth, they had decided, was to be groomed as a future premier danseur, a prince rather than a villain or a jester. He was destined to be the romantic Poet in *Les Sylphides* or Siegfried in Act II of *Swan Lake*. In a *Ballet Annual* essay in 1950 entitled 'English Male Dancers: A Curious Prophecy', he was singled out from his fellows as a potential 'notable danseur noble'.

Such physical typecasting overlooked his comic abilities, as his friend John Cranko had recognised. Cranko had chosen Kenneth for a witty role in his *Morceaux enfantins*, created for the RAD Production Club in 1947 and then taken into the Theatre Ballet repertoire in April 1948 with a new, English, title, *Children's Corner*. All the characters were dolls, in a ballet reminiscent of Leonide Massine's *La Boutique fantasque*. Kenneth was a Massine-like dago with a smarmy moustache, the Great Admirer of Mlle Piquant, pretty Patty Miller's empty-headed ingénue.

Cranko had already been transferred to the main company at Covent Garden in September the previous year, so that he could gain experience by working with established choreographers. He continued, to make works for the Theatre Ballet, of which he was to become resident choreographer in 1950. De Valois was carefully pacing his progress. He was fortunate, as a South African, in not being eligible for National Service in the United Kingdom armed forces. The two-year compulsory military service was to interrupt many of his fellow artists' careers until it was abolished in 1960.

De Valois believed that her young men should not claim exemption without good cause. No one now remembers why Kenneth did not do National Service. He must have received his call-up papers by the end of 1947, when he turned eighteen, and have been required to undergo a medical examination. There were, however, sympathetic balletomane doctors prepared to issue exemption certificates on medical grounds. Michael Hogan, for example, was let off National Service as unfit for service life because he was 'a nervous wreck after being caught in a bombed house in Battersea'. Kenneth could have claimed exemption on much the same grounds – and he had highly arched insteps, considered a liability for army boots and parade grounds. Whatever the reason he was excused, he would never have resorted, as Peter Darrell boldly did, to a declaration of homosexuality, which was taboo in the armed forces.

Kenneth was to join Cranko at Covent Garden in September 1948, when he became one of the stream of dancers graduating from the second company to the first. He still had a long tour to complete, before van Praagh would agree to release him. He went on the company's longest-ever tour – fifteen weeks – from the end of April to August 1948. Extended to sixteen towns, the tour was referred to as 'Hell, Hull and Halifax'.

Most of the theatres were poorly heated and maintained, run down after wartime privations. Dressing-rooms were cramped and bleak, hot water hard to come by. Daily class and rehearsals usually had to take place in drill halls, school gyms or pub function rooms. For Kenneth, conditions of life on the road as a professional dancer were no improvement from his days as a youthful amateur hoofer in Retford or Yarmouth.

Still, he enjoyed the theatrical-gypsy life of travelling with a close-knit group of friends. Leo Kersley, nine years older than Kenneth, remembered him at this time as a 'tall, extremely thin, rather gawky youth with observant eyes in a lantern-jawed face, often to be seen holding hands with Greta Hamby, never talking very much or using a great deal of unnecessary energy rushing about, but watching the world with a slight smile that served to conceal fairly well whatever he was thinking'. Other dancers, closer to Kenneth in age, were party to their gang's shared laughter. They developed running jokes into a code of their own so that the mere mention of a key word, usually one of Kenneth's, would set them off into hysterical giggles.

On tour, the dancers spent most of their waking hours together. They were both allies and competitors, hoping to step into each other's shoes. Their lives were largely organised for them, though they had to be self-disciplined within that imposed structure. They had to find their own digs in each town, turn up on time for train calls, be at the theatre several hours in advance to prepare for a performance; yet they were also treated like children whose opinions were of no significance. They were expected to do as they were told, to accept their rank within the company without question. Their teachers and coaches were strict and somewhat aloof: no one dreamed of discussing personal problems with the ballet staff or of drawing the management's attention to one of their number with psychological problems or domestic difficulties. There was a conspiracy of discretion that protected the frailer members of the company but which could also result in their isolation. Kenneth was not alone in feeling an outsider in the midst of a crowd.

By now, some of the youngsters were beginning to pair off rather more seriously, to the alarm of those in charge who dreaded emotional crises and unwanted pregnancies. A strict look-out was instituted (somewhat belatedly) for couples who disappeared in search of privacy. There were few opportunities, in any case, to escape from the pressures of being constantly together on tour. Company members had to develop survival techniques in order not to drive each other mad, especially during the interminable Sundays when they travelled slowly, in unheated stopping trains, from one provincial centre to another. Even the most innocuous ploys to pass the time by playing games could have unintended consequences: on one train journey, Greta Hamby remembers, a word-association game seriously upset Kenneth when he kept coming up with the word 'Mother'.

A long-running canasta craze meant that a group of card-players always gathered in the same train compartment, ignoring the others. Peggy van Praagh usually sat with the more mature members of the company, including the two South Africans, Cranko and David Poole, with whom she felt at ease. The younger ones were the gigglers, sending up the landladies of their digs or reciting dialogue from films they had all seen. Kenneth might have been laconic but he managed to be at the centre of his own clique. 'He didn't shut himself off,' says Greta. 'At least, not at this stage. He wasn't a loner – he joined in everything.' His skills in knitting and sewing, learned from his maternal grandmother in her Ormesby cottage, came in useful on long, tedious journeys. He would sew on the ribbons for Greta's pointe shoes and undertake commissions to knit leg-warmers and crossover woollies for the girls.

The 'Hell, Hull and Halifax' tour finally ended in Ireland in July, with two weeks at the Grand Opera House in Belfast and one at the Gaiety Theatre in Dublin. De Valois, who came from an Anglo-Irish family and was born in Northern Ireland, came out to see a performance in Belfast and was pleased by the dancers' standards and the audience's appreciation. She confirmed that Kenneth was to be promoted to the Covent Garden company in time for the start of the 1948–49 season. Greta was told that she would follow later, when a place became available in the female corps de ballet. Their ambitions to be regarded as dedicated, grown-up professional dancers were about to be realised.

Kenneth's most pressing task was to get himself a passport, so that he could travel with the Covent Garden company to Paris, Düsseldorf and Hamburg in September – his first trip abroad. Aged eighteen, he declared himself to be exactly 5ft 10¾ in. tall (his eventual full-grown height was 6ft 1in.), with a scar on his left temple as a distinguishing mark. The scar came from a blow with a saucer that Michael Hogan had thrown at him during an argument whose cause neither of them could recall. The passport photograph shows a long, solemn face with defensive dark eyes – a face that could almost be his father's, pictured in his World War I uniform.

The senior company had travelled extensively in Europe since peace was declared, first sent abroad by ENSA to entertain the Allied troops and then by the British Council to restore cultural links with war-torn countries. The dancers had endured Spartan conditions on their tours, their reward the gratitude of the artists and audience members they encountered. This tour, from 21 September to 3 October, was to be a more pleasurable one, thanks to ten days in Paris at the Théâtre des Champs-Elysées, the art-deco theatre where Nijinsky's *Le Sacre du printemps* had its notorious premiere in 1913. The Sadler's Wells Ballet had performed there on previous visits, so veteran members were able to advise newcomers such as Kenneth what to expect, where to eat and what to sight-see. He was thrilled by his first experience of Paris. Under German Occupation, the buildings had been largely undamaged, unlike the bomb-blasted towns on the German leg of their tour, Düsseldorf and Hamburg.

There, Kenneth appreciated what Allied bombing had done to the cities and people he had thought of as 'the enemy', far away in an unknown country. Now, as the company travelled by military train through the shattered industrial landscape, he saw how they, too, had suffered. Gilbert Vernon vividly remembers waking in the small hours of the morning at an unscheduled stop in the Ruhr valley and seeing lines of hollow-faced, poorly dressed Germans staring resentfully at the train, the station in which they stood nothing but twisted girders. When the company reached firestorm-flattened Hamburg, they performed in a garrison theatre for the benefit of the Allied Army of Occupation: no other theatre was still standing and the audience consisted of soldiers, not local civilians.

When the company returned to the Royal Opera House in mid-October, the pattern of Kenneth's daily life had changed. Instead of going to Sadler's Wells, his journeys were now to Covent Garden or to the dance studios at Baron's Court in West London. Because there was insufficient space in the Opera House to accommodate the company's dancers, most of their classes and rehearsals took place in the studios at the ballet school, which had been relocated in 1947. The dancers' performance schedule meant that they had to commute between the Baron's Court and Covent Garden underground stations – a ritual journey that ended only when the Royal Opera House was substantially rebuilt in time for the Millennium. Though the nineteenth-century opera house, with the tiers of seats and boxes in its horseshoe-shaped auditorium, would have seemed glamorous to Kenneth in comparison with dingy Sadler's Wells, it was to remain in need of restoration for many years to come. The interior was still dark and shabby, with no funds to replace stained carpets and wallpaper or repair the peeling plasterwork. Backstage dressing-rooms were cramped, the plumbing and electricity unreliable.

The theatre, facing Bow Street Magistrates' Court, was an integral part of Covent Garden market, where fresh produce – fruit, vegetables and flowers – was assembled for sale in the early hours of the morning. Ballet and opera staff and artists mingled with the market-porters as their professional paths crossed; they drank in the same pubs, one lot of workers going off duty as the other workforce started. Fans queuing for tickets overnight outside the Opera House would share the spoils of fruit dropped from the baskets the porters carried stacked on their heads. Covent Garden was a democratic, hard-working environment, not a temple to the arts. But the theatre held out the promise of beauty and excitement, an escape from the greyness and austerity of post-war London.

(Performers and ballet-going regulars referred familiarly to the Royal Opera House as the Garden. The nickname fell out of use once the market had moved in 1973 to Nine Elms in Battersea, and the piazza behind the opera house became a popular tourist destination synonymous with 'Covent Garden'.)

Now that he had joined the senior company, Kenneth was demoted from soloist to corps-de-ballet member. He was nonetheless selected to learn as an understudy one of the four secondary male roles in Ashton's *Scènes de ballet*, which had received its premiere earlier in the year. Set to an acerbic Stravinsky score, the neoclassical choreography is technically demanding, for Ashton was challenging the ability of his dancers in their grand new Opera House setting. He was also testing his own ingenuity by composing choreographic patterns based on geometry. The score, a seductive mixture of jazzy conceits, swooning melodies and a triumphant peal of bells, was Stravinsky's response to the ending of the war in Europe. Kenneth responded rapturously to his first exposure to danced Stravinsky. By learning *Scènes de ballet* as well as observing it closely in performance, he was absorbing Ashton's craftsmanship as a choreographer. It would always be his favourite Ashton work.

Cinderella, Ashton's first three-act ballet, was meanwhile in preparation for the Christmas season. Premiered on 23 December 1948, four months after Kenneth had joined the company, it was part English pantomime, part Petipa *ballet féerie*. Ashton and Robert Helpmann, still the company's leading man, made an irresistible spectacle of themselves as the Ugly Sisters. Kenneth and the other male members of the corps had little to do, their main task being to escort the ladies at the ball during which Cinders meets her prince. (He soon graduated to the demi-soloist role of one of the Prince's four friends.)

Kenneth frequently said that he was 'a terrible partner – really terrible'. He claimed to have broken the ribs of a corps-de-ballet girl as he lifted her in the ballroom scene. None the less, as he gained experience, he was in demand to partner the taller women in both companies. Peggy van Praagh invited him back to dance the sole male role in *Les Sylphides* on tour with the Theatre Ballet, and he later performed the role at Covent Garden, with one of the senior ballerinas, Beryl Grey, who does not remember having any complaints about his partnering skills.

In May 1949, the Covent Garden company paid its first visit to Florence, where they performed in the Maggio Musicale festival at the bomb-damaged Teatro Communale. The weather was glorious and wine was cheap and readily available – a complete contrast to cold, bleak Britain, which was still in the grip of rationing. The dancers were given a grand reception at the British Consulate. Greta Hamby, who had recently been transferred to the senior company, went to the party with Kenneth. 'A bit squiffy' by the end of the evening, on her own admission, she inspected the formal guest list. There she found the name of Lady Ada MacMillan. She promptly ripped the page in two, declaring, 'This time, Kenneth, you've gone too far!' A real Lady Ada had indeed attended their party – and Kenneth took her name back with him to Britain. All the boys in the ballet had girls' nicknames, camp soubriquets acquired by the straight men as well as the gays. Kenneth would eventually swap Ada for Zelda, bestowed on him years later in Stuttgart.

Kenneth and Greta were back together in the same company, after being separated for seven months. His initial concern that she might be lost in the big company proved unfounded. She was maturing from a skinny shrimp into a beauty, well able to look after herself. He was meanwhile moving up within the ranks, being tried out in the virtuoso role of the Bluebird in the last act of *The Sleeping Beauty*, with Rowena Jackson as his Princess Florine. He loathed the spectacular pas de deux, preferring to be cast in the pas de trois that opened the Act III wedding divertissement. Choreographed by Ashton in 1946 to the sparkling music originally designated for the 'Jewels' dances, it was known to the Royal Ballet as 'Florestan and his Two Sisters'. The male dancer escorts and supports the two women, and shows off his elevation in a series of darting grands jetés. Kenneth was particularly good at these, describing a clear arc in the air as he leapt. Ashton advised him to turn his head sharply towards the audience at the apex of the jump, for added impact.

He was chosen for the role of Florestan when the Covent Garden company took *The Sleeping Beauty* to New York in October 1949. De Valois was about to present her Sadler's Wells Ballet for the first time to American audiences, touring through the United States and Canada. The impresario for this momentous visit was Sol Hurok, who had agreed that the grand gala premiere should be *The Sleeping Beauty* – a potentially risky decision, since Americans were unused to three-act, three-hour-long ballets. De Valois selected her opening cast carefully, for she knew that reputations would be made or lost on that first night: the company's international name depended on its success, as did Margot Fonteyn's. As Aurora in *The Sleeping Beauty*, she would be showcased as a ballerina to rival any other in the world. Moira Shearer, in spite of her movie fame in America in *The Red Shoes*, would appear only briefly in the Bluebird pas de deux (with Alexis Rassine) in the opening performance; she would assume the leading role on the second night.

Elaborate preparations were under way, for the company was to be presented as a proud flagship of post-war Britain. Arrangements were made for the women to be dressed by British couturiers, including the highly fashionable House of Worth. 'We had day and evening dresses, and silk stockings, which most of us had never even seen,' remembers Greta Hamby. 'We were told to wear white gloves with our dresses and lectured about how we were representing England.' The men's outfits were evidently regarded as less important, for they were expected to provide their own. Ashton's society-hostess friend and patron, Alice Pleydell-Bouverie, regarded this as unfair. She arranged for the men each to be given two free shirts by a Fifth Avenue men's outfitters when they arrived in New York.

The company crossed the Atlantic in two separate chartered planes on 4 October 1949, the men in one BOAC Super Constellation, the women in another. The VIPs had left earlier, on a scheduled flight: that group included Fonteyn, Helpmann, Ashton, Leslie Edwards and David Webster, General Director of the Royal Opera House. De Valois, who was meant to be with them, postponed her journey because of a migraine and travelled later with the men instead. This enabled her to keep an eye on Constant Lambert, the company's Music Director, who was liable to arrive the worse for wear after a long journey. Flights were arduous in the days before jet engines, with several stops *en route*. (Appalling weather conditions stranded the VIPs' plane in Reykjavik, delaying their arrival at La Guardia airport by fourteen hours.) The transatlantic journey was Kenneth's first experience of flying, about which he was to develop a crippling phobia.

Fortunately, a week had been allowed for rehearsals, giving the company an opportunity to recover from the flight and the change of time before the opening night, 9 October, at the Metropolitan Opera House, which was then on Broadway between 39th and 40th Streets. The Hurok organisation had launched a massive publicity campaign about the Sadler's Wells Ballet, suggesting that the glorious mantle of the Russian Imperial Ballet had fallen on the British company, gallant survivors of the war. There was record advance booking for the New York season, but de Valois was still nervous whether American audiences would sit through the three acts, plus the long prologue, of *The Sleeping Beauty*.

The Sunday night of the premiere was stiflingly hot. Inside the packed Met (not yet air-conditioned), which seated three and a half thousand, were members of both governments and diplomatic corps, as well as the Mayor of New York and his entourage. 'The atmosphere . . . was like a jungle minutes before a tropical storm,' wrote Fonteyn in her autobiography.

Applause greeted the Oliver Messel decor before anyone danced a step. When I ran out on to the stage there was a burst of sound. It drowned out the music and also some part of my mind, for I have never been able to remember anything between those first minutes of deafening applause on my entrance and the incredible reception after the third act pas de deux.

At the start of the third act, when the fairy-tale characters enter to celebrate Aurora's wedding, the applause drowned out the music for Florestan and his two sisters. Kenneth, standing in the wings while Pamela May and Nadia Nerina danced their variations, missed the music cue for his entrance in the coda. He dashed on late, leaving out his speciality – the spectacular grands jetés that had won him the role. He did them impeccably in subsequent performances, with his colleague, Gilbert Vernon, giving him a hand signal from the wings for his entry, just in case.

After the tumultuous applause on the first night had finally ended, the company was escorted by police outriders to an official reception at Mayor O'Dwyer's residence, Gracie Mansion. Kenneth was photographed there, in the company of Greta Hamby, Moira Shearer and her fiancé, Ludovic Kennedy. Also present were famous figures from American ballet companies: George Balanchine, Jerome Robbins, Lucia Chase, Nora Kaye and Agnes de Mille. Parties abounded that night: Kenneth had disjointed recollections of dancing down Broadway with John Cranko and Alfred Rodrigues (another South African member of the company) and then attending yet another party with Alexandra Danilova.

Danilova had left Russia in 1924 with George Balanchine and, after joining Diaghilev's Ballets Russes, had a glittering career as an international ballerina, including dancing with the Sadler's Wells Ballet at Covent Garden during the 1948–49 season. Balanchine had meanwhile established the School of American Ballet and the New York City Ballet, thanks to the foresight and generosity of Lincoln Kirstein. Kirstein, a great Anglophile, was keen to set up a transatlantic exchange of ballet companies, dancers and choreographers. The arrival of the Sadler's Wells company in the States and its triumph in New York made the *entente* easy to arrange.

Kirstein invited Ashton to create a work for New York City Ballet the following year, while Balanchine staged one for the Covent Garden company. City Ballet would pay its first visit to London in 1950; Sol Hurok made the Sadler's Wells Ballet's tour of the United States and Canada a biennial (sometimes annual) event. British and American dancers came to know each other well, although Ballet Theatre members tended to be more regular visitors to London than City Ballet ones.

New York's excitement over the Sadler's Wells dancers (and Fonteyn in particular, with *Time* magazine putting her face on its front cover) helped ensure the success of the rest of the tour. After four weeks in New York, they went on to Washington, Chicago, Richmond, Philadelphia, East Lansing and Detroit; then they continued to Canada – Toronto, Ottawa and Montreal – flying home in time for Christmas. The dancers were lionised wherever they went. 'We were used to post-war austerity and now suddenly everything was available,' comments Greta Hamby.

It was like a hellishly rich box of chocolates opening up all at once. Not just food but all sorts of luxuries. We were plied with alcohol at parties and everything tended to go a bit peculiar. People showered us with presents. Kenneth was given cuff-links by stage-door admirers – men, inevitably: all the boys got cuff-links, it was par for the course.

Inevitably, heads were turned by all the attention. Some dancers disappeared for assignations, returning in the small hours in a limousine. Others bedroom-hopped within their hotels, encountering company members doing the same thing as they passed on the iron fire-escape ladders between floors. (In New York, most company members stayed at the Bryant Hotel, in the theatrical centre of Broadway, while the principals were in the grander Hotel St Moritz, at the edge of Central Park.) 'But some of us were still very innocent,' says Hamby.

We were taken to one party in a coach. There were lots of good-looking men to dance with – I was having a lovely time until somebody said, 'You do realise they're all women?' And I just said, 'Don't be so stupid. You're just jealous.' But they were women in drag. So we insisted on getting back into the coach, where our butch ballet mistress was looking very sad and uncomfortable.

The company travelled across America and Canada by steam trains with freight-pulling locomotives. For one-night stops in the smaller cities, everyone slept on board, travelling overnight to the next town. There were plenty of opportunities for in-train entertainment. The dancers would squeeze, as many as possible, into one bunk of their Pullman coaches for impromptu parties. For a birthday celebration, they would take over one of the washrooms, fill the handbasins with gin and decorate the mirrors with loops of lavatory paper. Guests were invited to bring a bottle and pay an entrance fee of ten cents, as a tip for the obliging porter. The cabaret was usually provided by Kenneth MacMillan, Kenneth Melville, Peter Clegg and Ray Powell. They were licensed jesters, joined by anyone else who wanted to let off steam. Peter Franklin White, who kept a diary of the American tours, which he later turned into a book, *Sadler's Wells Ballet Goes Abroad*, noticed that Kenneth never liked being on his own. He might not have been as naturally extrovert as his fellow jesters, but he was not going to be left out.

His letters about the tour to his sisters back in Yarmouth were 'reticent', according to Betty, but were evidently exciting enough for her to have read out details to a local reporter from the *Eastern Evening News*. The article, published on 18 November 1949, was headlined 'Young Yarmouth Dancer Fêted in US'. Betty, identified as 'Mrs V. E. Harmer of 12 Stanley Terrace', assured the reporter that nineteen-year-old Kenneth would send a telegram to her the moment he returned, as 'he always lets her know as soon as he is back'. The article mentioned the famous dancers with whom he was now associated: Margot Fonteyn, Moira Shearer and Robert Helpmann. 'He seems bemused by the fact that he is being fêted by stars of the stage and screen who, a few months ago, were only names to him. He mentions Danny Kaye and many others, and he has attended a reception given by the Mayor of New York.'

The article likened the local boy's rise to fame in the ballet world to 'the metamorphosis of Cinderella herself'. In its account of Kenneth's career to date, there was no mention of his Retford dance teacher, Joan Thomas. Credit for his ballet training went to Miss Phyllis Adams of Yarmouth, 'who describes him as "absolutely exceptional"'. Betty told the reporter that she had not seen Kenneth dance since he was fourteen, tap-dancing in summer talent competitions. Although he had performed in Norwich with the touring company the previous year, she said she had been unable to attend because she had two small children to look after.

Since Yarmouth is not far from Norwich, Betty could surely have made babysitting arrangements in order to see her brother perform as a professional dancer. She had been the one, after all, who had accompanied him to London for his audition for the Sadler's Wells Ballet School. But Betty had suffered badly from depression in the aftermath of the war and had undergone electro-convulsive therapy; she might not have been able to travel on her own, and her husband, Victor (by now earning a living as a builder), was unlikely to have accompanied her to a ballet matinee. Betty was probably deluding herself that 'when Ken gets back to England in December he will come down to his home in Yarmouth as soon as possible [where] his two nephews are looking forward to his visit, for just as in his own childhood he taught his playmates to dance, so now he tries to teach them'. This sounds like a sentimental invention by a journalist, with or without Betty's connivance, since Kenneth rarely visited his former home town. Whenever he did, he stayed with his favourite sister, Jean, at her boarding house but spent most of his time with Phyllis Adams's family.

Greta Hamby confirms that although Kenneth kept in contact with his sisters, sending them photographs of her with him as his girlfriend, he never took her 'home' to Yarmouth: 'He didn't go back often. He felt wrong, out of place.' He liked staying with Greta's family in Teddington, near London. They took care of him, making an appointment for him with their family doctor because he was convinced he had something wrong with his heart: 'He used to get terrible palpitations and he couldn't breathe. It was nothing to do with going on stage – that came later. But our doctor couldn't find anything wrong with him.'

Kenneth was evidently suffering anxiety attacks from this early stage in his career. They were to become overwhelming later, impelling him to seek psychiatric help. It is now thought that there may be a genetic cause for some panic disorders, which are often associated with depression. The underlying causes of chronic anxiety, like those of depression, are complex and at this point in Kenneth's late adolescence, no one diagnosed his symptoms. He did not seem neurotic or unhappy; his palpitations appeared to be a purely physical aberration. Ballet dancers tend to breathe shallowly, using the top of the lungs instead of their full capacity; any nervous tension can then lead to hyperventilation, the rapid breathing characteristic of hysteria. The heart speeds up, the brain races, sweat pours off and the sensation of panic takes over, which is often identified as stage fright. Performers who recognise the onset of stage 'nerves' can learn ways to calm themselves down, starting with slow, unrushed breathing, followed by relaxation techniques. Such basic practical advice was not available to Kenneth at the time; nor was any psychological counsel about the possible causes of his palpitations.

He must have been worried about the similarity of his symptoms to those of his parents' ill-health. His father's damaged lungs, burned by mustard gas in World War I, had meant that William's breathing was impaired; he was prone to bronchitis and died of pneumonia. Kenneth's mother suffered from seizures, but since he never mentioned her fits, a family secret, to Greta, she had no key to his apparently groundless obsession about his own health. The company ethos, instilled by de Valois, was that dancers kept any personal problems to themselves and 'got on with it'. If they had injuries or serious health conditions during the ballet season, de Valois sent them to see a doctor at Bart's Hospital. The company's preferred doctor was another cause for concern, however, for Greta suspected he took a more than professional interest in Kenneth: 'He was a very handsome, charismatic man and he rather took Kenneth under his wing. He said he wanted to "groom" him, which made us a bit dubious about the whole thing.'

9

Back at Covent Garden by the start of 1950, Kenneth was involved as a dancer in several new productions. Balanchine arrived in London in March to start mounting his 1941 *Ballet Imperial* for its British premiere in April. (He also created a new work for the Sadler's Wells Theatre Ballet, *Haydn Concerto*.) Although the company quickly grasped the formal grandeur *Ballet Imperial* required, the speed and energy of Balanchine's neo-classical choreography to Tchaikovsky's Second Piano Concerto were harder to assimilate. Moira Shearer was considered by balletomanes to have had greater success than Margot Fonteyn in the leading role; Beryl Grey was acclaimed as the second ballerina, partnered in the pas de trois by two tall men, Kenneth and John Field. Kenneth was impressed by the sophistication of the choreography but did not feel he or the company had fully grasped the essence of Balanchine's style. When New York City Ballet came to Covent Garden a few months later, Kenneth gave up his summer holiday in order to stay in London and watch its dancers in action. Fascinated to the point of obsession about what ballet could do (and having already seen a number of Balanchine ballets performed by other visiting companies, such as American Ballet Theatre and the de Cuevas troupe), he wanted to study how dancers trained by the choreographer himself executed his style.

Before City Ballet arrived, however, Kenneth had been chosen for a new work by Roland Petit. During the Sadler's Wells Ballet's season at the Met in New York, Petit's company, now called Les Ballets de Paris, had been performing near by. De Valois had seized the opportunity to invite him, as well as Balanchine, to choreograph for her dancers. Petit had eagerly accepted a commission for May 1950. The ballet turned out to be *Ballabile*, a suite of dances for five men and five women, to music by Chabrier, arranged by Constant Lambert. The fantastical designs were by Antoni Clavé, who had designed Petit's sensational *Carmen* the previous year. For his first 'English' ballet, Petit insisted on casting dancers with considerable stamina. According to Gilbert Vernon, one of the select few along with Kenneth, 'De Valois told us to think of it as "our *Symphonic Variations*" but it wasn't anything like as good.'

Ballabile was a quirky divertissement with no through story line. It opened with dancers doing their daily exercises at an improvised barre and continued in a series of unrelated scenes, for which the cast had to keep changing costumes: a circus interlude; 'Sunday on the river', with bicycles, a boat and a fisherman; a Spanish fiesta; a comic funeral with umbrellas in the rain and a glamorous widow, who went off happily with one of the mourners. Kenneth was antagonised by Petit's expectation that he should prove himself. He was to tell Susan Crow, 'He said "What can you do?" which I thought was awful, so I answered "Anything".' As a consequence of this boast, Petit made him try out and endlessly repeat a difficult combination of steps that never, in the end, appeared in the ballet. According to Vernon:

Kenneth had these long, supple legs and Roland made him go right down in a full plié, come up with a huge developpé at head height, spin round and go right down again. He had to do it over and over, a killer on the knees. It was the first time I saw Kenneth really angry. He felt that Roland was amusing himself at his expense.

Vernon, too, suspected that Petit was a bit of a sadist with his English cast. As the Ringmaster in the circus scene, Vernon had not succeeded in moving his head in the way Petit wanted, and had almost had his ears yanked off as a result. So he and the rest of the cast were not surprised when the choreographer told them all to be 'very nervous' on the opening night. 'We already were,' said Vernon. 'But then Constant [Lambert], who spoke good French, explained that Roland meant *nerveux* – all spiky and alert. That we could do. Interestingly, it's the quality that was to be typical of Kenneth's early ballets.' Clavé's vivid, angular designs – 'perfectly enchanting', according to Richard Buckle – might also have influenced Kenneth's taste in decors for his own early ballets.

His disappointment over his role in Petit's creation might have been sharpened by his longing to dance like Jean Babilée, the macho French leading man of Petit's various companies. Instead, he was required, yet again, to show off his long legs and elegant line. Babilée had been a revelation to English dancers when he first arrived with Les Ballets des Champs-Elysées: he was the Nijinsky or Nureyev of his day, with a magnetic, animal appeal. He had been the angst-stricken, dungaree-clad protagonist in Petit's *Le Jeune homme et la mort*, driven to suicide by his female muse, Death. In the fund-raising galas for Nijinsky at the Empress Hall the previous year, Babilée had danced the role of the priapic faun in *L'Après-midi d'un faune*, with a young Rambert dancer, Margaret Hill, as the chief nymph. Like Hill, whom he was to know later, Kenneth had been bowled over by Babilée's charisma, telling Susan Crow, 'He was the first man I saw really jump high. Even when he did Bluebird, all the women fell for him.' Kenneth rued the fact that his own dancing was likened to Alexis Rassine's: the company's slender danseur noble, Rassine had fine legs and feet but was hardly a sexual icon.

April Olrich, who danced with Kenneth in *Ballabile*'s Spanish fiesta finale, insists that by now he was a good partner. They giggled together over his imitations of Petit's French accent and shared a running gag about Kenneth's legs. When she first joined the company, Olrich had been awed by a seance Kenneth had conducted with a ouija board one rainy weekend: the lights had dimmed, the table levitated and every message from the spirits was pertinent. During *Ballabile* rehearsals, he confessed that he had manipulated the seance, raising the table with his knees. Either of them had only to refer to his knees for the giggles to start all over again.

Balanchine's New York City Ballet arrived in July 1950 for a six-week season at Covent Garden (10 July–19 August). A welcoming first-night party had established instant friendships and reaffirmed existing ones. Because the season was so long, many of the American dancers had rented flats rather than stay in a hotel. Kenneth and a group of ballet enthusiasts happily took up the open-house invitation of three corps-de-ballet girls: Ruth Sobotka, Arlouine Case and Una Kai, who shared a flat in Ryder Street, near St James's Park. Together with male City Ballet dancers Brooks Jackson and Shaun O'Brien, they went around together as a gang all summer long. Instead of being on his own during his holiday break, Kenneth found himself at the heart of a transatlantic family, caught up in the gossip and intrigues of any company on tour. It was a heady atmosphere in which to absorb the ballets NYCB had brought to Covent Garden.

The repertoire was predominantly American, with ten works by Balanchine and ballets by Jerome Robbins, Todd Bolender, William Dollar and Lew Christensen. Also included was Ashton's *Illuminations*, recently created for City Ballet as part of the reciprocal arrangement between the two companies that Kirstein had brokered. The Balanchine ballets in the season spanned a wide range, from neo-classical works (*Serenade, Symphony in C, Concerto Barocco, The Four Temperaments*) to dramatic ballets (*The Prodigal Son, Firebird* and *Orpheus*, to the Stravinsky score Kenneth would eventually use in 1982). There were also some of his light-hearted pieces: *Bourrée Fantasque*, coincidentally to some of the Chabrier music Petit had chosen for *Ballabile*, and *Jones Beach*, for which Balanchine shared the choreographic credit with Robbins.

Jones Beach apart, the Robbins ballets were intense ones: *The Age of Anxiety*, based on the Auden poem of the same name (to Leonard Bernstein's Second Symphony), featuring four lonely, insecure people; and *The Guests*, in which two young lovers from different social groups dare to go off together, despite the disapproval of the other guests – 'our old friend, the problem of minorities' sniffed the anonymous *Ballet Annual* reviewer. Kenneth was impressed by both ballets – *The Age of Anxiety*, in particular, because it showed how ballet could reflect the apprehensions of a generation living in the shadow of war.

He was also affected by Lew Christensen's *Jinx*, to Benjamin Britten's *Variations on a Theme of Frank Bridge*, which MacMillan would use seven years later for his first ballet for an American company, *Winter's Eve*. The title refers to an unlucky clown, shunned by the other circus performers for constantly causing mishaps; one of them turns on him and beats him to death, with the connivance of the troupe. The clown returns to haunt them, for a jinx cannot be killed. It is a dark version of the performing-troupe scenario used in many ballets, from Fokine's *Petrushka* to Petit's wistful *Les Forains*, Walter Gore's *Carte Blanche* – and MacMillan's later *Noctambules* (1956) and *The Poltroon* (1972). The New York City Ballet season had a lasting effect on him, once he came to choreograph.

Further influences were the dramatically charged ballets brought not long afterwards by American Ballet Theatre. The company came to the Royal Opera House (28 August–9 September) before its return to the States after performances at the Edinburgh Festival. By now, the summer break over, the Covent Garden company was rehearsing in London, preparing to set out on its second American tour on 6 September. There would have been time for Kenneth to see *Fall River Legend*, Agnes de Mille's dance-drama about axe-murderess Lizzie Borden, and two Antony Tudor ballets, *Pillar of Fire* and *Romeo and Juliet*. Nora Kaye, as on the company's previous visits to London, was the outstanding dance-actress of the ABT season.

Once on tour in the United States, the Sadler's Wells Ballet dancers were too busy performing to be able to see what their American colleagues were dancing. The company's second American tour was its longest ever, lasting for five months. Sol Hurok, their impresario once again, reckoned de Valois's company was a guaranteed money-spinner, and the Royal Opera House was eager to earn all the dollars it could. The dancers would not return until after Christmas, by which time Kenneth would have turned twenty-one. Accounts of him during the tour make him appear more carefree than he would ever be again. He looked jaunty and cheerful in a 'Farewell to the Ballet' publicity photograph reproduced in *Ballet Annual*, in which the dancers were lined up in front of the big, double-decker BOAC Stratocruiser that would fly them to New York. This time, the male dancers as well as the women had been equipped in advance with English-manufactured clothes, serving as a shopfront for British industry. Anne Heaton remembers John Field was kitted out with a ginger-coloured suit, 'well made but absolutely vile'. In contrast,

Kenneth was lean and elegant in a light-grey suit, waving conspicuously as he stood next to smartly dressed Greta Hamby.

The three-week season at the Met opened on 10 September with
Swan Lake, with Fonteyn and Somes in the leading roles. The company was apprehensive in case the opening night proved an anti-
climax after the delirium during *The Sleeping Beauty* the previous
year. New York audiences proved as warmly appreciative as before,
although they managed to contain their outbreaks of applause until
the Black Swan pas de deux. Admirers fêted the dancers with parties and presents. There were plenty of opportunities for amorous
adventures, without too many questions being asked: flings on tour
didn't count.

After New York, the company (a hundred and twenty strong,
including staff, orchestra and stage hands) travelled by dedicated
trains, known as the 'Ballet Special', for twenty-one thousand miles
through America and Canada. For the five-week journey through
the Midwest, they had a dining car and lounge cars, as well as six
Pullman sleeping coaches. The stage staff were in one coach, sleeping during the day and getting up early to unload the scenery for the
next performance. The orchestra was allocated two Pullmans and
the dancers three – two rowdy ones and a 'sedate' coach for those
who needed to sleep. Journeys were slow and jerky, with long
delays: their steam train had to give precedence to faster diesel
trains transporting American soldiers to the Korean War.

Some stops were more glamorous than others. In Atlanta, the
dancers were invited to a lavish Southern breakfast party – eggs,
bacon, peaches and grits – on a cotton plantation. In New Orleans,
they toured the jazz clubs and went skinny-dipping in the sea;
arrested for indecency, they were let off after special pleading by de
Valois. In St Louis, they appeared simultaneously with a circus in
the auditorium next door. At the first of their joint performances,
the tragic ending of *Swan Lake* was disrupted by the climactic big
bang of the human cannonshot, which hurled a small man and his
aunt across the circus ring. After pleas from the ballet staff, the circus hands kindly agreed to postpone the explosion until *Swan Lake*
was over. The dancers then ran next door in their tutus to witness
the cannonball act that had so unnerved them the night before.

Towards the middle of the tour, the company was temporarily free
of the train in Los Angeles, staying for two weeks in the luxurious

Ambassador Hotel on Wilshire Boulevard. Sold-out performances at the Shrine Auditorium were attended by a galaxy of movie stars, a prospect that intensified the dancers' nerves. 'What's the matter with you lot?' asked de Valois. 'They're only a lot of old pros who've made it in Hollywood.' She was singularly unimpressed by the British colony's plans for a Hollywood opening-night party. The hosts, film actor Ronald Colman and his wife, Benita Hume, had invited only the principal dancers: de Valois put her foot down and vetoed the party because the whole company was not included. It was a principled stance Kenneth would always remember.

Sol Hurok threw a party instead at the Coconut Grove. Among the film stars present were Greer Garson, Gene Tierney, Joseph Cotton and Cyd Charisse. Charlie Chaplin acted as master of ceremonies for a dance competition. According to Greta Hamby, she and Kenneth were having one of their tiffs when the music for the charleston started, and Kenneth declared, 'Come on, we've got to do this.' (The charleston had been added to Ashton's *Façade* for the second American tour, performed by Kenneth and Anne Negus, so he was well rehearsed.) He grabbed Greta and danced her onto the floor without either of them realising it was a competition. Although Kenneth's supple legs broke the rules for the maximum height of the kicks, they won, to their mutual surprise. The man's prize was an alarm clock, the woman's a voucher from the Niemann Marcus store. 'I went with Kenneth and bought an orange dress,' remembers Greta.

During the Los Angeles stay, the company was taken on a visit to the Hollywood film studios. Peter Franklin White photographed Doris Day on the Warner Brothers lot as she tried to strike ballet positions; Kenneth and Greta sat next to her in the studio canteen. Moira Shearer was fêted, thanks to *The Red Shoes* and plans for her involvement in future films. By the end of the fortnight, the British dancers had become quite accustomed to Danny Kaye and Gene Kelly, who came to see the ballet nearly every night.

San Francisco was next, followed by five gruelling weeks of one- or two-night stops through the Midwest. All but two of the journeys were made overnight, the dancers, musicians and stage staff joining the train after each performance was over. Orchestra members tended to stay up late into the night, playing cards and gambling ferociously in their two coaches. The dancers, who were supposed to catch up on their sleep before daily class at the next stop, would often join them. The corps de ballet slept in the upper bunks of the three dancers' coaches, with soloists and principals in the more comfortable lower ones. As Fonteyn commented in her autobiography, 'Very soon romances, serious and fickle, erupted and evolved in complicated patterns. Dramatic eternal triangles inevitably formed, bringing bliss to one compartment and tears to the next.'

By the time the company reached Chicago on 19 December, they rejoiced in being able to stay put in the Sherman Hotel for a fortnight over Christmas. They were given a series of parties by generous locals, by the British Consul and by David Webster, General Manager of the Royal Opera House, who sent money for a celebration at the hotel after the Christmas-night performance. Alfred Rodrigues organised a cabaret, which featured Kenneth, Leslie Edwards, Ray Powell and Rodrigues himself, dressed in jeans, check shirts and *Swan Lake* head-dresses. They rushed on stage, then slumped on their luggage in despair at having just missed the 'Ballet Special' train. To the tune of 'Everything's Up-to-date in Kansas City' from *Oklahoma!*, they sang, 'We're the swans they left behind in Kansas City'. Kenneth then put on pointe shoes and appeared as a tall Fonteyn lookalike. 'He could do her smile – the curl of her lips. He was a wicked mimic,' remembers April Olrich. The entertainment also included a duet by Kenneth and Anne Negus, 'Poor Chloe', sending up Ashton's forthcoming ballet for the company, *Daphnis and Chloe*. Ashton, perhaps fortunately, had just left Chicago, to be home in time for Christmas.

The company's fortnight at the Sherman Hotel coincided with a trade convention of salesmen carrying mysterious little boxes. 'You know what they are, don't you?' Kenneth said to April. 'They're undertakers, selling miniature coffins to each other. I got in the same lift and showed them my Bryant & May box with dead matches inside. That gave them a shock.' Olrich, who was young enough to believe everything Kenneth told her, collapsed in hysterics of horror and laughter. 'You could never be cross with Kenneth, even when he played practical jokes at your expense. He was just naughty and charming.'

Although he and Greta had still been regarded as a couple at the start of the tour, she had by now outgrown their relationship.

Glamorous and confident, she was much pursued by American admirers. She had caught the eye of the famous show-business photographer, Maurice Seymour, who was based in Chicago. Practically every star in films, the theatre and ballet had his or her publicity photographs taken by Seymour. He loved ballet dancers, and declared that he wanted to make Greta Hamby 'the most photographed woman in America'. When she came down, unromantically, with chickenpox and had to be left behind in Chicago, she was flattered that Seymour comforted her with fruit and flowers. Kenneth was in no position to compete.

The tour finally concluded in Montreal at the end of January 1951. It had been too long, according to Ludovic Kennedy, who had followed Moira Shearer (by then his wife) on the 'Ballet Special' by car for much of the five-month trip. 'I cannot help wondering whether such a very long tour, without any break in the middle and with but a short holiday at the end, was in the company's best interests,' he wrote in his account of the trip. Exhausted, the dancers succumbed to illness and yet more injuries on their return. The tour had earned the company half-a-million dollars in profit, taking over 2 million dollars at the box office. By the time of the next tour, two years later, Kenneth was no longer a member of the Sadler's Wells Ballet.

Back in London, Kenneth moved out of his digs near Sadler's Wells into a series of rented flats. In one disastrous experiment, he shared 22 Gloucester Place Mews with a moveable feast of dancer friends, most of them gay: Peter Darrell, Gilbert Vernon, Brian Shaw, Tom Douglas and Anthony Manning. They moved in with a housewarming party that never ended – so much so that Tom Douglas, who had first found the flat, decided to live elsewhere. He and Manning set up home at 32b Sinclair Road in Shepherd's Bush, where Kenneth soon joined them. Gloucester Place Mews, filled with bodies, had become known as 'The Snake Pit', after the film starring Olivia de Havilland in which a mentally ill patient in an asylum is exposed to swarming snakes as shock treatment.

When Jeffrey Solomons, who was to become a close friend, first met Kenneth at one of the overcrowded dancers' flats, he was sprawled in an armchair, one leg draped over the arm, a cigarette dangling from his lips, knitting. 'He didn't say anything – he never did, in front of strangers. I rather dismissed him as a wimp. And he couldn't stand me being brash and loud.' Later, they met by chance on Waterloo Bridge, going to the National Film Theatre, which they both attended regularly.

We started talking to each other properly for the first time. He knew I had a brother who was retarded and who had epilepsy. He had to be put in a home (he died in his early forties). Kenneth asked me, 'Does it worry you?' I said, 'Do you mean, am I afraid of going mad? If so, "Yes" is the answer. Why, does it worry you?' And he said, 'Yes, it worries me very much.' That started our friendship: we could understand each other's fears.

They were both obsessive about the war:

Our boyhood had been dominated by it. We grew up in an atmosphere of anxiety and unease – me, because I'm Jewish, Kenneth because he was nervous anyway. I had decided I was going to win the war for Britain by being a heroic fighter pilot. When it ended, I felt relief as well as disappointment because I was never going to be a hero. And I think Kenneth shared those mixed feelings.

They developed a private language about the apocalyptic horrors of war, calling anything they feared and dreaded 'polythycalithic'. Newsreel footage of the Nazi concentration camps had been seared into their consciousness, as they had watched, in the cinema darkness, magnified images of emaciated bodies, corpses and traumatised survivors.

Solomons was a dedicated music-lover, so he took Kenneth to concerts as well as endlessly playing records in his company. He was largely responsible for extending Kenneth's range of musical experience beyond the works to which he was exposed in ballets. If Solomons developed an enthusiasm for a particular composer or type of music, Kenneth was obliged to follow suit, although he had his own preferences: he liked twentieth-century music – Stravinsky, jazz, quirky French composers. The two of them fell into a habit of frequenting the same record shops (usually on Saturday mornings), listening to music in the soundproof booths provided for potential customers, but rarely having the money to make a purchase. The EMG Hand-made Gramophones store behind the old Shaftesbury Theatre was a favourite haunt, until the staff came to recognise them as habitual browsers, not buyers. They also went to exhibitions and art galleries together: Solomons, who had a good eye, was later to become a successful art dealer.

Cinema-going was a ritual, with Kenneth the more obsessive. 'If you wanted to find him, you went to wherever the latest film was showing,' says Solomons. 'He'd often go to three or four films a day – on his own or with people, it didn't seem to matter. It was his escape from life, but it was also his future source of inspiration.' Films had fed Kenneth's fantasies since he was small, attending children's matinees with his mother or brother. Annie Selby, his foster-mother in Retford, had taken him with her on twice-weekly visits to the cinema, so his habit was an ingrained one. He was certainly not unusual in his addiction, for films were the main form of entertainment for dancers on tour, eager to avoid their dreary theatrical digs. At the time, B-movies were the equivalent of modern daytime or late-night television, as well as having their own collector's charm. Kenneth was effortlessly building up an expertise in the as yet unacknowledged area of film studies, outshining his friends in his recherché knowledge of actors, directors and plot twists.

As Solomons remarked, the huge range of films Kenneth saw fed his imagination as a future choreographer. He thought visually, not verbally or analytically. Ideas for his ballets came more often from films than from books or plays, marking him out from earlier generations of choreographers who were less exposed to the cinema. Although he was an avid reader, his introduction to a writer's work (for example, the novels of Carson McCullers, which inspired two early ballets) was made initially through the movie version of a book. He saw the story in vivid images, as he would later 'see' the moves and shapes he wanted dancers to make, as though capturing an emotion in flight.

Above all, film served Kenneth as a drug, a compulsive distraction from his nagging anxieties, which reading might fail to do. He could lose himself for a few hours, sitting in the dark following someone else's story. Cinema-going on his own was also a way of avoiding the pressure of constant contact with others – an intimacy he both craved and resisted. Disappearing into a cinema provided an ideal alibi for avoiding people until he needed them again. His reputation as a film fanatic meant that no one could take offence. Margot Fonteyn once joked, when her plane was delayed by a couple of hours before landing in Lisbon to join the rest of the company, 'I bet Kenneth's had time to see at least two films.'

10

By the 1950s, the relief and optimism of the immediate post-war period had given way to impatience and resentment at the slow pace of change. Britain, still suffering the economic consequences of the war, was reluctant to take on the challenge of radical new ideas. The Angry Young Men were building up a head of steam to denounce English society, politics and culture as hopelessly hidebound. The shake-up in thinking was just beginning to threaten social and theatrical conventions: outright rebellion would make itself felt later in the decade, in plays, novels and films. The theatre was still subject to censorship by the Lord Chamberlain, and would be until 1968. Ballet was exempt, probably because its non-verbal nature was considered inoffensive. But British ballet, led initially by Ashton, was daring to test sexual boundaries, influenced by visiting companies whose frankness shocked and delighted audiences in equal measure.

London had seen the premiere of Roland Petit's *succès de scandale*, *Carmen*, at the Prince's Theatre in 1949. Gilbert Vernon remembered standing in the back row of the stalls with Kenneth on the first night and realising that Zizi Jeanmaire, Petit's future wife, was a star. They had not rated her highly as a classical dancer:

We'd always thought she had no neck, lousy arms and that she'd never make it as a ballerina. But when Zizi seduced Roland as Don José, the audience held its breath throughout the pas de deux. I swear you could hear men's trouser buttons popping when she ended up on top of him, those wonderful legs arched upwards.

The pas de deux was the most extended, graphic depiction of a sexual act yet seen on the stage. It showed how bold ballet could be, both through stylised convention (for Carmen never removed her pointe shoes) and in realistic detail (Don José wiping his hands on the curtain in the bedroom scene). Petit's tame *Ballabile* for the Sadler's Wells Ballet the following year had been a let-down for his fans and for the sensation-seekers who had flocked to the Prince's Theatre. The management there had followed up *Carmen*'s success with Birgit Cullberg's *Miss Julie*, advertised on posters as 'the ballet that shocked Stockholm – at every performance'.

Birgit Cullberg (famous in her own right and as mother of the future choreographer Mats Ek) brought three of her dramatic modern ballets to London in February 1951 for the first – and last – time: *Miss Julie*, based on the Strindberg play; *Medea*; and *The Stone Portal*, a version of Kafka's *The Trial*. They were performed by a troupe of a dozen dancers calling themselves the Swedish Ballet (which had nothing to do with the Royal Swedish Ballet from the Opera House in Stockholm).

Cullberg received such scorn from British dance critics that she swore never to return. Arnold Haskell, writing in *Ballet Annual*, called *Miss Julie* 'unpleasant in the what-the-butler-saw manner; shocking is too strong a word'. *Medea* 'seemed to me a skit from the moment we saw the happy family at home to the bloody climax when Medea carted the corpses around in a wheelbarrow'. *The Stone Portal*, which lasted just fifteen minutes, was 'the longest ballet I have ever seen'. Such pursed-lipped disapproval was misplaced. *Miss Julie*, with its steamy seduction scene on the kitchen table, became a modern-dance classic, taken into the repertoire of numerous companies. Kenneth, who had seen the Swedish Ballet season in 1951, was to choreograph his own version of *Miss Julie* for the Stuttgart Ballet in 1970.

Meanwhile, Ashton, by now in his late forties, had been more explicit than ever before in *Illuminations* (1950) for New York City Ballet, which that company had included in its first London season. Set to Britten's song-cycle on poems by Arthur Rimbaud, it contrasted romantic fantasy with risqué realism: the hero Poet masturbated, grappled sexually with his Profane Love and relieved himself behind a pissoir. While New York audiences had received it with equanimity, some spectators at its London performances had taken offence. Undeterred, Ashton, in his next work for the Covent Garden company, *Daphnis and Chloe*, had included a shuddering moment of climax for Daphnis and Lykanion, the woman who introduces the naive shepherd-boy hero to vertical sex.

Ashton was to go further in his next ballet for the company, *Tiresias*, given in July 1951. It dealt with the argument between the gods, Zeus and Hera, over who enjoys sex the most – man or woman. A Cretan youth, Tiresias, who is changed into a woman and back to a man, is blinded by Hera for agreeing with Zeus that the woman gains most satisfaction. Michael Somes was the male Tiresias, Margot Fonteyn the female one. Kenneth was in the corps de ballet of Cretan youths, looking unhappily embarrassed in a photograph of the ensemble on the cover of Richard Buckle's *Ballet* magazine.

The hour-long ballet was not well received by the critics, nor by the Royal Family, who attended the gala premiere as part of the Festival of Britain celebrations. *Tiresias* was hardly suited to such an occasion, and the gala audience was unenthusiastic. Like the critics, they found the subject matter distasteful, the ballet long and tiresome. Constant Lambert, who had prepared the scenario as well as composing the score (his wife, Isabel Delmer, had designed the ballet), died six weeks later. He was an undiagnosed diabetic who drank to excess. His death, however, was attributed by many to the critical onslaught that *Tiresias* had received, without a single favourable notice.

Richard Buckle, writing in the *Observer* on 15 July 1951, had started his derisive review of *Tiresias* by questioning the Covent Garden Ballet's directorial acumen. Along with other recent commissions, *Ballabile* and *Daphnis and Chloe* (coolly received at its premiere, though it earned its place in the repertoire), *Tiresias* had not been a success. Buckle damned every aspect of *Tiresias*, from Ashton's treatment of the story to Lambert's music and his wife's designs, and berated de Valois for allowing the travesty of a ballet to be put on. The company's 'blind mice', he declared, had no idea where they were going. 'Did you ever see such a thing in your life? Sadler's Wells has three artistic directors. See how they run. Ninette de Valois is too busy to supervise every detail of production; Frederick Ashton is too easily reconciled to compromise; Constant Lambert, one imagines, looks in occasionally with a musical suggestion.' In response to an outraged reaction to his remarks (including a letter from Lambert's solicitor), Buckle expanded his views in two further articles discussing the malaise at Covent Garden. The gist of his argument was that there was no one person supervising the creation of 'the masterpieces of today'. De Valois was so preoccupied with administrative duties, committee work, lecturing and propagandising abroad that most of the ballets created in recent years – coincidentally the period since Kenneth had been transferred to the main company – had been disappointing. The company had grown complacent, in Buckle's view, with de Valois reluctant to take advice or admit that she could be wrong.

Though the timing of his attack was unfortunate in that Lambert died so soon afterwards, Buckle had touched a raw nerve. After the challenge of proving the ballet company worthy of its Royal Opera House home, its staff had accepted all too readily that it was now a national institution: they assumed that audiences would oblige by admiring whatever was put in front of them. American adulation on tour had reinforced that opinion. Meanwhile critics at home had started sniping that the Arts Council subsidy was being wasted on inferior work. Buckle's broadside was the first move in what was to develop into familiar hostilities over the years to come between the Royal Ballet's administrators and its critics and rivals.

Kenneth, meanwhile, was no longer enjoying being a member of the company he had so longed to join. His concern was not so much with its artistic policy as with his own future. He was finding it harder and harder to go on stage. Greta Hamby remembers standing near him in the corps de ballet for *Daphnis and Chloe* and realising he was shaking uncontrollably. She and the others practically had to hold him upright. Frank Tait, a child psychiatrist who lived with John Cranko in Pimlico, said that Kenneth had the worst stage fright he had ever seen: 'He had palpitations and couldn't breathe. He was anxious about going on stage in case something awful might happen to him. So I offered to stand in the wings as reassurance. He knew that, as a doctor, I could get help if necessary. Then he'd go on and dance beautifully.'

Dr Tait was at the ballet most nights in any case. He accompanied Cranko, who was absorbing all the information he could, now that he had been made resident choreographer of the second company. Tait was not in a position to treat Kenneth as a patient at the time, nor was he prepared to diagnose Kenneth's phobic anxiety state and depression later, for the present author. He did speculate, however, that Kenneth felt increasingly alienated from the audience:

Stanislavsky's theory was that the reason people enjoy performing is that they're applauded for expressing an aspect of themselves that they might otherwise feel ashamed or guilty about: for example, an emotion that is 'unworthy' but which they can safely express in performance. But Kenneth didn't feel rewarded by the audience any longer. He didn't believe they enjoyed or approved of what he was doing.

The solo roles in which he was cast in the Covent Garden company were the 'white tights' ones, in which he had no disguise to hide behind: Florestan in *The Sleeping Beauty*, the Poet in *Les Sylphides*, the trio in *Ballet Imperial*, the peasant pas de deux in *Giselle*. These were the roles for which his apprenticeship in the junior company had prepared him, and which he danced so well that he had not, initially, been given any character parts. Even as a member of the corps de ballet, he had come to feel inhibited and embarrassed at passing himself off as a Greek or Minoan youth, a peasant boy or ballroom guest.

His comic abilities in the company's cabarets on tour, however, had not gone unremarked. After Helpmann abruptly left the company in 1950, Kenneth was drafted in to replace him as the bossy Ugly Sister in *Cinderella*. He made his debut, a lanky foil to Ashton's smaller, dithery Sister, when Nadia Nerina first danced the leading role in March 1951. The *Times* review of his performance (21 March 1951) commented, 'He plunges with inventive gusto into [the role's] ungainly farce, aided by his height as well as his feeling for the ridiculous.' The double act was deemed so successful that it became a fixture: Kenneth was less of an outrageous scene-stealer than Helpmann, but had plenty of ideas of his own, which Ashton would then appropriate for himself.

The monstrous Ugly Sister was the only role in which Kenneth could take any pleasure. Once he started losing his nerve in other ballets, he dreaded failing to live up to his own high technical standards. He felt very exposed on the big Covent Garden stage, knowing that ambitious dancers were vying for his roles. He claimed later, in 1963, that he was not particularly good as a purely classical dancer: 'I never would have danced any of the big parts.' None the less, Clive Barnes had picked him for the 'Dancer you will know' slot in *Dance and Dancers* magazine at the end of 1951, claiming that young Kenneth MacMillan could develop into 'the leading dancer in any company':

He has an excellent all-round technique, remarkable elevation, and is a good partner. He is a very easy, fluent dancer (e.g. in *Ballabile*) and a gifted comedy mime (e.g. in *Cinderella*). After giving a very fine performance of *Les Rendezvous*, no part since has really demanded his best. When one does, everyone will be surprised.

Kenneth's stage fright had little to do with a realistic appraisal of his performances. He was suffering anxiety attacks out of all proportion to what he was required to deliver on stage. He was candid about the full extent of his stage fright only towards the end of his life, confessing in the television documentary *Out of Line* in 1989 that it had become 'an absolute nightmare to go on the stage'.

The panic would start really in the morning of the day of the performance, and it would mount and mount and mount. I was very reluctant to go into the theatre because by the time the performance came I was really shaking. The most difficult thing I found during that period was actually to look at the audience because I was very aware that they were all looking at me, and I didn't want them to see that I was shaking from head to foot, and I couldn't wait to get off the stage.

Not being able to look the audience in the eye seems a strange admission from someone who had spent his youth competing in talent competitions, and who had defied his father by insisting on becoming a ballet dancer. It may be that, having reached his early twenties, Kenneth had started seeing himself through his father's imagined eyes: a willowy young man in a revealing costume, exposing himself to potential ridicule if his fancy footwork failed. He did not like who he was. His body rebelled against him, robbing him of his hard-won control over it. He was drenched in cold sweat, heart palpitating, muscles in spasm, scarcely able to breathe, let alone dance demanding steps. Will-power, and the fear of humiliation if he made a fool of himself, kept him going – but only just.

He was caught in a bind. He had achieved what he most wanted to do and yet he could not be happy. If he could not perform, he would no longer be wanted. He needed to belong, to be part of a tight-knit group, yet his stage fright was showing him up as a misfit. He contemplated resigning but was uncertain what other career choices were available to him. He wrote to the Brandon-Thomas organisation, producers of the popular *Charley's Aunt* farce, applying for the lead in their forthcoming musical *Where's Charley?* The original *Charley's Aunt*, written in 1892 by Charles Brandon-Thomas, involved an Oxford undergraduate dressing up as his maiden aunt in order to get himself out of a scrape, only to fall into yet more trouble. A cleverly constructed farce, it was exploited by the Brandon-Thomas family in various forms until its copyright ran out. Kenneth evidently hoped that his Ugly Sister experience might qualify him for the comic transvestite role until he received a kindly letter of rejection from Charles's son, Jevon Brandon-Thomas, saying, 'I think it is a sin for you to desert the ballet for musical comedy.'

Thwarted, Kenneth struggled on through the 1951–52 season. He had a small part in Leonide Massine's new ballet for the company in December 1951, *Donald of the Burthens*. Although Kenneth had danced in Massine's *Mamzelle Angot*, this was his first experience of working with the choreographer himself. Massine, who had made his name with Diaghilev and the various Ballets Russes companies, had been invited to Covent Garden because de Valois thought his vivid narrative ballets would suit the English dramatic temperament.

Donald of the Burthens told the *Faust*-like story of a Scottish shepherd who struck a bargain with Death so that he could realise his ambition of becoming a physician. The shepherd failed to keep his side of the pact and so paid the penalty. The story was told humorously (apart from the imposing role of Death, danced by tall Beryl Grey) in a balletic version of Scottish folk dance. Massine brought in a so-called expert instructor to teach the cast Scottish dancing: Kenneth and other Scots who had learned it as children resented the waste of their time. They were right in suspecting that the ballet would turn out to be a flop.

Massine choreographed the ballet using his own notation system. He asked the dancers to combine various sequences that he had prepared in advance. Kenneth told Susan Crow, 'He'd teach us A, B, C, etcetera, then he'd say, "I'd like A with half of D, all of E and a bit of C." It was absolutely hair-raising. A lot of hard work, and then all the Bs and Fs you'd been doing for hours were out of the window.' Kenneth had no sympathy with the systematic method of choreographers such as Massine and de Valois, who worked out their ballets well before coming to the rehearsal room. He preferred the intuitive approach of Ashton, who responded to whatever his chosen cast offered him.

For a dancer with imagination, such as Kenneth, collaborating in the creative process is far more rewarding than simply obeying instructions. The dancers tune themselves to the choreographer's wavelength, supplying suggestions for steps and solutions for problems, while their own particular qualities help determine the way a role evolves. The choreographer needs to be confident and experienced enough to trust the dancers. Kenneth himself, once he started making ballets, learned to rely more and more on his cast's contributions instead of demonstrating precisely what he wanted.

At this stage, handicapped by stage fright as a performer and without yet knowing where his future would lie, he was already more interested in how ballets were created than in how they were danced. Frustrated by the repertoire he was reluctantly performing, he wanted to know what other options were available. He latched on to the newly established Ballet Workshop evenings at Rambert's little Mercury Theatre in Notting Hill Gate. Marie Rambert's son-in-law, David Ellis, together with Rambert's daughter, Angela, had set up the choreographic workshop in January 1951. The intention was to give professional artists – dancers, musicians, designers – creative opportunities by presenting ballets in a small theatre to a select audience:

Here they will be able to watch young choreographers learn their craft, making mistakes, no doubt, but practising all the time and so finding their feet. In addition Ballet Workshop will provide a stage for experienced choreographers who feel they have something to say which, for various reasons, is for a small stage and theatre.

Rambert's Ballet Workshop functioned as a club, offering perform-ances on three Sundays a month, with the fourth used to rehearse ballets for the next month's programme. The Ellises provided admin-istrative support rather than artistic guidance. Choreographers and performers came from a variety of backgrounds, including the com-mercial theatre. Sadler's Wells dancers were not permitted by de Valois to participate. They were supposed to be too busy with their own company commitments – though the real reason was the rivalry between de Valois and Rambert, the two grandes dames of British Ballet.

Peter Darrell, by now a freelance dancer (mostly in musicals), soon started creating ballets for the Workshop. Kenneth, eager to be involved, designed the costumes and rudimentary sets for two of Darrell's early experiments, disguising his contribution by adopting the name of Kenneth Aadams. The double A was a ploy he had first mentioned to Gilbert Vernon years before, when their names started to appear on Sadler's Wells Theatre Ballet cast lists as junior soloists. De Valois had decreed that the lists should be alphabetical, so Kenneth joked that he would change his surname to Adams. Vernon declared that he would be Abrahams, so Kenneth threatened to trump him with Aadams. The proposal was never a serious one, so Vernon was amused when he spotted Kenneth's unlikely pseudonym in one of Ballet Workshop's simple, cyclostyled programme sheets.

At the start of Ballet Workshop's five-year run at the Mercury Theatre, the works tended to be, according to Lionel Bradley, writing in *Ballet Bulletin*, 'slight but charming'. Darrell's first attempt, *Midsummer Watch*, first performed on 10 June 1951, was a pastoral episode for country girls and their shepherd lovers. Kenneth's decor consisted of 'a sky cloth and tree trunk, a stile, and a cut-out in brown and green suggesting a hillock'. Their next joint effort, *The Telltale Heart* (8 June 1952), was more dramatic, not to say melodramatic. Based on a story by Edgar Allen Poe, its plot revolved around the murder of an old man by a youth, who hides the body under the floorboards. When the police arrive to investigate, the overwrought young man seems to hear the still-beating heart of his victim and confesses his crime. For this, Kenneth concocted a stark, modernist decor with pieces of newspaper stuck at angles across the furniture. 'We were all very influenced by Wakhevich, Roland Petit's designer,' says Vernon. 'I don't think Kenneth particularly wanted to be a designer. We thought of ourselves grandly as "men of the theatre" along Continental lines. One day you direct or act, the next day you sweep the stage or design.'

Kenneth's last stab as a designer, still disguised as Aadams, was for Darrell's first professional commission. London Festival Ballet had asked for a work for its Christmas season in the newly built Royal Festival Hall in December 1952. Darrell played safe with *Harlequinade*, featuring the usual *commedia dell'arte* scrapes and romances. Since the concert-hall stage could not accommodate elaborate sets, Kenneth had to curb his ambitions. His conventional costumes were bright, the set consisting of 'cut-outs to suggest a garden with box hedge, fountain and pots of flowers', as Lionel Bradley described it.

The Ballet Workshop evenings, meanwhile, were rapidly becoming more challenging in their subject matter. Michael Holmes's *Palisades*, for example, performed on 16 March 1952, started with a (non-specific) political prisoner being thrown into a cell. His fears were embodied by figures done up in bandages – 'sort of barbed-wire spectres'. At the end, a warder brought the hallucinating man back to reality, before he collapsed from exhaustion. *Palisades* was commended by Mary Clarke in *Ballet Annual* as 'a ballet of torment and suffering (mental as much as physical), which showed an extraordinary ability to convey strong emotion through movement'.

'We were all Angry Young Men before the term was coined', says Holmes.

I was interested in trying to push classical technique into dealing with today's themes. I did another ballet for the Workshop, *Common Ground*, based on a murder very much in the news. A boy and a girl on Clapham Common were attacked by a gang of thugs, who killed the boy. In my ballet, they kept blaming each other, pointing the finger at other members of the gang. One of them was made the scapegoat, left alone with the corpse. I was told that it was not a fit subject for ballet. But I thought, 'Bugger the audience wanting to be entertained. I want to frighten them, wake them up.'

Kenneth was to use virtually the same words once he started to make his name as a choreographer. He was still waiting in the wings, observing what others were doing. Although he was to be acclaimed as the first ballet choreographer of his generation to address contemporary issues, he was of his time – the post-war 1950s that were about to erupt into the kitchen-sink plays at the Royal Court, John Osborne's vituperative tirades, the new wave of grittily realistic British cinema, the defiant novels of John Braine and Kingsley Amis. Radical young choreographers were part of the same movement, but they lacked a prominent platform for their work. Sunday evenings at the tiny Mercury Theatre in Notting Hill made little impact on the outside world. As Clive Barnes commented in a 1953 guide, *Ballet in Britain since the War*, 'Ballet Workshop has performed some valuable work in the discovery of new talent, but so far there is no indication that any of this talent is going to be used by ballet companies.'

De Valois had grown cautious after the critical panning *Tiresias* and other recent works, her own among them, had received; Ballet Rambert was struggling to afford new productions; other small companies were playing safe. The flowering of daring ballets around the start of the 1950s had been a brief one, soon abandoned by audiences and financial backers. Most of the choreographers who showed promise at early Ballet Workshop evenings either gave up or sought work abroad, as did Michael Holmes, Michael Charnley and Jack Carter. Those, like Kenneth, who came later, when the cultural climate had been shaken up by Angry Young Men in other fields, were the lucky ones.

By March 1952, Kenneth had dropped out of a new ballet by Andrée Howard, *A Mirror for Witches*, in which he had been cast to appear. Based on the true story of the 1692 Salem witch hunt, it was a dramatically charged ballet, dealing with bigotry and possession. Kenneth did not get on with Howard, who had slapped his face during rehearsals for one of her earlier ballets. She was a highly strung woman who later committed suicide and her nervous tension probably exacerbated his own. He had attended rehearsals but was unable to face the opening night. He did, however, appear in John Cranko's comic *Bonne Bouche* (Cranko's first work for the Covent Garden company) in early April and he was included in the main company's tour to Lisbon and Oporto later that month.

On Kenneth's return, de Valois sent him to the second company, the Theatre Ballet, to appear in its new production of her 1935 work, *The Rake's Progress*. He danced only minor roles – the fencing master, the violinist in the asylum where the Rake ends his life – but Peter Wright remembers him being tortured by nerves: 'We sat together on the stairs and I remember asking him what the matter was. He said, "I can't bear to go on stage. I start to shake so badly I can hardly move." I asked if he'd like to see a psychiatrist because I knew of one, and he said he'd think about it.'

Kenneth evidently did consult a psychiatrist at that time. Greta Hamby was invited to meet him over dinner: 'I was too nervous to take in whether he was an analyst or whatever. I think Kenneth saw him for talks on a fairly regular basis. But our relationship was pretty well at an end anyway, so it was all too late as far as I was concerned.' Their long, close friendship had always been platonic. She was aware that he had had sexual experiences with men, 'but that wasn't his scene. He didn't like it. He wanted to be "normal", to get married eventually and have a family. So I was so pleased for him when he did.'

Whether Kenneth's stage fright was connected with his ambivalence over his sexuality was a matter he never discussed outside the sessions with psychiatrists and analysts he continued to consult during his career. As far as de Valois was concerned, the immediate practical step was for him to take time off dancing. She offered him three months' leave over the summer. When the new season started in the autumn of 1952, he could return to the Theatre Ballet, where the pressures on him would be less than with the Covent Garden company. However sympathetically she presented his options, it was a kind of demotion. Aged twenty-two, he had seized up as a promising danseur noble: he had to find an alternative route if he was to make his mark in the theatre.

2

The Making of a Choreographer

1952–1966

At the start of his three-month 'rest' from performing, Kenneth went back to Great Yarmouth, where he stayed with his sister Jean and linked up with his former ballet teacher, Phyllis Adams. By now, she and her family had moved into a large, bow-fronted Victorian house, grandly named 'Eaglehurst'. It had an unruly garden at the back and enough room upstairs for a dance studio. Kenneth joined in ballet classes with her pupils, impressing them with his ability. According to Mary Miller, by now one of the senior girls, they were told that Kenneth had been sent home to recover after an unexplained accident. Wendy Roche, Miss Adams's fourteen-year-old daughter (who subsequently became a dance teacher herself), also accepted the injury alibi for his return to Yarmouth.

Kenneth volunteered to choreograph dances for Wendy and Mary for the school's annual display. He enjoyed working with the girls, who found him full of fun and nonsense, though proper young Wendy was rather shocked that he smoked and drank. Her comic number was to the mocking song, 'Life upon the Wicked Stage'. She had a cloak with pockets in which disguises were stored – funny noses and spectacles. Mary recalls two further dances: a trio to 'There's a chance I might fall back on you' and a duet for her and Wendy to 'I love a piano, a grand piano, I love to hear somebody play', both with sharp, quirky movements. Kenneth teased Mary later, when she had become an actress, by introducing her to Margot Fonteyn as the person for whom he done his first choreography.

His dilemma, now, was whether he might be able to make a career as a choreographer. If he was unable to perform as a dancer, de Valois was unlikely to employ him simply as a would-be choreographer: he had no track record, unlike John Cranko, who had stopped dancing soon after proving his worth as a creator in the early days of the junior company. If Kenneth resigned and went freelance, how would he live? His hope was that he might recover from his fear of performing and keep going as a dancer, while he waited for the chance to try his hand at 'proper' choreography.

Back in London at a loose end, Kenneth was walking through the Covent Garden area with Jeffrey Solomons when a red car screeched to a halt beside them. It was John Cranko, 'the world's worst driver', according to Solomons. Cranko proposed that Kenneth should join him and a group of dancers in a short summer season at Henley-on-Thames, the picturesque setting of the annual rowing regatta in May. Solomons remembers the look of hope on Kenneth's face as Cranko assured him the show was going to be a small-town, small-group affair, intended to save a local theatre from extinction. Only locals and friends were expected to attend, so Kenneth had no reason for nerves. Cranko had already discussed Kenneth's involvement with de Valois, who agreed that it might do him good to take part.

John Piper, the artist and designer, who lived near Henley, had rediscovered the old Kenton's Theatre, hidden behind a garage in a side street near the River Thames. The garage owner had shown the disused building to him, knowing that he was a theatre designer. Piper and his wife Myfanwy took on the task of restoring and redecorating the tiny theatre, which is still in use today. They had asked Cranko to stage a show during his summer holiday in order to bring the theatre fully back to life. Piper, who had collaborated with Cranko before on his ballets, would design the sets and costumes, together with Osbert Lancaster, the cartoonist and painter (and designer of Cranko's *Pineapple Poll* and *Bonne Bouche*).

Cranko recruited dancers willing to give up their summer-holiday plans. Some he knew already; others he had spotted taking class with a well-known ballet teacher, Audrey de Vos, who had a studio in West London. He chose Margaret Scott from the Ballet Rambert, later to be a founder of the Australian Ballet School, who was retraining at de Vos's studio after a year off with a back injury; Yvonne Cartier (who after a performing career as a dancer and mime artist, was to teach ballet in Paris) and Sonya Hana, who were both soon to join the Sadler's Wells Theatre Ballet; Peter Wright, who was about to leave the company; Geoffrey Webb, a pal from Festival Ballet; and Kenneth, as the third male dancer. The idea was for them all to have fun preparing and appearing in a kind of ballet cabaret.

Shortly before rehearsals started, Cranko had taken the other five dancers aside. 'I want you to be kind to Kenneth,' he said. 'He's been through a very difficult stage. I think he's going through a transition to becoming a choreographer.' As Cranko created dances for the show, he would deliberately find an excuse to leave sections unfinished and ask Kenneth to finish them. Generously, Cranko was setting his younger colleague on the path that he had already taken. There was no pressure: they were aiming merely simply to entertain.

The dancers were put up in an empty farmhouse on the Stonor Park estate owned by Lord Camoys, whose family were friends of the Pipers. 'It was more of a manor house, with a baronial hall where we ate at a long trestle table', remembers Margaret Scott.

We were all allocated chores. Kenneth and I were in charge of the Aga stove, which supplied us with hot water. We had to ensure that it was stoked up before going to bed and we were alarmed by its gurgles and splutters. So we waited up late into the night, talking for hours. That's when I became aware how much he wanted to be a choreographer. It was all he talked about.

For the brief season, originally scheduled for one week in mid-July, Cranko mounted existing pieces of his own and added new ones, tailored to suit his ad hoc company. Kenneth danced the dashing role of Captain Belaye in a trio from *Pineapple Poll*; he was also the leading man in *Dancing*, a new ballet to end the programme. It was set in an attic, furnished by Piper from bits and pieces he had found in the derelict theatre. Kenneth was its solitary occupant, whistling as he wandered about, exploring. Finding an ancient gramophone-player with a horn, he put on a record and began to dance. Each new record (of music by George Shearing, the jazz composer and pianist) brought on different members of the cast as figments of his imagination, in duets, trios and a group finale. Kenneth's make-believe partner was Sonya Hana, in a duet that he largely devised (and whose steps he would adapt for later use in his own jazz ballet, *Elite Syncopations*). The piece ended as it had begun, with Kenneth on his own again, whistling.

Myfanwy Piper described Kenneth's role as 'lonely, imaginative, a natural clown, puzzled by the appearance and disappearance of the other dancers, and longing to be one of them'. Although the part was primarily a linking device, the personification caught Kenneth's nature very perceptively. Friends and former cast members stress that he was far from morose in Henley. He might have been troubled by the underlying causes of his stage fright but he was essentially an optimist, convinced that he could surmount his problems.

Besides, he loved making people laugh, and he was safe among a friendly group of fellow clowns.

Margaret Scott kept a faded snapshot of Kenneth and Geoffrey Webb playing the fool in a raspberry patch. They were gibbering, with their jackets pulled up over their heads, doing their ghoul double act from one of the new ballets, *The Forgotten Room*. In it, Peter Wright was the leading romantic figure, with the other two phantoms in supporting roles, carrying him about. Kenneth pretended to be affronted by his loss of status from soloist in *Dancing* into a mere porter for Wright. His double act with Webb continued offstage as well as on. When the actor Denholm Elliott came to Henley to see his girlfriend, Sonya Hana, he turned up in a dashing open-topped sports car. Kenneth and Geoffrey would hang out of the dickey seat at the back of the Triumph Roadster, screeching like *Forgotten Room* banshees as they surfed above the road at 70 mph. Elliott would race along the Fairmile, a famously straight stretch of road linking Henley with the Stonor estate where the dancers were staying. Wright recalls their foolhardiness with amazement: 'That was before Kenneth lost his nerve and dreaded travelling by car ever again. After that, he hated going fast and he absolutely refused to learn to drive.'

Everybody was madly in love with handsome Denholm Elliott, sharing erotic fantasies about him as they longed for his visits. They were also crazy about modern jazz. Geoffrey Webb was sitting in a Henley tea shop with Kenneth when they heard a jazz record being played in the room above. When they asked the shop owner what it was, she told them vaguely, 'My son is playing his music.' They went upstairs and discovered 'this boy with an enormous cock and thousands of jazz records', as Webb reported excitedly to Jeffrey Solomons. They cultivated the boy and his collection throughout the summer. He introduced them to the music of Stan Kenton, the British jazz composer and band leader, whose record they had first heard in the tea shop. Kenneth promptly went record-shopping with Margaret Scott to buy his own Stan Kenton collection. 'If you want to choreograph,' she had urged, 'go out, buy some music and start.'

She was unaware of his stage fright, which he never mentioned during their late-night chats around the Aga. His panic attacks had abated in the carefree atmosphere, even though the names of Piper, Lancaster and Cranko inevitably attracted visitors from London, curious to see what they were up to. The week's season at the restored

Kenton Theatre was extended to a fortnight to accommodate the demand for tickets. The show was a hit with audiences, guaranteeing the survival of the theatre. Every night after the performances, the cast would go back to the Pipers' house and get 'rather pianola' around the piano as they and visiting friends and colleagues sang together. Myfanwy Piper would make pies for the dancers to take back to their Spartan farmhouse, where they slept on camp beds, Kenneth's long legs overhanging the end of the canvas.

Cara Lancaster, Osbert's young teenage daughter who acted as wardrobe mistress, would have her meals with the cast. One of their running jokes, whenever anyone said 'Pass the Primula', referring to small triangles of processed cheese, was to pick up Cara and pass her round the trestle table. She was their mascot, their good-luck charm. Osbert Lancaster was horrified when he walked into the dressing room one night to find Cara mending the ghouls' netting outfits, in the company of almost naked men in jockstraps. Neither Cara nor the ballet boys could understand his alarm.

The successful season had an unexpected afterlife. *Dancing*, the hit of the show, was filmed for television later in the year, leading a TV reviewer in the *Manchester Evening Chronicle* of 29 September 1952 to mention 'a young artist of distinction, Kenneth MacMillan'. The Henley programme was then adapted and expanded for the Aldeburgh Festival in 1953, at the request of Benjamin Britten. Britten had met Cranko through Piper; as a result of their introduction, Cranko had collaborated on productions of Britten's operas, *Gloriana* and *Peter Grimes*. The Henley team reassembled for the Aldeburgh Festival, supplemented by dancers from the Sadler's Wells Theatre Ballet. For Cranko's *Beauty and the Beast*, Kenneth and Peter Wright had been relegated to bit parts as rosebushes, entangling Beauty in their thorny branches. They were hidden behind an archway, extending only their green-gloved arms. During one performance, the archway fell over, revealing Kenneth in his dressing-gown and Wright in jockstrap and boots: 'I bowed to the audience, gave my arm to Kenneth and we marched off together, to tumultuous applause.'

The hot, happy summer in Henley marked a turning point in Kenneth's life. He no longer feared that he would have to abandon his ballet career. He had lost his paralysing dread of performing and he was resolved to try his hand seriously at choreography. He declared to his colleagues that he was going to make ballets about real life, instead of creating an artificial world of their own. He was also about to fall in love and have his first heterosexual affair with the woman who would influence his early ballets. They were brought together by an accident that could have ended in disaster.

As soon as the Henley season was over, Kenneth rejoined the Sadler's Wells Theatre Ballet, with the rank of soloist, in time for its Edinburgh Festival appearances in September 1952. The company was to give the premiere of Cranko's *Reflection*, an ambitious, tortuous work very different from his light-hearted Henley ballets. Cranko offered to drive three of the dancers from London to Edinburgh in his red car. Unwisely, as it turned out, Kenneth accepted the lift, along with a new company member, Margaret Hill, and Pirmin Trecu, a Spanish Basque dancer whose family were refugees from the Spanish Civil War. Driving through the Midlands, Cranko took a hump-backed bridge too fast and lost control at a sharp bend in the road immediately after it. The car rolled over five times, landing on the roof. Trecu, fifty years later, paled at the memory: 'Somehow we were all in different places, upside-down, from where we'd been sitting. John managed to climb out through the space where the windscreen had been but the rest of us were stuck. We were yelling, "Let me out, let me out", terrified the car was going to blow up.'

An AA patrolman helped them scramble out, bruised but otherwise unscathed. The car was a write-off. They were taken to hospital to be checked over and released after being given cups of sweet tea. Trecu recalled the aftermath: 'Somehow we got to a local station, where we waited for a train to Edinburgh. It was a Sunday, so nothing was open: no pubs, no hotels, nothing to eat or drink. The platform was empty, except for us. Kenneth, John and Maggie sat silent on a bench; I walked up and down. We were like zombies, in shock. Nobody said anything for hours until the train came.'

Trecu had a delayed reaction the next day but did not recall the others' aftershock. 'We had to get on with the dress rehearsal of John's ballet, so there was no question of time off.' Kenneth's phobia about most forms of travel was to develop later, though Cranko's car crash cannot have helped his nerves. Margaret Hill was as highly strung as he was; their shared experience in the overturned car strengthened the bond between them.

She was to become an important figure in Kenneth's life during his twenties. The same age as he was, she had started her professional career early, joining Ballet Rambert at fifteen. She had been the youngest member on the company's lengthy Australian visit, which lasted for eighteen months, instead of the intended six, between 1947 and 1949. Deprived of Arts Council funding, Ballet Rambert was keeping going by performing abroad. While on tour in Australia, Hill had married, at the age of nineteen, Leonard Donnett, a violinist who played in the company's pick-up orchestra. The marriage was short and unhappy. Although Margaret was reluctant ever to discuss with her friends what went wrong, they received the impression that the relationship had been a violent one. Donnett elected to stay in Australia, while she went back to Britain with Rambert's much depleted company. Soon after her return in 1949, Hill had danced with Jean Babilée in the Nijinsky benefit gala that Kenneth had seen at the Empress Hall.

Tall and dark, with an impressive stage presence, she had been moulded by Marie Rambert into a dramatic dancer–actress rather than a purely technical dancer. She had been given a wide range of roles in the company's repertory. She danced leading roles in Antony Tudor's ballets, *Jardin aux Lilas*, *Gala Performance* and *Dark Elegies*, as well as Odette in Act II of *Swan Lake* and the title role in *Giselle*. David Paltenghi, a senior dancer who had turned to choreography, chose her for his first ballets at the start of the 1950s. He had been a member of the Sadler's Wells Ballet as well as of Ballet Rambert, and was extending his career by choreographing for films as well as the stage. Far more worldly than Hill, he swept her into a tempestuous relationship, in which he was very much the dominant partner. Marie Rambert was rumoured to have encouraged their affair, even though Paltenghi was a married man, in order to keep him in her company.

He was known to be a rake, unable to keep his hands off the girls in any company, and was a heavy drinker, prone to violence. Alexander Bennett, a dancer who lived in the same boarding house as Hill, was attacked by Paltenghi, drunk and jealous, after a performance: 'He threw me against a wall and said, "If you don't get out of that house, I'll kill you." ' Paltenghi finally overstepped the mark as far as Marie Rambert was concerned when she discovered him in Hill's dressing-room before a Saturday matinee, shouting drunken abuse and beating her up. Rambert, outraged, promptly sacked him, summoning Ronald Hynd to take over his role in the matinee at a moment's notice.

Hill then left Ballet Rambert, initially on a temporary basis, 'owing to illness'. Some of the Rambert dancers knew that she had had an abortion, arranged by Paltenghi's doctor wife; she might also have suffered from chronic depression, for she was subject to nervous breakdowns for the rest of her life. By the time she joined the Sadler's Wells Theatre Ballet in August 1952, she was a damaged person, albeit a resolute one. Her youthful marriage had failed and her abusive affair had ended in disaster. The theatre was her life, however, and she was determined to dance, no matter what her personal problems might be.

Sadler's Wells Theatre Ballet dancers found her decidedly odd. They noticed that she hid herself under great sloppy sweaters in class and rehearsal, insisting that they made her feel comfortable rather than hot. She blinked nervously, a facial tic that vanished once she was on stage facing an audience. 'She'd be convulsed with nerves in the wings, twitching away, then make her entrance, totally serene, as Prayer in *Coppélia* or the Queen of the Wilis in *Giselle*,' remembers Ronald Hynd. She was theatrically camp, talking in an elaborate jargon with nicknames for everyone and everything. People she favoured were her 'bag carriers'; others were known by sets of initials: BLF (brash little fucker) for a self-confident male dancer, SLP (simpering little pisser) for a pretty ingenue. She let Kenneth in on her private language, which he relished; he, too, had his own codes with all his intimate friends. Like him, Maggie was a people-watcher: she would spot and mimic behavioural mannerisms, storing them in an imaginary pouch for use when she created a character on stage.

She had her own peculiarities. One of her treats was to eat meringues on the underground-station platform at Notting Hill Gate, 'getting off' on the smell of passing trains. 'She had a thing for coal – she liked its taste but because that seemed so odd, she ate black-and-white humbugs instead, non-stop,' remembers Sara Neil, a New Zealander who had recently joined the Theatre Ballet. 'We reckoned she ate more than her weight in mints in a year,' says Gilbert Vernon. She smoked like a chimney: 'We all did, so that wasn't unusual'; Sara Neil again. Droll and mild-mannered, she could none the less be passionate in her opinions and vehement about expressing them. Annette Page remembers Maggie's infatuation with the film actor Rock Hudson, whom she had never met in person: 'We had to go and see every film he was in. We'd seek them out on tour on Sunday nights.

Then when she discovered he was gay, from one of the dancers who'd spent the night with him, she minded so much she threw up.'

The Sadler's Wells dancers, who had never met anyone like her, were uncertain whether she was eccentric, neurotic or traumatised by the years she had spent in the Rambert company. Marie Rambert had a reputation as a possessive termagant who routinely undermined her dancers' self-esteem. Survivors were able to overlook or forgive her cruel remarks; the more vulnerable fled to other companies, bearing tales of their mistreatment. De Valois's dancers regarded these refugees with a mixture of awe and pity. They were also inclined to patronise Rambert dancers, believing that they had not been as well trained as the Sadler's Wells products. Margaret Hill was always to remain something of an outsider as far as the Theatre Ballet dancers were concerned. 'She was very self-contained, with a loneliness about her. Not a lot of people could get close to her,' says Sara Neil.

She and Kenneth, however, soon became inseparable. They recognised each other as soulmates, sharing many of the same obsessions. They even looked rather alike, dark-eyed, slender and long-legged. Their relationship was a physical as well as an emotional one. Margaret had none of the inhibitions that had daunted the girls Kenneth had first known as a teenager. She appreciated his gentleness after Paltenghi's violence, and she took away his anxieties about expressing his affection physically. He moved to live close to her, renting a bedsit in the same building in Queensborough Terrace in Bayswater, originally chosen by Hill for its proximity to Rambert's base in Notting Hill Gate. She invited Sara Neil to share a double bedsit with her.

'Ken was always up in our flat, listening to music with us and talking about ballet,' says Neil.

He was totally wrapped up in dance – we all were. He never mentioned his family or where he came from. He didn't want to talk about the past. He and Maggie would stay up all night playing canasta or mah jong or whatever the current craze was. At weekends, we used to travel miles across London to catch up with films that he or Maggie wanted to see.

On tour, Neil and her future husband, Walter Trevor, became a foursome with Margaret and Kenneth, staying in the same digs wherever they could. The girls were equipped with wedding rings in case landladies objected to unmarried couples sharing a room. After about a year, Neil thinks, Kenneth and Margaret moved out of Queensborough Terrace to live together in the house owned by Margaret's mother at 94 Westbourne Park Road in Notting Hill. It would remain his address for the next four years.

'They were as close as a hand in a glove,' remembers Yvonne Cartier, who had joined the Theatre Ballet the same time as Hill. Cartier thought they were more like twins than lovers, sharing the same neuroses and sense of humour. They talked endlessly, exchanging views on everything they saw. 'I don't know any mind that met Kenneth's as sharply as Margaret's,' says Michael Boulton. 'She had a very strong influence on everything he did. She was a highly intelligent artist.' When Kenneth came to make his first ballets, the principal female role would be a combination of himself and Margaret Hill, a vulnerable figure at odds with the world.

12

Kenneth's official debut as a choreographer came six months after he had rejoined the touring company. Peggy van Praagh had just been promoted from ballet mistress to Assistant Director, so she now had greater responsibility for the Theatre Ballet, under de Valois's overall direction of both Sadler's Wells companies. Van Praagh had always been closer to Cranko and his fellow South Africans, Alfred Rodrigues and David Poole, than to Kenneth; she had spent more time with them (Cranko in particular), while Kenneth was still, in his own words, 'a very neurotic teenager'. She had rather lost touch with his development during the four years he had been with the Covent Garden company, in spite of his occasional guest appearances with the Theatre Ballet. She welcomed him back as a performer, without knowing whether his choreographic ambitions might amount to anything.

Cranko had been her first successful protégé as a choreographer; Rodrigues was set to be her next, with two commissions for the 1952–53 season. The first, *Ile des Sirènes*, was given at Sadler's Wells on the company's return from the 1952 Edinburgh Festival. Kenneth, having only recently rejoined the company, played no significant role in it. He was cast as the lead, however, in a new ballet by Margaret Dale, to be given its premiere in January 1953. Dale, still a member of the Covent Garden company, had started to try her hand at choreography. She had done children's ballets for BBC television, and had been invited to create a work for Rambert's Choreographic Workshop at the Mercury Theatre, provided de Valois agreed. When she sought permission, de Valois responded, 'Why don't you do a ballet for us instead?' It was an offer Dale could not refuse, though she was pushed into trying something far more ambitious than she had intended. She was presented, as a fait accompli, with a subject proposed by the composer Richard Arnell, a friend (and former lover) of van Praagh's. He wanted to write a Sherlock Holmes ballet. Dale immediately thought of Kenneth as its hero because of his resemblance to Basil Rathbone, the tall, saturnine actor who played Holmes on film.

She invented her own scenario for *The Great Detective*, in collaboration with Arnell. Kenneth was required to be Moriarty, Holmes's arch-enemy, as well as play the pipe-smoking detective, complete with caped coat and deerstalker hat. As Holmes, he had a 'Dance of Deduction' to solo violin before setting off in pursuit of the villain. In the elaborate chase sequence of himself, Kenneth was instantly transformed from one character into another while passing behind a screen. 'His length of leg, hand and leap are particularly valuable in allowing him to be in all places at once', declared a reviewer in the *Dancing Times*. Speaking on the BBC Home Service, Ivor Brown commented, 'Holmes appears markedly as a man of action – there's very little of the idle, drug-taking dresser about him . . . as Professor Moriarty, he does a sort of dance of Mephistopheles, demonstrating the power of evil in a few well-chosen pirouettes, grands jetés and tours en l'air.' Margaret Dale, with hindsight, thinks it significant that she cast MacMillan as a dual personality: 'Though Kenneth's dark side hadn't shown itself then. That came later. He looked a bit young for Holmes but he and Stanley Holden as Watson were very funny together.'

The production received such faint praise (Richard Buckle dismissing it as 'a silly muddle' in the *Observer*) that Dale abandoned any further choreographic attempts. Kenneth relished his comeback role as a comic character, but was still obliged to do his fill of danseur-noble duties on tour: van Praagh needed to make the most of every soloist in the company. He was Prince Siegfried to Doreen Tempest's Odette when she made her debut in *Swan Lake* (Act II) with Kenneth as her partner. She was aghast when he said to her in the wings, 'Oh, I don't want to do this, do you?' 'Being so young and inexperienced, I didn't dare contradict him, but it was such an off-putting thing to say, especially since I was so nervous.' Tempest found him perfectly fine as a partner, though she was aware he was struggling against his own reluctance to appear on stage.

He kept going because de Valois had decided to set up a Sadler's Wells choreographic workshop to rival Rambert's Sunday evening try-outs. Dancers from both the Wells companies would be encouraged to experiment with making ballets: if promising, their attempts could be developed for inclusion in the Theatre Ballet repertoire. De Valois found the money for her Choreographers' Group by endorsing an advertisement for Craven A cigarettes, declaring that she smoked the brand exclusively. Later, when more funds were needed, she suggested endorsing yet another cigarette brand, failing to see any inconsistency in reselling her name 'exclusively'.

She and van Praagh entrusted the organisation of the Sunday-night workshops to David Poole, who, on Cranko's advice, asked Kenneth to take part. De Valois advised Kenneth not to get involved; in the *Out of Line* documentary he remembered her saying, 'Oh, I don't think you should do anything because you haven't been well. You've just joined this company and I think you should settle down and do nothing except dance.' She feared he might over-stretch himself, since Poole's first programme was planned for 1 February 1953, less than a fortnight after the premiere of *The Great Detective*. But with only a week to go, one of the would-be choreographers dropped out and Kenneth agreed to fill the gap.

He had to work fast, drawing on ideas that he had been mulling over since the summer in Henley. He selected music from his collection of Stan Kenton records, choosing enough pieces by Kenton and Peter Rugolo to last for twelve minutes. He called his ballet *Somnambulism*: its theme was the effect of dreams on human behaviour. Three dancers – Margaret Hill, David Poole and Maryon Lane – were discovered restlessly asleep, sprawled across a small flight of stairs leading to a shallow rostrum. In turn, each dancer had a solo variation depicting the state of mind suggested by their dreams, categorised as Anxiety, Premonition and Monotony. A corps de ballet of six provided a suitably ominous context, wearing black masks to transform them into the faceless fantasies of the three dreamers.

Kenneth's inspiration obviously came from his own experience of anxiety attacks, as well as from Margaret Hill, who, he confided to Greta Hamby, had extraordinarily vivid nightmares that troubled them both. He was also strongly influenced by films, in particular *The Cabinet of Dr Caligari*, with its sinister Expressionist shadows and even stranger characters. In Robert Wiene's 1920 film, the audience, like the film's narrator, can never be sure where dreams and reality begin and end.

For the workshop presentations, De Valois had stipulated that sets and costumes were to be kept simple. *Somnambulism*'s cast wore practice dress, their only props black masks and white gloves. Maryon Lane, who danced Premonition, was menaced by gloved hands reaching out from the wings. When she grabbed at a hand, a body fell dead at her feet. She believed herself responsible for the man's death, watching in horror as his corpse was carried across the stage in a mock funeral procession. (The device of a body falling out of the wings was similar to one Cranko had used in *The Forgotten Room*, as several of the Henley cast noted.) Kenneth had little time to elaborate his own ideas, although he knew the dramatic effects he wanted. He worked out the steps in advance, teaching Lane her Premonition solo in a cramped corridor leading to the lavatory because no rehearsal space was available. 'The beginning of my solo was heel, toe, heel, toe – Kenneth's sort of intricate "talking with the feet" was original, not something other choreographers were doing at that time,' she said.

In the solo representing Monotony, 'a study of a young man rocked by conflicting emotions, as if in a brainstorm, being mentally tortured', as the *Dance and Dancers* critic described it, David Poole danced the same step over and over. As well as saving choreographic time, the tedious repetition was probably an echo of Kenneth's own frustration as a dancer, waiting for Roland Petit or Andrée Howard to make up their minds which moves they wanted in their ballets. In Hill's solo, Anxiety, she had to pick her way on pointe like a tightrope-walker fearful of falling into a yawning chasm. When she hurt her ankle on the day of the performance, Kenneth took over her role, his improvisation adding to his own nervous tension at his choreographic debut. He danced as if in a trance.

The ballet concluded with an ambiguous awakening coda: the dancers, rubbing their eyes, realised that their sufferings had been only a dream. They grasped at each other in relief, only to recoil in fear, covering their faces with their hands, as they failed to shake off their nightmares.

Somnambulism made a powerful impact as the last work in the programme. The inaugural workshop had opened with Cranko's whimsical *Umbrellas*, first performed in the Henley season; in between came short works by Pirmin Trecu, Peter Franklin White and Ray Powell. Sadler's Wells, far larger than Rambert's tiny Mercury Theatre, was packed with friends, supporters and balletomanes. Critics were not invited to review, although writers for specialist publications – *Dancing Times, Dance and Dancers, Ballet Annual* – were present as observers. Clive Barnes commented later, in *Dance and Dancers*, when *Somnambulism* was taken into the company repertoire in 1956, on the lasting impression its first performance had made: 'Coming at the end of an evening of experimental try-out ballets by inexperienced choreographers that had been more interesting than startling, *Somnambulism* was obviously the work of a new choreographer potentially of the first rank.'

A woman had laughed during one of the *Somnambulism* solos, disconcerting Kenneth, who feared his ballet was being misunderstood. To his surprise and relief, the cast's curtain calls were greeted with cheers and wildly enthusiastic applause. Margaret Scott, who had come with Cranko as a loyal member of the Henley team, would never forget the excitement: 'It was the first time I'd ever had the feeling of being in a theatre when a star was born.' Peter Franklin White acknowledged, 'Everyone recognised that here was a choreographer – a big, daring talent using modern jazz instead of pretty piano music.' Margaret Dale generously recognised that his talent was greater than hers: '*Somnambulism* was astonishing, different, original, brilliant.' She summed up his achievement in a book of photographs of the Royal Ballet: 'In his first attempt he had revealed himself as a potential choreographer with not only a contemporary approach, a sense of humour and a highly individual style, but most important of all, real choreographic invention.'

Margot Fonteyn came backstage and congratulated him in his dressing-room. So did Cranko, who was so elated by Kenneth's success that he forgot all about his promise to drive Margaret Scott home. When he rang her later to apologise, he told her that de Valois had boasted, 'I always knew Kenneth was a genius. You could tell by the shape of his head. Now we know he is.'

Kenneth was taken by a group of friends to celebrate at Le Petit Club Français in St James's Place. It was a convivial dining club frequented by writers, publishers, artists and actors. Membership, far from strict, was largely a ploy to get round restrictive licensing laws. 'The French Club was our idea of the pinnacle of success, where our famous betters were to be seen,' Jeffrey Solomons recalls.

After *Somnambulism*, we all went in, sat down and there was total silence. Kenneth said flatly, 'Somebody laughed.' One of our group, I think Stella Claire, volunteered, 'Nervous laughter.' We nodded solemnly in agreement. More silence. I was immersed in Gertrude Stein at the time and I said, 'Well, here we all are, sitting.' Everybody repeated the words after me. We caught each others' eyes, started laughing and from then on it was a very jolly celebration.

When Solomons eventually returned home, he was telephoned by Peter Darrell, who had been unable to attend the performance. After Solomons had told him the good news about *Somnambulism*, Darrell asked whether Kenneth's choreography had been quirky, twisty, spiky. 'How did you know?' asked Solomons. 'He's tried out things like that in class ever since I can remember,' replied Darrell. Sharp-eyed, he had long ago spotted another choreographer in the making. Other colleagues, less observant, had assumed Kenneth would try his hand at creating something much more classical, like the roles he usually danced.

Kenneth claimed later, in a 1972 interview with John Gruen, that he had no idea what *Somnambulism* was going to be like: 'I thought when I started doing choreography it was going to be like things everyone else had done. In point of fact, it came out unlike anything anybody else had ever done. This is what surprised me as well as everyone else.' In an interview for his sixtieth birthday, however, he admitted that he had set out 'to be different enough for people to take notice of me, and I think I succeeded in that. Of course, it wasn't that different – we all have to learn from other people. It had traces of other choreographers in it. It wasn't until later that I really started to develop my own style.'

None the less, what astonished observers of Kenneth's first choreographic attempts was his already distinctive 'signature'. Yes, he was influenced by choreographers he admired – Roland Petit, Jerome Robbins, Antony Tudor, Frederick Ashton, John Cranko. But his debts were not blatant and his work already seemed more individual than the efforts of other tyro choreographers in the Sadler's Wells and Rambert workshops.

The magazine *Dance and Dancers* hailed his achievement by featuring him as Personality of the Month in March 1953: 'Reason: for having done a number of things well but for having found himself in something quite different.' The (anonymous) writer commented that *Somnambulism* was the first step towards 'something he could do superbly . . . His remarkable invention of movement, understanding of mood, sense of theatre and how to use a stage, make this one of the most mature first works we have seen.' Kenneth was also proud to have been acclaimed by *Melody Maker* magazine, whose coverage featured his use of 'Progressive Jazz' for a ballet. Its reviewer enthused, 'MacMillan is an asset to ballet and to jazz. More surprising was his acclamation by the typical ballet audience – for this jazz fan received more applause than his colleagues.' He told the magazine grandly, 'You can call me a modernist.'

Ballet Annual sounded a cautionary note: 'It is said that everyone can write one interesting book and it is equally true that every experienced dancer can put on one interesting ballet if it is in terms of his own body. It is with the second and third works that one can truly form an opinion.' The comment was evidently aimed at Kenneth as the discovery of the evening, lest the success of *Somnambulism* go to his head. He had no worries, however, about running out of inspiration: he was already looking forward, overflowing with ideas for future projects.

There was very little time to prepare for the second choreographic workshop on 14 June 1953, since the company would be on tour in the Netherlands, Belgium and Germany between 6 April and 3 June. Kenneth had planned a ballet to Gershwin's Piano Concerto in F major. The work's projected title was *Solitaire* but rehearsals had to be abandoned a week before the performance when Margaret Hill was taken ill. Kenneth filled the gap in the workshop programme with another quickly created piece, *Fragment*, to a recent Stan Kenton record, 'Taboo'. *Fragment* was a trio for Sara Neil, Annette Page and Donald Britton, all of whom he was to use again in his next ballets. Plans for *Solitaire* were shelved for the time being, to re-emerge three years later to a different choice of music.

Fragment appeared on the same programme as a repeat showing of *Somnambulism*. This time the workshop (whose name had been changed to the Sadler's Wells Choreographic Group) was reviewed. *Somnambulism* was once again admired as 'the best first ballet by any choreographer for many years'. Predictably, *Fragment* was regarded, by the same critic, Peter Williams, writing in *Dance and Dancers*, as 'a tiny chip off the old block'. Joan Lawson also found that 'his original ideas are limited to the modern jazz-style classicism he has originated', although she thought that the solo for Donald Britton 'showed interesting possibilities for MacMillan to develop his dance along more classical lines'.

Kenneth then used his Kenton record collection yet again in order to concoct a variety-show number for Peter Darrell. He and another ex-Theatre Ballet dancer, Hermione Harvey, had linked up as a duo, promoting themselves as 'Darrell and Harvey', a versatile dance version of silent-film comics Laurel and Hardy. Darrell evidently accepted Kenneth as a fellow choreographer, asking him to create a duet to extend their repertoire. He chose Kenton's jazz version of 'The Peanut Vendor' for an acrobatic music-hall routine, performed at the Empire Theatre, Walthamstow, in the East End of London.

De Valois had meanwhile instructed Kenneth to choose something other than jazz music for his next 'proper' choreographic attempt. While he was contemplating what he might do, he was busy dancing solo roles in the company's repertoire. He was a debonair Captain Belaye in Cranko's comic *Pineapple Poll*, and a soulful Moon in Alfred Rodrigues's new ballet, *Blood Wedding*, which was given its premiere on 5 June 1953. Rodrigues based his ballet on Federico García Lorca's play, *Bodas de sangre*, in which a girl, about to marry a man she does not love, flees with her lover into the woods. The bridegroom and his friends follow, and the two rivals fight to the death. Kenneth's role was as the pale, chill Moon, craving blood to warm his heart; Death aided him by bringing the lovers together, setting the tragedy in train.

Rodrigues selected Kenneth for his lyrical quality of movement: 'He had a softness without being feminine and those wonderful high extensions, which most men didn't have then. I wouldn't say he was melancholic but there was a sadness in him that was right for the Moon.' Margaret Hill had a powerful role as the bridegroom's mother, ending the ballet with the woman's decision not to seek vengeance for the death of her son. Although *Blood Wedding* was a popular success, remaining in the repertoire until the late

1960s, Rodrigues was obliged to wait for his chance to make more ballets for the company. Cranko came first – and MacMillan was starting to lay down his challenge as a contender.

A month after the Sadler's Wells premiere of *Blood Wedding*, the company flew to Rhodesia, to take part in the national Rhodes centenary celebrations. The flight was a long one, involving several stops *en route*, and a transfer to a smaller plane capable of landing at Bulawayo airport. Nervous flyers, including Kenneth, were aware that Louis Yudkin, the much loved Stage Director of the Royal Opera House, had been killed in a plane crash on his way to Bulawayo earlier in the year. He had been flying out to Rhodesia to check on staging arrangements for the opera and ballet performances. Dancers who knew him well from the long American tours, travelling with him on the 'Ballet Special' trains as Kenneth had, felt his death especially keenly.

Performances, scheduled between 6 and 18 July 1953, took place in a huge temporary structure seating three and a half thousand people. Nights were cool in the African winter and heating was inadequate in the hangar-like hall, resulting in a spate of colds and injuries. The Theatre Ballet gave sixteen performances of ten ballets, alternating with the opera company, the Hallé Orchestra and a company of actors from Britain, including John Gielgud. Many performers stayed on after the two-week season was over, planning to see more of the country. Kenneth and Margaret Hill, together with Peter Wright and Sonya Hana, had intended to hire a car and drive through the Wankie Game Reserve to the Victoria Falls.

In the event, Wright and Hana (she had joined the company after Cranko's Henley season) travelled on their own. As a result, they decided to set up life together, marrying the following year. To their recollection, Kenneth and Maggie had dropped out of the game-reserve trip in order to return to England with the company. Jeffrey Solomons, however, vividly remembers Margaret Hill summoning him to her aid after she had arrived back alone in London, in the midst of a nervous crisis: 'She called me from a restaurant in Notting Hill, near where she lived, saying she couldn't move, couldn't do anything. So I took a taxi to the café and there she was, hidden behind a newspaper which she wasn't reading, helpless. She dreaded going home.' He escorted her back to her mother's house; since Kenneth was not around, Solomons assumed he must have stayed on in Rhodesia. •

The incident implies a rift in the relationship between Kenneth and Margaret, although Solomons does not recall it being a break-up. Margaret was a volatile creature, prone to violent mood swings. Kenneth kept his feelings tightly contained. They leaned on each other for support at this stage in their affair, continuing to live together in her mother's house. Whatever had happened to distress Margaret after the Bulawayo trip had been put behind her by the time the company reassembled in London to prepare for the Edinburgh Festival in September. She and Kenneth appeared still to be very much a couple. They rehearsed together, both cast to dance in *Blood Wedding*, Cranko's *Pastorale* and Walter Gore's new circus ballet, *Carte Blanche*. An *Edinburgh News* photograph of the dancers arriving at Waverley Station for the start of the Festival shows Kenneth and Margaret standing side by side, smartly dressed (as van Praagh, like de Valois, insisted). Their private lives remained private and they were evidently fond of each other.

During the autumn season of 1953, the Theatre Ballet dancers started learning John Cranko's new ballet, *The Lady and the Fool*, scheduled for the end of the year. Because of various difficulties, including Cranko falling ill, the premiere was postponed until 25 February 1954, when the company was on tour in Oxford. Cranko had cast Kenneth as the taller, more romantic of two clowns, Moondog, with Johaar Mosaval his small sidekick, Bootface. They were Chaplinesque figures rather than circus clowns, social out-casts gazing wistfully at a society beauty, La Capricciosa (Patricia Miller). She encounters them in the street and invites them to accompany her to a ball, where she dances with her wealthy suitors. At the request of each one, she removes her mask only to reveal another one underneath. Alone, she takes off the last mask and is discovered, sad and vulnerable, by Moondog. They fall in love, to the horror of the party guests, who spurn them both. La Capricciosa departs with Moondog, who returns at the last minute to retrieve his friend Bootface. An epilogue shows all three com-rades together, contentedly asleep on the bench where they first met: the lady has become a clown, like her companions. (In later versions of the ballet, she exits arm-in-arm with them both.)

When Cranko outlined the story to his cast, explaining their roles with infectious enthusiasm, they were as excited as he was. Kenneth, however, told Jeffrey Solomons that he was disappointed by how sentimental the ballet turned out to be. Cranko realised that the initial version of *The Lady and the Fool* was incoherent and unsatisfactory. The following season, he revised the choreography for the corps, and subsequently reworked the ballet for the Covent Garden company in 1955, when it had greater success.

At its Theatre Ballet premiere in Oxford, the critics' laurels went to the two clowns. Andrew Porter in the *Financial Times* commended 'the shy, awkward, tender love of the [Moondog] clown, excellently danced by Kenneth MacMillan'. Arnold Haskell commented in *Ballet Annual*, 'The physical contrast between MacMillan and Mosaval and the manner in which they exploited it, their timing and their restraint are among the best things I have seen at Sadler's Wells.' In *Dance and Dancers*, Clive Barnes analysed the different approaches of the two performers to their roles: 'MacMillan is essentially an intelligent dancer, while Mosaval is an instinctive one. MacMillan's brains practically tick on stage, as with careful brilliance he conveys his characterisation . . . With MacMillan one thinks, "That's clever!", with Mosaval, "That's right!"'

The Sadler's Wells Choreographic Group had presented its third programme on 24 January 1954, a month before *The Lady and the Fool*'s postponed premiere. It was obviously no coincidence that Kenneth's new work, *Laiderette*, featured a waif-like heroine whose true self is hidden from society behind a mask. The ballet's invented title was coined from the French word 'laideronnette', which means 'little ugly one'. The heroine, wearing white-face make-up like a clown, is totally bald. Her appearance was apparently based on that of a child with a deformed head whom Kenneth had seen with her family while on holiday. His scenario concerned a group of itinerant clowns (shades of Petit's *Les Forains* and the pierrots in Ashton's *Illuminations*) who abandon one of their number, Laiderette, on the steps of a grand house where a ball is taking place. A Mask Seller places a mask over the sleeping girl's face. One of the male guests discovers her and goes inside to tell the others. The host invites the mysterious stranger to join the party. He falls in love with her, until she is unmasked by the guests; her cap comes off as well and she is revealed to be bald and ugly. Mocked and reviled, she is mournfully reclaimed by her clown family. They hold up a mirror and she sees herself as she truly is. She runs back up the steps to the house, where the host rejects her. He returns to the gaiety of the ball and Laiderette is left sobbing as the curtain falls.

For the workshop Sunday evening, the set of the house's façade was borrowed from the Sadler's Wells Opera company's production of *Eugene Onegin*; the costumes came from the ballet wardrobe. Kenneth had chosen music by the contemporary Swiss composer Frank Martin, the *Petite Symphonie Concertante* for harpsichord, harp, piano and orchestra. The plangent, percussive music, which he had first heard in Jeffrey Solomons's company, was the nearest alternative he could find to jazz, vetoed by de Valois. In the ballet, a recording of the *Petite Symphonie* appeared to originate from a hand-wound gramophone, trundled in a barrow by the sinister Mask Seller. At one point, when Laiderette was alone with the host of the party, the gramophone record compelled her to dance a frenzied solo: 'The strange, eerie chords of the harpsichord and harp seem to awaken fears in Laiderette, and she dances until her body is grotesquely shaken with hysteria,' wrote Clive Barnes in *The Decca Book of Ballet*. Laiderette's violent trembling was reminiscent of Kenneth's mother's fits. Like his mother, she had a secret to hide. No one must know that she was not like 'normal' people.

The choreography for the ugly little heroine, danced by Maryon Lane, was intricate and strange. She moved at first with the gaucheness of a child, swivelling her knees sideways, turning her toes in and out, beating her flexed feet together then arching them in quick relevés on pointe. In her signature step, a flowing arabesque was distorted into an angular position for the raised leg. Her arms were held behind her, hands clenched or splayed out in anguish. Lane said later that she recognised her character as a projection of Kenneth, scared that the world would reject him if people knew what he was really like. (Lane believed that her character, as well as being Kenneth in disguise, was inspired by Giulietta Masina as Gelsomina, the pathetic little clown in Fellini's film *La Strada*. Masina was the waif par excellence of the time but *La Strada* was not, in fact, released until later in 1954. It is possible, however, that Lane's role in a later MacMillan ballet, *Noctambules* (1956), owed something to simple-minded Gelsomina and her little drum.)

Kenneth, outwardly presentable, feared that he, like Laiderette, was a freak. His calm exterior was a front hiding his uncontrollable panic attacks. The emotions other people expected him to show, including grief over his parents' deaths, were alien to him. Laiderette's inconsolable tears at the end of the ballet might have been because, as Kenneth's alter ego, she knew she deserved to be found out and rejected. There is an otherwise inexplicable incident where, after her public unmasking, her father holds up a mirror to show her, as if she needed reminding, that she is bald and ugly. This version of the Cinderella story ends with ashes in the mouth.

Laiderette received such acclaim that de Valois wanted to take it immediately into the company's repertoire. 'Here was a work of near-genius,' declared Peter Williams in Dance and Dancers in March 1954. 'If this and his first work, Somnambulism, are fair examples of what we can expect from MacMillan, we have a choreographer of major dimensions.' Williams, founder editor of Dance and Dancers, was an enthusiast, a propagandist for artists whose work he admired, rather than a dispassionate critic. He became a good friend and patron of Kenneth and other choreographers and dancers, entertaining them to tea in his Ebury Street flat and guiding their choices of designers and composers.

Kenneth's joy at Laiderette's reception was soon tempered, however, by the news that de Valois had changed her mind about including it in the Theatre Ballet's repertoire. The Musicians' Union insisted that Frank Martin's music, instead of being played on a record, would have to be live and de Valois thought a harpsichord impractical to take on tour with the rest of the orchestra's instruments. Marie Rambert, however, had no such problems because Ballet Rambert, unlike the larger Sadler's Wells companies, was able to perform some ballets on tour to recorded music. Marie Rambert might have approached Kenneth, requesting Laiderette for her company, or, as Jeffrey Solomons recalls, Kenneth might have taken the initiative in telephoning her. Either way, Laiderette was given its first full-scale production by Ballet Rambert the following year, on 4 July 1955, when it was performed during Rambert's summer season at Sadler's Wells.

Soon after Laiderette's triumph in the third Choreographic Group evening, two visiting companies arrived in London, bringing works that would affect Kenneth's development as a choreographer. The pioneer of American modern dance, Martha Graham, gave her company's first London season at the Saville Theatre in March

1954. A previous season, scheduled to take place in 1950, had been cancelled, disastrously, at the last moment, and Graham had been apprehensive about trying again. When she did, London audiences were slow to respond. She and her work were an unknown quantity, outside a small circle of enthusiasts: audiences for the three-week season were embarrassingly small, with only a dozen people at one matinee. Most ballet critics, unimpressed, damned the 'constant grovelling on the floor'. Richard Buckle's enthusiastic reviews in the *Observer* were an exception: 'Everything she does is true and essential . . . she has enlarged the language of the soul.' He commented later, in 1963, 'I had the impression that theatre people – as opposed to ballet people – were fascinated, because I got fan letters from actors and directors for what I had written.' Kenneth was among the few ballet dancers who went to the performances. He was particularly impressed by Graham herself in her role as the young bride in *Appalachian Spring* (Graham was sixty at the time). At one point in the work, to Aaron Copland's joyous score, she rolled up and down the steps of the porch in ecstasy. It was the most extraordinary thing he had ever seen a dancer do, 'rolling on the floor in a long taffeta dress, making emotion real', he told Robin Howard, who sponsored the Graham company's visit to the Edinburgh Festival in 1963, which was followed by a successful London season at the Prince of Wales Theatre. Howard was to set up the London Contemporary Dance Theatre company in the mid-1960s, staffed by Graham teachers. MacMillan was always interested in LCDT's activities, eventually making work for some of its dancers. He never identified with ballet purists who felt she had little to offer them.

Soon after the Graham company had completed its first London season, Janine Charrat's Ballet de France arrived at the Stoll Theatre, giving performances from 6 to 24 April 1954. A former dancer and choreographer with Roland Petit's company, Charrat had set up her own group in 1951. The talking point of the London season was her latest creation, *Les Algues*. It vindicated Kenneth's belief that ballet (as well as modern dance) could deal with controversial, contemporary subjects. Themes and devices Charrat had used would resurface in different forms in his own works. *Les Algues* was set in a modern mental hospital, where a young man had gone to find his loved one, Catherine. He had met her at a masked ball and drawn her into an abusive relationship that 'had proved disastrous for her romantic and hypersensitive character', as a programme note put it. The bal-. let opened with the effect of an ambulance drawing up to the asylum gates, the amplified sound of its siren and a jumble of voices relayed over a loudspeaker. The hero had feigned madness in order to be admitted to the asylum. There he encountered deranged inmates, including the 'King of the Snake Pit', an 'Erotomaniac' couple and the 'Outwardly Happy Man', and risked losing his own sanity. He danced a memorably tortured solo with his arms constrained by a straitjacket. In the end, he was free to go, leaving Catherine (Charrat herself) in her shadowy dream-world.

Somnambulism was televised by the BBC on 1 April 1954, re-titled *The Dreamers*. Videotape was not yet in use, so the performance had to be transmitted live, with Stan Kenton's music played in the TV studio by Ted Heath and his Band. The soloists were Maryon Lane, David Poole and Pirmin Trecu, in the role originally intended for Margaret Hill. The television director, Naomi Capon, made full use of the technology of the time. According to one review, there were 'inserts, fades, dissolves, superimposing one picture on another and even shots through a narrow slot in a back wall . . . Skeletons floated into the heads of the sleepers. It was all as modern as this morning.' An elaborate set, designed by Michael Yates, suggested a vast, empty hall, 'with long unexplored shadowy passages, leading off into the unknown darkness'.

The broadcast was well received, with reviewers expressing surprise that ballet did not have to involve fairy stories and classical music. One writer decided that MacMillan was reflecting the spirit of the age: '*The Dreamers* aimed to show the frustration and torment of youthful dreams. As danced last night, it did more – it symbolised the yearning for peace and quiet which afflicts this generation of the children of the atom bomb.'

A week after *The Dreamers* had been transmitted, the Sadler's Wells Theatre Ballet set off by sea on a three-month tour of South Africa. The boat journey took a fortnight, during which the dancers did daily class on the upper deck under Peggy van Praagh's supervision. Down below, travelling steerage, they put on cabarets in the evenings and won all the prizes in the ship's fancy-dress ball. 'The first-class passengers came down to our cabarets because we were having all the fun,' remembered Valerie Reece. David Gill, a senior dancer who later became a film director, passed the time making an amateur film in which Kenneth was cast as a thief stealing jewels from a passenger's cabin.

On 22 April 1954, the ship docked at Cape Town, where the company was given a series of civic receptions. The South African dancers on the tour included three principals, Maryon Lane, Patricia Miller and David Poole. Two others, John Cranko and Alfred Rodrigues, were represented by their choreography. The company then flew to Johannesburg for the start of the tour proper. Tickets sold so fast that the Johannesburg season was extended to seven weeks – the longest run for a visiting company in the city's history so far.

Kenneth was to dance the last role ever created on him in *Café des Sports*, Rodrigues's new ballet. The action took place in a town square in the South of France, through which passed the Tour de France cycle race. The café of the title was filled with a clientele of pseudo-intellectuals: described in the cast list as Hedonists, Essentialists and Absinthe-drinkers, they duly shocked the local bourgeoisie passing through the square. Kenneth was the leader of the 'Essentialists', a caricatured group of Existential poseurs. Doreen Tempest and Sara Neil, who danced a pas de trois with him as members of his group of followers, remember he hated doing the role. Photographs show him looking lanky and weedy in black, pretentiously clutching a skull; it was the kind of persona he despised.

South African audiences enjoyed *Café des Sports* as an entertaining piece of popular theatre. (London critics were sniffier when the ballet was shown at Sadler's Wells, with Arnold Haskell opining in *Ballet Annual*, 'To poke fun at existentialism in 1954 is completely pointless.') The company was greeted with great enthusiasm wherever it went. For a change, no comparisons could be made with the senior company, which the South Africans had never seen. A cult of hospitality grew up around the dancers, as local party-givers vied with each other to have them as star attractions.

Among the company's most devoted fans was a nineteen-year-old student, Christopher Nupen. He had gone backstage in Johannesburg, spotted a party invitation on the theatre's bulletin board and gate-crashed it in order to meet dancers. He was immediately drawn to a pair sitting slightly apart from the others – Kenneth and Margaret Hill:

'They had an air of vulnerability about them. They weren't stand-offish; they were very engaging.' Nupen succeeded in carrying off Maggie, with whom he had a holiday romance, unaware of her long-established relationship with Kenneth.

Kenneth, however, knew about Margaret's affair with her hand-some young admirer from the start. So did the rest of the company, including Peggy van Praagh, to whom Margaret boasted of her conquest. Nupen was accepted by all of them:

I loved the easy straightforwardness of the way Maggie and the other dancers lived. To me, at nineteen, they seemed to know enough about who they were and what they were doing to have no inhibitions, no hypocrisy about sex. They just enjoyed themselves. Kenneth and Maggie had this tremendous companionship, with shared jokes and laughter, but it didn't seem an overtly sexual one. Maggie didn't tell me how complex it was till I followed them to London. I was the only one who didn't know what I was getting involved in.

After Johannesburg, the tour had continued to Durban, for that city's centenary celebrations, and ended in Cape Town. Peggy van Praagh had given an undertaking to British Actors' Equity that performances would be to 'mixed' audiences of all races. The South African Theatres management group, which presented the company, reneged on the deal. In spite of van Praagh's pleas, performances were given in 'Whites Only' theatres.

The tour made a profit for the company, fuelling dissatisfaction among the lowly paid dancers. The Theatre Ballet was still regarded back home as the junior group, so salaries were accordingly low. The corps-de-ballet rate was only £8 a week, with no differentiation between newcomers and those who had been with the company for years; the top principals' salary was £18, far less than Covent Garden soloists received. Yet on a foreign tour such as the South African one, dancers were expected to be smartly dressed for offi-cial receptions, paying for suits and party clothes out of their mea-gre touring allowance of £3 a week. Several couples in the company were now married or about to be, wanting to set up home instead of living in digs. The senior dancers approached van Praagh as the tour ended, asking for a bonus in recognition of the hard work they had put in to ensure the company's success. She advised them to approach the Sadler's Wells management on their return.

The company travelled back, once again, by ship from Cape Town. The South African members stayed behind for a holiday with their families, while van Praagh flew to Italy for her summer break. During the two-week sea voyage, an action committee led by David Gill met to discuss the dancers' pay claims. There was plenty of time for heated discussions about the unfairness of the 'junior' company's treatment. The committeee resolved that instead of a bonus on top of the regular salary, the dancers should insist on a flat-rate increase of £2 a week. Yvonne Cartier, a soloist at the time, spoke up for the longer-serving members of the corps de ballet, insisting that they should be paid as much as junior soloists, instead of being treated as newly graduated 'kids'. Valerie Reece, one of the kids, accepted that they must all stick together: 'All for one, as a force to be reckoned with. It was all rather exciting and frightening.' The dancers decided to ask Equity to support their case before putting their demands to Stephen Arlen, General Manager of the Sadler's Wells Trust.

There was bound to be trouble, for de Valois's dancers had never before challenged the judgement of their 'betters'. Pirmin Trecu, who was to be transferred to the Covent Garden company after the South African tour, feared his chances would be spoiled if he went to action committee meetings: 'I knew Madam would be furious. She said to me afterwards, "Good boy. Do as I tell you and you'll get on." ' He cannot remember whether Kenneth and Margaret Hill were involved and nor can anyone else on the tour. Friends from the time think it unlikely, for their interests were so bound up in ballet that they would be very reluctant militants. If they did attend shipboard meetings, they were not among the vocal campaigners.

Trouble duly ensued on the company's return. The management was prepared to offer an increase in salary only according to individual merit, not on a flat-rate basis. De Valois invited the dancers to see her but found their demand to meet her at the Equity headquarters, in the presence of Equity officers, unacceptable: 'She was outraged. We were told our jobs were on the line. She said she could get rid of us at a stroke,' remembered Valerie Reece. Sara Neil was shocked because the dancers were accused of threatening to strike, an action they had never discussed: 'It was Madam who said we were on strike. She cancelled our season at Sadler's Wells, so we were stranded, without any money.'

De Valois held van Praagh responsible for the dancers' militancy because she had not accompanied them on the voyage home and had been unable to defuse their demands. The crisis escalated as the press became involved, sympathetically comparing the dancers' low pay with the higher wages earned by chorus girls in revues. Equity made the point that the Theatre Ballet was less well paid than the Sadler's Wells Opera company under the same management. Then, to add to the drama, the Soviet Communist Party sent a message of solidarity, signed by Russian ballet dancers such as Galina Ulanova, to their British comrades, mentioning (to their intense embarrassment) the names of David Gill and Yvonne Cartier. By mid-August there was talk of the Sadler's Wells Theatre Ballet being disbanded.

The dancers, meanwhile, were penniless. De Valois had no compunction about withholding their salaries. Kenneth and Margaret had to cut short a holiday with Jeffrey Solomons in West Sussex because they had run out of money. They were reduced to collecting abandoned soft-drink bottles in Hyde Park in order to pick up a few pence in refunds. In despair, Margaret contacted Marie Rambert to find out if she would be welcomed back to her former company. Rambert responded enthusiastically, writing to Kenneth, 'We all want her back.' Hill rejoined the company on a six-month contract. In her letter of 2 October 1954 addressed to Kenneth, Rambert had proposed an appointment with 'each one of you'. She might have wanted to see Kenneth to discuss plans for mounting *Laiderette* the next year; he could also have been keeping his options open for a job with her company.

By September, however, the Sadler's Wells stand-off had been resolved. The dancers did not receive anything like their full demands, although their salaries were raised a grudging amount, with the promise of a further review of the wage structure. De Valois insisted that the second company was still the junior one, to be paid accordingly: a Wells soloist, she decreed, had no more status than a member of the Covent Garden corps; a principal at the Wells was merely the equivalent of a soloist at Covent Garden. By now, it was evident to Theatre Ballet dancers that many of them had fought a lost cause. They had either to accept de Valois's terms or leave the company.

Kenneth, unlike Margaret Hill, was in a strong position. He had proved himself a promising choreographer, so de Valois would be keen to keep him from going elsewhere. He knew his own worth and he also knew how to negotiate, using Rambert's interest in him as a bargaining counter. First, he was immediately promoted from soloist to principal dancer, earning £14 a week. Then, on 2 September, he received a letter from the director of the Sadler's Wells Theatre, Norman Tucker:

This is to confirm what I told you this morning, that we would like you to do a new ballet for us to be produced next January. I understand you have been offered choreography at Glyndebourne next year, and we will release you as necessary to do this. In addition, if other opportunities for choreography arise during the course of this next season, we will do our best to make it possible for you to undertake the work.

One such opportunity was a commission from the BBC, thanks to the acclaim for *The Dreamers*, to create the choreography for a three-part television series explaining ballet to young viewers. The series would go out in November. From collecting empty lemonade bottles in August, he was about to be in the money, his reputation growing as a choreographer, by the time he turned twenty-five on 11 December 1954.

13

Steps Into Ballet, Kenneth's first commission specifically for television, was transmitted live on three successive Monday evenings, starting on 29 November 1954. Naomi Capon, who had directed *The Dreamers*, was in charge. Each programme was introduced by Peggy van Praagh, whose explanations about how ballet works were first demonstrated by the dancers, then incorporated into a 'serial ballet' in three parts, choreographed by Kenneth. The music was Richard Arnell's ballet score, *Punch and the Child*, which had first been choreographed in 1947 by Fred Danieli for Ballet Society, the forerunner of New York City Ballet, which kept it for a while in the repertoire. Kenneth stuck closely to Arnell's and Danieli's scenario about a Victorian child at the seaside, for whom Punch and Judy come alive.

Arnell had been the composer of Margaret Dale's *The Great Detective*, as well as Cranko's *Harlequin* in April (1951). *Punch and the Child* had been his first ballet score. He had subsequently had two young daughters who learned ballet and he was a regular ballet-goer himself. He was quoted in the BBC's *Radio Times* of 26 November 1954 as saying, 'It is apt that *Punch and the Child*, which is about a child's fantasy, should have its British premiere on children's television. There is something hugely satisfying in having a juvenile audience.'

Van Praagh opened the first *Steps Into Ballet* programme by demonstrating how everyday walking and jumping steps are turned into ballet. She explained that the way the steps are performed to music can convey character and emotion. Kenneth's choreography then introduced Mother (Maureen Bruce), Father (Donald Britton) and the Child (Susan Saloman, a twelve-year old ballet student) through their manner of walking. Although the device had to be spelt out in simple terms for children, it was one that Kenneth was to adopt when he created narrative ballets. A hallmark of his style is the way that his leading characters – women in particular – declare themselves by how they step onto the stage even before they launch into dancing proper: his Juliet, Manon, Anastasia, Mary Vetsera and many others reveal first who they are, then how they have changed during the course of a ballet, by placing one foot in front of the other in their own signature walking sequence.

Kenneth developed the device from his own observation rather than from van Praagh's instruction. He was a good actor–dancer, as was Margaret Hill. Both specialised in spotting and mimicking people's mannerisms, as well as studying the techniques used by actors on film and in the theatre. Dancers instinctively look at other performers' feet and posture as a way of sizing them up. For Kenneth, the exercise of having to illustrate his tradecraft for children's television would have reinforced the importance of making his characters' traits clear from the outset.

He played a role himself in the succeeding two television programmes as the heavy-footed policeman who pursues Punch, 'in what can only be described as seven-league boots', as *Dance and Dancers* put it in February 1955. The three-part ballet tells how the child, on holiday at an English seaside resort, becomes caught up in the antics of the puppet-show characters, before being reclaimed by her parents. The beach setting was designed by Michael Yates, who had collaborated with Kenneth on the television version of *Somnambulism*.

A reviewer in *Dance and Dancers*, Nicholas Barker, regretted that the *Punch and the Child* ballet could not be given a complete run-through at the end, instead of being shown in consecutive parts. He wrote that there had apparently been contractual difficulties over using recorded music. Arnell's score was played from a recording conducted by Sir Thomas Beecham, while John Lanchbery (the Theatre Ballet's conductor) accompanied van Praagh's demonstrations, live, on the piano. The BBC's tortuous agreement with the Musicians' Union over the use of live and recorded music was to cause problems when Kenneth came to create his next television commission, in October 1955.

While *Steps Into Dance* was being transmitted, Kenneth was preparing his first Sadler's Wells Theatre Ballet commission for January 1955. He was following in the footsteps of Cranko and Rodrigues as an in-house choreographer. De Valois insisted that he now use 'proper' music, to be played by the company's orchestra, not jazz. His first choice was Stravinsky's *Divertimento* from *Le Baiser de la fée*. He had bought a record of *Le Baiser de la fée* in New York when he was on tour with the main company in 1950. (New York City Ballet had been performing Balanchine's ballet to the Stravinsky score at the time.) Kenneth was haunted by the music, but de Valois warned him that the rights would be very expensive: in any case, the score required too large an orchestra for the touring company's resources. So he opted instead for the music on the reverse side of his *Divertimento* record: Stravinsky's *Danses concertantes*, which requires just twenty-four instruments. Jeffrey Solomons had sent Kenneth a laconic postcard (the equivalent between friends of a text message or email today) saying, 'Turn the record over.'

Solomons was aware that Kenneth's taste in modern music had not evolved beyond early-to-middle-period Stravinsky. They had both recently been to an avant-garde concert in Forbes House in Knightsbridge, where the ballet critic Richard Buckle had remounted a magnificent exhibition, first displayed at the Edinburgh Festival, about Diaghilev's Ballets Russes. In a concert during the exhibition, John Cage and David Tudor played their own compositions on 'prepared' pianos: the piano wires were adapted to make far-from-usual percussive sounds. Solomons remembers he and Kenneth trying desperately not to laugh, since they were in full view of Andrée Howard sitting solemnly opposite them. Kenneth hissed to Jeffrey, 'Thank God it's over. I was dying to light a cigarette – but I was afraid if I scratched a match someone would think it was part of the performance!' Solomons commemorated the occasion with two cartoons: one was of the radical pianists; the other depicted languid Kenneth, cigarette in hand, standing in front of Stravinsky's portrait in the exhibition, saying, 'That's my composer, you know!!'

Stravinsky's *Danses concertantes* was first performed in 1942 as a concert piece for chamber orchestra, not as a ballet score. There is evidence, however, that he had conceived it with Balanchine in mind and Balanchine did indeed choreograph a ballet to it two years later. Unlike *Le Baiser de la fée*, Stravinsky's homage to Tchaikovsky, it has no narrative content. It appealed to Kenneth as playful, restless, acerbic, twentieth-century music, with more than a hint of jazz. John Lanchbery, the company's Music Director and Principal Conductor, made his own piano reduction of the score for Kenneth to work with in the rehearsal studio – the first of a fruitful series of collaborations between the two men. Lanchbery confirmed dancers' memories that Kenneth needed no help in analysing the music. 'When we had difficulty with it, he used to say, "Just listen – quietly, quietly", and everything began to make sense,' remembers Sara Neil.

By taking on a plotless ballet this early in his choreographic career, Kenneth was deliberately breaking the mould of dance-drama that shaped the touring company's repertoire. He was moving into a different league, inviting comparison with Ashton's *Scènes de ballet*, to a slightly later Stravinsky score. The lessons he had absorbed while learning Ashton's choreography for *Scènes de ballet* were bearing fruit. His response to Stravinsky, however, differed from Ashton's. Where Ashton contrasted the sharpness of his dancers' footwork with soft, languorous usage of the upper body, Kenneth kept the movement consistently jagged and restless, fingers stiffly pointed. There are overt Ashton quotes, however, in the way the leading woman exits, once with a shrug addressed to the audience, once running off with her arms twisting around her head. Looking back after a revival of *Danses concertantes* in 1989, he remarked, 'I tried to match the spikiness of the music and its sort of off-beat, jazzy quality. I saw it recently and I think it still stands up.'

He chose Maryon Lane for the central role, but this time, instead of exploiting her urchin qualities, he took her strong, speedy technique to new, sophisticated extremes. She was to distort her pure classical line by wiggling her hips, splaying her fingers and even breaking into a kind of tap routine in her pointe shoes. His understanding of how versatile pointework could be was unusual for a young male choreographer. His early experiments in trying on girls' toe shoes were coming in useful, as was his observant eye for other choreographers' innovations: Petit's use of parallel positions and flexed feet, Balanchine's play with off-centre balances.

The principal male soloist was Donald Britton, who had a near-infallible sense of rhythm. According to Michael Boulton, 'Donald was the only one of us who could cope with the music that our pianist, Dmitri, used to play in class. It was terribly complex stuff and I think he did it sometimes just to test Donald. Kenneth really used Donald's musicality in *Danses concertantes*: I've never seen anyone else do those solos so well – they were killers.' Kenneth was stretching his cast's skills, adapting the Cecchetti enchainements they had been taught in class and adding quirky touches of his own. One of the angular arm positions in Britton's role, for example, came from the gesture of drinking wine from a leather bottle hooked over a shoulder.

To add an element of mystery, Kenneth devised a mask effect for Lane by showing her different ways of twisting her wrists and fingers around her eyes. 'It was entirely his idea,' she said. 'He had it all worked out. He was delighted when de Valois asked him after the dress rehearsal how I'd got rid of the mask so cleverly.' From a distance, the oddly angled fingers in black gloves uncannily resemble a mask, framing the dancer's glittering eyes and then magically disappearing. The impression of a disguise echoes the multiple masks La Capricciosa wears in Cranko's *Lady and the Fool*. Abstracting the idea for *Danses concertantes*, Kenneth had the leading lady's five suitors appear to stamp masks shaped by their fingers all over her body while she smiles enigmatically, looking through her own fingers.

Six corps-de-ballet women sit behind the soloists, poised coquettishly on chairs with one leg crossed in front of the other like a revue chorus line. In an early, cramped rehearsal in the Sadler's Wells foyer, while the single studio was in use, the girls waiting to take part in the ballet had perched along the drinks-bar counter in order to leave space for the soloists. Kenneth saw and exploited their natural elegance by lining them up in the same positions, the three soloists perched on the men's shoulders, arms linked, the others on throne-like chairs. His ballets often feature the poses dancers fall into at rest or while stretching their muscles as they wait for instructions. Their presence in the rehearsal room became for him part of the architecture of the ballet he saw in his mind's eye.

Having decided how he wanted to treat Stravinsky's *Danses concertantes* choreographically, Kenneth was ready to choose a designer for the first time in his new career. He was confident enough to reject de Valois's suggestions, which included Andrée Howard (who designed as well choreographed). 'She's trying to palm off on me all the designers she feels guilty about,' he told Gilbert Vernon. 'But I said I wasn't having any of them.' He proposed going to the Slade School of Fine Art to look at the work of students on the theatre-design course. De Valois insisted on going along too, so that she could introduce him to the Slade's Principal, Sir William Coldstream, who had recently become a member of the Royal Opera House Board.

She summoned a taxi, which dropped them near the art school in Gower Street. De Valois hustled him along the corridors of the first building they entered. 'She wouldn't listen to me when I kept saying, "Madam, there are *nurses* everywhere." We were in the University College Hospital instead of the Slade next door.' When they found the right building, Coldstream took them into his office and showed them the portfolios of students he had selected. Kenneth was impressed by the work of Nicholas Georgiadis, a postgraduate student who had studied painting and architecture in his native Greece and then in New York before coming to the Slade on a British Council scholarship. Aged thirty-two, he had already designed for the theatre in a distinctive style of his own, using stark structures and vivid Mediterranean colours – very different from the paler palettes of English stage designers.

'Nico' Georgiadis was duly commissioned. 'Kenneth said he wanted something in a neo-classic manner. So I gave him neo-classicism pared to the bones – the skeleton of classical buildings, to match the spikiness in the score. He saw the sketches and model as they progressed and he was content.' The architectural features were painted across the backdrop and wings; slender sphinxes with fingerlike wings appeared on the chairs as well as the backcloth. Barbed arrows on the men's brilliantly coloured bodytights (turquoise, yellow, lime green, burnt orange) were visual counterparts of the musical accents in the score. Men and women alike wore black chokers around their necks and cropped black gamin wigs crowned with head-dresses, pyramid-shaped for the men, bird emblems for the women. The vivid designs were unlike anything seen in a ballet before. To one commentator, Cormac Rigby, speaking on the Third Programme, their costumes suggested 'interplanetary nobility, dancing out a witty, sparkling courtly life . . . The princess brings her fingers up towards her face in what could be a mask to emphasise her mystery or could be glasses through which to watch the earthbound mortals beyond the wrought ironwork of her planetary palace.'

To other reviewers, the dancers looked like brightly plumaged birds, prinking, dipping and turning in an elaborate aviary. The 'cocked heads, flashing hands and sudden scatterings' described by Alexander Bland, might have been suggested by birdcalls in the score. They were also elements in a brittle, unpredictable dance vocabulary that Kenneth was to explore in his next work, *House of Birds*. *Danses concertantes* swiftly established him in the eyes of *Ballet Annual* as a 'genuine choreographer of a rare kind', although a warning note was sounded by A. V. Coton in the *Spectator*: 'A fine talent in danger of smothering by over-forcing: in this work he has thought out everything imaginable that can be done with fourteen bodies in twenty-five minutes.'

Clive Barnes, in a review for *Dance and Dancers* in February 1955, predicted his future judiciously:

MacMillan needs now the same opportunities as were given to Cranko. Sadler's Wells has seen its first entirely local boy make good, yet his final testing must come in his next half-dozen or so ballets, and, in a sense, the National Ballet is as much on trial as the choreographer. MacMillan has a talent which, if properly used, can add quite a few paragraphs and probably an important chapter in the history of British ballet.

Mary Clarke in the *Dancing Times* paid him the compliment of calling him 'one of the very few English choreographers who can be witty in movement, without props or situations to assist him, and in this respect, *Danses concertantes* belongs to the same school as Ashton's *Les Rendezvous*'.

Ashton evidently recognised the tribute and the challenge (and the borrowings from his own choreography) without yet feeling threatened. Kenneth was still his protégé, as well as being a companion Ugly Sister in his *Cinderella*. After the first night of *Danses concertantes* on 18 January 1955, he invited Kenneth to bring a friend to dinner at his house in Yeoman's Row. Jeffrey Solomons accompanied Kenneth. Ashton put himself out to entertain them with his celebrated impersonations of Ida Rubinstein and Bronislava Nijinska, as well as of the ballerinas he was going to use in his next ballet, *Birthday Offering*. He played jazzy 1920s recordings that he thought Kenneth would like – and which, according to Solomons, he did not.

The acclaim for *Danses concertantes* gave Kenneth the courage to inform de Valois that he wanted to stop dancing and become a full-time choreographer. She was not prepared to agree. She had allowed Cranko to stop performing, but MacMillan was too useful a dancer to let go at the age of only twenty-six. John Lanchbery recalled the confrontation scene in the Sadler's Wells canteen: 'Madam was lecturing him in a corner and he was losing his temper. We were so impressed that he could stand up to her like that. Then she noticed we were all listening and glared at us. We crept out of the canteen like ashamed schoolchildren.'

Kenneth won the day. De Valois, who respected those who dared defy her, took him off the dancers' payroll and put him on a resident choreographer's contract. His salary dropped by a pound a week to £13, but he received notional royalties. He kept among his papers the first royalty statement he received for *Danses concertantes*: for the seven performances on tour following its Sadler's Wells premiere he received just over £10. The ballet would remain in the Royal Ballet's repertoire, standing the test of time in successive revivals.

14

Now that Kenneth was no longer performing, he stopped attending daily class. Instead of his hours being determined by the dancers' busy schedule, he had time on his hands. He had no need to tour with the company unless he was working on a ballet that had to be rehearsed on the road. He was still living at the Westbourne Park Road house leased by Margaret Hill's mother. Margaret, during her six-month return to Ballet Rambert, was often away on tour. She had resumed many of her former roles as a principal dancer with the company, which had welcomed her back. Van Praagh had asked her to make a brief appearance with the Sadler's Wells Theatre Ballet in Rodrigues's *Café des Sports* (as Madame Flora, the café owner) at the start of 1955, so she would have been present at Kenneth's opening night of *Danses concertantes* on 18 January.

Her affair with Christopher Nupen was over. On coming to London, he had discovered that Maggie's enduring relationship with Kenneth was far more complex than he had realised. He appreciated he was out of his depth in trying to understand what was going on. She and Kenneth were emotionally bound together, even though they felt free to have sexual flings elsewhere. Nupen, just twenty, could not handle the complications of continuing his affair with Maggie while remaining friends with Kenneth. Fascinated by them both, he wanted to remain part of their world without feeling an interloper: 'They were a gang of two. Maggie told me how Kenneth had rescued her from a bad relationship and how she'd thrown a lifeline to him. They were so bound up together, they even shared the same way of speaking. And Kenneth was the first creative artist I became close to, which influenced the course of my life.'

Nupen went on to become a highly respected film and TV director, specialising in the lives and performances of artists and musicians. He likens Margaret Hill to the young Jacqueline du Pré, whom he came to know while making a celebrated documentary film (*Trout Quintet*, recorded in 1969) about her for BBC Television. According to him, Hill, like du Pré, had an engaging openness about her, a capacity for uninhibited enjoyment that masked her pain and insecurity. Hill, too, exposed her soul in performance with a frankness that could be frightening: Sonja Roberts in *Ballet Today* wrote of her Giselle (with Ballet Rambert), 'She has the power to make me want to crawl under my seat, rather than witness the extraordinarily realistic mental crack-up going on before my eyes.' Such vulnerability in a performer comes at a price, paid not only by the artist but also by those close to her.

While Hill was on tour with Ballet Rambert, Kenneth spent most of his free time with male friends. He established his own routine of eating in the same places with much the same group of habitués. The

French Club in St James's Place was a regular haunt, as was a favourite Greek Street restaurant known as Lena's (after a waitress who worked there). Lena's was run by Madame Maurer, a stout Bavarian woman with a ghastly dog. Madame Maurer served generous helpings of heavy German food, charging low prices for people she liked and exorbitant sums for those she wished to drive away. Her restaurant was a useful meeting place for dancers and actors from commercial shows in the West End and roving freelances such as Peter Darrell and Jack Carter. Jeffrey Solomons joined the ad-hoc group on Saturdays, when he was free from work and could spend all afternoon over lunch before going on to the cinema.

Solomons remembers Kenneth announcing rather grandly one day, 'My designer is coming to lunch.' Then he added, 'He's older than us and he seems to know more about everything than anyone I've ever met.' Nico Georgiadis soon became a regular at Lena's. Tall and imposingly handsome, he spoke softly with idiomatic Greek inflections and wry, impish humour. His manner was confiding until he took a view from which he would not be budged, supremely confident that he was right. He was a gifted teacher, willing to impart what he knew without pomposity. Widely read and cosmopolitan in outlook, he was far better informed about the world outside dance than Kenneth and his friends, who were six or seven years younger than Nico – a considerable gap at their age. Like them, he loved the theatre, in which he was to play an important role as a designer for plays, operas and ballets in Europe and America. He was to transform the way sets were designed (especially for ballet), giving them greater architectural substance in place of painted drops and gauzes. He brought his scholarly knowledge of period to the creation of props and costumes; his musicality informed his use of colour for more abstract works. He and Kenneth would continue to collaborate for the next thirty-five years.

During the lunches at Lena's, Kenneth was deliberating what kind of ballet he should do next. A new work for the company had been agreed after the success of *Danses concertantes* and de Valois had started passing on to him scenarios that writers had proposed for her companies. She received many such unsolicited offers, to which she was notoriously slow in responding. Kenneth dumped the scenarios at the bottom of a drawer. He accepted instead a suggestion by

Cranko, who was too busy working on a commission from the Paris Opéra Ballet to make use of the idea himself. Kenneth wanted to try his hand at a romantic, fantastical ballet: Cranko's proposal of a Brothers Grimm story, 'Jorinda and Joringel', fitted the bill.

The fairy tale, not unlike that of Hansel and Gretel, concerns the two children of the title, who are enticed into the house of a mysterious Bird Woman. The exotic birds trapped inside are bewitched human victims of the wicked woman. The girl is captured and the boy, coming to her rescue, releases the birds from their cages. They peck the witch to death, breaking the spell. The enchanted creatures resume human form for a happy ending. Kenneth envisaged the children of the story as young lovers for his ballet, which he called *House of Birds*.

Sinister as the Grimm story was, Kenneth made it even more nightmarish. He aimed to show a painful metamorphosis from human into bird for his helpless heroine, as the Bird Woman takes possession of her. In revenge, the witch's horrid death, stabbed by her victims' beaks, becomes the earliest instance of collusion in a killing that figures in later MacMillan ballets, such as *My Brother, My Sisters, Métaboles* and *The Judas Tree*. The murder is a collective act, with no one person accepting responsibility. In *House of Birds*, where the death is ordained in the fairy story, no guilt is implied.

John Lanchbery proposed music by the contemporary Catalan composer Federico Mompou, whose work he had heard while on holiday in Spain. Lanchbery played some of Mompou's compositions to Kenneth on the piano, selecting those he thought might fit the draft scenario. 'I don't think he made any alterations,' said Lanchbery. 'I had to track down the publishers and get permission to orchestrate the piano pieces. Mompou, who was quite unknown in Britain at the time, came to the first night at Sadler's Wells. He came again when we toured *House of Birds* to Barcelona later – I think he was very intrigued by the ballet.'

Kenneth turned, once again, to Georgiadis as his designer. The *Times* reviewer noted that the decor was

the most striking element in *House of Birds*, brightly coloured but impregnated with cruelty, nature red in tooth and claw. He [Georgiadis] is preoccupied with structure; from the outside of the Bird Woman's aviary we see the façade and, as it were, an X-ray plan of the interior; and the analytical method is repeated in the Bird Woman's macabre costume.

Doreen Tempest, the first-cast witch, remembers the avian skeleton being painted onto her black bodytights by Georgiadis himself. Her face was suffocatingly covered by a predatory bird's bill. Presented as a kind of pterodactyl, the Bird Woman seemed the more frightening because of her lack of human emotion.

The enchanted creatures had birdcages enclosing their heads, and wings attached by a harness to the small of their backs: these they flapped by working their elbows, arms akimbo. Clive Barnes commented in *Dance and Dancers*: 'His birds move awkwardly, often holding their sides as if racked with pointless laughter, and their heads poke forward, pointlessly inquisitive.' Kenneth had long ago registered how bizarrely birds walk: his Yarmouth schoolmates remember his demonstrating, in the context of a school play, how chickens scratch and strut.

The captive creatures also wore plumed masks, as did the heroine (Maryon Lane) when she was turned into a bird, tethered by a rope held by the Bird Woman. 'My transformation was a kind of agony,' Lane recalled. 'It was like being taken over by an irresistible force – shaking with the effort of finding your arms and hands didn't belong to you.' When the young man (David Poole) tried to dance with her after the metamorphosis, the girl found she could no longer respond to him with her strangely articulated body, her limbs rigid with fear. The boy was horrified to find she had become an alien creature – an echo of the Host's response to Laiderette, when she was exposed as a weird misfit.

After the spell was broken and the lovers reunited, they danced a romantic pas de deux – Kenneth's first attempt at choreographing complicated lifts. David Poole was a strong, experienced partner, so Kenneth was able to try out ideas with him and Lane, beginning to develop the erotic pas de deux that were to become a MacMillan hallmark. The waltz finale, in which the lovers were joined by the former prisoners, now restored to human shape, was the most conventional section of the ballet. Finding it unsatisfactory, Kenneth would revise the closing section when *House of Birds* was given a new production seven years later in 1963.

The 26 May 1955 premiere was on the night of the General Election, which did not, as feared, prevent a packed house at Sadler's Wells. (A Conservative government was returned to power, for the second time since the post-war Labour Party was ousted in

1951.) The Theatre Ballet's rudimentary publicity machine had gone into overdrive to sell *House of Birds* to the press. Kenneth was required to participate in photo opportunities, 'assisting' ballet girls in birdcages to sip soft drinks from a straw poked through their bars. He posed self-consciously for the camera, a cigarette dangling louchely from his lip, his dark hair arranged in a fashionable quiff. The *Glasgow Evening News* proudly claimed that young MacMillan from Dunfermline was 'rapidly becoming one of the big names in British ballet'.

House of Birds received extensive coverage in the national papers and magazines. The *Illustrated London News* devoted a full-page picture spread to scenes from the ballet, treating it as a major event. In *Dance and Dancers*, Clive Barnes started his appraisal by declaring, 'Kenneth MacMillan is brilliant and odd . . . following a spiky plotless ballet, he has produced a chilling fairy tale for grown-up children, and like his earlier work, it leaves behind a tremendous impression of originality, power and compelling oddity.' The *New Statesman*'s reviewer rated him with Roland Petit as the only other choreographer since the war 'to create new forms of expression in ballet suitable to the times'. An exception among the enthusiastic reviews was Richard Buckle's attempt in the *Observer* to deflate what he saw as exaggerated praise for an as-yet-unformed choreographer, whom he nonetheless acknowledged was 'promising'. Buckle used sarcastic italics to describe the ballet and its contributors: 'The music is by the latest *Catalan* composer, my dear, and the decor is by that divinely clever young *Greek*. The name of Grimm, whose Fairy Tales provided the theme, is, alas!, *faintly dowdy*, and so has quite rightly been suppressed.' Sir Kenneth Clark, in his capacity as Chairman of the Arts Council, wrote a letter for publication to the *Observer*, protesting at Buckle's 'silly parody of smart conversation, as though to imply that the ballet was not worth criticising'.

The letter was not published, so Clark sent a copy to Kenneth to let him know that Buckle's review was not appreciated by those who mattered in the culture hierarchy. Clark (who had not met Kenneth) congratulated him on a 'beautiful and moving work', which he had compared in his letter for publication to the thrill of witnessing the emergence of a new creation by the Diaghilev and de Basil companies over thirty years previously. Clark's letter was given pride of place in Kenneth's cuttings book alongside one from Fonteyn, on Panamanian Embassy notepaper, congratulating him on *House of Birds*. Although she signed the letter 'Margot', she was writing very much as Señora Arias, the Panamanian Ambassador's wife. She had recently returned from her honeymoon, after marrying Tito Arias in Paris, and she wrote on his behalf as well: 'We were very much impressed by it. Tito and I both want to congratulate you and wish you good luck with your next ballet.'

Before Kenneth could start work on a new ballet, he was involved in mounting *Laiderette* for Ballet Rambert, in time for its Sadler's Wells season in July. The Rambert dancer chosen for the role of Laiderette was Patricia Ashworth, 'the latest of a long line of sensitive artists inspired and moulded by Mme Rambert', as Richard Buckle described her in the *Observer* of 10 July 1955. Ashworth was a soloist, not a principal, but MacMillan insisted on having her for the leading role. Margaret Hill, who might have danced it instead, had rejoined the Sadler's Wells Theatre Ballet: it was on tour in July, leaving the Wells Theatre free for Rambert's season.

Instead of the rudimentary set in which *Laiderette* had originally been given in the Sadler's Wells Choreographic Workshop the previous year, it now had designs by an Australian artist, Kenneth Rowell. The decor had an air of fantasy, as though the events might have been a dream. The lights of a down-at-heel fairground twinkled at one side of the stage, while the grand house with its ballroom chandeliers beckoned at the other. Clive Barnes commented approvingly in *Dance and Dancers*, 'Properly dressed and produced, the dramatic implications of the ballet have become clearer and what at first sight seemed like a bizarre anecdote now appears as a bitterly poetic realisation of the Wilde-like idea that only the lovely can be loved.'

Laiderette was enthusiastically received by Ballet Rambert's audiences. Patricia Ashworth remembers fourteen curtain calls after the first night.

Kenneth was very demanding with us. We found his spiky choreography very difficult because we were used to being more lyrical. Every step had to be done with perfect line, as if caught in a freeze frame. He'd watch us intently, one leg draped over the other, smoking. He was quiet, enigmatic, rather elegant. I was in awe of him because he was already a Big Name. But there was a great sweetness about him, a certain grace.

Once Ballet Rambert took *Laiderette* on tour, it was renamed *Mask and Face* in order to avoid confusion with 'launderette'. Rambert dancers had already nicknamed the ballet after the do-it-yourself laundries that had caught on in Britain by the mid-1950s. *Laiderette*'s original title was restored for Rambert's first-ever visit to the United States, when it was given at the Jacob's Pillow Festival in July 1959 in a double bill with *Giselle*. Ballet Rambert kept *Laiderette* in its repertoire until 1967. By then, the taped music, made from the record Kenneth had first used in 1954, with Ernest Ansermet conducting, was of unacceptably poor quality: a later recording could not be used because the tempi would have been different, so *Laiderette* was finally abandoned. (A film of the Rambert production, made in 1966, is held in the New York Public Library for the Performing Arts and the Rambert archives.)

The Sadler's Wells Theatre Ballet was about to undergo major changes in the mid-1950s, although the dancers were kept in the dark about their future until the start of the autumn 1955 season. The company had been accustomed to giving twice-yearly seasons in London, performing in repertory with the Sadler's Wells Opera company. The dancers appeared, when required, in the opera ballets as well as in their own programmes. The combined seasons, however, were proving too expensive for the Sadler's Wells Theatre management. The plan under consideration was to send the ballet company out on tour for most of the year, leaving its home base at the Wells fully available for the opera company, which earned more money for the theatre. Extensive touring would also serve the Arts Council's need to ensure its subsidised clients were more widely seen around the country. The pressure was on the Theatre Ballet to comply, since the Covent Garden company was committed to touring abroad, mainly in the United States and Canada, which greatly helped its finances.

De Valois summoned Peggy van Praagh to dinner on 10 June 1955 to give her the news. She began by asking van Praagh, 'How would you like to go to Norway?' To van Praagh's surprise and dismay, the offer was one she was not meant to refuse. She was being given notice that she would no longer be Director of the Theatre Ballet by the end of the year. Her sole option was to serve as roving ambassador for de Valois's growing empire, mounting ballets from the British repertoire for overseas companies, such as the National Ballet of Norway.

There was a strong suspicion that de Valois was jealous of van Praagh's reputation as another pioneer woman director. Under her guidance, the 'junior' company had already produced two notable choreographers, Cranko and MacMillan, as well as providing opportunities for freelances such as Rodrigues, Gore and others to develop their talents. The Theatre Ballet had a more impressive creative record than the stagnant Covent Garden company at this point, largely thanks to van Praagh's nurturing. But de Valois took the view that van Praagh had become too familiar with her dancers, too lax in discipline. There had been mishaps on tour, from girls getting pregnant to disasters in theatres (a fire that damaged costumes, a gas leak that hospitalised four dancers), which de Valois had learned about too late, in her opinion. Worst of all the dancers had been 'allowed' to go on strike against the management the previous year, implicitly challenging de Valois's authority. Van Praagh's copybook had been well and truly blotted.

Rumours flew throughout the summer. A few dancers had been offered transfers to the Covent Garden company, including Maryon Lane and Annette Page; others would have to decide whether they wished to remain with a company without a London base. When the news broke in September, a number of senior soloists resigned, unwilling to endure the rigours of constant touring. Margaret Hill, who stayed on, was now one of the most experienced dancers in the company. Kenneth was not directly affected, though van Praagh's departure in December would mean the loss of a friend and mentor. Further changes in the company's structure the following year would have greater impact on his development as a choreographer.

His immediate concern was his second television commission from the BBC. Margaret Dale had invited him to create a thirty-minute divertissement for a regular Sunday-night slot, *Music at Ten*. Dale, who had recently become a producer in the BBC's Music Department, was trying to introduce more ballet on television, using her own experience as a dancer to ensure that choreography was recorded with proper understanding. She faced an uphill struggle, especially since de Valois resisted the televising of her companies' ballets. She considered that they belonged in the theatre, not on the small screen. Within a year, however, Dale had succeeded in convincing her that wider audiences could be reached through the medium of television: MacMillan's ballets would be among the first to benefit from de Valois's change of mind.

In the meantime, Dale had won the support of a senior BBC producer, Christian Simpson, who enabled her to commission specially created work from choreographers who saw the possibilities of the medium. Since her budget was too small to afford musicians as well as dancers, she gave Kenneth the task of choreographing to recorded music for which the BBC already held all the rights. This was mostly the kind of light, upbeat music used to fill time between radio programmes. She took Kenneth into the BBC's gramophone library, where they played through stacks of records. He chose a polka, a charleston, a square dance, a couple of medleys and a popular tune, 'How High the Moon'.

The selection was reminiscent of the records Cranko had juxtaposed in *Dancing* for the Henley season. Instead of jazz, though, the tunes were much like those to which Kenneth had performed in his youth. It was a straightforward, enjoyable assignment, involving a group of friends mostly from the Sadler's Wells companies. The cast of nine was made up of dancers not otherwise occupied on tour: they included Julia Farron, Gilbert Vernon and Sonya Hana (by now married to Peter Wright). One of the youngest members was John Stevens, later, as Ben Stevenson, to become Artistic Director of the Houston Ballet. Another was Sheila O'Neill, a dancer from musicals and the only female member of the cast not on pointe. Kenneth nicknamed her Gypsy Dangle, after the gold ear-rings she wore for her flapper routine to the charleston. 'It was a joy to be in,' O'Neill says. 'Kenneth used to tell everyone that they should work in a musical, like me, because it gave a pizzazz to ballet.'

Dale decided they needed a star attraction. She and Kenneth chose Violette Verdy, the bubbly blonde French ballerina who had charmed London audiences in performances by Roland Petit's Ballets de Paris. After that company disbanded, she had toured with London's Festival Ballet and would later dance as a guest artist with Ballet Rambert. She already knew Kenneth, Cranko and many of the Sadler's Wells dancers: 'I used to do class with them and we went to each others' performances,' she recalled. Whenever she came to London, she used to stay with her mother at an eccentric lodging house run by White Russian refugees. Kenneth and Cranko, who were to remain lifelong friends with Violette, loved visiting her at the 'Pension Voronine' at 23 Weatherby Gardens, where each over-furnished room, filled with stuffed birds, contained a grand piano and a coin-in-the-slot meter for heat and hot water. Mme Guillerm, Violette's mother, would do Tarot-card readings for her daughter's friends. She had a reputation for uncannily accurate predictions, based on her assessment of their characters.

Verdy and the rest of Kenneth's ad-hoc company assembled at the Espinosa studios in Barnes, south-west London (later the headquarters of the British Ballet Organisation). 'The choreography just poured out of Kenneth,' remembered Verdy. 'He had so much charm but he was so shy. He seemed uncomfortable in his own skin – looking at himself and not liking himself. But when the choreography started speaking in him, he listened to that voice.' He was seizing the chance to create his own mini-revue, just as Cranko was doing at the same time with *Cranks* – a cabaret show that was about to make his name in the world outside ballet. According to Verdy, 'They were great friends, John and Kenneth, more accomplices than rivals at that time.'

Kenneth's contribution to BBC Television's *Music at Ten* was called *Turned Out Proud*, a tortuous word-play on a ballet dancer's turned-out legs and a well-dressed appearance. The suite of dances was linked by a compère dressed in top hat and tails, around whom the cast swirled. The role was taken by John Neville, then a svelte and glamorous young actor at the Old Vic. The show was performed live in Studio G, the BBC's big television studio in Lime Grove, on Sunday 23 October 1955. Dale invited Kenneth to sit with her in the recording suite, watching the camera monitors. He was fascinated by the process and would for ever after take an active interest in the filming of his work.

The transmission went without a hitch. Kenneth and Cranko, who had come to the Lime Grove studio to watch the performance, rushed to Verdy's dressing-room to congratulate her. 'They were very sweet, saying, "We must have you in the Sadler's Wells Ballet." And John said, "I'll marry you if I have to", because that was the only way I could stay, as a foreigner. I was very gratified but I declined, "Thank you very much, but no." ' She was well aware that Cranko was gay but did not think that Kenneth really was: 'He told me then that he didn't know sexually what he was. He had this great closeness with women and we had a romantic friendship. I was both in love and in admiration with Kenneth – but I tended to fall in love with all my choreographers!'

Turned Out Proud was well received, although Dale was telephoned at home after the transmission by the BBC Music Controller, Cecil McGivern, asking, 'What was all that about?' 'He was not unsympathetic,' says Dale, 'simply bewildered by ballet.' Such television reviews as there were in the daily papers enthused about the 'youth, vitality and originality' of the programme: 'It had more than life and verve. It had rare courage and flair.' Mary Clarke commented in *Ballet Annual*, 'The programme was the liveliest half-hour of television dancing that has been seen for a long time and the greatest merit of all was that it had been created specifically for television.'

The Musicians' Union promptly protested about Dale's ingenious way round their live-music agreement with the BBC and she was warned never to use records again. She made her case to the management about inadequate budgets and was allocated enough money to televise Kenneth's *House of Birds*, with an orchestra, the following year. She also persuaded Kenneth to appear on television in the clowns' duet from Cranko's *Lady and the Fool* in a *Music at Ten* programme on New Year's Day 1956. Although he had stopped dancing, he could still perform his created role as Moondog, arguing over possession of a rose with Ray Powell as Bootface. The excerpt, retitled *La Commedia*, preceded Ashton's *Les Patineurs*, which was not quite long enough to fill the half-hour slot.

Cranko's revue, *Cranks*, at a tiny theatre club near Charing Cross Station, had meanwhile become a cult hit, not least because Princess Margaret and her in-crowd went to see it several times. After three months, it was transferred to the West End, becoming an award-winning popular show. Its success meant that Cranko no longer needed to make himself available as an in-house choreographer for operas. That job was now consigned to Kenneth, whose first-ever commission for the Covent Garden Opera House was the 'Venusberg' ballet at the start of *Tannhäuser*, in a new production designed by Ralph Koltai.

Caryl Brahms, reviewing *Tannhäuser* in the *Dancing Times*, commented that she could have wished MacMillan a more hopeful baptism at Covent Garden than this much disliked opera production, though he 'at least and almost alone, did nothing to detract from his growing reputation'. The ballet, in which Venus tries to keep Tannhäuser in her kingdom by diverting him with dancing and other delights, had been added to Wagner's opera in 1861 to please Parisian audiences. Rather than a romantic bacchanal, Kenneth had devised a frankly sexual orgy. His leading couple were Julia Farron and Gilbert Vernon, with a corps of twelve recruited from the ballet school and the Covent Garden Opera Ballet company. They were gratified by the attention drawn to their enthusiastic revels by the *Daily Mirror*, whose front-page banner headline screamed, 'Has the Lord Chamberlain Seen This?' Kenneth had achieved his aim of being noticed. The official censor did not, however, rise to the bait by requiring changes to the production.

15

The year 1956 was to prove momentous for Kenneth, as well as for de Valois's ballet companies. There was a bumper crop of anniversaries to be celebrated: twenty-five years since the Sadler's Wells Theatre became the home of the original Vic–Wells ballet company in 1931; ten years since that company moved into the reopened Royal Opera House after the war; ten years since the founding of the second, touring company. It was a period of stocktaking and of transition. Ironically enough, the first of the galas, at Sadler's Wells on 6 January, marked a break with the past. The Theatre Ballet's dancers were still reeling from the shock of losing their home base and their founder director, Peggy van Praagh. John Field, a principal dancer at Covent Garden, had taken over from her the day before the Sadler's Wells celebration. Since the company was about to be perpetually on tour, another group had been formed, once again named the Sadler's Wells Opera Ballet, to appear in the opera company's productions.

The gala performance was given by dancers from all three companies connected with the theatre. *Danses concertantes*, MacMillan's first commissioned work for the touring company, opened the programme. Margot Fonteyn, who had just been made a Dame in the

New Year's Honours List, then danced the Act II pas de deux from *Swan Lake* with Michael Somes, both representing the theatre's first resident ballet company. Finally, youngsters from the new ensemble performed dances from the Sadler's Wells Opera company's productions of *Hansel and Gretel* and *The Bartered Bride*. Among their number were two students from the ballet school, Lynn Seymour and Christopher Gable, who were to play an important part in Kenneth's life.

His friend and colleague, Peter Wright, had been put in charge of the new small Opera Ballet group, which was intended, like its 1946 predecessor, to give young dancers stage experience. Although students initially feared that being taken into the Opera Ballet could be a blow to their ambitions of joining the 'proper' companies, Wright proved expert at finding and nurturing unconventional talents that were then snapped up by other directors. Seymour and Gable were among his early protégés.

De Valois had decided to enliven the repertoire of the Covent Garden company by commissioning works from her two young resident choreographers: a three-act ballet, *The Prince of the Pagodas*, from Cranko, and a one-acter from Kenneth, his first opportunity to choreograph a ballet for the senior company. She regarded him, even more than Cranko, as her product, the result of her system of training in the ballet school and of apprenticeship in the junior company, both as a performer and choreographer. She had known Kenneth since he was a boy of fifteen and she was determined to mentor him, now that he had proved his creative talent was more than a flash in the pan.

She had not intervened in his early work for the Theatre Ballet, leaving him to find his own voice under the supervision of Peggy van Praagh. De Valois wanted her own quality control, however, over what was shown at Covent Garden. She could not entirely achieve this with Ashton and already established choreographers from outside the company, such as Massine and Petit. She was still smarting from Buckle's 'Three Blind Mice' criticism that she had become too busy to take personal responsibility for the (unsuccessful) ballets she had commissioned. Kenneth must have appeared her best chance of moulding an up-and-coming choreographer, passing on her own experience of how to make well-crafted ballets. She insisted he draw up a scenario for his new ballet and discuss it in detail with her before he showed it to the company's musical adviser, the composer Humphrey Searle.

Kenneth's scenario for *Noctambules* was his own invention. It owed something to German Expressionist films as well as to other fairground or circus ballets, such as Petit's *Les Forains* and Lew Christensen's *Jinx*. A magician in a huge cloak (rather like the Charlatan in *Petrushka*) entices spectators into the small back-street Théâtre des Noctambules. Once inside, the show begins with the magician hypnotising his female assistant, who has been hiding within the folds of his cloak. At first she plays her role obediently, then rebels and refuses to carry on the performance. The magician throws her to the ground and turns his powers on the angry crowd.

In the next scene, the hypnotised spectators act out their fantasies: a soldier imagines he is a general, a poor girl dances with a rich suitor, a faded beauty recovers her charms, surrounded by admirers. The magician falls in love with the rejuvenated woman; she recoils from him and tries to escape but he takes her with him down a trapdoor. In his absence, the crowd returns to its senses and disperses. The young girl and her suitor are still happily together, for love has its own enchantment. The magician's doll-like assistant is left alone. Without her master, she loses her reason for existence. She circles the stage in a demented dance, mechanically banging her little drum, and drops down dead as the curtain falls.

De Valois noted her comments on the scenario in a letter to Kenneth, trying to clarify his somewhat muddled ideas by analysing the ballet's possible meaning: 'I see the effect on everyone, after the magician's departure, as a release from some strange dream. The crowd symbolises a return to what they were. They gradually isolate in their midst the 3 characters who symbolise the positive and negative result [the two lovers and the mad assistant].' The assistant's distracted run around the stage at the end should 'symbolise emptiness'. De Valois evidently did not want to restrain Kenneth's imagination by requiring him to rethink the scenario. She was prepared to accept its illogic – some of the spectators are affected by their experience, others not – even though the unresolved ending was likely to puzzle audiences.

As instructed, Kenneth sought the advice of Humphrey Searle on the kind of music he should choose. They listened to numerous records, until, as Kenneth recalled in an interview with *Ballet Today*, 'I asked if he hadn't something of his own. He turned up a composition of his own, among stacks of records, which with very little rearrangement proved to be exactly the sort of thing I had in mind.' Kenneth was therefore able to hear in advance how the fully orchestrated score was likely to sound; he was not yet taking the risk of commissioning a score from scratch. Reviewers, however, including Andrew Porter in the *Financial Times*, assumed that the music was specially composed and commended its aptness:

Mr Searle's score conveys through the 'real' music, which is the notes Robert Irving's orchestra is playing in the pit, the imagined music to which the noctambulists are dancing and dreaming. This double-planned score, in which scraps of popular waltz drift through sonorities of a Berg-like compelling power, is amazingly skilful.

Kenneth chose Georgiadis, once again, as his designer, asking him to come up with a stage within a stage, and costumes that would indicate different layers of fantasy and 'reality'. Georgiadis produced a striking set in bright colours – acidic yellow, vivid violet, blues and greens accented by black. Leslie Edwards as the Magician wore a fright wig, his white hair standing on end as though electrified. Georgiadis took the idea from the famous shot in Fritz Lang's horror film, *Dr Mabuse the Gambler*, of the doctor's head gleaming in the darkness, eyes fixed hypnotically on the audience.

In an interview for a Royal Opera House publication, *Ballet* (no. 15), Kenneth was quoted as saying:

Although it might not have been very obvious at the time, I was deeply interested in Petipa's structural devices. I even provided a pas de cinq for [Nadia] Nerina [as the Faded Beauty] and the four men, which was my adaptation of the 'Rose Adagio'. In fact, *Noctambules* was essentially a dramatised last act of *The Sleeping Beauty*: its form was very much that of a divertissement – and I learned clearly that this could not work as a narrative: I had used the wrong construction for a dramatic work.

Nerina (who danced the role of Aurora in de Valois's production of *The Sleeping Beauty*) had recognised the reference to the 'Rose Adagio', but told Kenneth that she 'felt artistically dissatisfied and frustrated, as somehow the scenario seemed to have no conclusion, with my Beauty left strangely in limbo'. She and Kenneth did not see eye to eye on her role, 'which was a pity for both of us'. Kenneth's retrospective self-criticism about using the wrong construction for *Noctambules* must have been reinforced by the critics' comments that the ending was unsatisfactory. De Valois's attempts to clarify the scenario's symbolism had evidently been in vain.

Fortunately for Kenneth, John Martin, the dance critic of the *New York Times*, was in London during a visit to Europe and caught *Noctambules* 'by traveller's luck'. In his account of the ballets he saw, Martin gave *Noctambules* pride of place at the top of his column, favouring it over Ashton's *La Péri* on the same programme. He praised Kenneth's eerie imagination and strangely inventive choreography, analysing its virtues, which he saw as the obverse of its vices: 'Because he is young, he is inclined to give us too much, in a key that is too nervous, too high strung, too determinedly off the beaten track . . . but dull moments there are not.' Martin concluded, 'Not for a very long time indeed has one come across so completely talented a new work. Young Mr MacMillan is really somebody.'

Martin was the influential critic of a highly regarded newspaper, so his views would have been taken into account on both sides of the Atlantic. His preference for Kenneth's ballet over Ashton's *La Péri* must have been galling for the older choreographer. So must Andrew Porter's praise in the *Financial Times* of *Noctambules* at the expense of *Scènes de ballet*, when the two works were paired later in March, with the same principals (Nerina, Brian Shaw and Desmond Doyle) appearing in both. Porter commented that the dancers shone in the new work but were below their best in the established piece. As a result, *Scènes de ballet* appeared old-fashioned and diffuse, and 'the unfavourable comparison with MacMillan's *Danses concertantes* [also to Stravinsky] cannot be avoided any longer'. Porter must have been dazzled by novelty, for *Scènes de ballet* has stood the test of time and many changes of cast as generations of dancers have succeeded each other. None the less, Ashton had cause to worry that a talented young choreographer was coming up fast behind him.

While *Noctambules* was being given its first performances, de Valois and David Webster, General Administrator of the Royal Opera House, had flown to Moscow to negotiate the details of a long-proposed exchange of ballet companies: the Bolshoi would come to Covent Garden for the first time in October 1956 and the

Sadler's Wells Ballet would perform in Moscow and Leningrad in November. A chink in the Iron Curtain between the Soviet Union and the West had opened, with ballet smoothing the way. Three 'technical representatives' from the Bolshoi Theatre had arrived in London in March to check out the Royal Opera House. They were introduced to MacMillan after seeing a performance of *Noctambules.* According to one report, 'They were impressed by the technical strength of the dancers of the company, and were enthusiastic about *Noctambules*, whose choreography, decor and music lie far outside the experience of the Bolshoi repertoire.'

During the early part of 1956, balletic and state diplomacy appeared to be proceeding smoothly, though the Iron Curtain would slam closed before the end of the year. In April, the Soviet President Bulganin and First Secretary Nikita Khrushchev paid an official visit to London and attended a Royal Opera House gala in their honour. Small groups of soloists had already appeared under the auspices of the Anglo-Soviet Friendship Society, which put on annual concerts composed of folk dance, singing and ballet pas de deux; two of the Bolshoi's leading dancers, Raissa Struchkova and Alexander Lapauri, had danced at the Royal Albert Hall on 16 November 1954. Excitement began to mount in Britain at the prospect of the first-ever visit to the West by the Bolshoi Ballet, with its complement of over a hundred dancers.

By May, there had already been so many galas that the Covent Garden company's Silver Jubilee celebration on the 5th was treated more as a family affair than a formal public event. At the end of the anniversary gala, all the company assembled on stage for an address to the audience by de Valois. British ballet's 'Royal Family' occupied the centre: de Valois, Ashton, Helpmann, Fonteyn, Somes and the conductor Robert Irving. Kenneth was placed between Cranko and Rodrigues in a group near the front. His inclusion in the celebration confirmed him as a member of the first eleven. He would now be entitled to move between the two companies, choreographing for both of them.

The touring company was about to present a programme made up entirely of the ballets he had created for it. A signal honour, this would be the first time the ten-year-old company had devoted an evening to the work of one choreographer. He had been commissioned to create a one-act ballet for the occasion, as well as revive his apprentice piece, *Somnambulism*, for its first professional production. Stan Kenton had been persuaded to allow his music to be rearranged by John Lanchbery so that it could be played by the Theatre Ballet's orchestra on tour. (One audience member, who disliked Kenton's reorchestrated music, sent an anonymous note to the stage door, addressed to John Lanchbery, Kenneth MacMillan and Stan Kenton, saying simply, 'This is my opinion of it', and enclosing a halfpenny.) *Somnambulism* would head a programme that included *Danses concertantes* and *House of Birds*, as well as the new ballet, *Solitaire*.

Solitaire was Kenneth's celebration of Margaret Hill's talent and personality: according to people who knew them both, the leading role in *Solitaire* was how he perceived Maggie – and his younger self. He described the theme as 'a very simple one, or so I thought, of a lonely child unable to make friends – but happy in the memories of the past times that people had befriended her'. According to Donald MacLeary, who partnered Hill in the central pas de deux in *Solitaire*, her affair with Kenneth, in the sense of a sexual relationship, was over by the time she rejoined the Theatre Ballet, though the two of them still shared the same address. They spent much of their time apart, now that their careers took them in different directions. *Solitaire* was to be Kenneth's enduring gift to the girl he had loved, a role that defied de Valois's dictum that 'tall girls are never lonely'.

De Valois, petite herself, had rarely favoured tall dancers (Beryl Grey and Svetlana Beriosova were notable exceptions). She would have preferred Kenneth to cast a small dancer in the role, such as Maryon Lane, who was by now in the Covent Garden company. *Solitaire*, however, was tailormade for Hill, showing off her long, elegant legs, her quirky personality and the distinctive way she held her head. According to an account of the ballet's creation in a souvenir booklet, MacMillan had a very particular vision of the central character: 'In Margaret Hill, I found the perfect interpreter and the role lived through her.'

His ambition to create a ballet for Hill went back to 1953, when he had first planned one to Gershwin's Piano Concerto in F, shortly after he had created *Somnambulism*. His inspiration for *Solitaire* came from the 1952 film of Carson McCullers's novel, *The Member of the Wedding*. He identified strongly with the confusions of the central character, a young girl called Frankie Addams (a surname very similar to the one he had assumed as a designer, Aadams). An adolescent growing up in a small town in the American South during the war, she wants to belong to the older, self-assured groups she sees around her, though she is still caught up in her own childish semi-fantasy world.

The ballet's subtitle is a dictionary definition of 'solitaire': 'a kind of game for one'. A lonely girl (Hill) encounters a band of carefree young people, whose playful dances she watches wistfully. They let her join in some of their activities before they dash off elsewhere, leaving her alone once more. They may be real youngsters or figments of the girl's imagination. There are echoes here of Kenneth's role in Cranko's Henley ballet, *Dancing*, which captured his dreamy isolation, as well as of him as a boy in Yarmouth, trying to make friends with local children of his own age or anxiously striving to keep up with his older brother's gang. Margaret Hill had had similar experiences as a lonely adolescent. Joining Ballet Rambert at fifteen, she had been its youngest and lowliest member, longing to be regarded by her elders as an equal. Then, when she had made her way to the top, she had had to start again with the Sadler's Wells Theatre Ballet. Thanks to her Rambert background, she had remained something of an outsider in the Sadler's Wells touring company, forming her 'gang of two' with Kenneth.

For all its wistful theme, *Solitaire* was airy and witty, without the threatening undertones of Kenneth's previous work. The leading girl was hopeful, not disfigured or neurotic. Hill embodied the tenderness with which Kenneth had constructed the role, a delicate balance between melancholy and resolute gaiety. The light-hearted atmosphere was to some extent determined by the pre-existing decor, designed by Desmond Heeley. The backdrop had been intended for Cranko's next creation for the touring company, *The Angels*, postponed while he worked on the long-delayed *Prince of the Pagodas* for the Covent Garden company. De Valois had requested that Kenneth make use of the decor – a painted backdrop of silvery scaffolding against a turquoise-blue sky. In the context of *Solitaire*, the setting served as 'one of those secret playgrounds in the mind of every child – a paradise of half-finished buildings, swinging ropes, half-dug trenches and the hundred and one unromantic and ordinary things that children so delight in'.

Following Kenneth's prescription for the costumes, Heeley designed attractive, ragged-skirted tutus with velvet, plum-coloured bodices for the women and similar waistcoats for the men, worn over full-sleeved white shirts and white tights. Hill, in an orange and pink tutu, was further distinguished by a bathing-cap head-dress of roses of many colours that she had devised herself. The massed flowers compensated for what van Praagh had told her was a defect – the smallness of her head in relation to the rest of her body. The overall effect of the hat's petals, enhancing Hill's large, dark eyes, was similar to Giulietta Masina's 'artichoke' crop of hair as the forlorn girl in *La Strada*, one of Kenneth's favourite films at the time.

As the music, he had chosen Malcolm Arnold's *English Dances*, which Jeffrey Solomons had first heard on the radio during a bout of flu and had commended to Kenneth. 'It was very youthful, charming and witty, and the ballet was about young people,' MacMillan told Allen Robertson in a 1991 interview. He and Solomons tracked down Arnold's music in one of their favourite record shops, Imhof's on New Oxford Street. They played the *English Dances* in a listening booth and debated what to do because the suite was too brief for Kenneth's purposes. Too shy to approach Arnold himself, he asked de Valois to contact the composer (who had written the music for Ashton's *Homage to the Queen* in 1952), requesting more music in the same vein to make a half-hour ballet. Arnold generously obliged with two extra dances, the *Sarabande* that Kenneth had specified, and a *Polka*.

The *Sarabande* was used for the central pas de deux between Hill and Donald MacLeary, as idealised young lovers. Kenneth gave Margaret the kind of lyrical choreography that she, as a tall, dramatic performer, did not usually dance. MacLeary, still only eighteen but dashingly handsome, was already an accomplished partner. He recalls that when the rest of the company saw the finished pas de deux for the first time, they burst into delighted applause. They had never seen Kenneth choreograph anything so purely romantic before.

The rest of the cast was given giddy, playful choreography, a mixture of classical steps with naturalistic movements: gestures of awakening from sleep, shaking hands in greeting, fingering a flute or a typewriter, with gymnastic cartwheels and tumbles for the men. The soubrette role of the perky *Polka* soloist went to diminutive

Sara Neil: she temporarily seized the limelight from Hill's quieter character, who could only stand aside during her antics. 'We had a laugh creating the polka solo,' Neil recalls. 'The steps were so zany and quirky. They had nicknames, like "Cat on a Hot Tin Roof". He let you get on with it, using your own personality.' The *Polka* girl was the cute one of the bunch – the confident player who would always be first choice in a team, whereas Hill's girl would be the leftover. 'We developed this game carrying the long flute, two boys and me,' says Neil. 'Maggie ran from one end to the other, trying to join in, and we wouldn't let her.'

The ballet, however, belonged to Hill, who linked what was essentially a series of divertissements into a bitter-sweet commentary on the loneliness of not belonging. Clive Barnes called it 'one of the finest characterisations in the brief history of the Royal Ballet', noting that Hill, childlike rather than childish, captured the girl's paradoxical pleasure in her isolation. She is content, by the end, to be on her own. Kenneth commented later (when *Solitaire* was revived for the Houston Ballet in 1991) that the ballet ended happily, 'and my ballets don't usually have happy endings'. There was another, solipsistic, aspect to the ballet, which perhaps only someone who knew its creator well would fully have appreciated. Jeffrey Solomons interpreted *Solitaire* as a self-portrait of Kenneth: 'A solitary person who creates his own world – that's Kenneth all over; a solitary who created all of us to be his chums. We existed to entertain him.'

16

Kenneth gave an interview at this turning point in his life to a Scottish newspaper, the *Glasgow Evening News*, which headlined the article published on 7 June 1956, 'Crew-cut Scot Breaks Ballet Record'. It was illustrated by a Sadler's Wells publicity shot by Denis de Marney of Kenneth seated on a stool, hands on knees, looking disdainfully at the camera with a cigarette drooping from his lips. His Teddy-boy quiff was inaccurately described as a 'pie-dish crew-cut'. He drawled in what the interviewer, Tom Olsen, considered 'a rather dreamy voice', remarking that he had indeed been fortunate in making a career as a choreographer, since those who had could be numbered on the fingers of one hand.

The 'ballet record' to which the headline referred was twenty-six-year-old Kenneth's achievement in having four of his ballets simultaneously presented at Sadler's Wells while a fifth, *Noctambules*, was given at the Royal Opera House. Kenneth told Olsen that he took about six weeks to make a ballet: 'At first I felt rather nervous. I had to direct people I had grown up with in the company as a dancer myself. Choreography is not like writing a book or composing music. You can't do it alone and you have to have a room full of people. But I don't find it so difficult nowadays.'

Olsen asked if he had had 'any nibbles' from Hollywood. Kenneth replied confidently, 'The nearest at the moment is a New York suggestion. But I'd certainly be ready to consider Hollywood. At the moment I'm thinking on television lines. I had a half-hour on TV last year called *Turned Out Proud* and it turned out quite a success.' The BBC was to transmit *House of Birds* on 16 September 1956, with casting different from the original production. Margaret Hill was the sinister Bird Woman; Maryon Lane's role as the leading girl was taken by Sara Neil, with Michael Boulton instead of David Poole as the young man. The director, once again, was Margaret Dale, who remembers that the Theatre Ballet was so unused to the demands of television that they sent Georgiadis's set without any accompanying technician to advise on its construction. 'We wasted hours of valuable time trying to assemble it,' she says. 'The dancers pulled the show together in time for the live transmission but it was a nail-biting experience.' Television was still in black and white, so Georgiadis's searing colours could make no impression.

The New York 'suggestion' to which Kenneth had referred in his interview would come to fruition at the end of the year, after he had been introduced to decision-makers at American Ballet Theatre in September. Evidently, some kind of proposal had been made earlier, perhaps as a result of John Martin's laudatory review of *Noctambules* in the *New York Times* in March.

Meanwhile, there was nothing on the horizon at home for Kenneth after his all-MacMillan accolade. A ballet to Bartók's *The Miraculous Mandarin* music had been a possible project, for de Valois had told the Ballet Advisory Panel in April 1955 that Kenneth was interested in the Bartók score, as was Alfred

Rodrigues. In the event, Rodrigues was given the go-ahead for a *Miraculous Mandarin* ballet for the senior company's Edinburgh Festival visit in August 1956. Kenneth was being kept in his place, obliged to wait his turn. His only scheduled new creation in 1956 after *Solitaire* was a *Fireworks* pas de deux for Nadia Nerina and Alexis Rassine, to Stravinsky's early *Feux d'artifice*. Nerina and Rassine, who were going on a concert tour of the provinces during their summer break, needed a bravura piece to spice up their 'Ballet Highlights' selection. Kenneth swiftly concocted an intricate, virtuoso pas de deux, making good use of Nerina's speed and attack. A review of the concert programme in *Dance and Dancers* in September commented that *Fireworks* was by far the most interesting item, 'rather in the manner of the solos from *Noctambules*', with shooting, flamboyant movements appropriate for a pyrotechnical display.

Then (American) Ballet Theatre came to London in September, on its third visit since the war. The company had yet to adopt the full title by which it is now known internationally, American Ballet Theatre (ABT). The change was made after it returned to the States in February 1957, following a European and Middle Eastern tour, of which London was the first leg. The repertoire was selected for the tour rather than specifically for London audiences, which were disappointed by the choice of ballets, most of which had been seen before. The only works new to London were Antony Tudor's comic *Offenbach in the Underworld* and Valerie Bettis's version of *A Streetcar Named Desire*, essentially a vehicle for the company's dramatic ballerina, Nora Kaye. Mary Clarke commented regretfully in *Ballet Annual*, 'We have known for some years that the company was living on its past reputation, flogging old favourites and picking up as novelties works of minor importance from other repertories . . . on balance the two-week season was rather sad.'

Lucia Chase, Ballet Theatre's Co-Director with Oliver Smith, was well aware of her company's shortcomings, due as much as anything to its precarious funding in the States. She was looking to acquire a new, not too expensive, ballet by an up-and-coming European choreographer, made specially for the company. She asked the advice of Peter Williams, editor of *Dance and Dancers*, who proposed MacMillan. By now Williams knew Kenneth well, as a regular member of the tea parties at his flat for dancers, designers and an eclectic collection of friends. Williams had written an editorial in *Dance and Dancers* in June the previous year about the growing internationalisation of ballet, in which he put forward the suggestion: 'Why not send Kenneth MacMillan to mount a new work on an American company?'

Williams introduced Kenneth to Lucia Chase backstage at the Royal Opera House on 31 August, near the end of the company's season there. Kenneth was eager to choreograph a ballet for Nora Kaye, whom he much admired. He proposed Georgiadis as his designer, showing Chase his designs for previous ballets. She then organised a dinner at the Savoy so that the two of them could meet Nora Kaye. Although Kenneth was his usual quiet self, reluctant to sell his ballet idea over the dinner table, he hit it off with both powerful American women. Lucia Chase left for New York the following day to talk to 'the money-bags', as she called Ballet Theatre's sponsors, about raising funds for a ballet by her latest find. Nora Kaye joined the rest of Ballet Theatre on its European tour, satisfied that she had met her next choreographer.

Kaye's career had been built around choreographers who could put her exceptional talents to good use. She did not have the right physique for a purely classical dancer but she could convince audiences that she was indeed a ballerina. The British critic Caryl Brahms described her succinctly as 'the Helpmann of the American Ballet' in *A Seat at the Ballet*. Like Helpmann, she was so compelling a dramatic performer that any imperfections of physique or technique were unimportant. Although she was more than capable of dancing the classics, her forte was the kind of meaty role, tragic or comic, that only a modern choreographer could create for her. She had a vital, earthy, wise-cracking personality that made her seem invincible, though she was vulnerable enough to have suffered a nervous breakdown at the end of the 1940s. By then, she had two failed marriages behind her, first to Michael Van Buren, great-grandson of the eighth president of the United States, and then to the violinist Isaac Stern.

Born in January 1920 of Russian-Jewish parents (her real surname was Koreff), she was nearly ten years older than Kenneth. She had decided early on in her career that her future lay with the choreographer Antony Tudor, who had joined Ballet Theatre after leaving Britain at the start of the war. He created *Pillar of Fire* for her in 1942, and she inherited Maude Lloyd's roles in the English ballets Tudor revived for Ballet Theatre. Kaye forged a strong bond with Tudor and Hugh Laing, the British dancer who was his close companion for most of their lives. By the time Ballet Theatre first came to Covent Garden in 1946, Kaye's triangular relationship with them had been disrupted by another American dancer, Diana Adams, who married Laing, briefly, in 1947.

Kaye had by then transferred her affections to Ashton, whom she knew to be basically gay. To ingratiate herself with Ashton, she helped further his affair in 1947 with Dick Beard, the inspiration behind *Valses nobles*, in which Kenneth had danced as a seventeen-year-old. Ashton, however, never made a ballet for her, so she threw in her lot, once again, with Tudor and Laing, leaving Ballet Theatre with them in 1951 to join New York City Ballet.

There she had an affair with Jerome Robbins, another bisexual man who was fundamentally homosexual. That relationship resulted in *The Cage*, in which Robbins cast her as a predator, an adept of an all-female insect cult who killed men after copulating with them. It was a formidable role for Kaye – and her successors, for the 1951 ballet continues to be performed by companies around the world. Once no further created roles were forthcoming from Robbins, Kaye returned to Ballet Theatre in 1954, still in search of a choreographer. By the time she met Kenneth two years later, she feared she was running out of options.

When Ballet Theatre's fundraisers in New York gave the go-ahead for Kenneth's commission, the plan was for the new ballet to be tried out on tour in January, shortly before the company returned to New York. Kenneth was to join the dancers for their season in Monte Carlo in December, after their Middle East tour was over. He would choreograph the ballet in Monte Carlo, whose theatre workshops would make the sets and costumes from Georgiadis's designs. The ballet's European premiere, however, was to be in Lisbon, Ballet Theatre's final date. After that, all being well, Kenneth could travel with the company to New York for its American premiere in February. De Valois agreed to give him leave of absence for three months so that he could make the most of his international opportunity.

While pondering his plans for the new work, he had plenty of time to attend the Bolshoi Ballet season at Covent Garden in

October. The much awaited visit had very nearly been cancelled at the last minute. Eighty tonnes of scenery had already arrived at the London docks when Soviet officials suddenly refused to authorise its clearance. A Russian discus-thrower, Nina Ponomarova, had been charged with shoplifting hats from an Oxford Street department store. She had received a summons to appear in court but had failed to do so. No doubt spurred on by the Soviet authorities, leading members of the Bolshoi, including the company's senior ballerina, Galina Ulanova, had sent a letter for publication in *Izvestia*, expressing fears of similar 'provocation' if they visited Britain.

Over the next ten days, the stand-off between Moscow and London made headline news. Diplomatic negotiations dragged on until three days before the first-night curtain was due to rise at Covent Garden, with the ballet scenery still on the dockside. The resultant publicity ensured that when the Bolshoi season went ahead, it was treated as an event of major significance. It was, in any case, the first time the two-hundred-year-old ballet company had ever performed abroad. (A proposed visit to Paris in 1954 had been cancelled because of Cold War politics.) Ballet-lovers had queued for three days and four nights outside the Royal Opera House to be sure of obtaining tickets; the black-market price went as high as £175 for a pair – a vast sum at the time. Opera House insiders like Kenneth had ways of securing a pass, if only for a standing place backstage.

The opening ballet was *Romeo and Juliet*, first created sixteen years earlier by Leonid Lavrovsky to Prokofiev's score. Lavrovsky's production, originally for the Kirov Ballet in Leningrad, had been reworked for the Bolshoi in 1946. A film of the Bolshoi production, with Ulanova as Juliet, had been shown at the Royal Festival Hall in March 1956, whetting appetites for the ballet's first appearance in a Western theatre. The eagerly awaited performances fully lived up to expectations. The staging was spectacular, with action-packed crowd scenes and a huge cast that included mature character dancers of the kind that no English company was yet in a position to provide.

'We were transported into that incredible evocation of rich, Renaissance, provincial life,' remembered Fonteyn in her autobiography. 'The very weight of the production, criticised by some as old-fashioned, was what impressed me. No doubt it was just such realism that Diaghilev had discarded when he presented his innovations early in the century, taking Europe by storm. Now it burst upon me as new and completely valid.' Kenneth and Nico Georgiadis were just as impressed by the opulence and dramatic realism of the production, so different from the much sparer ballet stagings favoured by British and French companies.

The Royal Opera House management looked enviously at the production, knowing that the Covent Garden company had no hope of emulating it – yet. The Sadler's Wells Ballet did not have sufficient money or manpower to mount an epic three-act Shakespearean ballet: the realisation of such an ambition would have to wait for almost a decade. Where the Opera House had assumed that the Soviets would be impressed by Western production values, the reverse turned out to be the case. True, the Russians were desperate to acquire Western fabrics (firm elastic for the male dancers' jockstraps was at the top of their shopping list) but their confidence in the supremacy of their performance standards remained unshaken.

The Covent Garden company was scheduled to pay its exchange visit to Moscow in November. De Valois had already put measures in train to enhance the status of her national ballet institution. She had proposed a new title in place of the misleading Sadler's Wells one, bringing her companies together within a single organisation that would also include the ballet school. She had compiled a list of six possible titles, all of them prefixed by 'Royal' rather than 'National'. On 31 October 1956, Queen Elizabeth II duly granted a charter 'with perpetual succession, creating one body corporate with the name of "The Royal Ballet" '. As far as the visit to the Soviet Union was concerned, the about-to-be Royal Ballet (the name change was not announced publicly until 15 January 1957) would appear to have so many dancers, just like the huge Bolshoi, that it could afford to leave a sufficient number at home to entertain domestic audiences.

International affairs intervened, however, before the visit to Russia could take place. Scenery, costumes and scores had already been sent ahead to Leningrad for the planned opening on 14 November when news came of the uprising in Hungary against Soviet domination. The Bolshoi Ballet arrived back in Moscow just as Soviet tanks rolled into Hungary on 4 November 'to restore order'. On 7 November, David Webster announced that the Royal

Opera House, in consultation with the British Foreign Office, had cancelled the tour to Russia. Webster had sent a cable to his counterpart at the Bolshoi, stating, 'In view of public opinion in this country which strongly condemns the renewed suppression by Soviet forces of Hungarian liberty and independence . . . it has been unanimously agreed that in present circumstances the projected visit of the Sadler's Wells Ballet to Russia cannot take place.'

There was great anger and concern in Britain over events in Hungary, as well as a feeling of shame that Prime Minister Imre Nagy's broadcast appeal for help from the West had gone unanswered. However complex the political and military options might have been, in simple human terms it was the kind of betrayal that deeply affected Kenneth, as the Tiananmen Square crisis in Beijing would do towards the end of his life, influencing the creation of his final ballet, *The Judas Tree*. In 1956, Kenneth was too young and inexperienced as a choreographer to absorb his political feelings into his work. The Soviet repression of Hungary was, in any case, soon to be overshadowed by fevered debate about Britain's role in the Suez crisis, which followed a few weeks later.

When a fundraising gala for Hungarian Relief was organised at the Sadler's Wells Theatre on 10 December, Kenneth's contribution had nothing to do with the uprising and its repression. *Valse eccentrique* was a comic trio for Alexander Grant, Brian Shaw and Anya Linden to music by Jacques Ibert (the *Divertimento* from *The Italian Straw Hat*). They were dressed as Edwardian bathers, in striped costumes borrowed from Ashton's seaside ballet, *Les Sirènes*. Two solemn, mustachioed gentlemen manoeuvred a sweet young thing between them: 'Danced with perfect seriousness, it won louder laughter than has ever been lavished on the Crazy Gang,' reported *Ballet Annual*.

Kenneth had meanwhile been co-opted into reassuming his Ugly Sister role at Covent Garden. Because the company's Russian tour had been cancelled, a season was hastily organised at the Royal Opera House, starting with Ashton's *Cinderella*. He and Kenneth wickedly sent up the Bolshoi's more extravagant ballerinas in their Ugly Sisters routine at the ball, with Kenneth flinging in some abandoned Russian-style grands jetés. Unfortunately for Ashton the choreographer, his use of Prokofiev's music for *Cinderella* provoked invidious comparisons with Lavrovsky's treatment of the composer's score for *Romeo and Juliet*, so recently admired in the same theatre. 'With Prokofiev's *Romeo and Juliet* fresh in our minds, his *Cinderella*, as staged by Frederick Ashton, was bound to seem thin, unconvincing dramatically and at times almost amateur,' wrote Mary Clarke in *Ballet Annual*.

Such damning criticism discouraged Ashton from thinking of mounting his *Romeo and Juliet* at Covent Garden, at least for the time being. He had created his ballet to the same Prokofiev score for the Royal Danish Ballet in Copenhagen in 1955, before he had seen the Lavrovsky version. The Royal Theatre in Copenhagen is intimate in scale, its dancers renowned for their naturalistic acting. Ashton's *Romeo and Juliet* was essentially a chamber ballet, without the tumultuous crowd scenes in which the Bolshoi excelled. Ashton's protective feelings about his 'modest' ballet were to prevail against the Royal Opera House Board's urging that the Royal Ballet, once it had the resources, should have a *Romeo and Juliet* of its own. The impact of the Bolshoi's first visit to the West was to have a long-lasting effect on British ballet and on MacMillan's career.

17

Kenneth's preparations for his American Ballet Theatre commission were disrupted by the 1956 war in the Middle East over the Suez Canal. Britain and France had invaded Suez, in support of Israel, to seize back control of the Canal from Egypt. America and the United Nations opposed the invasion and Britain and France eventually withdrew their troops. The immediate effect of the Middle East conflict for Kenneth was that Ballet Theatre's tour of Israel, Syria and the Lebanon was abruptly cancelled. Stranded, the company might have had to return immediately to the United States, abandoning the remainder of its European dates. His ballet was in jeopardy.

Lucia Chase hastily arranged for extra performances to be added in Italy and the Netherlands to keep the company paid and occupied until its allotted Christmas season in Monaco. Kenneth was therefore able, after all, to start working with the dancers early in December. He and Georgiadis travelled by train to Rotterdam, joining the company during its performances there, before going on to Monte Carlo.

His ballet, to be called *Winter's Eve*, was inspired by yet another Carson McCullers story, *The Heart is a Lonely Hunter*. In the novel, the central character is a deaf mute who communicates without words. The theme had obvious resonances for Kenneth because of his sympathy for his deaf sister Jean. For the ballet's purposes, the heroine's affliction was transmuted into blindness. The designs and lighting effects could therefore suggest the world as she imagined it – an opportunity that Georgiadis relished. Lucia Chase was excited about the proposals Kenneth and Georgiadis had outlined to her, and gratified to have such a strikingly original European designer involved with her company.

Kenneth was eager to begin creating the central pas de deux between Kaye and John Kriza, as the young man who falls in love with the heroine without realising she is blind. There were echoes here of *Laiderette*, but Kenneth was well aware that Nora Kaye was no pathetic pierrette. He needed to work intensively with her and Kriza to discover how her role might evolve. American Equity, however, restricted the hours dancers could rehearse while they were performing on tour. With Kaye's and Kriza's connivance, Kenneth secretly arranged to use dance studios, after hours, in the Rotterdam ballet school at which his former colleague Leo Kersley was now a teacher. Kenneth and the two dancers could work in seclusion to a recording of the music he had chosen, Benjamin Britten's *Variations on a Theme of Frank Bridge*.

He had initially wanted to commission a score from the French composer Henri Dutilleux (who had written the score for Roland Petit's ballet, *Le Loup*) but the rehearsal schedule was too tight and complicated for such an undertaking. Britten's attractive music had previously been used by Ashton and Cranko, as well as by Lew Christensen for *Jinx*, already performed by Ballet Theatre. None the less, since Britten's *Variations* suited Kenneth's purposes, Lucia Chase raised no objections. She did, however, veto his proposed title of *Winter Garden*, with its echoes both of Tudor's *Lilac Garden* and the New York theatre of the same name.

Most of *Winter's Eve* was created during the company's three weeks in Monte Carlo, in the opera-house rehearsal rooms used by Diaghilev's Ballets Russes in the early years of the century. Even before the ballet was fully completed, a run-through was given at the end of December for the benefit of Lucia Chase and members of Monaco's royal family, the Grimaldis. A photograph of the occasion, reproduced in *American Ballet Theatre News* in February and in *Dance and Dancers* in March, shows Kenneth sitting, one crossed leg dangling over the other as in all his rehearsal photographs, next to Princess Antoinette, Prince Rainier's sister. The three young Rainier children are watching in a solemn line with their elderly governess.

Although the choreography for the two principals and sixteen corps-de-ballet members was proceeding on schedule, Georgiadis's sets and costumes could not be made, as intended, in the opera-house workshops. The staff were too busy preparing for the next opera season. The costumes were made instead in a suite at the Hôtel Excelsior in Monte Carlo, with Svetlana Beriosova's step-mother, Madame Lilyne, coming to the rescue. The scenery was made in Paris, and Georgiadis was none too happy with the results. The company flew to Lisbon for the dress rehearsal, while Kenneth, who by now dreaded air travel, went by train. He had not flown since the Sadler's Wells Theatre Ballet's tour to Rhodesia three years previously, and his nervousness about flying had since grown into a phobia.

Unaccustomed to making his own travel arrangements, he had not secured the necessary visa to pass by train through Spain *en route* to Portugal. The long journey was delayed by a day's wait for a visa at the Franco-Spanish border. Nora Kaye had elected to accompany Kenneth on the train, and it was during this protracted journey that their affair started – an affair of which the company soon became aware when they finally arrived in Lisbon. Kaye set out to seduce her choreographers as an inevitable part of her creative intimacy with them. The often repeated story went that Ashton had predicted, 'She'll have Kenneth for breakfast' – as indeed she did.

Kenneth was flattered, proud to be involved with a famous American woman ten years his senior. Besides, she could make him laugh, which was just as important as sex, and she understood his ambivalence about his own sexuality. Violette Verdy commented, 'It must have been a passionate affair because Nora was passionate. She was a continuation, no, an enlargement of Maggie Hill: funny, witty, with a poignancy and a charisma about her that was riveting.' Kaye and Hill had a similar liberating quality as far as Kenneth was concerned, though Kaye, by 1956, was a happier, more self-confident woman than Hill. Nora would be Kenneth's key to America, his guide and protector in cultural and social situations. A vital, loving and generous person, she would always remain close to him and look after his friends, family and dancers whenever they visited the States.

Winter's Eve did not make full use of Kaye's dramatic talents, although it emphasised her very individual qualities. The young man who falls in love with the vulnerable heroine gradually realises she is blind when she starts to stumble into her unaccustomed surroundings at a ball. She attempts to flee, stops for a brief solo of defiant courage, then runs away again. Striking out wildly, she accidentally blinds her lover; she tries to help him, teaching him how to walk when he cannot see. In their mutual distress, they lose each other in the crowd before the curtain falls. The girl is left alone, as in so many early MacMillan ballets, to face a desolate future. Her fears and emotions are represented by birds that only she (and the audience) can perceive. They flutter around her, first as symbols of hope, then as savage tormentors.

The birds, less substantial than those in Kenneth's Grimm ballet, *House of Birds*, were dancers dressed in black, only their hands visible in white gloves with feathers around their wrists. In one scene, the girl's exhilaration at finding herself loved was expressed in a dance in which she appeared to soar through the air, borne by white doves. Lighting effects behind the lacy appliqué patterns of Georgiadis's set made her 'blind' world seem magically phosphorescent. One critic, Ann Barzel, writing in *Ballet Annual*, interpreted the cut-out shapes as 'dilated pupils, unseeing eyes'. Kaye wore a simple white shift dress, splashed with colour, while the ballroom guests were dressed in 1830s period costumes in black and purple, the women with full sleeves and skirts and large hats, the men in tight-fitting frockcoats.

Using Kaye's strong technique, Kenneth was exploring the expressive possibilities of pointe work. The girl's hesitant steps, picking her way blindly on the tips of her toes, were emblematic of her insecurity. The young man supported her protectively, lifting her in a way that freed her to stride forward weightlessly – a device Ashton often used in his love duets. Kaye was adept at being able to bourrée backwards swiftly and smoothly, feet carrying her in directions she apparently could not foretell, as though her emotions were tugging her against her will. That 'involuntary' ability on pointe was to become a requirement for future MacMillan heroines.

After a fraught dress rehearsal, *Winter's Eve* was given an appreciative reception at its premiere in the Teatro San Carlo on 16 January 1957, an 'espectaculo extraordinario' attended by the President of Portugal and the diplomatic corps. The ballet was enthusiastically applauded, with Kaye and Kriza called back on their own at least a dozen times. The Lisbon critics praised their performance and MacMillan's ingenuity, claiming that the work was 'worthy of the artistic direction of Diaghilev'. Kenneth travelled back to London by train and then set out for the American premiere of *Winter's Eve* on 10 February, crossing the Atlantic by sea rather than air. Lucia Chase had requested another ballet from him, so he intended to remain in the United States for several months. He had not, however, secured de Valois's permission to make a second work for Ballet Theatre. She fired off a cable to him in New York, followed by a letter on 4 January, insisting he came back as soon as possible: he was scheduled to do his Ugly Sister role with Ashton in *Cinderella*, and she proposed that he should create another ballet for the Covent Garden company.

Kenneth, however, had no intention of returning to London after the first performances of *Winter's Eve* in America. He stayed in Nora Kaye's apartment in New York on East 55th Street, where he shared her bed, as he shyly indicated to Gilbert Vernon who was to visit him at the apartment a few weeks later. 'He showed me round her place and quite obviously there was only one bedroom. "Oh, fine!" I said, and he smiled.' Kenneth's position was well understood by Ballet Theatre members. Ray Barra, a dancer who was to become a good friend of Kenneth, recognised what was going on:

Nora had Kenneth in her grip. He was very nice, very gentle, extremely shy and withdrawn, so she took care of him. Nora adored the Royal Ballet at that time – she fell in love with them all. That's why Kenneth ended up with us in 1957: we thought he was going to join Ballet Theatre. He said he felt he wasn't getting enough opportunities to develop within the Sadler's Wells Ballet, and I think Nora fed that belief.

Winter's Eve was given a high-profile gala premiere at the Met, with a party afterwards to welcome the company back from its foreign tour. From now on, it was to be dignified with the national title of American Ballet Theatre. 'Flag-bedecked boxes told of the presence of American officials, embassy and United Nations dignitaries representing the nations visited by the company on its travels abroad,' reported the *New York Herald Tribune*. The Sunday gala was the sole New York performance before the company set out on a five-week tour of the United States. New York critics did not greet Kenneth's ballet with the unqualified approval for which Lucia Chase might have hoped. John Martin in the *New York Times* found the ballet 'callow, cruel, capricious – and yet there still remains the indubitable evidence of Mr MacMillan's talent. Invention is at present his greatest asset and his greatest danger, for he can turn out an endless amount of original movement without developing any of it.' Walter Terry in the *New York Herald Tribune* felt that the tragic elements in the story were overemphasised: 'The anguish here is over-extended, the moments of emotional release not fully exploited, the buffetings of fate administered too often. These are negative points. The positive values of *Winter's Eve* are many and the scale swings in their favour.' Terry went on to praise much of the choreography, which he found 'richly imaginative . . . wonderfully fresh, an unusual and peculiarly affecting combination of gentle sensitivity and glowing sensuality'.

On tour in Chicago, Detroit and Boston, review headlines ranged from 'Ballet stars twinkle in *Winter's Eve*' to 'Provocative *Winter's Eve* proves dreary one'. These were the worst reviews that Kenneth had received in his three-year career as choreographer. Over-sensitive, he regarded *Winter's Eve* as a failure, a betrayal of Lucia Chase's trust.

De Valois sent him a consolatory letter after the New York premiere, telling him not to

feel so unduly depressed about your Press. It was fair enough considering that they did not appear to like the ballet, but your abilities were never for one moment overlooked. You are only suffering the disappointments of all at your stage, and that applies to composers, writers, etc. You must expect to do a certain amount of good work that is not fully realised; it will be like this until your choreography is suddenly harnessed to a ballet that is, in its essence, really worth while. This unity is the hardest thing to achieve – and can only be achieved every now and then – hence the difference between a masterpiece and a good work. It is essential for you to realise that every time you execute a good work, it is one step further towards that goal of the occasional perfect unity.

She was advising him in her role as mentor – an experienced choreographer and director addressing a younger colleague whose work she respected. Then her tone switched to that of exasperated administrator, refusing to prolong his leave of absence until 10 May so that he could make a second ballet for 'some form of "workshop" ', which she had first heard about as a rumour, not from Kenneth himself: 'I do not feel this is necessary for our choreographers. After all, we have always shown ourselves willing to give you opportunities.'

She was doing all she could to ensure that he came home. The bait was her promised commission for a new ballet for Covent Garden, to be included, along with *Noctambules*, in the company's next American tour, from September 1957 to February 1958. She wrote to Kenneth in New York on 21 February, insisting that the new work would have to be ready in time for a final dress rehearsal in June, before the company's summer break. She therefore wanted him back by March, in order to decide on music and designs; she was not prepared to let him start creating the new work only in May, without having talked it over beforehand with her: 'I cannot find time to come over to you and discuss it in detail and I do not think it is possible with you at your present stage and myself so busy, that this can be achieved by correspondence.' By the end of the letter, she was cracking the whip: 'I do wish to emphasise that the question of time is really worrying me and I just cannot give you a production [for London and New York] if your second production for Miss Chase runs as late as May, giving you no time to collect your wits for your work with us.' She signed off, 'Yours affectionately, Madam'.

When Kenneth held out, refusing to return in March, she wrote, 'A pity, but nothing to be done. We must leave your ballet until later in the year.' She was not going to let him get away with a rushed creation for her company. He had hoped to talk to her in person, explaining the advantages for him of staying longer with ABT, when she and the company came to New York in April. It was to be a flying visit in order to film Ashton's *Cinderella*, with Fonteyn in the title role, for NBC Television. Since Kenneth was already in New York, he was required to perform alongside Ashton as the tall, haughty Ugly Sister. Although he was in disgrace with de Valois, the recording would reinforce the fact that he was still a member of her company. In the event, she decided not to travel to New York but to leave Ashton in charge. He directed the filming as well as performing in it, making sure that close-ups of the Ugly Sisters favoured himself rather more than Kenneth. Although the three-act ballet had to be shortened for American television schedules, the 1957 recording of *Cinderella* (issued as a DVD in 2004) still endures as a testament to both men's understanding that the travesty roles need not be grotesque to be effective.

De Valois, realising that she was not going to see Kenneth, wrote him a long piece of advice, warning him not to discuss the contents of her letter with anyone. She had wanted to alert him in person to the 'balletic blunderings' perpetuated by Lucia Chase's press campaign over *Winter's Eve*. A long article had appeared in the London *Times*, explaining how Kenneth's commission had come about. The writer, Peter Brinson, had not mentioned that the talented young choreographer was a staff member of the Royal Ballet – an omission that 'very naturally displeased us – as it was rather lacking in common courtesy'.

Even worse, according to de Valois, was the article's assertion that Kenneth had been approached because ABT's two new productions shown in London (Tudor's *Offenbach in the Underworld* and Bettis's *A Streetcar Named Desire*) had been 'failures'. This dismissive remark, she wrote, had probably got the backs of the American press up. 'You would be the last person to want such stupid things said, I know.' She warned him to be on his guard with the American press: 'Just work and keep out of things; you are quite sensible enough to understand and reason it all out calmly.' The subtext of all de Valois's letters to Kenneth during his New York stay was that he would be better off making ballets for her in London: she was the right mentor for him, not Lucia Chase. Her 6 March letter ended with comments on *Winter's Eve*, based on what she had picked up from the American press: 'I imagine that your scenario was really too sinister for your choice of music . . . at least that is how I visualise the chosen subject matter with this particular music – they would not really "belong" to each other.' In other words, she was telling Kenneth, don't go making ballets without consulting me.

The next communication from Covent Garden was a cable from David Webster on 27 March, announcing that *Solitaire* as well as *Noctambules* would now be taken on the company's American tour in the autumn: 'Essential you make arrangements return London directly after premiere for immediate rehearsal stop please confirm stop de Valois writing.' Her follow-up letter explained that they had decided to 'lift' *Solitaire* into the Covent Garden repertoire: 'This does not mean that we are removing it from the second company . . . we will give it in both companies.' If he was back by May, he would have four weeks to mount *Solitaire* on the Covent Garden dancers – 'a much quicker job naturally than a new work' – before the company took its summer break. She asked for his views on casting, while suggesting, far from tactfully, 'Someone small for the central figure . . . as the ballet is so light I think that the figure in the centre should not be in any sense statuesque – it gives the wrong twist to the humour, and for that matter, any moment of pathos.'

De Valois proposed 'little Merle Park, who has a sort of hopeful vivacity about her'. Anya Linden, she thought, would be good in the Sara Neil secondary role. Kenneth stuck to his guns and insisted on a tall, lyrical dancer for Margaret Hill's role. In her next letter, de Valois agreed that, in that case, Linden would be the right choice. She played Kenneth like a fish, allowing him slack over decisions concerning his existing ballets while keeping him on the hook with proposals for a new work over which she intended to exercise control.

None the less, Kenneth remained in New York to fulfil Lucia Chase's commission for a workshop ballet in May. The workshops had been set up by the Ballet Theatre Foundation to encourage creativity, like the more modest Rambert and Sadler's Wells ones. Four programmes were to be given on successive Monday nights at the small Phoenix Theatre on lower Second Avenue in downtown Manhattan. The evenings, called 'previews', would be a mixture of works by established and first-time choreographers: the most successful would be taken into ABT's repertoire. Kenneth's new ballet, *Journey*, appeared in the same programme on 6 May as Alfred Rodrigues's *Blood Wedding*. Rodrigues, who had left the Sadler's Wells Ballet to work independently as a choreographer, arrived in New York to mount his ballet on the American dancers.

Kenneth, who was delighted to see him, helped coach Scott Douglas as the Moon, the role he had himself originated.

Journey was based on the German poem 'Death and the Maiden' by Matthias Claudius. Kenneth had been fascinated by an American exhibition of Edvard Munch's paintings illustrating the poem. Instead of the obvious Schubert music, he chose Bartók's *Music for Strings, Percussion and Celesta*; he entitled the four movements *Premonitions, Three Messengers of Death, Journey* and *Judgment.* Nora Kaye was the Maiden, accompanied to her fate by Erik Bruhn, John Kriza and Scott Douglas. Ray Barra was one of the supporting ensemble of twelve men and three women. 'We sat on chairs and passed the girls like swimmers over our heads from hand to hand,' he remembers. 'Nora scarcely touched the ground. At the very end, we all made a circle and picked her up with our hands around her waist. We dropped her, so that she vanished down a hole among the men and we all watched her go, boom, with our heads down.'

The costumes, designed by Georgiadis, were simple bodytights for both sexes in ox-blood red, with black lines drawn across them. Photographs of the ballet's groupings look very like MacMillan's later *Rite of Spring* (1962), for which he appropriated some of the moves Barra described. David Vaughan, reviewing *Journey* for *The Times* in London, noticed resemblances to Kenneth's *Somnambulism*, which he had seen in London. Vaughan dismissed *Journey* as

a protracted piece of foolishness in which Nora Kaye was persecuted by fifteen men (in revenge for *The Cage?*). The choreography . . . came up to the choreographer's usual level of invention only in the solos for Bruhn, Kriza and Douglas. Otherwise the ballet resembled rather closely the kind of modern dance that fortunately is going out of fashion here now.

Other critics, however, found greater virtues in *Journey* than in *Winter's Eve*; Arthur Todd, writing in *Dance and Dancers*, claimed that its workshop production had 'some of the most inventive and unusual movement to be seen in several seasons in New York'. *Journey* was regarded as enough of a success to be taken into ABT's repertoire; it was eventually given at the Met in September 1958.

After the 6 May premiere, instead of returning immediately to London at de Valois's command, Kenneth stayed on in New York with Nora Kaye to see the second workshop programme the following week. There was a buzz of excitement about a ballet by Herbert Ross based on Jean Genet's play *The Maids*, using music by Darius Milhaud. At the time, Ross was working as an independent choreographer and director, mainly in musicals and television. He was determined to make a big impact on the workshop season, having fallen out of favour with Ballet Theatre in the past. He was going to mount three ballets, with *The Maids* as his manifesto: 'I'd saved up money from my commercial work and rented a studio to work on *The Maids* for six months or more prior to the workshop rehearsals,' Ross recalled. 'I had my group of dancers and Kenneth had his. Yes, we were rivals, though Kenneth had Nora, and she was a formidable weapon. They'd come sweeping in to my rehearsals, saying, "Do you mind if we just watch?" But I wasn't in a position to do the same to them.'

The Maids duly scandalised critics for its sexual perversity – 'a real shocker . . . completely pornographic' wrote Arthur Todd – but it impressed Kenneth. Fourteen years later, he would invite Ross to mount *The Maids* for the Royal Ballet New Group. Ross had cast Kaye in his second, less controversial work, *Paean*, later in the workshop season. The story goes that *Newsweek*'s dance critic, Emily Coleman, had rung Kaye before *Paean*'s premiere, wondering whether, after two tragic MacMillan ballets, Nora was going to suffer yet again in Ross's latest. To which Kaye replied, 'Emily, I die in the end, but I have sex first, so it's not so sad.' *Paean*, to verses by Sappho, received a rousing ovation and was taken into the repertoire.

With these two ballets, Ross had succeeded in usurping Kenneth as the white hope of the company, and was invited to become a resident choreographer. He was also to replace Kenneth as Nora Kaye's live-in choreographer. They would marry two years later and set up their own company, the Ballet of Two Worlds. After it folded, Ross became a renowned Hollywood film choreographer and director. His extensive output included a number of ballet-related films, such as *The Turning Point*, *Dancers* and *Nijinsky*, for which Kaye shared the credit as producer. Nora Kaye died in 1987; Ross, who then married Jackie Kennedy's sister, Lee Radziwill, died in 2001.

Until May 1957, however, Kenneth was still in residence with Kaye, weighing up whether his future lay in America with Ballet

Theatre. He was greatly enjoying living in New York, in the company of one of its best-loved ballerinas who had the entrée to wherever she wanted to go. But de Valois had a strong hold over him. Ray Barra commented, 'She offered him enough not to lose him – and maybe the Royal Ballet was more secure for him than the American way. I think security was very important to him. There was talk at the time of Ballet Theatre closing for a year to save money – and he didn't want to risk starving to death. So he went home.'

Kenneth bade farewell to American Ballet Theatre and to Nora Kaye in mid-May, and sailed to England on board the *Queen Mary*. He was apparently incapable of going by air to save time, even though Margaret Hill had sent him a cable on 13 May that read as an urgent cry for help: 'At home nervous breakdown Maggie.' Hill had abandoned the Sadler's Wells Theatre Ballet's spring tour to Spain and the Low Countries while the company was performing in Barcelona. According to Sara Neil, Margaret either left or was sent home to London: 'She was devastated about Kenneth. She didn't confide in me but I know she was pining for him and she didn't think he'd come back.' The cable alerting him to her crisis was sent to ABT's offices in New York, not to Kaye's apartment (as de Valois's letters had been), although Margaret presumably knew of their relationship. She might have accepted it initially as a short-term adventure, like her affair with Christopher Nupen; but Kenneth had been away for nearly six months, apart from his stopover in London *en route* for New York. She and Kenneth had been soulmates for five years, even if they were no longer lovers: she must have despaired of seeing him again. Margaret had a volatile, unstable temperament, and Kenneth's apparent defection seems to have pushed her over the edge into one of the breakdowns from which she suffered all her life.

When Kenneth did return from America, he joined Hill at her mother's house in Westbourne Park Road, where they had lived together from the early days of their relationship. It remained his address for the rest of the year. By July, Margaret had recovered sufficiently to dance her created role in *Solitaire* during the touring company's season at Sadler's Wells. De Valois seems to have sympathised with Hill's troubles: she took her into the Covent Garden company in time for the American tour in the autumn, enabling her to alternate with Anya Linden in her *Solitaire* role. Hill's sudden promotion to a leading role in the senior company must have surprised her and pleased Kenneth. 'Margaret seems well and happy,' de Valois reported in a letter to him in October.

By the end of 1957, both Margaret and Kenneth had accepted that their futures lay in different directions. They were both approaching thirty. Margaret knew that she wanted to get married and have a family of her own; Kenneth was not ready for such a commitment. 'It hadn't all gelled for him yet,' says Gilbert Vernon. 'Like a lot of us, he was bisexual. We took it for granted – we didn't talk about it a lot. Most of us probably wanted to have families eventually but when we were young, we were too busy having fun to settle down.'

Margaret became involved with Michael Boulton, by now with the Covent Garden company. He had stayed a friend of Kenneth's since their student days. He had recently broken up with Anya Linden, and once he fell in love with Margaret, he wasted no time in proposing. They married in 1959 and left the company to start a family. No longer involved with the theatre, they nonetheless followed MacMillan's progress as a choreographer, regularly attending his ballets. *Solitaire*, the ballet Kenneth made for her, has been danced by companies around the world and remains in the repertoire of the Birmingham Royal Ballet, the original touring company's successor.

18

Kenneth had arrived back in London to find the newly named Royal Ballet in a state of upheaval. De Valois's intention, in securing a Royal Charter for her companies and school, was that their status should be clarified. Instead, the resulting organisational changes led to confusion – not for the last time in the tortuous history of the Royal Opera House. In theory, from 21 May 1957, there was to be one Royal Ballet. Dancers from both companies would be interchangeable: one group would go on tour while the other performed in London, until they swapped around. The two groups would share the same productions instead of having separate repertoires.

De Valois acknowledged in an article for the *Dancing Times* in January 1958 that there were problems attendant on this merger. Reshuffling dancers and repertoires would take time, money and careful planning: 'Until fusion is complete and understood by everyone, we shall most carefully distinguish between [the companies].'

Fusion never happened. After initial attempts at exchanging ballets and dancers, the two companies reverted to their previous activities, with much the same troupe as before going out on tour. The immediate effect of the unsuccessful merger was that audiences for the touring group, now encumbered with the title of 'The Royal Ballet, formerly the Sadler's Wells Theatre Ballet', were no longer sure which company they were watching. De Valois called it the second company in her letters to Kenneth, though that was officially taboo: both wings of the supposedly integrated Royal Ballet were meant to be equal.

Kenneth's first commission on his return was a ballet for the touring wing. By defying de Valois, he had forfeited his chance to create one for the resident company. He was now to share a triple bill with new works by John Cranko and Peter Wright, to be given during the company's Christmas season at Sadler's Wells. It would be an opportunity to show how much he had matured, thanks to his experience abroad: eighteen months had passed since he had last created a ballet in Britain. He had agreed a new contract as resident choreographer with the officially unified Royal Ballet. He was to be paid £1,000 a year for up to three ballets or one full-length one (for either company), with permission to work elsewhere without taking a cut in salary. Royalties were set at £3 per performance by the 'first' company and no more than £2 for the 'second' company. He would be entitled to a living allowance of an extra £4 a week whenever rehearsing a ballet on tour.

Cranko, who went freelance in October 1957, had up to this point been paid £750 a year (with royalties of 3 guineas for one-act ballets and 10 guineas for each performance of his three-act *Prince of the Pagodas*). He had protested in the *News Chronicle* that he was grossly underpaid: 'They expect you to sit on your behind at the Wells for £14 a week [*sic*] and turn out masterpieces every year.' Thanks to Cranko's insistence, fees had gone up and a standard contract for choreographers had been put in place, after decades of ad-hoc negotiations. The terms of the contract allowed the Royal

Ballet to have exclusive licence to a ballet for three years, after which its ownership would revert to the choreographer, who could then mount it for other companies (with the Royal Ballet's agreement). Kenneth would soon profit from this new dispensation, as his reputation spread abroad.

For his new work, Kenneth had set his heart on Stravinsky's ballet score for *Le Baiser de la fée*, having forgone the *Divertimento* from the suite two years earlier, when he choreographed *Danses concertantes*. On Kenneth's behalf, the Royal Opera House had started trying to secure the music rights from Stravinsky's American publishers. David Webster, General Administrator of the ROH, had engaged to negotiate in person while he was in New York with the Covent Garden company. De Valois wrote to Kenneth from New York in August to break the bad news:

I am deeply distressed to tell you that, for the present, negotiations over *Baiser* are at a deadlock. The publishers are being extremely unreasonable and Webster cannot yet come to terms with them. Even when he does it will undoubtedly be on terms for Covent Garden only – therefore I feel that we may as well accept that you eventually do the work, on a large scale, on the bigger company. Have you anything else that you were interested in? I would like to talk to [Sir Adrian] Boult, our Music Director here, tomorrow and send you a telegram of any suggestions. Did Searle give you any help? I wish I was not so far away – I advise you to stick to Kenneth Rowell [as designer] anyway – Have you thought of Sibelius? Ask Searle if he has any ideas in this direction . . . Believe me, Kenneth, when I tell you that I and Mr Webster are as disappointed as you may well be. My only consolation is that I feel *Baiser* is too big an undertaking for the second company as it stands today. I hope that by next year I will not be writing that view ever again!

She signed off 'Love, Madam'.

Putting his ambitions for *Le Baiser de la fée* on hold, Kenneth decided to invent his own scenario for the new ballet. 'Ken poured out ideas for ballets, at least one a week,' remembers Gilbert Vernon. 'He had an incredibly fertile imagination. To me, what he lost later in his literary ballets was that originality. As a young man, he'd never have accepted somebody else's scenario.' The story he came up with concerned a group of people trapped claustrophobically in a room. He scrawled his outline of the ballet in pencil on a sheet of scrap paper: 'They are herded together trying to live normal lives. All have one thing in common. Fear. They all fear the unknown terror that lies beyond the door of the room.'

Kenneth handed the draft scenario to Nicholas Georgiadis in preparation for the designs. He had specified a set with a single door and a window, covered by a curtain:

There should be only one source of light, a naked bulb that flickers and goes out halfway through the ballet. In scene two, candles illumine the room until the light goes on again. The end of the ballet comes when the group of people hear a sound from without and stand, rooted to the spot, desperately listening. There is a knock at the door.

'We'd been having difficulties with the design – lots of sketches, lots of ideas,' said Georgiadis.

He said he wanted something less 'fantaisie', less abstract than I had proposed. When he saw some of my discarded drawings lying about on the floor, he picked one up, a dun-coloured room with white scratches on the wall and said, 'That's it, that's the Burrow' – which became the name of the ballet. The title didn't exist before that design.

Commentators have speculated that MacMillan had Kafka's short story of the same name in mind. If he did, either he had never read the story or he had forgotten it when he repeated the assertion in interviews that Kafka's *The Burrow* 'was about rabbits being pursued underground. I changed that into a sort of metaphor for people who were persecuted during the war . . . a group of people hiding in a place that could have been a burrow.' Kafka's terrifying last story, written while he was dying of tuberculosis, concerns a solitary, paranoid creature (evidently a mole, although the first-person narrator is never identified). The underground burrower fears that death has already invaded his tunnels, in spite of his frantic precautions, and is coming ever closer. Kafka-the-mole is a very different animal from anthropomorphised rabbits living in terror of the hunter's feet.

By alleging that Kafka's *The Burrow* was his inspiration, Kenneth was trying to draw critics and audiences off the scent of *The Diary of Anne Frank*. The book, first published in English in 1952, had made a tremendous impact in post-war years because it was a first-hand account, by an artless adolescent, of what it felt like to be part of a threatened community in an occupied country, in constant dread of discovery. The 'unknown terror that lies beyond the door of the room' was known in its full horror by the time the diary was published. Anne Frank had died in a Nazi concentration camp, like millions of other Jews and persecuted people. Kenneth did not want to appear to be retelling the enormity of her story in a ballet. He claimed in interviews that he had neither read the published diary nor seen the 1956 stage adaptation, which had opened in London before he had left for America. He told the ballet's cast, however, to read the book before rehearsals started. They assumed that the underground room was a version of the attic in Amsterdam in which Anne Frank's family and other Jews had hidden from the Nazis. (One of the lifts in the ballet was known as 'the swastika'.) But the dancers understood that in Kenneth's scenario, the inhabitants' fear of discovery by the Gestapo had been universalised to a dread of an imminent, brutal future.

The ballet began in silence, with the twenty or so inhabitants of the single room asleep or resting. When a girl pulled aside the curtain covering a window, the group attacked her for endangering their hiding place. To relieve the tension, individuals began to dance, revealing their characters as they did so. There was a young couple caught up in the wonder of first love; an embittered outcast; a crassly cheerful joker; a neurotic woman on the verge of giving way to the hysteria they all felt. Halfway through the ballet, the flickering light bulb went out and the dances took place in candlelight. Even in the semi-darkness, however, there could be no escape from the presence of other people. The light returned for the climactic ending, when the panic-stricken woman, driven to breaking point, slapped the joker's grinning face and the outcast broke into mirthless laughter. Caught up in their private drama, they were momentarily oblivious to the sound of the long-dreaded knock at the door.

Kenneth, who lived with the fear generated by his own capacity for acute anxiety, was quick to recognise incipient hysteria in others. He projected that understanding onto the central role of the highly strung woman, danced by Anne Heaton. It was a dramatic, Nora Kaye kind of role, a nightmare version of the *Winter's Eve* girl trapped in a situation from which she could not escape. Other roles contained elements of Kenneth as well as of the dancers he chose. Ted Miller was the Outcast, a tortured misfit who served as a sombre foil to Donald Britton's Joker. Britton the man was an ebullient practical joker, the kind of extrovert personality who could be transformed into an unbearable irritant in the claustrophobic context of *The Burrow*. This buffoon, the would-be entertainer who gets his timing wrong, reappears in a number of MacMillan's ballets. His insufferableness reflected Kenneth's mistrust of his own ability to make people laugh; he could stand outside himself, cringing at his own facility.

The characters' interactions sprang from his close observation of group behaviour. The cooped-up creatures in *The Burrow* were partly based on his own family in Great Yarmouth and his ballet family on tour. He knew what it was like to crave privacy and resent the predictable responses of people he saw every day. He used his knowledge of the dancers' personal lives and idiosyncrasies to portray recognisable types of humanity under stress. Some of his cast found his perceptions uncomfortably close to the bone, but they were prepared to endure any embarrassment for the sake of having a role tailormade for them.

They were not Kenneth's only source of inspiration: he was also drawing on John Osborne's angry plays about characters trapped by society in hopeless situations, among mean-spirited people they hated and despised. 'Kenneth told me that *The Burrow* was about England, as much as about oppressed people in a police state,' says Jeffrey Solomons.

It had a similar sort of claustrophobia to *Look Back in Anger* and *Epitaph for George Dillon*. Osborne was writing about the society we knew, class-ridden, timid and hypocritical. That's why we went to all the Royal Court plays. They were speaking directly to us: Kenneth even recognised, from his childhood, the East Anglian dialect Arnold Wesker used in his plays. *The Burrow* was Kenneth's 'Royal Court' ballet – I'm not saying it was directly influenced by any one play but it had the same rage at having to conform, at 'keeping up appearances', which got on all our nerves.

Kenneth wrote in a letter to Osborne years later, in May 1992, that *Look Back in Anger* had 'an enormous influence on me, not least because it made everything else in the theatre seem so trivial. Certainly it made me look at what was happening in dance, and your bombshell made me see that everything in my world was merely window dressing.'

The Burrow was to be his manifesto that contemporary ballet could deal with contemporary themes. He was expressing the fear and despair of the generation in Europe who had grown up during the Second World War and who lived with its consequences: the knowledge of its atrocities, the dreariness of economic austerity, the threat of nuclear warfare. All these would be implied within a one-act work lasting only twenty minutes.

The brevity was due to his choice of music, Frank Martin's 1949 Concerto for seven wind instruments, timpani, percussion, and string orchestra. He had used Martin's music before, for *Laiderette*, and de Valois was keen for him to try a different composer. She was away, however, on tour with the Royal Ballet in the United States until November 1957, so she was resigned to accepting the music he had selected in her absence. None the less, he was not to go ahead with the ballet until she had overseen his plans. Because of the delay in securing her approval, Kenneth managed to postpone the premiere of *The Burrow* from December to early in January 1958, thereby taking it out of the earlier triple bill of new ballets. Intentionally or otherwise, he had ensured that his ballet would be reviewed separately from the others, receiving its own publicity.

The touring company's Christmas season, originally planned for Sadler's Wells, was to take place for the first time at the Royal Opera House. Since the resident company was still on tour in America, the use of its theatre was intended to emphasise that both companies now had equal status. The bar had therefore been raised higher than expected for the newly commissioned works – a tough call for Peter Wright, who had to make his apprentice ballet, *A Blue Rose*, for exposure on the much larger stage. Among his cast was his young Canadian protégée from the Sadler's Wells Opera Ballet, Berta Lynn Springbett, who had just become a member of the touring company, aged eighteen. She was soon to change her name to Lynn Seymour.

She had been singled out while still a student at the Sadler's Wells Ballet School to be one of two youngsters on whom Ashton choreographed testing solos for the Royal Academy of Dancing's senior examination. She had caught Kenneth's eye in one of Wright's rehearsals for *The Blue Rose* and he immediately chose her for the role of the adolescent girl in love in *The Burrow*. The girl was not intended to be one of the central characters in the ballet, but the impact Seymour made was unmistakable. Small, with a round, vivid face, she was both childlike and lusciously feminine; her warmth and vulnerability were ideal for the part, making the lovers' fragile happiness a key element of hope in the story.

Seymour was unaware of her potent appeal. Still unformed as a dancer, she had plushly rounded limbs, a natural suppleness that she found hard to control and a vital, headstrong personality. She moved with an eager freedom that was unlike the more rigorously disciplined English girls in the corps de ballet. Above all, she was musical, responding instinctively to the pulse and shape of the music's phrases. Kenneth recognised in her some of the qualities he had had as a dancer, before he had become inhibited by stage fright.

Since she was still unaccustomed to being partnered, he let her find her way with the help of the more experienced Donald MacLeary. Their pas de deux was intentionally gauche, with the enamoured girl clinging to the boy's back rather than embracing him face to face. Determined to learn, Seymour asked MacLeary to rehearse extra hours with her. As a result, they became increasingly absorbed in their roles. 'The touching, hesitant ardour they brought to the adolescent lovers was immensely moving,' wrote Clive Barnes in *Dance and Dancers*.

MacMillan has created fragmentary dances, tender in their observation, unsentimental in their honesty. The first frightened kiss, seen but not really noticed by the others, and the lyrical dances which follow are simple and direct. In an ugly, squalid world love remains triumphant, with, on MacMillan's part, a praiseworthy diffidence. It would have been tempting to have pointed his moral with a grandiose pas de deux, but how much more effective are these reticent embraces.

Berta Lynn Springbett had never up to then been kissed, she claimed in her autobiography, except once, chastely on the cheek, by a Canadian boy.

The Burrow's Royal Opera House premiere at the start of the New Year received extensive coverage in the press, not least because Princess Margaret attended the opening night. 'Fashion note at Covent Garden,' cooed the *Daily Mail*, 'Princess Margaret wore diamond butterfly brooches in her hair . . . and a dress which drew murmurs of admiration from the crowds.' Kenneth and the cast were presented to the Princess in the interval. According to Oleg Kerensky's *Daily Mail* review, she told him, 'We were all sitting on the edge of our seats. I had shivers down my back watching it. My hands were quite worn out with clapping.'

Reviews in the national papers were enthusiastic, but no critic went as far as Clive Barnes.* In the *Daily Express*, Barnes prophesied, 'Controversial and stimulating, this piece seems a landmark destined to do for ballet what *Look Back in Anger* did for the theatre.' Reality had broken through into the fantasy world of ballet at Covent Garden, he claimed, thanks to 'the first British ballet to deal, albeit obliquely, with post-war life'. Helpmann's *Miracle in the Gorbals* and *Adam Zero*, created in the 1940s, had been regarded as 'tragedies of our own time', according to Audrey Williamson in *Contemporary Ballet*, but MacMillan was speaking for a younger generation: his challenge was, above all, to Ashton. By the 1950s, Ashton had taken to drawing on myths and legends for his ballets – *Daphnis and Chloe*, *La Péri*, *Sylvia*, *Ondine* – rather than contemporary concerns. Ashton had celebrated the Coronation of Queen Elizabeth II in 1953 with *Homage to the Queen*, and choreographed *Birthday Offering* in honour of the company's Royal Charter in 1956. He was identified with the Establishment that Kenneth, like John Osborne and the Royal Court playwrights, was rebelling against.

19

After *The Burrow*, Kenneth rented a flat of his own in Dover Street, the first time he had lived alone. According to friends, he was scarcely ever there, finding endless excuses to stop over at their places. He maintained his routine of eating meals at the same restaurants with much the same group of people: Nico Georgiadis, Jeffrey Solomons, Gilbert Vernon, Geoffrey Webb and Peter Darrell, whenever he was in town. The group was not exclusively male: women would sometimes join them, provided they knew how to be entertaining dining companions. Lynn Seymour decided to try her luck.

---

* Clive Barnes wrote about dance for *The Times* and the *Daily Express* concurrently, as well as for *Dance and Dancers*. He was to become the *New York Times* critic in 1965.

She had developed an intense crush on Kenneth during the *Burrow* rehearsals. He had travelled with the second company while he was creating it, so they had attended the same parties on tour and shared the nervous excitement of the premiere at Covent Garden. She wrote home to her parents in Vancouver, 'Kenneth MacMillan was on tour with us and he is the one that's been making life worthwhile for me . . . He liked me – fancy someone liking me! I'm a sucker for anyone who pats my head!' He treated her indulgently, recognising in her the loneliness and insecurity that had plagued his own youth. She was an odd little person, her myopic brown eyes needing powerful glasses when she was offstage. Her Canadian accent marked her as an out-sider and her very evident talent made it difficult for her to find friends who did not resent her rapid advancement.

Hungry for knowledge, she saw in Kenneth and his circle of inti-mates a tantalising source of information and guidance. She deter-mined to find out more about him, since his life in London was a closed book to her. She waylaid Solomons one day in Covent Garden, on the pretext of talking to him about *The Burrow*, and established that the in-group met on Saturdays for lunch at Madame Maurer's – Lena's – in Soho. She nerved herself to gate-crash the meal, reckoning that if her intrusion was resented, she would soon be away on an extended tour with the second company in Australia. Eight months would surely be long enough for her faux pas to fade into insignificance.

She walked in on the group and handed them souvenirs of a trip she had made to San Francisco. Her token gifts were saucy beer mats from a saloon bar with a drag-act cabaret; 'Lola Montes', pic-tured on the cork coasters, commanded 'Bring on the Dancing Girls!' In the silence that followed, Seymour blushed and turned to leave. The male diners, intrigued by her kittenish courage, insisted she join them: according to Solomons, she had 'smiled so beguil-ingly, it was almost sad'. She had staked her claim on their attention and they would include her in future meetings. 'It was such a big thing for me when they invited me to tea or lunch,' remembers Seymour. 'I wouldn't say I was in Kenneth's close circle then – I was a protégée, not yet a friend. And anyway, I was going away soon, so I wasn't part of the group for long.'

Kenneth, meanwhile, was preparing his next ballet for the Covent Garden company. De Valois had reported to the Ballet Sub-Committee in May 1958 that MacMillan wanted to create a ballet to Stravinsky's recently composed score for *Agon* and that he proposed doing it for La Scala Ballet (which had previously danced works by Cranko and Rodrigues). De Valois moved swiftly to pre-empt La Scala by commissioning Kenneth to create his new Stravinsky ballet for her 'first' company instead.

Agon's music had been a commission from Balanchine for New York City Ballet, which had given the premiere in December 1957. Stravinsky had collaborated closely with Balanchine, who wrote in his programme note:

Agon . . . is planned by Stravinsky and myself for twelve of our ablest technicians: it has no story except the dancing itself; it is less a struggle or contest [the meaning of the Greek title] than a measured construction in space, demonstrated by moving bodies set to certain patterns or sequence in rhythm and melody with multiple ingenuities.

There are famous photographs by Martha Swope of Stravinsky and Balanchine poring together over the score in a New York City Ballet rehearsal room, both gesticulating while the Russian pianist Nicholas Kopeikine waits with his fingers on the keys. Dancers are visible in the background, ready to take their place as the choreographer's and composer's instruments. The collaboration resulted in the twelve dancers being part of the score, making the music visible. They are the equivalent of the twelve notes in the dodecaphonic composition; their black-and-white practice dress matches the piano keys. *Agon* is a Balanchine–Stravinsky classic, acutely receptive to the avant-garde experimentalism of the 1950s.

Although Stravinsky, always interested in earning money, soon released his score for other productions, none could compare with Balanchine's account and choreographers stopped trying. Kenneth, unaware of what he was taking on some six months after the New York City Ballet premiere, did not even have the advantage of the one British ballet conductor who understood Stravinsky's music – Robert Irving, who had recently left Covent Garden for New York. MacMillan was going to have to create his *Agon* without musical guidance; the dancers would perform to an orchestra that had no idea how to play Stravinsky's latest music.

Since Kenneth could not read music, unlike Balanchine, he listened exhaustively to the recording, conducted by the composer himself, in the Dover Street flat. He interpreted the music in his own way, adding two dancers to the twelve Stravinsky had prescribed. The extra pair served to link the three sections of the work by their more or less continuous presence. The roles were taken by Deirdre Dixon and Ronald Hynd. 'There was a suggestion [by Clive Barnes in *Dance and Dancers*] that we were brothel-keepers, presiding over a bordello,' says Hynd. 'But Kenneth never told us anything. He showed us what he wanted – he was still a very good dancer, so he could demonstrate. I think he and Hilda Gaunt, the company pianist, worked out counts for us, until we got used to the music. It was very perplexing at first.'

Even though Kenneth gave the dancers no context for the ballet, he and Georgiadis had decided that the performers were *commedia dell'arte* characters, a travelling theatrical troupe who had arrived in a town with an arena (and a bordello) in the centre. Georgiadis's colour scheme was Mediterranean: burnt orange for the set, with black cut-out figures standing watch along the edge of the arena. Their stylised outlines were repeated on chairs scattered about the stage, as though the performers were perpetually under observation – contestants watched by spectators or voyeurs. The costumes for both sexes had Harlequin-diamond patches on them; the bounce of the girls' full skirts, short at the front and longer at the back, was incorporated into the choreography, as were their plumed head-dresses. The effect could not have been more different from the monotone practice dress and bare stage of Balanchine's austere *Agon*. Nor could the emotionally charged atmosphere of MacMillan's ballet: a pungent mix of pathos, irony, frustration and resignation.

The central pas de deux was danced by Anya Linden and David Blair as Columbine and Harlequin figures. 'We each sat on a chair, side by side,' says Linden. 'I had to put my hand across on David's knee and take it away. Kenneth gave me no clues, so I did it mechanically. Suddenly, it seems I got it right and the whole pas de deux came from that. It was sexy and ambiguous: is she seducing him or he her?' According to Hynd, 'It was like watching somebody being picked up in a cinema and making love in the back row with a stranger.' Linden remarks of her twenty-five-year-old self, 'I discovered something in myself that I didn't know. Kenneth could do that for his dancers.'

He had an unerring instinct for picking dancers with what in the 1950s was labelled as sex appeal – often before the person in question was fully aware of it. Anya Linden's beauty was still cool and virginal, like that of Botticelli's Venus, whom she resembled, as many admirers noted. By setting her in a brothel, without her knowledge, Kenneth was spotlighting her innocent sexuality. The ballet, however, mystified audiences, who sensed that something was going on without knowing what. A. V. Coton, reviewing the ballet for the *Daily Telegraph*, found, 'Unintentionally the *agon* (or conflict) of the title can be seen as reflecting the three-part struggle between choreography, music and decor – a contest which has not yet been clearly resolved.' In the *Financial Times* Clement Crisp* commended MacMillan's 'almost dazzling virtuosity in the creation of movement' but disliked Georgiadis's eye-catching designs: 'The ballet is so closely written, so filled with invention both musical and choreographic, and makes such intellectual demands of its audience, that the ingenuities of decor go for nothing.'

On the opening night, 20 August 1958, the Royal Ballet's orchestra battled with the score, while the dancers concentrated their efforts on keeping pace with the erratically conducted music, under the baton of Emanuel Young. The ballet's lukewarm reception meant that it was only ever given nineteen performances, nine of them on tour. Clive Barnes commented in *Ballet Annual* a year later that it was

dropped after the barest number of performances, unliked by the audiences, unloved by the critics, and so far as I can tell, unrespected by most of its dancers. I am never quite sure whether MacMillan himself had much faith in *Agon* . . . bedevilled by fiendishly bad orchestral playing and never particularly well danced, *Agon* was a hopeless struggle from the first.

Agon was Kenneth's first work for the Royal Ballet that had met with less than enthusiastic acclaim. He was on the defensive, feeling unappreciated. No future commission was scheduled for the Covent Garden company's next season and the touring company was about to leave on its eight-month visit to Australia and New Zealand. Since there was nothing for him to do at home, he was tempted to approach companies abroad. The critic Noel Goodwin wrote in his *Daily Express* column, 'I predict that ballet choreographer Kenneth

---

* Clement Crisp was Andrew Porter's deputy until 1970, when he became the *Financial Times*'s principal dance critic.

MacMillan, white hope of Britain's younger dance creators, will join his senior colleague, Antony Tudor, in artistic exile in America, because of lack of encouragement at home.'

De Valois evidently decided that she could not risk Kenneth defecting to American Ballet Theatre or taking his talents elsewhere. She told him that he should travel round Australia with the touring company, overseeing his ballets and creating two new ones that would be put into production on the company's return. She knew of his fear of flying – the flight to Sydney took four days, with five refuelling stops *en route* – and had booked him a return voyage by sea. The additional expense of shipping a spare choreographer to Australia for many months must have been considerable, but there was no sign of objection in the ROH Board minutes. Perhaps the Board members were unaware of how indulgent de Valois was being towards Kenneth; maybe they accepted that the extra cost might be absorbed by the Australian promoters of the tour.

The main reason for sending the second company abroad for so long – September 1958 to May 1959 – was to save money. The Royal Opera House, having relieved Sadler's Wells of the financial responsibility of the touring company, found itself encumbered with a troupe it could not afford. The Arts Council had yet to agree to increase the Royal Opera House subsidy to provide for the second company's touring obligations. Impresarios and theatre managers in Australia and New Zealand were required to foot the bill for as long as possible. The eight-month Antipodean tour eventually made a profit of £15,000.

The dancers were excited and apprehensive about the prospect of the long tour. They would be joined by principals from the Covent Garden company, including Margot Fonteyn and Michael Somes, and by dancers returning to perform in their home countries, such as Alexander Grant and Rowena Jackson from New Zealand. Youngsters would be given the chance to prove themselves in ballets they had not yet danced in Britain: Lynn Seymour, for example, was to learn and then perform the role of Odette/Odile in *Swan Lake* on tour. In a letter to a friend, she confided how pleased she was that Kenneth would be coming with the company for part of the tour: 'Ken MacMillan is showing promise! It still may be a crush but I feel like a goner ... He's a person fantastically aware of other people's emotions – almost psychic, amazingly kind and gentle.'

Her hopes were to be dashed. One night, Alexander Grant (who was to join the tour much later on) encountered Kenneth in the Nag's Head, the pub across from the Opera House stage door: 'He was sitting in a corner, looking absolutely miserable. I asked, "What on earth's the matter?" and he said, "I've got to go to Australia tomorrow and I don't want to." I sympathised because I knew he hated flying, but he said, "Madam's got me a passage on a boat that's going to take a month – I'll be on my own and I'll hate it." '

The next night, Grant returned to the Nag's Head after a performance and saw Kenneth sitting in the same corner: ' "Why are you still here?" I asked. Kenneth said, sadly, "I took a taxi almost to the gangway and I couldn't go up. Now I've got nowhere to stay because I've let my flat." ' Grant put him up in a spare room in his house in Rosenau Road in Battersea. Kenneth, who loathed being on his own, was grateful for Grant's hospitality and the company of his many guests. He was to remain in Grant's house for almost a year.

Having funked the trip to Australia, Kenneth was at a loose end. He knew that de Valois (who had flown with the touring company for the start of the Australian tour) would be furious. There was no chance of his working with the resident company to keep himself occupied. One possible project had already fallen through. Fonteyn and Somes had been hoping to commission a pas de deux for a concert in Monte Carlo in January 1959, before they set off for New Zealand. Kenneth had planned an Orpheus and Eurydice pas de deux to music by Milhaud – an early indication of his enduring fascination with the Orpheus myth. He would have relished the opportunity to work with Fonteyn but, in the event, she and Somes had no time to rehearse a new pas de deux. They were too preoccupied with the creation of Ashton's latest ballet, *Ondine*, to Hans Werner Henze's ballet score.

Kenneth had met Henze at Grant's house. Henze was the first German he had got to know and like, he told Grant. Henze remembered MacMillan, along with John Cranko and Alfred Rodrigues, watching stage rehearsals of *Ondine* from the back of the stalls before the first night on 27 October 1958. After that, the prospect of a long and dreary winter stretched ahead for Kenneth, until salvation of a kind came with a script sent to him in December 1958.

It was John Osborne's first and only attempt at a musical, *The World of Paul Slickey*, and he was looking for a choreographer.

MacMillan's name had been suggested by Jocelyn Rickards, who was to design the costumes; the set was entrusted to her friend, the architect Hugh Casson. She was a self-confessed ballet groupie, who had seen Cranko's Henley show in 1952. She had got to know Kenneth through Peter Williams, with whom she shared a flat, along with an ex-lover, Alec Murray, in Eaton Square – 'so there were choreographers and dancers in and out all the time'. She introduced Kenneth to Osborne, who wrote years later in the second volume of his autobiography, *Almost a Gentleman*, 'The happiest and most valuable recruit was the choreographer, Kenneth MacMillan.'

Kenneth was immensely flattered to be chosen as a collaborator by Osborne, readily acknowledging the influence of the plays on his own work. Choreographing for a musical was something he was confident he could do. As well as performing in amateur revues in his youth, he had watched countless musicals on stage and on film. He had ambitions to emulate Jerome Robbins's work on *West Side Story*, which had transferred from Broadway to London not long before, integrating dance as part of the narrative action.

He was shocked to find that most of the musical-theatre dancers who turned up at auditions for *The World of Paul Slickey* were incapable of doing what he wanted. So he recruited ex-ballet dancers whom he knew already: they included Geoffrey Webb, Patricia Ashworth (Rambert's *Laiderette* girl) and former colleagues from the Sadler's Wells Theatre Ballet, Stella Claire and Jane Shore. The stage manager was to be an ex-Opera House colleague, John Copley, who later became a celebrated opera director. Unwisely, as it turned out, the director of the musical was Osborne himself. He proved reluctant to cut any of his songs or scenes, even when the show was running at four-and-a-half hours.

During the initial rehearsal period in London, Osborne, Rickards and Kenneth spent most evenings together. 'We'd stay up and talk until the small hours. Kenneth never wanted to go home. He hated being on his own,' said Rickards. One night, a thick, yellow fog gave Rickards the excuse to remain overnight with Osborne, while Kenneth made his way cautiously back across the river to Battersea. 'When I told him John and I had been to bed together,' Rickards said, 'he asked me, "How could you?" "Very easily," I said. Then he asked, "Why him and not me?" "You never asked," I told him.' Kenneth had told her about his affair with Nora Kaye, saying, 'You see, I'm not homosexual.' 'And he showed no sign of it, apart from not fancying me,' Rickards said. She was Osborne's mistress for the next two years, and remained his friend and confidante for the rest of his life.

Osborne described *The World of Paul Slickey* as being a satire about 'the disagreeable exploits of a newspaper gossip columnist'. The character was based on two such columnists: William Hickey of the *Daily Express* and Paul Tanfield of the *Daily Mail*. Their catty comments were widely read and deeply resented by those whose privacy they invaded: upper-class 'society', nouveaux-riches social climbers and hangers-on, newly celebrated film stars, performers and playwrights, such as Osborne himself. He dedicated the published text to 'the liars and self-deceivers; to those who daily deal out treachery; to those who handle their professions as instruments of debasement; to those who, for a salary cheque and less, successfully betray my country; and those who will do it for no inducement at all'.

Osborne's bile was excessive, his lyrics hit and miss, the music by Christopher Whelen patchy. Peter O'Toole was supposed to take the leading role (for which Sean Connery had auditioned): when O'Toole walked out, he was replaced by Dennis Lotis, a South African with a fine voice who had no acting ability whatsoever. According to the actress Adrienne Corri, who played a debutante, the best bits in the show were Kenneth's dance numbers. To Kenneth's distress, Osborne used them as set pieces that did little to advance the action. 'Kenneth rehearsed and re-rehearsed us,' says Corri. 'He was a tower of strength because he knew what he was doing as far as the staging was concerned. Some of the show might have been good, but it was far too long and limp and John wouldn't cut it. He couldn't be objective. He took all our suggestions as criticising him personally.'

The show opened in Bournemouth on 14 April 1959 and then toured before coming to the Palace Theatre in London on 4 May. Word of mouth preceded it: 'We knew audiences were waiting to hate it,' says Jane Shore, who remembers crying furiously in the girls' dressing-room before going on. Adrienne Corri gave weekend parties at her house in order to keep the cast's spirits up and the show more or less afloat. 'No performers want a show to fail. We made some lasting friendships thanks to *Slickey* – it was like surviving the

Titanic.' Kenneth and David Pelham, the show's backer, had taken her aside during the tour and asked her to distract Jocelyn Rickards while they tried to persuade Osborne to make extensive cuts. 'He was being obstinate and Jocelyn was supporting him,' says Corri. 'I invented a dilemma about my love life and asked Jocelyn's advice for hours in the ladies' loo. But the men still couldn't convince John to cut.'

The cast took to placing bets on when each audience would start to boo. The coffin dance at the end of Act I was guaranteed to set them off, if they hadn't already erupted. On one occasion on tour, after the booing had begun, Corri stopped the show: 'If you're going to do this,' she shouted at the audience, 'let's get this organised. You'll boo in sections – this half first, then that half.' Quelled, the audience shut up. Corri pushed Osborne on stage at the end to face the hostile reaction: 'If we had to put up with it, he could too. But he was crying; he wasn't used to failure. Kenneth was all right; he knew it wasn't his fault. We all knew what was wrong, except John.'

Osborne wrote in his autobiography that the London first-night audience, primed by press reports of the tour, was particularly cruel: 'At the curtain call, John Gielgud was booing, not waving. So was Noël Coward . . . I must be the only playwright this century to have been pursued up a London street by an angry mob.' From the stage, Osborne had given a two-fingered salute to the gallery, whose members wanted revenge. Their angry contempt was because he had failed to deliver the satirical scourge they expected from his work; *Slickey* was merely a failed revue, embarrassingly amateurish and an easy target for disappointed critics.

In spite of terrible notices, the show ran for six weeks in London. MacMillan had received the only favourable mention, in a review by Mollie Panter-Downes in the *New Yorker*: 'The choreography, by Kenneth MacMillan, is a witty decoration for these goings on.' According to Corri, it had started to become fashionable among young people (who sat in cheap seats in the gods) by the time it finally closed. Osborne and MacMillan remained in contact for years, exchanging good-luck cards and telegrams for first nights and going to see each other's productions. A proposed collaboration towards the end of both their lives, which might have brought their working relationship full circle, could not happen because the timing was wrong for MacMillan. He was too busy working on *Carousel*, the only other stage musical he was to choreograph, long after *The World of Paul Slickey*.

20

After *Slickey*, Kenneth's agent secured another commercial contract for him, to fill in the time until the touring company returned from Australia. He choreographed the dance sequences in the film version of *Expresso Bongo*, a 1958 rock-and-roll musical that had been a big hit in the West End. Kenneth had originally been introduced to *Expresso Bongo*'s composer, Monty Norman, as a potential choreographer for the stage show. In the event, the dance routines for the West End musical were devised by William Chappell, who co-designed it with Jocelyn Rickards. *Expresso Bongo*, on stage, was a darkly sardonic exposé of corruption in the early British pop scene (the leading role was taken by Jimmy Kenny); the film version, directed by Val Guest and released on New Year's Day 1959, was sanitised as a launchpad for the young, squeaky-clean Cliff Richard and had little of the original's impact. Kenneth put together some rock-and-roll sequences and the big striptease number, for which he was paid far more money than his annual Royal Ballet salary.

The touring company returned towards the end of April, in time for Lynn Seymour to make her London debut in *Swan Lake* on 6 May 1959, dancing with the Covent Garden company. Alexander Bland wrote in the *Observer*, 'The grapevine from Australia had been tingling with the news that an exceptional young dancer had emerged . . . Rumour had not outrun the truth. Seymour is exceptional – in fact it is safe to say that, barring accidents, a legitimate heir to the dynasty of top British dancers has been born.'

She had been welcomed back by Kenneth and the in-group of diners, who congratulated her on how much more sophisticated she appeared. Robert Helpmann, who had joined the touring company as a guest artist in Australia, had befriended Seymour after seeing her in *The Burrow* in Melbourne. He took her in hand, encouraging her sense of theatre and advising her on how to dress stylishly. An extravagant dresser himself, he told Seymour that she should always wear high heels to show off her legs, and a hat for a touch of mystery. A head-turning hat was to become a Seymour trademark.

She put on her finery to impress Kenneth when he invited her to dinner at the French Club to celebrate her Covent Garden debut in *Swan Lake*. His opinion was what mattered to her; she had little sense of her own worth and she could not trust the comments of her peers. She was in the awkward position of being a member of the second company, invited, briefly, to dance at Covent Garden and then being sent back on tour. Like Margaret Hill before her, she would never quite belong. She was rootless and lonely – a condition Kenneth understood. Her appeal was that she needed him, and because she was still so young and unformed, he could bring out in her the qualities he required in an interpreter. Both recognised their mutual curiosity and attraction without appreciating that the relationship could develop into an obsessive one.

Kenneth knew that Lynn had nowhere to go when the touring company took its summer break in June. He proposed a holiday in St Tropez, where he been before with Margaret Hill. The invitation was not an overly intimate one, for Donald MacLeary was coming too, and Lorna Mossford, the second company's ballet mistress, had been asked to make up a foursome. The fortnight's holiday was to be a treat, carefully planned in advance. Kenneth had money to spend from his *Expresso Bongo* earnings; Seymour's parents sent her a cheque from Canada, so that she could keep her end up. The quartet opted to travel in style, booking *wagon-lit* compartments on the overnight Blue Train from Paris to the South of France. They crossed the Channel and joined the train in Paris in the evening, enjoying the luxury of dinner in the restaurant car, with its pink lampshades and fine crystal and cutlery. Their sense of occasion was completed by the sight of the American film star and comedienne Rosalind Russell, svelte and self-assured, dining at the next table.

Their hotel in St Tropez was not particularly grand, but for Seymour the whole trip was an exotic adventure. She wore a bikini for the first time, hoping to emulate Brigitte Bardot, whose appearance in Roger Vadim's film *And God Created Woman* had made St Tropez a popular resort. Holiday snaps, however, show Lynn looking very much the baby of the group. The glamorous hats and high heels Helpmann had recommended had no place on a beach. Lorna Mossford, in her thirties, succeeded in looking sophisticated with her bleached blonde hair and strapless tops. Seymour, small and dark, resembled an urchin in her striped matelot T-shirt and shorts. In one group shot, she straddles her hired bicycle like a child, her pose reminiscent of a photo of Kenneth as a small boy, standing alongside his taller brother and his bike. She wasn't just tagging along, however: 'I must have fitted in,' she says of her role in the group, 'contributed to the fun in some way.'

They did have enormous fun. When they weren't bicycling, they spent the day on the beach, taking snapshots of each other toasting in the sun. Kenneth and Donald, in sun hats and bathing trunks, showed off their long, elegant legs; 'Mossie' posed as a siren; Lynn, round-faced and freckled, cuddled between the men. The foursome ate all their meals together, talking about films, books and ballet. Kenneth was happy to discuss topics and ideas but revealed nothing personal about himself, his family or his childhood. They gossiped about other people's sex lives but tried to keep their own urges out of the equation. When Lorna Mossford made a pass at MacLeary during an afternoon siesta at the hotel, they succeeded in turning the grapple into farce. When Lynn confided to Donald that she thought she was desperately in love with Kenneth, he told her avuncularly to keep quiet about it. Kenneth was going to make a ballet for them both and there was no point in burdening him with her emotions. She took the advice to heart and the holiday ended cheerfully, with cha-cha-cha and champagne in a nightclub.

On their return to London, Kenneth finally accepted that the time had come to move out of Alexander Grant's Battersea house into a place of his own. He took over the lease of Anya Linden's basement flat near Marble Arch, at 23 Seymour Street – an address that caused giggles among the in-group. Though the central location was convenient for cinemas, theatres and the Opera House, the place had no life of its own. Traffic and crowds swirled past in busy Oxford Street to the south but the side streets to the north were largely empty of local shops, pubs and pedestrians. On Sundays, when the Oxford Street stores were closed, the place was dead. Kenneth's building faced the unlovely back of a large hotel, while his basement prospect was of a dank area below street level.

Without realising it, he had elected to live in *The Burrow* on his own.

He had little experience of home-making, having stayed mostly in digs or other people's houses. Visitors to the small dark flat reported that it was sometimes without electricity, either because Kenneth had forgotten to pay the bill or because a fuse had blown and he had no idea how to fix it. Although he hated being alone, he was beginning to dread going out: like the mole in Kafka's story, he would withdraw increasingly into his underground chamber, fearful of the world outside. The move to Seymour Street marked the start of his descent into the depression and agoraphobia that would almost cripple him.

Initially, however, all appeared to be going well. He was stimulated by his independence and supported by his surrogate family of friends. Lynn was now very much part of the group, although she had expected to be away on tour for most of the rest of 1959. After the summer break, both companies had presented their first joint season at the Royal Opera House, fulfilling de Valois's ambition to have over a hundred dancers at her disposal. In fact, the two groups performed their own repertoires, with just a few large-scale ballets, such as *Swan Lake*, combining their casts. The touring company did *The Burrow* and *Solitaire*, with Seymour dancing Margaret Hill's role as the wistful girl, coached by Kenneth. He encouraged her to read the Carson McCullers novel that had inspired him, knowing that she would identify with the young heroine. She then wrenched her foot and was unable to go on the company's autumn tour of the provinces. She stayed behind in London, worrying that she would never be able to catch up with those who taken over her roles. She had also lost MacLeary as her partner. He had been transferred from the second company to become Svetlana Beriosova's partner at Covent Garden. The only consolation for injured Lynn was that both Donald and Kenneth were in London.

She had moved into the same house as Clover Roope, a dancer friend who had been at the Royal Ballet School with her and who later joined Peter Darrell's Western Theatre Ballet. The house, owned by Roope's parents, became yet another meeting place for Kenneth's gang. On wet Sundays, they held impromptu musical soirées in the sitting room, calling themselves the Lesbos Ensemble (after a contemporary music group, the Melos Ensemble). Clover had a tape-recorder on which they registered their *musique-concrète* efforts. These included a disrespectful *hommage à* John Cage, whose musical experiments were discomfiting traditionalists.

The group laughed themselves silly playing on makeshift instruments: Seymour's was the vibrowumph – a suitcase bashed with a wooden spoon. Solomons rolled pennies down a chute into a bowl of water; Ronald Emblen played the spoons; Kenneth conducted proceedings from the piano, its strings 'prepared' to make unpredictable noises. They composed and recorded a twelve-minute opera, *Fanny or the Demon Barber of Fleet Street*. Once they were satisfied with their performance, they played *Fanny* back on the tape-recorder and held an earnestly intellectual discussion about its merits in the style of the BBC Third Programme's *Critics' Forum* (nicknamed 'Critic's Foreskin').

Seymour's more serious exposure to the arts was meanwhile taken in hand by Georgiadis and Solomons, as well as by Kenneth. They escorted her to concerts, plays and exhibitions, enjoying her company and enquiring mind. Like Kenneth before her, she was making up for an education that had been eclipsed by intensive dance training. If he was going to use her in his ballets, they needed to be on the same wavelength. From now on, she would share his reference points as they went to the same films and plays and listened together to the music he was considering for his next ballet.

While Kenneth and his friends were immersing themselves in the radically changing cultural and political climate of the late 1950s, the Royal Opera House was moving in a different direction. The previous Chairman of the Board, Lord Waverley, had been succeeded after his death in January 1958 by Garrett Moore, Earl of Drogheda. He had been the Board's Secretary for seven years and was eager to make his mark as its new Chairman. It was a role he combined with being Managing Director and subsequently Chairman of the *Financial Times*. His first move was to pack the Board with music- and opera-lovers, most of them acquaintances who could be trusted to go along with him. They included Jack Donaldson, his oldest friend, and Burnet Pavitt, a businessman who was Lady Drogheda's piano partner at private recitals. Both men, who knew little or nothing about ballet, would later make decisions that affected Kenneth's career as a choreographer.

The Royal Ballet's interests were represented on the Board by Mark Bonham Carter, a well-respected member of a political dynasty. The eldest son of Violet Asquith and Sir Maurice Bonham Carter, he was elected a Liberal Party member of parliament in 1958. He soon lost his seat, although he was to remain active in Liberal politics. He was a director of Collins, the publishers, and was later to become the first Chairman of the Race Relations Board. Bonham Carter was a ballet-lover, unlike the rest of the Opera House Board, and briefed himself fully on the Royal Ballet's affairs. It would begin to be superseded by the opera company, which Drogheda was determined to bring up to international standards. The opera company, which still usually sang in English,* had nothing like the reputation of de Valois's longer-established ballet troupe. By the start of the 1960s, there was a worldwide explosion in the fees singers of international status could command. In order to afford them, money needed to be raised to supplement the Arts Council subsidy to the Royal Opera House.

Drogheda's plan was to appeal to rich individuals and corporations, who would gain social cachet by attending fund-raising galas and taking boxes or rows of top-price seats at Covent Garden. He initiated the Society of the Royal Opera House: an inner core of patrons, who would contribute substantial sums towards new productions of operas and ballets. (The Society gave way to the ROH Trust in 1973.) A social and financial coterie of supporters grew up, very different from the egalitarian post-war spirit among ballet- and opera-goers. The trend towards elitism was encouraged, paradoxically, by the Friends of Covent Garden organisation, which was modelled on the Metropolitan Opera Guild in New York. Members paid – and still pay – a subscription that entitles them to certain privileges, such as booking in advance and access to dress rehearsals. In return, their money helps pay for productions and revivals, as well as providing scholarships for students. The idea, put forward by its Organising Secretary, Kensington Davison, was not intended

---

* Under Drogheda, the opera policy began to change to giving performances in the original language, sung whenever possible by top-ranking singers in the leading roles – although Maria Callas and Victoria de los Angeles sang in Italian in the 1950s. Some operas – Tchaikovsky's *Eugene Onegin* and Janáček's operas among them – continued to be sung in English for decades.

to be at all exclusive: 'We genuinely want to make a large number of people feel that they have a personal stake in their national opera house.' But although the annual subscription was not, initially, a hefty sum of money (5 guineas, or a 30 shilling membership for students), it nevertheless brought about a distinction between ordinary members of the public and an inner circle of opera and ballet lovers – some five thousand in 1962 – however extensive that circle eventually became.

In order to attract big money, the Royal Opera House was turning itself into the seemingly snobbish institution that was so to enrage its critics in years to come. The relationship between the Board, the Opera House administrators and the Artistic Directors of the opera and ballet companies was always a tricky one, its balance shifting with the personalities involved. A further complication was the Opera House's negotiations with the Arts Council and the Treasury, as it sought an ever bigger increase in its subsidy.

The ballet and opera companies were now answerable to their own sub-committees, supposedly composed of experts, including Opera House staff. The sub-committees took decisions that were then referred to the Board for approval. Board members, with some notable exceptions, were amateurs of the arts with little professional experience of the theatre, whatever their intellectual or financial acumen might have been. Kenneth was about to experience their views on his proposed choice of music for his next ballet.

De Valois told the Ballet Sub-committee in September 1959 that she was prepared to 'defer' the ballet she had intended to create for the next season in favour of a new work by Kenneth MacMillan. *The Lady of Shalott*, to music by Arthur Bliss, would have been de Valois's swansong as a choreographer: instead, she gave way to the young man she hoped would be her, and Ashton's, eventual successor as the company's principal choreographer. She was well aware that if MacMillan's ambitions were thwarted, he might return to Lucia Chase's American Ballet Theatre. At a subsequent committee meeting, on 22 October 1959, she endorsed his proposal for a ballet to *Das Lied von der Erde*, Mahler's final song-cycle, which, she said, could amount to 'a considerable artistic event'. David Webster, however, worried about finding the right singers and conductor for such a difficult piece of music, let alone the expense involved. There would be savings on designs, de Valois replied, because MacMillan

envisaged the performers in practice clothes against a plain cyclorama. The Sub-Committee decided to refer the matter to the ROH
Board, which was due to meet the following week.

Kenneth's proposal was an audacious one, especially for a choreographer not yet turned thirty. Mahler's music was not often performed in Britain at the time, in spite of the respect in which he was
held in Europe, especially his native Austria. In any case, ballets to
vocal music were a rarity: the notable exception was Antony
Tudor's *Dark Elegies*, created for Ballet Rambert in 1937, to
Mahler's *Kindertotenlieder* song-cycle. Tudor's later attempt in the
United States at a ballet to *Das Lied von der Erde* was regarded as
a failure: *Shadow of the Wind*, created for American Ballet Theatre
in 1948, was only ever performed six times. Kenneth could not have
seen it, although Nora Kaye, who was in the cast, would have told
him about it.

Kenneth had first heard *The Song of the Earth* at a Festival Hall
concert to which Jeffrey Solomons had taken him in 1958.
Solomons so loved *The Song of the Earth* that he wanted Kenneth
to share the experience of hearing it live in performance. As they
walked back together over Hungerford Bridge across the Thames,
Kenneth suddenly stopped and asked, 'Do you think I could do a
ballet to that?' Surprised at the idea, Solomons replied, 'I don't
know – but if anyone could, you could.' Kenneth immediately
bought a recording of Mahler's music and sketched out a scenario.
His idea of a simple setting might have been a reaction to criticism
of the elaborate designs for his *Agon*, whereas Balanchine's ballet
was performed in practice dress against a plain cyclorama.

The Board's deliberations were divided between those who fore-
saw the practical difficulties and expense of mounting a Mahler ballet and those who objected to the composer's music being used at
all. In the latter group's opinion, ballets should not be mounted to
great music that was not written expressly for that purpose; choreography would impose an interpretation upon music that was
better left to the mind's eye. The Board, made up mainly of opera-
lovers, had little awareness of the wide range of music used for
ballet since the days of Diaghilev's Ballets Russes. Although the
minutes do not record who the principled objectors were, they were
known to be led by Lord Drogheda and his old friend Jack
Donaldson. After long discussion, the Board decided to seek Sir

Adrian Boult's opinion, as music adviser to the Royal Opera House, and to inform MacMillan about the doubts expressed by their members. They were prepared to offer him a sop: 'If he decided not to go ahead, he could perhaps be offered *Le Sacre du printemps* as a consolation prize,' the minutes noted, adding, 'There was reason to believe that he would welcome such a proposal.' Jerome Robbins had proposed choreographing *The Rite of Spring* for de Valois's company in 1953 but had been informed that Leonide Massine was going to mount his version. Nothing came of either proposal, but the ROH management was evidently interested in a *Rite of Spring* ballet.

Sir Adrian Boult duly handed down his judgement. He advised against *Das Lied* as a ballet and MacMillan had to drop the idea. He would try again six years later, in the vain hope that the Board had changed its opinion. The Royal Opera House would eventually realise what a mistake its advisers had made.

Thwarted in 1959, he rejected the offer of *Le Sacre du printemps* for the time being and returned to his postponed ambition to choreograph Stravinsky's *Le Baiser de la fée*. This time, the Royal Ballet succeeded in securing the rights to the music and de Valois agreed that MacMillan should create his ballet for the Covent Garden stage, using dancers from both companies: Lynn Seymour from the touring group, Donald MacLeary and Svetlana Beriosova from the resident company. It was to be Kenneth's first attempt at a classical ballet in narrative form, requiring divertissements for a large corps de ballet as well as a variety of solos and pas de deux for the principals. He wanted to prove how versatile a choreographer he could be.

According to Alexander Grant, Ashton, who had created his own *Baiser de la fée* in 1935, with the very young Margot Fonteyn as the forsaken Bride, warned Kenneth that Stravinsky's scenario was intractable. It had encumbered both his and Balanchine's ballets to the same tempting score, in which Stravinsky paid homage to Tchaikovsky. Ashton's *Baiser* was not revived after 1939; Balanchine revised his 1937 version, mounted it for several companies, including New York City Ballet in 1950, then adapted it into a plotless *Divertimento from Le Baiser de la fée* in 1972. Kenneth prepared his own account of the story, only to have it vetoed by Stravinsky and his publishers, who would permit no alternative version.

Stravinsky had derived his scenario from Hans Christian Andersen's story, *The Ice Maiden*, in which a fairy imprints her magic kiss on an infant boy. Twenty years later, when the young man is about to be married, she reclaims him with another kiss and carries him off to the Land Beyond Time and Place. Stravinsky's adaptation was intended to be a poetic allegory of the divine discontent of the true artist, whom no mortal love could satisfy. It could also be interpreted as the story of Tchaikovsky himself, marked out by his genius and his covert homosexuality. Tellingly, the music in the score for the final pas de deux between the Young Man and the Fairy is based on Tchaikovsky's setting of Goethe's song 'Nur wer die Sehnsucht kennt' ('Only one who has known yearning can understand my sorrow', more familiarly known as 'None but the Lonely Heart').

The problem for a choreographer is that the score does not recognisably match the action that the scenario prescribes: Stravinsky deliberately avoided the theatrical scene-setting and climaxes that Tchaikovsky supplied so liberally for his choreographers. Music and story line meander over an hour's duration, with the tricky requirement that the ballet must lead up to an apotheosis showing the hero somehow striving for the unattainable.

Kenneth's instinct was to focus not on the Young Man and his destiny but on the Bride he abandons on their wedding day. Innocent and uncomprehending, she is the one to suffer, in a more human way than her apparently unfeeling lover. She was to be left alone to a lifetime of loss while he follows his icy fate. As in all MacMillan's ballets so far, the emotionally damaged protagonist is a young woman. He had spotted in Seymour, inexperienced though she was, an unusual quality of directness, both as an actress and a dancer. Her Bride would be no wistful waif but a girl as recognisably real as the desperate young lover in *The Burrow*.

For the Fairy of the title, he had the advantage of Svetlana Beriosova, with her ethereal, wide-eyed Slav face and Russian-trained technique. He could exploit her flexible back and high-arching arabesque in choreography that made her appear an other-worldly creature, both imperious and desirable. She would prove an ideal foil for Seymour's earthier fiancée. However, Kenneth had never worked with Beriosova before, and she had difficulties in adjusting to his demands.

De Valois, who came to see the unfinished ballet in rehearsal, sent Kenneth notes of advice, suggesting he adapt some of the lifts for the tall Beriosova in her pas de deux with MacLeary. She remarked that the Fairy's role was a difficult one, with all the sympathy going to the Bride: 'Beriosova is still feeling her way – but she has two weeks alone with you now and you must work her hard.' De Valois ended her letter by commending the ballet as 'a very beautiful work, deeply musical, refined and clearly stated'.

The designer was Kenneth Rowell, who had done the Ballet Rambert production of *Laiderette*. Kenneth and he agreed that the setting for *Le Baiser de la fée* should have nothing to do with traditional fairyland. Rowell proposed a harsh, rocky mountainscape of cliffs and gorges in dark, mineral colours. For the difficult final scene, when the Fairy takes the Young Man to the Land Beyond Time and Place, vast, iridescent veils swept in front of an eerie backdrop, concealing the couple from the bride, searching forlornly for her lost love. The ballet ended with a spotlit tableau of the man in the Fairy's embrace, his hands raised to the heavens in an intimation of the allegory Stravinsky intended.

Le Baiser de la fée was given its premiere on 12 April 1960, a few months after Ashton's popular success with *La Fille mal gardée*, his sunny ballet of young love fulfilled. MacMillan came in for inevitable criticism that the structure of his ballet was flawed, its finale mystifying. His choreography, however, was admired for its range and fluency, even though Mary Clarke in *Ballet Annual* protested, 'No ballet can be sustained throughout at such a peak of ecstatic invention.' He had shown that he could fulfil the conventions of a classical ballet, albeit in the space of one act: fantastical dances for the Fairy's attendants, folk dances for the villagers, lyrically romantic pas de deux, a concluding apotheosis. His choreography for the Bride and her retinue of female friends was a graceful tribute to Ashton and the way he grouped dancers in his ballets, as reviewers noticed.

Lynn Seymour was singled out in all the reviews for special mention. Philip Hope-Wallace commended her in the *Guardian*:

Her dancing has a rich fluency, like a sustained line drawn by some master draughtsman or like a long musical theme, modulated, altered, but wonderfully unbroken. That is her special enchantment and it is much to Mr MacMillan's credit that he should be the first of our choreographers to have given such perceptive expression to it.

Le Baiser de la fée was taken to the Edinburgh Festival in August 1960, as part of a Stravinsky triple bill by the Royal Ballet for the festival's opening night. The other two ballets were MacMillan's *Danses concertantes* and Fokine's *Petrushka*. Conditions were dire in the old Empire Theatre, with its wide, shallow stage and inadequate lighting. There had been too little time for music rehearsals with the conductor, John Lanchbery, and the City of Birmingham Symphony Orchestra, which struggled with the unfamiliar Stravinsky scores. During a hurried technical run-through in the morning, some of the stage hands had not been available. At the first performance of *Le Baiser de la fée*, part of the scenery in the village scene fell flat on the stage, nearly braining one of the dancers. She skipped out of the way just in time, leaving one of the stage hands, as described by Noel Goodwin in the *Scottish Daily Express*, 'mournfully surveying the wreckage in full view of the audience'. Two of the male dancers came to the rescue, shifting the collapsed set into the wings. Reviewers made light of the mishap since no one was hurt, but MacMillan was outraged. He fired off a furious letter to de Valois in London: 'I can only describe this as the most amateur show that I have ever seen on any stage . . . It was only the quick reaction of the dancers that saved what might otherwise have been a disaster.'

He informed her, 'As there was not one member of the administrative staff here in authority, I took it on my head to call a technical rehearsal with full lights the next day to go through *Baiser* again. Nothing fell down at the second performance but I would hardly call the performance satisfying.' Shy, taciturn MacMillan had no qualms about defending his ballets, as he was to demonstrate in the years to come. He also came to the support of his young star. Lynn Seymour's name had not been included in the list of company members, nor was she acknowledged as a guest from the second company. In high indignation, MacMillan reproved the company's management: 'As far as the audience was concerned she could have been from anywhere. I know for a fact that they were very perplexed as to who she was.' Seymour was always to feel that she was regarded as an interloper by the Covent Garden company, but at this stage, at least, she had MacMillan fighting her corner. He was confident enough of his value to the Royal Ballet to threaten to resign: 'My list of grievances is so long that I feel I must sever my connections with the Royal Ballet . . .' Then he added the rider: 'after my next production'.

A Scottish reporter had sat in on the vexed *Baiser* rehearsal, noting in his Festival gossip column that 'Dunfermline-born MacMillan was clearly a perfectionist'. Kenneth was quoted as saying that he planned to create a new ballet with a Scottish theme, along the lines of a 'classical *Brigadoon*'. He had been offered a scenario by the Scottish actor Sean Connery, proposing a ballet based on a legend involving a chieftain's family and a white swan. Connery, who had yet to make his name in films as James Bond, very much wanted to develop his Scottish *Swan Lake* idea. After MacMillan failed to take it up, Connery later, at the height of his fame, approached Balanchine with the same idea, without success.

Kenneth had decided to keep away from myths and legends for his next ballet, and return to the real-life, gut-wrenching experiences he had begun to explore in *The Burrow*. 'I'm sick to death of fairy stories,' he declared categorically in an interview with *The Times* published on 29 December 1960. 'I want people to go to the theatre to be moved by something they can recognise.' He was about to take ballet further than anyone had dared before.

21

The Invitation, Kenneth's next work for the touring company, was to be his first to a commissioned score. De Valois had been urging him to collaborate with a composer; it would be a testing experience, since he did not read music and would not be able to hear the fully orchestrated score in advance. He would have to work to a piano reduction of the music. He had been attracted by a radio broadcast of music by Mátyás Seiber, a Hungarian émigré living in Britain. Although Seiber had never written a ballet before, he had composed for films and was used to working to a script. De Valois approved of Kenneth's choice, instructing him to draw up a detailed scenario with suggested durations for each part of the action, known as a minutage. The choreographer briefs the composer on the main themes of the ballet and how long the ensemble dances, pas de deux, solos and other variations are expected to last. Precise timings for the music are further negotiated in collaboration.

Kenneth drafted his scenario for *The Invitation* from two different sources. Both were novels: *The Ripening Seed* (*Le Blé en herbe*)
by Colette and *House of the Angel* by the Argentinian writer Beatriz
Guido. His inspiration came initially from films of the books, which
sent him back to the originals. Both deal in different ways with the
awakening awareness of sexuality and the loss of innocence. The
young girl's story in the ballet is drawn from *House of the Angel*, in
which a repressed woman's life is blighted by the memory of her
first love affair; the boy's story, based on Colette's novella, is of his
sexual initiation by an older woman. In the French film the role was
played by Edwige Feuillère: Kenneth and his friends relished the
scene in which she called the boy 'garçon', looked down at his
crotch, smiled knowingly and said, 'Pardon, monsieur.'

He set his ballet in a tropical country at the start of the twentieth
century. The strict moral code of a different era and country would
make the forbidden passions in the story rage the more fiercely, with
dire consequences. The final version of his scenario features a house
party arranged by a respectable widow with three daughters. The
two of marriageable age are strictly chaperoned; the youngest plays
with her boy cousin and a gaggle of friends, supervised by a governess. The girl is more innocent than her playmates, who mischie-
vously pull protective sheeting off statues in the garden to peer at
their nudity, and then jeer at her embarrassment.

During the afternoon, guests arrive and watch the children's
dancing class. Among the guests is an unhappily married couple.
When the girl is encouraged to perform a solo to entertain the visitors, she is flattered by the attention paid her by the husband. The
scene then changes to the evening, when the entertainment for the
adults is a cabaret in the garden by acrobats dressed as cocks and a
hen, in an atmosphere of unbridled sexuality. The husband and wife
quarrel yet again, and both become involved with the two adolescent cousins. The wife seduces the not-unwilling boy; the husband
ends up raping the girl. By the close of the ballet, the audience
witnesses the guilt and anguish of the older pair, as well as the acute
distress of the violated girl. Repelled by her boy cousin's attempt to
comfort her, she retreats into herself, staring out at a frigid future,
alone as the curtain falls.

Kenneth discussed the scenario at length with Seiber during the
first half of 1960, visiting him many times as the score progressed.

A copy of the final, heavily annotated scenario is filed with Seiber's manuscript piano score in the British Library. Included within the bundle of papers is an earlier draft of the scenario that, very surprisingly, makes no mention of a rape. Instead, an encounter in the garden between the married man and the young girl in a nightdress is described as a 'love scene': when the girl returns later, she is alone and 'enraptured'. Meanwhile, the boy has enjoyed his sexual initiation by the married woman. At the end of this draft scenario, the girl and boy leave together happily, while the disaffected older couple remain apart on either side of the stage.

This version is so unlike the final ballet, with its catastrophic ordeal for the girl, that MacMillan might have intended to hoodwink de Valois with the first scenario to secure her approval. However, Seymour, who danced the role of the girl, finds it hard to credit that MacMillan set out to deceive de Valois: 'He wouldn't have dared – he was far too in awe of her.' He might have appreciated that his initial scenario needed heightening as he talked over his ideas with Seiber, clarifying what the ballet was about. He might then have decided to defy balletic convention by portraying an explicit, and brutal, act of sex on stage. Ashton had been daring about depicting consensual sex, incurring disapproval for his frankness; MacMillan would go further in showing the physical and psychological realities of rape. It seems unlikely that the first draft without the rape, with a minutage and detailed annotations in Seiber's hand in preparation for composing to it, was simply a dummy copy. Since no one involved in the ballet was aware of this previous, alternative version, the mystery remains.

Certainly, by the time MacMillan gave interviews to publicise *The Invitation*, he was adamant that it concerned the loss of innocence, which 'can be a shattering experience without resolution'. The theme would recur so often in his ballets that it evidently meant much more to him than a dramatic device. If he suffered a traumatic sexual initiation himself, however, he kept it a secret. The end of his own childish innocence and optimism seems to date back to his mother's death when he was twelve. The repugnance he felt at having to kiss her dead body in her coffin, combined with his guilt and confusion about his feelings, might have scarred him for ever. As he wrote in his draft memoir, 'A darkness settled on me like a cloak.' The girl's devastation in *The Invitation* was his strongest expression yet of a young person's life blighted by an experience that cannot be accommodated. In his earliest ballets, the defenceless heroine, ugly or blind, was already damaged in some way: in *The Invitation*, he showed the full impact of the damage happening to a naive, trusting adolescent.

Kenneth knew he had the ideal interpreter for the role in Lynn Seymour. He had already used her natural acting abilities in *The Burrow* and *Le Baiser de la fée*. Now, wanting to take her further, he set out to teach her 'what I had learned [about dramatic dancing] from such artists as Nora Kaye and Margaret Hill and Robert Helpmann'. Seymour was coming and going between the two companies, with a flying visit to New York to appear in *Le Baiser de la fée* at the Met, when Edwin Denby in *The Times* described her as 'adorable in an odd way'.

Casting the other roles would come later, once Kenneth started creating the ballet for the second company while it was on tour. The first performances would be given in Oxford in November, before the ballet's London premiere in December 1960. Anne Heaton had recently retired from dancing but returned, at MacMillan's insistence, to perform the role of the disillusioned wife. As the husband, he chose Desmond Doyle, who had recently joined the touring company, replacing MacLeary. Doyle soon became an intimate, a member of the MacMillan inner circle, cast in cruel, overbearing roles because of his height and narrow face, as lethal as a knife blade. MacLeary would have been the obvious choice for the boy cousin, but since he was not available, Pirmin Trecu was selected instead.

Trecu then badly injured his knee, so an alternative had to be found. On tour in Belfast before the summer break in mid-June, Seymour suggested Christopher Gable. They had started their careers together, and she was about to take him to Canada as her partner for two dance concerts in her home town of Vancouver. MacMillan watched them preparing the pas de deux they were going to perform there and agreed to consider Gable for the role. When they returned after the holiday break to start work on *The Invitation*, Kenneth realised he had found another ideal interpreter. Gable, like Seymour, was an instinctive actor and a very musical dancer. He had a gauche charm and blunt boyish looks that could convey his character's transition in *The Invitation* from immaturity to a knowledge he could scarcely bear. Annabel Farjeon in the *New Statesman* described his 'unformed nose as enquiring and responsive as a dog's'.

Mátyás Seiber had completed his piano score, including the four-minute rape scene, by June 1960, and the orchestration by the beginning of August. Kenneth's choreography was still in its early stages when Seiber was killed in a car crash on 24 September – a tragic end to their collaboration. Seiber's death appears to have affected the structure of the ballet. Although the manuscript scores, which mention two 'scenes', are in a finished state, Seymour says that MacMillan intended there to be two acts with an interval, rather than two scenes without a break. MacMillan appears to have confirmed this in an aside during a *Dancing Times* interview five years later with Clement Crisp.

After Seiber's death, the ballet seemed too short at 58 minutes to warrant an interval. Kenneth had already requested additional music for the first scene and might have wanted yet more. The cockerel cabaret dance, which initiates the distinction between day-time and night-time events, was to have opened the second act. When the two scenes were run together, the acrobats' divertissement had to continue for long enough to cover costume changes to evening wear for the central characters. As a result, it held up the story instead of raising the erotic temperature. The rude, crude activities of the befeathered entertainers were both risible and tedious, a clumsy and otherwise inexplicable chunk of padding. Although cuts were subsequently made to the acrobats' dances, MacMillan never fully succeeded in resolving the structural problem when he mounted *The Invitation* for other companies later on.

MacMillan had asked Seiber to lengthen the music for the young cousins' first pas de deux in the opening scene. After the composer's death, the addition was supplied by Don Banks, a colleague and former student of Seiber. Banks extended material from Seiber's existing music, *Pastorale* and *Burlesque* for flute and strings, which the composer had used for the entry of the children and their opening games. Quotations from the *Pastorale* and *Burlesque* appear later to contrast innocence with experience. Seiber had provided pastiche Strauss waltzes for the scene where the children are taught social dances of the period. John Tooley remembered the composer William Walton overhearing the music in rehearsal at the Opera

House, asking what was being played and, on being told it was Seiber's score for *The Invitation*, snorting, 'Ought to be ashamed of himself.'

Seiber's death did not delay preparations for the production for long. Georgiadis had already designed the set, a series of painted gauzes evoking a colonial mansion with a lush, tropical garden. His Edwardian costumes, with huge hats for the women, provoked the arguments he and Kenneth would habitually have over the size of headgear dancers were capable of wearing. MacMillan was forever insisting on smaller head-pieces, usually in vain. The adult women were corseted, restricted; Seymour's white dress, with lace and flounces, was evidently a young girl's party frock. For the second scene in the moonlit garden, she wore a demure nightdress, as though she had stolen out of her bedroom.

In spite of the stylised period setting, MacMillan wanted the performances to be realistic. He said of Seymour, in *About the House*, the glossy Royal Opera House magazine, 'I felt that, besides her enormous talent, she could act as a dancer as well as anyone in the legitimate theatre, and this made me want to do the most with her. I wanted *The Invitation* to move the audience in the way one is moved at a cinema or a play.' He and Lynn had been to see a Royal Court production of Ionesco's *The Chairs*, with Joan Plowright as the old woman. Seymour remembers being fascinated by Plowright's feet and how, shuffling in carpet slippers, she managed to convey great age. By making 'young feet' just as telling, Seymour exposed the girl's awkwardness when she flirted naively with the husband in her solo dance, stopped and didn't know what to do next. Her uneasy feet gave away her apprehension that she was out of her depth.

The relationship between the husband and wife (Heaton and Doyle) was based on the behaviour of couples Kenneth had observed. There were plenty of philandering men in a ballet company filled with tempting young bodies and plenty of wives who had seen it all happen before. The tensions between the married pair were also revealed through body language Kenneth had picked up from Antony Tudor's *Lilac Garden*. As in that ballet, gestures and glances, the way people hold themselves and touch – or refuse to touch – others were choreographed as meticulously as the steps they danced.

MacMillan appears to have had no problems working with the piano version of Seiber's score, even though he was unable to listen to it over and over, as he did with recordings. Heaton recalls that the encounter between her older woman and Gable's young man took just over an hour to complete in the rehearsal room: 'It just fell into place. We all looked at each other in amazement and said, "Good grief, we've finished it." ' The rape scene between Doyle and Seymour needed much longer consideration. Seymour protested that MacMillan expected the physically impossible from her. He had a mental image of a position he wanted, which supposed that her knees could hinge backwards: 'But something came out of that, simply because your knee doesn't bend in that way and so another movement evolves.' The man flings the girl violently against his hips, her legs splayed, and twists her so that she arches backwards into a knot around him; she hangs on to her feet as she slides slowly to the ground. While being extraordinarily apt for the girl's state of horrified rictus, the hooped position and descent down the man's legs echo the end of the sexual act in Balanchine's *Prodigal Son*.

Seymour's acting ability made the rape scene appear even more graphic than it was. No one from the company had been allowed to watch it in rehearsal until the final run-through on stage. Her portrayal of the girl's desolation was so compelling that her fellow dancers, astonished, assumed she must have experienced something similar. She had not. She was drawing on her imaginative understanding of how a young person could feel an outcast after such an experience, crippled by guilt and fear.

De Valois came to see the final rehearsal in Oxford before the opening night on 10 November 1960. Evidently unprepared, she was aghast at the rape scene. She suggested to Kenneth that the 'seduction' (she avoided saying 'rape') should take place offstage. He objected: either some minor character, a gardener, perhaps, would have to come and mime what he had witnessed – which would be obscene – or the audience wouldn't know what had happened to so distress the girl. When he declared that the brutal act was essential, since everything in the ballet was leading up to it, she gave way. 'It's your ballet,' she said as she left, ready to do battle on his behalf with protesting letter-writers and objections from the Opera House Board.

Critics had been asked not to review *The Invitation* until its London debut at Covent Garden on 30 December. Seymour wrote to her mother in Canada, 'Kenneth has undoubtedly produced a masterpiece – one of the most staggering works ever created and we all know it, but we also have a feeling that on its official press debut in London it will be ill-treated by the critics.' *The Invitation* was for the most part enthusiastically received. A rave review from Clement Crisp in the *Financial Times* proclaimed it 'a ballet of poetic truth and understanding, unsentimental and without romantic falsification'. Other critics had reservations, however much they praised the performances. Several wondered why MacMillan had chosen to set his sexually graphic ballet in the Edwardian period, thereby inviting comparison with Tudor's restrained masterpieces, *Lilac Garden* and *Pillar of Fire*. Richard Buckle (by now writing in *The Sunday Times*) was disconcerted by the contrast between the raw immediacy of emotions in the ballet and the stiffly conventional behaviour of characters such as the governess, the mother and some of the guests. Whose society was being shown in moral decay, he wanted to know: theirs, safely in the past, or ours?

Some confusion, perhaps deliberate, was caused by the fact that Georgiadis's Edwardian costumes for the men resembled the clothes currently in fashion for Teddy boys in the late 1950s and early 1960s. *The Invitation* therefore seemed less of a period piece at the time than in later revivals, when contemporary fashions had changed. Clive Barnes, writing in the *Spectator*, hazarded,

It is possible that MacMillan is trying to look 'unsentimentally' at the falling moral standards of our time . . . Into a world of smutty juvenile prurience and hypocritical adult lasciviousness come two young innocents; the girl is raped into feminine submission while the boy is seduced into masculine insensitivity, and the ballet's copious copulation is apparently enjoyed by no one.

Barnes, like the rest of the critics, had nothing but praise for the performers, 'practically dissolved into the ballet, and carrying conviction like an act of faith'. Annabel Farjeon, in the *Evening Standard*, summed up Seymour as 'wonderfully impressionable as the young girl, so nearly plain, so serious, so wrapped in her inner dreams'. The depiction of the rape did not upset the reviewers' sensibilities, though it did that of some audience members. Buckle, on the receiving end of letters from agitated readers, congratulated MacMillan on having made a work controversial enough to have aroused debate about an art form often considered safe.

The Invitation remains a compelling dance-drama some fifty years after its creation. Its hot-house intensity might have been difficult for some companies to convey, with the cockerel cabaret an obstacle few can surmount. But the choreography contains such insight into its characters' predicaments that a succession of dancers has been able to give individual accounts of roles once thought indelibly stamped by their original cast.

Its choreography has survived intact because it was the first of MacMillan's ballets to be written down while it was in the process of creation by the Benesh method of movement notation.* The Benesh system had been adopted by de Valois for her company and school in 1955, in preference to the longer-established but more complex Labanotation, developed by Rudolf Laban and his colleagues from the 1920s onwards.

The Royal Ballet had just appointed its first full-time notator (or choreologist, as the profession is also called) in 1960. Faith Worth was a graduate of the Benesh Institute of Choreology, which trained notators, mostly ex-dancers, in Benesh's 'shorthand' method of recording movement on musical staves. She travelled with the touring company from August 1960, making a written record of *The Invitation* as it was being choreographed.

MacMillan soon appreciated the advantages of working in conjunction with a choreologist. He and the dancers no longer had to remember every sequence of steps they tried out: they could refer instead to the notator's pencilled record, which would later be written up in ink when the choreography was confirmed. MacMillan was the first choreographer to disseminate his work abroad through the use of professionally notated Benesh scores.

Nora Kaye came to see *The Invitation* soon after its Covent Garden premiere. Recently married to Herbert Ross, she was in London with Ross, who was choreographing and co-directing a film vehicle for Cliff Richard, *The Young Ones*. The Rosses invited

---

* Kenneth's *Solitaire*, created in 1956, had been notated in 1958 by Elphine Allen, one of the first Benesh-trained graduates. Faith Worth then notated Kenneth's *Danses concertantes*.

Kenneth and the dancers round to their rented flat for dinner, and Kaye befriended Seymour, presenting her with pearl ear-rings for her outstanding performance as the girl. She was gracefully acknowledging Seymour as Kenneth's muse, her much younger successor as a dramatic dance-actress. 'Nora was a great admirer of Lynn's,' confirmed Ross. 'She thought she was a wonderful artist. We had her to stay with us in New York not long afterwards. Lynn had given a disastrous performance of *Giselle* at the Met and Nora had to comfort her for about four hours, convincing her that she must persevere. She was so unsure of herself.'

Before then, Seymour had danced a leading role in Ashton's new ballet for the touring company, *Les deux pigeons* (its title soon anglicised to *The Two Pigeons*). Its premiere was on 14 February 1961, six weeks after *The Invitation* was given in London. In choosing Seymour for the role of the heroine whose lover abandons her (temporarily) for a gypsy temptress, Ashton had been influenced by seeing her in a somewhat similar role in MacMillan's *Le Baiser de la fée*. Like the jilted Bride, the *Two Pigeons* girl would vie for her lover's affection with a formidable rival. Ashton had already cast Seymour as his Cinderella in the 1960–61 season and knew how affecting she could be.

The story of *Les deux Pigeons*, based on a La Fontaine fable, is a warm-hearted one with a happy ending, very different from the bleak conclusion of most of MacMillan's ballets. Ashton, now in his late fifties, belonged to an era of British theatre that was being elbowed aside by the Angry Young Man generation. Since he had no desire to compete by resorting to angst and violence, he fought back with the sweetly piercing romanticism he could do so well. His blissful bucolic ballet, *La Fille mal gardée*, had been a great success for the Covent Garden company in 1960; *The Two Pigeons* would be his gift to the touring company a year later.

Ashton had warned Seymour before rehearsals started that he would bully her in order to mould her into the kind of dancer he wanted. In fact, they worked together very harmoniously. Seymour was already used to the collaborative approach that MacMillan had learned from Ashton; she soon adapted her contributions to suit Ashton's style and sensibility. When Donald Britton, her intended partner, was injured, she prompted Ashton to consider Christopher Gable. Because she and Gable were such good friends, they were able to play off each other as Ashton's endearing youngsters, finding true love in spite of themselves. With the same partnership as in *The Invitation*, the contrast between the two choreographers' view of the world could not have been more marked.

Seymour worried that Ashton was encouraging her to be too winsome, so she asked Kenneth to sit in on a *Two Pigeons* stage call, out of sight in the balcony, to give her his opinion. He agreed that she should remove some of the girl's pouts and flounces, making her more wilful. Ashton would not have known that the subtly changed interpretation had been endorsed by his rival; what mattered was that the ballet worked. It did, though it was not to every critic's taste. Annabel Farjeon called it 'a sentimental piece of pseudo-Victorianism' and Richard Buckle mercilessly sent up its gypsy-camp activities.

Ashton was aware that for all his skill, his latest production had not trumped *The Invitation*. He was on the defensive, fearful of seeming hopelessly dated while protesting that he was entitled to mine his nostalgic seam of young love fulfilled. The Royal Ballet was not, after all, the Royal Court, dedicated to the new. To fuel Ashton's anxieties, MacMillan, not he, had been invited to redo the choreography for the Royal Opera's revival of Gluck's *Orfeo ed Euridice* in January 1961. Ashton had created the dances for the original production in 1953, when an ailing Kathleen Ferrier was a memorable Orpheus. It had been her swansong, for after just two performances she was unable to appear on stage again. Ashton's dances for the Furies in the Underworld were now considered too tame to revive, so MacMillan was asked to replace them immediately after he had finished *The Invitation*. Though the opera commission was not a major one, it was nonetheless a slap in the face for Ashton.

MacMillan was now Ashton's principal challenger, for Cranko had recently left Britain to become Artistic Director of the ballet company in Stuttgart at the Württembergische Staatstheater. He had been head-hunted to take it over in January 1961, after mounting his *Prince of the Pagodas* for the Stuttgart company, which was then directed by Nicolas Beriozoff, Svetlana Beriosova's father. Cranko had been growing increasingly frustrated by his lack of opportunities within the Royal Ballet, where he and MacMillan both had contracts as resident choreographers. While Kenneth had created two works in the previous year, there had been no new ballet from Cranko. Tempted by the Stuttgart offer, he had discussed his options with de Valois. She accepted that he should go, promised to give him her advice whenever he needed it, and told him he would always be welcome back.

Cranko was eager to get away from Britain. He had been arrested in 1959 for 'importuning men for an immoral purpose' in Chelsea, cautioned in court by a magistrate and fined £10 when he pleaded guilty. According to friends, he had been reckless, half hoping to precipitate a crisis that would disrupt the stagnation he was experiencing in his life. A crackdown on prominent homosexuals had been engineered by police and public officials who objected to reforms proposed in the Wolfenden Report. Sir John Wolfenden, chairman of a Home Office committee, had recommended in his report, published in 1957, that homosexual acts between consenting adults should no longer be considered a criminal offence. The change in the law took nearly ten years to come into effect. In the meantime, a campaign against reform had been mounted by the popular press, led by the *Daily Express*.

The *Express* seized on Cranko's arrest as 'the latest on the list of famous stage names who have been found guilty of this squalid behaviour'. The editorial of 9 April 1959 declared:

The private lives of people, whether they are a brilliant ballet designer and author like Cranko or an ordinary office worker on the 6.15 should, according to the Wolfenden Report, be their own business. But this question is public business. It has become a sour commonplace in the West End theatre that unless you are a member of an unpleasant freemasonry your chances are often lessened. For the theatre is far too full of people belonging to a secret brotherhood.

The article could be read as an implicit threat to expose homosexuals in the Royal Opera House 'establishment', which was even more concerned about its reputation than commercial theatre managements were. John Gielgud's acting career had not been affected for long by his arrest for importuning in 1953, but closeted figures in the Opera House, such as the General Director himself, David Webster, were apprehensive about witchhunts. They had good reason. During the Coronation year of Queen Elizabeth II, there had been a campaign to 'flush out' homosexuals from high-profile sections of society. A then Home Secretary, Sir David Maxwell-Fyffe, declared war on 'a vice infecting the nation'. The resulting court case, involving Lord Montagu of Beaulieu, Michael Pitt-Rivers and Peter Wildeblood, was the most sensational trial involving homosexuals since that of Oscar Wilde. Extensive coverage in the press had intimidated gay men from all walks of life, leading to jitters among those well placed enough to hope for a knighthood.

Cranko had not been ostracised after his arrest, but the continued snide references in gossip columns to his bachelor state, flamboyant clothes sense and association with Princess Margaret's bohemian circle, through his *Cranks* revue, meant that his future prospects for advancement within the Royal Ballet were questionable. He had been caught and criminalised, while others whose careers depended on the institution remained discreet. Fed up with British hypocrisy, Cranko was glad to move on to another country and start afresh.

Whether the publicity about Cranko's homosexuality had any effect on Kenneth's sexual behaviour is impossible to tell. His friends and colleagues assumed he was gay or bisexual, but whatever he got up to in private remained a secret. He did not court danger, unlike Cranko and other uninhibited gay friends. If there were suspicions that straight-seeming dancers might have exchanged sexual favours for roles in Kenneth's ballets, there was no evidence other than the gossip that always circulates in a ballet company. Kenneth would talk, in camp theatrical language, of a hopeless infatuation for some unattainable male figure. He startled Christopher Nupen on one occasion (long after Nupen's youthful fling with Margaret Hill was over) by complaining that he had suffered anguish throughout their friendship, fancying the unaware Nupen. It was a piece of information that Nupen didn't know how to deal with, but Kenneth evidently expected nothing from him. Ronald Emblen, who would come round to Kenneth's Seymour Street flat to bemoan the incorrigibly unfaithful behaviour of his lover, Peter Darrell, was aware of a 'frisson of attraction' between Kenneth and himself, but nothing ever happened.

Later, when Kenneth visited Cranko in Stuttgart, he distanced himself from his friend's late-night cruising in the town's gay bars. Most evenings, Cranko would surround himself with dancers (of both sexes) from his company, drinking and talking and drinking some more, until the dancers dropped away, conscious of class the next morning. Cranko would migrate in the small hours to rough-trade bars, from which he sometimes needed rescuing by loyal minders. Kenneth found Cranko's way of life exhausting, preferring to stay in Stuttgart with home-loving dancer friends, where he could talk and drink in private. He was going to spend a lot of time with the company, for Cranko invited him as a collaborator from the start, partly to maintain the Royal Ballet connection (which gave Stuttgart, then a minor though ambitious regional company, added prestige) but mainly because he genuinely admired Kenneth's work.

Solitaire was included in Cranko's very first programme, at the Liederhalle (the city's concert hall, not the main theatre) in March 1961, making up a light, entertaining bill with three of Cranko's own one-act ballets. Lorna Mossford staged *Solitaire* for the company, taking Cranko's advice in choosing a young soloist, Micheline Faure, for the leading role. Graeme Anderson, an Australian dancer who had recently joined the company, remembers how difficult he and the rest of the cast found MacMillan's choreography: 'John gave us steps that suited what we could do. Kenneth's stuff was made for technically stronger dancers and it nearly killed us.'

Peter Darrell was the next former colleague to request a ballet from Kenneth. Darrell had been making a living in the commercial theatre as a performer and choreographer for musicals, pantomime and television shows. Without a ballet company on which to experiment, he had continued to create ad-hoc pieces for workshop evenings and ballet clubs. Then he was thrown a lifeline by Elizabeth West, who had set up an adventurous small touring company, Western Theatre Ballet, based in Bristol. She co-opted Darrell as Co-Director and Principal Choreographer in 1957. Their policy was to build up their own repertoire entirely of dance-drama works using contemporary themes – something no other ballet company in Britain dared do at the time. Even Ballet Rambert, with its reputation for creativity, had to rely increasingly on 'the classics' as box-office staples.

Lord Harewood, then the Director of the Edinburgh Festival, was sufficiently impressed by Western Theatre Ballet's ambitions to invite the company to take part in the 1961 Festival. He proposed that it should present a programme of new ballets by Darrell and invited choreographers, with the participation of the Scottish National Orchestra musicians and singers. The music was determined before the choreographers were commissioned: Stravinsky's *Renard*, Milhaud's *Salade* and Kurt Weill's *The Seven Deadly Sins*, with its libretto by Bertolt Brecht.

Richard Buckle was asked to advise on the choice of choreographers and designers. He approached MacMillan, who seized *The Seven Deadly Sins*; Alfred Rodrigues selected *Renard*; Darrell was left with *Salade*. All three designers happened to be Australians. Barry Kay (who had collaborated with Darrell before) was to be responsible for the basic setting, a series of rostrums that remained in place throughout the triple bill; he was also the designer for *Salade*. Buckle recommended the painter Arthur Boyd for *Renard*, while Kenneth chose a young newcomer from the Slade School of Art, Ian Spurling, for *The Seven Deadly Sins*. Spurling was a style-conscious eccentric: he painted his face white with pancake make-up, dyed his bobbed hair jet black and sported a vast black cloak and broad-brimmed hat. His designs for Kenneth's project were similarly bold, incorporating large building-block cubes with letters of the alphabet on each side. They were manipulated by the cast to spell out each sin, ending with a tower that collapsed with a crash, spilling the blocks all over the stage.

In Brecht's caustic libretto, the sins punctuate the pilgrimage of the central character, Anna, as she travels through America in pursuit of a fortune for her family. The role is split into two: a singer, the worldly Anna, cynically advises her naive alter ego, a dancer, how to lay her hands on money. The singer in the original production, created for the short-lived Les Ballets 1933, was Brecht's wife, Lotte Lenya. Balanchine, who had done the original choreography, had involved Lenya once again when he reworked *The Seven Deadly Sins* for New York City Ballet in 1958.

Now, in order to add lustre to the Edinburgh Festival, Lenya was invited to appear in Kenneth's version. She flew from the United States to meet him at the Royal Opera House in London, where they discussed his ideas for the production. Kenneth introduced her to Anya Linden, who was to be her dancing counterpart, appearing with Western Theatre Ballet as a guest star from the Royal Ballet. 'This legendary woman inspected me, putting her hand under my chin to look at my face,' Linden recalls. 'Then she nodded, as if to say "She'll do." '

Lenya gave Kenneth her consent, and preparations went ahead without her. She was to arrive in Edinburgh for the last week of rehearsals in August, in time to familiarise herself with the staging. It turned out, however, that she had assumed the moves she was to make were the same as those she had done in Balanchine's version. The first impression she made on the Edinburgh cast was an indelible one. 'I am Lenya,' she announced in her deep voice, as she threw open the door to their rehearsal room, confronting ten nervous dancers and an apprehensive choreographer. 'Kenneth was quaking, as we all were,' remembers Brenda Last, an early member of Western Theatre Ballet. 'She sat down in her mac, the belt tied in front, next to Kenneth and we showed her what he had done. She stood up and said, "No, no, no, is all wrong – always I do here and here." She didn't understand that the choreography could be different. And she hated Ian Spurling's designs. So she walked out and flew back to America.'

Adrienne Corri, whom Kenneth knew from their fraught experience in *The World of Paul Slickey*, had stood in as the singing Anna during preparatory rehearsals. Harewood had been pressing for Corri to alternate with Lenya during the Edinburgh run; she was then to perform the role on her own in Western Theatre Ballet's season at Sadler's Wells the following week. She had been looking forward to working with Lenya but now found herself in a quandary. She chose to support Lenya's objections to the staging, to Kenneth's indignation. 'I did the dress rehearsal,' says Corri, 'and when Kenneth was petulant, I walked out. He could humiliate you in front of others and I'd had more than enough. I thought, "This is not worth being miserable for – you can always leave. So I did." '

Harewood, who tried in vain to mediate, was obliged to issue a press statement about 'artistic differences' being impossible to reconcile. Corri stayed on at the Festival, escorted by Harewood to performances and parties, and being cut by Kenneth whenever their paths crossed.

The day was saved by Cleo Laine, then a young jazz singer who had made her name in nightclubs. Kenneth was overjoyed when she agreed to come at once and to sing every night; she opted to use a throat microphone (then a comparative rarity) to amplify her voice in the large Empire Theatre. Percy Cater, a music reviewer, commented: •

You would never have suspected, from the ease and style with which she stepped into Lotte Lenya's celebrated role, that the star jazz singer was making her debut in this 'ballet with songs' entertainment . . . in a voice sometimes heavily charged with 'blues' emotion, sometimes rich and smooth as a cello and sometimes ringing like a trumpet.

Laine's throaty blues voice suited Kenneth's conception of the piece as a jazz revue rather than a savage social satire. Her youth made her a good foil for Anya Linden's Anna, both of them wearing identical black 1920s-style wigs. Once again, Kenneth exploited Linden's seemingly innocent sexiness and gamine elegance. Andrew Porter countered the views of critics who found the production too light-hearted when he wrote in the *Financial Times*, 'It is not *The Seven Deadly Sins*, one feels, that Brecht and Weill intended. On its own terms, however, if not on theirs, MacMillan's choreography is filled with brilliance and invention, and the whole presentation, in Ian Spurling's extremely clever set, is exciting.'

When the triple bill transferred to Sadler's Wells, *The Seven Deadly Sins* had to be placed last in the programme: an extended interval enabled Cleo Laine to reach the theatre after her other, previously booked, singing commitments in jazz clubs. She was worth the wait, according to the critics, who agreed that the final section of the bill deservedly won the most applause.

It cannot have been a coincidence that both MacMillan and Rodrigues had premieres coming up at the Royal Opera House at the same time as their Western Theatre Ballet commissions. Richard Buckle commented in his *Sunday Times* column, tongue in cheek, on the Royal Ballet's strange forward planning: 'Without in the least meaning to be possessive, it was suddenly found absolutely necessary that both choreographers should have to rehearse new ballets for Covent Garden during the same brief weeks when they were rushing round the country after the covered wagons of the plucky little western pioneers.' De Valois had chosen to open her senior company's season in September with a double bill of novelties: MacMillan's *Diversions* and Rodrigues's *Jabez and the Devil*.

She had asked Kenneth for a plotless work to complement the narrative ballets in the season's programmes, which included

Ashton's new *Persephone*. She suggested music by Sir Arthur Bliss, who had asked to be involved with the Royal Ballet again: his music had previously been used for ballets by de Valois and Helpmann. De Valois, who had forgone choreographing Bliss's score for *The Lady of Shalott* in 1959 in order to let MacMillan do *The Invitation* to Seiber's music, evidently felt that she owed Bliss a ballet. Kenneth, who had no time to find any other music, agreed to use the composer's late-Romantic *Music for Strings*, which was far from his taste. *Diversions*, his first non-narrative ballet since *Agon*, was to be an exercise in swift, demanding, neo-classical dancing for a technically strong cast of twelve.

He commissioned designs from Philip Prowse, who was later to become well known as a theatre director as well as a designer. The set consisted of disjointed architectural features suspended in mid-air; costumes in brown, gold and black resembled Etruscan paintings. The action revolved around a noble central couple (Svetlana Beriosova and Donald MacLeary) and their exuberant alter egos (Maryon Lane and Graham Usher). The main couple's trance-like duet was based on a device MacMillan would develop in later ballets. The pair remained at arm's length for much of the time, the woman cantilevered into slow balances and promenades. The smaller, nimbler couple were like taut springs, releasing and recoiling in speedy jumps and pirouettes.

An ensemble of four subsidiary pairs framed the various pas de deux, sometimes serving as an animated frieze. The taxing choreography for this supporting cast required considerable stamina over the piece's half-hour duration, though its intricacies tended to be lost against the fragmented set. The critics, in the main, found *Diversions* a bloodless, claustrophobic experiment to an uninspired choice of music. They had come to expect something more from MacMillan than craftsmanship for its own sake. Clive Barnes, however, writing in *Dance and Dancers*, remained an admirer of his talent, calling *Diversions* 'a very good ballet. Exciting, coherent, neat, and swiftly flowing in MacMillan's own very personal variation of Ashton's (call it British school) neo-classical style, *Diversions* is a feast for the eye, a balm for the heart and a challenge for the mind.' Alexander Bland, in the *Observer*, admired the way in which 'the consistency of style which holds the choreography firm was matched by perfectly modulated dancing . . . There is no echo of his early, jerky, perky style.' MacMillan was paying homage to Ashton, as he had done in *Le Baiser de la fée*, proving that he came from the same classical lineage as the older choreographer. Rodrigues's *Jabez and the Devil* on the same bill was given short shrift by the critics and never taken into the repertoire, unlike *Diversions*.

Had Kenneth elected at this stage to leave the Royal Ballet to work elsewhere, as Rodrigues, Cranko and Darrell had already done, he would have lost access to dancers whose technical standards were reaching new heights. The Royal Ballet's ranks were filled with promising dancers competing for roles, ambitious to take over from Fonteyn, now in her forties and considered likely to retire soon.

Then Rudolf Nureyev defected to the West in June 1961. Aged twenty-three, he was eager to experience the world outside the Soviet Union. Frustrated by the conservatism of the Kirov Ballet and the constraints on his private life, he had claimed political asylum on tour in Paris in order to avoid being sent back to Russia. He was looking for a Western ballet company with a good, classically based foundation that would welcome what he had to offer. He was determined to dance with Margot Fonteyn, whose international reputation intrigued him. Within a year, he joined the Royal Ballet as 'permanent guest artist', forging his famous partnership with its prima ballerina assoluta, Fonteyn's honorary position with the company. She and the Royal Ballet were about to enter a new phase in their joint history and Kenneth MacMillan would be part of it.

22

Kenneth's reputation as a choreographer was spreading abroad. The Royal Danish Ballet had been particularly persistent in asking for a new work. When he had been too busy to provide one, the Director and principal dancer, Niels Bjorn Larsen, proposed an all-MacMillan evening of existing ballets for the company's season at the Royal Theatre in Copenhagen in December 1961. The Danes were expanding their repertoire, dancing modern works by Balanchine and Robbins, Petit, Béjart and Cullberg, as well as their own nineteenth-century ballets by August Bournonville. Appreciation of their

Bournonville repertoire had eventually extended to the rest of the ballet-loving world in the 1950s, and the company now toured internationally, making its first visit to the Royal Opera House in London in August 1953. At home in Copenhagen, they continued to maintain the academic technique Bournonville had passed down through his classes, while Vera Volkova, who joined the company in 1951, had introduced her Russian-based training method as well. It was she who had been pressing the Royal Danish Ballet management for the past three years to invite MacMillan to work with the company.

Kenneth went to Copenhagen in September 1961 to get to know the company. He was pleased to see Volkova, his former teacher, and sought her advice about which dancers he should choose for his ballets. He watched the Bournonville classes with a choreographer's eye, relishing step combinations that were rarely seen outside Denmark. Attending performances, he loved *La Sylphide*, the Romantic-era Bournonville ballet that has continued to be a staple of the Royal Danish Ballet's repertoire, and he was impressed by the company's productions of ballets by Roland Petit, particularly admiring Erik Bruhn's performance as Don José in *Carmen*. Realising what fine actors the dancers were, he decided that they should do *The Burrow* as well as *Danses concertantes* and *Solitaire*.

He returned to Denmark for six weeks at the end of the year to stage the ballets. It was the longest time he had spent with another company since his return from American Ballet Theatre. Faith Worth, the Royal Ballet's notator, had gone ahead to reproduce *Danses concertantes* from her Benesh score, while he supervised his other two ballets. Because there was a span of ages in the company, with older performers traditionally staying on as character artists (something the Royal Ballet in Britain was only just beginning to accommodate), he could broaden the range of the cast in *The Burrow*. The ballet's theme of oppression and terror would have extra resonance for the Danes because of their experience of German Occupation during the war.

He worked with senior artists such as Kirsten Simone, Inge Sand and Niels Bjorn Larsen himself, as well as with young dancers at the start of their careers: Lise La Cour, Annette Armand, Anna Laerkesen. Eva Kloborg, who took the role of the child in *The Burrow* (she was thirteen, still in the Royal Danish Ballet School), remembers him as very intense, watchful, smoking all the time, 'but we all liked him a lot'. Faith Worth remarked on how well Kenneth was looked after by the Danes: 'He was never left on his own. Mind you, Kenneth was an expert at finding people to take care of him. He was very charismatic in his quiet way. He always managed to have a second- or third-favourite person around as a back-up if his first choice wasn't available.'

Thanks to the friendships Kenneth made in Denmark, his work became widely known in Scandinavia. When Erik Bruhn was appointed Artistic Director of the Royal Swedish Ballet in 1967, he urged Kenneth to mount a ballet for that company: it was to be the first outside Britain to perform MacMillan's *Romeo and Juliet*.

The influence of Kenneth's stay in Denmark was apparent when he was asked to make a piece for the Royal Ballet School's annual performance at Covent Garden in the summer of 1962. He choreographed a Bournonville-style ballet for the students, *Dance Suite*, to Milhaud's *Suite provençale*. It was an intricate work with fast footwork, designed to challenge an exceptional group of graduating students. They included Vergie Derman, soon to be one of his favourite dancers, and a talented American, Richard Cragun, who would become a principal dancer with Cranko's Stuttgart Ballet.

Dance Suite's staging was preceded by Kenneth's ambitious new work for the Covent Garden company, won by default in 1962. Jerome Robbins had been due to mount his own version of Stravinsky's *Les Noces* for the Royal Ballet in May, a work he had long wanted to choreograph.* There were objections, however, to his requirement of two grand pianos on stage, and he pulled out. The Board agreed that the projected budget should be allocated to MacMillan instead. He seized the opportunity to propose *The Rite of Spring*. He had been tempted by Stravinsky's *Sacre du printemps* in 1959, when the Board suggested it as an alternative to Mahler's *Das Lied von der Erde*, but the scale of the undertaking had daunted him then. He was confident now that he could do justice to Stravinsky's earth-shattering music.

Visitors to Kenneth's flat in Seymour Street remember hearing a recording of *The Rite of Spring* pouring out of the basement day and night. Jeffrey Solomons, who turned up while Kenneth was

---

* He eventually created his *Les Noces* for American Ballet Theatre in 1965; the Royal Ballet mounted Nijinska's *Les Noces* in 1966.

painting a wall to tone with one of Georgiadis's paintings, with the record at full blast as an accompaniment, was informed, 'Actually, after a while, you can hum it – it's full of tunes.' He told Solomons that he had researched accounts of Nijinsky's notorious, short-lived version in 1913 and of the 1920 Massine ballet to the score. Both choreographers had depicted a sacrificial ritual carried out by an ancient Slavic people, dressed in tribal costumes by the Russian historical painter Nicholas Roerich.

Kenneth, too, wanted the movement to be primitive: 'But with a primitiveness of my own invention rather than any attempt at an imagined pre-history . . . I believe that the actions and feelings that are shown may still be observed in people today.' Popular dances in vogue in the palais de danses and nightclubs of the early 1960s often resembled 'tribal' dances. Social dancers linked up in conga lines or gyrated wildly in the Twist, the Monkey and various forms of jive and rock and roll. MacMillan recalled their rhythmical mass movements when he came to invent his spring ritual. He also drew on traditional dances he had seen performed by visiting troupes in London from the Philippines, Haiti, Guinea and Senegal. His own concerns were reflected as well: the sacrificial victim, the Chosen One, was the outcast who had appeared in different forms in many of his ballets.

He chose Monica Mason, a twenty-year-old South African still in the corps de ballet, for the leading role instead of an established soloist. He explained his choice to an interviewer for *About the House*: 'For one thing, she has tremendous power . . . rare in English dancers, who tend to be more elegant and refined. But she has a real athletic quality, which struck me in rehearsal – also, she is tremendously musical.' He had cast her in previous ballets in subsidiary roles; now she was to be the focus of his *Rite*. Mason, later to become Artistic Director of the Royal Ballet, remembers being conscious of him watching her going wild at a party and 'showing off a bit because his eyes were on me'. He told her to buy and listen to a record of *The Rite of Spring*, and asked her to come to the first rehearsal in soft ballet slippers instead of pointe shoes.

He began work on the ballet with her concluding solo in which the Chosen Maiden dances to death – the climax of the music and the ballet. He arranged for her to leave the morning company class early so that they could squeeze an hour's rehearsal time into the tight schedule. The two of them worked in concentrated bursts for ten days in a small studio in Baron's Court, with Anthony Twiner playing the piano over and over. Twiner (known to dancers by his given name of Donald) had broken the music into counts so that they could follow Stravinsky's rhythms. Mason showed Kenneth her recollection of the Zulu dances she had seen as a child in Natal, when she had watched black legs pounding on red soil and had joined Zulu children in a stamping circle. She felt that she was making up her own sacrificial dance, and then realised Kenneth was tailoring the solo to fit her body. She understood that the Chosen One was possessed with the tribe's collective power: 'But in her dance, she is desolate, involuntary. Her arms dangle, suspended as if from a clothes line by her elbows. She has no will of her own.'

Although the Chosen Maiden's final solo is a long one, she is not a victim dying of exhaustion. Exalted, she dances to the point of orgasm and her heart stops: her death will be the earth's renewal of life. She is sacrificed by the will of the mass, all obeying a single impulse as they watch her die. The *Rite of Spring* sacrifice is a necessary, impersonal one: the choice is made swiftly and arbitrarily by the tribe's elders, who select one of six identical-seeming youngsters. The designated virgin falls into a trance and then has to find the inner resources during the 'Dance of Death' to embrace her fate.

MacMillan constructed the rest of the ballet to build up to the final solo. The choreography for the tribe involved most members of the company. Large groups of dancers were divided, as Stravinsky's score indicated, into Adolescents and Elders, men and maidens, before they came together as a single group to witness the sacrifice. He worked with the mass of dancers for three weeks, producing 'fiendishly difficult choreography', and then bravely scrapped everything he had done because he sensed it was wrong. He went for simplicity instead, basing the group formations on geometrical structures and reusing some devices from *Journey*, his 'Death and the Maiden' ballet for American Ballet Theatre: the girl being passed overhead along a line of men, the cluster of figures surrounding her, arms pointing towards her, so that only her head can be seen in the centre of their circle.

For the section shortly after the girl has been chosen by the Elders, he adapted a traditional dance he had seen done by a visiting company, the Bayanihan troupe from the Philippines, using bamboo poles. He asked the dancers to lie face down in straight lines, grasping each other's ankles instead of manipulating bamboo sticks. To Stravinsky's ominous beats, the dancers' limbs scythed open and closed as the Chosen One hopped down the lines, avoiding tripping as if by divine guidance. Richard Buckle compared her progress to the flight of a rook skimming over furrows of ploughed field. Another memorable mass effect was a long serpentine line in which the dancers held each other round the hips, falling backwards in sequence into a sitting position on the ground, like a row of dominoes being knocked over.

The designs were by Sidney Nolan, whose setting suggested a parched Australian outback inhabited by an Aboriginal tribe. MacMillan had initially hoped to use landscape paintings by Dubuffet, whose work he had admired in Paris. He asked de Valois to look at some Dubuffet paintings at the Marlborough Gallery in London, where Jeffrey Solomons worked. When she discovered the high price Dubuffet commanded, she took the gallery owner's advice in choosing Nolan, a new Marlborough client, instead. Nolan, Australia's most celebrated painter, had been living in London since the early 1950s.

Nolan committed himself completely to the ballet, attending rehearsals for six weeks and experimenting, in close collaboration with MacMillan, with schemes for the costumes and decor. For the first scene, Nolan reworked one of his paintings acquired by the Tate Gallery. He transposed its desert-like surface, criss-crossed with lines, onto a backcloth, wings and floorcloth. For the second and final scene, he enlarged a shape he had used as a motif in other paintings: a spherical blob on a stalk that could represent a human head, a phallus, a tree of life or an atomic explosion cloud.

MacMillan had requested costumes that revealed the shape of the human body. When he went round to Nolan's London studio, he was startled to see the painter's wife, Cynthia, modelling the proposed effects stark naked, with an outsize phallus strapped between her legs. Even he balked at the idea of choreographing a corps of penises for a Royal Ballet gala premiere. The compromise was bodytights for all the dancers in shades of ochre, red and brown, daubed with hand prints. Mason remembers standing on the Opera House stage with Nolan and his wife pinning newspaper cutouts of their hands all over her to show Kenneth how the designs would look. Only years later, when Mason saw Australian prehistoric cave paintings in Kakadu National Park, did she fully appreciate the source of Nolan's inspiration: 'There was *The Rite of Spring* on the walls of the cave – real goosebumps time.'

Nolan devised the tribal markings the cast were to wear as make-up, with wigs for the celebrants and masks and head-dresses for the Elders. The women's wigs were of pale raffia strands, tipped with black, that they lashed back and forth to the music; the men's black wigs were like Sumo wrestlers' topknots. When the dancers lay on their backs, one leg raised, they resembled plant sprouts reaching for the light. Upright, their slender bodies made them look more like a tribe of spider monkeys than primitive homo sapiens. They were far removed from the weighty early Russians in bulky clothing imagined by Nijinsky and Roerich.

The gala context for the first performance of MacMillan's *Rite of Spring*, on 3 May 1962, was somewhat incongruous: 'The Queen Mother, Princess Margaret and Lord Snowdon watched from under the blue-and-gold canopy of the Royal Box. The socialite charity audience (seats up to 10 guineas, programmes 10s) glittered with famous faces,' reported the *Herald*. Clive Barnes, in the *Spectator*, described the choice of fare as 'a glorious folly: the programme, though disastrously planned, triumphed on nothing more than its merits'. It opened with Erik Bruhn's staging of bright and bouncy Bournonville divertissements, starring Bruhn and Nadia Nerina; then came Ashton's *Raymonda* pas de deux for Beriosova and MacLeary to music by Glazunov; *Les Sylphides* followed, with Nureyev and Yvette Chauviré as guests in the leading roles. The easy-on-the-ear selection of music meant that Stravinsky's *Rite* at the end had the shattering impact the composer intended. Colin Davis had been invited to conduct as a Stravinsky specialist, and he drove the ballet to its climactic finale, leaving audience and performers stunned, gasping for breath.

'There could have been no bigger contrast to all that went before,' wrote Oleg Kerensky in the *Daily Mail* in an overnight review. 'But it is a powerful and exciting spectacle.' 'The choreography glitters with MacMillan's customary sophistication. There are no savage writhings and gyratings,' A. V. Coton reassured readers of the *Daily Telegraph*. With a few exceptions, the national dailies and Sunday papers enthused, led by the *Financial Times* in two long reviews by Andrew Porter, one of the gala, the next devoted solely to *The Rite of Spring*: 'The basic images – the tight, massed circle, the open ring of spectators seizing, violating, leaping, stamping, whirling, shaking – are used to create a spectacle that is hair-raisingly exciting.' Although Stravinsky had come to the conclusion that his *Rite* should not be performed outside the concert hall, Porter judged that 'MacMillan, aided by his collaborators, persuades one respectfully, and after almost fifty years, to disagree'. (Stravinsky continued to revise his opinion about the *Rite*'s performability until the end of his life.)

John Percival, writing in the *New Daily*, declared, 'The choreography is perhaps the most masterly MacMillan has yet produced . . . Brilliantly organised, it gives the illusion of spontaneous happenings yet matches at all points the structure and development of the music.' Praise was given to Colin Davis for his contribution in making Stravinsky's score danceable, and to Monica Mason for her tireless commitment as the Chosen Maiden. The *Dancing Times* noted that although higher prices were charged for the triple bill because a row of stalls had to be removed to accommodate the enlarged *Rite of Spring* orchestra, 'The very warm reception given to the ballet by the public suggested that the production of such an expensive work, even at higher prices, had been welcomed.'

The Rite of Spring was extensively reviewed in West German newspapers, the *Deutsche Zeitung* announcing an end to English ballet's 'teacup gentility'. A long account by Horst Koegler in the *Stuttgarter Zeitung* spread the word that Cranko's colleague in London was another name to watch. MacMillan's reputation preceded his forthcoming visit to Stuttgart.

In July of 1962, Cranko invited several of his former Royal Ballet colleagues to Stuttgart's Ballet Week festival, which concluded with a gala. MacMillan went to watch the company perform, deciding whether to make a work for its dancers. De Valois was in Stuttgart as well; Cranko was seeking her guidance on how to develop his company and enable it be seen outside Germany. Two Royal Ballet dancers, Georgina Parkinson and Gary Burne, had been invited to appear as guest artists during the festival. Erik Bruhn, who partnered Parkinson in Cranko's new *Daphnis and Chloe* at the start of the week, was due to dance in the Saturday gala. The unexpected arrival of Rudolf Nureyev threw him off course. Nureyev, who had been performing with Fonteyn and the Royal Ballet at the Nervi festival in Italy, had impulsively caught a train to Stuttgart in order to see Bruhn, his lover at the time.

Nureyev's presence caused a huge stir. Ray Barra, who had left American Ballet Theatre to become a principal dancer with the Stuttgart company, recalls that when Nureyev joined in the company's daily class, 'the whole city tried to watch through the windows'. Cranko couldn't resist inviting Nureyev to dance in the gala, even though he was bound to take the limelight away from Bruhn. Disturbed and appalled by the gossip surrounding his relationship with Nureyev, Bruhn refused to dance. Members of the company overheard 'one huge row between Erik and Rudi' before Bruhn walked out of the theatre. He took to his hotel bed, claiming to be ill. Cranko, strongly suspecting that there was nothing physically wrong but embarrassed to challenge an invited guest, asked Barra and MacMillan to go and talk to Bruhn. When they questioned his decision not to perform, Bruhn ordered them out of his room and fled the country.

Nureyev stayed on in Stuttgart, dancing in the gala with Yvette Chauviré. This was MacMillan's first opportunity to meet Nureyev in a context other than the Royal Ballet. After performances, they dined and drank with Cranko and some of the dancers. Nureyev was the kind of dancer Kenneth would have liked to have been: virile and virtuoso, with a highly charged sexual appeal that attracted both women and men. Although Nureyev was always looking for choreographers to create a work for him, his schedule was too crowded for MacMillan to consider anything for him – yet.

The conviviality of the Stuttgart company greatly appealed to Kenneth. Cranko's management style was informal, to say the least: he had no office, preferring to conduct the ballet's business from the canteen. He was always accessible to his dancers, who had started to flock to Stuttgart from all over the world. Eventually, it was reckoned that nineteen languages were spoken in the canteen, with English, rather than German, the one in common. Because so many of the dancers came from outside Germany, they tended to stick together as an extended family. They socialised easily with Cranko, both because they liked him and because they wanted to be cast in his ballets. Their friendliness extended to Kenneth, who recognised the kind of intimate, creative atmosphere he had enjoyed with Cranko in Henley. Peter Wright had now joined the company as ballet master, so Kenneth was confident his ballets would be well danced and well looked after. He agreed to create a new work for the Stuttgart Ballet in a year's time.

Kenneth returned from gregarious Stuttgart to his solitary Seymour Street flat, which was beginning to depress him deeply. Or, rather, he was sinking into a dark state of depression that his isolated existence in the basement flat did nothing to alleviate. His chronic anxiety was exacerbated by the Cuban Missile Crisis in October 1962, with the world seemingly poised on the verge of nuclear warfare between East and West. He and Jeffrey Solomons stayed up for night after night, discussing the stand-off between Khrushchev and Kennedy and speculating on what the worst outcome might bring. They turned for advice to Gilbert Vernon, whose grasp of political affairs they trusted more than their own, and were profoundly relieved when his prediction that Khrushchev would back down proved right.

Afterwards, without an external cause to justify his panic attacks, Kenneth became mired in helpless gloom. Now in his thirties, he was dissatisfied with the way his life was turning out. He needed to work, to be kept busy creating and rehearsing his ballets, but he was frustrated by the sparse opportunities offered by the Royal Ballet. Lacking the stimulus of creation, he turned in on himself, aware how lonely he was. He agonised over his infatuations for 'straight' men, in emotional pain rather than in love. He did not want to think of himself as homosexual: he told friends he didn't really enjoy sex with men. He felt under conflicting pressures to conform: to marry, as his brother and sisters had, and his parents would have expected of him; or to accept that he was indeed as queer as men in ballet were assumed to be. Sexual liberation was proclaimed in the 1960s, a revolution after the hypocritical prudery of the 1950s. If Kenneth couldn't liberate himself, there must indeed be something wrong with him.

His depressive tendency might also have been an inherited condition. His sister Betty had a breakdown after the war, severe enough to be treated with electro-convulsive therapy. His father, a deeply morose man, had become an alcoholic. Kenneth was drinking more and more as he grew older during the 1960s, the period when youthful idealism and cannabis flourished. He drank on his own, relying on whisky to enable him to leave his flat and face the outside world; he needed to be numbed by yet more alcohol, in the company of others, before he could return. He dreaded going to sleep because he knew how awful he would feel when he woke up and his anxieties crowded in again.

'People in the company were beginning to get impatient with him because they didn't know if he'd make it to rehearsal – sometimes he just didn't turn up,' remembers Hilary Cartwright. His close friends and colleagues colluded with his drinking, bringing him bottles of whisky: 'We knew he couldn't control his nerves and we had to keep him going,' Hilary Cartwright said. 'What he had to offer was so important to us and the company.' He relied on his surrogate, ballet family to keep him company, but now, as they grew older, the once tight-knit group was dispersing.

Even Lynn Seymour, ten years younger and hitherto available whenever she was in London, had gone in search of a life and love of her own. On tour with the second company in the Far East during 1961, she had grown close to Colin Jones, a dancer in the corps who was taking photographs of everything he saw. 'I didn't meet her – she met me,' says Jones. He wouldn't have dared approach her, since she was one of the stars of the company and he was low down the hierarchy. 'She was fascinated by photography and by the places we saw on tour.' He took her to areas the other dancers did not visit, such as the slums of Manila and Hong Kong, and talked of things other than dance. 'I was beginning to lose the faith,' he says of his ballet career. 'I was already thinking of leaving and starting up as a photojournalist.'

When the company next went on tour in the autumn to Baalbek, Damascus and Athens, Lynn introduced him to Kenneth. MacMillan, who had joined the tour in Athens, usually dined with the group the company called 'the Royal Family' – the senior staff and principal dancers, including Margot Fonteyn as guest artist. (Jones had earlier snapped Fonteyn and Seymour walking barefoot, shrouded in cloaks, in the Great Mosque in Damascus.) Lynn invited Colin to join her at the rooftop restaurant in Athens where the 'Royals' ate after the performance; he remembers, marvelling, that he sat next to Lynn at the privileged table for five days in succession. She was making the point that she now had a boyfriend;

she also knew that Kenneth would be attracted by Colin Jones, as she was. He was interesting, gentle, good-looking, with a mop of soft brown curls. Although Kenneth's extravagant infatuations were for more butch, overtly masculine types, he would be drawn to Colin because he was a lot like himself as a young man.

Kenneth's spiral into depression, and his jealousy of Lynn's happy relationship with Colin Jones, might have been at the root of the problems he had in creating his next ballet with Seymour. He had not worked with her since *The Invitation* at the end of 1960. She had been unavailable, either on tour or injured, during a long, frustrating period. By November 1962, she had moved into a flat at John Cranko's former address in Pimlico and was about to become engaged to Jones. She had dropped out of the in-group meetings in Soho – 'the Diners' Club', as they had come to be called – because her intention of marrying Jones 'had gone down like a lead balloon' with Kenneth's circle of intimates. Kenneth, however, would come round to the Pimlico flat nearly every day and night, to talk about his next ballet or whatever else was on his mind. Jones comments wrily, 'I gradually realised I was going to have to marry Kenneth as well.'

Symphony was to be another plotless work for the main company, following on from *Diversions*. The music, Shostakovich's youthful First Symphony, had been suggested by John Lanchbery, who had loved it since his student days at the Royal College of Music. Although the symphony appealed to Kenneth, he struggled to find the right choreographic form to contain the ideas the music suggested to him. He did not want to introduce a narrative line, though he could not resist the dramatic elements in the score. He used a larger cast of soloists than usual, with four principals, six demi-soloists and a corps of twelve who often danced as individuals. He told Jeffrey Solomons that *Symphony* was his Jackson Pollock ballet. At the time, Pollock's densely spattered 'action' paintings were being given their first British commercial exhibition at the Marlborough Gallery, where Solomons worked. Kenneth said that, like the artist, he was experimenting with Abstract Expressionism, throwing the ballet together in bits and pieces and seeing what came out of their juxtaposition with each other and with the music.

He packed *Symphony* with images from unrelated sources: 'Football provided some germinal images because I had been watching matches and looking at photographs, so that certain of the horizontal dance lines were suggested by the way that players dash past and collide and glance off each other.' Many of the jumps for the eleven men involved kicks and scissor-like slices. The leading woman (Seymour) reached with her arms outstretched in front of her as though she were throwing a ball back into the game. Then, in one unrelated sequence, she crouched on the ground, resting on her elbows like a sphinx, while two men confronted her. The pose came from a painting by an artist, Martin Battersby, who featured sphinxes and sylphides in an exhibition at the Arthur Jeffress Gallery in Davies Street. MacMillan would try out ideas, struggle to combine them and then despairingly scrap everything he had done the following day.

Seymour remembered the creation period as 'agony to work on. It seemed as if Kenneth was assailed by demons. It was a very difficult, dark time. We'd go for days, weeks even, without making any progress. He'd say, "I'm wasting your time, you might as well go home." He was blocked, really in torture.' They never discussed what the problems were, but she understood the emotional import of the ballet: 'All those Carson McCullers novels he liked, and the film of *The Loneliness of the Long Distance Runner* – I was the unwanted one, trying to make contact. I was him, his first person singular.' He choreographed a sequence in which she was involved with two men (Donald MacLeary and Desmond Doyle) who were rivals for her attention – a mirror of what was happening in her life and Kenneth's. The men, one introvert, the other extrovert, were also the two sides of Kenneth's divided self, a duality that appears over and again in his ballets.

Clive Barnes, in a review for *The Times*, noted 'sudden shafts of desolate poetry' among the physical turbulence, and picked up themes of 'private loneliness amid public triumph, of virginity and love, of tenderness and violence'. Expanding on these themes in a longer article for *Dance and Dancers*, Barnes suggested:

At times, the ballet might well be about loss of virginity, at others loss of identification, at others still loss of human contact . . . This desolate undertow finds its final expression in the closing sculptural group. Here you find the two men locked in a sort of combat, with the [main] girl emerging from the group with her empty arms outstretched for contact and the [other] girl at the back, her arms raised aloft in despair or even horror.

MacMillan reacted edgily to attempts at reading a story line into the ballet: 'To me it was simply a ballet of mood, rather as Balanchine's *Serenade* is. *Symphony* is certainly less "abstract" than my earlier *Diversions*, which was a pure dance piece not aimed at creating a mood, but it should be considered as "non-representational" all the same.'

None the less, he was aware that his persistent theme of the outsider underlay the ballet. While *Symphony* was still being created, he gave an interview to Clement Crisp for *About the House* that summed up his work to date: 'The more I look at my work, the more it seems that, unwittingly, I choose the lonely, outcast, rejected figure . . . I don't set out to do it, but it always seems to happen unconsciously – as a sort of leitmotif.' He was aware that in addition to his personal loneliness, he was set apart by his creative gift. If inspiration failed him, he was letting down the dancers who depended on him for roles. He had no way out; he had to keep on exploring what his subconscious suggested, however much it isolated and distressed him.

He must have known the much quoted title of Colin Wilson's book of essays, *The Outsider*, whether or not he had read the book in full. When *The Outsider* was first published in 1956, Wilson, then twenty-four, was regarded as one of the new breed of Angry Young Men. The title of his book became a handy term of reference, seized upon by every sensitive soul who identified with his analysis of the outsider at odds with society. In his essays, Wilson cited numerous examples of writers and artists who were conscious they didn't fit in, from Kafka and Camus to Van Gogh and Nijinsky; he set out to examine their effect on society and society's treatment of them. 'The Outsider' was used increasingly often to describe alienated characters in MacMillan's ballets, and was sometimes applied to Kenneth himself.

As the designer for *Symphony*, he had chosen a former pupil of Nico Georgiadis's at the Slade, Yolanda Sonnabend. She had designed Peter Wright's first ballet, *A Blue Rose*, when MacMillan and Georgiadis were working on *The Burrow*. For *Symphony*, she offered Kenneth a variety of bold abstract shapes, 'very Russian' in feeling to suit the Shostakovich music. He selected two potential backdrops: one was turbulent blue, black and orange, the other 'huge slabs of molten orange rock rent asunder by white hot flame'.

Sonnabend remembers the ballet as 'very violent and strong – too passionate for people to take'.

From now on, she would alternate with Georgiadis as MacMillan's most frequently used designers. While Georgiadis eventually came to be associated with the full-length narrative ballets, where his knowledge of period design, social history and architecture was invaluable, Kenneth preferred Sonnabend's painterly evocations of mood for his more personal, one-act works. 'He liked to feel he'd generated the designs, though he didn't tell you much in advance,' says Sonnabend. 'I'd do lots and lots of sketches, listening to the music – and then do as my assistant told me: "Put the one you really like face down on the floor, so Kenneth will pick it up and think he found it." '

Symphony's premiere at the Royal Opera House was on 15 February 1963. A few days before, Seymour came down with raging influenza. Like Kenneth, she suffered acutely from nervous tension before a first night: increasingly often, she would fall ill or be injured in the run-up to an important performance. In the years to come, her premieres would frequently be threatened by last-minute accidents, injuries or infections – an unpredictability that fuelled Kenneth's latent anxiety. For *Symphony*, the start of this pattern, her role was taken by Antoinette Sibley, the same age as Seymour and regarded, then, as a more purely classical dancer than Lynn. She was coolly assured, projecting, in Clive Barnes's words, an 'understated waif-like quality – a delicate sense of a character that was not so much a characterisation as a transiently held mood'. When Seymour took over, her performance deepened and darkened the ballet: 'Her isolation from the rest, her trembling, almost angry efforts to make contact are more clearly pointed,' wrote the *Times* critic.

Critics were divided in their opinions, uncertain whether to interpret *Symphony* as an Expressionist or an abstract ballet. Mary Clarke dismissed it at first as 'Balanchine-and-water' in the *Guardian*. She changed her mind after seeing Seymour in the leading role:

A passionate and troubled little person . . . [she] is so much a part of the ballet that everything she does communicates an emotion or an idea to the audience. Leave out any suggestion of meaning and do it in practice clothes and it would be an enthralling if exhausting demonstration of pure dance. When Sibley dances the principal role it is almost this. But when Seymour burns up the stage with affection, experimentation, fury and frustration the other dancers become unnecessary.

Clement Crisp saw the ballet as an extension of the lyrical classicism MacMillan had started to develop in *Le Baiser de la fée*: '*Symphony* remains one of his most important and critical dance statements: it was a work of extreme emotional power despite its "abstract" form and it contained some of his most beautiful choreographic ideas (later to reach fuller realisation in *Song of the Earth*),' he wrote in *About the House* in August 1967. Barnes gave it the strongest endorsement he had given a MacMillan ballet to date: 'If there are any ballet-goers who still doubt that Kenneth MacMillan can be numbered among the half-dozen or so major choreographers of the world, they are recommended to see his ballet *Symphony* . . . what marks it out from the ordinary run is MacMillan's unforced invention, musicality and robust craftsmanship.' (Tantalisingly, *Symphony* has disappeared from the repertoire: it has not been performed since 1976.)

The Royal Ballet took *Symphony* on its next visit to the United States and Canada, opening at the new Metropolitan Opera House in New York on 17 April 1963. The repertoire for the tour included two other MacMillan ballets, *The Invitation* and *The Rite of Spring*, as well as Ashton's *The Two Pigeons* and his new vehicle for Fonteyn and Nureyev, *Marguerite and Armand*. Ashton fretted in a letter to Tony Lizzul that MacMillan's ballets would receive all the attention, because they were 'more sensational' than his own. He need not have worried. The overwhelming sensation of the tour would prove to be Nureyev and his partnership with Fonteyn. *Marguerite and Armand* was a guaranteed hit: ballets without Nureyev paled into insignificance.

None the less, Seymour's performances in *The Invitation* and *Symphony* were commended. She had travelled to New York filled with excitement at the prospect of marrying Colin Jones at the end of the three-month tour. They were to meet up in her home town of Vancouver, where her family was busy organising the wedding. Jones, who had stopped dancing in order to start his new career as a photographer, intended to fly out to join her in July. To her surprise, he arrived in New York in time to see her perform at the Met in April.

He had come by sea with Kenneth on board the liner *France*, a five-day voyage from Southampton to New York. MacMillan, terrified of flying, had offered Jones a first-class ticket to travel with him in the same cabin on the passage out. The SS *France* was the flagship of the French shipping line, priding itself on its luxury and the quality of its meals. Jones excuses himself in retrospect: 'I shouldn't have accepted such intimacy, but Lynn was there in New York, you see, and I had very little money. The ship was unbelievable. We met James Baldwin over drinks – there were thirteen bars and first-class passengers could use every single one of them.' For Jones, the ship was a kind of limbo, a floating world out of touch with reality. He suspected that for Kenneth the shared voyage and cabin was a way of insinuating himself into the envied closeness between Colin and Lynn, ensuring that he too would be part of their marriage – 'a member of the wedding', the title of the Carson McCullers novel Kenneth liked so much.

When the *France* docked in New York, Colin joined Lynn in the Rosses' house in Greenwich Village. So did Kenneth. Nora Kaye and Herbert Ross, who had been looking after Lynn from the start of the Royal Ballet's Met season, left for London just as Kenneth and Colin arrived, so the three of them had the house to themselves, a *ménage à trois*. According to Colin, it was an emotionally unsettling arrangement until Kenneth returned to London on his own. Lynn then continued on tour with the Royal Ballet and Colin occupied himself with photo assignments he had fixed up in Alabama and Mississippi. Two months later, they were married in Vancouver and spent their honeymoon in the Canadian countryside.

Winifred Edwards, Lynn's most trusted teacher at the Royal Ballet School, had written perceptively and hopefully about the marriage to Mrs Springbett, Lynn's mother. Ever since Lynn's schooldays, Miss Edwards had reported regularly to her parents, keeping them in touch with her personal development and the progress of her career. In the letter, she said reassuringly,

I believe the loving companionship and security of marriage will give her what she has lacked so much through all these years. Colin Jones is a likeable, manly young man. He was a tough, rather naughty boy in the ballet school. Then he went into the opera ballet and touring company. Realizing he would not go to the top as a dancer, he wisely decided to leave the ballet and return to 'real life'. I think they will start life together as comrades, on a level with each other, give and take. Lynn will no longer have to wear the armour these children build who are proud, reserved and lonely.

Miss Edwards had no idea how complicated and crowded the marriage would turn out to be. Lynn and Colin moved into a flat of their own in Baron's Court, near the company's rehearsal studios. The four-roomed flat in Charleville Mansions had belonged to Anya Linden, who had just married John Sainsbury, the food-store millionaire and future ROH Board member, who later became Chairman of the Royal Opera House. Christopher Gable and Carole Needham, also newlyweds, lived near by. Kenneth soon came to regard the flats in Charleville Road as his refuge from Seymour Street. If Lynn and Colin weren't available, Christopher and Carole might be. He could be a cuckoo in both their nests, demanding attention, food and very often a bed for the night. In his depressive state, frightened of being alone, he had become more and more needy.

The young couples did not resent him, except very occasionally. Dancers were used to sharing their lives and they felt rather privileged to have him around, since he was likely to make ballets for them. They had been instilled with the Royal Ballet mystique that creative people were special and must be indulged: the future of the company, as well as their own careers, depended on Kenneth MacMillan. Besides, it was the period of the 'Swinging Sixties' in London, when all kinds of unconventional relationships could be experienced without judgements being made. It was cool to be open to pretty well anything.

Kenneth, however exigent, could be very entertaining, once they had cheered him up. He always brought half a bottle of whisky with him, 'but I don't think it dawned on us at the time how reliant he was on alcohol'. Looking back, with an insight she did not have at the time, Seymour thinks that Kenneth wanted to be the child in a close, accepting family group. 'I don't think he fancied any of us, really, in a sexual way. He was bonding with us, casting me and Colin as Mummy and Daddy – and I didn't want to be Mummy.'

In the summer of 1963, as Lynn and Colin were getting married, Kenneth started work in Stuttgart on his commission for Cranko's company. Peter Wright, there as ballet master, feared that MacMillan was on the verge of a nervous breakdown. Wright, who knew his old friend's moods well, sensed that he was even more than usually fraught and anxious. This he put down to MacMillan's having had a difficult year, with his sole new work, *Symphony*, regarded as an anti-climax after *The Rite of Spring*. Perhaps, too, Kenneth was apprehensive about working with Cranko's dancers, who might expect too much from him. Once the new ballet was under way, however, Wright found MacMillan a changed man, inspired with a sense of purpose that invigorated him and the cast he had chosen.

The suggestion for *Las Hermanas* had come from Nico Georgiadis, who had just read Federico García Lorca's play, *The House of Bernarda Alba*. 'I had never seen the play, but I knew that, as a ballet, it was very Kenneth,' said Georgiadis. In choosing the title of *Las Hermanas*, 'The Sisters', MacMillan was possibly thinking of his own family. Instead of two sisters, the play deals with five, in thrall to a Spanish matriarch not unlike his own Scottish grandmother. A prospective husband is brought to the Alba household, in order to set up a marriage with the eldest sister: the others cannot wed until she does, and he is lured by the prospect of her dowry. The man, a bold Hispanic cockerel introduced into a hen coop, returns later at night, determined on a sexual rendezvous. His first encounter is with the eldest sister, repressed but longing to surrender to him. The jealous middle sister interrupts them, and the man then has his way with the youngest one; their duet is so swiftly sensual that they must already be lovers. (A BBC Television film of the ballet two years later, broadcast on 21 February 1965, directed by Peter Wright in collaboration with MacMillan, revealed in a silent prologue that the man and the youngest sister were indeed lovers.) The spiteful middle sister, who has spied on them, rouses the household: the man is banished and the disgraced girl hangs herself. The others face a life of sour spinsterhood.

Lorca's themes were also Kenneth's preoccupations. He could empathise with the shy, spurned older sister as well as with the youngest, who is punished for her sexual hunger. The role of the suitor was almost a parody of the type of man who aroused his own shameful feelings. The ending, with one girl sacrificed and the rest trapped in a sterile non-future, was *The Invitation*'s conclusion writ large. MacMillan, like Lorca, feared being forever the outcast, as barren and bitter as their desolate female characters.

For the role of the eldest sister, Kenneth chose Marcia Haydée, Cranko's Brazilian-born ballerina. Haydée, the same age as Seymour, had been at the Royal Ballet School with her. As a foreigner from outside the Commonwealth, Haydée had little chance at the time of becoming a member of the Royal Ballet; she was, in any case, too idiosyncratic a dancer to be accepted into the company. Cranko had spotted Haydée's potential the moment she auditioned for him in Stuttgart; he went on to provide her with roles that would develop her into a great dramatic dancer. MacMillan had scarcely seen her dance, but he soon recognised her ability to convey emotional truth. He was also very taken with eighteen-year-old Birgit Keil, whom he cast as the eager youngest sister. Keil had been given leave of absence from the Stuttgart company to take up a scholarship at the Royal Ballet School; Kenneth had asked for her early return to Stuttgart so that she could be in his ballet. Ruth Papendick, a formidable character dancer, was the mother and Ray Barra the suitor. Strong and darkly handsome, he had a powerful, virile stage presence. As the male intruder into an all-female household, he conveyed a feral intensity, both compelling and repulsive.

Georgiadis designed a two-tiered house, with shutters and tropical plants that suggested the oppressive heat outside. The women vented their frustration by knitting and rocking in unison on bentwood chairs. In a memorable, surreal image, the five sisters sat in a line, each cupped against each other until the last was on their mother's lap, as if they were growing out of her, buds along a single stem. MacMillan once again chose music by Frank Martin, his Concerto for harpsichord and small orchestra. The ferocity of the harpsichord's strumming well expressed the women's pent-up emotions.

The premiere, on 13 July 1963, concluded a programme that began with *House of Birds*, in a revised version that MacMillan had recently expanded for the Royal Ballet touring company. There was a more elaborate divertissement at the end to show off the dancers' abilities. The macabre fairy tale, even though it came from the German Brothers Grimm, went down less well with Stuttgart audiences (who found it slight and childish) than the expressive dance drama of *Las Hermanas*.*

---

* Faith Worth, who had notated *House of Birds* for the Royal Ballet, taught the work to the Stuttgart dancers. She notated *Las Hermanas* during its creation in Stuttgart, and also taught it to the cast for the later film directed by Peter Wright. The film's *Las Hermanas* cast combined dancers from the Stuttgart and Royal Ballet companies.

Cranko then took *Las Hermanas* to the Edinburgh Festival in August, for the Stuttgart Ballet's first visit abroad. The programmes consisted entirely of works made for the company under his direction. His own choreography was not seen to good effect on the shallow stage of the Empire Theatre; MacMillan (who was present at the Edinburgh performances) stole his thunder. Cranko's intention had been to present his own big success from 1962, his three-act *Romeo and Juliet*, which served as a showcase for the entire company. The Empire Theatre, however, could not accommodate its scene changes. Had British audiences enjoyed it then, the Royal Ballet's repertoire might have developed very differently.

23

Behind the scenes at the Royal Opera House, the Royal Ballet was enmeshed in plans to mount a *Romeo and Juliet* production of its own. The fourth centenary of Shakespeare's birth was to be celebrated in 1964, and the Royal Ballet wanted to play its part in the national tributes with a ballet based on his best-known romantic tragedy. Protracted negotiations over which production to choose had affected the timing of Ninette de Valois's retirement. She wanted to secure the company's future by handing over the reins once she was sixty-five, in June 1963. The institution she had created must be able to survive her, and she intended to keep a discreetly watchful eye over her chosen successor, Frederick Ashton. She hoped that he would mount his *Romeo and Juliet* (created for the Royal Danish Ballet in 1955) for her company before she went. She informed the Board that she was prepared to postpone her retirement while he worked on adapting the ballet, which was scheduled for January 1964.

Ashton, as we have seen, was wary of redoing his chamber production for the Covent Garden stage, for fear of comparison with the epic Russian *Romeo and Juliet* that had so stunned London audiences. He procrastinated. To push him into committing himself, de Valois had started negotiations to bring a ballet master from Copenhagen in September 1963 to help restage the Danish *Romeo*, in exchange for Ashton's mounting *La Fille mal gardée* for the Danes, which went ahead in January 1964. But then came news that the Bolshoi was going to return to London in the autumn of 1963, bringing Lavrovsky's *Romeo and Juliet* with them once again. Ashton cancelled his tentative plans and de Valois told the Board that she was going ahead with her retirement. Ashton would replace her in September 1963.

Since Ashton would be fifty-nine shortly after he took over, de Valois must have been thinking even further ahead. The most likely candidate to succeed Ashton would have been Cranko, were it not for the unfortunate publicity over his arrest. The stain on his record, at least as far as the Board was concerned, might be overlooked if he proved to be an outstanding director in Stuttgart, as he showed every sign of becoming. He could bring that valuable experience back to the Royal Ballet in six years' time. MacMillan would not, at this stage, have appeared promising director material: he was reserved and neurotic, but de Valois respected his ambition as a choreographer and his ability to stand up for what he wanted. She would continue to monitor him closely.

MacMillan had had no new ballets scheduled for either of the Royal Ballet companies since *Symphony* in February 1963. The next year would be more fruitful, with one for the touring company in February 1964 and another for the Covent Garden company's Shakespeare celebrations in April: instead of Ashton's *Romeo and Juliet*, there was now to be a triple bill of Shakespeare-themed ballets for the poet's 400th birthday.

After *Las Hermanas* for Stuttgart, MacMillan had kept himself occupied with small-scale commissions. Rudolf Nureyev had asked him for a solo for the Royal Academy of Dancing's annual gala in December 1963. Nureyev's first appearance in London had been at an RAD gala two years previously, in a solo Ashton had created for him. To Scriabin's *Poème tragique*, Nureyev had rushed on stage, eyes blazing, trailing a red cloak behind him. The effect was electric, although Nureyev had blanked out Ashton's dramatic choreography and improvised his own. MacMillan intended something very different, choosing Bach's Fantasia in C minor for an intricate, challenging solo that eschewed the usual male virtuoso steps. The result, in its one and only gala performance, was a puzzle. No one could be sure whether Nureyev, dressed in a chunky white sweater and grey tights, was mocking or serious. He nearly fell at one point and lost a shoe at another. He stopped, removed the other shoe and 'with devastating sang froid' tossed both slippers into the wings. Once again, he improvised the rest of the solo. 'It could have been called "Impromptu in B flat" – very flat and best forgotten quickly,' wrote Peter Williams in *Dance and Dancers*. The signs were not promising for any future creative collaboration.

MacMillan had meanwhile been able to try out some ideas he had been incubating in a piece for television. A pas de deux entitled *Dark Descent* was broadcast on 29 September 1963 as part of a series called *Tempo* for ABC Television, based in Birmingham. In the introduction, Kenneth was seen working with his invited dancers, Marcia Haydée and Ray Barra from the Stuttgart Ballet. He then answered, rather hesitantly, questions about how he went about choreographing for the camera. His story line was based on the Orpheus myth, using music by Milhaud that he had first intended for a Fonteyn–Somes pas de deux. The Orpheus legend was one of his preoccupations, reappearing in various forms in many of his ballets.

Dark Descent opened with a man mourning his dead wife. Her corpse seemed to vanish from the open coffin and, in his imagination, the husband followed her to the underworld. He danced with her, lost her, and in an epilogue found himself back in his room, his wife back in her coffin. The TV designer James Goddard, a former student of Georgiadis at the Slade, came up with an ingenious setting accommodating the two worlds. MacMillan, who was much taken by Goddard as well as by his work, asked him to design his next ballet for the touring company in February.

Kenneth, who turned thirty-four at the end of 1963, had decided the time had come to catch up with contemporary popular culture. Peter Darrell had just had a big success with his trendy *Mods and Rockers* ballet to Beatles music for Western Theatre Ballet and although MacMillan did not intend to jump on that particular music bandwagon, he did want to acknowledge the modish visual taste of the time. His subject matter was the creation myth, *La Création du monde*, to Milhaud's score of that name for a daringly radical work for Les Ballets Suédois in 1923. It was the result of a close collaboration between Milhaud, the painter Fernand Léger and the Swedish choreographer Jean Börlin, telling the creation story as a primitive tribal myth. There were obvious parallels with *The Rite of Spring*, so to avoid inventing another tribe, Kenneth turned to children's games and 'naive' pop-art images. His *Création du monde* was to be a modern allegory of original sin, appropriating cartoons and advertising slogans in the way contemporary artists did: David Hockney and Peter Blake in London, Roy Lichtenstein and Andy Warhol in New York.

The ballet began with dancers dressed as children selecting costumes from a dressing-up box. A butcher's boy (Adrian Grater) circled round them on his delivery bicycle, carrying small Ronald Emblen, who elected to be God, in his basket. Emblen started out in an oversized dinner-jacket and top hat; he removed these to reveal white bodytights with a circular red-white-and-blue Union Jack on his front and back. The top hat was replaced by a paper one in the shape of a boat. As Kenneth remarked, 'If a little boy wants to make himself out an important person, what better way than to stick a flag on himself and wear a paper hat?' The children then performed a Genesis charade, each scene introduced by slogans projected onto the backcloth. Emblen's Great Deity was heralded by 'For my next creation . . . new instant people', as he produced Adam and Eve (Richard Farley and Doreen Wells).

Stripped down to bodytights plastered with trendy slang words for man and woman (guy, bloke, fella; bird, bint, doll, filly), Adam and Eve danced an innocent pas de deux that became erotic once the serpent had intervened. Elizabeth Anderton ('I was a Teenage Snake') slithered in, sucking her thumb as a Lolita temptress. She persuaded Eve to take a bite out of Adrian Grater, dressed in a blow-up apple costume ('Granny Smith') that deflated as he was eaten. All the characters joined in a serpentine knees-up conga before reverting to being children playing with their dressing-up box as the curtain fell. Emblen, the Deity, was left alone, rejected by his creatures, his playmates.

The ballet was created swiftly, in just three weeks, while the touring company was performing in Stratford-upon-Avon. Milhaud's score lasts for only eighteen or so minutes and MacMillan was not trying to make a profound statement. He would take the idea of children's games as a distorted mirror of reality a great deal further in later works. Milhaud, aged seventy-two, visited Stratford for the first night and enjoyed the pop-art account of his ballet music, saying it was the best version he had seen. (Among previous ballets to his *La Création du monde* had been one by de Valois in 1931 and another by Todd Bolender in the US in 1960.) Audiences, however, were bemused by the ballet's switch between dancers pretending to be children and their roles in the creation scenario. 'One groped around for an explanation, one asked one's friends, one even asked the dancers themselves; no one knew, one retired baffled,' wrote G. B. L. Wilson in the *Dancing Times*. The designs tended to dominate the action, especially when things went wrong: the apple developed a slow puncture and the bicycle was hard to control on steeply raked stages on tour.

MacMillan dismissed *Création du monde* as a failure and changed his mind about using Goddard as the designer for his next Covent Garden commission, *Images of Love*. Kenneth had been besotted with him, pursuing him relentlessly. Most of the cast, according to Elizabeth Anderton, were all 'a little bit in love with Jimmy because he was so gorgeous and jolly – a heterosexual hunk'. Kenneth's gay friends recognised a sexual infatuation and predicted, rightly, that once Kenneth was over it, Goddard would be dropped from the MacMillan inner circle.

Barry Kay was brought in instead for MacMillan's contribution to the Royal Ballet's Shakespeare tribute. While the touring company was in Stratford, Richard Buckle had been setting up an extravagant commemorative exhibition in Shakespeare's birthplace. Kenneth had been surrounded by theatrical Shakespeareana as he planned his new ballet. It was to be part of a triple bill at the Opera House in April, along with a new work by Ashton and a revival of Helpmann's 1942 *Hamlet*. Ashton created *The Dream*, a concise and witty précis of *A Midsummer Night's Dream*, to Mendelssohn's incidental music. He retold the lovers' dilemmas in dance and mime, transposing the story to a Victorian setting so that he could use ballet conventions of the Romantic period, with Shakespeare's fairies as sylphides.

Instead of following Ashton's path by adapting one of the plays, MacMillan opted for a suite of nine dances inspired by Shakespearean quotations about love. The brief quotations came from an anthology, though MacMillan told an interviewer he had trawled through all the sonnets and plays in search of inspiration. (He might recently have read or seen *The Two Gentlemen of Verona*, since four of the nine quotes come from its second act.) The characters in the various sections were not drawn directly from their Shakespearean sources: they were universal, contemporary lovers, based on the personalities of the dancers. 'I wanted to show them in a different light from their public image,' he told an interviewer. The linking theme throughout the ballet was to be provided by Nureyev, as a solitary wanderer in a world of unsatisfied loveless couples. He was meant to appear in, or between, each of the scenes.

Nureyev, however, was too busy with other commitments to give MacMillan the time he needed. His participation, apart from brief appearances at the beginning and end, was limited to a trio with Lynn Seymour and Christopher Gable – the most memorable scene in the ballet. Nureyev was the poet torn between two loves 'of comfort and despair' (from the opening line of Sonnet 144). Seymour was his profane love, the Dark Lady of the sonnets, and Gable his fair, angelic love. The choreography was exotic, ritualised. 'Because of Nureyev's very plastic movement, I began to think of Kabuki theatre,' MacMillan told an interviewer. Lynn had intrigued Kenneth with her description of Kabuki performances she had seen during the second company's tour of the Far East. He portrayed her as a wild black-maned demon haunting the poet (Shakespeare calls the Dark Lady in the sonnet 'my female evil'). Barry Kay devised a fiendish Kabuki-style wig for her, and dressed the men in brief tunics wrapped with cummerbunds. All three looked arrestingly beautiful as rivals for the others' affections.

The stylisation of movement and costume was intended to convey that the angelic and demonic loves were present in the poet's imagination, not in reality. They could be aspects of the poet himself, his male animus and his female anima; they could equally well represent the conflicts experienced by a bisexual or homosexual man – possibly Shakespeare, certainly Nureyev and MacMillan. (A *Ballet Today* critic saw the trio as 'a very kinky modern interpretation of the situation hinted at by Shakespeare'.) MacMillan was not, however, making ballets *à clef*, even though he used his own and his dancers' experiences as raw material.

He cast Nadia Nerina and Alexander Grant as humorously ill-matched lovers in the fourth section of *Images of Love*, knowing that as youngsters they had once been a couple, until Ashton lured Grant away for himself. Svetlana Beriosova appeared in two scenes with Donald MacLeary, both depicting a woman adrift in different kinds of unsatisfactory relationships; in spite of her beauty, she seemed destined to be unhappy. Usually considered a cool, statuesque dancer, she was able to reveal herself as a wounded woman. In a 'Love is blind' duet for Gable and Seymour, Lynn was a cruel seductress, torturing her bewildered lover with elusive, slow-motion caresses. One critic described them as 'drowning in a sea of sensuousness', a phrase that Kenneth thought aptly summed up the pas de deux. The ballet ended with the familiar opening lines from *Twelfth Night*: 'If music be the food of love, play on; give me excess of it' – a finale for the entire cast, with Nureyev isolated as the lonely, unwanted lover.

Music proved the ballet's downfall. MacMillan had hoped to commission a score from Richard Rodney Bennett; when he was unavailable, John Lanchbery suggested another British composer, Peter Tranchell, a lecturer in music at Cambridge. Tranchell had written musicals, an opera and several ballet scores, including one for Ballet Rambert, *Fate's Revenge* (1951). MacMillan briefed him, apparently to the satisfaction of them both, and choreographed *Images of Love* to a piano reduction of Tranchell's score. He heard the orchestrated version only at the final rehearsals, by which time it was too late to alter anything. MacMillan had been expecting an astringent, jazzy score, but found himself encumbered with slick Broadway-style arrangements at odds with the often bitter themes in the ballet's loosely related episodes. 'Tranchell's method seems to be "when in doubt, throw in something extra" . . . so we get xylophone decoration splashed around like glitter-dust, liberal reinforcements of percussion and even counter-melodies dredged up on the tuba to make sure that nothing in the way of thematic material is ever left alone,' wrote Noel Goodwin in *Dance and Dancers*. In despair, MacMillan avoided commissioning music for future ballets for another seventeen years.

He had not had an unqualified success with his work for either of the Royal Ballet companies since *The Rite of Spring*. Ashton, who had replaced de Valois as Artistic Director at the start of the 1963–64 season, was dismissive in his report to the Ballet Sub-Committee about *Images of Love*: 'Not one of his best,' he decreed, secure in the knowledge that his own *Dream* was far superior. MacMillan himself was dissatisfied with the trajectory of his career after his much-lauded debut as a choreographer twelve years previously. His stalwart supporter, Peter Williams, commented in *Dance and Dancers* in June 1964 that *Images of Love* and *La Création du monde* marked a down period, while adding encouragingly, 'Such periods occur in the creative life of almost every important choreographer and the great thing is that they should happen in middle periods rather than late periods – from a late "down" period there is seldom a chance to pull back.' The critic James Kennedy, assessing MacMillan's progress in an article for the *Guardian* a month after the *Images of Love* premiere, commented,

He does not seem to be a fulfilled or confident artist, at ease with himself. Outside a small group within the Royal Ballet, he is the shyest of men. Within the coterie, he is communicative and is recognised as a genius, but the image presented to a less circumscribed world is one of gentle, monosyllabic, slightly melancholy, slightly awkward elusiveness. It is, on public occasions particularly, the image of a conspicuously tall, neo-Edwardian figure visibly wishing it could shrink into invisibility.

MacMillan's manner in a BBC Radio interview recorded in the spring of 1964 and broadcast on 17 April fitted Kennedy's description, although he was trying his best to be communicative. Obligingly, he outlined the way he choreographed ballets, even though the process was probably almost as much a mystery to him as to his unseen audience:

I go into a room and show the dancer movements by doing the movement myself . . . I experiment in the studio rather like a sculptor – one is shaping things in space, rather than with clay . . . I know, dramatically, what I want to happen on certain bits of music, but I have no idea of the movement until I'm in the room with the dancers, which is what makes it so difficult.

The voice is diffident, rather fey, though the drawl is not as pronounced as it would be in later interviews.

Kennedy concluded that MacMillan's main weakness was a lack of rigour and stamina: 'Although distinctive, the quality is usually short-winded and the originality sometimes seems a bit febrile – half-hearted too – rather than the fruit of a really strenuous artistic imagination.' The ballets, he considered, lacked the sinews of true craftsmanship; their construction was tenuous and indulgent. He hazarded an absence of tough artistic discipline within the Royal

Ballet – an implicit reproach to Ashton's leadership, echoing Buckle's remarks about the 'three blind mice' in charge of the company thirteen years earlier.

Some of Kennedy's criticism was fair. As de Valois had pointed out in her letters to Kenneth, his narrative ballets, such as *Noctambules, Le Baiser de la fée* and *The Invitation*, had unresolved elements that made their structure unsatisfactory: the confused ending to *Noctambules*, the cockerel cabaret in *The Invitation*, an unexplained gypsy woman in *Le Baiser de la fée*. However, in *The Burrow* and *The Rite of Spring*, he had succeeded in building the tension in both ballets to a masterly conclusion. Kennedy had not taken into account MacMillan's intention not to create well-made story ballets (like Ashton's *The Dream* or *La Fille mal gardée*) but to disturb and disconcert audiences, as the new wave of playwrights and film-makers had done. Meanwhile, in his plotless ballets, he was trying out different styles and ways of approaching music, from the early *Danses concertantes* through to *Symphony* and *Diversions*. Had the Royal Ballet still been served by a music director of the calibre of Constant Lambert or Robert Irving, MacMillan might have developed his innate musical understanding yet further. As it was, he had been let down by his first commission from Tatchell and betrayed by conductors and musicians who struggled with 'difficult' modern scores, such as Stravinsky's *Agon*.

He was not, however, about to be abandoned as a lost cause by the management. Another ballet was planned for early 1965: probably *Lulu*, Ashton informed the Committee, to music by a contemporary German composer, Giselher Klebe. MacMillan had Seymour in mind as Lulu, a role she would have seized upon with relish. She had now been officially transferred to the Covent Garden company, which meant that she was performing less frequently than she had on tour and was longing for roles.

Without the demands of regular touring, she had put on weight; she was eventually discovered to have a thyroid problem. Her compact, rounded physique showed any weight gain very rapidly, although her legs remained impeccably shaped. As Elizabeth Anderton, a similarly afflicted dancer, commented, 'It's not fair. Tall, lanky dancers can get away with a few extra pounds, but if you've got a short neck and torso, you look fat instantly.' Margaret

Dale, who had intended to film *The Invitation* for BBC Television, thought Seymour looked 'too matronly', at twenty-five, to be convincing for the cameras as the young girl in the ballet. Dale proposed Doreen Wells (who had taken over the role with the touring company) instead. Kenneth flatly refused to allow *The Invitation* to be filmed without Lynn. 'He wouldn't budge,' says Dale, 'so we cancelled, even though the set was already being built. The BBC wasted a lot of money but nobody complained.' *The Invitation* was pulled from its transmission slot on 17 May 1964 and replaced, at short notice, by Peter Wright's *Quintet*. Kenneth was prepared to sacrifice the recording of his work in order to stand up for Seymour. Whether or not he regretted the decision, it was not a choice he would be willing to make again.

By April 1964, he was seeing a psychoanalyst on a regular basis. The first bills covered the period immediately after *Images of Love*. Dr H. E. W. Hardenberg, whose rooms were in Upper Wimpole Street, close to Seymour Street, was a Freudian analyst whose fees amounted to a considerable investment for Kenneth. In April, for example, his 19 sessions cost £56 14s, a large chunk out of his monthly earnings.

Dr Herman Hardenberg was recommended to Kenneth by Barry Kay, who underwent psychoanalysis himself. Kenneth was fascinated by Freudian theory, although initially he feared his creativity might dry up if he examined its sources too closely by undergoing analysis. He realised, however, that he did need professional help. He had exhausted the patience and understanding of his friends and colleagues, who could not meet the demands he made on them. 'He expected you to be available at all times, and we had schedules to keep and lives of our own,' says Seymour. 'He was putting us in a position where we were bound to fail him, as he saw it. That gave him permission to have a resentful feeling of dislike that he didn't want to have about himself: "Poor me, look how nasty they've been – I've got a reason to feel angry." Whatever we did wasn't good enough and we didn't know how else to help.'

Her marriage was undergoing difficulties as her husband Colin adjusted to his new profession as a photographer. He, too, went to see Dr Hardenberg for the short time he could afford the analyst's fees. 'Kenneth urged us all to undergo analysis once he'd discovered it,' Colin Jones recalls. 'For him, it was like going to church – if he missed a session, it was disastrous. He tore himself inside out. That kind of analysis was all talking in the 1960s, so it took a very long time. The analyst wouldn't intervene to move things along, but for Kenneth Dr Hardenberg was his prop.'

Having started analysis, Kenneth had to interrupt his sessions in order to travel to Stuttgart, where he oversaw the mounting of his *Diversions* (by the notator Faith Worth) for the company's Ballet Week at the end of May 1964. Birgit Keil, Richard Cragun and Egon Madsen were soloists in *Diversions*; young John Neumeier, future choreographer and Director of the Hamburg Ballet, was in the ensemble. Cranko had invited Lynn Seymour as a guest artist during the Ballet Week: she was to dance the role of his Juliet, with Ray Barra as her Romeo.

It was the first time Seymour had been to Stuttgart, and she flourished in the theatre's friendly atmosphere. She stayed with Marcia Haydée, whom she knew from their days at the Royal Ballet School; Kenneth lodged with Ray Barra and his boyfriend. 'We were like family for Kenneth,' says Barra. 'We cooked for him, cut his hair, played Monopoly with him and giggled like schoolkids. It was a nice way for him to relax.'

The Stuttgart company had developed its own private language of code words, much like the in-jokes the early Sadler's Wells Theatre Ballet had enjoyed when Kenneth was a young dancer. The favourite Stuttgart adjectives were Hilda (hideous), Monica (even more so, named after the monthly menstrual cycle) and Riva (worst of all). A performance described as 'Hilda Monica Riva' was utterly damned. All the men had girls' nicknames, a camp convention introduced by Gary Burne, a Royal Ballet guest artist who stayed on in Stuttgart because he liked the company so much. Cranko was known as Crystal (after Joan Crawford's character in George Cukor's 1939 film *The Women* – summed up in *Halliwell's Film Guide* as '135 women with men on their minds') and his house in Neue Weinsteige, inevitably, became the Crystal Palace; Ray Barra was Theda, in tribute to the silent movie star Theda Bara; Kenneth was renamed Zelda, not after Scott Fitzgerald's neurotic wife but in mocking reference to the title of a pulp novel, *Zelda, Goddess of Love, Wanted by Ten Men, Dead*.

The Stuttgart Ballet was camp and cosy, its members mutually supportive. 'They were like a group of vagabonds in the midst of a grim provincial German town – at least, that's how Stuttgart was then,' says Seymour. 'They played together as much as they worked together, like a jolly, cosmopolitan family. There were a lot of flamboyant characters, who were much more exotic and daring than the English types in the Royal Ballet.' Since they had few inhibitions about what they did and said, they assumed Kenneth had little to confess in exchange. Dancers of the period remember him as more likely to enjoy gossip about the previous night's entertainment than to get involved himself: he rarely went with them to bars or clubs. Cranko accused Barra of 'taking over' Kenneth, about whom he felt possessive, but Cranko's style of life did not suit MacMillan. '[Kenneth] and John liked to drink until they'd had the last drink in the small hours, to ward off the fears of the night. But Kenneth preferred to drink his Scotch where he felt at home, instead of staying up in public,' comments Graeme Anderson.

MacMillan watched the rehearsals of *Romeo and Juliet*, as Haydée taught her role to Seymour. Lynn danced just one performance with Barra as Romeo on 26 May 1964, to great acclaim; both Cranko and Kenneth told her how good she had been, to her immense relief. She believes that Cranko's ballet gave Kenneth the courage to think about undertaking his own *Romeo and Juliet*. He had not yet attempted a full-length narrative ballet and Lavrovsky's famous account of Prokofiev's music would be a hard act to follow. Yet Cranko had dared do it, so successfully that he had already mounted an early version of his *Romeo and Juliet* for La Scala Ballet and the later Stuttgart one for the National Ballet of Canada.*

As soon as Kenneth returned to England, his first task was to rehearse a pas de deux for Fonteyn and Nureyev to dance at Yehudi Menuhin's annual Bath Festival in June. Kenneth had choreographed the *Divertimento* pas de deux two months earlier, before Fonteyn and Nureyev went on tour to Australia. Menuhin was to play Bartók's Sonata for solo violin to accompany the duet; it would be given as part of a programme by Western Theatre Ballet at Bath's Theatre Royal.

---

* Alfred Rodrigues had done one for La Scala as well in 1956, and Ashton for the Royal Danish Ballet in 1955, so Kenneth was to be the fourth 'British' choreographer to attempt a *Romeo and Juliet*.

1 George and Mary Anne Shreeve, outside their Ormesby cottage, East Anglia
2 Jane and David MacMillan, Kenneth's Scottish grandparents
3 William MacMillan in his army uniform, Dunfermline, 1915
4 Edith Shreeve, Kenneth's mother, as a young girl about to enter service

5 About to become an evacuee
6 Kenneth with his mother and older brother George
7 Kenneth, aged 11, in his new Great Yarmouth Grammar School uniform
8 Joan Thomas, his first ballet teacher in Retford
9 Phyllis Adams, his ballet teacher in Great Yarmouth, as a performer in her youth
10 The Empire Orpheans, Great Yarmouth, 1943–44. Kenneth seated right, next to Queenie Cannon, with Edward Bowles, manager of the troupe, behind them

11 With Greta Hamby in Granchester, on tour in Cambridge, 1947
12 On the beach at Brighton, on tour with the Sadler's Wells Theatre Ballet
13 With Nadia Nerina in Granchester, 1947
14 In Ashton's *Valses nobles et sentimentales*
15 Kenneth with his eldest sister Jean and nephew Barry Harman

16 Greta Hamby, growing into a beauty
17 MacMillan as an intense young dancer, taken by his landlord, Paul Wilson
18 The Sadler's Wells Ballet departs for the United States, 1950. Kenneth, waving, stands beside Greta Hamby
19 *The Sleeping Beauty*, Act III, for BBC TV. Beryl Grey as Aurora, MacMillan as Florestan with Gerd Larsen beside him, John Field seated

20 John Cranko's *Dancing*, with Kenneth in the leading role, Kenton Theatre, Henley-on-Thames, 1952
21 & 22 As Moondog in Cranko's *The Lady and the Fool*, for BBC TV, 1956
23 MacMillan the young choreographer
24 Rehearsing his first ballet for Covent Garden, *Noctambules*

25 Margaret Hill as Anxiety in *Somnambulism*
26 Margaret Hill
27 Hill in *Solitaire* with Donald MacLeary

28 Nora Kaye in *Journey* for American Ballet Theatre, 1957
29 MacMillan rehearsing Nora Kaye and John Kriza in *Winter's Eve*, 1957

30 The team behind *The World of Paul Slickey*, 1958. John Osborne, seated centre, with
Jocelyn Rickards beside him, Dennis Lotis behind, MacMillan left
31 With Kenneth Rowell, designer of *Le Baiser de la Fée*, 1960
32 Rehearsing Lynn Seymour and Desmond Doyle in *The Invitation*, 1960
33 Nico Georgiadis, MacMillan and Seymour in the early 1960s
34 Lynn Seymour in *The Invitation*

Conveniently, Fonteyn and Nureyev had just been in Stuttgart for the Ballet Week, dancing the leading roles in Cranko's production of *Swan Lake* and appearing in the closing gala. MacMillan was able to remind them of the *Divertimento* choreography before they met up again in Bath, shortly before the premiere. The pas de deux, the only one he created for the famous pair, showed them as glittering, mythical creatures (skimpily costumed by Barry Kay) in a dream world. Nureyev, the questing male, was in thrall to his female alter ego, attracted and repelled in turn. There were echoes of the choreography MacMillan had devised for Nureyev in the recent *Images of Love*.

The night before the premiere on 9 May 1964, Fonteyn received the news that her husband, Roberto Arias, had been shot and badly hurt in Panama. MacMillan and Barry Kay, who were staying in the same hotel as Fonteyn, sat with her, Nureyev and other friends while she waited in high anxiety for a telephone connection to Panama to learn more about what had happened. They all debated whether she should fly out as soon as a flight could be booked for her. After hearing that Tito was apparently out of danger in hospital, Fonteyn decided to stay for the opening night of the Bath Festival and then leave for Panama. Kenneth would always remember her fortitude.

The dress rehearsal for *Divertimento* was tense, with a distracted Fonteyn forgetting the steps she was meant to be dancing. MacMillan helped her through the section she had temporarily blanked out and she regained her composure. By the evening performance, she was professional enough to perform the pas de deux with Nureyev twice, as the audience demanded an encore. 'That a gala audience in the English provinces, faced with a modern-dance arrangement to a bit of unaccompanied solo violin by Bartók, should respond not with an icy rattle of gloved hands but with determined shouts for an immediate encore is surely a signal worth noting . . . Most credit must go to the choreographer of this short piece,' wrote Alexander Bland in the *Observer*. Fonteyn flew to Panama the next day and *Divertimento* was dropped from the programme, never to be danced again. Lynn Seymour came from Covent Garden to replace her in a different pas de deux with Nureyev for the remaining Bath performances.

Fonteyn discovered on her arrival in Panama that Tito Arias had been shot three times: a bullet in his neck, pressing on the spinal cord, had paralysed him from the neck down. Whether the assassination attempt had been by a political rival or aggrieved husband was a matter of contention. Once Tito's condition was stabilised, after two weeks, he was flown to Stoke Mandeville Hospital, an hour's drive from London, for rehabilitation. While there, he went into a coma as the result of an infection and very nearly died. He remained in Stoke Mandeville Hospital for two years and eventually returned to Panama, still paralysed and barely able to speak in a whisper. Fonteyn took on the responsibility of caring for him and of supporting him financially for the rest of his life. (He died in 1989, not long before she did.) Her need to keep earning money by dancing meant that she prolonged her career as long as she could: she continued until she was sixty, still performing occasionally until 1986. She was forty-five when her husband was paralysed: eight months later, she would dance a role in MacMillan's next ballet that would have profound repercussions for her and for the Royal Ballet.

MacMillan's first opportunity to try out his *Romeo and Juliet* ideas came when Seymour asked him for a duet that she and Christopher Gable could perform for Canadian Television in Toronto in September. CBC intended to celebrate her as a Canadian ballerina in a programme featuring contrasting kinds of pas de deux. She wanted to perform a brand-new romantic one, so Kenneth chose the balcony scene between Shakespeare's young lovers. Instead of the lovers being separated as in the play, unable to touch, their courtship would be shown in physical terms, as Juliet awakened to the realisation of what love, and being in love, could be. He would build in hints of the tragedy to come for such headstrong youngsters. The choreography was completed in just three sessions, although the pas de deux is a long one. Kenneth Rowell, who had designed *Le Baiser de la fée*, devised the costumes, which Seymour and Gable took to Toronto for the television recording. CBC paid MacMillan $2000 (then the equivalent of £665, a gratifying amount) for what was prophetically described as 'Excerpts from *Romeo and Juliet*'.

On the way back to London, the two dancers stopped off in New York to see Nora Kaye and Herbert Ross. They talked excitedly of how marvellous it would be if MacMillan could create the complete *Romeo and Juliet* for the Royal Ballet. During the brief New York visit, Lynn felt faint and nauseous: she confided to Kaye that she thought she might be pregnant. Back home in London, her doctor confirmed that she was. The timing could hardly have been worse. Colin was still making his way as a photographer, his earnings unreliable. Lynn was battling to establish herself in the first company, in competition with other ballerinas of her generation. She could not afford to have a child at this stage in her career. Then came the telephone call from Kenneth, announcing delightedly that the Royal Ballet had commissioned him to create his full-length version of *Romeo and Juliet* at Covent Garden in a few months' time – in February 1965.

24

MacMillan owed his *Romeo and Juliet* opportunity in part to Soviet Cold War cultural politics. The Royal Ballet's protracted negotiations with the Soviet Ministry of Culture had failed to pin down a date for Lavrovsky to mount his version for the Royal Ballet. De Valois had meanwhile been frustrated in her efforts to persuade Ashton to stage the *Romeo and Juliet* he had choreographed for the Royal Danish Ballet in 1955. He had been brought round to the prospect by the end of 1962, only to change his mind when the Bolshoi declared its intention of including Lavrovsky's production in its 1963 season at Covent Garden. Ashton feared the comparison with his chamber version would be invidious.

Lord Drogheda had announced at the end of the 1963 Bolshoi season that agreement had been reached for the Royal Ballet to do Lavrovsky's production 'in the near future', in exchange for Ashton's *La Fille mal gardée* for the Bolshoi. The announcement, however, turned out to be premature. By January 1964, the formidable, stonewalling Minister of Culture, Ekaterina Furtseva, had declared that the Russian choreographer would not be available for another two years.

Lavrovsky, who was fifty-nine, had just been supplanted as Artistic Director of the Bolshoi Ballet by Yuri Grigorovich and sent to run the Moscow Ballet Academy instead. He was out of favour with the influential Mrs Furtseva, and might in consequence have been deprived of the privilege of working outside the Soviet Union. In addition, after several tours by the Bolshoi and Kirov ballet companies to the West, the Soviet authorities had realised the financial value of big Russian ballets: they were unlikely to allow Lavrovsky's *Romeo and Juliet*, one of the jewels of the Soviet repertoire, to be duplicated by the Royal Ballet, especially on its regular tours to the United States. Mrs Furtseva sidestepped saying so outright, but the Royal Ballet understood that there would be no point in waiting for Lavrovsky much longer. (Ekaterina Furtseva was the only woman in the Soviet Union to have achieved Politburo status. She remained Culture Minister until 1974, when she was sacked for misappropriation of public funds and committed suicide. She had been Nikita Khrushchev's mistress.)

Ashton had suggested that the Royal Ballet should do Cranko's *Romeo and Juliet* instead. This was vetoed by Lord Drogheda on the grounds that it would antagonise the Russians: he and the Board evidently hoped to hold out for Lavrovsky's popular 'classic' production. An in-house version might be less provocative, and if it was not a success, there was always the chance that Lavrovsky's might replace it in a few more years' time. Ashton duly reported to the Ballet Sub-Committee on 22 September 1964 that

he would welcome a *Romeo and Juliet* from MacMillan. He needed a big opportunity of this kind and had already done the Balcony scene for Seymour and Gable, who were performing it in Canada . . . The ballet might be performed at Covent Garden in February, and as Fonteyn wanted a new ballet for the visit to the USA, this could be included in the repertory.

Magnanimous though Ashton appeared, he confided to Gerd Larsen, the dancer and company teacher who was an old friend, 'I've given in.' His judgement was sound: the time had come for a new challenger to take on Prokofiev and Lavrovsky.

The Board yielded as well, agreeing to the February 1965 date. MacMillan was therefore asked to complete his first three-act ballet within five months. Time would have to be found for his preparatory rehearsals in an autumn–winter season filled with already scheduled works. The reason for the rush was that the company's next American tour started in April 1965 and *Romeo and Juliet* had to be tried out at home first. Ashton's comment to the Sub-Committee in September that Fonteyn 'needed a new ballet for America' contained the assumption that she would be cast as Juliet. She and Nureyev had immense pulling-power at the box office, so their involvement in the risky enterprise could ensure its success. MacMillan, however, had as yet no inkling that casting conditions would be attached to the decision to let him realise his *Romeo and Juliet*.

In a fever of excitement, he, Seymour and Gable read and re-read the play and listened over and again to the Bolshoi orchestra's recording of Prokofiev's score. MacMillan had requested a special screening of the Bolshoi film of *Romeo and Juliet* as soon as he had received the go-ahead to choreograph his own account. There was no question in any of their minds that Christopher and Lynn were to be Kenneth's Romeo and Juliet: the balcony scene pas de deux already contained the germ of their ideas about how the characters would develop.

Lynn was not going to miss the opportunity to create the role of Juliet because of an unintended pregnancy. She reasoned that she could have a baby at a later time. Abortions were not uncommon among dancers in an era when motherhood for a ballerina was still unusual. Fonteyn, the Royal Ballet's role model, did not have children, and those dancers who did usually chose to postpone their pregnancies until their careers were well advanced. Lynn and Colin were in no position to look after a child. As she saw it, the decision that confronted her was not a sacrifice for the role of Juliet but a practical necessity.

Colin accepted that the abortion was inevitable, though he dreaded the outcome for his marriage. 'I don't think I actually said anything about it. It was so weird between the three of us – like something Kenneth might have invented for one of his ballets.' Jones was due to leave on a photographic assignment in Leningrad, taking pictures to illustrate a book by Nigel Gosling about the city. Gosling was the *Observer*'s art critic; he also wrote about dance in collaboration with his wife, Maude Lloyd, under the nom de plume of Alexander Bland. The Goslings dropped in at Charleville Mansions to talk about the book project with Colin; Lynn was in bed, unwell, with Kenneth sitting beside her. 'He looked like Svengali, brooding over his Trilby,' remembered Maude.

Nigel couldn't understand why Colin was so distracted when they got to Leningrad. It was a big commission and Colin wasn't taking any photographs. Eventually he told Nigel what was wrong. He was desperately concerned about Lynn and whether she'd gone ahead with the abortion. When he finally managed to get through by telephone to London, which was very difficult at the time, Colin learned she'd done it.

Lynn had approached several doctors before resorting in desperation to underhand help from a Royal Ballet administrator, who supplied the address of a 'clinic' and advanced Seymour £500 against her salary of £40 a week. Kenneth stayed with her as she recovered, talking of the ballet they were going to create together. *Romeo and Juliet* was his primary preoccupation and any guilt he felt about Lynn's decision was suppressed, for the time being. Although the abortion was her choice, he had colluded with her for the sake of his ballet, and as his most personal works would reveal, guilt by complicit association would be a persistent theme throughout his life.

When Colin returned from Leningrad, the abortion became an unmentionable topic between the three of them. Colin spent more and more time in his darkroom, while Lynn and Kenneth were absorbed in Juliet's dilemma. Kenneth had decided that Juliet was to be the driving force in the ballet: like Lynn, she would be headstrong, vulnerable and stubborn; she would also have to take all the important decisions – marrying Romeo, taking the sleeping potion and then killing herself to join Romeo in death – on her own. Even within the bosom of her family, Juliet is an outsider: 'a tender child marooned in a sea of grown-ups', as Nigel Gosling described her. She and Romeo are both made exiles from their society. Kenneth's ballet would finish with their deaths in isolation, without the reconciliation between the feuding clans at the end of Shakespeare's play.

Franco Zeffirelli's radical production of *Romeo and Juliet* for the Old Vic Theatre (with the young, unknown Judi Dench and John Stride in 1960–61) influenced the way MacMillan, Seymour and Gable thought about their Verona in the ballet. Zeffirelli had depicted Italian early Renaissance society as violent, power-seeking and ruthless. His Capulets lived in an intimidating fortress designed to keep foes at bay and to defend the family's treasures, including the virgin Juliet. The teenage lovers were real, hot-blooded youngsters rather than romantic sonneteers. MacMillan wanted to create a similar *verismo* atmosphere in his ballet, distinguishing it from the more stylised approach of Cranko's and Lavrovsky's productions. His lovers would be sexually passionate and die painful, ugly deaths instead of arranging themselves in pretty positions.

MacMillan's options in determining the pace and structure of his ballet were largely determined by Prokofiev's score. Composed in 1935, the original score had been altered by the Soviet authorities before its first production by Lavrovsky for the Kirov five years later. By then, the scenario had been edited to correspond with Shakespeare's tragic ending, and the music rearranged and reorchestrated much like a film score. (Prokofiev's 1935 score was recently rediscovered in a Russian archive by an American musicologist, Simon Morrison, complete with a happy ending: Friar Lawrence prevents Romeo's suicide and Juliet wakes up to be reunited with him. Mark Morris choreographed the score in full as a ballet in 2008.) The printed scenario sets each scene, describes the action in it and provides motifs for the characters. Lavrovsky had already stamped key episodes (Tybalt's death, Lady Capulet's grief, the clandestine wedding) with his memorable choreographic effects; Cranko had claimed other high moments. MacMillan had to avoid duplicating their stagings, in so far as he could, though he was undeniably influenced by Cranko's staging. Kenneth's instinct was to narrow his focus on the lovers' emotions, gradually excluding the crowded public world around them as the ballet progressed. Some critics would complain that, by the last act, the performers were more like actors in an intimate play than dancers in a large-scale ballet, which was exactly what Kenneth intended.

He, Seymour and Gable explored the lovers' feelings, drawing on their own experience and imagination. Then they tried to find steps and gestures to express the characters' state of mind. MacMillan chose to make full use of ballet's classical vocabulary instead of devising steps of his own, though the lifts they worked out together were far from conventional. They experimented all day in the rehearsal room and rang each other up at night with urgent new suggestions. As had become his practice, MacMillan started with the key pas de deux in each act and built the ballet around them. Thus, the youngsters' first encounter in the Capulet ballroom would lead up to their ecstatic declaration of love in the balcony scene; the bedroom pas de deux would show its consequences. Both Juliet and Romeo would be transformed by their brief wedding night together and by their imminent separation. The final pas de deux in the tomb scene would be a shockingly grotesque one, as Romeo manhandled Juliet's insensible body, forcing her in his distress to appear to respond to him.

MacMillan knew that he could trust Seymour's instincts as a dance-actress. As he said in an interview, 'She brings a sense of reality to an art that is very unrealistic. Quite simply, you believe in her.' When they came to the scene where Juliet, after Romeo's departure, is in a quandary over her impending marriage to Paris, they thought her natural reaction would be to sit, numb, on the end of her bed, while the music surged with Romeo's theme. Her stillness would last for what seemed like eternity before she made up her mind to seek Friar Lawrence's help. 'Shall we dare?' asked MacMillan, apprehensive about the long wait. 'Why not?' responded Seymour. 'If you're in a predicament like that, it's very hard to think. Something's got to happen. It's just like squeezing yourself together until suddenly you snap your fingers, you find the only thing to do.' They tried out the immobile sit in rehearsal, realising that it would work. On stage, the effect is that of a film close-up, drawing the audience in to share the girl's agonising tension.'

The use of complete stillness to heighten drama has extraordinary potency in ballet, where motion is the means of expression. Frozen moments occur at key times in MacMillan's *Romeo and Juliet*: when the lovers' eyes first meet at the ball; at the start of the balcony-scene pas de deux as they gaze at each other; Juliet discovering, when she wakes up in the family vault, that Romeo is dead. Her immobility is followed by a flurry of runs, as she impels herself into action: she hurtles down the stairs from her balcony; flies to the Friar for help; stumbles into the corpses in the vault. MacMillan had absorbed the lessons of Tudor, Ashton and Cranko in conveying emotional truth through the language of the body. Seymour and Gable brought their own insights: their exploration of Romeo's and Juliet's motives and reactions contributed to the way the ballet evolved. To a significant extent, the roles were portraits of them.

The collaborative approach must have helped free MacMillan's ideas, for he had never communicated so extensively with his interpreters before. Performers in his previous ballets had protested that he never told them anything about the work. By now, he, Seymour and Gable were on the same wavelength, so the lovers' scenes together were quickly completed. He expanded Romeo's role, giving him solo variations by appropriating music from elsewhere in the score. Then he moved on to Juliet's duets with her official suitor, Paris: her debutante dance with him in the ballroom and its distressing reprise in her bedroom when she has to consent to marry him. The key to Juliet's rebellion, Kenneth and Lynn believed, lay in her relationship with her parents and their insistence on an advantageous arranged marriage. For the intimate family scenes he had chosen performers he knew to have powerful stage presences: Derek Rencher as Paris; Gerd Larsen as Juliet's Nurse; Michael Somes and Julia Farron as the Capulet parents. (Farron had given up performing in favour of teaching, but returned at Kenneth's insistence.)

Once he had established the Capulet family context, he concentrated on the choreography for Romeo and his two friends, Mercutio and Benvolio. Although he later arranged attractive ensemble dances for the girls who were Juliet's friends and potential bridesmaids, this was to be a ballet that showed off the prowess of the company's male soloists; there were virtuoso steps for the men that he had hitherto avoided as too conventionally balletic. Then came the largest crowd scenes MacMillan had ever attempted to characterise, amplified by numerous extras brought in to populate Verona's market square. He intended the action to appear spontaneous, with dances evolving from the bustle of everyday life. There were to be no set pieces like the ones Cranko had choreographed for his *Romeo and Juliet*, which concluded in a picturesque pose for applause. Instead, the performers would go about their business without directly acknowledging the audience.

MacMillan did, however, follow Cranko in resorting to three hard-working harlots to animate the crowd scenes in the piazza. In place of Cranko's *commedia dell'arte* entertainment in Act II, he introduced a mandolin dance for acrobats who were part of a passing wedding procession, a device that Zeffirelli had used in his Old Vic production. To make the street brawls and duels more realistic, MacMillan enlisted the help of an experienced theatrical fight arranger, John Bardon. Royal Ballet dancers were not yet routinely trained in sword-fighting, so Bardon's moves had to be simplified by MacMillan to avoid injury. The thrusts and parries were timed to the music, which made them easier to learn but less convincingly realistic than less tightly structured theatrical brawls and duels. (However, one American reviewer, John Chapman in the *Daily News*, was to comment of MacMillan's version in 1966, 'I have never seen such dazzling swordplay in a ballet or in any other kind of theatre.')

In the years since its creation, MacMillan's *Romeo and Juliet* has been performed so frequently that its innovations are hard to recognise. James Monahan declared in the *Dancing Times*, shortly after the premiere, 'There has been nothing quite like this *Romeo and Juliet* in the two decades of the Royal Ballet at Covent Garden'. The mix of conventions, *verismo* drama and dance, was unusual for its period. Although the choreography draws on classical-ballet technique, only Juliet and her six girlfriends are on pointe; the other members of the cast, apart from Romeo, Mercutio and Benvolio, are in heeled shoes or boots appropriate for their Renaissance costumes. (Exceptions are the mandolin troupe, who wear ballet slippers for their acrobatic dances.) Coded ballet mime gestures are kept to a minimum in favour of naturalistic acting. Instead of miming 'I love you', Juliet takes Romeo's hand and places it on her breast, against her beating heart.

MacMillan also downplayed the entrances of his leading characters, keeping them out of any expected spotlight. Romeo is first seen as Rosaline's anonymous suitor, then as one of the lads, only gradually emerging as their leader. Juliet is denied a grand entry in the ballroom in her party dress; nobody pays her any attention when she first arrives with her Nurse, so she has to retreat and try again, until her parents turn and acknowledge her. She and Romeo are merely youngsters on the periphery of adult society until their love match takes centre stage and the ballet belongs to them.

MacMillan had taken pains to place the tragedy in a formal historic context. His preparations for the ballet had involved studying Italian Quattrocento paintings, as Georgiadis had done for his costume designs, in search of appropriate period poses and groupings. The massed might of the Capulets and their guests in the ballroom scene struts and sways in formal dances he devised to convey the household's social standing in fifteenth-century Verona. The ball makes clear that Juliet, the intended bride in an arranged marriage, is being initiated into a powerful patriarchal society.

On the streets, life is more raffish and disorderly. After fights between the rival clans, casualties are piled unceremoniously into a heap, like so much litter. Tybalt's important death, however, is grotesquely prolonged: in the original choreography (since modified), he hurls himself repeatedly at Romeo, thrashing in his final throes to Prokofiev's blaring chords and thumping drumbeats. His corpse is extravagantly mourned by Lady Capulet, beating her breast and throwing herself to the ground. Naturalistic responses have been overtaken by Expressionism.

By the final scenes, dancing has almost entirely given way to acting. Juliet forces herself to swallow the sleeping potion, gagging on its bitterness; she hauls herself onto her bed as she falls into a death-like coma. When Romeo finds her in the family tomb, he flings her seemingly lifeless body about in a necrophiliac pas de deux that is profoundly disturbing. When he realises he cannot make her respond, he pulls her across the floor by her wrists like a piece of dead meat. The image Gable had in mind was of a gorilla at London Zoo whose baby had died: she refused to relinquish its corpse, trailing the body behind her for days. 'I used to drag Lynn around the stage, and she'd just let her legs fall apart, all open and exposed and vulnerable and ugly . . . and I used to rock, the way you rock when you go into that bad, grief place.'

Reprovingly, James Monahan was to write in his *Dancing Times* review that 'she overdid the naturalism . . . so turning anguish into an occasionally unstylised ugliness'. That was precisely the brutal effect Seymour and MacMillan intended to make. When Juliet kills herself with Romeo's dagger after finding him newly dead, Seymour chose to stab herself symbolically in the womb before crawling in agony towards Romeo. Juliet expires on her sepulchre (recognisably her bed, stripped of its coverings) without quite reaching Romeo. MacMillan wanted no suggestion that they would be united in death. 'So they die apart, not touching. Two beautiful young lives have been totally wasted. Nothing's been achieved, nothing's better, and they're not united. They're just dead. Just two dead things,' Gable told Barbara Newman.

The harshness of MacMillan's vision undoubtedly stemmed from his own youthful experience of the deaths of his parents and of wartime casualties. His unsentimental account of the lovers' suicides, however, was first and foremost an artistic choice: the ending of his *Romeo and Juliet* was to be different from the pathos of the ballets that had gone before. He could not avoid similarities with Lavrovsky's and particularly with Cranko's versions, but the final impact of his ballet would be all his own. John Osborne wrote to him admiringly, 'I thought the Tomb scene was a miracle, unlike any other sort of experience. You really are a genius!'

There is a much repeated story about Cranko's awareness of how much MacMillan owed to him. Cranko had been watching a performance of MacMillan's ballet when a fellow spectator said to him, 'I wish I'd seen yours.' 'You just have,' replied Cranko.

Before the ballet even reached the stage, however, Kenneth had lost important battles, both personal and political. Company members of the period remember their collective shock at learning, in their recollections seemingly at the last moment, that Fonteyn and Nureyev would be the first-cast Juliet and Romeo instead of Seymour and Gable. It was unheard of for a ballet's premiere to be allocated to anyone other than the performers on whom it had been created. Only in cases of illness or injury would an alternate cast take over the first performance. Fonteyn herself would have been reluctant to usurp Seymour as the first Juliet, especially since MacMillan had conceived the role as that of a very young, headstrong girl. Nureyev, however, would have expected to dance the premiere and Fonteyn knew that her partnership with Nureyev needed the oxygen of a fresh challenge. Ulanova had danced Juliet with the Bolshoi in her forties and so could she. 'Margot was calculating in the nicest possible way,' said Peter Franklin White, who played Lord Montague. 'She had an iron will and she got what she wanted.'

As Ashton had told the Ballet Sub-Committee, what Fonteyn wanted was to appear in a new ballet on the forthcoming American tour. The company's fortunes, and her own, depended on their joint acclaim in the United States. According to her friend, the photographer Keith Money, Fonteyn did not want to dance the first Juliet in London: she would have preferred to ease herself into the role later in the run, once the production had settled in. But Sol Hurok, who had been the company's American impresario since its first visit to the United States in 1949, was adamant that Fonteyn must dance the London opening night in order to generate publicity before the ballet's New York premiere in April. The Royal Ballet had never before offered a brand-new production at the outset of a US tour and Hurok was not prepared to promote an expensive, untried ballet unless it was already associated with her and Nureyev.

Keith Money, at Fonteyn's insistence, accompanied her to a lunch in New York in November 1964 to persuade Hurok to relent. She said that although she was willing to perform as Juliet later in the season, she did not wish to dance as the first cast. She came away from the meeting confident that she had succeeded, until Hurok swiftly overruled her by cabling an ultimatum to the Royal Opera House: Fonteyn and Nureyev or no *Romeo and Juliet* in America. According to John Tooley (then Assistant to General Director David Webster), there was strong opposition to letting Hurok having the final say but Webster caved in and agreed. 'Such demands should have been refused; however, artistic and moral considerations were discarded and the knee was bowed to the box office,' wrote Tooley in *In House*.

Fonteyn and Nureyev duly arranged their international schedules to ensure that they would be free to dance the two first performances in London, on 9 and 11 February 1965, and two more later in the run. It is unclear exactly when MacMillan learned that they would be his first-cast Romeo and Juliet. Julia Farron, the first Lady Capulet, comments, 'I suspect the Opera House were really shifty. They let Kenneth carry on working with Lynn and Christopher and be happy with what he'd done – and then the bombshell was dropped pretty late. It came as a terrible shock to all of us,' One version of events has Webster calling a meeting at his own house 'not long before the first night', at which he informed an appalled MacMillan of the Fonteyn–Nureyev casting for the premiere – 'a decree against which there was no appeal'.

There is evidence, however, that Kenneth and the company must have known about the decision months before the opening night. The information was made available to the public in November 1964, in 'throwaways', leaflets released to encourage early booking (which opened for *Romeo and Juliet* on 16 December 1964). The flyers announced that tickets for Fonteyn and Nureyev performances, higher priced than for the four later casts, would be rationed to two per person because of the expected demand. According to the throwaways, Fonteyn and Nureyev would be dancing twice in the first week, on Tuesday 9th and Thursday 11th; next came

Annette Page and Donald MacLeary the following week, on Wednesday 17th; MacLeary was to dance the Saturday 20th matinee with Merle Park, while Lynn Seymour and Christopher Gable made their debuts that evening. The fifth pair was scheduled to be Antoinette Sibley and Gable on Monday, 22 February.

Seymour has never forgotten her horrified disbelief at reading the rehearsals calls on the company notice board. She knew by then that she had lost the first night to Fonteyn, but no one had warned her that she would be way down the list as the fourth-cast Juliet. Her memory is that she was fifth and last, after Sibley. In fact she was scheduled, with Gable, for the fifth performance: a Saturday night, more prestigious (with the press invited to review) than the matinee, but none the less at the end of the second week of the new ballet's run. In the flurry of alternating casts, her account of Juliet, the role she had created, might be overlooked and her special partnership with Gable be dissipated when he danced with Sibley two days later.

Seymour has never been able to understand why she was so publicly humiliated – and why MacMillan was unable to stand up for her. Even if she had to accept the management's decision that Fonteyn was given priority with Nureyev, why were she and Gable so low down in the casting order? MacMillan could not give a satisfactory explanation to his devastated favourites: the matter, it seemed, was out of his hands.

It was indeed, according to John Hart, one of the company's two assistant directors, along with Michael Somes. Hart organised all the performance and rehearsal schedules, along with the casting order:

From the moment we knew that Margot and Rudi would be available for the first night, we had absolutely no choice. Once the production of a full-length *Romeo and Juliet* became a Company Ballet and not a 'work in progress', I was responsible, with the assistance of the ballet staff, for the dancers and all rehearsals and performances – as always for the past ten years.

Romeo and Juliet had been appropriated from MacMillan's control in order to become a Royal Ballet brand product, a showcase for the company at home and abroad. Hart and Ashton therefore insisted that casting should be done in order of seniority, according to a hierarchy that had become established on the American tours. Fonteyn (who had officially been a guest artist since 1959) was first cast in all the ballets in which she appeared. Annette Page would be the next Juliet because she was a long-established principal dancer at Covent Garden, followed by Merle Park. Seymour was regarded as an incomer from the second company; Gable was similarly junior in status, unless a senior ballerina requested him as her partner – as Fonteyn sometimes did, most recently as Daphnis to her Chloe. Hart's view (which reflected Ashton's, as Artistic Director) indicates that the official merging of the two companies was a façade. The Covent Garden company's culture prevailed and dancers whose careers had started in the lower-rated touring company were kept in their place. The fact that MacMillan had begun work on *Romeo and Juliet* with Seymour and Gable evidently carried no more weight than a choreographer trying out ideas on a couple of apprentices before moving on to the real thing.

Although Seymour had been a principal dancer for six years and a member of the senior company since 1963, she was often sent out on tour with the smaller group, and neither she nor the Covent Garden dancers felt she truly belonged in the resident company. Gable was also resented because he (and members of the touring group) had been given prominence in a recently published book of photographs and sketches by Keith Money called *The Art of the Royal Ballet*. The senior company had been away on tour in America at the time the photographs were taken and the second troupe was felt to have stolen their thunder in their absence: only 'real principals' should have represented 'The Art of the Royal Ballet'. There could therefore be no question of a pair of arrivistes taking pride of place in an important new ballet at the Opera House. *Romeo and Juliet* was, after all, only the fourth three-act British ballet in the company's history. (The others were Ashton's *Cinderella* (1948) and *Sylvia* (1952)* and Cranko's *The Prince of the Pagodas* in 1957.)

Even though Hart cited box-office and company protocol as the straightforward reason for the casting decisions, conspiracy theories abounded, and continue to do so. One was that Seymour was being punished for having an abortion. This was unlikely on moral

---

* Ashton's *La Fille mal gardée* (1960) is given in two acts at the Royal Opera House, though the touring company, now Birmingham Royal Ballet, performs it with two intervals instead of one.

grounds alone, since abortions were not exceptional in a ballet company, especially in the years before the contraceptive pill became readily available. However, some company members believed that she was implicitly being punished for being different and difficult. She refused, for example, to take the advice of company coaches who she believed were set in their ways, such as Michael Somes. 'Other people toed the line and she didn't. She danced in her own way and certain people in the organisation weren't happy about that. She had problems with her weight and Fred couldn't bear her looking fat. She was being punished for not fitting in,' comment Annette Page and Ronald Hynd.

Another theory was that the powers-that-be feared the rise of a younger star couple to rival Fonteyn and Nureyev. As John Copley put it:

The buzz around Lynn and Christopher was so enormous that Covent Garden may have been afraid they'd eclipse the status quo. It was difficult enough to deal with Margot and Rudi, let alone another partnership everyone wanted to see. Plus Lynn would be a threat to Margot, who was getting on, and Kenneth was a threat to Fred as a choreographer.

Ashton was indeed apprehensive about being supplanted by MacMillan, even though he had agreed to stand aside for him over *Romeo and Juliet*. As Director of the company, however, Ashton needed the ballet to be a triumph. He had inherited de Valois's vision of the Royal Ballet as a company of world standing, and he was its curator. Accordingly, his advice for MacMillan was: 'If he wants a local success he should use Seymour and Gable, but for an international success he must have Margot and Rudolf.'

Ashton was in any case ambivalent about MacMillan's protégés. He had admired them enough to have created *The Two Pigeons* on them for the touring company in 1961, and had considered them suitable understudies for Fonteyn and Nureyev in *Marguerite and Armand*, though they were never to dance the roles. Once in the Covent Garden company, though, they tended to be regarded as members of MacMillan's clique. During the creation of *Romeo and Juliet*, the three of them had been inseparable, arousing jealousy among less-favoured dancers. Reports of ill-feeling within the company had no doubt reached Ashton's ears. He was, in any case, coming to prefer Sibley and Dowell, following *The Dream*, as his

kind of dancers, casting them more and more frequently in his ballets. The decision to downgrade Seymour and Gable to fourth-cast
Romeo and Juliet ultimately lay with Ashton. By insisting on a hierarchy of seniority, he could assert his authority over his rival's aspirations. He could also avert any future protests about casting
decisions for other ballets by pointing out that no exceptions had
been made for *Romeo and Juliet*. Ashton hated company rows,
so he was content to hide behind the smokescreen of a protocol
administered by Hart.

The question still remains why MacMillan did not put his foot
down and defy the casting decisions about his ballet. He had stood
up to de Valois in the past, when he was much younger and less
experienced; Ashton was a less formidable figure, though he was
supported by tough lieutenants in John Hart and Michael Somes.
Ashton, however, could pass the buck to David Webster and the
Board of Governors, on the grounds that the Royal Opera House
had become a corporate institution whose requirements overruled
the demands of a mere salaried employee. MacMillan, under the
terms of his contract as resident choreographer, received no separate fee for *Romeo and Juliet*: it was therefore not his ballet but the
Opera House's. He was in no position to defeat the system. 'He
tried and tried – he persisted very hard – but he couldn't win,' said
Nico Georgiadis, to whom Kenneth agonised.

MacMillan's anxiety levels were already soaring as he panicked
over finishing the choreography on schedule; he had to be ruthless
in betraying both Lynn and Christopher in order to concentrate all
his efforts on the final stages of his ballet. He also knew, deep down,
that having Fonteyn and Nureyev as his first cast would give a
tremendous boost to his career. Cranko had originally wanted the
famous pair to dance his *Romeo and Juliet*; Kenneth would have
them instead. If the ballet was as good as he thought it was going to
be, New York as well as London would go wild for Margot and
Rudi as the lovers. *Romeo and Juliet* would become the ballet
everyone had to see. His reputation would be made in America,
Britain, the world. He was hugely ambitious – and for the time
being, he could blind himself to the compromises he was making by
blaming forces beyond his control. He had championed Lynn
against Margaret Dale and the BBC over the television casting of
The Invitation, and lost the chance to have that ballet reach a wider

audience. He was not going to imperil *Romeo and Juliet* by fighting for her again when even higher stakes were involved.

He had already sacrificed Kenneth Rowell, who had assumed he was to be the production's designer. Rowell, who had designed the costumes for the Canadian Television recording of the balcony pas de deux, had been involved in MacMillan's early discussions of how he envisaged the complete ballet. The Opera House Board, however, preferred Georgiadis, who had just designed Nureyev's grand-scale production of *Swan Lake* in Vienna and who now had an international reputation. Kenneth gratefully endorsed the choice of his favourite designer. Georgiadis remembered MacMillan telephoning him in Vienna with a plea to accept the commission, even though it meant that Nico had only twenty days available in his already busy schedule. Rowell was deeply upset by what he felt to be MacMillan's betrayal: it was the end of their friendship.

Georgiadis designed a monumental structure with an upper arcade of pillars that remained in place throughout the ballet. (The two-tiered classical structure was similar to one he had designed for the Old Vic's *Julius Caesar* the previous year, which he considered the best thing he had done.) The architectural setting could be adapted to serve as Verona's central piazza, the Capulets' ballroom, Juliet's bedroom and the balcony outside it. Its solidarity gave an oppressive sense of place and of power. Juliet, whenever alone on stage, was dwarfed by the set's towering proportions. 'It is doubtful whether ballet has seen such splendour since the days of Leon Bakst,' wrote Peter Williams in *Dance and Dancers*.

Georgiadis had to draw on his considerable reserves of stubbornness to get his ideas across: 'It was a fight to the death with the technical staff and the administration. They thought ballet decor should be painted wings and backcloth, not constructed. There was great antagonism – you felt from the moment you walked into the Opera House that they wanted you to fail.' The management balked at the expense of the final tomb scene, with gigantic statues of pensive angels looming above the Capulet family's grandiose mausoleum. The vault was an elaborate structure for such a brief scene, though it contributed greatly to Juliet's horror when she awoke from her drugged trance. Arguments over the angels continued almost to the first night, with Georgiadis threatening to withdraw his designs from the production.

Tension mounted even further when Fonteyn and Nureyev finally arrived to learn the leading roles in the run-up to the premiere. It was feared that Nureyev might not make the first night. He had injured his leg in a confrontation with a motor bike and had not been able to rehearse properly before the dress rehearsal. Only days before the opening night, Keith Money wrote in his diary record of the production, 'Margot said she hadn't been shown all the steps yet; when there is a session, if Rudolf nurses his ankle and doesn't work fully, she can do nothing much about it.'

Seymour, instead of concentrating on 'her' role, had been obliged to teach it to Fonteyn and the other Juliets. Gable was similarly galled by having to pass on his interpretation of Romeo, especially to Nureyev, who insisted on elaborating the choreography. MacMillan and Gable had kept Romeo's dancing relatively unflashy, aiming for telling imagery. In the balcony pas de deux, for example,

We very, very consciously devised a series of steps that were all slightly off balance and turning and reeling. You know that minute when you know that you are hugely, deeply attracted to somebody and when you realise that they're feeling the same way? You can't believe it's happening . . . Which is why I was so distraught when Rudi cut all that and put in a big, virtuoso manège because he felt Romeo needed big dancing steps there.

MacMillan deeply resented anyone changing his choreography without his agreement but he had no control over Nureyev. He had retreated into nervous misery, hating what was happening to his ballet and incapable of doing anything about it. He did not even know how Nureyev intended to perform on the first night because the dress rehearsal had been a debacle. Gable had been asked to partner Fonteyn at the final stage call in case Nureyev's injury prevented his dancing. (Gable had already replaced him at very short notice in the *Kingdom of the Shades* scene from *La Bayadère* just a few days before). Nureyev turned up at the last moment and took offence that the rehearsal was being watched by large numbers of people: the Friends of Covent Garden have the privilege of attending final rehearsals, seated upstairs in the amphitheatre. He refused to fulfil expectations of a full-out performance and Fonteyn, helpless, was unable to dance properly in the pas de deux. 'They mucked about and behaved badly so that the ballet fell apart. They pulled it together for the first night, in their way, but it was never Kenneth's way,' says Annette Page.

Although Page was listed as the second-cast Juliet, with Donald MacLeary as her Romeo, she had known all along she would be unable to make her scheduled performances:

I was injured from the start of rehearsals, so I sat at the back, watching. An ankle tendon had got stuck within its sheath. They tried injections, then putting me in plaster – in the end I had to have an operation and miss the whole of the season. I think my name was still down as Juliet for status reasons: I was between Fonteyn and the younger generation – Park and Seymour and Sibley.

Since Page's injury was not responding to treatment, the management must have realised fairly early on that someone else would need to take her place as the second Juliet. Seymour might have been intended all along, provided that Gable could still be scheduled as her Romeo. If so, nobody, including MacMillan, told her to ease her disappointment about her fourth-place casting. Her recollection is that she learned she would be the second Juliet, with Gable as her partner, only shortly before the ballet's run started.

By the first night on 9 February 1965, queues had formed around the Opera House for three days and nights, with people sleeping on the pavement in their determination to secure the remaining tickets for the Fonteyn and Nureyev performances. Press interest had been stirred to fever pitch. According to Nicholas Tomalin, writing a preview piece in *The Sunday Times* two days before the premiere, 'The attraction is not just Fonteyn and Nureyev, but choreographer Kenneth MacMillan. This is his eighteenth ballet, and probably his most eagerly waited . . . he has the sort of international reputation no other British choreographer has ever had at his age.' Tomalin, who had witnessed Nureyev's shouting match with the orchestra at the dress rehearsal, noted that MacMillan, 'tall, with a boxer's build and a jutting chin, looks pretty rough'. When Kenneth obligingly posed, smiling, for a photograph, Tomalin added, 'At second glance he doesn't look rough. He's like a soft brown-eyed Freddie Trueman' – the best-known (and burliest) English cricketer of the time.

In spite of the disastrous dress rehearsal, the opening night was an outstanding success. There were forty-three curtain calls and the applause lasted for at least forty minutes, ceasing only when the safety curtain was brought down: 'one of the most tumultuous finales the Royal Opera House has ever seen' (*Daily Express*); 'a spectacular asset to the repertoire . . . altogether a milestone for MacMillan' (*Observer*); 'Kenneth MacMillan takes his place as one of the world's leading choreographers' (*Daily Mail*). There were inevitable comparisons in the first reviews with the Bolshoi's version, not unanimously in MacMillan's favour, though he was congratulated on the scale of his vision: 'His recent work may have prepared us for the ease of flowing classical invention. But one could not have foretold that he would be so powerful and big a choreographer and producer' (Andrew Porter in the *Financial Times*). Georgiadis was praised for the grandeur of his sets: 'High and deep and handsome, the stage looks enormous, and the company glamorous. When the lights finally turn up on the Knight's Dance [in the ballroom] the scene gives off the genuine glow of the Renaissance, a moment when solid money bore fruit of gold' (Alexander Bland in the *Observer*).

Fonteyn's Juliet was appreciated for 'her inimitable mixture of elegance and naivety' (Bland again); 'all trust and purity, grace and gentleness, radiance and puppy love' (Edward Mason in the *Sunday Telegraph*). There had been no mention in previews (including a long article by Clement Crisp about the making of the ballet in the *Dancing Times* of February 1965) that the roles of Juliet and Romeo had been made on Seymour and Gable. But some of the critics were in the know: Andrew Porter was the first to comment, in his overnight review of the premiere for the *Financial Times*, that the choreography for Juliet was not shaped in Fonteyn's image: 'Juliet is plainly a role conceived for Lynn Seymour, and so until we have seen her dance it we cannot be precise about MacMillan's intentions.' Nureyev received qualified praise as Romeo, with allowances made for his injury. Porter found that 'he seemed to bring a generalised romantic intensity rather than any conception of a particular character'. The message was being relayed that the real Romeo and Juliet were yet to come, though the ballet was already a triumph.

The *Daily Express* immediately sent its star reporter, Ann Leslie, to catch up with the man behind the ballet everyone was talking about. She tried to paint a picture of an interesting 'loner' overwhelmed by his success, but the snapshot of MacMillan that comes through her breathy report is a revealing one of the choreographer trapped in his burrow. She had expected to meet him in a trendy Chelsea flatlet. Instead, she wrote, 'To find the man . . . you must fight your way to his door through a labyrinth of dustbins and back alleys. The view from the basement flat where he lives gazes upwards through railings at a corps de ballet of one-eyed parking meters.' No. 23 Seymour Street evidently lived down to its reputation as a deeply gloomy dwelling: 'The lack of anything obviously glamorous or pretty about MacMillan's basement flat is typical of his work,' Leslie concluded. He told her, 'I'm trying to get some of the toughness back into ballet. Most of it is so "snob", so far removed from daily life or the experience of the average man.' He said that he had found the closely knit, claustrophobic world of ballet too much for him: 'It's one of the reasons I wanted to leave it. I mean, they all talk a completely private language – they even make up words that no one else understands. I'm not a "group" person myself.' This was rich indeed from the man who coined much of the private language his intimates spoke, and who gave his own nicknames to the steps in his ballets.

Ann Leslie described him as a big, shy man with dark, smudgy eyes, looking younger than his thirty-four years, although she noted that his mop-top Beatle haircut was already greying. The telephone was ringing with congratulatory calls throughout their interview. 'MacMillan was beginning to look frantic. "I must get out of here. The phone is sending me out of my mind. After all this I want to go off somewhere and just collapse." As I left, the sound of the telephone bell was ricocheting off the dustbin lids. MacMillan was still answering it.'

A week later, on Wednesday, 17 February, Seymour and Gable made their debuts and the press enthused all over again. The *Daily Mail* carried a photograph of Lynn sitting up in bed with a mug of coffee and the papers spread out on her lap: 'The new Fonteyn wakes up to read all about it.' The intimate (though posed) photograph was by Colin Jones. The accompanying article quoted the view of the *Mail*'s ballet critic, Oleg Kerensky:

It isn't often that the second cast gives a new ballet greater depth and significance than the first one, especially when the first one was Margot Fonteyn and Rudolf Nureyev. But that is what happened . . . Seymour gave Juliet a youthful tenderness and a dramatic poignancy which combined to make this a great interpretation. It also makes Seymour a great ballerina.

Alexander Bland in the *Observer* summed up the difference between the two pairs:

In the Fonteyn–Nureyev version Juliet was a shy, fey little creature carried away unwillingly by the force of a lively young cynic suddenly struck down by genuine passion. Seymour's Juliet is innocent in a different way. She surrenders to her feelings with complete and guileless abandon. Her whole life is freely offered, and when she is baulked she plunges into desperate measures with equal violence. You feel that she would sacrifice her nurse, her parent – anything or anybody – in her determination, and in the end she reaches death as naturally as a sexual climax.

Bland (a committed Nureyev enthusiast) found Gable's wholesome Romeo 'somewhat more loved against than loving', but commended his acting, like his dancing, as consistent, well timed, easy and sympathetic.

Seymour and Gable were acclaimed by many as the ideal pairing, which went some way to alleviate the initial blow to their self-esteem. 'If ever a pair of dancers made dance be the natural servant of drama, these two have done so in this work: dance just happens to be the language in which they tell their story,' wrote James Kennedy in the *Guardian*. They overshadowed the casts that followed, though they too received enthusiastic reviews and had their own following of fans. Official press nights indicate that the seniority protocol had broken down. Antoinette Sibley (originally fifth cast) was reviewed next on 22 February, with Anthony Dowell; Dowell, who had originally been cast only as Benvolio, stepped into his first three-act leading role as Romeo at short notice. He replaced Gable, who was reserved as Seymour's partner. The last press night, for Merle Park and Donald MacLeary, was nearly three weeks after the premiere. (Their first performance at a Saturday matinee had not been offered to the press.)

MacMillan's new ballet and its various casts were given extensive coverage in the national press and the dance magazines. In the end, Seymour and Gable danced four of the twelve performances in the run, the same number as Fonteyn and Nureyev and more than the other couples. Their achievement had been acknowledged but they knew that when *Romeo and Juliet* was taken on tour to the United States, they would be overshadowed once again by Fonteyn and Nureyev. The ballet had been such a success that the company and its impresario opted to take the risk of opening the season in New York with it rather than a familiar 'classic'. It would be the first American tour under Ashton's directorship and the first to start with a brand new ballet. Sol Hurok set to work publicising Fonteyn's and Nureyev's appearances in advance as those of 'ballet's fabled pair'.

According to Walter Terry in the *New York Herald Tribune*, they were 'nothing less than fabulous' at the Metropolitan Opera House opening gala on 21 April 1965. Terry asserted that Fonteyn had probably never given a more perfect portrayal in her illustrious career. He commended Nureyev for his acting, 'beautifully woven into the dramatic fabric of Dame Margot's characterisation', even though he had (apparently) few opportunities to show off his dazzling technique. Allen Hughes in the *New York Times* noted that 'those who attended the performance hoping to see Dame Margot and Mr Nureyev in a succession of pyrotechnical displays were doubtless disappointed'. Few in the gala audience even recognised Nureyev at first: no applause greeted his appearance, unlike Fonteyn's. (Romeo is discovered on stage from the start, a cloaked figure serenading Rosaline, before revealing himself as a market-place roisterer with his two companions, Mercutio and Benvolio. It was MacMillan's deliberately low-key introduction of the hero.) Instead of Nureyev making his presence felt, as he was accustomed to doing, he remained in character: 'There is less flamboyance, less of the ham about him . . . in the new discipline of his dancing he has put art before display,' declared the *New York World Telegram and Journal*.

Terry commended the second cast, Seymour and Gable, in his next review, on 23 April 1965: 'Upon them fell the terrible burden of following the world's most famous duo. Let us not pretend that they can electrify an audience as Dame Margot and Mr Nureyev can, but let it also be said that in their own youthful terms, they are wonderful as Romeo and Juliet . . . sweetly scared but oh, so eager to live only for each other.' Terry's somewhat tempered praise indicated that Hurok's well-honed instincts were justified: American audiences were more likely to succumb to big stars than up-and-coming ones. Hurok held back announcements of which casts would be performing in cities on tour in the expectation that eager fans would buy multiple tickets to be sure of seeing the celebrated pair. To Seymour's and Gable's chagrin, they were regarded by fame-struck spectators as Fonteyn's and Nureyev's understudies: 'If they're this good, what must the real ones must be like?' a spectator was overheard to say.

MacMillan had travelled to New York by ship to enjoy the accolades for the first American performances of his ballet. 'Rudimania' had reached new heights of excitement, fuelled by media publicity about the Royal Ballet's famous couple and by the mid-1960s' fascination with 'Swinging London'. MacMillan was caught up in the hysteria, taking curtain calls with the cast as audiences leapt to their feet, screaming and ripping up their programmes into a snowstorm of confetti. He was given a standing ovation in Sardi's show-biz restaurant and fêted at the trendy new discothèque, 'Arthur', launched by Sybil Burton. The former wife of Richard Burton, who had left her for Elizabeth Taylor, she made a point of inviting the Royal Ballet to her nightclub, along with other theatrical luminaries. Though she was photographed dancing with Nureyev, Kenneth became her favourite catch, as they enjoyed each other's company out of the limelight as well as in it.

Then, while the company continued the tour, he returned to London, wondering what to do next. The Board had congratulated him on 'one of the most remarkable achievements seen at Covent Garden since the House opened'. Lord Drogheda had written him a personal letter of appreciation, saying,

You have achieved a masterpiece. Your problem now is going to be how to live up to it next time. What musical score can come up to the brilliance of Prokofiev's and how can you match Shakespeare's tale? I have a feeling that you ought to think about commissioning a modern composer. But who? Britten is terribly tied up . . . what about Henze? Do you have a feeling of sympathy for his music?

The composer whose music most attracted Kenneth was Mahler. His desire to create a ballet to *Das Lied von der Erde*, first expressed in 1959, had been rejected yet again in April 1964. The Board member, Jack Donaldson, who had objected to Kenneth's initial proposal in 1959, was still holding out against the 'imposition of some other man's permanent visual images' on musical masterpieces that had not been written expressly for ballet and that were concerned with matters of greater import than dancing. Donaldson and the rest of the Board had already refused to countenance Cranko's proposal to create a ballet for Fonteyn and Nureyev at Covent Garden to music from Tchaikovsky's opera *Eugene Onegin*. Cranko had made his *Onegin* ballet for Stuttgart instead, in April 1964, using an arrangement of other music by Tchaikovsky. When Cranko repeated his open invitation to MacMillan to choreograph whatever he wanted for the Stuttgart company, Kenneth seized the opportunity the Opera House was determined to deny him.

As soon as *Romeo and Juliet* was launched in New York in April, he telephoned Cranko in Germany. They arranged to meet up in Spoleto, where the Stuttgart Ballet was appearing in the annual arts festival in June. Kenneth watched the dancers in class and performance and discussed plans for his *Song of the Earth* in the late autumn of 1965.

When the Royal Ballet returned home from the four-month North American tour, ready for a holiday in August, Kenneth went to Positano with Donald MacLeary, Georgina Parkinson and her husband, Roy Round. Lynn had stayed on in California, where she was joined by Colin in a vain effort to repair their marriage. *Romeo and Juliet* had come between them and Lynn's long absence on tour had further estranged them.

Deeply unhappy on her return to London, Lynn consulted Kenneth's analyst, Dr Hardenberg. She, too, was suffering panic attacks, terrified of venturing out from the flat where she and Colin had started their married life so hopefully. In spite of the acclaim she had received as Juliet, she was pessimistic about her future with the Royal Ballet. When Kenneth came back from holiday, he was unable to be of any support. Angry and resentful at the way his *Romeo and Juliet* had been wrested from him by the Opera House, he was as perilously near the edge as she was, though he could ward off his depression by working. He was about to go to Stuttgart for three months to create and rehearse his *Song of the Earth*.

In his absence, *Romeo and Juliet* was filmed by the director Paul Czinner, who pioneered the use of multiple cameras when filming ballet for the big screen. He had recorded the Royal Ballet in 1959, dancing *Ondine*, *Firebird*, and *Swan Lake* Act II, all with Fonteyn in the leading role. Czinner insisted on Fonteyn and Nureyev as the star-crossed lovers, even though Fonteyn was rightly apprehensive that close-ups would reveal she was at least thirty years too old for

Juliet. The film, shot at Pinewood Studios as though it were a record of a live performance at the Royal Opera House, was released in October 1966, first in the United States and then in Britain, with a gala screening at the Royal Festival Hall. MacMillan accepted a £3,000 fee for his choreography but otherwise washed his hands of the film, which he thoroughly disliked. He felt that his choreography had been betrayed by Czinner's preoccupation with Nureyev and Fonteyn at the expense of the rest of the dancing. It was not how he wanted his *Romeo and Juliet* to be seen by cinema audiences.

Once in Stuttgart, liberated from the pressures of the Royal Opera House, MacMillan was a different person. Cranko gave him first choice of the dancers he wanted and as much rehearsal time as he needed. *The Song of the Earth* was going to be on the same programme as *Danses concertantes* (which Kenneth would oversee) and a new piece by Cranko, *Opus 1*, to Webern's Passacaglia No. 1. The two choreographers did not watch each other's work in preparation, though they shared some of the same dancers and even a similar theme: the recurring cycle of life and death, as individuals struggle and then submit to fate. Both men were in their mid-thirties and aware that time was passing increasingly swiftly. Although their careers had taken off, their emotional lives were unstable and unrewarding. Both were subject to black depression. Yet so long as they could create, inspired by the dancers patiently waiting for them in the rehearsal room, they found fulfilment. They relied on alcohol to get them through the day – and night. As one of the (former) Stuttgart dancers, Reid Anderson, later to be Artistic Director of Stuttgart Ballet, commented, 'John and Kenneth couldn't choreograph without alcohol and cigarettes. When I was young, that's how I thought all choreographers were, fuelled by drink and nicotine. They seemed catalysts to let the choreography happen.'

Marcia Haydée, who took the leading female role in *Das Lied von der Erde* (as the ballet, like the music, is known in Germany), remembers that MacMillan came well prepared to the first rehearsals. 'He knew the words to all the songs and what they meant. He knew exactly the movement he wanted and how it should be. Of my role, he said, "Marcia, it's you, as a human being. What you are, that's what I want." So that's what I did.' Hers was one of three principal roles: the Woman, the Man and 'Der Ewige' – the Eternal One (called the Messenger of Death in English cast lists). The rest of the cast are young people going about their lives, happily oblivious of the fact that death will claim them one by one.

The text of the songs is taken from verses by Chinese poets of the T'ang dynasty, freely adapted into German by Hans Bethge. The poems are bitter-sweet recollections of human joys, ending with a poignant farewell to the world. Mahler composed *Das Lied von der Erde* after a series of cruel blows, the last of which was the diagnosis that he had incurable heart disease; he was distancing his dread of dying by contemplating the inevitable through music and poetry. Each symphonic movement is based on one of the Chinese poems except the last, *Der Abschied* ('The Farewell'), in which Mahler combined two verses and added a coda of four lines of his own.

MacMillan introduced a narrative thread as a visual link between the songs, without illustrating the text in slavish detail. Quoted in *About the House*, he said, 'My interest was to create movements to describe the essence of the poems.' Creating the ballet in Germany, he assumed that audiences would make the connections between the German text and any specific references in the action on stage. 'The theme of the ballet is quite simple,' he said. 'A man and a woman; death takes the man; they both return to her and at the end of the ballet, we find that in death there is the promise of renewal.'

He started by choreographing the duet between the man and the woman at the start of the final section, to the orchestral interlude that precedes the song of farewell. The man has been present from the start of the ballet, when he enters shadowed by Der Ewige. The woman appears in the second song, *Der Einsame im Herbst*/'Autumn Solitude', in which the words reveal her apprehension of death and her longing for a companion to end her loneliness. In their final duet, she finds her lover only to lose him to death: the pas de deux encapsulates the story of *Romeo and Juliet*. The original feeling of the pas de deux was 'like a ritual – impassive, as if they're in the grip of fate', says Reid Anderson, adding the comment: 'It's usually danced more prettily now as a love duet but actually she's held as if she's in a straitjacket with her arms behind her.'

Der Ewige intervenes to claim the man, in a pas de trois with echoes of the *Images of Love* trio, 'Two loves I have, of comfort and despair'. When the two men leave the stage together, the woman, bereft, dances on her own in a long solo requiring great reserves of stamina. She has to reach an acceptance of her loss, the return of her loneliness and the inevitability of death. 'Kenneth wasn't sure of how the solo should end,' remembers Haydée. 'On the day of the premiere, when he was stuck, I said, "What if I just bourrée?" and he said, "Go", and that's what I did.' The woman is driven diagonally backwards across the stage in speedy runs on pointe, like a leaf tugged by a force outside her control. She is rejoined by the man, now wearing a white half-mask symbolising death, and Der Ewige, both of whom link hands with her; they step forward serenely in slow motion as if into eternity. The curtain falls on the pacing figures and the final words Mahler added to the song: 'Ewig . . . Ewig . . . for ever and ever.' Combined with the ecstatic closing music, it is one of the most moving endings in ballet, and it came about almost by accident.

'Kenneth said to us, "Go on walking, go on walking." Then he changed it from small steps to much bigger ones, like flying away from the earth. He didn't start out with this in mind – we discovered the ending on stage,' says Egon Madsen. Madsen, who danced the role of Der Ewige, says that there were many discussions about whether he represented Tod (death) or a more benign Hereafter. At just twenty-three, Madsen was a slight, romantic dancer, younger than Haydée and Ray Barra, her partner as the Man. 'Kenneth chose me, I think, because I had a gentle way of dancing – I was not hard or threatening. So we agreed that Der Ewige was not a cruel culler of souls. He is among the people and he lets them go to their places. He stays with them. If he was Death, he would pick them out and dictate what happens.'

MacMillan commented in his *About the House* interview, 'The Death figure is not at all evil. In fact, he is rather a nice guy, just there, always hanging about. He wears a colourless mask without any marks on it, and from out front it makes him look like the others, only that much different.' Although Der Ewige is Other, he is not entirely the MacMillan misfit, the Outsider. That role belongs to the woman, conscious of her isolation from her first appearance; in the final 'Farewell' section, she picks her way among her companions like the Chosen Maiden in *The Rite of Spring*.

Since Der Ewige was never intended to be a melodramatic memento mori, MacMillan did not introduce him into every single episode. He was not originally present in the fourth song, *Von der Schönheit*/'Of Beauty'. In 1990, the last revival of *Song of the Earth* (for the Royal Ballet) in MacMillan's lifetime, he added a brief appearance for Der Ewige, stepping out of the wings in the fourth song's last moments. It completed a pattern audiences had come to expect.

The Stuttgart dancers found the movement MacMillan devised with them unusual and initially uncomfortable, until they adjusted to the tilted torsos, turned-in positions and flat-footed walks. The women's arms were often bent at the elbows and wrists, adjusting imaginary kimono sleeves or picking flowers. Some of the shapes were orientalisms, echoing the ancient Chinese poems; others were modernist curves and angles, influenced to some extent by the stark movements in Antony Tudor's *Dark Elegies*, to Mahler's *Kindertotenlieder*.

German dance-goers saw a resemblance to *Jugendstil* or art nouveau in the curling, organic shapes and continuous free-flowing movement – 'rhythmic, linear lines in space, with floral ornaments and the youthful dynamism which carried the whole art nouveau movement', according to Horst Koegler's review in *Dance and Dancers*. MacMillan commented later, in *About the House*, 'This was certainly not intended by me, but I suppose that the combination of an oriental background, a composer writing during the height of Viennese *Jugendstil*, and my new free-flowing, organic movements, may have lent support to the notion, however remote, of a streamlined, cleaned-up art nouveau.'

He went on to refute any connection with Martha Graham or other modern dance choreographers. Haydée says that Graham's name was never mentioned and that she and the other Stuttgart dancers had no experience at the time of American contemporary dance technique: 'The choreography was just Kenneth responding to Mahler and that's how it came out. It had nothing to do with Graham – it was his own creation.'

MacMillan had, however, seen Graham's company dance in London in 1963, and he had watched Seymour experimenting with Graham exercises while she warmed up for rehearsals of *Symphony* the same year. The technique was being taught in London by the time *Song of the Earth* was later performed at the Royal Opera House, and British dance students were convinced they could recognise the Graham influence on MacMillan's choreography, whether he was conscious of it or not. Richard Buckle's *Sunday Times*

review of the first British performances of *Song of the Earth* commented on the 'Grahamish deep *plié à la seconde* with knees pressing ever further open . . . the moan of the unfertilised womb, as it
were'. The male dancers in particular were using the floor in an
earthy, gravity-bound Graham way that was alien to ballet's classical vocabulary.

The choreography's unusual elements were all the more exposed
in plain outfits that replaced the intended costumes. When
MacMillan had first proposed *Song of the Earth* for the Royal
Ballet back in 1959, he had suggested simple practice dress as a way
of keeping expenses down. Given free rein in Stuttgart, he had
asked Georgiadis to design costumes with an oriental feel, though
not too literally Chinese. Georgiadis obliged with floating chiffon
garments. When the dancers wore them at the dress rehearsal, he
and Kenneth found them 'vomit-making'. 'So we agreed, "Let's get
rid of them and just dye tights and T-shirts for the boys and put
tunics on the girls." ' The Stuttgart wardrobe staff dyed the clothes
in bluey-green and purple shades overnight and the ballet was given
against a plain cyclorama, its colour changing through blues to pale
green-yellow. Der Ewige wore dark grey with a flesh-coloured half-
mask; the Man had a white mask for his return after death. Shorn
of adornment, Georgiadis considered *Song of the Earth* 'the acme of
Kenneth's abstract ballets'.

For the Stuttgart company, *Das Lied* was far from abstract. They
had invested themselves in its creation: 'It was a love relationship
between us and Kenneth – there was an emotional charge that you
don't get ever again. It was special to us and I don't think it's ever
been recaptured the same way,' insists Haydée. They were all aware
that dancing to Mahler's song-cycle was an audacious thing to do in
Germany, where the composer was a cult figure (far more so than
in Britain at the time). Cranko, as ballet director, had to convince
the Württemberg State Theatre to enable its orchestra to play
Mahler's music and to engage two fine singers (Margarethe Bence
and James Harper) who would agree to be placed far apart on
opposite sides of the stage. He knew that the risk would be justified
as soon as he saw the first run-through. MacMillan had asked him
to bring a libretto to the rehearsal to check that there were no infeli-
cities between the German text of the songs and the choreography.
By the time the dancers had reached the *Abschied*/'Farewell',

Cranko had put the score aside and watched the dancers with tears in his eyes.

German critics were divided between those who thought MacMillan's ballet a masterpiece and those who believed Mahler should be left alone. Two British critics, Andrew Porter for the *Financial Times* and John Percival for *The Times*, went to Stuttgart for the premiere of *Das Lied von der Erde* on 7 November 1965 and wrote glowing accounts of it. 'London must acquire it too without delay; for it is a major work and a beautiful one,' enthused Porter. Members of the Royal Opera House Board were still not convinced it should be considered for the Royal Ballet until 'a representative of Covent Garden' had seen the work in person. Since *Das Lied* was no longer in performance in Stuttgart over the New Year, no one could go. The diehards gave in, however, when the Ballet Sub-Committee urged in January 1966 that the Royal Ballet must have it: a deciding factor was Sol Hurok's insistence, thanks to favourable reports, that it should be included in the company's next US tour, which was scheduled for 1967. Magnanimously, Cranko agreed that the Royal Ballet could mount it in May 1966, while Stuttgart continued to perform the original production.*

Both Cranko and MacMillan relished making the ROH Board climb down from its purist position over music too 'good' for ballet. 'I crowed inside,' MacMillan confessed later in the *Out of Line* television documentary. He was now in a position to dictate terms to the Royal Ballet. He had been invited, at Ashton's suggestion, to join the Ballet Sub-Committee, which gave him added status. He announced that he wanted Marcia Haydée to dance the opening performances of *The Song of the Earth* with the Royal Ballet. Reluctantly, the Committee agreed, noting that a company ballerina would thereby lose out. The minutes do not record whether MacMillan rubbed in the fact that no objections had been raised when Fonteyn, as a guest artist, displaced Seymour as Juliet.

Haydée came to London and danced her role as the Woman, with Donald MacLeary as the Man and Anthony Dowell (at twenty-three, the same age as Egon Madsen) as the renamed Messenger of Death. Seymour then replaced Haydée, followed by Monica Mason.

---

* *Das Lied von der Erde* had been notated by Faith Worth, with additions by Stuttgart Ballet's notator, Georgette Tsinguirides.

Georgiadis had slightly altered his designs, darkening the background cyclorama from blue to black and shades of grey, and dressing the cast in grey and black instead of blues and purple. The Woman was in white, the Man in silver-grey and the Messenger in black. The ballet was hailed as a major achievement and Haydée's 'darkly dramatic personality' was much admired. 'She faces death as she faces love, not as a victim but as an equal,' wrote Alexander Bland in the *Observer*. Richard Buckle commented in *The Sunday Times* that MacMillan had clearly been living with – married to – Mahler's music for years: 'He has had time to work out what movements can be put with it and he has made no mistakes.' Clive Barnes, who had been appointed dance (as well as theatre) critic for the *New York Times*, reported, '*The Song of the Earth* is very probably the best ballet of his career ... Ideas first tried out, occasionally unsuccessfully, in earlier works here reappear, and the result is choreography of great richness of texture and scope of imagination.' Noel Goodwin remarked in *Dance and Dancers* that the delay between the Board's original rejection of a Mahler ballet and its creation might have been to MacMillan's advantage, in that his choreography had greatly developed in the interim. David Webster made the same point, from his own mixed motives, in a personal letter of congratulation: 'I honestly don't think that in being the means of holding it back for a bit we have done you any kind of damage, indeed very much the reverse.'

MacMillan said, years later, that *The Song of the Earth* was the ballet he would like to be remembered by: 'It was the first ballet I was satisfied with. It had great unity of style, which until then had eluded me.' He might have been quoting de Valois's heartfelt approval of *The Song of the Earth*, which inspired her only poem with a ballet as its subject. Entitled 'Dancers in Action', it was an attempt to capture 'movement's ecstasy ... challenging all the formal laws of form' in the paradoxical stillness and symmetry of performance. The poem concluded with a evocation of 'that strange moment of great power/Which was the body's exploration of/A unity that this instant ceased to be'. De Valois published numerous poems in her collected writings, distinguishing 'Dancers in Action' by its dedication to 'Kenneth MacMillan and the dancers of the Royal Ballet in Mahler's *Song of the Earth*'. Her conviction had grown that he should be her company's next artistic director and chief choreographer once Ashton retired.

MacMillan had very mixed emotions as he took his curtain calls at the end of the first Royal Ballet performance of *The Song of the Earth*. He was rejoicing in his triumph at home while bidding farewell to the company and his British audience. He had decided to accept an offer to direct the Deutsche Oper Ballet in Berlin on a contract expected to last at least three years.

Richard Buckle started his ecstatic review of *Song of the Earth* in *The Sunday Times* with a description of its creator receiving his plaudits on stage:

His hair was grey like ours, but he was grinning in his nice childish way; and we remembered him in younger and perhaps unhappier days, soaring across the stage in Florestan's pink jacket with feet wonderfully arched (and we must have been rather mad about him, for we put him on the cover of *Ballet* magazine). This was a thought from the past; and MacMillan's future lay in Berlin and in battling to create a great company there and a glorious repertory for them, so he was lost to us; and at present he was grinning rather collusively, we thought, sharing a joke with us two thousand lovers out here, but a bit pleased no doubt, but not entirely, for there is even something sad about having created a masterpiece.

before MacMillan headed to Berlin, there was another television ballet to choreograph for the BBC. The subject and treatment were once again typical of his preoccupation with sex and death. Based on Barbey d'Aurévilly's *Le Rideau Cramoisi*, the ballet tells the story of an army officer billeted in a house where a young girl, Albertine, makes advances to him. She goes to his room at night, passing through her parents' bedroom. She dies during sex and the officer has to carry her body back to her room without waking her parents. He then leaves. Lynn Seymour and Desmond Doyle were the two principals and the piece was transmitted on 13 May 1966, with Peter Wright directing.

3

Berlin: Divided City, Divided Self

1966–1970

25

By the mid-1960s, Berlin was the most extraordinary of German cities. Already divided politically between the Allies after the Second World War, it had been physically split in two in 1961 by the wall separating East from West. East Berliners were forbidden to cross to the West; many of those who tried were killed in the attempt. While foreigners and some residents in the Western sector were able to travel, with restrictions, to or through the Eastern part, they needed visas to do so. Geographically as well as politically, West Berlin had become an enclave within Communist-ruled East Germany. The simplest way to travel in or out was by air. Going by train (as MacMillan would insist on doing) required form-filling for permits in advance. The narrow corridor of rail to Berlin through East German territory was cordoned off with barbed wire and patrolled by soldiers; border guards searched the trains for anyone without the correct papers. Checkpoint Charlie, the crossing point by road between the two halves of the city, was heavily manned by armed guards; inspection of travel documents was as rigorous and time-consuming there as at the underground, S-Bahn and railway stations. The presence of the military on both sides of the frontier was an ever-present reminder of the hostility between East and West.

Cold War politics, combined with the revolutionary fervour of the 1960s, meant that Berlin was a fevered place in which to live and work. Students and radicals in the Western sector demonstrated against what they perceived as imperialism of all kinds: America's war in Vietnam, the autocratic rule of the Shah of Persia, capitalist oppression, illiberal foreign policies. For some years, protest was openly expressed on the streets and in the theatres of West Berlin. The Schaubühne and Freie Volksbühne put on challenging plays about Auschwitz, the bombing of Dresden, America's intervention in the Far East, each of which aroused heated discussion and yet more demonstrations. Then the West German authorities started to crack down. A student was killed by police, protesters were arrested, demonstrations banned. By the 1970s, frustrated revolutionaries would turn to terrorism, spawning the Red Army Faction and the Baader–Meinhof Gang.

MacMillan had no awareness of what he was letting himself in for when he accepted the job of Ballet Director at the Stadtische Opernhaus (the Municipal Opera House), known as the Deutsche Oper. West Berlin was competing with the East for cultural prestige. The division effected by the Wall had left two of the city's important opera houses, the Staatsoper and the Komische Oper (the State Opera House and the Operetta Theatre), in the Eastern sector near the Brandenberg Gate. Both had impressive reputations for opera (or operetta) and, to rather a lesser extent, for ballet. The Staatsoper ballet company could draw on Soviet-bloc performers and coaches to keep its technical standards high; the Komische Oper's Intendant, Walter Felsenstein, had appointed Tom Schilling as Ballet Director in 1965 to introduce a policy of dance-theatre.

West Berlin's response had been to build a brand new, state-of-the-art theatre on Richard Wagner Strasse to house its own opera and ballet companies. Generously funded, the Deutsche Oper was now the responsibility of the West Berlin Senate, or local government, which allocated its budget and appointed its Intendant, whose role combined that of general manager and artistic director. Gustav Rudolf Sellner, Intendant since 1963, had concentrated on raising the quality of the opera company. At the start of his appointment, he had left the ballet in the hands of Tatjana Gsovsky, the company's principal choreographer. Born in Moscow in 1901, she came to Berlin in 1925 with her then husband, Victor Gsovsky. She opened her own ballet school there, teaching many dancers who would go on to have distinguished careers. She had been ballet mistress and Chief Choreographer for the State Opera in Berlin, as well as working in opera houses elsewhere in Germany and in Buenos Aires and Milan. In the 1950s, she became Ballet Director of the Frankfurt Opera Ballet and the West Berlin Municipal Opera (renamed the Deutsche Oper in 1961). With Gert Reinholm, she had founded a chamber group, the Berlin Ballet, made up of her former pupils and invited artists. Partly subsidised by the Berlin Senate, it toured widely, eventually becoming the official touring wing of the Deutsche Oper Ballet.

Gsovsky was a prolific choreographer of dramatic ballets, usually to contemporary music. She had, for example, devised her own

Agon to Stravinsky's music in 1958, some months before MacMillan had created his version. She collaborated with avant-garde German composers, such as Boris Blacher, Hans Werner Henze and Giselher Klebe. Under her direction, the Deutsche Oper company had built up a fair reputation as a versatile ensemble, its emphasis on dramatic interpretation rather than purely technical standards. By now in her mid-sixties, she had entrusted more and more of her administrative duties as Director to Gert Reinholm, who had been a well-known principal dancer in both her companies, creating leading roles in her ballets before retiring as a performer at the age of forty in 1966.

When Sellner turned his attention to the ballet company, he intervened in the productions, crediting himself as the director of each work Gsovsky choreographed – an offensive loss of face that led to her resignation. Sellner cast around for a big name, preferably an international one, to replace her (and Reinholm) as ballet director. Cranko was the obvious choice, but he was reluctant to leave his Stuttgart company. Various options were suggested, including the merger of the Berlin and Stuttgart Ballets into one national company with Cranko as its artistic director. He still demurred, proposing MacMillan for Berlin in his place. Sellner, who had visited the Stuttgart Ballet Week in November 1965 in order to persuade Cranko to change his mind, had been impressed by MacMillan's *Das Lied von der Erde*. He sent his deputy, Egon Seefehlner, to see MacMillan in London at the end of the year, offering a co-directorship with Cranko of the Deutsche Oper Ballet in Berlin. MacMillan replied that if he were to consider taking the post, he would have to have sole responsibility.

When the Deutsche Oper then offered him the job on his own, MacMillan asked to see Ashton to sound out his opinion. According to MacMillan's old friend and colleague, Gilbert Vernon, Kenneth had not made up his mind about the directorship in Berlin. While he admired and even envied what Cranko had achieved in Stuttgart, he believed his own future lay with the Royal Ballet. He intended to use the Berlin offer to impress the Royal Opera House management with his value, and thereby secure more frequent commissions for new ballets. (He had nothing scheduled for at least two years following *Romeo and Juliet*.) Vernon recalls Kenneth returning from the brief interview white and shaking. Ashton had said at once that it was a good idea for him to go to Berlin, without urging him to reconsider. There was no discussion of the pros and cons, or any suggestion that he was essential to the Royal Ballet. Ashton simply recommended that he accepted the Berlin offer and then showed him the door. 'It was the off-hand way Ashton did it that so upset Kenneth,' says Vernon.

He felt that his whole life had been thrown out of the window, that he'd been rejected as worthless. I tried to tell him it wasn't so. Ashton probably meant that it was a good idea for him to get some administrative experience, but Ken wouldn't be convinced. He felt that his position at the Royal Ballet had become untenable, so he took Berlin.

Ashton's motives might well have been mixed. He was jealous of MacMillan's recent big successes with *Romeo and Juliet* and *The Song of the Earth*; with Kenneth out of the way, Ashton would no longer be under pressure to give him yet more opportunities. His previous encouragement of the younger man had given way to an uneasy resentment as he realised that Kenneth was likely to be his successor, eventually, as Artistic Director. On the other hand, de Valois had always impressed on Ashton the necessity for planning ahead; she had stepped aside when she reached sixty-five to give him his chance. She was still a powerful force, in a position to remind him and the Opera House administrators that MacMillan, the heir apparent, should be prepared for his future responsibilities. Ashton's advice to him was sound: the West Berlin directorship would widen his horizons by giving him the experience of running a large ballet company.

As a chronically insecure artist himself, however, Ashton must have been aware that by withholding praise and reassurance, he was wounding his vulnerable rival. He had been generous enough to write 'Dearest Kenneth' a warm letter for the first night of *Romeo and Juliet*, wishing him 'the greatest triumph that you can possibly have. It is very beautiful and should seal your reputation as a major choreographer. All love and kisses, Fred.' Now he was appearing to devalue his company's first entirely home-grown creator by letting him go elsewhere, just as Cranko had been encouraged to leave for Stuttgart.

MacMillan, always inclined to paranoia, took Ashton's coolness as rejection. The Royal Ballet had replaced his family since he left home at fifteen. He had a huge, possibly exaggerated respect for the ballet culture and sense of tradition that de Valois had inculcated in a comparatively young establishment. He shared her and the company's collective belief that the Royal Ballet was among the best in the world. He was ambitious, but however much faith he had in his own abilities, he must have doubted that he was equipped to take over the company from its parental founders, de Valois and Ashton. In his mind, especially in his darkest moments, there was no guarantee that he would be welcomed back from Berlin. He was being obliged to cut himself off from his artistic life-support system to go it alone in a foreign country.

He evidently turned to his analyst, Dr Herman Hardenberg, for support. Bills from the first half of 1966 show that MacMillan was attending Hardenberg's Wimpole Street rooms every weekday. During these sessions, MacMillan must have talked himself round to making the most of the opportunity offered to him. Anger over the perceived humiliations the Royal Ballet had inflicted on him – overriding his choice of cast for *Romeo and Juliet*, refusing Mahler's music for *Song of the Earth*, failing to offer him regular commissions in spite of the big successes he had achieved – gave him the strength to accept the Deutsche Oper challenge. He would show the Royal Ballet what 'they' had lost. Like Cranko, he would transform a hitherto insignificant company into his vision of an important classically based ensemble that could do justice to his work. Berlin would give him control over his own ballets and those he intended to commission from choreographers he admired. Instead of being a hireling of the Royal Ballet, he would gain the status he deserved.

The Royal Opera House issued a blandly worded press release announcing his departure 'for a period' as Director of Ballet at the Deutsche Oper, which the announcement crassly placed in East instead of West Berlin. The error, a minor one as far as the management was concerned, revealed how little they understood the divided city and the Cold War politics of the country to which MacMillan was moving. The press release gave the impression that he had been granted leave of absence, though he let a sympathetic journalist from *Dance and Dancers* know, 'That was the diplomatic way we agreed to put it. My contract with the Royal Ballet has expired.'

By now committed to leaving in July 1966, MacMillan sounded out friends and colleagues he hoped to take with him to Berlin. He wanted a core group of trusted intimates to support him. His key requirement was for a ballet master who could take charge of company classes and rehearsals. Peter Wright, who had been Cranko's ballet master in Stuttgart for several years, turned down MacMillan's invitation to do the same job in Berlin. Wright was now working as a BBC Television director in London, having chosen to bring up his young children in Britain rather than Germany. Kenneth then called on his old friend Gilbert Vernon, offering him the post, but Vernon wanted to pursue his luck as an actor. 'I didn't realise at the time it was a cry from the heart or I might have changed my mind,' he says. He believes that Kenneth never really forgave him: their friendship foundered as a result. MacMillan finally succeeded in luring Ray Barra from Stuttgart to be his ballet master, to Cranko's regret. Injury had recently ended Barra's performing career and Cranko wanted him to remain with the Stuttgart company as his assistant. Barra, torn between the two, realised that Kenneth had most need of him. He had the great advantage of being fluent in German, so he was sent ahead to Berlin to organise living quarters. Ashley Lawrence, a New Zealander who was conductor for the Royal Ballet touring company, agreed to accept the post of Music Director and Conductor (as well as rehearsal pianist) of the Deutsche Oper Ballet.

Kenneth had already approached Lynn Seymour, who was despairing of her prospects with the Royal Ballet. She was about to lose Christopher Gable as her favourite partner, for he had decided to stop dancing in favour of a career as an actor. (Kenneth would otherwise have invited him too to join the Berlin company.) Seymour, depressed after the break-up of her marriage, was putting on weight again and being offered fewer and fewer roles. Ashton's interest, as director and choreographer, was focused on the partnership between Antoinette Sibley and Anthony Dowell, who were being brought on as potential English successors to Fonteyn and Nureyev. Kenneth's proposal to Lynn to join him in Berlin as prima ballerina of the Deutsche Oper company could hardly have come at a better time. (The Board minutes noting her intended departure recorded merely, 'The company would not be short of ballerinas.')

When Kenneth heard that Vergie Derman had resigned from the Royal Ballet, he immediately proposed that she should pursue her career in Berlin instead. He had always liked the way she danced, choosing her and Richard Cragun as students for leading roles in

Dance Suite, his work for the Royal Ballet School in 1962. Four years later, she had felt she was going nowhere in the company. She accepted Kenneth's invitation to become a principal dancer with the Deutsche Oper Ballet on a whim, not convinced that he meant it; she was surprised the next morning to be rushed by him to the West German Embassy to get a work visa as fast as possible. On being told they needed an official's signature authenticating Derman's photograph, they left the building for Kenneth to fake one. There was no time to be lost and he took the same pragmatic approach as he had when he forged his father's name on his letter applying to join the Sadler's Wells Ballet School.

With his team assembled around him in Berlin, MacMillan was ready to begin his new job and new life. Ray Barra had rented a large apartment at 107 Reichsstrasse, off the former Adolf Hitler Platz, in an art-deco building once occupied by German stage and film actors in the 1930s. There were ten rooms on two floors at the top of the building – more than enough for the first occupants, Kenneth, Lynn and Ray, as well as any guests from London and Stuttgart. Kenneth occupied the two rooms on the upper floor that were like a separate flat with its own staircase. Barra had chosen the very back rooms, beyond the main sitting room, next to the kitchen. But when Seymour arrived, Barra had to yield his quarters to her and move all the furniture he had installed:

I remember dismounting my huge bookcase while everyone else was at a party and it fell on top of me, this monstrous thing. I was mad at having to move because I was the one who had to run the apartment – find the cleaning lady, buy the food, fix everything that went wrong – because none of the others spoke German.

Barra soon appreciated, however, that his new rooms by the flat's entrance at least afforded him some privacy. The drawback to the otherwise desirable rear section, now Seymour's domain, was that the occupant's comings and goings were evident to everyone else. Kenneth would install himself in the kitchen, his nerve centre, monitoring what time, and with whom, she returned. 'He wanted to control our lives,' says Barra. 'He was very possessive of the people he liked and loved. That apartment was going to turn into Hell's Kitchen.'

Initially, however, all went well. Holding court, as he had done since his student days in Miss Coe's café, Kenneth entertained his ballet family with mimicry and wild speculations. He imagined what their stolid cleaning lady must make of the odd threesome in the flat; he cast Lynn as Sally Bowles (from Christopher Isherwood's Berlin story, *Goodbye to Berlin*). Seymour flourished in her flamboyant new role, wearing her trendiest outfits from London boutiques. 'Oh, she was the rage of Berlin,' says Barra admiringly. 'She had this big red fox-fur coat with a bottom half that zipped off and could be used as a stole. And she wore the shortest skirts.' She was making the most of her enhanced prestige as the company's leading ballerina. Instead of moping, low and lonely in London, she could reinvent herself in a foreign city.

Seymour points out that she (Canadian), Barra (American) and Derman (South African) were accustomed to being transplanted to another country, whereas MacMillan had never been an émigré. Though he had spent some months at a time in New York, Copenhagen and Stuttgart, mounting his ballets, he had not had to fend for himself. He had, in fact, been better cared for on his stays abroad than in London, where he was inept at living on his own. He soon discovered that in Berlin he was helpless – not least because he made no effort to learn German. Unlike the polyglot Stuttgart Ballet company that Cranko had assembled around himself, the Deutsche Oper staff and dancers had German, not English, as their common language, leaving MacMillan dependent on English-speaking colleagues. Largely deprived of his habitual solace, the cinema (apart from a select number of English-language films), the Reichsstrasse flat became his source of comfort and entertainment, on condition he was not left alone for long.

His immediate concern was the ballet company. Tatjana Gsovsky had chosen to stay on as a teacher and répétiteur (rehearsal director), along with Gert Reinholm, who had been accustomed to running the company. Both were now answerable to MacMillan, although any resentment they felt at being usurped by an outsider appeared to be contained: they were prepared to respect him as a renowned choreographer who would raise the company's reputation to a new level. The dancers' union was meanwhile vigilant in protecting its members' interests. Their numbers had been reduced the previous year from 83 to 59 dancers and the union was bitterly opposed to further losses. MacMillan was obliged to leave the company untouched, except for the introduction of Seymour and

Derman as principals. Under the German opera-house system, the ballet company performed only three or four times a month, if that: opera took pride of place. MacMillan had been assured there would be more performances during his directorship, including Ballet Week festivals, with concluding galas, like those Cranko had made such a success in Stuttgart.

In later interviews that MacMillan gave to the British press, he misrepresented the state of ballet in Berlin and (West) Germany. He claimed to the *Guardian* that 'The Germans are bitterly opposed to classical ballet . . . they've had no education in it.' In fact, Berlin had been a leading centre of ballet in the nineteenth century and at the start of the twentieth. After the Second World War, there had been a resurgence of interest in Germany in classical ballet, thanks to visits by foreign companies and the appointment of artistic directors from countries with strong ballet traditions. From Britain alone, Walter Gore had gone to Frankfurt and Alan Carter to Munich (where he would be followed by Ronald Hynd), as well as Cranko to Stuttgart. 'Classics' such as *Swan Lake* and *Giselle* were in many German repertoires: the Deutsche Oper's production of *Giselle*, for example, had been mounted by Antony Tudor in 1964. Tatjana Gsovsky had staged her own productions of *The Sleeping Beauty* and *Don Quixote* for opera-house companies, and always included classical-ballet divertissements in her touring group's programmes, danced by invited guests as well as her ballet-trained former pupils.

Indeed, ballet in the 1950s and mid-1960s had largely eclipsed Germany's own pre-war school of Ausdruckstanz, modern Expressionist dance. Among its chief proponents, Kurt Jooss and Rudolf von Laban had fled to Britain in the 1930s. Jooss had returned after the war to set up his school and company in Essen, where Pina Bausch started her career. Through her and others, Ausdruckstanz would re-emerge as a considerable force as Tanztheater, flourishing by the 1970s. Berlin had Mary Wigman, the famous pre-war performer and choreographer whose dance school in Dresden had been proscribed by the Nazis. She had re-established her school in Berlin in 1949: by the time MacMillan arrived, she was eighty and the school was about to close, depriving the city of a centre for modern dance. Wigman had been a guest choreographer in several German opera houses, including the Deutsche Oper. Although the company had danced her *Rite of Spring* and *Orpheus and Eurydice*, ballet was what mattered in an opera house that aspired to national and international prestige.

Intendant Sellner's hope was that his newly appointed Ballet Director would create critically acclaimed ballets for the Deutsche Oper, as well as mounting existing works such as *Das Lied von der Erde*. Among MacMillan's priorities, however, was his own production of *The Sleeping Beauty*, a ballet he believed, like de Valois and Ashton before him, should be the keystone in any reputable company's repertoire. If the dancers could accomplish Petipa's classical choreography, they would be capable of managing whatever else was required of them. But first he needed to find out what their abilities were. In programming the forthcoming season, starting in September, he kept Tudor's production of *Giselle* going and selected triple bills of ballets already in the repertoire (including three by Cranko and one by Tatjana Gsovsky), while preparing the first evening of his own works for November 1966.

For this, he made *The Invitation* the centrepiece, thereby providing Seymour with a strong dramatic showcase. He cast Falco Kapuste opposite her as the young cousin (Gable's role), Rudolf Holz as the brutal husband and Vergie Derman as the wife. Performed by the Deutsche Oper company, the ballet took on a Germanic flavour reminiscent of Wedekind's *Spring Awakening*. MacMillan seized the opportunity to cut and rethink the acrobats' dance, and Georgiadis redesigned the set along simpler lines. (The costumes were on loan from the Royal Ballet's production.) An Austrian dancer in the company, jealous of Seymour, took out an unsuccessful injunction against the ballet on the grounds that it was 'overtly sexual' – a minor scandal that did no harm to the box office.

The Invitation was framed by two new works, the first of which was undermined by a last-minute difficulty. MacMillan had set his choreography to Ravel's *Mother Goose Suite* but shortly before the premiere Ravel's estate, notoriously reluctant to release his concert music for any other kind of performance, refused copyright permission. As a rapid resort, MacMillan adapted the choreography to fit the same composer's *Valses nobles et sentimentales*, which had already been used several times for ballet: he had danced as a very young man in Ashton's *Valses nobles* for the Sadler's Wells Theatre

Ballet. MacMillan had devised a slight narrative of a youth (Falco Kapuste) yearning for a girl (Didi Carli), narcissistically absorbed in her hand mirror. The man gradually weaned her from her reflection as four couples waltzed on and off. Seymour was aware that MacMillan could scarcely sleep before the premiere, gnawed with anxiety. 'He was so meticulous about every nuance in his work and to fit all these steps to another score was just a mind-boggling sort of task,' she said in the *Out of Line* documentary. 'To do all that and the rest of the programme within three months of arriving in Berlin . . . if that isn't enough to make anyone suddenly go "Help!" I don't know what would.' MacMillan later dismissed it as 'an awful ballet, created in a panic'.

The closing work, *Concerto*, to Shostakovich's Second Piano Concerto, was MacMillan's carefully considered primer for the company. He had previously intended to use the score, written in 1957, for a work for the Royal Ballet's touring company, so he already knew the music well. Fresh, witty and exhilarating, it had been written for Shostakovich's nineteen-year-old musician son Maxim and the Moscow Youth Orchestra. Full of cheek and mischief, the score might have been a character study of Maxim, whom his father hoped would be a concert pianist: Maxim became a conductor instead. MacMillan envisaged the ballet as an ensemble piece for as many of the Deutsche Oper dancers as he could fit on stage. Phalanxes of young people march and swivel in the first and last *allegro* movements, constantly changing direction. They move *en bloc*, so any errors or weaknesses are immediately evident. Since the girls' feet on pointe have no traction on the stage, they must use their inner thigh muscles to effect the swift changes; sloppy dancers are soon exposed. MacMillan was deliberately devising choreography that would improve the company's technical training, while giving soloists a chance to shine.

In addition, he was acutely conscious of Germany's Nazi past. The corps's massed drill is mock-militaristic, like a *jeu d'esprit* in response to its music, full of march rhythms. A comic marching exit for the women, arms swinging forcefully at the close of the first movement, is a parody of soldiers on parade. Since they are dressed in bright yellow and orange ballet tunics, the military reference is a light one, with no threatening overtones. The drill could simply be the aesthetic discipline of a corps de ballet, rehearsed to keep in line, on the beat. (The costumes, with white socks for the yellow-clad boys, were by Jürgen Rose, Cranko's preferred designer, as was the plain grey set.)

The second, soulful *andante* movement opens with a pas de deux based on warm-up stretches MacMillan had watched Seymour doing in a ballet studio as she readied herself for rehearsal. 'I used to become fascinated by what she was doing rather than what I was supposed to be doing, and I decided to incorporate the idea of the barre work into the choreography,' he recalled. The ballerina (Seymour, in the first cast) uses her male partner's arm for support as if she were holding on to a barre. Balanced on pointe in a fourth position that shows off the curves of her legs and feet, she stretches luxuriously forwards and backwards in a series of sweeping arcs. The man continues to support and promenade her throughout the pas de deux, balancing her at the end across his knees. The two dancers appear to be watching themselves objectively in a studio mirror, trying out shapes and angles, at the same time as enjoying the sensuality of their encounter. When their eyes meet at the beginning and end of the duet, a frisson of acknowledgement passes between them. Meanwhile, three couples have passed slowly behind them in silhouette, a moving frieze responding to Shostakovich's romantic melody.

Duets in the rest of the ballet are playful, with partners dancing alongside each other as youthful equals. The girl who leads the third movement originally had a partner: he was injured before the first night, so the woman's role was danced as a marathon solo, and has been ever since. *Concerto*, which remains a taxing ballet for any company, received a standing ovation at its premiere. Lucia Chase, present at the first night, asked if American Ballet Theatre could have it as soon as possible; Ashton (on the recommendation of David Webster) requested it for the Royal Ballet touring company; the Royal Swedish Ballet wanted it as well. MacMillan had thus launched his Berlin directorship with an instant international success. German critics noted enthusiastically that an exciting new era seemed to have dawned for the Deutsche Oper Ballet.

David Webster had flown to Berlin to represent the Royal Opera House at the first all-MacMillan evening. He had told his Board that he hoped to secure a new work from MacMillan for the following year at Covent Garden. After the Berlin performance, he assured

Kenneth privately that when Ashton retired in 1970, he, Kenneth MacMillan, would be the Royal Ballet's next director. Webster was envisaging a change of regime at the Royal Opera House when he himself retired in 1970. He had already privately told Clement Crisp, who had fulminated in the *Spectator* about the Royal Ballet letting MacMillan leave for Berlin, 'Don't worry, I'll have him back in three years.' Kenneth kept Webster's information to himself, telling no one in Berlin about it. There was to be no hint in later renegotiations of his three-year contract with the Deutsche Oper that he intended leaving at the end of it. On the contrary, his ambitions for the company appear to have been long-term ones, and his angry despair when he was thwarted indicated that he regarded his Berlin directorship as more than a stop-gap post. Webster's promise might have come to seem a mirage once things turned sour in Berlin.

They soon did. The atmosphere in the apartment was growing increasingly oppressive. Deutsche Oper schedules meant that the ballet company rehearsed after class in the morning until one o'clock, with time off in the afternoon; on non-performance days, rehearsals resumed at five and continued until ten at night. MacMillan expected his inner circle to return to the apartment with him for dinner, which he cooked as a way of winding down. It was a protracted process, according to Ray Barra: 'He'd say "I'm going to make fishcakes" and he'd put on his robe, get his tea (which was half whisky) and chain-smoke. We'd have to wait hours to eat, way after midnight. It could be agony, much as we loved Kenneth – he didn't have to get up as early as we did.'

When the flat's inmates were eventually able to retire to their beds, others, such as Vergie Derman and Ashley Lawrence, had to return to their 'pensions', their boarding houses near the theatre. Kenneth would wait up, unable to sleep, until Lynn Seymour was back in the flat. He was exasperated by her attitude towards her new life. She had launched on an affair with Falco Kapuste, her partner in *The Invitation*. She saw no reason why not: Kapuste was handsome, personable and eager to show her round Berlin; through him she was learning German and integrating herself in the city. She had put her broken marriage behind her and wanted to prove herself a liberated woman of the 1960s. Staying cooped up in the apartment, talking ballet shop, was not her idea of fun.

Kenneth complained bitterly about the affair to Ray Barra: 'How can she, with him? And she comes home at all hours, when she's meant to be fresh for class in the morning.' Kenneth was rapidly turning into his father, who had waited up, jealously and suspiciously, for his daughter Jean to return at night. Like his father, Kenneth suspected his authority was being challenged: Lynn was rejecting the family home he had set up, refusing to supply the utter loyalty he required. 'He wanted unconditional love,' says Seymour. 'But his love was conditional: "Be entirely available to me when I need you, otherwise you're betraying me."'

Seymour's availability became increasingly unpredictable. She scalded her leg by knocking over a coffee pot in the theatre and Kapuste rushed her to the emergency wing of a hospital. Rumour spread that the accident had happened while they were engaged in sex in her dressing-room. Although the story was false, the injury to Lynn's leg, while Kenneth was depending on her as his ballerina, further disturbed him. He turned vengefully on Kapuste, who, realising that his career was at stake, ended the affair. Seymour sank into lethargy and put on weight, as she did whenever she was low. Berlin was icy cold in winter and she developed a flu she could not shake off. Desperate to escape the claustrophobic flat, she flew back to London after Christmas and sought refuge with Georgina Parkinson and her photographer husband, Roy Round.

Seymour's doctor in London diagnosed a bad case of glandular fever and sent her to hospital to recover. While she was in London for six weeks, she went to see her and Kenneth's psychoanalyst, Dr Hardenberg. She described the situation in Berlin and told him that Kenneth was convinced she was malingering, deliberately letting him down. Hardenberg was concerned enough to write a letter to Kenneth in February 1967, assuring him that Lynn had indeed had a debilitating illness and that her depression before she left was largely due to the onset of glandular fever. He asked Kenneth to come and see him when he next returned to London.

MacMillan meanwhile remained in the Reichstrasse flat, having invited Vergie Derman to move in while Seymour was away. Derman did her best to keep him cheerful, as he fretted about the pettiness of German bureaucracy. The Opera House finance department had refused to pay for his numerous long-distance telephone calls from the apartment (instead of his office) and objected to the expense of travel fares for the people he had brought with him. He felt his new-found status as Director was being undermined. More importantly, he was confronted with financial problems over his plans for the company's future. He and Intendant Sellner had been in accord that it should develop into the National Ballet of Germany. For that to happen, MacMillan believed that it needed its own school to train its dancers in a unified style. He proposed transforming Tatjana Gsovsky's private school into the official Deutsche Oper Ballet School.

He had invited de Valois to Berlin to launch the school and advise him on his planned production of *The Sleeping Beauty*. Her proposed fee and expenses had been discussed, but in the absence of any confirmation from the Deutsche Oper, she had gone instead to look after the Turkish State Ballet on its first ever foreign tour to Bulgaria. She had helped found the Turkish company and ballet school, and was a very active artistic adviser. As well as ballets by her, the Turkish company's repertoire contained MacMillan's *Solitaire* and *The Burrow*. She wrote chattily to MacMillan, addressing him affectionately as 'Kenneth, dear' and apologising for being unavailable. 'What is Lynn up to?' she asked. 'I hear stories of boiling kettles pouring themselves over her knees. Not possible – except in her ever accident-prone case.' At the end of her letter, de Valois offered a possible later date for her visit. British dance writers had evidently been informed of her plans, for both Andrew Porter in the *Financial Times* and Alexander Bland in *Dancing Times* mentioned at the start of 1967 that she was due to start up a ballet school in Berlin.

Nothing, however, was reported in the Berlin press and nothing came of the scheme for a company school. Instead, Gsovsky, with Reinholm, re-established her private school on Fasanenstrasse as the Berlin Dance Academy: both she and Reinholm taught there. The Deutsche Oper's subsidy from the Berlin Senate was not as generous as MacMillan had supposed and the municipal authorities were reluctant to take on the cost of a training establishment. Disquiet was also being voiced early in 1967 about the probable cost of the *Sleeping Beauty* production. The opera company was doing new productions of Wagner's *Ring* and Stravinsky's *The Rake's Progress* in the spring; the budget would not stretch to an expensive ballet as well.

MacMillan, however, had already commissioned Barry Kay as the designer and invited him to stay during the planning stages in the Reichstrasse flat. Kay, an Australian who had studied art and design in Paris, was a good friend as well as an experienced theatrical designer. They had met through Peter Darrell, when MacMillan had done *The Seven Deadly Sins* for Western Theatre Ballet in 1961. Kay had designed Darrell's *Salade* then, and *Images of Love* for MacMillan three years later. His most recent ballet designs had been a much admired palatial white-and-gold setting for Nureyev's production of *Raymonda* Act III for the Royal Ballet. That kind of splendour was what MacMillan had in mind for *The Sleeping Beauty*. Germany, he believed, had never experienced a production that did justice to Tchaikovsky's music, Petipa's choreography and the magnificence of the original Mariinsky setting in St Petersburg.

Together, he and Kay conjured up images of imperial grandeur, recalling the court of Tsar Alexander III at the time the ballet was first performed in 1890. West Berlin's production of *Dornröschen*, as *The Sleeping Beauty* is known in German, should evoke the Tsarist era, thereby challenging East Berlin's claims to be inheritors of the Russian ballet tradition. The Deutsche Oper management, however, did not see why such opulence was necessary for an old fairy-tale ballet. Sellner and his deputy, Seefehlner, were taken aback by the grandiose maquette Kay produced in February 1967. They asked for modifications to make the sets less expensive and easier for stage hands to dismount before opera performances. MacMillan was outraged. He wrote an angry letter to Sellner on 4 March 1967, saying that he felt betrayed and disappointed. He had been led to believe that he would have the full support of the management for everything he required, since they were using his name and reputation to build up their theatre: 'I do *Dornröschen* not out of personal interest but to help the Deutsche Oper. My time and ideas are precious to me, and I cannot waste my ideas in Berlin if they are not really needed.' In the first of a series of threats to resign, he said that since he was not prepared to make the sacrifices the management required, it would be better he left.

Sellner wrote back in alarm, pleading budget constraints and lack of time for forward-planning. He stated that he was fully committed to supporting MacMillan and was trying to find more money for *Dornröschen* and more performances for the company. The correspondence is preserved in an official file MacMillan retained after his departure from Berlin. The tone of his own letters, dictated in English and then translated into German, is peremptory. Sellner's responses are placating, asking for MacMillan's understanding of the administration's difficulties. Although Sellner writes in formal German, he signs off warmly (and he took pains to send Kenneth birthday greetings for 11 December each year). There is no indication on record that he opposed MacMillan's plans for the company. Hostile letters appear only towards the final dates in the file, and they are from other management figures, not Intendant Sellner.

A budget for *The Sleeping Beauty* was eventually agreed in April 1967: DM 183,000 for the sets, DM 200,000 for the costumes, on top of Kay's fee. The production therefore cost far more than the DM 160,000 allocated for the opera's entire *Ring* cycle, designed by Fritz Wotruba. There was insufficient time to prepare for *The Sleeping Beauty*'s projected premiere on 7 May, so the production was postponed until the annual Berlin arts festival in October. MacMillan put in writing his insistence to Sellner that the production must be 'perfect'; there must be no further demands that Kay compromise his designs. Sellner guaranteed that the workshops would have everything ready well in time for technical rehearsals in September, and that the premiere would definitely take place on 9 October 1967. He regretted that *Das Lied von der Erde*, originally planned for the company to perform in the Berlin festival, would have to be abandoned.

MacMillan's letters show that he was backing Kay to the hilt, as he had done with Georgiadis over the *Romeo and Juliet* designs. His other motive in fighting for an opulent production might have been to outdo the scale of the Royal Ballet's *Sleeping Beauty*: he would show de Valois and Ashton what he could accomplish, staged in a theatre far better equipped than the Royal Opera House. He was also safeguarding himself and the company against inadequate performance standards in a technically demanding ballet. Audiences would be overwhelmed by the setting instead of scrutinising the dancing.

His victory over the bureaucrats was a pyrrhic one. The Deutsche Oper management (like many of the German ballet critics) would rather he spent his energies and budgets on his own works, preferably ones unique to the Berlin company. The expensive, postponed *Sleeping Beauty* meant that there was little money left for other ballets scheduled for that season. MacMillan now needed to supply a ballet without a design budget within the period originally scheduled for the *Sleeping Beauty* performances in early summer.

He told Sellner that he had an idea in mind but was worried about the legal implications. He was intrigued by the story of Anna Anderson, the woman who claimed to be Grand Duchess Anastasia, youngest daughter of Tsar Nicholas II. The imperial Romanov family had been executed in 1918 but there were persistent rumours that one or more members had managed to escape. False Romanovs abounded, promoted by people who hoped to lay their hands on supposedly hoarded riches. The woman calling herself Anna Anderson had been rescued from drowning in a Berlin canal in 1920 and taken to a mental hospital. There she convinced (or was convinced by) White Russian exiles that she remembered details about imperial court life only an insider would know. Her supporters encouraged her to pursue a series of court cases in Germany over the years to establish her right to be recognised as a Romanov.

Gert Reinholm recalled discussing a newspaper report of her latest legal appeal in Hamburg over a meal with MacMillan in early 1967. Kenneth was fascinated by the woman's determined quest to prove her identity. He had read her 'autobiography', *I, Anastasia*, and was inclined to believe Anna Anderson was indeed the Grand Duchess. In any case, as he confirmed later in a 1971 piece in *About the House*, 'I found in her story a theme that has sometimes appeared in my work before: the Outsider figure. Anastasia seems to me a supreme example of this.' He intended to base a ballet on Anderson's claim to be Anastasia, but Reinholm warned him that she and her supporters, notoriously litigious, might sue if he used episodes from her book. Sellner's opinion was sought. He advised MacMillan to trust his own creative instincts and not to worry about lawyers: ballets were hardly likely to be regarded as chronicles of historical truth.

MacMillan duly went ahead. Seymour had recovered from her glandular fever after a long period of physical weakness, barely able to struggle through daily class with the company. She had reinstalled herself in the Reichstrasse flat and, despite the tension between her and Kenneth, she was determined to be involved in his new work. She had read *I, Anastasia* and seen, as he had, romanticised films about the Grand Duchess's supposed fate. With Seymour in the role of Anna/Anastasia, MacMillan intended to evoke the woman's nightmarish experiences in a dramatic work that took advantage of the Deutsche Oper's modern stage machinery. When he mentioned his ideas to Ashley Lawrence, the Music Director swiftly came up with the proposal of Martinů's *Fantaisies symphoniques*, 'which bowled me over. I will never forget his smile of pride and pleasure at having helped me so quickly,' Kenneth recalled in his memorial tribute to Lawrence in 1990.

The one-act ballet, like Anderson's account of her life, starts in a clinic. Anna/Anastasia sits with her nurses, backs to the audience, watching a screen on which the (real) Imperial family appears in black-and-white snatches of film. The Romanov home movies came from a documentary compilation called *Vom Zaren bis Stalin* ('From Tsar to Stalin'). In the ballet, the film clips are supposed to be part of Anna/Anastasia's therapy, though their disconnected, flickering images also serve as a dramatic expression of her mental turmoil. The Berlin Technical University provided a tape of *musique concrète*, made in the students' sound laboratory, which sets the opening scene in a timeless limbo.

When the orchestra joins in with Martinů's restless, fragmented Sixth Symphony, the 'woman who calls herself Anastasia' is now seated alone on her bed (like Juliet), trying to hang on to her few certainties. Her feet trace the line of the floorboards; she inspects her hand, shows it urgently to her warders and visitors – 'Look, this is me, here is my life story written on my palm.' Her hand held in front of her face could also be a mirror, reflecting her identity. She places her hand on her heart, its thumping beat heard in Martinů's music. She confuses past and present, reliving incidents at the Imperial court and on her escape journey, helped by Russian peasants, as she tries to convince her royal 'relatives' of what she remembers. They reject her but cannot ultimately shake her core belief in who she is. At the end of the ballet, she stands like a ship's figurehead at the prow of her bed as it sails round the stage, a small defiant figure floating on a sea of darkness.

Since there was no design budget, Barry Kay selected and adapted costumes from the opera wardrobe; others were hired from a German television company that had done a play from the right period. The performance area was extended beyond the upstage trapdoors to the rear wall, making it a deep, dusky void, 'like the inside of Anastasia's head', according to Seymour. The bed was placed on the stage's sliding revolve. Copious onstage rehearsal time originally scheduled for *The Sleeping Beauty* meant that MacMillan, Kay and the stage staff could experiment with a technically avant-garde production. Instead of looking makeshift for lack of a budget, the concise, one-act *Anastasia* was to be MacMillan's best-realised Expressionist work.

While he was still creating *Anastasia*, MacMillan had taken a weekend off to visit Stuttgart, for the first time since he had moved to Berlin. His experience *en route* was to feed directly into the work-in-progress. Cranko had invited him to see new works performed by the Stuttgart company during its May Ballet Week. Kenneth asked Vergie Derman, who had remained a flatmate after Seymour's return, to go with him by train. They set off without taking into account the requirement for visas to travel through East German territory. MacMillan's previous travel had been arranged by the Deutsche Oper staff, who assumed that, by now, he knew about East Germany's visa regulations; Derman, who had so far flown in and out of Berlin, had yet to travel by rail. After starting their journey, they were removed from the train by East German border guards and told to wait while their papers were examined. Since neither of them spoke German, it took some time to establish that they had to return to Berlin and obtain the necessary visas from the East German authorities there. Armed soldiers with dogs watched over them while they sat waiting for the next train back. Kenneth kept whispering to Vergie that he was in a panic and had an urgent desire to get up and run. She told him that he risked being shot and warned him not to reach for cigarettes or his hipflask of whisky.

She succeeded in restraining him from bolting until the train back to Berlin arrived. It was rigorously searched by armed guards before the two frightened foreigners were allowed to board. Once back in West Berlin, they obtained travel visas by crossing to the Eastern sector through Checkpoint Charlie. They then faced an interminable queue for a taxi to return to the Western sector, so they walked the long way back. Kennneth had insisted on returning to the familiar safety of the Reichstrasse apartment, where he passed out with stress and exhaustion. Derman, refusing to be deterred, bought tickets for the late-night train to Stuttgart and persuaded him to risk the journey once more. They clutched their precious visas as they sat up through the night, glared at by other passengers in the crowded compartment if Kenneth so much as dared open a cigarette packet.

He was in no state to appreciate the ballet performances when they eventually arrived in Stuttgart. Cranko nonetheless secured a promise from him to make a work for the company, which seemed an oasis of warmth and goodwill after the trials of Berlin. On his return to resume work on *Anastasia*, MacMillan intensified the heroine's terror of soldiers, who threatened to kill her as they had executed her family. The starched nurses in the Berlin clinic became even more overpowering authority figures, casting doubt on her identity. Like Anna/Anastasia, Kenneth felt adrift in a foreign land, hemmed in by an officialdom whose arbitrary demands he did not fully understand.

Anastasia's premiere in June was threatened by yet another Seymour disaster. Soaping herself in her bath one morning in May, she noticed that one arm was swollen and severely discoloured. During the previous week, she had been repeatedly rehearsing a lift with powerful Rudolf Holz as her character's peasant husband, who gripped her upper arm as she struggled. She showed the alarming bruise to Ray Barra over the breakfast table. They watched in horror as the congested arm ballooned before their eyes. Barra hastily telephoned for a doctor, who was unable to tell what was wrong. When the swelling grew even worse overnight, a second doctor diagnosed a thrombosis in her arm that might easily travel to her heart: he called an ambulance to take her immediately to hospital. She had to remain there for weeks while the blood clot was dissolved with drugs. She was warned not to take her arm out of its sling and not to think of dancing until she was out of danger.

While Seymour worried about missing her forthcoming performances of *Anastasia*, MacMillan went into a tailspin of anxiety about his ballet. He telephoned frantically in search of Georgina Parkinson to stand in for Lynn; he did not feel he could communicate well enough with a German understudy. He eventually located Parkinson on tour with the Royal Ballet in Montreal and secured Ashton's agreement for her to leave the tour and fly to Berlin. (The

Deutsche Oper finance department, once again alarmed at the cost of the long-distance calls and airfare, insisted he paid all the bills from his own salary.) Parkinson stayed in the Reichsstrasse flat for two and half weeks while she rapidly learned Seymour's role. She and Vergie Derman shared the responsibility of reassuring Kenneth so that *Anastasia* could be completed on time. It was to be in a programme with two of his earlier ballets, *Diversions* and *Solitaire*, whose entry into the company repertoire he needed to supervise.

Faith Worth, the Royal Ballet's notator, had also been staying in the flat while she taught *Diversions* and *Solitaire* from their Benesh scores to the Berlin casts. She remembers the atmosphere in the apartment as being 'absolutely poisonous' before Parkinson arrived:

Kenneth was criticising people behind their backs, taking out his tensions by badmouthing his friends to each other. He could be very manipulative. I was sleeping on a settee in the central living room and he'd keep me up until 4 a.m., complaining. Then I had to get to the theatre in the morning while he stayed in bed.

Parkinson's friendly presence in the flat distracted Kenneth for a while, though she, too, was alarmed by the state he was in:

He couldn't sleep, he was drinking far too much and eating fatty fried comfort food. He disguised the drinking by putting whisky in his tea all day but people around him knew. Nobody could do anything. He was a very complicated man who couldn't deal with his emotional side. He was demanding too much of people, straining the limits of their friendship, and then pushing them away, complaining that he was lonely.

He was deeply resentful of Lynn for imperilling the premiere of *Anastasia*, even though the thrombosis was hardly her fault. She had grown bored and restless in hospital, craving distraction from her worries about her health and career. Gossip reached Kenneth that she had started another affair and was planning to move out of the flat. Determined to perform her role, she defied her doctors' advice and returned in time for the final rehearsals. MacMillan asked Parkinson to step aside and dance the lead girl in *Solitaire* instead. He refused to speak to Seymour directly, so Parkinson tried to mediate between them. She left for London in relief, glad to escape but worried about those left behind. She assured Kenneth that he could seek refuge with her and her husband whenever he needed to come to London.

Anastasia was given in a tense political context. Three weeks before its premiere, students had demonstrated outside the Deutsche Oper theatre in protest at the visit of the Shah of Persia to an opera performance on 2 June 1967. The demonstration was dispersed by police but the violence escalated and later the same evening, a Berlin student, Benno Ohnesorg, was shot dead. Ohnesorg quickly became a martyr of police brutality, fuelling hostility between protesters and state authorities. Although one commentator later claimed that the disparity between riots on the streets and the illusionary world of ballet inside the opera house had rarely been more blatant, *Anastasia* was not remote from reality. The accusation might have carried more weight had the ballet in question been the fairy-tale *Sleeping Beauty*, as originally scheduled. Audiences for *Anastasia* were exposed to the fear and confusion of a flesh-and-blood woman at the mercy of forces beyond her control. MacMillan was, on his own terms, in tune with the turbulent spirit of the time.

26

By the summer of 1967, the Reichstrasse flat had been deserted by its occupants. Vergie Derman had gone back to London to marry her television-producer boyfriend, David Harrison. Ray Barra had moved out in order to live with his boyfriend, Maximo, a dancer from the Stuttgart company who had the same surname (though Ray's had been shortened from Barrilobre). Seymour found the prospect of remaining in the flat without Barra as a buffer between her and Kenneth too awful to contemplate. She was now involved in a relationship with Eike Walcz, a dancer in the Deutsche Oper corps de ballet. Half German, half Polish, he had come to dancing late after a chequered early career. Lynn found him interesting and fanciable; Kenneth disapproved of him. She and Walcz set up house together in the suburb of Grunewald in order to escape from the claustrophobia of the ballet company. MacMillan's substitute family had dispersed in order to lead their own lives, unable to bear the tension of living under the same roof as him. The rent on the big, expensive Reichsstrasse flat would still have to be paid until the end of the lease but their freedom was worth the price.

MacMillan abandoned the empty apartment and went to London during the summer break. He stayed with Georgina Parkinson and Roy Round in their house in Battersea, and resumed his psychoanalytic sessions with Dr Hardenberg. These were the last occasions on which he was able to see Hardenberg, who died in September 1967. When MacMillan returned to Berlin, he moved into a small canalside flat on Helgoländer Ufer, living on his own. He never completed his unpacking, camping like a squatter among boxes and suitcases, the debris of his hopes of a life in Berlin to match Cranko's in Stuttgart.

There had been no conspiracy to leave MacMillan to his own devices. 'We didn't discuss it among ourselves,' says Seymour. 'He'd started to make life so unpleasant for us that we just had to find our own ways of dealing with it as best we could.' She believes that he needed someone to blame for how bad he was feeling: he did not want to admit that the blackness was within himself. 'Leaving the Royal Ballet did something fundamental to him,' she says.

The powers-that-be in the company had always exerted great influence over him. Their opinion of him meant a great deal to him because he didn't have a very high one of himself. And when they freely let him go, he thought it was because they didn't value him, which made him feel unbelievably shitty. He went to Berlin without a leg to stand on and he just perched there, dying to be called back.

He had been drinking heavily even before he was obliged to live on his own, when his alcoholism became acute. 'It had become hard to cover up for him when he didn't show up at the theatre,' says Barra. 'We'd know he was still in bed in his dressing-gown, drinking a bottle and a half of whisky and missing the morning rehearsal.' On one occasion, when MacMillan had failed to arrive for a morning rehearsal and Barra had taken charge in his place, their working relationship was strained to breaking point:

We had a limited amount of time on stage for rehearsal. Class was over, everyone was on stage ready to start. No Kenneth. Gert Reinholm said we couldn't waste time. I was First Ballet Master, so I started the rehearsal. Kenneth came in later, very upset and wouldn't speak to me. Gert told me

Kenneth was out of his mind that I'd gone ahead without him: 'Who did I think I was?'; 'I wanted his job.' It was the bottle talking.

Both Barra and Seymour believe that MacMillan could not have lasted as Director without Reinholm's support. Kenneth genuinely liked and trusted him, sensing, perhaps, that here was a fellow loner. Reinholm, a strikingly handsome man, kept himself aloof from the dancers: he had been in charge of them, alongside Tatjana Gsovsky, and would become their director some while after MacMillan had left. The company's interests were his own, and he did not want to see it, or Kenneth, brought down. In Seymour's opinion,

Gert was very clever at reading people. He understood his own strengths and weaknesses and knew he wasn't a creator. He recognised Kenneth's great talent, but he also saw the small vulnerable boy there. He looked after him and jollied him along. He was Kenneth's liaison man with the Oper management, trying to get him what he wanted.

Reinholm remained loyal to MacMillan to the end, never acknowledging that he knew how much Kenneth drank: 'He was not openly drunk while he was working. I never saw him drunk.' He humoured Kenneth, inviting him to his summer home in Bavaria, where they walked in the woods with Gert's dog. Snapshots of the holiday show MacMillan at ease, playing chess with Reinholm on the chalet's terrace or cuddling the dog. In 1982, in the *Sunday Express* colour magazine, he would claim, 'In three years in Berlin I only once went into someone's home and I was really desperately lonely.' Reinholm did what he could to keep MacMillan on an even keel, but Kenneth was locked in his sense of isolation.

He evidently wrote despairingly to his eldest sister, Jean, who tried to comfort him in her letter in reply: 'I'm sorry you should hate it so, Ken, you will have to alter your way of life somehow and get more happiness from it.' She admitted, however, that her solution was unlikely to appeal to him: 'I have visions at times of you having a big country house here and you have all the family and your friends around you, but I suppose that is just a pipe dream of mine.' Jean was busy running a boarding house in Great Yarmouth with her husband, Arthur, keeping in regular touch with the rest of the family there and in Scotland. Their brother George, who now had two daughters, also ran a boarding house in Yarmouth with his wife, Frances. Betty was already a grandmother, and Jean was to be godmother to one of the new babies. Jean's regular news of supper-dances, weddings and christenings must have reinforced Kenneth's sense of alienation from his past, as well as from the city in which he was now living. 'I just feel that you don't really want to come home at all now,' Jean wrote, adding, 'However, I still love you.'

His most pressing concern was to mount the postponed produc-tion of *The Sleeping Beauty* for its 8 October premiere. Vergie Derman had returned after her wedding to dance the role of the Lilac Fairy; Seymour was the first-cast Aurora, with Rudolf Holz as her Prince. MacMillan was still refusing to speak to Lynn directly. His instructions were conveyed through Barra and others: 'Why is she doing that?' he would ask; 'Tell her to do such and such.' Seymour put up with the indignity because she had no option. 'He'd started doing that during *Anastasia*. I thought it was because he was in a bad way and that he'd get over it. We'd uprooted, he and I, to come to Berlin because we wanted to be productive creatively – and we were. You concentrate on what you have to do and that's all that matters.'

Seymour had danced Aurora with the touring company (though not the Covent Garden one), so she knew the role well. MacMillan, in his production, remained faithful to the Petipa choreography that had been passed on to the Royal Ballet by the exiled Russian répéti-teur Nicholas Sergeyev in the 1930s. In an article for the *Deutsche Oper* magazine, he wrote:

Some variations I have cut entirely and some ensemble numbers I have shortened or rechoreographed after the style of Petipa. With the collabora-tion of Barry Kay, I have set this production in a very Russian setting . . . to me, the music epitomises all that is grand and traditional in the time of the Tsar. It is amazing that this ballet has survived all these years since its conception, but it must be proof of the durability of the brilliant inventions of Petipa that this is so. I hope the German public will see and appreciate the beginnings of all modern classical ballet.

MacMillan's own choreographic contributions came mainly in the third act, which took place in a glittering imperial palace that Anastasia might have recognised. Reverting to Petipa's original scheme of variations for Jewel Fairies near the start of the wedding celebrations, he devised a pas de sept in place of the Florestan and his Sisters pas de trois he used to dance in de Valois's production.

He aimed to conclude the celebrations with a large-scale mazurka, bringing on thirty dancers for a grand finale. Dissatisfied with what he had set in rehearsal, he asked Tatjana Gsovsky to help arrange folk-dance choreography for the mazurka in the flamboyant style of the Soviet Moiseyev troupe. He then adapted her arrangements into the effects he wanted. The mazurka, which started out as a stately procession, developed into a spectacular parade-ground wheeling ensemble, its tempi accelerating as it progressed.

Kay's elaborate set designs featured a huge curving staircase placed on the stage's revolve, which turned to suggest the Prince's journey in search of the sleeping Princess. The staircase then became part of a wedding-cake structure, down which entered the fairy-tale characters attending the marriage of Aurora and her Prince, blessed by a Russian Orthodox priest. Clement Crisp, who travelled to Berlin to review MacMillan's production for the *Financial Times*, described it as

impossibly opulent, imperially fantastic. Kay's sets glow in gold and cream, his stupendous costumes, encrusted with jewels and embroidery, complement this scheme in muted colours that reflect back gold on gold . . . This is a real court, packed with real aristocrats – the Berlin supers have a tremendous time, and the stage is big enough to use them properly – and into it the Fairies appear as brilliantly magical beings.

The drawback to the opulence was that the heavy sets took at least forty minutes to change between acts. Barra suspects the management told the stage hands to be brutal, both to save time and to damage the props and sets so they could not be used for long: 'They got rid of half of it by the time Kenneth left, or just did the third act as *Aurora's Wedding* – it was a completely impractical production.' The impracticality might have been MacMillan's deliberate defiance of an opera-house system that favoured elaborate opera productions and expected ballets to fit discreetly into the schedule. It should be remembered, however, that he had no experience of accommodating an opera-house repertory system: his only previous large-scale ballet, *Romeo and Juliet*, had been the Royal Ballet's responsibility, not his own. He and Kay might not fully have appreciated what a liability their grandiloquent *Sleeping Beauty* would prove to be.

Descriptions of the designs dominated the reviews. Although British critics who came to see the production (Crisp for the

Financial Times, John Percival for *The Times*, Noel Goodwin for the *Daily Express*, Alexander Bland for the *Observer* and *Dancing Times*) were impressed by their splendour, German critics felt that they were an end in themselves and distracted from the choreography. Seymour's performance as Aurora met with only qualified praise. She was not in good shape after her glandular fever and thrombosis, and the testing role exposed her weaknesses. She told her biographer, Richard Austin, that years later, 'I wake up in the night, quaking, thinking of it.' She sensed that Kenneth blamed her for the disappointing response to his hard-fought production. After the first performances in October, she abdicated the role in favour of Didi Carli, the young Argentinian dancer of whom MacMillan had high hopes.

Although the German critics' views of *The Sleeping Beauty* were muted, they were far from hostile. MacMillan claimed, however, in interviews in Britain a few weeks later that his efforts were unappreciated. He might not have had the reviews properly translated: he misunderstood a critic's remark that the Deutsche Oper would be better served by MacMillan's original work than by his production of a traditional Petipa ballet. Klaus Geitel in *Die Welt* was making the point that Berliners had been hoping for 'their' full-length MacMillan ballet to rival Cranko's creations for Stuttgart. They wanted something up to date, not a reproduction of a ballet other companies performed. MacMillan thought, wrongly, that Geitel was disparaging Petipa's choreography and that he and other German critics were dismissive of what Kenneth had achieved for the company by bringing them his vision of *The Sleeping Beauty*.

During a break at the end of October, MacMillan and Seymour returned to London, and were jointly interviewed by Sydney Edwards in the *Evening Standard*. Relieved to be back in England, however briefly, both made statements they would later regret. Seymour said that she was intending to abandon ballet, and Berlin, for Broadway. She had been offered the chance to appear as the leading lady in a musical that would then be transferred to the screen. The idea was being developed by Herbert Ross and Ray Stark, who had worked together on the musical, *Funny Girl*, which was soon to be released as a film starring Barbra Streisand. Ross had recommended Seymour for the lead in the new musical, and had flown her to New York during the summer to meet Stark and the proposed scriptwriter, the playwright Terence Rattigan. 'I'm trying to keep cool about New York,' Seymour said to the *Standard*. 'I told them I would accept the role. It will probably open next June. It is all about a dancer. All I have to do is speak and dance – other people do the singing.'

Her proposed defection to showbusiness had not improved her strained relationship with MacMillan, who had counted on her to be his star in Berlin. In her view, though, the future seemed so uncertain that she needed to manage her own career. She could not believe Kenneth would remain in Berlin for long and, as she told Sydney Edwards, there was nothing for her at the Royal Ballet. In the event, she heard no more from Broadway or from Hollywood. The Deutsche Oper Ballet remained her best option, at least for the time being.

MacMillan was undiplomatically candid in his interview with Edwards about Berlin, the Deutsche Oper and the Germans. He said that he was glad he had gone to Berlin but did not want to stay. He recounted his frightening experience of being 'hauled off a train at gunpoint and surrounded by big dogs because I did not have the right kind of visa'. The Germans, he said, were very cold and formal, without spontaneity. 'There is a great deal of resentment that I'm English but I can't do much about that. The ballet company is attached to the Opera House and I've got more money out of them than anyone else, mainly through threats. They are now slowly understanding what having a good ballet company involves and they are not liking it very much.'

His remarks were reported back in Berlin, where they did not go down well. Nor did his quoted criticism of the dancers' union for being

appallingly difficult to work with. If two of the corps de ballet are in an opera then I can't use the rest of the dancers at a rehearsal: the union say, 'The corps de ballet are working tonight.' They fix the working hours . . . so there's no social life. I haven't been to a play or a movie since I've been there. And I haven't spoken to anyone in English except Lynn and Vergie Derman.

In complaining about his life in Berlin, he was effectively damning himself for failing to learn German and to make the most of what the city had to offer.

He had come to London to discuss a new work for the Royal Ballet and to secure Ashton's approval for the Deutsche Oper to perform his *Scènes de ballet* during the Ballet Week in March 1968. Ashton was willing to let the work be taught from its notated score and hoped to visit Berlin to supervise the final rehearsals. He evidently had no inkling of Webster's plan to make MacMillan his successor by 1970 – news that would break sooner than anyone involved suspected.

Back at the Helgoländer Ufer flat over the 1967 winter, surrounded by unopened packing cases, Kenneth was sinking further into depression. He was looking puffy and unwell; for the photograph with Lynn in the *Evening Standard*, he had refused to take off the dark glasses he had worn to hide his eyes. His sister Jean wrote to him for Christmas, saying, as ever, 'I wish you could come home but I know that doesn't appeal to you – So Happy Christmas, dear.' Jean's wistful urgings merely made him more aware than ever that he had no home, either in Britain or Berlin.

He brooded over his battles with the Deutsche Oper administration, who had informed him that, because of *The Sleeping Beauty*'s expense, there was no money for sets for the next season's repertoire. *Scènes de ballet*, for example, would have to be danced in black tutus against a plain background, instead of in its original André Beaurepaire designs. Ashton sent a telegram of regret that he was unable to visit Berlin, but gave his permission for the spare setting. He evidently put considerable faith in MacMillan's judgement as a director, for this was the first time an Ashton ballet had been mounted in the choreographer's absence, entirely from notation. At MacMillan's urgent request, Monica Parker, a former dancer and teacher of ballet who was employed by the Benesh Institute of Choreology, had been sent to Berlin by Joan Benesh. Faith Worth was no longer available and MacMillan could not function without a notator. The Deutsche Oper had reluctantly agreed to fund a resident notator, provided she also taught as a ballet mistress at Gsovsky's school.

When Monica Parker had visited Berlin earlier in 1967 to audition for both posts, she had seen *Anastasia* in performance and was bowled over by the ballet and its creative team. She readily agreed to move to Berlin, even though the hours she would have to work left her without any free time. Only twenty-three, she was already experienced at working with notated scores. She soon became MacMillan's trusted aide and the principal teacher and producer of his ballets. He knew he could depend on her formidable memory, accurate eye and speedy notation; above all, she was totally loyal, the safest recorder of his intentions.

Soon after arriving in Berlin, she mounted *Scènes de ballet* and started notating his latest ballet, *Olympiade*, due for March 1968. Set to Stravinsky's *Symphony in Three Movements*, it favoured the company's male contingent, who otherwise had little to do in the rest of the programme: Fokine's *Les Sylphides*, Ashton's *Scènes de ballet* and the first Berlin performances of *Las Hermanas*. MacMillan's response to Stravinsky's vigorous music might have been inspired by television coverage of preparations for the Olympic Games, held in Mexico later in 1968. The choreography was full of sporting metaphors, with suggestions of liaisons between the male athletes and the select handful of women. Since there was no money for designs, he chose the outfits himself, putting the men in T-shirts and gym trousers, and the women, who included Seymour, in short pleated tennis skirts. Tennis had yet to be accepted as an Olympic sport, but the ballet nonetheless included a mixed-doubles match.

Olympiade met with an unenthusiastic reception from the German press, who found it and the Ballet Week programme disappointingly drab. The only vivid designs were those for *Las Hermanas*, the set and costumes borrowed from the Stuttgart Ballet. MacMillan wrote a formal letter to Sellner, declaring that he wanted to end his contract and listing the reasons why. (The letter was dictated in English to his German secretary, who then translated it.) He rehearsed many of the same complaints as the year before, saying that he had not been given the opportunity to create 'a real international ballet company'. 'I heard only, "You can have everything you want" . . . the fact that you promise everything to me personally and not the ballet company I find one of the biggest problems.' He felt that although his name as a choreographer was being used to build up the company's reputation, he was given no real responsibility as a director: 'The position is that of a secretary.'

'As I see it, the only real interest you have is to avoid problems leaking out to the public. After all the talk about the cost of *Dornröschen*, I made a sacrifice with the March premieres at your wish and in the end we showed everybody this sacrifice, which helps neither you nor I.' He was presumably referring to the spare settings for *Olympiade* and *Scènes de ballet* and poor performances of the new works. He blamed the 'bad spirit' of the dancers on the *Gewerkschaft* attitude of the union and the management's lack of interest in the ballet company.

He voiced his criticisms publicly in an interview with *Der Tagesspiegel* published on 1 May 1968. It was one of the few times he spoke to the German press, in an attempt to present the problems he faced with the management and with the audience's expectations. The article was headed 'Disappointed in Berlin'. A member of the public wrote to the paper in response, claiming, 'Berlin is disappointed in this artist from Great Britain.' In her published letter, Ingrid Seidel said that she resented MacMillan's disparaging remarks about Berlin audiences, and she took him to task for failing to interest Intendant Sellner sufficiently in ballet to secure the budgets and number of performances he wanted. 'Why blame Berlin?' she asked. 'Where are the great ballets by Mr MacMillan we were promised? Why could he not prove his ability with more of his own ballets instead of so often inviting guests? Is the Chief Choreographer of the Deutsche Oper aware of the fact that Berlin is also disappointed in him?'

MacMillan might have been spoiling for a fight because he knew he had little to lose. The Royal Ballet was about to announce that he would become its Artistic Director in 1970, when Ashton retired. The timing of the announcement on 26 April 1968, over two years in advance, took many people by surprise: it had been precipitated by rumours within the Royal Ballet, started by Ashton and his supporters – rumours that were spreading like wildfire. According to Gert Reinholm, the Deutsche Oper staff had been kept in the dark: 'Nobody in Berlin had heard that the directorship of the Royal Ballet was under discussion. I had advised Kenneth to stay in Berlin for a long period, to set the foundation for future achievements, such as the creation of a wider repertoire, a training school, and touring to other theatres. I did not think he intended to leave so soon.' Kenneth had, however, informed Monica Parker back in December 1967 that he intended to leave Berlin in mid-1969, without telling her why.

As far as MacMillan was concerned, the promise David Webster had made to him at the start of his stay in Berlin was no longer a mirage. He had already threatened to resign as Ballet Director of the Deutsche Oper several times before in order to get what he wanted; now he meant it. He had not mentioned his future post with the Royal Ballet in his latest resignation letter to Sellner, probably because it would have blunted the impact of his complaints. He was not, however, in a position to leave at once: he still had to serve out the year's notice required in his contract. He simply handed over his administrative responsibilities to Gert Reinholm for the rest of his time in Berlin. MacMillan retained the title of Chief Choreographer, while Reinholm, at his own request, was billed as Deputy Ballet Director. 'It was strange that nobody commented on the lack of a ballet director, merely a deputy for an imaginary position,' noted Reinholm. 'But I did not want a title that made me seem MacMillan's superior.'

27

The Royal Ballet was thrown into disarray by the abrupt announcement that MacMillan was to replace Ashton in two years' time. The lack of preparation (the company was on tour in New York when the news broke) was the result of David Webster's mishandling of a sensitive situation. Ashton had apparently been totally unaware that he would be required to retire once he turned sixty-five. He had often said how much he looked forward to retiring, but as he told his biographer, Julie Kavanagh, he had wanted everyone to beg him to keep going. As de Valois commented to Kavanagh, 'He was always boasting that he was off as soon as his time was up. To such an extent that we all believed him. He'd pretend he didn't want to stay on; and he rather overplayed it and misled a lot of people.' Ashton craved reassurance that the Royal Ballet needed him, but his bluff was called, just as he had called Kenneth's two years earlier when he let him go to Berlin.

John Tooley, who was to be David Webster's successor as General Administrator, believes that Webster had privately determined there would be a clean sweep at the Royal Opera House in 1970 when he retired. Webster would then be sixty-seven, but he had been asked to stay on past the official retirement age in order to smooth the period of transition, even though he was not in good health. Georg Solti had warned the Board in 1967 that he would not be renewing his contract as Musical Director of the Opera House in 1970; Colin Davis had already been designated his successor. Davis was expecting to work in tandem with Peter Hall as Artistic Director of the opera company, a new post created specifically for Hall. (He pulled out of the arrangement in July 1971, leaving Davis in sole charge.) That left only Ashton as a member of the *ancien régime*, and de Valois was exerting her influence behind the scenes for him to be obliged to make way for MacMillan sooner rather than later.

Matters came to a head early in 1968 when Webster learned that John Field, Director of the touring company, was being head-hunted to run London Festival Ballet. Donald Albery, who was to announce his resignation as Festival Ballet's Director on 18 March, had approached Field to be his replacement. Field had long felt out on a limb, in charge of a 'second' company that was not regarded as a priority by Ashton and the Royal Opera House. He was growing restless, greatly tempted by the Festival Ballet offer. Webster asked him to be patient for a short while longer: he was to be offered the co-directorship of an enlarged Royal Ballet, both companies united into one, alongside MacMillan on an equal footing. Ashton's departure would have to be cleared first, so that preparations could be made to reorganise the administration of the two companies.

At Webster's request, these schemes were not formally discussed at Board meetings or committed to paper in the Royal Opera House files. Instead, Lord Drogheda had discreetly sounded out the views of Mark Bonham Carter, Chairman of the Ballet Sub-Committee, and Lionel Robbins, on the same committee, along with other colleagues. According to Drogheda's memoirs, *Double Harness*, they all accepted that Ashton was ready to retire: they left it to Webster to sort out the arrangements for his departure and the appointment of his successor. Webster summoned Ashton in March 1968, and informed him brusquely that they would both be leaving at the end of the 1969–70 season. Ashton was aghast. Tooley remembers entering Webster's office just after he had made the announcement, to be told glumly by Ashton, 'It's all over, I've been sacked.' Ashton had dramatised the situation into a *fait-accompli* dismissal, rather than due notice of a handover in two years' time. Rumours that he was being forced to resign spread through the company. Ashton told his Assistant Directors, John Hart and Michael Somes, that he had not been consulted about his retirement or his successor: he had simply been informed that Kenneth MacMillan and John Field would replace him as Co-Directors.

Lord Drogheda, in his memoirs, reproached himself for not intervening to speak to Ashton more diplomatically. He had assumed that Ashton was longing to retire, having been told so several times by Ashton himself: 'I had taken him at his word.' Drogheda also claimed that de Valois knew nothing about the timing of Webster's bombshell meeting with Ashton, since she had been in Ankara at the time, on her annual visit to the Turkish Ballet company. Richard Glasstone, however, who was teaching at the ballet school in Ankara, knew that she was frequently on the telephone to London, urging that MacMillan's appointment be confirmed in order to ensure an orderly changeover in 1970.

The way the announcement was handled at the end of April 1968 was far from orderly. The news had already leaked out, thanks to Ashton's wounded pride. Kenneth's sister Jean commented in a letter to him that she had seen Fred Ashton on television during the interval of a transmission of *The Nutcracker* on 10 March, saying that he would be retiring and that 'Mr MacMillan would be his successor'. Jean expressed her surprise that Kenneth hadn't let her know. The two companies, however, had not yet been formally told. An indignant head of steam had built up in support of Ashton, with staff and dancers protesting that he should remain for longer. He had been their Director for only five years so far: it was surely not right that he should go so soon. Fears were voiced that a changeover would mean that Somes and Hart, Ashton's Assistant Directors, would lose their jobs and that lots of the dancers would be sacked.

Tooley urged the Royal Opera House Board to agree that a press statement should be released as soon as possible, even though the Covent Garden company (and Webster) would be away on tour in New York in April. When some Board members objected to the timing, Tooley said both Royal Ballet companies were so unsettled that the situation needed to be clarified as soon as possible. The announcement to the press on 27 April said simply, 'In two years' time, in the summer of 1970, Sir Frederick Ashton will retire from his post as Director of the Royal Ballet. His place will then be taken by a joint directorship of Kenneth MacMillan and John Field . . . It is hoped that Sir Frederick will continue to create new ballets for the Royal Ballet after his retirement.'

Webster had meanwhile called a company meeting in New York and made the same brief announcement, with Ashton by his side. The dancers were in shock, according to Antoinette Sibley:

> We were in the middle of one of the most successful seasons ever at the Met, when Webster told us that the person leading us to this triumph was to leave. Why? We couldn't understand it – lots of us were in tears. It was overwhelmingly obvious Fred shouldn't go and we couldn't believe all our protests would just be ignored. Yes, Kenneth was his natural successor – but not yet. It was too soon. Losing Fred would be like having a leg cut off.

Ashton kept silent throughout the meeting, so John Hart leapt up to make the point that Ashton had known nothing of the plan to replace him in two years' time and had not been consulted about his successor. Hart told Webster as he left the meeting that he felt he had to speak out on Ashton's behalf. 'Later that day I saw Sol Hurok who told me that Sir David had sat alone in his office for two hours without speaking to anyone. Then, about 1 a.m, Sir David called me at my hotel and said he would ring London and cancel the announcement. He called again about 4 a.m and told me it had already gone to the press.' Tooley confirmed that Webster was in a terrible state of indecision. 'He was constantly on the phone: "What will I do, what will I do?" He wasn't well and I think this was one of the reasons why it was so badly handled.'

Webster was suffering from a heart condition that caused his death within nine months of his retirement. Poor circulation meant that he sometimes blacked out and lost his grasp of affairs at this troubled time of transition for the Royal Opera House. None the less, the decision that Ashton should retire to be replaced by MacMillan and John Field was not his alone. MacMillan's succession had been instigated by de Valois and agreed by Drogheda; the joint appointment had been accepted at Board level. Radical changes would affect the two ballet companies in two years' time, though these were yet to be decided. What now seems spectacular misman-agement of the end of an era was due only partly to Webster's ill-health: the blame lay with the culture he had inculcated in the

House, in which decisions were habitually opaque and badly communicated. Webster was known to certain members of the Board as the A.D. (Artful Dodger) or A.P. (Arch Procrastinator) because of his evasions and refusal to commit anything to paper. In his attempts to 'tidy up' before his own departure, he was badly damaging the morale of the company MacMillan was to inherit.

The Berlin press greeted the news of MacMillan's intended departure from the Deutsche Oper in 1969 with equanimity. Although German dance critics had hailed his arrival, they were growing disillusioned with his inability to transform the company into a creative powerhouse. So far, his only new work for the company to have met with enthusiastic approval was the one-act *Anastasia*.

MacMillan planned to confound their criticism with an ambitious Ballet Festival lasting eleven days in November 1968. It would be the longest unbroken run of performances under his leadership, concluding with a gala featuring international stars. He would create a new ballet and mount a retrospective of all the works he had introduced into the repertoire, showing Berliners the range of ballets the company now possessed.

His assumption that Seymour would be available to dance her leading roles was confounded by her announcement that she was pregnant. She and Eike Walcz had been trying for a baby because she wanted 'something positive' to come from her Berlin experience. Even though the longer-term future was uncertain, she was entitled to maternity leave on full pay as a member of the Deutsche Oper company. To her and Eike's surprise, the 'something positive' proved to be twins, due in the autumn of 1968. Under German law, she would be on leave from three months into the pregancy until at least three months after the birth. MacMillan would therefore be deprived of his principal ballerina for the rest of 1968.

Lynn claims she does not recall how Kenneth reacted to her news. He was no doubt furious with her for making herself unavailable, yet again, as his principal dancer. He might have been profoundly envious that she could be happy and optimistic about creating her own family. She had ended a pregnancy in 1964, in part, at least, because of his *Romeo and Juliet*; now she was going to have two babies, at the expense of further ballets he might have made for her in Berlin. The twin boys, who were born six weeks early at the end of August, were named Adrian and Jerszy: Kenneth became one of their godparents, along with Rudolf Nureyev, Vergie Derman and Georgina Parkinson.

MacMillan had meanwhile turned to Cranko, asking whether he could borrow Marcia Haydée for Lynn's roles in the November festival. In return, he would create a one-act ballet for the Stuttgart company's Ballet Week at the start of June. He agreed to take over an assignment that Cranko was unable to complete before June for lack of time. Cranko's plan had been to pair two short works, one serious, one comic, to music by Darius Milhaud, choreographing them both himself. He had already commissioned designs for both ballets from Elisabeth Dalton, Georgiadis's assistant at the time. Cranko telephoned her in London to ask if she would mind collaborating with MacMillan on the 'serious' piece (to Milhaud's *Five Small Symphonies*), while he concentrated on the comic suite from *Salade*. Dalton, who had already prepared the designs for both pieces, took them to Berlin to show MacMillan.

Her experience of Berlin was vastly more entertaining than the gloomy picture painted by previous visitors from Britain:

Ken and Ray Barra met me at the airport and took me to a pension Ray had found by the Kurfürstendamm. It was run by Frau Sheïra, who looked like Mae West with bleached hair and a tight blouse pulling open across her substantial chest. Kenneth lurked because he didn't speak much German – Ray did it all. They ushered me into a huge room with bas-relief ladies holding hoops for the ceiling lights, and the biggest bed you've ever seen. Frau Sheïra turned out to have an Arab lover, who came in while I was unpacking to remove his coat from the bedroom. Kenneth was enchanted. It was straight out of *Goodbye to Berlin*.

He asked to have a look at the other rooms, which were all themed. The one he adored was like Ludwig of Bavaria's palace, all swans. Frau Sheïra's room next door opened into the well of the building, which was full of plants, just like the set for *Las Hermanas*. That set Ken off giggling, so he decided to move into the pension once he got back from Stuttgart. Later on, an awful thing happened to the Arab lover. One night he came back and jealously thought Frau Sheïra was in bed with someone else. So he climbed out of a window to spy on her and fell to his death. His body was found among the plants below her room. It was a truly bizarre place to stay.

Lis Dalton was the kind of companion Kenneth craved: earthy, zany, able to entertain him and make him see Berlin through someone else's eyes. 'Every day he came rushing over to the Kurfürstendamm to find out what had happened in the pension the night before. He loved my stories of what was going on.' Her memory of him was not of a depressive but of how funny he could be. She noted, however, that she usually met him when she was part of a creative team, a theatrical family with him at the centre. They travelled together to Stuttgart, where he started work on the new ballet.

He so envied John Cranko's set-up at Stuttgart. Berlin was very different. John's Intendant, Dr Schaefer, actually wanted a ballet company – and Stuttgart was such a boring place that the company did nothing but work and be with each other. Of course there was a rivalry between John and Kenneth because each could do something better than the other: John could do the choreography for the corps in his ballets and Kenneth was best at the pas de deux for his. But they were good friends and Kenneth loved being in Stuttgart, without any worries except making his choreography.

MacMillan liked the designs Dalton had already prepared for the Milhaud ballet, which Cranko had envisaged as being about the sphinx, half woman, half lioness. Since Dalton's sketches were based on Minoan themes and colour schemes, MacMillan kept the sphinx idea, casting Marcia Haydée as the mythical creature of the title. *Der Sphinx* depicted the legend of the Theban monster who asked all travellers the same riddle: What is it that goes upon four legs in the morning, two in the afternoon and three in the evening? The answer (as Oedipus worked out) was man – growing from crawling infancy to adulthood, and then declining into old age, with a stick as the third leg. Haydée posed the question by holding up four, two and three fingers. In the ballet, all the Sphinx's challengers (Heinz Clauss, Richard Cragun and Egon Madsen) failed to find the answer: they were despatched by a scissor-like split of Haydee's legs, seeming to chop off their heads.

John Percival, writing about *The Sphinx* in *Dance and Dancers* in August 1968, noted the icy alienation of the ballet: 'The dancers go through it like observing a ritual, with Haydée as a perversely smiling and yet so very distant Coptic Turandot, who, alas, is sentenced never to meet her Kalaf.' Percival confessed that neither he nor his fellow spectators understood at the time what the constant signalling of 4–2–3 fingers meant. His wry solution was to identify the sphinx monster with the Deutsche Oper and the three victims with the succession of 'frustrated ballet masters and choreographers who tried in vain to master its complex ballet problems'. MacMillan might well have agreed with this alternative interpretation.

Der Sphinx was given only once in Stuttgart, in the Ballet Week gala programme (on 1 June 1968). It was not notated, so no record remains. Some of the multiple partnering was recycled in a later ballet, *Triad*, in 1972. The Stuttgart cast did, however, perform *Der Sphinx* in Berlin during the Deutsche Oper's Ballet Festival in November, when MacMillan invited them to give the Berlin premiere of Cranko's *Opus 1* as well.

On his return from Stuttgart, MacMillan had moved his packing cases from the lonely Helgoländer Ufer flat into Frau Sheïra's eccentric pension. He claimed the swan-themed room as his own and persuaded Monica Parker to stay in the same pension so that he would have company after rehearsals ended at night. He cooked supper for them in the kitchen, whisky glass in hand. 'Frau Sheïra soon banned him from making scrambled eggs because it cost her too much to have the pans cleaned. So we had fish fingers instead, burnt on the outside and cold on the inside.' Parker knew how dependent Kenneth was on alcohol: he required her to buy him a bottle of whisky a day to top up his own supply. He carried on drinking alone in his room when she left to work on the notation she had made during the day. He rarely went out, his world narrowed to working and drinking.

He was greatly cheered by the arrival of Marcia Haydée from Stuttgart to learn Seymour's roles for the Ballet Festival programme. She stayed in the Pension Sheïra, along with Richard Cragun. Lis Dalton remembers:

Marcia and Ricky were in the room next door to Kenneth's mad swan chamber, and I remember us all piling onto Ken's bed, laughing at Marcia's cloud of hair, which she'd just washed. He needed that warmth and affection, which he didn't get in Berlin. For example, when Marcia came into the rehearsal room, she sat on Kenneth's lap, pretending to read a notation score, and the other dancers were shocked. They'd never have dreamt of doing that.

Haydée admitted to being surprised at how different the atmosphere in the Deutsche Oper Ballet was from Stuttgart's informality:

Berlin was more hierarchical but also Kenneth felt he must be distant from the dancers. He wasn't like John, the father of his company. When I arrived, with the old relationship I already had with Kenneth, the Berlin dancers couldn't quite understand.

Haydée's view is that MacMillan was miscast as a director:

He didn't have the right kind of charisma. He was a choreographer, not a director. His problem in Berlin was that he needed to be tough with the management and the dancers, and he wanted to put his choreography first. He wasn't so interested in building a company. If he had stayed in Stuttgart as a guest choreographer, with John taking all the responsibility, he could have been happy. Berlin was not for him.

MacMillan poured his tortured sensibilities into his new work for the Berlin Ballet Festival in November. *Cain and Abel* was the last one-act ballet he was to create for the Deutsche Oper company. (Tatjana Gsovsky had choreographed a ballet, *Kain*, on the same subject, for the Berlin Ballet chamber group in 1957.) With Seymour out of the picture, he had found a male dancer as a vehicle for his inspiration. Frank Frey, at twenty-one, was an idealist, a free spirit swayed by passionate convictions. He came from Munich, where he had trained as a dancer. In 1967, he had been visiting his friend Eike Walcz in Berlin when he happened to meet MacMillan at Eike's and Lynn's Grunewald apartment. Frey was on his way to try to join the National Ballet of Cuba, and was intending to secure a Cuban visa in East Berlin. MacMillan suggested he audition instead for the Deutsche Oper Ballet and recruited him as a potential soloist. Frey was a powerful though unpolished dancer, with a soaring jump that enabled him to seem to hang in the air. Tall and strong, with a helmet of straight blond hair, he had a compelling presence on stage: Elisabeth Dalton compared him with James Dean on film. Klaus Geitel, critic for *Die Welt*, wondered if MacMillan saw him as 'the German Nureyev'. Above all, Frey represented the kind of supremely virile dancer Kenneth would like to have been in his youth: he had an athlete's muscular physique and a dancer's ability to subsume effort into ease, in spite of his lack of technical refinement.

MacMillan had become fixated on Frey, in a way that many took to be a homosexual infatuation. Frank was straight and unattainable, which might have played a large part in his attraction. He was gratified by Kenneth's attention, even though he was uncertain how to handle the choreographer's passion for him as a person as well as an interpreter. He chose to understand MacMillan's obsession with him as an artist's desire to be taken over by his muse, a choreographer's need to identify himself with the being through whom he could create. Frey quotes Goethe: 'Die schönste Form der Seelenwanderung ist sich im anderen wieder auftreten zu sehen.' ('The most beautiful form of spiritual recognition is to see oneself in the other.') Kenneth had spotted qualities that Frank did not even know he had, investing him with an artistry he might not otherwise have developed so fully. Like the young Lynn Seymour, Frey was an instinctive actor, capable of expressing emotions he could not yet have experienced.

Frey did not believe that MacMillan was truly homosexual. Instead, he thinks Kenneth at this stage in his life felt threatened by women, whom he feared would demand more from an erotic relationship than he felt he could give. In his profoundly insecure state, he preferred women to be confidantes and carers, not sexual partners. A foreign straight man was a safe fantasy object – especially someone as young and vital as Frank, who was making the most of his time in Berlin. Kenneth could live an alternative life through him, hearing what was happening in the streets, cafés and clubs, finding out where the political debates were heading. Monica Parker remembers being taken on a protest march by Frank, and shouting, 'Ho, Ho, Ho Chi Minh', without being quite sure what cause they were supporting. Frey's rebellious nature would lead him into trouble sooner or later; for the time being, he was happy to be available as a companion, easing Kenneth's isolation. He was a frequent visitor to the Pension Sheïra, sharing his latest enthusiasm for clothes, music and films with a naivety that Kenneth took as teasing flirtation – or so he complained, in frustration, to Ray Barra: 'He tries his new clothes on in front of me. I don't know where to look.'

Lynn Seymour thinks that Frank, in his early twenties, was genuinely naïve:

He was offbeat, completely taken up with whatever theory he held at the time. He was a bit of a bull in a china shop, who didn't know how big he was. His gaucheries were mocked by some of the Berlin dancers, who thought of him as 'that oaf of a Bavarian'. Berliners were very snobbish about Bavarians. They couldn't understand why Kenneth favoured him as a dancer, which led to much resentment.

Lynn and Eike saw a lot of Frank, since he lived near them in Grunewald and he and Eike continued to remain good friends. Unlike the stand-offish Berliners, they and Kenneth enjoyed his combination of earnestness and good humour.

Frey remembers eating regularly with MacMillan at Peppino's, an Italian restaurant near the Deutsche Oper where theatre people (and political spies) would gather after performances:

Kenneth ate always the same thing, scampi and salad. He would ask for the back room to be opened for him, so he could be out of sight of the other people. My bad English made him laugh – he'd take my words and use them as running jokes – but he didn't really try to learn German. Enough people spoke to him in English, and in his head he never abandoned the possibility of going back 'tonight' to England. He never unpacked his things – something seemed to have paralysed him.

MacMillan cast Frey as Cain, the murderous elder brother in his new ballet; Daniel Job, dark and slight, was Abel, the younger son favoured by his mother, Eve. Set to two pieces of music by Andrzej Panufnik, the *Sinfonia Sacra* and the *Tragic Overture*, the ballet examined the brothers' rivalry for the love of their mother. Cain's growing envy set him apart from the rest of the tribal family, over which Adam ruled as a tyrannical father. The family's closeness was symbolised by ribbons binding them together in a spider's web. The Serpent (Gerhard Bohner) insinuated himself into every encounter, the embodiment of poisonous jealousy and the forbidden knowledge that had driven Adam and Eve out of Eden. Cain was goaded unmercifully into killing Abel, and then had to face the enormity of what he had done. Frey, resembling one of Michelangelo's monumental figures, crouched over the dead body, hunched in the anguished posture of a condemned sinner in *The Last Judgment*. Cain's punishment was to be sent into exile, dragging the corpse of his brother with him wherever he went.

Clement Crisp, who came to Berlin to review the new ballet for the *Financial Times*, recognised that MacMillan had split himself in two, his dark destructive side murdering his sensitive self:

We realise how great has been Cain's love for Abel despite their rivalry; the killing seems like an orgasm that both consummates and destroys this love, and the final section shows Cain isolated in his guilt. He treats the dead Abel with an almost uncomprehending tenderness . . . His guilt has a kind of innocence, he must carry its weight with him for ever, but in a curious way it seems that he knows he has killed the best part of himself, and his grief is not only for himself but for his love for Abel. The ballet offers the purest and most intense expression yet of a recurrent theme in MacMillan's creativity, that 'outcast' figure, the personality driven into isolation; and the dance language is magnificently expressive of the theme.

As well as portraying his conflicting feelings about his own family relationships, MacMillan had found a way of externalising his agonies over his sexuality. For him, the act of sex with a man was associated with guilt, brutality and a longing for expiation. His scapegoat in the ballet, Cain, had to carry the burden of his pent-up emotions, condemned to loneliness. Apart from the brief role for Nureyev in *Images of Love*, the characters in his ballets with whom MacMillan had previously identified had been his vulnerable heroines. Now, in Berlin, he had a male dancer strong and arresting enough to be his protagonist.

Frey received rave reviews for his performance in a work that was much admired for its searing intensity. German critics, in general, were impressed by MacMillan's mastery of his archetypal material, biblical and Freudian. A notable exception was Horst Koegler (writing for the *Stuttgarter Zeitung*), who found *Cain and Abel* 'a disgusting, unappetising ballet, weighed down by its sweaty, body-building style, groaning with sex and fratricide'. Koegler's preference was for ballets that relied on classical technique. There were no balletic steps in *Cain and Abel*, and few sustained passages of dancing apart from those for Frey as Cain. Nigel Gosling, one of the British critics who followed MacMillan's activities in Germany, writing as Alexander Bland in *Dancing Times*, noted how radically his choreographic idiom had changed since he had been in Berlin, from *Concerto* to *Anastasia* to *Cain and Abel*: 'MacMillan has always been sensitive to the ambience round his work and to the dancers he was working with. He seems to be moving away from what could be called the Anglo-French (Ashtonian) world of his youth towards a more Anglo-German one . . . much nearer to the world of modern dance.'

Barry Kay's stark, metallic decor, which featured a huge suspended eye reflecting the action below, was seen as placing the work in the German Expressionist tradition of cinema as well as theatre. *Cain and Abel* was certainly more to the taste of Berlin audiences than Balanchine's *Ballet Imperial* on the same Festival programme. MacMillan had acquired the Balanchine work for the Deutsche Oper company because he had enjoyed performing it as a young dancer, and he hoped to extend the dancers' and audiences' appreciation of neo-classical choreography. *Ballet Imperial*'s formal conceits, inadequately danced, met with tittering, ironic applause, whistling and cat-calling. When the pianist took his bow, he was mistaken for Balanchine and loudly booed. Monica Parker believes the booing and cat-calling was a political protest at the double-headed Imperial Eagle on the backdrop for the ballet. MacMillan, however, took the audience response as yet another indication that he had wasted his time trying to educate the Berlin public.

For his final Ballet Festival, the manifesto of his artistic beliefs, he had programmed an impressive range of twentieth-century works (nine of them his own), as well as his production of *The Sleeping Beauty* and Tudor's account of *Giselle*. (Although MacMillan had intended to include all his Berlin creations, *Olympiade* had to be dropped when one of its principal dancers, André Doutreval, was injured.) He had invited a group of dancers from the Stuttgart Ballet to give the Berlin premieres of Cranko's *Opus 1* and his own *Der Sphinx*. Marcia Haydée took the leading role in *Las Hermanas*, as well as replacing Seymour in *The Sleeping Beauty*, with Richard Cragun as her Prince. Gosling, writing as Alexander Bland in the *Observer*, praised their 'firm focus' in a dazzlingly opulent production that demanded strong dancing. 'The company emerges with credit,' he concluded. For the concluding gala, MacMillan was able to call on Fonteyn and Nureyev, Yvette Chauviré and Flemming Flindt. The Deutsche Oper was now in a different league from the company he had taken over two years earlier.

At the end of the gala, Axel Springer, the rich and influential newspaper proprietor based in Berlin, invited MacMillan and the guest stars to a private party at the top of his company's opulent headquarters, near Checkpoint Charlie. MacMillan refused the invitation unless all the dancers were included. He was not going to condone an elite group being fêted while the corps de ballet was ignored. He was following the example of de Valois's principled stand for her company during their tour of the United States in 1950: he, too, was prepared to stick up for his dancers. After heated argument, Springer gave way and extended the invitation to all the performers: Nureyev had meanwhile invited all the stage hands, so Springer's party was far from the exclusive treat he had intended.

As soon as the festival was over, MacMillan went back to London, staying with Georgina Parkinson and Roy Round at their house in Battersea. He said he was exhausted and needed to get away from Berlin. Gert Reinholm was left in charge of the company, reporting to Kenneth by phone and letter. John Cranko, who had been in Berlin during the festival with his Stuttgart dancers, had coined a nickname for Reinholm: 'the Black Nun', a neat and naughty description of his aloof appearance and scrupulous correctness. Although Cranko was among those who found Reinholm a sinister figure, MacMillan continued to trust him as his friend and liaison officer with the management. The responsibility for planning the ballet company's tour of West Germany and Austria at the start of the next year was left entirely in Reinholm's hands.

Kenneth remained in London until after Christmas, being looked after by the Rounds, who tried to wean him away from the tea-and-whisky that rarely left his hand. 'He was in a bad way and we were his support system. He'd talk his problems out with us but he didn't necessarily take our advice. He was in a state of constantly frustrated neurosis – about the Berlin ballet management, about Frank Frey, about his lonely life, everything,' remembers Georgina Parkinson. He cost the Rounds a fortune in long-distance telephone calls to Berlin, for which they later had to ask for reimbursement, since it did not occur to him to offer payment. He was negotiating, unsuccessfully, for German Television to film *Anastasia*, as well as preparing his final production for the Deutsche Oper Ballet: *Swan Lake*, scheduled for May 1969, before his departure in June.

He was also discussing future plans with the Royal Ballet, which hoped for a new work from him before he took over as Artistic Director. Nureyev, who wanted to remake a working relationship with him, had meanwhile proposed the company acquire *Cain and Abel* in February 1969: he had seen the work during his gala appearance in the Deutsche Oper's Ballet Festival and wanted to perform the leading role. MacMillan insisted that if the Royal Ballet were to acquire the piece, Frank Frey must be invited to take his created role as Cain. Kenneth was not going to have his interpreter usurped by Nureyev, as Christopher Gable had been in *Romeo and Juliet*. Ashton refused to invite Frey as a guest artist, on the grounds that he was only a soloist, not a principal dancer, let alone one of international standing. Neither Ashton nor MacMillan would give way in this clash of wills, so *Cain and Abel* was abandoned. (Frey was the only dancer ever to perform the role of Cain.) Roland Petit was swiftly commissioned instead to create a vehicle for Nureyev and Fonteyn, which turned out to be an insubstantial piece, *Pelléas et Mélisande*. MacMillan blamed Nureyev for sabotaging his ballet and Frey's chance of dancing with the Royal Ballet, when in fact the decision was Ashton's.

The company still needed a ballet from MacMillan for later in the season and for the next American tour. A new work by him had been provisionally scheduled, and since he was not going to provide one in time, Ashton agreed to take on *Olympiade* (spelt in its English incarnation without a final 'e'), even though no one from the company had seen it. The result was a setback for MacMillan's reputation. This was the first ballet from his time in Berlin to be performed at Covent Garden since the announcement that he was to be Ashton's replacement. *Olympiade* had been created as a somewhat makeshift display piece (with no budget for designs) for the Deutsche Oper's male contingent, its then topical Olympic Games references a pretext for showy dancing. MacMillan had rechoreographed the final section to accommodate his new cast but the Royal Ballet's men were not as powerfully athletic as their German counterparts, and the ballet, danced without conviction, looked risible, failing to match the strident power of Stravinsky's *Symphony in Three Movements*. In *Dance and Dancers*, Peter Williams, MacMillan's champion in the past, berated the Royal Ballet management for putting it on:

Had it been a new ballet that failed it would have been sad but forgivable . . . but this wasn't new and surely must have been seen by somebody responsible for this revival other than MacMillan himself. Anybody from the front of the stalls to the back of the amphitheatre could have told the administration that *Olympiad* simply would not do. What a sad waste, and what a lot of leeway MacMillan now has to make up. This was the time for him to re-establish himself here with an exciting overture to what we all hope will be the main body of his life's work.

Olympiad was dropped from the Royal Ballet repertoire after six performances and omitted from the American tour. MacMillan's only consolation was that Petit's *Pelléas et Mélisande*, which did go on tour, was an even greater flop in the United States than it had been at Covent Garden.

Back in Berlin, MacMillan was preparing his last production for the Deutsche Oper. He had secured Sellner's agreement for *Swan Lake* on condition that it would be much less expensive than *The Sleeping Beauty*. Nico Georgiadis, commissioned as the designer, came to Berlin to present the maquette of the set he had discussed with MacMillan in London. He had devised a basic architectural structure with an imposing flight of terraced steps to frame the action. Sellner liked it. *Swan Lake*, in Georgiadis's designs, proved to be MacMillan's longest-lasting legacy to the Deutsche Oper; it would be performed more frequently over the next twenty years than any other production he had introduced into the repertoire.

He had his own vision of the Petipa–Ivanov ballet, keeping much of the extant choreography but adapting the original scenario to suit his purposes by adding a prologue and epilogue. In the English draft for his German programme note, he explained:

I have made the Prince a young, freedom-loving man, raised in a court that is suffocating him by the fact that his mother is arranging a marriage for him. To compensate for this the Prince retreats into wild fantasies and dreams. Therefore the whole ballet becomes a dream, in which he must struggle against forces that prevent him from reaching full maturity as a man, and the freedom of choice that he desires.

The hero, Prince Siegfried, thus becomes a MacMillan misfit, rebelling against the constraints of his society. The Prince is haunted by an evil genius, Von Rothbart, a sinister, cloaked figure trying to assert power over him in the court as well as in the fantasy lakeside scenes. In the last act, the Prince wrestles with this mysterious enemy, who is finally unmasked as Death. Siegfried awakes from his nightmare to find that his true love is not a swan but the real girl he met in the prologue.

MacMillan retained the traditional Ivanov choreography for the 'white' acts, taught by Monica Parker from the Benesh score of the Royal Ballet's production. He created his own dances for the court celebrations in Acts I and III (retaining Petipa's Black Swan pas de deux). Frank Frey was to be the first-cast Siegfried, Gerhard Bohner the deadly enchanter and Lynn Seymour Odette/Odile, a role she had danced with the Royal Ballet since her debut as a youngster. In spite of the deterioration in his personal relationship with her, MacMillan still needed her as the company's ballerina: he could not have mounted *Swan Lake* without her. Seymour had been working hard during the company's winter tour to recover her strength after the birth of her twin sons. She was willing to rehearse with Frey on their own, advising him how to partner her in the ballet's famous pas de deux in Acts II and III. Since he was not a danseur noble of the type who would normally be cast as a prince, his accession to the leading role caused much resentment among more senior dancers. According to Seymour, 'Kenneth could have smoothed things over by explaining how he saw the role and why he chose Frank for it, but he didn't. So there was a bad atmosphere.'

MacMillan had rethought the Prince in Frey's likeness, as a head-strong young rebel and wildly romantic idealist. *Swan Lake* became the Prince's psychological journey rather than Odette's tragedy. Ray Barra commented, 'You didn't know which one to look at, Frank or Lynn – they were both so interesting on stage, it almost didn't matter how they danced technically. You wanted to know more about them as characters, not whether they could bring off the virtuoso stuff – which they couldn't.'

Rehearsals were under way when Frey was arrested for taking part in a political demonstration. He was already in trouble with the theatre management for unpunctuality; his brush with the law nearly resulted in his dismissal. He had become involved in a protest by actors and students against the West Berlin Senate's decision to close down Peter Weiss's latest play, *Vietnam Discourse*, at the Schaubühne theatre. The play aroused heated debate and its actors had been collecting money to help American army deserters from the war in Vietnam. When their performances were cancelled, they invaded an unrelated dance-workshop evening at the Schaubühne, aiming to read out and distribute their pamphlets of protest at the Senate's action. The audience objected to the disruption, as did most of the dancers, who wanted to get on with their performance. The notable exception was Frey, who exhorted his fellow dancers to show solidarity with the actors' sit-down demonstration. The police were called and the protesters, including Frey, were hauled off the stage and into the cells.

After their release (thanks to a radical lawyer who later joined the underground Red Army Faction), the militants gathered at the

Pension Sheïra to discuss what action to take next. MacMillan was not involved, though Frey visited his swan room in high excitement to tell him what was going on: 'Kenneth was sitting in his huge bed, pulling at his hair. Almost crying, he said, "I'm losing all my hair." It was the stress with the ballet company and with me. For him, his hair falling out was a sign of losing his life and his potency.' Self-absorbed in his state of depression, MacMillan had no energy to spare for political causes or even for listening to Frey's angry indignation at the Berlin authorities.

Although his pressing concern was to finish *Swan Lake* on time, MacMillan had been missing rehearsals, incapable of leaving his room. He claimed that he was suffering from a long bout of flu, but he was also incapacitated by anxiety and alcohol. He knew he was damaging his health by drinking, but he had postponed his attempts to cut down until his Berlin exile was over. Frey believes that Kenneth's previous good intentions had been undermined by apparently sympathetic colleagues, such as Tatjana Gsovsky, slipping him bottles of whisky: 'They were deliberately making him powerless, and he robbed himself of power by staying in bed and not fighting for himself.'

Kenneth was brought to greater depths by the news that his sister Jean had been killed in a car crash on 3 April. Jean had told him in her letters how proud she was of passing her driving test at the age of fifty, though her deafness had made it difficult for her to pick up instructions. Their brother George had persisted in teaching her in spite of her slowness, she joked, and had advised her on buying a car. She wrote that she had driven several times between Great Yarmouth and Scotland to visit the MacMillan clan, shortening the (very long) time she took with each journey. Kenneth must have expressed his concern about her safety in his reply, for she reassured him in her letters that her driving had improved.

Betty, Kenneth's second sister, broke the news that on Jean's latest trip north, *en route* to Scotland, a truck had forced her into the path of an oncoming car. She and her husband Arthur had died instantly. Betty had telephoned Georgina Parkinson in London, asking her to inform Kenneth: a long-distance call to Berlin, probably with German being spoken in reply, was beyond Betty. Georgina managed to locate Kenneth, in bed at the Pension Sheïra, telling him as gently as possible that his favourite sister was dead. Jean had died at Easter time, as their mother had; he had been away, at a distance, on both distressing occasions.

He was unable to return in time for Jean's funeral. He was ill and in any case believed himself incapable of travelling by air. Had he been in a stronger state, he could have made the long journey by train, but he was in no condition to travel on his own and then to endure his family's grief as well as his own. *Swan Lake*'s first night, a month away, provided a pretext for not being able to leave Berlin. Frank Frey remembers discussions between Kenneth and Gert Reinholm about whether Kenneth should go to England, and whether he was in a fit enough state to cope with the demands of the *Swan Lake* preparations. Kenneth commented to Reinholm on how amazed he had been at Fonteyn's strength when she learned in Spoleto that her husband had been shot. She had fulfilled her commitment to perform, in spite of her distress. Remembering her stoicism, MacMillan assured Reinholm that he would devote himself to the final rehearsals for *Swan Lake*'s premiere on 14 May.

His absence from the funeral and apparent lack of involvement in family affairs deeply offended his brother and sister. For George and Betty, the circumstances of Jean's death were a matter of concern for the whole family. They retained lawyers who would dispute for years over who might have died first by minutes, Jean or her husband, since the inheritance of their Yarmouth boarding house was at stake. They had died childless and intestate, so the legal question was whether their estate should go to Arthur Sparham's brothers and sisters, or to Jean's. George and Betty insisted on being told the exact details of the car crash, the extent of Jean's injuries and which of the two occupants of the mangled car might still have been breathing when witnesses were present. The distressing information was formally passed on to Kenneth, who preferred to keep out of the legal wranglings. Reports on the slow progress of the court case continued to plague him for years, until he eventually received a small sum of money from Jean's estate, shared between him, George and Betty. Poignantly, Jean had left an envelope with her bank, noting, 'Owe Ken £600 less £10' – evidently a loan, which was duly returned to him by the family solicitors.

For Kenneth, the run-up to *Swan Lake*'s premiere was further bedevilled by disputes with the Deutsche Oper management. Upset and angry, he threatened to withdraw the entire production. The set was late in being built; Monica Parker had not been paid as his notator; and as the last straw, Frank Frey had been called for a disciplinary hearing in front of the theatre's management, thereby being made unavailable for a rehearsal. Frey had been threatened with instant dismissal if he did not obey the summons to account in person for his arrest. MacMillan had cancelled the *Swan Lake* rehearsal and fired off furious letters to Sellner and the technical director, demanding explanations and apologies. He received stiff replies from both men, stating that he was being unreasonable. Sellner pointed out that since MacMillan had renounced his position as Ballet Director, he had no right to challenge management decisions. His sole responsibility as resident choreographer was to supply two ballets per year; disciplinary matters involving Frank Frey had nothing to do with him. The Deutsche Oper had taken legal advice that he was not entitled to cancel rehearsals or imperil the opening night of *Swan Lake*: the management refused to be intimidated by any more ultimatums. Sellner very evidently had no further interest in trying to placate MacMillan. The time had more than come for a parting of the ways.

Swan Lake was a success, in spite of the bad feeling behind the scenes. German critics praised the production and its 'psychological subtext', though they were less admiring of the dancing. Seymour was considered below par technically and Frey too raw a dancer for a major classical role. There were comments that the corps lacked commitment, 'dancing like civil servants': Berlin critics were aware that the company was disaffected. As *Die Welt am Sonntag* commented, 'MacMillan has failed in his attempt to teach the dancers that art is more than exercising their duty. They simply refused to do more than they had to.' The orchestral playing was such a disgrace that the first-night audience booed Ashley Lawrence when he was brought on stage to take his bow. Although the conductor was not to blame for stand-ins replacing the opera-house musicians, the booing reinforced MacMillan's conviction that Berlin audiences were incapable of appreciating classical ballet and were glad to be shot of him.

Nigel Gosling and his wife Maude Lloyd attended one of the performances and went backstage to speak to MacMillan. They found him in the canteen, where the dancers habitually gathered, and noticed that no one talked to him. According to Maude Lloyd, 'The dancers didn't even say goodbye to him, though they knew he was leaving – it was very pointed and very disconcerting.' As far as most of the staff and dancers were concerned, MacMillan had concluded his choreographer's contract and had nothing more to offer the company.

Five days after the launch of his swansong production, MacMillan travelled to Munich, to discuss remounting *Der Sphinx* for the ballet company there. Cranko was by now Artistic Director of the Munich company (the Bayerische Oper Ballet), as well as the Stuttgart Ballet, and had invited Kenneth, as an official guest, to attend the Munich Ballet Week in May. The Stuttgart Ballet would be in Munich, performing *Das Lied von der Erde* during the festival, and Cranko wanted to talk about plans for a new ballet from MacMillan for the company. Frey went along too, since Munich was his home town. Kenneth then intended to return to Berlin to pack up his things and leave for London. His departure for Munich, however, turned out to be his farewell to Berlin.

Berlin, the divided city, had mirrored Kenneth's divided self, isolated in what he perceived as alien territory. The veteran German critic, Horst Koegler, who had savaged several of his works for Berlin, categorised him, years later in *Ballett International* in December 1989, as 'nowhere at home'. In his assessment of MacMillan's period in Berlin, Koegler contrasted him with Cranko, who had successfully transplanted himself, first from South Africa to London and then to Stuttgart. Where Cranko had re-created in Stuttgart the supportive, nurturing culture he had known in the Sadler's Wells touring company in the 1950s, MacMillan had been defeated by the hierarchical opera-house system in Berlin. He had made little impact on the Deutsche Oper's set ways: although he had enhanced the status of its ballet company, he had not managed to win it significantly more performances each season. In Koegler's view, Cranko had triumphed and MacMillan had failed, even though he would go on to greater things in the rest of his career.

For his part, MacMillan had believed himself betrayed, let down by Intendant Sellner's unfulfilled promises. It is evident, however, both from the accounts of those who were present at the time and from the correspondence files, that he was the wrong man to do battle with Sellner, whose initial goodwill he failed to exploit.

MacMillan was not a diplomat or a strategist; he became stubborn when he didn't get his way, issuing threats because he felt himself to be threatened.

He had set himself at loggerheads with the technical staff and unions by criticising them instead of winning them over. Unable to speak German, he found few allies apart from Gert Reinholm (who was eventually asked to take over the company after MacMillan's immediate successor, John Taras, had quit, serving from 1972 to 1990). The German critics and journalists who had welcomed MacMillan's appointment lost faith in him, disappointed that he had not brought about the 'ballet miracle' that Cranko had achieved in Stuttgart. In fairness to MacMillan, no subsequent ballet director of the West Berlin company effected such a miracle. The Deutsche Oper continued to favour opera over ballet through the 1970s and 1980s, frustrating a series of ballet directors who hoped to transform the company into one of Europe's leading troupes. By the time the Berlin Wall came down in 1989, the Deutsche Oper ballet was not the most outstanding of the companies from East and West that the unified city struggled to support into the next millennium. All three state-funded classical ballet companies were amalgamated in 2004.

Although the Deutsche Oper and MacMillan ended up mutually disillusioned, both had gained from the experience. When he left, most of the repertoire the ballet company performed was either created by him or had been chosen by him. He had made two enduring one-act ballets for it, *Concerto* and *Anastasia*; *Cain and Abel* was performed some twenty times after his departure. He had introduced works he admired, from Petipa's *Sleeping Beauty* to Ashton's *Scènes de ballet* and Balanchine's *Ballet Imperial*, even if Berlin audiences did not take to them whole-heartedly. His production of *Swan Lake* remained in the repertoire until the 1980s. What he had learned by staging the classics and experimenting with new influences on his own choreography would continue to inform his work in the future. Had he stayed with the Royal Ballet instead of going to Berlin, he would have been frustrated by his lack of opportunities.

None the less, he thought of his three years in Berlin as the worst period of his life. He had spiralled downwards into a slough of bitter depression and alcoholism, alienating his friends and undermining his health. Blanked off by his self-absorption from the outside world, he had scarcely been aware of the political protest movements that had challenged governments in the United States, Britain and France, as well as in Germany. Profoundly miserable, he narrowed his focus to the one thing he could do: create. His limited energy was expended on forcing himself into the rehearsal room to make ballets. Once there, even though he was confronted by a sea of expectant faces, the dance studio was the place he felt safest. Outside it, he was virtually help-less, unable to manage his own life, let alone run a company. He blamed Berlin for his misery, convincing himself that his future role as Director of the Royal Ballet would be far less onerous. He had a year, from mid-1969 to September 1970, in which to prepare for his new post; meanwhile, his ballets were much in demand by other compa-nies, which he proposed to visit during the interim.

What happened to MacMillan in Munich disrupted all his plans. He, Cranko and Elisabeth Dalton were all staying at the Hotel Splendide as guests of the Ballet Week festival. They had planned a day out in the mountains with Frank Frey as their guide. When Dalton went to fetch MacMillan from his room in the morning, she found him slumped against the bathroom door. The washbasin was overflowing and there was broken glass on the floor. He was semi-conscious and as she struggled to haul him to his bed, he muttered, 'This is a pas de deux and a half.'

Dalton telephoned Cranko, who assumed that Kenneth was drunk and told her to leave him to sleep it off. Frey arrived and realised something was seriously wrong. Kenneth had recovered sufficiently to refuse absolutely to see a doctor, so Frey asked his own G.P. to come to the hotel in the guise of a friend. 'Kenneth was fearful of doctors in white coats, so I asked my doctor, who was a homoeopath, to come wearing his off-duty clothes,' says Frey. The doctor succeeded in reassuring Kenneth, while arranging for him to be admitted at once to the new Harlachinger Hospital south of the city. Tests showed that, as the doctor had suspected, MacMillan had suffered a stroke.

He was told at the time that a severe vascular spasm had con-stricted the flow of blood to his brain. (Twenty years later, after he had suffered a heart attack in Australia, a technically advanced scan confirmed that the spasm had indeed been a stroke.) The left side of his body was markedly weakened, though the temporary paralysis he had experienced in the Munich hotel soon passed. His speech remained slurred for twenty-four hours. The German doctors told him never to drink again and strongly advised him to stop smoking. His friends wondered whether his last attempt to give up alcohol completely just before he left Berlin had in fact brought about the stroke. Whatever the probable cause – stress, depression combined with acute anxiety, alcohol and nicotine abuse – Kenneth's body had sent out a drastic alarm signal.

He was discharged from the hospital two weeks later. Monica Parker had been asked to come to Munich to visit him while the others were busy and to escort him back to Britain by train on 31 May 1969. 'He could walk all right, but he had a semi-paralysed left hand. I don't think a stroke was mentioned – it was passed off as stress and exhaustion.' He had expected to go directly to Battersea to stay with Georgina Parkinson and her husband, but when Roy Round and Elisabeth Dalton met the boat train at Dover, they drove him directly to Charing Cross Hospital. John Tooley, who was soon to take over from David Webster as General Administrator of the Royal Opera House, had insisted that British specialists checked MacMillan over. Their diagnosis corresponded with the German doctors': he had suffered a minor stroke from which he had recovered well, but he was warned to take life easy before beginning his Royal Ballet job. He was prescribed a cocktail of drugs: sleeping tablets, tranquillisers (including Valium) and a stimulant to counter drowsiness whenever he needed to keep his mind alert. He would come to depend on prescription drugs as a replacement for alcohol.

The onus of looking after him fell once again on Parkinson and Round. Kenneth stayed with them in Foxmore Street in Battersea for almost a year, regarding them as his surrogate family. He was, as ever, a demanding guest. A friend, Peter Hollamby, observed how Kenneth always managed to get what he wanted, or needed, from his close friends: 'He took over the Rounds' drawing room as his office, sitting behind a huge desk as king pin in their household. He could be daunting, putting on a front he'd hide behind.' He was covering up his profound shock at his illness, effectively a psychological as well as physical breakdown.

He had suppressed his grieving for Jean and been reminded of his own mortality. Like his damaged father, he was now scarred for life. His left side remained weaker than his right; although he managed to disguise the difference, he was hypersensitive about his frailty for a long while after his stroke, suspecting that people looked at him as though he were disabled. Turning to Georgina for support and reassurance, he became totally dependent on her and her husband. Despairing that he would ever leave of his own volition, she eventually persuaded Kenneth to move out, convincing him that once he was Director of the Royal Ballet (in which she was a principal dancer), he must have a place of his own. She helped him find a terraced house nearby in Worfield Street. She comments, 'It was like ours and near ours. He got the builders in to modernise it, but he didn't spend much time there when they'd finished. It wasn't the house he wanted but the family to go in it.'

At the same time, he bought a basement flat in Hove, near the seaside resort of Brighton, intending to use it as a bolthole at weekends to escape the pressures of London living. He ended up letting it or leaving it unvisited. His old friend Ray Barra suspected that Kenneth was trying to rival his siblings' canniness in the landlord business but he made no money out of the seaside flat.

Even when he had moved into the Worfield Street house, he continued to walk to the Rounds in Foxmore Street for daily meals and often stayed overnight. His Berlin belongings had been packed up and sent by boat to the docks at Tilbury, the nearest port to London. It took many months (and many persistent letters from Germany) before he arranged to pay the overdue storage bills and collect the possessions with which he could furnish his new place. On the advice of an interior decorator, he did it up with the William Morris Arts-and-Crafts wallpaper and fabrics that had become fashionable in the 1960s. Georgina had urged him to buy two dogs for company but, left for hours on their own, they destroyed the expensive wallpaper and had to go.

He spent as much time as he could with other old friends. Elisabeth Dalton, who had become a lodger in a South London house owned by Clement Crisp, remembered Kenneth's frequent visits, endlessly asking for cups of tea: 'He drank pints and pints of tea but never a drop of whisky. He was very strong-minded about giving up alcohol, though he couldn't yet renounce the smoking.' Crisp provided tea, gossip and encouragement 'but we never talked about his ballets. He never discussed them with anyone.' Jeffrey Solomons regularly met up with MacMillan for an evening meal, always at the same King's Road restaurant, Osteria 430. Although its menu was Italian, the friendly proprietors laid on English tea instead of coffee for Kenneth:

I'd try and cheer him up with jokes about Wallis Warfield [the maiden name of Wallis Simpson, for whom Edward VIII renounced his throne]. For example, every time he bought a picture for his house, we called it 'adding to the Wallis Collection'. But Kenneth often said nothing throughout the meal. Just sat there in silence and then walked back home across Battersea Bridge to Worfield Street.

Urged on by his friends, MacMillan acknowledged that he needed psychiatric help and once again sought the advice of Barry Kay, who had sent him to Dr Hardenberg. Kay recommended Marianne Jacoby, a Jungian psychotherapist in St John's Wood. He introduced Kenneth, who became a patient of hers in July 1969. She assessed him concisely in her notes as suffering from a combination of 'maximum ambition, maximum anxiety'. He was in a bad enough way for her to see him three or four times a week. He noted in his diary that she focused on his feelings about his mother when he was still a child. Mrs Jacoby believed that he had never been weaned psychologically from his mother: they had been too close and he feared he had forced his mother to love him because 'he couldn't live without sitting in her lap'. His stroke was interpreted as a delayed reaction to losing her. In a 1979 interview for the television profile of him, *Out of Line*, MacMillan said about his stroke (and the stammer might be revealing):

It wasn't a men-men- – certainly it wasn't a mental breakdown. It was a physical breakdown then . . . and I recovered from it. But I certainly didn't want it to happen, and I certainly had to look at my life and I went into analysis and saw psychiatrists to help me look at my life. It took me a long time to find the right psychiatrist because you can't shop around for them, really.

He continued to see Mrs Jacoby for two and a half years before parting from her abruptly. He felt that her mother-centred approach was not helping him in the long run and abandoned her for a psychiatrist whose methods suited him better. He would consult psychiatrists or psychotherapists for the rest of his life.

Before taking up his post as Artistic Director, MacMillan was persuaded by the Royal Ballet press office to give a few, albeit reluctant, interviews about his future plans for the company. He succeeded in putting up quite a few backs by declaring on radio that Britain's male dancers, unlike the German men with whom he had worked, were inferior to their female counterparts. The minutes of the next Royal Opera House Board meeting noted tersely that 'the implications were being considered by the Administration'. He was obliged to back down in a subsequent interview for *Move* magazine, claiming that 'far from planning to replace British boys with hardy Continental stock, he was studying the problem at Royal Ballet School level with Dame Ninette de Valois'. Telling the interviewer, Gemma Lee, that he had been deeply hurt by the criticism that followed his remarks, he said that he tried to avoid personal publicity – especially live interviews on air.

She had evidently caught him unawares at the Rounds' house:

Local intelligence had prepared me for his shyness but when we met I was the one who kept looking down at his feet. He hadn't intended to come to the door in socks, nor had he meant to catnap after lunch. The white towelling socks he was wearing so underlined his natural air of defencelessness that my instinct was to offer him rusks and National Health orange juice.

She described him as friendly but guarded, 'the eyes brown, black-coffee brown, quietly watchful'. He told her that he was listening to enough music, 'padding upstairs and downstairs with a tape-recorder tucked under his arm', to feed his choreography for the next two years.

He said he intended to create a new three-act ballet for his first Covent Garden season, and to include works by Ashton, Cranko and Jerome Robbins, while keeping a balance between the classics and modern ballets. His ambitions extended to the audience as well as the dancers:

I want audiences to feel involved in what is happening on the stage. I'd like them to see new ballets exploring problems they can identify with. They should be gripped, as one is gripped by a drama. I want the dancers to be better actors than dancers normally are. For instance, I'd like to see them being more interested in plays, in discovering how actors achieve their effects. Actors today are learning to dance, and I think it would be to everyone's advantage if dancers returned the compliment.

When pressed by Ms Lee, he gave a selectively edited account of his life and career, belying her claim that 'in one of his rare interviews, the real Kenneth MacMillan stands up'. He admitted, however, that he had suffered a mild stroke because of overwork and emotional strain in Berlin. Running the Deutsche Oper Ballet had not been a good experience and he was far from sorry to have left Germany. Revealingly he described West Berlin as a 'fake town, like a Hollywood movie set: if you go behind the houses there's nothing there'. He kept a paternal interest in his former company, he said, but his focus was now on his future with the Royal Ballet.

He returned briefly to Berlin towards the end of 1969 to settle his affairs. He continued to keep in contact with Ray Barra and Gert Reinholm but otherwise severed his connection with the Deutsche Oper and its ballet company. Frank Frey was an exception. Kenneth proposed that Frey should join him in Stockholm in November 1969, when the Royal Swedish Ballet would be preparing a production of his *Romeo and Juliet*. Erik Bruhn had become its Artistic Director in 1967, and had persuaded his Intendant, Göran Gentele, that the Swedes should obtain MacMillan's *Romeo and Juliet* rather than Cranko's. Agreement had been reached, with the Royal Ballet's permission, well before MacMillan had left Berlin. He wanted Frey to dance Romeo in Stockholm as a guest artist but Bruhn maintained that the company's male dancers were strong enough to undertake the main roles. To Kenneth's disappointment, Frey had to remain in Berlin.

Bruhn did, however, request a guest ballerina as Juliet for the company's premiere on 15 December. The obvious choice would have been Seymour, who was now dancing as an itinerant freelance artist. She had been dismissed from the Deutsche Oper after MacMillan left, but subsequently reinstated as a guest ballerina and was still based in Berlin with Eike Walcz and her baby sons. She wanted to resume her role as Juliet in Stockholm but Kenneth resisted inviting her, on the grounds that bringing her, the twins and their nanny would be too expensive for the Royal Swedish Ballet and too disruptive for him. He associated Lynn with bad times in Berlin, so he asked Georgina Parkinson to be Juliet instead. He owed Parkinson a major favour for having been prepared to stand in for Seymour at the time of *Anastasia*'s premiere; he was also grateful for her continued, unstinting care of him. Dancing a leading role with the Swedish company would boost her standing with the Royal Ballet, as well as providing extra money: she was also to be paid for coaching the principal dancers who would take over after she left.

MacMillan required Faith Worth (who had notated the *Romeo and Juliet* Benesh score) to drop other work commitments and teach the ballet to the company. Desmond Doyle was brought in to supervise the fight sequences. Surrounded by trusted Royal Ballet colleagues and new friends in Sweden, Kenneth enjoyed himself. 'He was extraordinarily relaxed and funny,' said Glen Tetley, the American choreographer who had been Co-Director of Nederlands Dans Theater since 1962. Tetley was in Stockholm to mount his *Ricercare* pas de deux for the Swedish company. It was the first time the two choreographers had spent any time together, though they knew each other's work and had many friends in common.

He told me about his affair with Nora Kaye, whom I knew well – he was very open, full of anecdotes. He didn't seem to me a troubled man. I took it for granted that he was basically gay – we talked as gay men do. He'd known my partner, Scott Douglas, from back in the 1950s when Scott was in Kenneth's *Journey* with ABT.

We talked about the problems of creating choreography and the difficulties of having relationships with dancers. One regularly 'falls in love' with ·a dancer one works with – until one gets down to reality. Then the person who has been the Muse gets hurt if they're replaced by someone else. I'd seen Lynn dancing with Frank Frey on tour with the Deutsche Oper, and she'd stayed at my house in The Hague with her twins on the way back to Berlin. She felt betrayed by Kenneth. He didn't want her to have the babies and he didn't want her as Juliet in Stockholm. But choreographers have to be ruthless. We put the work first.

MacMillan had by now conceived an infatuation for Jonas Kage, the young Swede who was dancing Romeo with Parkinson as Juliet, and whose girlfriend was cast as one of the three marketplace whores. 'Jonas was embarrassed by the teasing that went on within the company,' says Faith Worth. 'Kenneth's obsession was misplaced and he wasn't very nice to the girlfriend. He'd changed a lot since I last saw him in Berlin. He moved far more slowly after his stroke and his speech was a bit slurred. But at least he wasn't drinking.' Göran Gentele took charge of MacMillan, making sure that he had everything he needed. Gentele, 'a beautiful man', according to Tetley, 'helpful and genial, a very good friend', was about to leave Sweden to become Artistic Director of the Metropolitan Opera

House in New York. He was killed in a car crash on holiday in Italy shortly after the Royal Swedish Ballet's premiere of *Romeo and Juliet*. His death was a deeply distressing conclusion to one of the less troubled periods in MacMillan's life. The Swedish company had danced *Romeo and Juliet* with great gusto, making it such a favourite with audiences that it became a staple of their repertoire.

As soon as *Romeo and Juliet* was up and running, MacMillan returned to London to start preparing a new work for the Stuttgart Ballet, due for March 1970. At the time of Kenneth's stroke in Munich, Cranko had cheered him up by discussing his commission, assuring Kenneth that it would take place as soon as he was well enough. MacMillan had proposed a ballet based on Strindberg's *Miss Julie*, with Frey as Jean, the valet, and Haydée as Julie. Cranko was dubious about the idea, according to Elisabeth Dalton, but didn't want to discourage Kenneth. 'Kenneth was full of plans for *Miss Julie*. I remember thinking with relief that he can't have been too affected by his stroke because he'd overridden John's reluctance so quickly.'

Within six months, MacMillan had drafted a scenario for *Miss Julie* and commissioned a score from Andrzej Panufnik, whose music he had used for *Cain and Abel*. Panufnik lived with his family in Richmond, on the outskirts of London, so he and Kenneth were able to meet and discuss the scenario in person. They drew up an outline of the action, with a minutage for the music, to last 65 minutes in all. In order to make use of a number of Stuttgart's soloists, as well as the corps de ballet, MacMillan had expanded Strindberg's chamber play by adding roles for Miss Julie's parents, the Count and Countess, and her fiancé, a dour, formal man who would dance to the crack of her riding whip. The upper-class pairing of Julie and her suitor was therefore mirrored by the valet, Jean, and his fiancée, Kristin the cook. MacMillan was quoted in the *Stuttgarter Nachtrichten* insisting that the ballet, like the play, was primarily about 'the battle between man and woman' rather than class warfare. (Thirteen years later, MacMillan was to direct Strindberg's play of marital strife, *The Dance of Death*, at the Royal Exchange in Manchester.)

The corps de ballet were to be the ghosts of Miss Julie's stern ancestors, as well as drunken peasants celebrating Midsummer's Eve. For the revelling, Panufnik had drawn on folk songs and dances he remembered from his native Poland: the words would need to be translated into German, to be sung by the Stuttgart opera chorus. *Miss Julie* was going to prove a considerable drain on Cranko's budget for his ballet season.

Frank Frey had come to London, at MacMillan's invitation, to meet Panufnik and learn how plans for the ballet were developing. He stayed in Battersea with Georgina Parkinson and her husband, then accompanied Kenneth, by train, to Stuttgart. Once installed in the rehearsal room, MacMillan, as always, began with the key pas de deux – in this case, the seduction and act of sex between the valet and Miss Julie. In the draft scenario, where Panufnik had written '16 minutes of love-making . . . an extremely tender passage in the strings gradually builds to a very huge climax', MacMillan had simply scrawled 'Fuck'. The frenzied congress on the kitchen table was to have the avidity of the passionate duets MacMillan later took to extremes in *Mayerling*: a power-play as much as a mutual act of lust.

Reid Anderson, then a young corps dancer in the production, remembers what extraordinary performances Frey and Haydée delivered. The ballet, like the play, began and ended with the valet cleaning his master's riding boots. 'I have this image of Frank sitting downstage right, spit-polishing the boot with his arm inside the leg, moving the cloth up and down the leather. Marcia as Julie was practically suffocating with repressed sexuality.'

But although MacMillan had rapidly established the outlines of the ballet in early rehearsals, he hit a creative block that lasted for about three weeks. The main cause was the arrival in Stuttgart of Frey's new girlfriend, an actress with decided views of her own. MacMillan suspected that Frey was making a defiant bid for independence, as Seymour had done in Berlin, and was no longer fully accessible to him as an interpreter of his choreography. Sensing there were problems, the Stuttgart dancers became uneasy. 'We could tell it wasn't right between Kenneth and Frank any more – and it was hard for Frank to adapt to our constellation of dancers. Hard for us, too, to accommodate him,' says Haydée.

Monumental designs by Barry Kay were an additional complication. Kay had envisaged the kitchen, in which most of the action took place, as a boiler room dominated by vast metal pipes: in his view, it served as a portent of the industrial revolution that would end the old order. Cranko objected to the overpowering decor both because it was costly and cumbersome and because it had little to do with the ballet's emphasis on sexual power struggles. When Kay protested that the interlocking parts of the set had been shoddily made, Cranko refused to intervene, saying the opera's sets took priority in the workshop and there was nothing he could do.

Both Kay and MacMillan asked for the premiere on 8 March to be postponed, but Cranko was not prepared to change the scheduled programme. When the dress rehearsal went ahead, MacMillan discovered that Cranko had authorised changes to the costumes. Cranko believed that he was simplifying the action, but MacMillan found his interference intolerable. Kay, already in a rage about the execution of his designs, stormed out before the premiere, insisting that his name be taken off the programme credits. It was, but only after the first night.

MacMillan, too, left Stuttgart the day before the premiere, demanding that Frey drove him to the railway station. He had expected Frey to side with him and refuse to dance; he was angry and disappointed when Frank chose to stay on. *Miss Julie* marked the end of their relationship. The rows with Cranko led to an estrangement between the two choreographers that endured for years to come: MacMillan was not invited to work with the Stuttgart company again while Cranko was alive.

Cranko pulled *Miss Julie* from the Stuttgart season after just four performances. Haydée, torn between her loyalties to Cranko and to MacMillan, had become physically ill with misery. The theatre wrote off the production, in spite of its expense. Frey had to bring a legal case to receive compensation for not getting his contracted number of performances.

MacMillan was never willing to revive *Miss Julie* for another company, and Georgette Tsinguirides, Cranko's notator, did not finish its Benesh score. Kenneth preferred to put the bitter experience behind him, moving on to the next stage in his life. He was preparing to take over as Director of the Royal Ballet in September 1970, when a new era would begin in the history of the company and the Royal Opera House. Precisely what, and whom, that regime would involve, however, was far from evident. MacMillan was about to inherit a hornets' nest, brought about by bad planning, poor communication and clashing egos.

4
Artistic Director of the Royal Ballet
1970–1977

28

David Webster had led MacMillan and John Field independently to believe a different account of their future status as co-directors of the Royal Ballet. Kenneth understood the arrangement to mean that he would be Artistic Director and Field his Administrative Director. In an interview with Ian Woodward in the *Guardian* in March 1969, eighteen months before he took over the job, MacMillan asserted:

The whole point of this co-directorship is to allow me more free time for creative work, unlike Sir Frederick, who has had to look after everything, including the administrative side. Well, this aspect will be largely taken care of by John Field, leaving me time to create new ballets and commission outside choreographers to mount works.

Field, meanwhile, had been assured that he would be responsible for artistic decisions as well as managerial ones. During Ashton's reign as Royal Ballet Director, nominally of both companies, Field had been fully entrusted with choosing the touring company's repertoire and commissioning its choreographers. According to Field's widow, the former dancer Anne Heaton, Webster would never have been able to woo him away from the offer of the Festival Ballet's directorship if Field thought he was going to be no more than MacMillan's administrator:

Kenneth needed a good guardian angel, which John would have been, to give him time to choreograph. John had been told that they both would have a say over the rep., not that John would do the office work and never go into the rehearsal room, if you please. His life was with the dancers.

Both men seem to have been strung along from the start, in a deliberate confusion that Webster must have hoped would sort itself out. According to John Tooley:

David had got himself into a hole with John Field, making rash promises so that he wouldn't go to Festival Ballet. I'm not sure David ever said, 'You will be director', but he'd gone further with Field than he should have. So what with a promise to Kenneth in Berlin, a promise to John in London and another to Ninette de Valois in Turkey, David kept digging the hole deeper and deeper.

Webster even told John Hart, Ashton's Assistant Director, that MacMillan had asked for Field as his co-director – a request that seemed so unlikely to Hart that he wrote to 'Mac' in Berlin to ask if it were true. Hart must have been concerned about his own future. MacMillan replied that he had been presented with a fait accompli he had felt bound to accept: 'I hear that many people are unhappy at the prospect of this co-directorship, which makes me unhappy. I hope that we will be able to talk openly together regarding this when I am next in London.'

At the time MacMillan had agreed to the proposal in 1968, he was about to hand over all his administrative duties as Director of the Deutsche Oper Ballet to Gert Reinholm (whose official title became Deputy Director). He had realised how onerous such responsibilities were and was no doubt relieved that Field would shoulder them for him at the Royal Ballet. He had not appreciated that Field, unlike Reinholm, would resent being second in command.

Word would have reached the Opera House administration (and de Valois) that MacMillan had been making heavy weather of directing the Deutsche Oper Ballet company. The need for an experienced aide at his side once he took over the Royal Ballet was evident – even more so after he had suffered his stroke in 1969. He had stopped drinking but his health and lack of resilience under pressure gave cause for concern. To make matters worse, the Royal Ballet was about to undergo a period of major upheaval in 1970, just at the point when the directorship changed hands.

The Arts Council, which controls the Royal Opera House's subsidy from government funds, was concerned about its accumulating deficit. Demands for an increased grant could not be justified, the Arts Council decided, unless the Royal companies served the regions more comprehensively, sending their biggest stars on tour instead of reserving them for London. The Opera House Board, required to examine its touring provision and to cut its costs, opted to sacrifice the second ballet company as a separate entity, thereby saving an estimated £100,000 a year. Some of its complement of 70 dancers would be merged with the Covent Garden company, making a single Royal Ballet about 125 strong. Touring commitments would be met by the combined company in the summer and a smaller group of up to 25 dancers in autumn and winter (starting in November 1970). Large productions, including the classics, would be the preserve of the resident Covent Garden company: the small group would be more like the early Sadler's Wells Theatre Ballet, with a repertoire of one-act works such as *The Rake's Progress, Pineapple Poll* and *The Invitation*, supplemented by new, experimental ballets made specially for it. Principals and soloists from the main company would join the group on tour, thereby gratifying audiences in the regions who wanted to see the Royal Ballet's stars. In theory, all 125 dancers would be interchangeable, providing more opportunities for performances in a wider range of ballets.

The reorganisation plans, finally agreed by the Board in November 1969, were presented to MacMillan, Field and the rest of the ballet staff as a done deal with the Arts Council. Field was distressed at the loss of 'his' touring company but was prepared to make the new scheme work in his future role as Co-Director. Peter Wright, who had already been co-opted to take over Field's job as Director of the touring company, suddenly had to come to terms with a very different brief. Instead of a well-established company of 70 dancers, he would now be in charge of a variable group of around 20. MacMillan, for his part, positively welcomed the proposal for a smaller, predominantly creative group. He looked forward to choreographing ballets for it as well as for the newly enlarged main company. The drawback, though, was that at least 26 dancers would have to be made redundant, most of them from the touring company.

After the merger announcement was released to the press on 9 January 1970, the dancers' Equity representative, Kenneth Mason, voiced their concerns to a meeting of the Ballet Sub-Committee and members of the administration. Field was present but not MacMillan. Mason put on record that the dancers welcomed MacMillan's appointment warmly: their worry was about provisions for their future under the reorganisation. Equity was promised that the 'last in, first out' union rule would apply. Junior members of the corps would be the ones required to leave, not senior artists who failed to find favour with the new regime. As a consequence, the merged company was going to be top heavy with soloists expecting to be cast in roles they considered their due. By the time MacMillan took over in mid-1970, the official roster of dancers listed 40 principals and 25 soloists. Among the principals would be Lynn Seymour, relieved to renounce her freelance career and rejoin the company she had left four years earlier.

In spite of the management's attempts to reassure the dancers, morale in both companies was low from the start of 1970. The touring company faced dissolution at the end of the summer season. The Covent Garden company, which had been so appalled by the announcement of Ashton's retirement, devoted the first half of the year to bidding farewell to him. Its annual season at the New York Met ended on 31 May with a gala tribute to Ashton, complete with an onstage speech by Webster. As Ashton's last American season in charge of the company, it had been warmly appreciated, although Arlene Croce in *Ballet Review* had noticed 'signs of disrepair and demoralisation'. She commented that the new directors would have to decide what course the company took in the next decade: 'There is a lot for the Royal to do,' she warned.

When the company returned to the Royal Opera House, its summer season consisted largely of Ashton ballets, with 'the company and audience behaving as though it was the last time we would ever see them', as Leslie Edwards recalled in his autobiography. Ashton's frequent curtain calls became part of the performances, cheered on by loyal supporters who showered him with flowers. 'It must have been very difficult for MacMillan waiting in the wings,' commented Edwards. Michael Somes, with the help of Edwards and John Hart, masterminded a magnificent tribute to Ashton, with thirty-six extracts from his ballets, for his final gala on 24 July, which followed soon after David Webster's operatic farewell gala. Ashton's gala was a highly emotional occasion, its contents kept a secret from him until the performance was under way. He was overwhelmed, as were audience members who were aware that an era had ended and that Ashton had felt rejected. Yet more outpourings of regret attended the touring company's last-ever performance on 25 July in Wimbledon, at which Ashton and de Valois were present, as well as Field and the now-redundant ballet staff. Although the August holiday break would diffuse some of the fraught feelings, MacMillan was to inherit a very troubled company for his first season as Director – or rather, as Co-Director, for his and Field's responsibilities had still not been resolved.

Both men had been asked to outline their plans for the future at a Ballet Sub-Committee meeting in April. According to the minutes, MacMillan talked about the repertoire and Field discussed the shortage of good male dancers and 'the Fonteyn–Nureyev problem':

how to allocate their guest performances, what to do when Fonteyn finally retired. The presentation of the two Directors' spheres of interest seemed an amicable enough arrangement at this stage. MacMillan announced that he intended to create a three-act version of *Anastasia* for his first season, as well as a ballet for the new touring group. He was pleased to have secured Jerome Robbins's *Dances at a Gathering* for the main company in October and a new work from Glen Tetley for the small group in November. He had asked Cranko and Ashton for ballets: Cranko could not yet oblige but Ashton had agreed to a new work, probably for March 1971, in addition to his latest ballet, *Creatures of Prometheus*, which was premiered by the touring company in Bonn in June 1970.

It was a promising list of acquisitions, though there were inevitable hitches once the new regime started. MacMillan's *Anastasia* had to be postponed because of rehearsal scheduling difficulties (a new opera production of Michael Tippett's *The Knot Garden* took precedence); Ashton's *Prometheus* was a flop. Ashton went into a prolonged period of inactivity at the start of his retirement, unable or unwilling to create a ballet for his successor's company for the next five years, even though he had signed a contract to choreograph annually for the Royal Ballet. His works continued to be regularly performed under the guidance of Michael Somes, who stayed on in order to supervise the Ashton repertoire. But until *A Month in the Country* in February 1976, Ashton's only new contributions would be small *pièces d'occasion*. He would, however, continue to appear before the curtain to take his bows after performances of his existing ballets, 'as though in need of the reassurance he derived from the ovation that always ensued', as David Vaughan commented.

MacMillan's coup was Robbins's *Dances at a Gathering*, made for New York City Ballet the previous year and already regarded as one of his masterpieces. The two men were old acquaintances (not least through their continuing friendship with Nora Kaye) and Robbins was top of MacMillan's list of priorities for the company's repertoire. Robbins had previously made proposals for ballets to de Valois, and Ashton had requested a work when he was Artistic Director, but nothing had materialised. 'Of course I would love to do a work for the Royal Ballet,' Robbins had written to MacMillan on 6 August 1969. 'I have always wanted to but I am just as mystified as you are as to why it has never worked out . . . I would like to do a new work but I would also like to see the Royal Ballet dance my latest work, *Dances at a Gathering*. I think the Royal Ballet would dance it beautifully.' MacMillan, who knew how exigent Robbins could be about casting and rehearsal conditions, persisted with letters, telephone calls and telegrams to ensure his prize did not slip away. He nearly lost *Dances at a Gathering* on several occasions because of scheduling difficulties. (Robbins eventually sent him a reassuring cable in April 1970, saying simply, 'Relax, it's all working out.') By the time Robbins arrived in London in September 1970 to oversee rehearsals, MacMillan was willing to give him everything – and every dancer – he required.

Meanwhile, Kenneth had been wooing Glen Tetley, who was initially reluctant to create a ballet for the new group. Tetley was busy co-directing Nederlands Dans Theater in The Hague, choreographing for it and for Ballet Rambert, which had transformed itself into a contemporary dance ensemble in 1966. According to Tetley, 'My work in England was identified with Rambert, where there was a bit of animosity towards the Royal as being the old school, whereas Rambert represented the new frontier. So I debated whether I should work with the Royal when I was establishing myself internationally as a contemporary choreographer.' MacMillan despatched Peter Wright to the Netherlands to convince Tetley that the Royal Ballet was about to enter a new era. After eight long hours' discussion, Tetley agreed, insisting on his own terms: 'I'd do it very contemporary, I'd audition the whole company to pick the dancers I wanted, we'd rehearse in seclusion and I'd have total control.'

In agreeing to the conditions imposed by his two fellow choreographers, MacMillan was setting up logistical problems for himself and his staff. Wright remembers that no decisions could be made about the composition of the new touring group until Robbins and Tetley had chosen their casts:

Rehearsal schedules were a nightmare because there were so many dancers and nowhere to put them. There weren't enough studios at Baron's Court [the West London headquarters of the Royal Ballet senior school, where the company rehearsed since there were no ballet studios at the Royal Opera House until 1982] so we used the Donmar Studios in Covent Garden as an overflow. Robbins and Tetley were rivals, Jerry pulled clout over his rehearsals, Glen wasn't happy . . . Kenneth let them have their way because he was thinking like a choreographer, not a director.

Incipient chaos was further compounded by the dancers' need to be on call for the filming of *Tales of Beatrix Potter*.* The retirement package Ashton had negotiated with the Royal Opera House included a film project to swell his pension fund. He had been contracted to do the choreography for a film of Beatrix Potter's stories for children, using Royal Ballet members in elaborate animal masks and costumes as the creatures she illustrated in her books. In planning the reorganisation of the two companies, nobody in the Royal Ballet management seems to have taken into account the timing of the film. Although Ashton was freely available in September 1970, the dancers were not. MacMillan had assumed that Field would take into account the rehearsal requirements for the film, only to discover that Field wanted nothing to do with schedules and timetables.

Unfortunately for the new regime, John Hart, the Royal Ballet's expert organiser (in charge of class, rehearsal and performance schedules since 1962), had resigned at the end of Ashton's last season. Field's appointment as Co-Director and Adminstrator had apparently pre-empted Hart's role. The two men, who had been rivals as dancers, did not like each other. Hart was not prepared to work under Field and was in any case frustrated with his desk-bound post; he left to become an artistic director in his own right with the PACT ballet company in South Africa. (He also took up an academic post as Head of the Performing Arts Course at San Diego University.) His departure and Field's recalcitrance left MacMillan without an experienced right-hand man. Henry Legerton, Field's assistant and répétiteur with the former touring company, eventually assumed responsibility for the schedules; Desmond Doyle became ballet master and Jill Gregory continued as ballet mistress. MacMillan had, however, inherited an able secretary in Iris Law. She took over the organising required for the film on top of her regular work, while he nagged the management for an extra secretary to help her out.

As preparations for the new season intensified, MacMillan and Field were increasingly at loggerheads. They were both paid at the

---

* The EMI film, directed by Richard Goodwin, was released on 1 April 1971. *Tales of Beatrix Potter* was staged as a ballet after Ashton's death and remains in the Royal Ballet repertoire.

same salary level – £7,500 p.a. – but Field demanded (and got) an extra responsibility allowance of £500 for the work he had put in between April and July. He had suffered a coronary thrombosis in April; Peter Wright had taken charge of the touring company until its final performances while Field remained in London, recovering his health and overseeing the reorganisation plans. MacMillan, who had also been working hard during the same period, threw an angry tantrum on discovering that Field's name was printed above his on a leaflet advertising the Royal Ballet's forthcoming performances. He told the dancers that if they had any complaints about dressing-rooms or lavatories, they should address them to Field, who would deal with 'that sort of thing'. MacMillan had taken over Ashton's former office (with Iris Law near by) at Baron's Court, leaving Field without a base. When he found that Field was out of reach when he needed him, Kenneth made room for him in the Director's office. In an angry draft memo to John Tooley, Webster's successor, MacMillan described what happened next: 'A desk arrived, locks were put on the doors, an opaque window was set in one door and a tea service arrived. He [Field] made very few appearances, mainly arriving at 4.30 p.m. and staying approximately until 5.30 p.m.'

The situation was intolerable on every level, from petty complaints to vital decision-making. As Clive Barnes had prophesied in the *New York Times* in 1968, soon after the co-directorship was first announced, 'In any system of dual steering, there must be a doubt as to which hand is ultimately on the steering wheel. Ballet companies are like armies. There can only be one supreme commander.' MacMillan threatened to resign at the start of December, sending a letter to Lord Drogheda, Chairman of the Board, and was then persuaded to change his mind. Clearly, Field had to go. MacMillan, as a choreographer, was more valuable to the company and a replacement manager could be found.

The solution was to entrust Peter Wright with running both companies, the resident one as well as the small group, when Field resigned on 23 December 1970.* Wright tries to account for what had gone wrong:

---

* Field went off to direct La Scala Ballet, then London Festival Ballet, the Royal Academy of Dancing and finally the British Ballet Organisation. He died in 1991.

The appointments were all made at Board level. I suppose there was a feeling that Kenneth needed support as Artistic Director but nobody anticipated that he and John Field wouldn't be able to work together. Kenneth believed that Field wanted power, while Kenneth wanted someone to do his bidding without threatening his status. I was very close to him, so we could trust each other. He realised he didn't want to do the manager's job, especially in such stressful conditions. He wasn't a strong man – he had to reserve his energies to choreograph. He was always complaining that he didn't want to be bothered with admin stuff.

The mistake Webster and the Board had made was in choosing Field instead of Wright as MacMillan's aide. Wright had a more diplomatic personality than Field, who was a bluff, assertive figure, accustomed to being in charge. Field held decided views on what British audiences expected from the Royal Ballet companies; Wright was more open-minded, having spent much of his working life with foreign companies. He had been persuaded to abandon his freelance career as a television director, choreographer and stager of ballets to accept the non-specific title of Associate to the Directors. He had now been given the responsibility for coping with the administration of the Covent Garden company as well as the new touring group. The dual role was to prove more than one man could handle.

29

In spite of mismanagement behind the scenes, MacMillan's first season started well. The newly enlarged company danced mixed programmes of one-act ballets: revivals of the classics would have to wait until the corps de ballet, combined from the two companies, settled into a cohesive unit. Fortunately, Robbins's *Dances at a Gathering* proved a smash hit, as it had in New York. MacMillan paired it with ballets by Ashton: either *The Dream*, *Enigma Variations* or *The Creatures of Prometheus*.

Robbins had finally selected two casts that met his exacting requirements: the first included Rudolf Nureyev, Anthony Dowell, David Wall, Lynn Seymour, Antoinette Sibley and Monica Mason.

They gave greater dramatic emphasis to the roles than the New York City Ballet cast, making more play with implied relationships in the hour-long sequence of dances to Chopin piano studies. Royal Opera House audiences responded with rapt delight. Robbins himself had reservations.

He wrote to MacMillan from hospital in New York, on 2 November 1970, saying he had returned with a debilitating illness that turned out to be hepatitis. That might explain, he said, why 'I wasn't pushing for what I felt could be a more definitive version of the ballet and why I allowed many things to happen that did. Some of these you could take care of for me.' Some of the dancers, Robbins believed, had gone behind his back to the pianist, Antony Twiner, and asked him to play slower: 'I guarantee you that once the tempi have been picked up to the correct level for the choreography, the ballet will gain enormously.' Royal Ballet dancers were unaccustomed to the speed at which City Ballet's dancers were trained to move; Nureyev in particular liked to dictate the tempi at which he preferred to perform.

Robbins told MacMillan how much he had enjoyed the weeks of work while he was well and passed on his thanks to the dancers. He made no mention of creating a new ballet for the company and one never materialised (although four more of his ballets entered the repertoire during MacMillan's directorship). As soon as MacMillan ceased being Director, Robbins withdrew the Royal Ballet's right to perform his ballets. He relented over a few, but *Dances at a Gathering* would not be given again by the company until 2008, after Robbins's death and thirty-two years after its last revival in 1976.

Glen Tetley had been as exigent as Robbins in demanding rehearsal time for his work for the small group, *Field Figures*, to electronic music by Stockhausen. As requested, MacMillan stayed away for the first weeks, 'letting us get on with it'. Tetley had started with a pas de deux for Deanne Bergsma and Desmond Kelly, the only two dancers who had smiled at him when he was introduced to the company. The others, he felt, regarded him with suspicion, if not outright hostility. He required his chosen pair to stay intimately interlocked in what Tetley described as 'a kind of double yoga' – his way of challenging the Royal Ballet's habit of distancing itself from modern dance. When MacMillan arrived at the Donmar Studios to watch the work in progress, Tetley recalled, 'He folded himself up, as always, one leg draped over the other, arm on one knee, chin in his hand. After we stopped, there was silence. He turned to me and said, "Bitch." I couldn't have had a better compliment.'

Field Figures, herald of the new era, was given its premiere on tour in Nottingham on 9 November 1970, in a triple bill with Balanchine's *Apollo* and Ashton's *Symphonic Variations*.* The launch of the New Group (as it came to be known, since it had no other title) was an important occasion, attended in Nottingham by de Valois as well as MacMillan. Tetley was surprised to find there were no celebrations afterwards and that no one came forward to thank him for his premiere. The dancers suggested he went with them to a Chinese restaurant, where they found MacMillan eating with Wright and de Valois. 'Someone at their table told me later that Ninette instructed Kenneth to go and talk to me, tell me I was needed at the Royal Ballet and ask me to do another ballet. So then Kenneth came over bashfully and congratulated me.'

MacMillan's own ballet for the New Group, *Checkpoint*, was given later in the month in Manchester. Based on Orwell's *1984*, it was inspired by Kenneth's experiences in Germany: passing through Checkpoint Charlie in Berlin after being turned off a train to Stuttgart by armed guards, and hearing reports of lovers being separated by the Wall, of spies and informers on both sides of the divided city. Elisabeth Dalton was the designer, briefed by MacMillan to create a limbo land, an Orwellian dystopia where love was forbidden. In Kenneth's scenario, a guard holding a woman for interrogation falls in love with her. He slips away from his fellow guards to join her; their pas de deux becomes more passionate as they try to evade the surveillance spotlights and the all-seeing eye of Big Brother. Realising they have been discovered, they scramble up the prison wall, the only place the eye cannot detect them. But the guards have been alerted and the lovers are eliminated on the wall. Svetlana Beriosova and Donald MacLeary were cast as the doomed pair.

---

* *Field Figures* was later given in November 1971 at Covent Garden, where Nureyev asked to dance in it. The opening pas de deux, with Nureyev and Bergsma, was recorded in the Donmar Studios for the Nureyev film *I Am A Dancer*, with the dancers wearing a form of practice dress instead of the original costumes (for copyright reasons).

Dalton devised a claustrophobic set like a cell, with side walls and a black wall at the rear, overhung with huge metal spotlights. Sheets of heavy black corset elastic were stretched over a grid to form the wall, so that unseen figures standing behind it could grab hold of the fleeing pair. In the final *coup de théâtre*, the elastic wall engulfed them. Film was projected onto the wall, showing a series of slogans and instructions; a filmed eye kept watch and at the end a sinister mouth denounced the deviant lovers. (The mouth belonged to Cliff Michelmore, a well-known television presenter.) Dalton later expressed her regret that the ballet was ahead of its time technologically. Video and CCTV cameras were not yet in use and film projectors were cumbersome and unreliable. At the premiere in Manchester, the reel of film unspooled over the floor as it was being mounted. It had to be rewound by hand, protracting the interval before the ballet could start to over fifty minutes. John Tooley went out before the curtains to apologise to the audience, who then had to put up with the projector breaking down before the end of the very brief ballet. 'It was the worst, horrible night,' remembered Dalton. 'Svetlana and Donald were very brave to carry on because it was actually quite dangerous. Nobody could see what they were doing.' For the rest of the run, the theatre manager insisted on putting up a notice refusing to guarantee anyone's safety on stage during the ballet.

Wright believes that MacMillan deliberately defied restrictions imposed by the Opera House management on decor for ballets on tour. The New Group was intended to be a much less expensive operation than the disbanded touring company, so costs were meant to be kept to a minimum. 'That made Kenneth see red because he thought priority was being given to opera productions, not to his company's ballets. He could be incredibly obstinate,' Wright remarks. 'He didn't express himself readily in words but his actions told you a lot.' *Checkpoint* turned out to be the most expensive production of the year, way over budget. Many modifications had to be made on tour by over-stretched technicians, with little or no co-operation from headquarters back in London. Production notes detailing the problems leading up to the premiere make hair-raising reading. Beriosova had gallantly come to the rescue by sewing up tears in the elastic wall and helping backstage staff lash foam-rubber coverings into place.

As a further complication and expense, MacMillan's choice of music, Roberto Gerhard's *Collages*, had to be taped in order for the film to be precisely synchronised with it. This meant that, due to Musicians' Union regulations, the orchestra had to be paid both for the recording and for every performance of the ballet, even though they did not play live. As a result, *Checkpoint* was soon dropped from the New Group's repertoire, never to be revived.

By the end of 1970, when a profile of MacMillan appeared in *About the House*, he was about to turn forty-one. Nigel Gosling, writing under his nom de plume of Alexander Bland, pointed out that whether MacMillan liked it or not (and evidently he did not), he must expect to come under the spotlight as a personality, not just as a choreographer:

His work rhythms, his relationship with other people, his views on his own art and on that of others, his knowledge and social opinions, his courage, his cunning, his public presence and his private dreams, all become of vital interest to us. For they will be reflected in his company and tilt its growth this way or that.

Gosling added perceptively:

MacMillan is one of those large men who look as though they would like to be small. His appearance of Roman calm conceals an egregiously recessive personality. He often suggests an outsize mollusc driven by fate to live a few paces from its shell. He speaks softly and sadly and has big, watchful eyes and a gentle smile. To cope with the problem of the shy man who has to operate in public he has adopted the best kind of defence, an evasive charm which is proof against almost any aggravation (a sharpish claw can emerge on occasion).

Ninette de Valois summed him up in similar terms from her own perspective, in an essay published later in a collection called *Step by Step: The Formation of an Establishment*: 'On the surface I do not know a more reserved, unspectacular and sensitive person, nor do I know a more sincere, granite-like character underneath.' She commented from her knowledge of him as a private person, 'He has his own world, and within this world he lives, works and thinks. Small talk is unknown to him; if he has nothing to say of any interest he remains silent, aloof from the nattering ebb and flow, and totally unaware that his self-removal may be causing some embarrassment.'

MacMillan found the prospect of explaining himself to the Ballet Sub-Committee unsettling, especially when they started complaining, early in 1971, about the lack of forward planning for new productions of the classics. He and Peter Wright pointed out that the difficulties of merging the two companies were still largely unresolved. None the less, he intended to schedule Wright's production of *Giselle*, originally staged for Cranko's Stuttgart company, and to revise the existing production of *Swan Lake*. Fonteyn would therefore have familiar roles she could dance with the company; so would Natalia Makarova, who had recently defected from the Soviet Union to the West, and who was much in demand as a guest artist. The Committee agreed that Makarova should make six appearances in the following season, three in *Giselle* and three in *Swan Lake*.

MacMillan was meanwhile working on his own postponed three-act *Anastasia*, to be given its premiere in July, at the end of the 1971 summer season. Now that Seymour had returned to the Royal Ballet at his invitation, she could resume the role she had created in Berlin. The ballet would end with the Berlin act, as 'the woman who called herself Anastasia' tried to retrieve her identity in the mental asylum. He was about to add two preceding acts that would depict the events (or her version of them) that led up to her incarceration. Her recollections of life within the Imperial family until the outbreak of the Russian Revolution would not need to be historically accurate. This was a ballet, not a documentary account of the pre-Revolutionary period. In any case, MacMillan wanted to maintain an element of mystery about Anna Anderson's identity: her 'memories' of an idyllic childhood in the royal Romanov household might have been fantasy.

He was strongly inclined to believe Anderson's story. Royal Ballet dancers remember that he pinned up on the company notice board a recent newspaper report that an analysis of Anderson's ear shape had 'proved' she was indeed Anastasia. After MacMillan's death, DNA tests in 1994 showed conclusively that Anderson could not have been a Romanov. She was almost certainly Franziska Schanzkowska, a Polish-German woman who had tried to commit suicide in a Berlin canal. A private detective hired by the dead Tsarina's brother in the 1920s had discovered her probable identity but was unable at the time to verify his suspicions. 'Anna Anderson' died in the USA in 1984, still claiming she was Anastasia.

(When MacMillan's ballet was revived in 1996, four years after his death, new designs by Bob Crowley indicated that the world conjured up in the first two acts could not be relied upon. Angles were dramatically tilted, chandeliers hung askew, the interior of the Hermitage Palace ballroom confounded with the exterior. Audiences' foreknowledge that Anderson could not have been Anastasia turned out to make little difference to their appreciation of the ballet.)

The first two acts were to be seen as if through young Anastasia's eyes. The problem MacMillan faced was that the real Grand Duchess was an insignificant figure in the cataclysmic events that overwhelmed Tsarist Russia. As the second youngest of five royal children, her death or survival would have made no difference to the outcome of the Revolution. He needed, however, to establish his Anastasia at the heart of what would turn out to be her story in Act III. To evoke a picture of the over-privileged society in which she was growing up, he selected music by Tchaikovsky, the First and Third Symphonies: the choreography would recall the classical-ballet style of the period. Then Martinů's Sixth Symphony would follow for the Expressionist asylum scenes, the disjunction with the previous acts signalled by the *musique concrète* – garbled voices, dissonant squawks and scratches – recorded in the studio of the Technical University of West Berlin. Characters from the first two acts would reappear in the last act, some assuming different identities to indicate the confusion in Anna's mind. Like readers of a detective thriller, audiences were being given clues in the earlier parts of the work with which to unravel Anastasia's tangled nightmare at the end.

It would not be an easy ballet either to watch or to perform. Ideas for its unusual structure had been forming in MacMillan's mind for a long time: he now had the opportunity, and the dancers, to try them out. He also wanted to show that the Royal Ballet was set on a new, more radical course than under Ashton's leadership. *Anastasia*, his first full-length ballet since *Romeo and Juliet*, was to be a fresh challenge. Although the first two acts would prove that he was a classical choreographer in the Royal Ballet tradition, its audiences had never seen anything like the last act before. He was bringing together his two strongest influences: Petipa and German Expressionism. The discontinuity between the dance styles would reflect the cataclysms that exposed the faultlines in twentieth-century society.

Barry Kay, who was commissioned to design the entire ballet, produced a vortex of suspended curving screens as a metaphor for coils of memory winding into the past. The screens remained in place throughout the ballet, adapted to suit the settings of each act. The opening act, with a dappled effect on the overhanging screens, suggested a silver-birch grove by a lake. The Imperial family was shown at play, enjoying a picnic attended by naval officers and cadets. Kay's set indicated that all was not well: some of the trees had been reduced to stumps – a Chekhovian Cherry Orchard warning that the old order was about to change. By the end of the first act, World War I had been declared.

The second act, Anastasia's coming-of-age party, took place in the palace ballroom, a gilded metallic cage with a spiral staircase. Anastasia used the stairs as a vantage point from which to watch the convoluted relationships played out on the dance floor below. Her father's mistress before his marriage, the ballerina Mathilde Kchessinskaya, danced a 'command performance' pas de deux with her Imperial Ballet partner; she then joined the Tsar and Tsarina in a quartet with Rasputin, whose relationship with Tsarina Alexandra appeared sexually charged. Interspersed with the ballroom activity were scenes before a front cloth, showing the Tsar's rebellious subjects gathering in the streets outside. By the end of the second act, the Russian Revolution was under way.

The last act, set in the Berlin asylum some years later, was a reworking of the original Deutsche Oper production. At the start, the same film footage of the Imperial past, intercut with revolutionary violence, was projected onto the curved screens. People and events from Anna Anderson's 'memoirs' (her rescue from the family's massacre, her marriage to one of her rescuers, the removal of her child) intermingled with figures seen earlier in the ballet. At the end, when the woman reclaimed her self-belief, she toured the stage triumphantly in a remote-controlled bed – a substitute for the revolve in the original Berlin staging.

Seymour had had reservations about rejoining the company, even though she wanted to bring up her twins in London instead of Berlin. It was tricky for her to re-establish her place in the roster, resuming many of her former roles. Inevitably, other principal dancers resented the fact that MacMillan's first major creation as Artistic Director was to be based on her. She was convinced that he wanted her back essentially for the expanded version of *Anastasia*, and might never create another leading role for her. Uncertain of her long-term prospects, she accepted guest engagements while he was working on *Anastasia*. She seized the opportunity to take the flamboyant role of Janis Joplin in Alvin Ailey's new modern-dance work, *Flowers*, in New York; she travelled to her home town, Toronto, to dance *Giselle* with the National Ballet of Canada. In between performances, she flew back to London for rehearsals of *Anastasia*. Her absences did little to repair her strained personal relations with MacMillan.

As his interpreter of Anastasia, however, she brought her invaluable insight into the role and its context. She understood how he was working to make the first two acts lead up to the nightmare of the asylum act. It was her idea to turn young Anastasia in Act I into a tomboy to differentiate her from her sister Grand Duchesses. She suggested adopting the roller-skates and sailor suit worn by the real Anastasia in the Imperial family home-movie, now screened in Act III. Audiences would, she and Kenneth hoped, pick up the reference in the final scene. (Few did at first because the projected film was hard to see on Kay's curved screen.)

The middle act was the most problematic. Although it was supposedly Anastasia's party, she was sidelined in the ballroom dances. Tchaikovsky's Third Symphony, uncut, had too many repetitive passages; brief scenes on the forestage provided unconvincing accounts of the brewing Revolution; the incursion into the palace ballroom of angry peasants brandishing red banners was unmatched by any climactic effect in the music. The last act, with its Martinů score, was so stylistically unrelated to what had gone before that it seemed a different ballet, juxtaposing a woman's mental breakdown with the collapse of a privileged society.

The premiere on 22 July 1971 met with a mixed reception, including boos and catcalls from several parts of the house. Most critics, whatever their views, saluted MacMillan's boldness in undertaking such an ambitious subject and praised his inventive choreography. Seymour's powerfully sustained performance was universally acclaimed. A number of reviewers found the structure flawed and recommended drastic pruning of the longueurs. Nicholas Dromgoole in

the *Sunday Telegraph* was not alone in calling *Anastasia* an honourable failure, although Andrew Porter in the *Financial Times* gave
it unqualified praise: 'It is one of those rare and precious works of art
in which a major creator consolidates all that he has done before and
on this firm foundation goes on to build something new, larger and
stranger and more exciting than anything he has done before.' Porter,
while genuinely admiring MacMillan's achievement, also realised
that the choreographer needed authoritative support against his
detractors. A climate of hostility was threatening MacMillan's directorship of the Royal Ballet. It would not help if his first big production were dismissed as a flop.

The harshest criticism came from John Percival in *The Times*. He
described the first two acts as sheer padding, the choreography a mixture of Ashton's *Enigma Variations* and the Bolshoi's *Spartacus*, 'both
very insipidly copied'. The comparison with *Enigma Variations*, he
said, was compounded by casting some of the same performers in
similar roles:

Derek Rencher as the Tsar wears his puzzled, sad look, and Svetlana
Beriosova as the Tsarina does her dutiful, understanding wife once more . . .
But in Ashton's ballet the dancers were given real characterisations.
MacMillan allows them only simplified set attitudes: Rasputin, for instance,
looks perpetually costive.

Percival found fault with the use of Tchaikovsky's music and with
Kay's designs – 'the whole ballet is tastelessly Ruritanian in concept' –
and concluded that, as MacMillan's first creation since becoming
Director, 'it hardly augurs well for the future'.

The dismissive tone of the review provoked Derek Rencher into
writing a letter of protest to *The Times*, acknowledging that he was
'breaking the unwritten code that an artist must remain silent and
allow history to condemn or acclaim a work of art'. Published on
25 July 1971, the letter defended the ballet and the dancers' interpretation of their roles. Lord Drogheda, who had approved the letter, followed it up with his own private letter to John Higgins, Arts
Editor of *The Times*, whom he knew from Higgins's days as a journalist on the *Financial Times*. 'I hope you believe I have no personal
axe to grind,' Drogheda wrote. 'I do, however, mind passionately
about the effect upon the morale of MacMillan and of the Royal
Ballet of Percival's astonishing article.' Drogheda asked Higgins to

prevent *The Times* from being part of a campaign of hostility towards the Royal Ballet.

Higgins had no intention of censoring his paper's dance critic at Drogheda's request. He replied to the letter in guardedly friendly terms, writing that in his personal opinion 'MacMillan has not come up with the ballet we have all been waiting for during this first year of his directorship – but he has produced a work with admirable elements in it'. Higgins then assured Drogheda that *The Times* was not campaigning to have MacMillan replaced as Royal Ballet Director by Nureyev. Drogheda followed up this remark with a second letter to Higgins, saying (possibly disingenuously) that it was the first time he had heard Nureyev's name rumoured in such a context. What he had wanted to impress upon Higgins was his and the Board's fear that MacMillan, distressed by press criticism, might 'throw his hand in'. 'I really do not know who would be willing to take on the job, at any rate not anyone that we might want.' Drogheda had meanwhile written to MacMillan, expressing the Board's appreciation of 'your magnificent new ballet' and assuring him of its strongest and fullest support. In his reply of thanks, MacMillan was unusually forthcoming about his feelings: 'One feels so helpless at times like this and of course you can imagine how deeply depressed I am. Apparently time heals all, so I do hope it will – and quickly.'

He realised that he was spiralling downwards, as he had in Germany. He was very aware that although the dancers' spirits had risen during the creation of *Anastasia*, the public's and critics' lack of enthusiasm for his new work had dashed them once again. Mutterings of 'He'll have to go now' were widespread among the company and their fans, repeated by regular ballet-goers who gossiped among themselves. John Field's supporters further fuelled the discontent by claiming that the Royal Opera House had made a damaging mistake in favouring MacMillan over him.

Kenneth felt even more exposed than he had in Berlin, where he could at least attribute the hostility to his work to what he believed was the Germans' lack of appreciation for ballet. In London, he knew he was being invidiously compared with Ashton. 'I wasn't welcome at all,' he told an interviewer. 'Ashton had been a great, great favourite with everyone and everybody missed him and I think everyone was very suspicious about what I was going to do with the

Royal Ballet. I think they thought I was out to destroy it, but I wasn't.'

He had dedicated *Anastasia* to Ninette de Valois, tacitly acknowledging that he was her heir as a creator of dramatic narrative ballets. His tribute had, he felt, been disparaged by blinkered critics. There is no record of de Valois's opinion of *Anastasia*, though she must have appreciated the spirit behind the dedication to her. She was diplomatic in her comments on his ballets in her collected essays: 'His major works are on the grand scale, and that is rare today.' She added the rider that such works could benefit from revision after their first productions. 'A certain weakness springs, inevitably, from the very great facility of his choreographic inventiveness . . . his bridging and general stagecraft needs momentary attention.' Her view of the critical responses to his appointment as Artistic Director was typically forthright: 'Better, though, to live through controversy than to exist in an atmosphere of apathy.'

MacMillan, however, was in no condition to appreciate the value of controversy. His defences were low, his paranoid tendencies easily activated now that he could no longer numb his nerves with alcohol. He was isolated, with few allies in the company in whom he could trust. After *Anastasia*, he effectively had a nervous breakdown. He belatedly admitted as much in an interview eighteen years later: 'I didn't really work for about three months after that. I mean, nowadays I wouldn't take it so seriously, but then I did, you know. Unfortunately I took it very seriously and I lost confidence completely.'

At this crucial stage in September 1971, he had suffered a crisis of insecurity when his psychotherapist, Marianne Jacoby, was away on holiday in Switzerland in September. He dreaded being on his own in an empty house, terrified that in his heightened state of anxiety he might suffer a seizure or another stroke. He sent a concerned letter by express post to Mrs Jacoby in Arosa, receiving a reply assuring him that he was psychologically, not physically, ill: she wrote that he must not think he was suffering from the illness that killed his mother. Mrs Jacoby trusted that he would be all right staying with friends until she returned. Since he could no longer install himself with the Rounds in Foxmore Street (Georgina Parkinson was fully occupied with their baby son, Tobias), he moved into Clement Crisp's house in Lambeth for a week. Crisp was soon to become principal dance critic of the *Financial Times*, taking over from Andrew Porter, whose deputy he had been since the 1950s. The house's inhabitants, who included Peter Hollamby and Lis Dalton, made room for MacMillan, understanding that he was in a bad state but respecting his desire for discretion.

Hollamby noted in his diary:

Kenneth sleeps next door in the study and often has bad nights. He thought he'd better arrange things round the bed in case he sleepwalked during the night. I was amazed to see that he'd put chairs and suitcases all around the bed, which he said would wake him. Then he insisted on having his mattress on the floor in case he fell out of bed. I think he's frightened of suddenly falling and having another spasm.

Kenneth stayed indoors during the day, cutting himself off from the rest of the world. The house's inhabitants kept an eye on him, reassuring him by their presence that he was safe. If any guests came for dinner, 'he makes sure it is understood he has a virus'. His friends recall his endless tea-drinking, chain-smoking and obsessive crochetwork – the distraction therapy he had learned from his grandmother as bombs fell on Great Yarmouth.

'He didn't talk about what he was going through,' says Crisp.

We just let him be and kept him company when he needed it. He was gone, quite suddenly, one day when I returned in the evening. He'd left a note on the table saying he'd got back in touch with the Opera House and was going back to Worfield Street. He never mentioned the episode again and nor did we.

MacMillan continued his psychotherapy sessions with Mrs Jacoby on her return to London but remained unhappy and anxious. He was able to function well enough to deal with the start of the Royal Ballet's new season in October, a month after his crisis, although Peter Wright spoke for him at a press conference announcing the company's plans for the next year. MacMillan hid behind dark glasses and avoided answering journalists' questions.

The year ended with the annual Royal Ballet Benevolent Fund gala, for which he contributed a dance for seven of the company's female soloists, including his two close friends, Georgina Parkinson and Vergie Derman. The choreography for the *Pas de Sept* was not newly created: he had adapted the Jewel Fairies' variations from Act III of his Berlin *Sleeping Beauty* production. The gala included the company premiere of another Robbins ballet MacMillan had been eager to add to the repertoire, *Afternoon of a Faun* (created for New York City Ballet in 1953). Danced by Sibley and Dowell, the duet to Debussy's evocative music was a popular success.

It was trumped, however, by a pas de deux for the same two dancers by Ashton. Set to the *Méditation* from Massenet's opera, *Thaïs*, the pas de deux had been created not for MacMillan's Royal Ballet but for another occasion in March, a fundraiser for Friends of Fatherless Families at the Adelphi Theatre. Ashton made the most of audience applause for his reappearance on the Opera House stage when he took one of his famous curtain calls with the dancers. Holding up his hand for silence after numerous bows, he asked the audience if they would like to see the pas de deux again. A roar of enthusiasm indicated that they would. Taken aback and still breathless, Sibley and Dowell repeated Ashton's *bonne bouche*, ensuring that his was the triumph of the evening.

MacMillan was meanwhile working on a new one-act ballet for January 1972, using just three soloists and a small supporting group. Although he felt on trial as the company's choreographer as well as director, he still had the willpower to go into a rehearsal room and face dancers waiting for him to tell them what to do. In a preview statement about the new work to Rodney Milnes for *Harpers and Queen* magazine, he said cautiously, 'It seems, at the moment, to be about the breaking off of one friendship and the start of a new one . . . but it might develop into something quite different.'

He had chosen Sibley, Dowell and the young, still-inexperienced Wayne Eagling for *Triad*, to Prokofiev's First Violin Concerto. Sibley, gratified to have a leading role created on her by MacMillan, was disconcerted at not being able to see his eyes behind his dark glasses or read his expression. 'Kenneth obviously was in a bad way,' Sibley remembers. 'He didn't even come to most of the final rehearsals and stage calls. Anthony and I would ring each other up, trying to make sense of what we were doing in his absence and longing to have more time with him.'

He gave them few clues about the ballet, which was primarily a response to Prokofiev's music, infused with memories of his youth. It also had a literary source (not revealed in the programme note): L. P. Hartley's novel *The Go-Between*, made into a film in 1970 with a screenplay by Harold Pinter. Film and novel were set in

Norfolk, the county of MacMillan's boyhood. Like Hartley's book, the ballet depicts an adolescent boy's transition into manhood – a change of gender from MacMillan's previous rites-of-passage ballets. Because of Prokofiev's plangent, shimmering music, the events in *Triad* seem recollected in relative tranquillity, however painful they might have been at the time.

The two principal male characters are an older and a younger brother, whose close sibling relationship is disrupted by the presence of a girl. MacMillan asked Sibley to keep her blonde hair loose, as she had in Robbins's *Afternoon of a Faun*. There are further echoes of Robbins's (and Nijinsky's) faun in the way the men lie prone or sit, one leg bent over the other. The girl seems a nymph, as slippery to catch and hold as an ondine. The ballet's imagery suggests sea creatures, dolphins and otters, as well as birds in flight. Both Dowell and Eagling were unusually supple for Royal Ballet male dancers of the time, able to extend their legs as high as Sibley and to dive acrobatically to the floor. MacMillan, who had complained in press interviews that he found the company's men inadequately trained when he took over as Director, deliberately exploited the litheness of these two, emphasising their graceful virtuosity. The younger brother was Eagling's first experience of a leading role, three years after joining the company. He would develop into one of MacMillan's most frequently used dancers.

Soon after the start of the ballet, the girl enters, escorted by a gang of three young men who will return later to plague the brothers. She picks her way forward on pointe, typically introducing herself by the way she walks. Although her manner is demure, unconcerned, she disturbs the two brothers, who are already on stage. She chooses the older boy, whispering to him with an intimacy that sends the younger wild. The Dowell brother puts his hand over the boy's eyes, indicating, 'Don't look, don't tell, this is not for you, not yet.' MacMillan eventually acknowledged that the ballet's genesis was his memory of keeping watch while his older brother, George, seduced girls under a Yarmouth pier (a sexual prowess George denied, as we have seen, attributing it to young Kenneth's hyperactive imagination).

After the girl leaves, a strange, shadowing dance for the two brothers is a teasing forerunner of the duet to come between the elder boy and the girl. MacMillan had started work on the ballet by choreographing, as usual, the central pas de deux. He had happened to see Dowell practising his part to the music, marking the lifts in the absence of Sibley, temporarily off with an injury. MacMillan retained Dowell's gestures, raising his arms in enigmatic shapes (without a body to support) that the younger brother imitates, as if trying to experience his brother's feelings. Irritated by the boy's persistence, the Dowell brother throws him to the wolves – the three louche youths who first accompanied the girl.

They tease and torment him without doing him real harm: he is put in his place, under their knees. Although there is a reminder of *Cain and Abel* in the older brother's betrayal of the younger one's trust, the Dowell brother does eventually come to his rescue. He has been watching with half-contemptuous amusement, asserting his superiority until the time comes to see off the intruders. Left alone, the younger boy is then excluded from the increasingly erotic relationship in the pas de deux between his older brother and the girl. Bewildered and frustrated, the younger brother pushes between them like a child resenting sexual affection between his parents (or Hartley's go-between schoolboy, envious of the passion between the clandestine lovers in the novel).

His actions could either be taking place in his imagination or be distorted by memory, for the girl seems to become their mutual fantasy or responsibility. They carry her above their heads as though she is dead, grabbing her hands as she twists downwards between them. The ballet ends with the younger boy sobbing bitterly as he straddles his leg protectively over the entwined, supine bodies of his brother and the girl. His grief seems more than regret at his exclusion. In a return to the *Go-Between* story, he is somehow guilty of betraying them both, destroying them through his envy. He is mourning far more than his own lost innocence.

Triad is a water-colour painting in which MacMillan's often more lurid themes of love, treachery and death are inextricably mixed. The girl, virgin and siren, is provocative without fully realising what she is letting herself in for. Sibley was described by Annabel Farjeon in the *Evening Standard* as 'a strange blend of passivity and aggressive assertiveness', with 'a new sour-sweetness that gives her curling body a more sensitive character'. Like the girl, the two boys represented aspects of MacMillan himself, as well as replaying his youthful relationship with his brother. The tensions between the three main figures proved too enigmatic for some reviewers.

Richard Buckle in *The Sunday Times* spotted the *Cain and Abel* connection but suggested the programme's description of the two men as brothers was euphemistic. Oleg Kerensky made the same comment in the *New Statesman*. MacMillan indignantly denied the suggestion of homosexuality, and Eagling insists there was never any hint of it in the ballet: 'Kenneth told us from the start we were brothers. We used to joke about "Sibley-ng rivalry". I must say Antoinette was deliciously sexy – I daringly gave her a pair of frilly knickers as an opening-night present.'

Far too much hung on the critical reception of *Triad*. MacMillan was under fire for imperilling the future of the company he had inherited: his two previous one-act ballets, *Checkpoint* and *Olympiad*, had been savaged, and the full-length *Anastasia* was not regarded as a success. Before *Triad*'s premiere on 19 January, MacMillan had reached such a state of misery and tension that his friends were acutely concerned. He was obviously unstable and in need of more help than they could provide. When he turned up for meals at Crisp's Lambeth house, Peter Hollamby noted in his diary that Kenneth looked 'very upset and worried, with that sudden stretch of his forehead which sets back his hairline and widens his eyes. I'm sure the basis of his trouble is having no real other person to share his anxieties. We worry about him. He says, "If only I could feel well." '

MacMillan had walked out of a session with Mrs Jacoby, declaring that she was of no help to him and that he would never see her again (although in fact he did). He turned to his friends for support, ringing round with desperate appeals: 'Please talk to me.' They did, for hours. By Sunday, 16 January, two days before *Triad*'s premiere, telephone lines were constantly engaged as MacMillan rang Clement Crisp, Peter Wright, John Auld, Jeffrey Solomons and Georgina Parkinson, and they called each other, wondering what to do for the best. Crisp took urgent advice on a psychiatrist for Kenneth and arranged an emergency appointment for him on Monday, 17 January, with Dr Carl Lambert. 'The idea is to try and get some sort of relief for K from this anxiety,' Hollamby wrote in his diary. 'K is fearful of "being put into an asylum" and being given "electric shock treatment".'

Dr Lambert, like Dr Hardenberg, MacMillan's first analyst, and Mrs Jacoby, was a German émigré. Half German, one-quarter English, one-quarter Jewish, he had fled Berlin in 1939. Short and craggy, with a large head and drowsy eyelids, he looked rather like Aristotle Onassis. He ran a sexual impotence clinic at St Bartholomew's Hospital and saw private patients for psychoanalysis at his consulting rooms off Harley Street. Although he had trained as a Freudian analyst, he preferred to use unorthodox methods, including drugs, to hasten the therapeutic process – an apparent short cut appreciated by his patients. He was renowned as a 'society shrink' for his success in enabling his patients, many of them high achievers, well known and well connected, to cope with the pressures of their lives and work. He dealt with their symptoms first, before spending time examining the underlying causes. He believed that psychological disorders were often reinforced by habitual responses to certain triggers: if the response could be modified, the disorder could be held, at least temporarily, at bay. He had been recommended by Zoë Dominic, the theatre and ballet photographer who had known MacMillan since she was first assigned to photograph *The Burrow* in 1958. Lambert said to her, soon after seeing Kenneth and before knowing anything of his work, 'That's an extraordinary artist you've brought me.'

Lambert had made the appointment after securing Mrs Jacoby's agreement: she still regarded Kenneth as her patient but she was not qualified to prescribe the drugs and medical advice he needed. Crisp accompanied MacMillan in a taxi to Lambert's consulting rooms in Upper Brook Street. Whatever pills or injection Lambert gave MacMillan had an instant effect. He was able to take two curtain calls (which he had dreaded) after Tuesday night's premiere of *Triad*, looking 'very elegant in black velvet', as Hollamby noted in his diary. The reviews, though mostly cool, were kinder than he had feared.

Hollamby went with MacMillan to his next appointment with Lambert. 'Kenneth in dark glasses, calling the cab man "driver". It was like a strange expedition in search of some unknown phenomenon. Which it is. Kenneth kept saying, "I hope he has the pills for me."' When they arrived, they were disconcerted to find another man pacing up and down, expecting to see Lambert at the same time. Hollamby waited in a rather seedy ante-room until MacMillan's hour-long session was over and then took him for a cup of tea at a nearby café. 'Kenneth seemed to think he'd had a mind-altering injection. He took his pill and said to me, "What a life, Peter."'

Lambert might have given his new patient (as he did others) a relaxant to calm him and break down his defences. He put MacMillan on a regime of barbiturates and anti-depressants to ease his high level of anxiety, with vitamin injections to boost his energy. MacMillan cancelled his psychotherapy sessions with Mrs Jacoby in order to commit himself completely to Lambert's care, seeing him every day. Mrs Jacoby had wanted him to continue with self-analysis, but after two and a half years and a breakdown, MacMillan had had enough. He would try Lambert's methods instead.

Lambert set about tackling his patient's phobias one by one, taking a pragmatic approach. First, his terror of dentistry. The last time that Kenneth had had a tooth pulled out, as a child, he had thought he was dying. Ever since then, he had avoided dentists at any price and his teeth were in a terrible state of decay. Lambert arranged for a dentist to do all Kenneth's fillings in one go under a general anaesthetic. Instead of steeling himself to endure a drill during many sessions in a dentist's chair, he was out for the count, his teeth fixed. Next, a hypnotherapist was recommended to help him overcome his fear of flying. Lambert then proposed a similarly practical measure to resolve Kenneth's confusions over his sexuality. As a first step to end his celibacy, since Kenneth claimed he couldn't remember when he had last had sex, a call girl would be provided. Thanks to the impotency clinic at Bart's, Lambert had reliable contacts. Aghast, Kenneth was provoked into making his own decisions about how he wanted to lead his life. Dr Lambert's shock tactics were having their intended effect.

30

MacMillan had just met the woman who was about to set his future on a new course. She was Deborah Williams, a twenty-six-year-old Australian who had come to London two years before. She was striking to look at, with big dark eyes in an oval face, a determined chin and slender model's figure. When they met, she was down on her luck, scraping a living after the end of a relationship with the Australian who had brought her to Britain. She had no intention of returning to

Australia, having broken with her family and her past; she did, however, plan to leave London soon for Greece. Uprooted, she was an outsider, relying on her own resources. Unlike Kenneth, she was frank and open, confident that she could overcome the reverses she had experienced, including a failed marriage.

Deborah had been born in Boonah, Queensland, in 1944, a year before the Second World War ended: her doctor father finally returned home from working in New Guinea when she was three and her elder brother six. Dr Dudley Williams moved his young family to Manly, a Sydney suburb, where he ran a successful practice as a General Practitioner. Three more children were born – Roger, Julia and Simon. All five had a conventional bourgeois upbringing. They were expected to do well at school and to go on to become (or marry) a doctor or lawyer.

Growing up in a large, argumentative family, Deborah was happy enough until her carefree childhood ended when her brother Roger had a bad accident. He suffered severe burns after tipping a pan of hot fat over himself during a camping trip. His long, painful recovery marked the family. Deborah felt protective towards him in much the same way that Kenneth had felt towards his deaf sister, Jean.

Deborah was good at art and won a scholarship from Wenona Girls' School to the National Art School in Sydney. There she studied sculpture and painting and began to rebel against her straitlaced upbringing. She took up with a fellow student, Denis Allard, older than she was, and regarded as a wild card. An only child, he had been put in a home as a youngster when his parents split up, seeing his mother only during the school holidays. She worked as a cook at an institution where Deborah's father was the doctor on call. When she remarried, Denis's stepfather looked after the cars in Dr Williams's practice.

Denis Allard's working-class background did not recommend him to Deborah's parents as a suitable boyfriend for their daughter, and nor did his 'unreliable' reputation. He had driven across Australia on a motorbike, fraternised with Aborigines and provided them with alcohol – at that period, a criminal offence for which he was arrested. To earn money while he put himself through art school, he posed as an artists' model. When Deborah told her parents she was leaving home to live with him, they gave her an ultimatum: she had to end her relationship with this feckless man with a criminal record or never see her family again.

Reluctantly, she agreed to go away for a trial period of six months, staying with a former family nanny. There her resolve to remain with Denis strengthened and she returned to Sydney after two months for a final showdown with her parents. They cut her off, so that she could no longer afford to finish her final year at the National Art School. Her brothers and sister were told to ostracise her when she moved in with Allard. They married in May 1966, when she was twenty-two. None of her family attended the wedding, though she caught sight of her father standing outside the register office, before he walked away without speaking to her.

Deeply hurt by her parents' rejection, she relied on Allard for emotional support, which he became increasingly reluctant to give. They lived in a flat in the bohemian King's Cross area of Sydney, where soldiers on leave from fighting in Vietnam came for rest and recreation. Deborah supported them both by teaching art at a girls' school. After three increasingly unsatisfactory years of marriage, Allard abandoned her to 'find himself': 'I thought he was travelling around Australia on his own, but it turned out he was with a bunch of mates, surfing, drinking and doing drugs. He didn't want to be lumbered with a long-term commitment – though he did settle down later on with someone else.'

Deborah was determined not to turn to her family for support. She continued to teach, and set about earning extra money as a photographers' model. A girlfriend had introduced her to an agency: tall and slim, with vivid features, she was soon in demand to model clothes for fashion shoots. Her friends encouraged her to have fun, to start enjoying herself and to put behind her the hurt of her rejection by Allard and by her parents. In the evenings, she appeared in a cult drag-show cabaret at the Purple Onion club in King's Cross, master-minded by a gay friend, David Williams, who coincidentally shared her family name.

Although homosexuality was still illegal in Australia, the police more or less condoned Williams's gay club, on the grounds that 'at least they knew where three hundred faggots were at any one time'. Famous figures (including Robert Helpmann, Cecil Beaton and Dusty Springfield) would visit whenever they were in Sydney, along with actors and dancers winding down after evening performances.

Williams's shows were expertly arranged by Betty Pounder, a well-known Australian choreographer for musicals. Williams, six foot one before he put on high heels, was the star turn. He recruited Deborah for some simple routines, backed by towering drag queens, in *A Streetcar Named Beatrice*. ('Beatrice' was David's female persona.)

Williams fell for her and decided to try going straight. Since he had often been urged by showbiz friends to take one of his shows to 'Swinging London', he persuaded Deborah to join him on an adventure. He was confident that they could live together in a series of borrowed flats and make the most of London. Soon after arriving in July 1970, he mounted *The Sound of Mucus* in Toto's club in Kensington High Street. 'I was several Von Trapp children, a Nazi officer and a nun,' says Deborah. 'Because Toto's was a private club, we couldn't do any publicity except word of mouth, so the show didn't last very long – though it was quite a success.'

After the show's short run had ended, Deborah worked as a shop assistant at Harrods and as a waitress in various restaurants at night. Then, to escape the English winter, the two Williamses travelled through Europe in a Dormobile. They got as far as Morocco, where David abandoned her in favour of more exotic, gay pursuits. Stranded on Christmas Eve 1971, she returned to London, homeless and almost penniless. To go back to Australia would have been to admit defeat: Deborah would have had to ask her parents for the airfare – 'the last thing I wanted to do'.

Her plan was to take a course in teaching English as a foreign language and then work in Greece. While she did the course, she stayed in a cheap bedsit from which she was happy to escape to house-sit for friends. She had met up with a former fellow waiter, Brian Kinch (known as Bubbles), to whom she poured out her woes. He told his flatmate, Jeffrey Solomons, about her and they took her up as a lost soul. Solomons invited her to an art exhibition, liked her immediately and set about match-making.

He suggested she join him and Bubbles at a Fulham Road cinema to see Clint Eastwood in *Play Misty for Me*. Solomons had meanwhile invited MacMillan as well, pretending to both Kenneth and Deborah that he had forgotten the other was coming. He knew that Kenneth would never have turned up if he was required to meet a stranger. Deborah, who had no idea who Jeffrey's friend was, found his behaviour during the film intriguing. He kept going out during the violent episodes, so she assumed he was even more frightened than she was. In fact, he was making telephone calls to the Royal Ballet from public phone boxes.

The four of them went for a meal afterwards at Osteria 430, where Kenneth and Jeffrey regularly ate together. By then, Deborah had been rapidly briefed that MacMillan was Artistic Director of the Royal Ballet. She had been just once to the Opera House, to see a ballet dress rehearsal at the invitation of a friend of David Williams. She had noticed the back of MacMillan's grey-white head as he sat in the stalls, giving instructions to the dancers. The only ballet of his that she had seen was the film of *Romeo and Juliet*, which she told him she had much admired. He deplored her ignorance and offered to take her to a Royal Ballet performance. 'When he asked for my telephone number, I told him I couldn't remember it, which was true – I was house-sitting and I'd forgotten the number. But Kenneth took it as a major brush-off, so we nearly didn't get together at all.'

As they walked back in the direction of Solomons's flat for coffee, Kenneth peeled off to cross the bridge over the Thames to Worfield Street. 'What do you think of him?' asked Jeffrey. 'I think he's got real come-to-bed eyes and rather lovely blue lips,' Deborah replied flippantly. Jeffrey told her, 'He's convinced nobody fancies him, that he's so mixed up no one could find him attractive.' The telephone rang the moment they entered the flat. Jeffrey, guessing that it would be Kenneth, answered by saying at once, 'She likes you too.'

Deborah then invited Kenneth and Jeffrey to dinner at her temporary residence. She and Kenneth had by now spoken on the phone a few times, but this was only their second encounter. He arrived an hour early, disconcerting her while she was still preparing the meal. He sat in the kitchen and announced, 'I want to go to bed with you very badly, but not just yet.' She found this unusual seduction line irresistible. Then, as he told her about himself before Jeffrey arrived, she wondered what she would be letting herself in for. He warned her of his terrible depression and anxiety, and described the effects of his stroke in Munich. 'Now you know the worst,' he said, and asked for a photograph of her to take away with him.

Surprised, she gave him one from her modelling days. She suspects he showed it triumphantly to Carl Lambert, for Lambert had forced Kenneth's hand. 'I don't think he'd have had the nerve to make a move otherwise,' Deborah says. 'He laid all his cards on the table. It was very touching. After that, he courted me in such an old-fashioned way – he was enchanting.'

Cautiously, he introduced her to the ballet culture in which he worked. He gave her a ticket to see *Triad*, which told her rather more about him than he had revealed in their exchanges of confidences about growing up in very different backgrounds. Then she met members of the company. 'He never made me feel an outsider, I think because he felt an outsider himself and didn't want to identify completely with that world. He wasn't like some artistic directors who never leave the building, never miss a performance. His interests were elsewhere, like mine – films, theatre, art, music.' Deborah already knew the cliquish world of backstage gossip and theatrical shop from her time with David Williams, and had become disillusioned with it; although she admired the Royal Ballet dancers' beauty and discipline, she was not seduced by their society.

Dancers are very self-obsessed, which is how they have to be. They're the only people I know who, if you ask how they are, tell you in great detail. They take for granted that you're interested in their body parts. If they've got an injury, that's all that matters. When I first met the company, they had no curiosity about me or the life I led before I knew Kenneth. Everything revolved around him, because he could give them roles. He was the creator and the casting director, so he was waited on hand and foot.

She had more in common with his friends who had a wider range of interests: Nico Georgiadis, Clement Crisp, Nigel and Maude Gosling, who invited her to their Kensington house to meet Nureyev. Kenneth took her to see Georgina Parkinson and Roy Round and their new baby. 'Deborah had arrived on the scene like an angel from heaven,' says Georgina Parkinson.

Suddenly Kenneth had found what he wanted all along. I remember how proudly he told me he was seeing someone and how cross he was when I asked whether it was a woman or a man. He asked Roy and me to meet her as though he was seeking our approval. Of course we approved – and then he didn't need us any more.

When Deborah first met Carl Lambert over a lunch, he warned her and MacMillan that although Kenneth's friends and colleagues would seem happy for him in his new relationship, they were likely to resent the end of his neediness. However much they might have complained about the demands he made on their time and sympathy, they would not welcome being replaced by a newcomer, someone from outside their circle. MacMillan, at forty-two, had finally found the 'we of me', Frankie Addams's words from *The Member of the Wedding* that had so affected him in his youth. He stopped turning up on his friends' doorsteps for tea and company. As Lambert had predicted, most of them felt released and rejected in equal measure, which made life potentially difficult for Deborah.

31

Kenneth wanted Deborah to move in with him as soon as possible, but she had taken a job as an au pair for three months and was committed to staying with the family. She was also cautious of living with someone so soon after the start of a relationship, especially with an unhappy marriage and a doomed affair behind her: 'I'd had to grow up a lot, after having the rug pulled from under my feet. I didn't want to be dependent again, though it made Kenneth proud to be able to help me.' He bought David Williams's car for her, and transferred money to her bank account to secure her tourist visa when it came up for renewal. (She had to prove that she had means of support other than working, which a tourist visa did not entitle her to do.) When she tried to return the money, assuming it was only a convenient, very temporary, loan, he told her to leave it where it was: 'A girl needs a bit of money in her bank account,' he assured her, as if with the wisdom of long experience.

Kenneth tried to persuade her to come with him to Portugal, where the New Group would be performing his latest ballet, inspired by his first encounter with her at the Fulham Road cinema. *Ballade*, to music by Fauré, started with its cast seated on chairs, backs to the audience, as though watching a film. Brief and light-hearted, the work was a pas de quatre for a young woman (Vyvyan Lorrayne) and three men dancing attendance. The Lisbon season also included *Triad*, performed by a cast from the touring group.

When Deborah was unable to get away to Portugal early in May, he tempted her with a trip to New York later that month on board the *QEII*. The Royal Ballet was performing at the Met from 24 April to 3 June, for the first time since he had become Artistic Director. He had initially baulked at accompanying them because he still refused to fly: he claimed that he needed to work on *Ballade* and going by sea in advance would have taken too much of his time. His real reasons for avoiding the transatlantic trip were his fear of being out of touch with Dr Lambert for long and his anxiety about how Americans might receive him as Ashton's successor.

Once Lord Drogheda heard about his intended absence, however, he had fired off a stern letter on 19 April 1972:

Dear Kenneth,

I was dismayed to learn yesterday that it was not your intention to go to New York at all for any part of the Company's visit, let alone not being there for the opening. This seems to me most regrettable, and I should like to ask whether there is any chance of your reconsidering the matter.

The Company has paid twelve visits to New York since the War, and I am pretty certain that I am right in saying that this will be the first time the Artistic Director has not gone with the Company, not appeared at all at any time. Your absence is bound to be commented upon, and this surely cannot be good for the morale of the Company or for the standing of the Royal Ballet.

There is a further point, namely, we have just launched the American Friends of Covent Garden and the Royal Ballet and we had been hoping to recruit members in the United States during the course of the visit. Your presence would surely have helped greatly in this respect.

I look forward to hearing from you.

Yours sincerely,

GARRETT DROGHEDA

Thus reprimanded, MacMillan had to make his apologies: 'I am sure you will appreciate that this decision has not been taken lightly and is certainly not a wilful act on my part.' He assured Drogheda that he had now arranged to go to New York by sea as soon as he could. The *QEII*'s next sailing was not until 24 May, well into the company's Met season. It would give Deborah time to find an Australian girl-friend to take her place in the au-pair job. When Deborah agreed to accompany him, he insisted on telephoning her parents in Sydney to introduce himself and inform them of the trip, assuring her mother, 'My intentions towards your daughter are perfectly honourable' – a declaration that took Deborah by surprise. After knowing her only a few months, he was committing himself to a long-term relationship.

Before they left, he met John Tooley for a terse interview. Afterwards, prompted by Lambert, MacMillan wrote Tooley a letter of explanation and apology. A rough draft is written on the psychiatrist's headed paper, with emendations by Lambert. MacMillan prepared this account of himself to Tooley:

As you know I never speak very much when I am with you for the reason that I am intent on what you are saying and the reasons why you say it. In the past I know that at times I have been unreliable and a somewhat confusing character to all of you. This is now in the past and I hope that I will be able to continue in my post as the Director of the Royal Ballet for the second half of my innings.

The reviews that I personally have had both here and in America have been awful – but I shall rise above them. My critics will think it extremely arrogant of me to appear now in New York but my concern for the company and my relationship with it is my reason for going.

I am grateful for having seen you before I left and on my return I hope I will have had a chance to rethink the policy of the touring company and plans for the resident company for the next year.

By the time MacMillan and Deborah arrived in New York, the Royal Ballet's six-week season was nearly over. The transatlantic voyage had taken nearly a week because of bad weather. As an unmarried couple, even though they were travelling first class, there was no likelihood of their being invited to dine at the Captain's table. Instead, they were seated behind a pillar, which suited them both. Their romantic isolation ended when they stepped ashore and MacMillan met the hostility he had dreaded. His absence had indeed been interpreted as disregard for the Royal Ballet's American audiences. Clive Barnes had led the way with an article in the influential *New York Times*, asking 'What happened to MacMillan?' After saying that 'his absence strikes me as extraordinarily casual', Barnes lamented that although MacMillan was the most talented British choreographer since Ashton, 'his recent record has not been at all encouraging . . . Both of the new ballets he has shown in New York [*Anastasia* and *Triad*] have been embarrassingly feeble.' MacMillan had not been available for interviews to counter such criticism or defend himself against charges that he was neglecting the company's classical heritage. Loyal fans of the Royal Ballet, as well as the New York critics, were raring to let him know their displeasure.

The season at the Met had got off to an unfortunate start. Fonteyn and Nureyev, instead of dancing together in the opening gala, had appeared separately in ill-received pieces: Fonteyn in Cranko's *Poème de l'extase* (as an ageing diva dreaming of her lovers); Nureyev with Seymour in MacMillan's *Side-Show* (a burlesque duet for a circus strong-man and his 'ballerina' partner). Memories of Ashton's farewell gala, a reverential affair, were still strong; his American supporters were convinced that he had been unfairly ousted. His *Thaïs* pas de deux was greeted ecstatically, while MacMillan's *Triad* was barely applauded.

Anastasia, the main new offering of the season, found little favour with audiences or critics. Barnes damned it in the *New York Times* as

a bad and extravagant ballet. The real sorrow is that its inclusion in the New York repertory has meant the exclusion of works such as Ashton's *La Fille mal gardée* or *Ondine* that are basic to New York's view of the Royal Ballet . . . The falling off of MacMillan as a choreographer is one of the strangest aspects of European dance. He strikes me as a director in sore need of direction.

MacMillan had been roundly booed when he finally arrived to take a curtain call after *Anastasia*. Deborah was appalled to find that he had to run the gauntlet of stage-door balletomanes shouting 'Ashton, Ashton, Ashton' after each performance. 'A very deranged woman used to lie in wait for us at the hotel and follow us around about four paces behind, making vomiting noises. I thought the ballet world was completely insane.' Deborah was a staunch ally, giving MacMillan a refreshing perspective on his tormenters. He was also helped by Dr Lambert, who had flown to New York on the pretext of renewing contact with his American patients.

After Deborah and Kenneth had sailed back on the SS *France*, she agreed to move in with him. The Worfield Street house had been burgled the moment he left for America, and he couldn't face returning to it on his own. The New York trip had brought home to Deborah how vulnerable he was and how much he needed someone who would support him unconditionally. 'He was the first person who was totally on my side as well,' she says.

I knew he would never let me down. Not long after I moved in, I got the most dreadful flu – I had a temperature of 104 degrees for a month. Kenneth looked after me with such care, doing everything he could. Then he got in a nurse and eventually I had to go to hospital because my liver and kidneys were packing up.

The doctors ran a series of tests, including one for pregnancy, which appeared positive:

I was horrified because I'd been so ill. I was in floods of tears when I told Kenneth that evening when he visited me in hospital. I was afraid he'd be shocked but his reaction was like the sun coming out. 'I never thought I'd have a child,' he said – and I wailed because I thought it'd have three heads.

A second test proved negative and she was sent back to Worfield Street to convalesce.

'He said, "Look, I'm forty-two, you're twenty-seven. I want to marry you. Let's go ahead and have a baby." I got pregnant almost immediately and he was overjoyed.' They had known each other for less than a year and she was still legally married to Denis Allard. When she remarked to Lord Drogheda that their irregular situation might be awkward for the Royal Opera House, he replied, 'Don't be silly, this is England, not Australia.'

32

Deborah set about giving Kenneth some stability in his life.

When I first visited his house, it wasn't really lived in. It had been trendily done up with William Morris wallpaper and dark furniture, which was all right at night but gloomy during the day. I opened a cupboard in the kitchen and the only food there were twenty-seven Harvest pies and tins of Rosti [a pre-made Swiss potato dish]. Nothing else. He could cook, but he didn't know how to look after himself. He told me that during his breakdown, he couldn't do anything – not even go upstairs.

She persuaded him to eat cereal or porridge (made Scots-style with salt) for breakfast instead of subsisting on tea and cigarettes. It would be four years before she could convince him to give up smoking altogether.

He'd been seriously dependent on alcohol and he had an addictive personality. What I hadn't appreciated was that he'd be addicted to the drugs Carl gave him. I'm a doctor's daughter, so I was used to people being prescribed pills. It didn't worry me until later that Kenneth believed he couldn't function without them. And he couldn't, when we first got together. They were his substitute for alcohol.

Lambert continued to prescribe barbiturates for use at night, and sedatives during the day: Valium, Ritalin, Amytal. He also tried MacMillan on tricyclic anti-depressants, which came into use in the 1970s. At the time, psychiatrists did not realise how addictive some of the drugs would prove to be, nor what the side-effects might be of their long-term use. MacMillan hoarded pills, acquired from different doctors (when he changed GPs), so no one could monitor exactly what, or how many, drugs he took. He stockpiled them in apprehension that he might run out of supplies. His subsequent problems with ill-health and recurring depression might have been due as much to the cocktail of drugs he was prescribed and took over the years as to the chronic condition he was hoping to alleviate.

He couldn't, and wouldn't, drive, so a minicab came to fetch him each morning to take him to the Artistic Director's office in Baron's Court. (The Royal Ballet's administrative offices and rehearsal studios remained in the Upper School building in West London until the Royal Opera House was modernised in 1997–99; some studio and office space for the company had been added to the Opera House in 1982.) Once there, he had to deal with routine matters as well as supervising rehearsals; by late afternoon, he was tired, but with Deborah waiting for him at Worfield Street, he would return for tea with her before setting out again for a performance at Covent Garden. He began to feel, at last, that he had a home to which he could retreat.

Although MacMillan's private life was blossoming into happiness, his public role as Director of the Royal Ballet was still beset by problems. His hostile reception in New York had convinced him that there was a concerted campaign against him on both sides of the Atlantic, orchestrated by Clive Barnes in the *New York Times* and John Percival in *The Times* in London. (Both also wrote regularly for *Dance and Dancers* in Britain and *Dance Magazine* in the United States.) Although they had reviewed MacMillan's ballets favourably in the past, visiting Berlin independently of each other to cover his work there, they appeared to have turned against him once he became Director of the Royal Ballet. MacMillan suspected that they had lobbied for Cranko to succeed Ashton and were taking their disappointment out on him.

Both critics said the charge was unfounded. They believed that Cranko was better off in Stuttgart, where he had more freedom of action, and they had welcomed MacMillan's appointment. When it was first announced in 1968, Percival had written an article for *The Times* headed 'Just the man for Covent Garden': 'Here, it seems, is a man who ought to be able to keep the Royal Ballet at the eminence to which Ninette de Valois and Frederick Ashton have brought it, and add (as they did) something of his own besides.' Percival, however, was having doubts about the repertoire the company was dancing under MacMillan's leadership; and he considered that MacMillan's recent ballets had not lived up to expectations.

Barnes, who had been based in New York since 1965, returned to London at least once a year, usually during the summer. Writing for the *New York Times* on 10 July 1972, he appraised MacMillan's first two years in office from a dual perspective. He had recently been watching the Royal Ballet on its home territory, sounding out opinions about how it was faring; he had also attended a Covent Garden press conference about plans for its next season. His article started by explaining to American readers why

Britain's Royal Ballet should suddenly have become so controversial. Talking with people in London – critics, a few dancers, civilian audience members and the like – there seem to be certain fears for the company's future, fears that more than reflect those that were in evidence in New York when the company visited the Metropolitan Opera House this spring.

In Barnes's opinion, 'The fears are exaggerated but not necessarily groundless'.

He pointed out the difficulties MacMillan faced as director and choreographer, curator and innovator: a conservative institution, such as a large state-funded ballet company, was bound to be resistant to change. But, he reported, 'The morale of the company does not seem at all good. Dancers are malcontents by nature ... but disaffection, at least to my careful eyes and ears, appears too widespread to be entirely disregarded.'

He went on to raise questions over MacMillan's artistic policy, claiming that 'British observers fear the gradual Americanisation of the British repertory'. MacMillan had already introduced ballets by

Robbins and Tetley for the resident company, as well as works by his old friend Herbert Ross and another American, Joe Layton, for the New Group. A triple bill of Balanchine ballets – *Agon, The Four Temperaments* and *The Prodigal Son* – was announced for the next season, as well as another Robbins, *Requiem Canticles*. Although MacMillan would not defend his policy to the press at the time, he said in a retrospective interview, for the television documentary *Out of Line*, that America was where good choreography was coming from at the time. He was trying to broaden the experience of ballet-goers, at a period when American contemporary-dance choreographers – Paul Taylor, Alwyn Nikolais, and Martha Graham's disciples with London Contemporary Dance Theatre – were making an impact on less conservative dance audiences in Britain.

Barnes, writing for an American readership, reserved judgement about MacMillan's choice of repertoire. He ended his article by suggesting that, as the Royal Ballet's chief choreographer as well as Director, MacMillan needed more time to prove himself. If he 're-found his form' and created splendid new ballets for the company, all would be well. 'When we in New York next see the company . . . it may well be a very different company indeed.'

As Barnes had been informed, however, trouble was brewing within the Royal Ballet's ranks. A campaign was afoot to get rid of MacMillan. Dancers resentful of the merger between the two companies had been voicing their discontent in a series of meetings on their return from the New York season. A deputation handed a letter to John Tooley in October 1972, asking for MacMillan's dismissal and threatening to go on strike. Tooley told them, in effect, 'You can go. We're keeping him.' MacMillan responded in his own letter to Tooley, drafted on 18 October 1972: 'The whole business has had a profound effect on me and I feel that unless something is done very soon, I am afraid that the thing will get really out of hand.' He had experienced the same kind of petition from the Deutsche Oper dancers. On both occasions, he had demanded to know what had been said about him – a sign that his day-to-day communication with dancers was, to say the least, inadequate.

As Barnes had remarked in his *New York Times* article, dancers are malcontents by nature. Their work is physically demanding, their careers short: there will always be those whose expectations of roles are disappointed. Since a ballet company spends most of its time together, the group is readily roused to indignation. Dancers in European opera-house ballet companies have a long history of expelling directors they dislike by passing votes of no confidence in their leadership. In Britain, London Festival Ballet's dancers ousted Beryl Grey as their Director in 1979. The Royal Ballet has been, on the whole, less volatile, though petitions and strikes are not unknown. In 2002, the dancers rebelled against their new Australian Director, Ross Stretton. He was removed after only a year in office.

Ultimately, whether a director is obliged to leave depends on the views of the management, not of the dancers. The Royal Opera House Board gave apparently staunch support to MacMillan, whatever reservations its members might have had about their joint decision to stick by him. As Drogheda had written in confidence to John Higgins of *The Times*, no acceptable alternative was available. De Valois, if she could be persuaded to return, could only be a stop-gap; Michael Somes was too cruel and Drogheda had no faith in any other mooted candidate, such as Nureyev or Fonteyn.

The Chairman of the Ballet Sub-Committee, Mark Bonham Carter (who was also a Governor of the Royal Ballet), was asked to prepare a paper in October 1972 examining whether the company was really in deep trouble under MacMillan. Bonham Carter started his analysis with the statement:

The Royal Ballet is in a critical situation . . . the position of Kenneth MacMillan as Director is, as I know he recognises, different from and far more difficult than that of Frederick Ashton when he succeeded Ninette de Valois. MacMillan, despite his long association with the Royal Ballet, was regarded in some quarters as something of an outsider. He is not, as it were, a member of the Royal family, although he is what we hope to be the founder of a new dynasty.

Bonham Carter, briefed by Peter Wright and John Tooley, out-lined the intractable problems of the merged companies and the small educational offshoot, Ballet for All (six dancers and two actors). Some dancers were overworked, others were frustrated by their limited number of performances. Touring was unsatisfactory. The New Group, now with thirty-five dancers, had become too big to be purely experimental, but was too small to perform box-office favourites such as *The Nutcracker* and *Coppélia*. There weren't enough opportunities for tyro choreographers and young dancers to develop: the Opera House needed a second, smaller auditorium for try-outs. So far, new ballets created by company members (Geoffrey Cauley and David Drew) had not provided much hope for the future. Bonham Carter concluded that none of these problems was MacMillan's fault. They were endemic in a structure, and a funding system, that would continue to plague the Royal Ballet for years to come.

Ninette de Valois remained MacMillan's advocate: she had seen the company she founded endure many periods of hostile criticism. In the 1950s, she had attempted the merger of the Covent Garden company and the touring company, and had experienced much the same problems – which no one, apparently, had predicted the second time around. MacMillan had inherited a difficult situation, especially since he was the first Director to have come through the ranks. She continued to pin her faith in him as a choreographer of immense talent: there were no other contenders, now that Ashton had withdrawn into a prolonged sulk. Unfortunately, MacMillan, still recovering from his breakdown, was unable, and unwilling, to mount a charm offensive against his detractors.

He expressed his anger and frustration in his next ballet, *The Poltroon*, for the New Group, premiered at Sadler's Wells on 12 October 1972. The music was by a Hungarian composer, Rudolf Maros. Kenneth had been reading a book about the origins and continuing appeal of the *commedia dell'arte* characters – Pierrot, Harlequin, Columbine, Brighella, Pantaloon – who have appeared over the centuries in countless plays and ballets. He intended to show the dark, sadistic side of the familiar, often sentimentalised figures. Pierrot, instead of being a pathetic, white-faced scapegoat, would become a vicious coward, revenging himself on his tormentors, an unpleasant gang of fools. Columbine, usually depicted as a pretty tease, would get her comeuppance as a provocative harlot.

Brenda Last, small and feisty as Columbine, was handed around like a parcel among the men; 'mauled nearly to the point of being hanged, drawn and quartered, a Columbine of every misfortune', as Philip Hope-Wallace described her in the *Guardian*. According to Last, 'My character was insufferable, really. She flirted and mocked Pierrot, humiliating him until he strangled her. I wouldn't say she was a damaged innocent, unless you saw her as a victim of her circumstances. She couldn't beat the men so she joined them, behaved as badly as them.' After her murder by Pierrot, her body was callously dragged about – a parody of the way MacMillan's Romeo treats unconscious Juliet.

A lot of the mass partnering, Last says, was worked out by trial and error, while MacMillan sat and watched, chain-smoking. He did stand up to demonstrate what he wanted, but not nearly as much as he had before his stroke in Germany. He chose Donald MacLeary as Pierrot, the first time he had portrayed a male anti-hero in a work for the Royal Ballet. One of the critics, Fernau Hall in the *Daily Telegraph*, observed that MacMillan had returned to 'his obsession with forlorn little girls, while transforming this theme by changing the girl into a man and making him turn aggressive at the end'.

In the first scene, the *commedia dell'arte* characters enact one of their stock comedies; in the second scene, they are shown backstage as they really are. According to the programme synopsis, Pierrot's 'Lords and Masters are now symbolised by the businessman and administrator Pantaloon, the authoritarian Captain, Pulcinella the Fascist bully and the Doctor. Pierrot here faces his persecutors, looks in the yellow of their eyes, with dramatic results.' Pierrot slays the lot of them.

The viciousness was so savage that viewers speculated that Pierrot's massacre of his fellows was MacMillan's fantasy of destroying his critics – or Royal Opera House management figures. *The Poltroon*, dismissed by the critics and unsuitable for family matinees on tour, was soon dropped from the repertoire. Ashley Killar, who danced the role of the Doctor, commented:

It does seem, in retrospect, to have been an exercise in personal demon-exorcism. The tragedy is that the ballet's real virtues – the masterful study of grotesquerie, insightful character choreography and inventive pas de deux – are now dismissed. They were part of a ballet that was produced in the wrong programmes at the wrong time. It seems to me that Kenneth's need for truth to his own precepts was his own worst enemy.

Lord Drogheda remarked that *The Poltroon* was MacMillan's reaction to harsh criticism: 'a kind of "he who gets slapped" tragedy'. In Drogheda's view, 'He certainly never met anyone as much as half way. The rest of us had to make concessions. He is, though, a man of great artistic integrity, sticking almost mulishly to his beliefs.'

By the end of his second year as Director, MacMillan had done little to counter his critics. *The Poltroon* was an act of defiance that did not enhance his reputation as the company's chief choreographer. The New Group for whom it was made was considered to be floundering, with no sense of purpose. The latest Robbins ballet he had acquired for the main company, *Requiem Canticles* (created earlier in the year for New York City Ballet's Stravinsky Festival), was unpopular with Royal Ballet audiences; Glen Tetley's works to electronic music, *Field Figures* and *Laborintus*, were a minority taste. The only production that met with general approval was MacMillan's staging of *Swan Lake* – not a rethought version, like his Berlin production, but a rearrangement of previous productions by Helpmann and Ashton. He was, at last, credited with respecting the company's classical heritage – though his upcoming production of *The Sleeping Beauty* in the New Year would go badly awry. Doubts persisted over whether his contract should be renewed when his initial term as Artistic Director was up in mid-1973. But with Deborah's pregnancy confirmed by Christmas, he now had an added incentive to fight back.

33

The New Year of 1973 had started with a ten-day festival, Fanfare for Europe, celebrating Britain's entry into the European Economic Community. The Royal Opera House hosted the opening and closing galas, assembling a galaxy of British (and Commonwealth) performers alongside European guests. The opening gala was woven round readings by Laurence Olivier, Sybil Thorndike, Max Adrian and Judi Dench; singers included Janet Baker, Thomas Allen and Peter Pears, as well as Tito Gobbi, Elisabeth Schwarzkopf, Kiri Te Kanawa and Régine Crespin. The closing gala on 13 January was a ballet one, with the Royal Ballet as the core company: guests from the Paris Opéra Ballet, the Royal Danish Ballet, the Dutch National, La Scala and Cranko's Stuttgart Ballet danced mainly pas de deux.

It was the kind of formal occasion MacMillan would have dreaded only a year previously. He was required to be on parade, greet important figures, shake hands with royalty. Above all, he had to ensure that the Royal Ballet was presented as a standard-bearer for Britain's cultural aspirations. The success of the evening went some way to redeeming him in the eyes of the Establishment. The company danced Ashton's *Symphonic Variations* as the gala centre-piece, as well as extracts from *The Sleeping Beauty* and Cranko's *Lady and the Fool*. Fonteyn and Nureyev appeared in the pas de deux from *Le Corsaire*; Nureyev and Seymour clowned in *Side-Show*. MacMillan contributed a new pas de deux, *Pavane*, to music by Fauré, danced by Sibley and Dowell. A tender love duet, it is an adoration of the woman, who rarely leaves her partner's embrace; it has none of the acrobatic manipulations of his later pas de deux.

He had accepted the need to wear a formal dinner-jacket for the occasion, rather than his black velvet suit or one of his eccentric outfits. Deborah had been taken aback by a three-piece suit he had bought from a smart New York store on their first visit there together:

It was purple and yellow and mossy green, in big loud checks like American golfers wear. Actually, it was more like the kind of suit Max Miller [the brash English comedian] used to wear. Kenneth had it on at a dress rehearsal attended by the Friends of Covent Garden, and when he came out from behind the curtain, with a cup of coffee in his hand, just before the rehearsal started, there was a sharp intake of breath from the audience. He looked quite extraordinary.

Later on in Kenneth's directorship, Royal Ballet staff would implore Deborah to 'do something' about the casual clothes in which he took curtain calls. 'His trousers hung down with the crotch around his knees because he insisted on loosening them at the waist. There was nothing I could do about it – and he didn't care. All that mattered was his ballet, not his appearance after it had ended.'

In MacMillan's third season as Artistic Director, his main energies went into rescuing the Royal Ballet's new production of *The Sleeping Beauty* from a design debacle. The previous production, mounted by Peter Wright in December 1968, before MacMillan's arrival as Artistic Director, had medieval-gothic settings by Henry Bardon and elaborate, iridescent costumes by Lila di Nobili and Rostislav Doboujinsky. When the production had been taken to New York in 1970, it had been so disliked by Met audiences that the American Friends of Covent Garden had agreed to sponsor a new one. The premiere was to be at the Opera House in February; the production would then be taken on tour to South America in April and May 1973, and was scheduled for New York the following spring. Because of the touring requirement, there was no question of MacMillan attempting to remount his Berlin production, whose choreography had been arranged for Barry Kay's grandiose, untransportable settings. Instead, the new designs were to be by the veteran Italian stage designer Beni Montresor.

MacMillan had been required to use Montresor, who had pressurised the Opera House into giving him a commission after failing to use his designs in the past. (Montresor had been dropped in favour of Carl Toms as designer for Helpmann's production of *Swan Lake* in 1963. Then, although he had designed Nureyev's 1964 production of *Raymonda* for the Spoleto Festival, danced by the Royal Ballet touring company, the three-act production was never taken into the repertoire, to Montresor's disappointment.) Although MacMillan had reported to the Ballet Sub-Committee in October 1972 that he was satisfied with Montresor's initial ideas, by December he had reached the conclusion that Montresor was not taking the commission seriously: 'The designs were appalling – garish and ghastly. Even Walt Disney would have found them over the top,' Kenneth told Deborah. In desperation, he turned to Peter Farmer and begged him to come up with alternative designs in a matter of weeks. Rashly, Farmer agreed.

Pushed for time, Farmer restricted the range of colours in each act. 'A complete disaster,' declared Richard Buckle in *The Sunday Times*. 'The black background of the first scene is depressing, the red decor of the last, claustrophobic. The one excellent idea is the breeze-blown muslin curtains of Aurora's bedroom.' The billowing curtains for the awakening scene, when the Prince breaks the spell by kissing Aurora, proved more striking than MacMillan's contributions, which comprised a new Garland Dance in Act I, the *Polonaise* in Act III, variations for Aurora, the Lilac Fairy and the Jewel Fairies, and an innovation – a Hop o' my Thumb solo in the last act for the diminutive virtuoso Wayne Sleep. These were mainly replacements for choreography Ashton had added over the years, regarded by many (including Ashton himself) as integral to the Royal Ballet's 'heritage' production. Ashton was to claim that he had fainted in his royal-tier seat at the Opera House when he saw 'what Kenneth MacMillan had done to *The Sleeping Beauty*'. He had indeed fainted, though the reason was more probably a physical than an aesthetic malaise. The word soon got round that Ashton and his supporters considered the new *Sleeping Beauty* an unforgivable travesty.

It received short shrift from the critics and the management decided not to take it on tour to the United States the following year. The expense of the production (aided by American sponsorship) meant, however, that it could not be dropped from the repertoire. 'Had it been successful it could have been most helpful for the future,' Drogheda wrote reprovingly in his memoirs – yet another black mark against MacMillan's artistic directorship.

Although *The Sleeping Beauty* was to MacMillan (as to Ashton and de Valois) the pinnacle of ballet classicism, his own productions over the years brought him little gratification. The curse of Carabosse seemed to affect his designers, his budgets and his dancers. When Natalia Makarova and Nureyev performed together for the first time in London, in June 1973, they appeared in the Farmer-designed production of *The Sleeping Beauty*. Their partnership was far from harmonious, since neither of them liked the Royal Ballet's version and their temperaments were in any case at odds with each other. MacMillan's production was further discredited by their less-than-great performances, even though Sibley and Dowell, Park and MacLeary and other Royal Ballet pairings had no problems with it. Nor did Fonteyn, who was to dance her last Aurora in Brazil when the company left on the South American tour in April.

Since this was to be the Royal Ballet's first visit to South America, it was essential that MacMillan accompanied them. He would have to fly, leaving Deborah, four months pregnant, behind. Carl Lambert arranged for him to undergo an intensive course of hypnotherapy and supplied him with sedatives to calm his nerves. (He had to carry a letter on Lambert's headed notepaper certifying that the large quantity of drugs was for the patient's own use.) As a result, MacMillan was able to endure the long flight to Brazil, the first time he had been in an aeroplane since he toured with the company as a young dancer. The flight was made even longer by an unscheduled stopover of sixteen hours in Freetown, Sierra Leone. While the rest of the company made the most of the opportunity to go to the beach, MacMillan slept off the effect of the pills he had taken, curled up in a baking-hot corrugated-iron bus shelter by the sea.

He coped with the rigours of the three-week tour remarkably well, buoyed up with optimism about his relationship with Deborah and the prospect of their baby. Additional Brazilian dates had replaced a tour to Argentina, cancelled because of a strike. The weather was so oppressive in Belo Horizonte, experiencing its hottest April since 1909, that dancers collapsed on stage. The most memorable performance took place at the very end of the tour when the company was asked, at short notice, to inaugurate the brand-new sports stadium in Brasilia, the Ginasio. All went smoothly during the daytime preparations, for 1 May was a national holiday and the capital seemed deserted. 'No rehearsal could have seemed more relaxed,' reported John Higgins of *The Times*, who had travelled with the company. 'Kenneth MacMillan, whose black-and-white striped suit looked almost formal against the Ginasio's feminine colours, gently suggested a few minor alterations . . . [But] by 7.30 that evening, serenity and sunshine had disappeared.'

Thousands of spectators fought to get into the stadium to see Margot Fonteyn dance. A quarter Brazilian by birth, she was a national heroine: she had just been presented with a State Award in Rio de Janeiro, after the company's last performance there on Sunday night. Monday's hastily arranged performance in Brasilia was an unexpected chance for those who had missed her to see her dance with her famous British company. Tickets for the 19,000-seat arena had been massively oversold and the excluded mob outside the gates grew ugly when the performance started without them. The programme began with the *Kingdom of the Shades* scene from *La Bayadère*, with its notoriously difficult entry for the female corps, following each other down a ramp in repeated arabesques. Shouts of protest and voodoo chants against the impresario drowned out the music; when riot police waded in, MacMillan and the dancers thought a revolution was under way. Antoinette Sibley, dancing the leading role with Anthony Dowell as her partner, struggled to keep her composure: 'We didn't know if people were getting killed out there. We didn't know the tickets had been oversold. For us, it was just bloodcurdling screams.'

The crowd outside the stadium was ruthlessly cleared and the performance continued in relative calm. Fonteyn's eventual appearance in

The Sleeping Beauty (Act III) was ecstatically applauded. 'But the triumph belonged to the company,' reported Higgins. 'They had gone on in conditions they had never encountered before and will probably never encounter again . . . the evening was as sizeable a company milestone as that first performance at the Met in 1949 – *Sleeping Beauty* was the work again and Fonteyn the Aurora.' Fortunately, Higgins had been able to relay the company's triumph back to London, earning MacMillan respect, at last, in the management's eyes.

The journey back to Britain was uneventful. MacMillan returned with presents of jewellery for Deborah and a pair of hand-made black-kid bootees for their future baby. The tiny shoes had been an anonymous gift: later, they wondered whether the black bootees might have been presented with malevolent intent by a disgruntled dancer or stage hand who had had a voodoo curse put on them. That such an unpleasant idea should have occurred to Kenneth was an indication of his insecurity about his popularity within the company.

A month later, at the end of June, came the distressing news that John Cranko had died during a transatlantic flight from Philadelphia, where the Stuttgart Ballet had been performing on an American tour. On the return flight with the company, Cranko had taken a sleeping pill that quickly knocked him out, causing him to choke on his vomit. He was unconscious by the time his companions came to wake him up; he was pronounced dead on arrival at Dublin airport, where the plane had been diverted. He was forty-five, two years older than Kenneth.

The circumstances of Cranko's untimely death had horrible resonances for MacMillan, who had been able to endure flying only by dosing himself with sleeping pills. Although he was no longer as close to Cranko as he had been before the rift over *Miss Julie*, they had managed a rapprochement. He could not bring himself to fly to the funeral and mourn with the Stuttgart company. He would pay his own tribute to Cranko by choreographing a ballet in his memory – but not yet, not until the pain and anger had been absorbed into regretful acceptance. *Requiem* would lie dormant for another three years. In the meantime, he tried to secure more of Cranko's works for the Royal Ballet, including his three-act *Onegin*. Cranko's *Card Game* would be revived by the touring company later in 1973 for a tribute to him at Sadler's Wells, where he had spent his formative years as a choreographer in Britain.

The Royal Ballet moved into the London Coliseum for a month-long season, while the opera company occupied the Covent Garden theatre. Ballet was fighting back. The number of annual ballet performances at the Royal Opera House had fallen dramatically since the start of MacMillan's tenure as Director: from 142 in 1969–70 to 126 in his first full year, down to only 115 in 1971–72. Opera was hogging the stage; the Board, under Lord Drogheda, ruthlessly gave it preference over ballet. With the help of Bonham Carter and the Ballet Sub-Committee, MacMillan succeeded in rectifying the imbalance by adding 28 performances at the Coliseum while that theatre's resident opera company (still called the Sadler's Wells Opera, later English National Opera) was away on tour. The Royal Ballet benefited by attracting new audiences and giving regular ballet-goers a different perspective on the company's performances, in a bigger theatre with far better sightlines and lower prices.

MacMillan was meanwhile working on a new production of *The Seven Deadly Sins* for the company's summer season back at the Opera House for the rest of June and July. Its choreography would be almost entirely different from the 1961 version he had done for Western Theatre Ballet at the Edinburgh Festival, although once again he used Ian Spurling as his designer. He had chosen Georgia Brown, the jazz singer (who had been the first Nancy in the musical *Oliver!*), for the Lotte Lenya role and Jennifer Penney as the dancing Anna. Penney was an unexpected choice. Slender and pretty, with a doll-like face and long, beautiful legs, she had never danced a non-classical role and had no early training in tap or show-dance, which MacMillan was going to use. 'He saw something in me nobody else had seen. Nobody knew, including me, that I could be funny on stage.' She was to prove a gifted comedienne, later cast in comic roles in ballets by Ashton and Robbins, as well as in MacMillan's *Elite Syncopations*.

Lynn Seymour might have seemed the likely choice for Anna but she could no longer pass as an innocent young thing. In the *Side-Show* duet, the only role MacMillan had created for her since *Anastasia*, he had cast her as a raddled circus acrobat. In *The Seven Deadly Sins*, she had a very minor role as yet another over-the-hill burlesque performer, twirling tassels on her breasts as Queen of the Cabaret, illustrating the sin of Pride. MacMillan's casting could be cruel, if the artist concerned realised what he was up to. Seymour, who knew but was beyond caring, turned her backside to the audience during the opening-night curtain call. Despairing of her career in MacMillan's Royal Ballet, she was on the point of resigning and giving up dancing altogether.

The Seven Deadly Sins was one of the few creations for the Royal Ballet in which MacMillan drew on his youthful non-ballet dancing experience. Those of his cast who had done tap and jazz dance in their past (Vergie Derman and Christopher Carr among them) enjoyed performing cabaret-style routines in a work very unlike the rest of the Opera House company's repertoire. Although MacMillan's response to Kurt Weill's caustic satirical moralising was mockingly cynical, *The Seven Deadly Sins* was one of the seeds of his next ballet, *Manon* – an even darker tale of innocence corrupted by the need to survive in an avaricious society.

34

On 16 August 1973, Deborah gave birth to a girl, Charlotte. Her name was a thank-you to Carl Lambert, one of her future godparents. The birth was induced in the West London Hospital, with Kenneth present from the start. 'He arrived at the hospital first thing in the morning, having somehow managed to put his shirt on inside-out,' recalls Deborah. 'He was with me all the time, except for the actual forceps delivery, when they sent him out. The next morning he rang to say, "I can't come in, I can't move." He'd experienced every contraction with me and he was aching all over.'

They took the baby home to Worfield Street, and looked after her without any outside help. Deborah was gratified at how readily Kenneth adapted to the demands of a small baby, whom he loved unconditionally. He had proudly informed his relations in Scotland, as well as his brother and remaining sister in Great Yarmouth, that he was now a father. Deborah's parents came over from Australia to see their grandchild, thereby mending the rift with their once wayward daughter. They had agreed to help trace the whereabouts of Denis Allard back in Australia, so that Deborah could obtain a divorce. 'Actually, I wasn't sure that I wanted to get married in case it upset my relationship with Kenneth, but he was determined. It took five months after Charlotte was born for the decree nisi to come through.'

She had meanwhile set about house-hunting for their first proper home as a family. They needed a larger house with a nursery for Charlotte and a garden for her and their shitzu dog, Sid. They settled on a semi-detached Edwardian house in Lyford Road, near Wandsworth Common, in the area of south-west London in which MacMillan was accustomed to living. To afford the mortgage, they sold 19 Worfield Street to Australian friends and put Kenneth's Hove flat on the market. He had taken Deborah there at weekends while he was first courting her but they both decided it should be sold in order to invest in a family house.

Deborah organised the redecoration of the Lyford Road house while Kenneth worked on *Manon*, scheduled for March 1974. At a press conference announcing the *Manon* season, MacMillan was his usual silent self, adopting the position in which he habitually watched dancers in rehearsal. 'The Royal Ballet's apparently mournful director hunched on the platform under his shock of grey hair, with hand supporting head and ever-present cigarette holder.' The reporter, Robin Stringer, for the *Daily Telegraph* magazine, noted that Peter Wright outlined the ballet programme plans and John Tooley fielded questions: 'The meeting was embarrassed into silence by the brooding MacMillan presence.' In a later preview article for *Manon*, Stringer quoted MacMillan as claiming that he was no longer concerned about press criticism: 'It has taken me a long time to get over it. But I don't worry about my image with the press now, though I think Covent Garden still does.'

Lord Drogheda sought advice on ways to take the pressure off him. One useful suggestion was that Board members (and the press, if possible) should meet MacMillan on an informal basis, when he was less likely to be intimidated into silence. His perceived distance from the dancers could be eased if an intermediary was brought in to relieve Peter Wright, who was now fully occupied with the touring company. Peter Brownlee, the popular Company Manager of Festival Ballet, was head-hunted to become 'ballet co-ordinator' by the start of the new season (September 1975), liaising between the two companies and dealing with dancers' difficulties.

MacMillan was well aware that if he was to continue for a second term as Artistic Director when his contract came up for renewal, his new full-length ballet needed to please. The company could do with a big, operatic, story ballet, more conventional than *Anastasia*, with juicy roles for the leading dancers and plenty of ensemble scenes for the corps. The story of Manon Lescaut, taken from the 1731 novel by the Abbé Prévost, *L'Histoire du Chevalier des Grieux et de Manon Lescaut*, and adapted for operas composed by Massenet and Puccini, should fit the bill.

On the last night of the Royal Ballet's summer season at Covent Garden in 1973, MacMillan had left a copy of Prévost's novel in Antoinette Sibley's dressing-room. A note informed her, 'Some holiday reading for you – which will come in handy for March 7, '74. Much love, Kenneth.' Sibley, who had discovered the book just before her first entry as Aurora in *The Sleeping Beauty*, was intrigued but confused. The Everyman's Library edition of *Manon Lescaut* coupled the novel with Merimée's *Carmen*, which was illustrated on the dust cover. Which story did Kenneth mean? Urgently, Sibley whispered to Anthony Dowell in the wings, 'Could you find out before the interval?' Dowell, who had been given the same edition in his dressing-room, sought out MacMillan, who told him he would be Des Grieux to Sibley's Manon.

Though both were gratified to be given the leading roles in a new three-act ballet, casting them was essential for its success. They were the Royal Ballet's home-grown stars, their partnership by now almost as much an audience draw as Fonteyn's and Nureyev's. Sibley was lauded as a pure classical dancer, rather than a dramatic one like Seymour, but her sensuality had been subtly brought out by Ashton in *The Dream* and the *Thaïs* pas de deux, and revealed in Robbins's *Afternoon of a Faun*, as well as in *Triad*. MacMillan was confident he could now take her even further, in the first graphically erotic role created specially for her.

He had been tempted to use Natalia Makarova, according to Nicholas Georgiadis, who had proposed *Manon Lescaut* to Kenneth as a ballet. Georgiadis had been re-reading the novel, and pictured Makarova as Manon, capricious, maddening and irresistible. 'Russians can do French "camp" so much better the English,' he said. MacMillan, thinking as an artistic director, decided that his new three-act ballet should not serve as a vehicle for a guest artist. Fonteyn had held back the Royal Ballet's young stars for long enough; it was time he gave them a chance.

The idea of *Manon* as a ballet had been at the back of MacMillan's mind for some time. Jean-Pierre Gasquet, a professor of French who shared Alexander Grant's house in Battersea, had initially suggested Prévost's novel (a set text for his students) to Ashton. When Ashton turned Manon's story down as being too similar to his *Marguerite and Armand* for Fonteyn and Nureyev, Gasquet had mentioned it to MacMillan. Georgiadis had reinforced the idea, and Kenneth had then seen a French film, *Manon 70*, starring Catherine Deneuve in a modern-day version of the story. It was a remake of a post-war film with Cécile Aubry, which MacMillan had also enjoyed. In both films, Manon was depicted as a pragmatic, amoral girl who realised that the only way to a better life was to sell herself to the highest bidder.

When MacMillan went back to Prévost's novel to prepare his scenario, he identified from his own early experience the compulsion that underlay Manon's behaviour. In an interview for the *New Yorker* in May 1974, he said, 'My clue to her behaviour is her background of poverty. Manon is not so much afraid of being poor as ashamed of being poor. Poverty in that period was the equivalent of a long, slow death.'

He discussed his ideas with Georgiadis, whom he wanted as his designer. Nico suggested the ballet should follow Puccini's operatic structure for *Manon Lescaut* (which was in the Royal Opera repertoire). The opera's climactic duets would translate well as pas de deux and Puccini's tragic finale in Louisiana was more dramatically effective than the novel's inconclusive ending, in which Des Grieux survives to become an *abbé*. Puccini's music, however, was still in copyright – a cost consideration as far as the Royal Opera House was concerned.

When MacMillan proposed using Massenet's earlier *Manon* score instead, Tooley advised him to steer clear of the opera and go for an arrangement of less-well-known pieces by the same composer: it was the solution Cranko had adopted for his ballet *Onegin*, resorting to a selection of Tchaikovsky's non-operatic music. Tooley suggested as arranger Leighton Lucas, an experienced conductor for ballet, who had been a dancer himself in Diaghilev's Ballets Russes. Lucas had composed a number of film scores, the best known being for Hitchcock's *Stage Fright* (1950). Massenet's extensive range of music was still largely unfamiliar in Britain at the time, but Leighton was able to research and rearrange extracts from overtures, preludes, opera ballets and incidental music for plays, as well as orchestrate vocal music from then obscure operas and oratorios. The resulting collage, with repeated themes for characters and events, supports the ballet's action in the manner of a film score.

While Lucas diligently researched Massenet's music, MacMillan started work using piano transcriptions made by the Royal Ballet's rehearsal pianists, Hilda Gaunt and Philip Gammon. Very little of Massenet's music, apart from his *Manon* opera, had been recorded by 1973, so MacMillan depended on the company pianists for guidance. It was Gaunt who suggested which music would be suitable for the various pas de deux between Manon and Des Grieux, the starting point, as usual, for MacMillan's choreography. She had been company pianist throughout his career (she had played for the early Sadler's Wells Ballet from before the war and had willingly been involved in playing for Cranko's Henley season in 1952). Her name was added to the music credit for *Manon* – 'Music by Jules Massenet, orchestrated and arranged by Leighton Lucas with the collaboration of Hilda Gaunt' – as an acknowledgement of her invaluable assistance over the years.

MacMillan drafted his own outline scenario several times, determined to structure the story as clearly as possible. He greatly simplified Prévost's original plot, shifting the emphasis onto Manon instead of her besotted lover, Des Grieux. The final version evolved during rehearsals; some scenes were then cut or altered once the ballet was in performance. He had planned to start, for example, with a prologue depicting Manon's ambition to escape from penury into luxury. The stage was to be covered with an enveloping cloth through which the cast of key characters would emerge in a dream sequence. When this proved both confusing and impractical, he abandoned the cloth and replaced it with an inky cloak surrounding the seated figure of Lescaut, Manon's unscrupulous brother. After a moment's stillness, the action swirls around him, taking him, and the audience, into the ballet in full swing.

In Act I, Manon is on her way to enter a convent when her stagecoach stops at a wayside inn. Lescaut is there with a demi-monde crowd on an outing from Paris. He prepares to sell his pretty, virginal sister to the highest bidder, Monsieur G.M., but she runs off with a young student, Des Grieux, whom she has just encountered.

The naive lovers' penniless idyll in Des Grieux's lodgings is disrupted by Lescaut's arrival with Monsieur G.M. (Guillot de Morfontaine). A man of wealth and debauched tastes, G.M. offers Manon luxuries she cannot resist. Urged on by her brother, she abandons Des Grieux without a backward glance to become a kept woman.

Act II shows her on G.M.'s arm at a party in Madame X's *hôtel particulier*, a high-class brothel where every woman is for sale. Des Grieux is reluctantly present, brought by Lescaut. Manon, the belle of the louche proceedings, is torn between her material pleasures and her first love. She conspires in a scheme for Des Grieux to fleece Monsieur G.M. at a game of cards, in order to fund their future life together. His inexpert cheating is soon exposed and the reunited lovers make their escape in the mayhem that follows. They are discovered at Des Grieux's lodgings by Monsieur G.M. and the police, who have already arrested Lescaut. Lescaut is shot and killed and Manon is detained, to be deported as a prostitute.

In Act III, she arrives in the port of New Orleans, accompanied by Des Grieux, who has elected to share her exile. The gaoler of the penal colony (who, in the first draft of the scenario, was the colony's governor) seizes Manon and forces her to fellate him, contemptuously rewarding her with a bracelet. Des Grieux breaks in and kills the gaoler. While eluding their pursuers in the swamps of Louisiana, Manon collapses and dies in Des Grieux's arms.

MacMillan based the narrative structure on that of *Romeo and Juliet*, his most successful three-act work. In both ballets, hero and heroine, still young innocents, first encounter each other in a crowded party scene. Romeo/Des Grieux courts Juliet/Manon with a solo displaying his ardour, while she sits admiringly on a chair. Their love story is then revealed through a series of pas de deux: the first tells of their growing desire; their bedroom duet shows the aftermath of its gratification; both ill-starred affairs end with a necrophiliac pas de deux. In the swamp, Des Grieux hauls Manon's almost lifeless body about in his arms, much as Romeo manhandles the unconscious Juliet. The curtain falls on the tragic lovers, isolated in their suffering.

Ensemble dances for the corps de ballet in *Manon*, as in *Romeo and Juliet*, provide a social context for the story. Where MacMillan had resorted to three hard-working whores to animate his Verona piazza scenes, he invented an entire hierarchy of disreputable

Parisian characters for *Manon*, classifying the women as 'actresses, courtesans, harlots, skivvies' and the men as 'clients, gentlemen, beggars'.

He and Georgiadis agreed that the ballet's designs should reflect the precarious division between opulence and degradation: costumes could be lavish but the stench of poverty should be ever present. Georgiadis made his own dramatic contribution to the ballet by altering the period from the French Regency of the book to the pre-Revolutionary 1780s: 'a *fin de siècle* disrupted by the collapse of moral and financial values'. He looked at paintings and etchings of the era but took his main inspiration from a passage in the Goncourt Brothers' *Journal*, written much later in 1867, describing 'a picture of dereliction, with all its usurious exhaustion and tatty criminality, opening between burnt, ravaged, moth-eaten and rotten tapestry drapes . . . a sort of hole, full of bundles tied with string, piles of tow-ropes, unravelled silk and wool, a kind of cloth cesspit'.

Tiers of rags drape the background of the ballet's first two acts, half hidden behind the architectural settings. This 'cloth cesspit' is a reminder of what lies in wait for Manon, as is the presence of a sinister ratcatcher (a figure taken from an etching) who haunts her. Depending on the lighting, the rags can look as velvety as fur or as rank as unwashed clothing. In the Louisiana swamp scene, they are replaced by dangling strands of Spanish moss, through which characters from Manon's past emerge and vanish: the dream sequence MacMillan had planned as a prologue was transferred to the end, as Manon's feverish, dying recollections.

When the company returned in September 1973 from the summer break, MacMillan had to work fast. Sibley and Dowell had other commitments, made before *Manon* was scheduled for March 1974. After making their debuts in Robbins's *In The Night* at the start of the season, they appeared with the company in *The Sleeping Beauty* at the Théâtre de la Monnaie in Brussels from 17 to 21 October. Then they were due to leave immediately afterwards for Australia, dancing as guests on tour with the Australian Ballet, followed by yet more guest appearances in Japan. 'We wanted to make international names for ourselves, so we'd organised these tours abroad,' says Sibley. 'But Kenneth, quite rightly, was rather put out, so we just went to Australia, which we couldn't cancel, for a fortnight and pulled out of Japan.'

Before they left, in the ten days or so at his disposal, MacMillan had created three of the main pas de deux with them: the first encounter between Manon and Des Grieux and the two bedroom scenes, in the second of which, reunited, they plan to flee Paris but are caught by Monsieur G.M. 'I've never known anything like Kenneth at that time,' says Sibley.

He was raring to go after the holiday break, overflowing with ideas as if he'd imagined every step without anyone there. He knew the music inside out and he knew precisely what he wanted. He saw it and we had to make it happen. He was on top of himself, like a Mozart or a Beethoven. We'd finish one pas de deux and start on the next – it was all just flowing out.

The pas de deux were the most pleasurably carnal MacMillan had ever created. They revealed his sensual delight in the female body, expressed without inhibition. In both the bedroom pas de deux, MacMillan told Sibley that he wanted her to make seductive use of the inside of her upper arm. 'He loved that area, so Manon often twines her arms around her head. She lies down for Des Grieux with her arms raised – it's her special erotic zone,' says Sibley. Manon twines her arms suggestively in her only real solo, after she has entered the *hôtel particulier* in Act II, escorted by Monsieur G.M. She removes her elaborate outer garments and flaunts her finery – her arms, her dress, her jewels, herself – in a provocative little dance, briefly on her own before eight 'gentlemen clients' take hold of her, lifting her *en masse* so that she appears to be swimming in a sea of lust. 'Kenneth showed me the steps for the solo, doing them with those arched insteps of his. He was very particular about the sharpness of the feet, but when I instinctively put the musical accent in a different place, he accepted that. He wanted it to look right on my body.'

But he soon had to work with another body, that of Jennifer Penney. Sibley returned in November from her Australian tour injured:

I was tired and overworked, and I'd had a recurring knee problem since I was nineteen. No one could tell me what was wrong, and it ruined my career. During the *Manon* creation period when I couldn't dance, I consulted endless doctors and physios. I ended up staying for a month in Monte Carlo, where the treatment was supposed to be best, constantly on the phone to Kenneth and Anthony [Dowell] to find out what was happening.

I begged Kenneth to wait for me to get better, but he was pushed for time so he went ahead with Jenny.

MacMillan, who had recently worked with Penney on *The Seven Deadly Sins*, loved her highly arched feet and long, beautifully shaped legs. It is Penney's priapic leg that rises above the men in the brothel scene, as her skirts fall back in their joint grip. All the scenes in which Manon is involved with other characters in the cast rather than Des Grieux alone were choreographed on Penney, including Manon's first appearance as she descends from the coach in Act I. She introduces herself by the way she steps forward on pointe, placing each foot delicately in front of the other with a little shake – a rond de jambe. It is the balletic equivalent of Manon's first aria in Puccini's opera: 'Manon Lescaut mi chiamo' – 'My name is Manon Lescaut'. This signature step is repeated for Manon's entry in each act, revealing how much she has changed in the interim.

The final pas de deux in the Louisiana swamp was the only duet in the ballet devised around Penney's particular abilities. Sibley had earlier experienced problems with some of the lifts in the bedroom pas de deux because she had exceptionally frail wrists: 'Kenneth kept telling me he knew the lifts were possible because he'd worked them out with Marcia [Haydée] in *Song of the Earth*. But I couldn't push down on my wrists in that way, until Anthony and I found a way of managing it through timing alone.' Penney had no such difficulties, so MacMillan was able to take the last-act pas de deux to risky extremes. Since Manon and Des Grieux are meant to be at the limits of their strength, with Manon lifeless by the end, the strenuous lifts and body flips convey their emotional desperation rather than their physical condition – just as Violetta in *La Traviata* sings her heart out as she dies of tuberculosis.

The last act originally opened with a pas de deux between two new characters, the Governor of the penal colony in New Orleans and his mistress, a role for Georgina Parkinson. Their duet was interrupted by guards announcing the arrival of a new shipment of deportees from France. The scene then moved to the quayside, where MacMillan's depiction of New Orleans society included ensemble dances for the corps de ballet dressed in colonial finery. (The dances were categorised in a *Financial Times* review by Andrew Porter as 'a pas des soldats, a pas des mulâtresses, an entrée and pas triste des prostituées').

The Governor supervised the newcomers' disembarkation, picking out Manon to be his next resident mistress. It became obvious in performance that the indignant ousted mistress was a character too many at this stage in the story and Parkinson's role was dropped after the first London and New York seasons. The last act now opens at the quayside, with the ensemble dances considerably shortened. The Governor has been demoted to Gaoler; the jewels with which he intended to bribe Manon to abandon Des Grieux and live with him have become the contemptuous reward of a bracelet for her oral abuse.

In spite of the amount of work required to create a well-populated three-act ballet, MacMillan had almost finished it within four months, by the end of January 1974. He had built the characters around the personalities of the dancers he had cast, encouraging them to develop their roles. David Wall was a charismatic Lescaut, with Monica Mason his feisty, forgiving courtesan mistress: together they turned their duet in Act II, which MacMillan encouraged Wall to perform as though he were drunk, into a subtly comic tour de force. 'We laughed so much,' Mason recalls. 'Kenneth could be such fun in rehearsals, whatever his problems were outside the room. He was like two different people, most at ease as a creator.' Wall and Dowell would later alternate in the roles of Des Grieux and Lescaut, performing the roles with different casts.

Derek Rencher, the first Monsieur G.M., decided the character should not be an aristocrat but a debauched squire, 'who'd buy someone and discard them without scruple'. Gerd Larsen (who was frequently cast as Juliet's plump nurse) was well accommodated as the brothel madam. 'Gerd was always a party animal,' Rencher says wrily. 'She was very jolly in the brothel scene, getting drunk and silly with Lescaut, her favourite.' Among the *filles de joie* vying for clients, Vergie Derman was wittily competitive. The whore dressed as a boy in the brothel scene was Georgiadis's idea, based on a portrait of Mme du Barry, King Louis XV's last mistress, in pretty boy's clothes. The implication is that she is available for men with certain inclinations. When the dancer Jennifer Jackson asked MacMillan why she was dressed differently from the other harlots, he told her, 'You're more expensive.'

The corps of courtesans, harlots and clients were given considerable leeway in characterising their minor roles, provided they did not

distract attention from the main events. The Royal Ballet's crowd acting was put to good use, although MacMillan would be criticised for
resorting to too many unison dances for fuzzy-wigged whores raising
their skirts to expose their thighs. Such choreography *en masse*, castigated as 'padding', saved him the creative energy to concentrate on
the principal characters on whom the story-telling depended.

Three weeks before the 7 March premiere, Sibley was ready to
reclaim her completed role. She was shown the choreography by
Jennifer Penney, in an echo of the way Lynn Seymour had had to
teach the role of Juliet to Fonteyn nine years previously. Penney
danced as second-cast Manon, with Wayne Eagling as Des Grieux,
followed by other pairings. Nureyev would make his debut as Des
Grieux, with Merle Park as Manon, when the company took the
ballet to New York in May.

Peter Wright had been put in a difficult position when MacMillan
told him to keep de Valois away from the final stage calls for
Manon. 'It wasn't an easy thing to do tactfully, because she
expected to come to rehearsals for all his new works, which he
found very disconcerting. Often, he'd welcome what Madam had to
say, provided it was what he wanted to hear. But her last-minute
corrections in the studio run-throughs for *Manon* were driving him
mad.' De Valois bore no resentment. As a first-night present for
MacMillan, she had bought him one of Sidney Nolan's designs for
The Rite of Spring, using money from the Erasmus Prize she had
been awarded. She left it at the stage door for him, telling Deborah,
'He's not speaking to me, so tell him it's there.' On the back of the
package, she had written, 'I think this belongs to you.'

Shortly before the Royal Opera House premiere, MacMillan had
been interviewed by James Monahan (under his pen-name of James
Kennedy) for a *Guardian* feature. He was persuaded to remove his
by-now-habitual dark glasses for the accompanying photograph of
the ballet in rehearsal. Kennedy found him calmer and more self-
confident than in previous interviews, though his quiet manner was
unchanged:

He has always been diffident; the last thing he would want to be is an
assertive, dominating personality. But he now shows an awareness of
capacity and purpose, an inner equanimity, which I at least had failed to
notice before. The diffidence, it seems, of this very gifted choreographer
turned ballet director and administrator is now outward only.

MacMillan assured Kennedy that in *Manon*, he was, as always, 'firmly neo-classical. This awareness had grown with experience; he had become increasingly sure of what he wanted . . . much less blown about by other styles, outside influences'. Since *Romeo and Juliet* nine years earlier, he had learned more about dramatising the classical technique in his own way. Kennedy speculated that this might have been why he no longer relied on a typical 'MacMillan dancer' (such as Lynn Seymour) for his leading roles: 'He has perhaps become more confident in adapting the instrument to his style (and vice versa) . . . Perhaps there is some parallel here with Ashton's development; after years of making ballets almost exclusively for Fonteyn, he did a lot, rather late in his career, for others.'

Kennedy's judgement was premature, for it took a while before the character of Manon, created on two different dancers, was fully realised in performance. Initial interpretations were tentative rather than definitive, unlike Seymour's created roles. Reviewing the premiere, Alexander Bland in the *Observer* found that Sibley, with her light, lyrical English style, was not a natural Manon: 'She has flashes of real conviction . . . but a whiff of chastity clings to her.' In Bland's opinion, Dowell's role as Des Grieux seemed underwritten: 'His dancing is impeccably easy and graceful . . . but he spends an inordinate amount of time standing or sitting about and has little chance to assert himself.' David Wall as Lescaut, 'an overwhelming charmer', had almost stolen the show as the most fully rounded character in the ballet.

In a long review in the *Financial Times*, Andrew Porter described and assessed the ballet in detail (having seen a dress rehearsal as well as the opening night performance). Porter, who had become music critic of the *New Yorker* in 1972, had returned briefly to London. Clement Crisp, who had succeeded him as principal dance critic of the *Financial Times*, invited him to review *Manon* since he had covered MacMillan's previous full-length ballets. Porter declared it a success, praising the distinction of the choreography, dancing and designs and predicting that it would 'certainly reward repeated observation and generations of interpreters'. His main reservation was about the weakness of the score, a complaint echoed by other critics: 'By the end of the evening, you do get awfully tired of Massenet,' wrote Mary Clarke in the *Guardian*. Reviewers had strong reservations about the characters' development and the ballet's structure: 'Basically, Manon is a slut and Des Grieux is a fool and they move in the most unsavoury company,' wrote Clarke. 'However, MacMillan does not whitewash too much. The most effective character, in fact, becomes Lescaut himself.' She considered the ballet too long but eminently cuttable: 'MacMillan needs an editor . . . but for all his faults, he is one of the very few choreographers today who can write a big-spectacle ballet for an opera-house company that is developed entirely in the classical idiom and is done entirely through dancing.'

The general view was that the ballet's merits far outweighed its faults. The most vehement dissenting voice was that of Jane King in the Communist daily, the *Morning Star*. She deplored what she saw as MacMillan's misogyny: 'It is an appalling waste of lovely Antoinette Sibley who, as Manon, is reduced to a nasty little diamond digger. You do not have to be a militant feminist to resent MacMillan's repeated representation of the female sex as deceiver and destroyer of the male.' With the passage of time (and selective quoting from newspaper cuttings), King's comments have been taken as typical of critics' negative reactions to *Manon*. MacMillan added to the misapprehension that *Manon* was ill-received by claiming later that it had been a failure at its premiere, and that it took some seventeen years to find an audience.

Yet he received an ovation on the gala opening night and reviewers of subsequent performances, whatever their reservations about the ballet, noted that *Manon* was a hit with the public. Mark Bonham Carter, Chairman of the Ballet Sub-Committee, wrote a personal letter of congratulation to MacMillan, saying, 'All the evidence suggests you have a huge popular success on your hands.' Attendance figures for *Manon* performances during its first year at the Royal Opera House averaged 92 per cent, dropping only marginally, to 87 per cent, the following year. Over-exploitation by the Opera House management might have led to attendance falling off during some later seasons, but it is a myth that *Manon* was ever unpopular in its home theatre.

There were worries, however, about how American audiences would respond to it when the company went on tour to the United States in May, two months later. Clive Barnes, who had seen the ballet in London, had given interviews on US radio and television programmes warning that American ballet-goers unused to operatic ballets would not enjoy the length of *Manon*'s story development, though they might appreciate the quality of the dancing. In his opinion, *Manon* was a flop – 'a mediocre ballet with puerile music beautifully danced'. To counter this bad publicity, MacMillan was required to let a writer for the *New Yorker* watch a rehearsal in London. The anonymous preview piece that appeared in the 'Talk of the Town' section on 6 May 1974 described his apparently eccentric appearance: 'A tall, angular forty-three-year-old Scot, he has brown eyes, gunmetal hair, a neat black moustache, and a very shy disposition. He was wearing a green-and-red plaid suit and a long grey overcoat.' The writer noted that he smoked throughout the rehearsal he was taking. As a provocation, or inducement, for American audiences, MacMillan remarked languidly, 'You have a sixteen-year-old heroine who is beautiful and absolutely amoral, and a hero who is corrupted by her and becomes a cheat, a liar, and a murderer. Not exactly our conventional ballet plot, is it?'

Before setting out to face American reactions to his ballet, Kenneth and Deborah were married at the Chelsea Register Office. The brief ceremony was witnessed by Peter and Sonya Wright and Georgina Parkinson and Roy Round. Since photographs of the newlyweds were bound to appear in the press, Kenneth had informed his relatives in Great Yarmouth and Scotland at the last minute that he was going to be married. He confided to Deborah that had his sister Jean still been alive, she would have been extremely jealous of the woman he married: 'She wouldn't have been able to stand it,' he believed.

Since Deborah was still breast-feeding, the baby came with her and Kenneth to New York, this time travelling by air with the company. The tour marked the twenty-fifth anniversary of the Royal Ballet's first visit to the United States in 1949. A party was given in New York in honour of veterans of the original tour: MacMillan was one of the nine survivors present. The others were Alexander Grant, Gerd Larsen, Leslie Edwards, Michael Somes, Henry Legerton, Brian Shaw, Jill Gregory and former wardrobe mistress Joyce Wells. Fonteyn was not with the company on the latest tour, so most of the publicity featured Nureyev, and the Sibley–Dowell partnership.

Audience response for *Manon* was far more enthusiastic than Barnes had predicted, particularly for Nureyev making his debut as

Des Grieux. Even Barnes had to report that the New York season had been an enormous success for the company: 'frankly, its biggest yet', though he refused to reconsider his pronouncement that *Manon* was a flop. A thin house at the Met on a Memorial Day matinee convinced the Hurok organisation that *Manon* should be pulled from the forthcoming Washington schedule and replaced with Nureyev in additional *Swan Lake* performances. MacMillan, uncowed by Hurok's demands, threatened to withdraw the company and return with it to London on the next plane if *Manon* were dropped. He won. Its advertised performances went ahead at the Kennedy Center to an average 85-per-cent capacity.

Influential New York figures, however – particularly those ballet-lovers who preferred Balanchine and Ashton to MacMillan – condemned *Manon* as unworthy of the Royal Ballet. Arlene Croce, whose lengthy assessments of dance in the *New Yorker* commanded respect, was dismissive: 'It is neither as good nor as bad as advance reports had suggested, and its smooth mediocrity is alarming only because it seems to derive from a fear of offending public opinion.' She was disappointed by what she perceived as a lack of dramatic focus in MacMillan's choreography. Too much of it, she found, amounted to 'meaningless dancing' – especially in the various pas de deux, over-reliant on the performers' personal qualities:

Its stars are so busy dancing they haven't time to fill out their characterisations or advance the plot . . . On opening night, when Des Grieux introduced himself to Manon, he seemed to be saying, 'Madame, I am Anthony Dowell. Notice my turns, my perfect developpé into attitude front.' And her answer was: 'If you're Anthony Dowell. I must be Antoinette Sibley. Let's have a Sibley–Dowell pas de deux.' And they did.

The comments stung. So did Croce's main reproach, that MacMillan had lost confidence in his own vision of what ballet could do. She had respected 'the steely bravura' of *Anastasia*, in which he had 'produced a personal fantasy about a global cataclysm entirely from nothing'. Now she perceived that he was playing safe with *Manon*, trying to craft a conventionally well-made three-act ballet along operatic lines. What Croce could not foretell from early performances, however, was how dancers (including Sibley and Dowell) would develop the roles once they found the measure of the ballet. As their understanding of the choreography's structure deepened, performers were able to give richer (and very different) interpretations of the characters, making the ballet's dramatic trajectory clear. Manon was to become a role that ballerinas around the world aspire to dance; male principals vie to dance Des Grieux or Lescaut, some alternating the roles. (Croce was to modify her opinion of the ballet when reviewing later casts, such as Natalia Makarova as Manon and Irek Mukhamedov as Lescaut.)

Meanwhile, the Opera House management became convinced that the ballet was not the success for which they had hoped. Lincoln Kirstein had expressed his opinion in a letter to Richard Buckle in London that *Manon* was a disaster, the company was demoralised and that MacMillan as leader of the company was as impotent as President Nixon, about to lose office because of the Watergate scandal. Kirstein passed on his insider knowledge that Tooley had privately approached Nureyev to take over the Royal Ballet, while continuing to express support for MacMillan, whose contract renewal was under discussion. Nureyev, it seemed, was definitely interested. He intended to direct a classical company eventually and the Royal Ballet was dear to his heart. But he also wanted to carry on performing internationally to an extent that Tooley considered unacceptable. Kirstein revealed his information that Michael Somes would probably leave if Nureyev were appointed and Somes, it was generally agreed, was vital in keeping the company together. Nureyev, in any case, decided that he was not yet ready to take on the demands of a big, complicated national company. Leaving MacMillan in charge for another three years appeared to be the only option.

Unaware of these negotiations behind his back, though sensitive to the hostile gossip about him, MacMillan had been busy in New York setting deals in train for the next year. Jerome Robbins had agreed to create a 'substantial' work for the Royal Ballet, to be performed later by New York City Ballet. In return, Balanchine had asked MacMillan for a new work for City Ballet in spring 1975, when the company was planning a Ravel festival to mark the composer's centenary. 'So at least someone was impressed with me there,' MacMillan told Michael Owen of the *Evening Standard* on his return. The exchange plans fell through, and MacMillan's Ravel ballet was eventually done for his own company, not Balanchine's.

The Royal Ballet came back for its 1974 summer season at the Opera House with a sheaf of enthusiastic reviews for its dancers, if not for *Manon*, and a question mark hanging over MacMillan's head. He was defensive about his reputation in the *Evening Standard* article, which was accompanied by a photograph of him with arms crossed tight across his chest, cigarette, as always, between his fingers. The caption read: 'Misrepresented in Manhattan'. Deborah tried to reassure him that he was not being plotted against, though his suspicions were in fact justified. (Information about the Nureyev proposal was not published until long after MacMillan's death.) Lord Drogheda, a somewhat ambivalent ally who nevertheless supported MacMillan in public, was about to retire as Chairman of the Board after sixteen years. Its members would wait to see what decisions his successor, Sir Claus Moser, would take.

The Arts Council was flexing its muscles, demanding reforms and a clear vision of where the Royal Ballet was going in the future. Pressure would be put on the new Chairman to justify the annual Royal Opera House grant of £2,550,000 (in 1974–75) and its two ballet companies' outsize slice of the money allocated to dance of all kinds. Other companies, including the growing number of contemporary-dance groups, were complaining about the 'flagship of excellence' privilege awarded to the Royal Ballet, especially since its prestige appeared to be waning.

35

MacMillan's contract was renewed for a further three years, though it would be some time before its terms were agreed. Mark Bonham Carter had meanwhile been asked once again for a paper surveying the state the company was in, two years after his previous assessment. This time he laid the blame squarely at MacMillan's door: 'The Direction of the Royal Ballet is not matching its past achievements, nor is it building an exciting future.' The merger of the two companies was no longer sufficient excuse for a repertoire that was 'stale and unimaginative'. There had been a failure to involve distinguished international designers and to come up with good librettos for narrative ballets. This was a damning conclusion to reach after a season that had seen the premiere of *Manon*, with widely admired designs by Georgiadis. Bonham Carter's generalisation may, however, have been a dig at the substitution of Peter Farmer's designs for Beni Montresor's for *The Sleeping Beauty*.

The criticism of repertoire choices applied primarily to the touring company. In the four years of its existence, the New Group had nearly doubled in size (to 45 dancers) and was reverting to performing familiar ballets in order to attract audiences: *Les Sylphides*, *Giselle* and *Coppélia*. Its 'experimental' phase had been brief; few of its in-house creations had succeeded, and invited choreographers – Glen Tetley, Hans Van Manen – preferred to work with the higher-profile resident company rather than be relegated to the provinces. In order to keep up morale and maintain performance standards, Peter Wright was spending more and more of his time on the road with the touring group. What with his other duties as MacMillan's assistant, Wright was so overstretched that his health suffered. He warned the Board that he could not be expected to do two full-time jobs: one or other must go.

Bonham Carter posed the question in his paper of what to do if Wright gave up his administrative duties: 'What support does MacMillan need to give him strength and confidence and lead to improvements all round? How/who can provide it?' Bonham Carter was pessimistic: 'Perhaps no amount of support will help. To date that is the case.'

The eventual outcome of discussions with the Arts Council provoked by the paper was the decision to ask John Hart to return to the Royal Ballet in 1975 as its Administrator. Tooley flew to San Diego, where Hart was Director of the Dance Division of a new School of Performing and Visual Arts, and told him of the difficulties MacMillan and the Opera House were experiencing. Hart, if he accepted, would be responsible for the kind of forward planning he had done so efficiently in the past, and which had been missing in recent years. He would also be expected to improve relations with the ballet press, whose critical views were having a damaging effect on the box office. After long deliberation, Hart agreed to return for the start of the 1975–76 season in September.

Wright, meanwhile, was given full responsibility for the touring company, with John Auld as his second in command. They would soon have to deal with an Arts Council proposal to save money by merging it with the Manchester-based Northern Dance Company (later Northern Ballet Theatre), which was operating at a loss. Negotiations between the Arts Council, the Royal Opera House and Greater Manchester Council dragged on until 1976, demoralising both companies, until the merger idea was dropped. The continuing confusion over the touring company's future further undermined MacMillan's standing as titular head of both Royal Ballet companies.

MacMillan had returned from the American tour with an agonising pain in his left foot. An X-ray revealed that a spur of bone was cutting into nearby tendons, a not uncommon problem among dancers with highly flexible feet. He had the spur surgically removed during the summer break, hoping the incision would have healed by the time he started work on his next ballet for the company. He continued to hobble with a stick throughout the creation of *Elite Syncopations*, due for the start of the new season in October 1974.

He had wanted to do a ragtime ballet ever since revisiting Kurt Weill's music for *The Seven Deadly Sins*. Festival Ballet had unwittingly pre-empted his plans by commissioning Barry Moreland to choreograph 'The Prodigal Son (in Ragtime)' to music by Scott Joplin and others for March 1974. Joplin's catchy rhythms had meanwhile shot to the top of the pop charts thanks to the theme tune used in the film *The Sting* with Paul Newman and Robert Redford. MacMillan knew he would be accused of jumping on the Joplin/ragtime bandwagon, but he went ahead none the less. He had declared to the *New Yorker* that, after the travails of *Manon*, his next project was going to be 'Something short and light and funny, which I can toss off and walk away from.'

He envisaged a revue-style performance in which the band would be placed on stage as part of the spectacle, as if in a 1920s dance hall. Five of the twelve numbers were by Scott Joplin, including the title piece, *Elite Syncopations*; the rest were by his contemporaries, Joseph Lamb, Paul Pratt, James Scott, Max Nurath, Donald Ashwander and Robert Hampton. The choreography drew on social dances from the 1920s, such as the black bottom, cakewalk and charleston, as well as later disco-dancing moves. At one point, when the performers wore numbers on their backs, MacMillan might have been recalling the charleston competition he had won with Greta Hamby in Los Angeles in 1949.

He quoted moves from the duet he had danced with Sonya Hana in Cranko's *Dancing* at Henley. She recognised the wiggle the shy girl does in *The Golden Hours*, twisting her knees together sideways as she pulls down her skirt. 'Kenneth admitted I was right, he had "borrowed" it, but he said it had been his idea in the first place.' There are allusions to the 1920s dances in Ashton's *Façade*, and silent-movie comic routines by Charlie Chaplin, Harold Lloyd and Buster Keaton.

Diminutive Wayne Sleep was cast as the valiant small man in glasses and straw hat who has to cope with a tall, coolly elegant female partner (Vergie Derman). Their mis-sized duet to *The Alaskan Rag* has more than a hint of Lescaut's drunken pas de deux with his mistress in *Manon*. MacMillan included a vamping number for Monica Mason (*Calliope Rag*) and a show-stopper for Merle Park (*Stoptime Rag*) as a glamorous attention-grabbing girl who ends up with a mass of admiring partners. Ian Spurling dressed the dancers in lycra bodytights decorated with strategically placed stars, stripes, buttons and painted-on outfits, complete with jaunty headgear. The effect was both stylish and funny, a sly comment on the then ubiquitous unitards in modern-dance works.

The twelve-piece band was more soberly costumed in waistcoats, shirtsleeves and trousers, with flowers decorating their boaters. Members of the Royal Opera House Orchestra gamely agreed to perform on stage behind the dancers, though musicians for other companies could be less accommodating when *Elite Syncopations* was requested abroad. (Unions in Germany, for example, were able to claim that onstage appearances were not covered in orchestral players' contracts, entitling them to demand extra payments.)

Though *Elite Syncopations* seemed, at the time, little more than light entertainment to a passing musical craze, it was well crafted enough to endure. Audiences enjoyed seeing classical dancers using their technique to silly/sophisticated ends (even if the performers were not immediately recognisable beneath their headgear). Seymour and Sibley both danced as the *Stoptime Rag* girl, and Natalia Makarova, who became a 'permanent guest artist' with the company in the summer of 1974, made her debut in the role in a performance filmed by the BBC.

444

Makarova also danced the leading roles in *The Song of the Earth* and *Manon*, both of them roles she greatly valued. She remembers that MacMillan was very anxious for her to like *Manon* when she first saw the ballet in performance. 'I was surprised he was so pressing, but then I saw it at once as my role, that it fitted me exactly but I could have extraordinary freedom in doing it.' Georgiadis had been right in suggesting that she was a natural for the role. She forged a strong rapport with Dowell as her Des Grieux, establishing a partnership that illuminated other ballets in the repertoire.

The Royal Ballet was on a high as far as performance standards were concerned, for all Bonham Carter's concerns about the future. At the start of 1975, the corps de ballet was awarded the *Evening Standard* Award for Outstanding Achievement in Dance during the previous year. De Valois presented the award on stage after the 31 January performance of the *Kingdom of the Shades* act from *La Bayadère*, in which the corps plays a defining part. On the same programme was Hans Van Manen's new work, *Four Schumann Pieces*, featuring Dowell's particular qualities as a lyrical dancer. Van Manen, choreographer and ballet master with the Dutch National Ballet, had mounted several of his existing works for the touring group, but this was his first creation for the resident company. MacMillan was broadening its scope with more European as well as American choreography.

Jerome Robbins was evidently not going to deliver the substantial new work he had promised, so by March the company had to be content with a vintage Robbins romp from 1956, *The Concert*, and a new one-act ballet by MacMillan, *The Four Seasons*. By now more strategically astute than he had been at the start of his directorship, MacMillan planned a company display piece, using the award-winning corps de ballet and giving prominence to male soloists. He had criticised the poor quality of male dancing (compared with German standards) when he first took over; now he could show how dramatically the men had improved four years later. As he searched for appropriate music, Andrew Porter, who by now was music critic for the *New Yorker*, suggested Verdi's ballet music from his opera *Les Vêpres siciliennes* (*Sicilian Vespers*), a work MacMillan had never seen.

Verdi's music would be a change from the twentieth-century composers he usually chose for one-act ballets. To make a work fifty-five minutes long, the *Sicilian Vespers* seasons music was extended with dances from other operas, *Jerusalem (I Lombardi)* and *Don Carlos*. The setting, by Peter Rice, was of a turreted and balconied inn, with a sign declaring it 'Le Quattro Stagione'. Most of the cast were dressed as southern Italian peasants, in stylised versions of folk costumes; others were soldiers or passing travellers. Several critics took the tavern to be the house of ill-repute familiar from other MacMillan works, with a madame at the door and 'an inexhaustible supply of girls' as John Percival put it in *The Times*.

The ballet opened with a prologue in which wayfarers arriving at the inn joined the locals in a drink while local girls performed for them. Though the prologue served mainly to give the corps de ballet something to dance, it also provided a choreographic platform on which the 'seasons' would be built, starting with winter. Snow fell on a scarlet-clad hussar and two *vivandières*, the subjects of his gallantry. The lights then brightened for spring, an explosion of high spirits by three men and a girl in Neapolitan outfits. Summer was hot and languorous, a pas de deux (for Monica Mason and David Wall) full of yawns and sultry surrender. Autumn started with a dazzlingly fast solo for Wayne Sleep, followed by a pas de deux for Penney and Dowell which repeated in a light-hearted fashion the *Manon* Act III acrobatics in which he threw her, spinning several times in the air, before catching her. Dowell then had the last of the virtuoso solos before the whole cast returned for an exhilarating finale.

The choreography was full of invention, as MacMillan set out to show how masterfully he could combine ballet's classical lexicon with fresh ideas. Clement Crisp commented in the *Financial Times*, '*The Four Seasons* looks like a tribute from a choreographer immensely proud of his artists' technical brilliance, and they reward him with a reciprocal dazzle.' Its fireworks, however, were dampened by the cumbersome set and fussy costumes. Even when the prologue was shortened, the seasons outstayed their welcome; their narrative interest was insufficient to entertain those not prepared to enjoy dance for its own sake. The critic for the *Daily Mail*, David Gillard, who enjoyed the ballet, noted that 'the anti-MacMillan booers were still mutedly in evidence last night'.

The ballet was only sporadically revived after its first year in the repertoire. For its last Royal Ballet performances in 1980, it had new, sparer designs by Deborah MacMillan, under her maiden name of Williams. Extracts have subsequently been given at galas and by the School and other companies. The Paris Opéra Ballet would have its own version, mounted by MacMillan, in 1978.

In April 1975, the Royal Ballet undertook a four-week tour of Japan, stopping off *en route* in South Korea. MacMillan, who had a routine medical examination before travelling with the company, suddenly found his life insurance premium heavily loaded. In a panic that a life-threatening condition had been discovered, he asked to be referred to a heart specialist in Harley Street. The consultant's report, following another examination, reassured him that there was no sign of cardiac or vascular disease: the insurance loading was presumably because of his previous history of a 'vascular spasm' in 1969. Cleared to travel, he flew with the company, while Deborah took Charlotte, eighteen months old, to visit the Williams family in Australia.

The tour was the first time the Covent Garden company had visited the Far East, though the Sadler's Wells company (including Lynn Seymour) had toured to the Philippines, Hong Kong and Japan in 1961. Seymour's accounts of Kabuki performances she had attended then had stimulated MacMillan's interest in Japanese theatre, which he was eager to experience in its proper context. He and members of the company saw Kabuki performances in Osaka, as well as traditional Bunraku puppet theatre. He was delighted by a Takaratsuka music-hall show, in which all the performers were young women, some *en travesti* in male roles. In Nara, during a visit to see the biggest statue of the Buddha in Japan, ten of the dancers met up with a friendly Japanese schoolteacher, who took them home to meet her father, a renowned Nō teacher. He instructed them in the Nō conventions of walking and holding a fan, which Monica Mason then demonstrated to MacMillan on their return to the hotel.

This exposure to aspects of Japanese theatre was to influence his next work for the Royal Ballet. He had already chosen Bartók's Sonata for two pianos and percussion, music that interested him because of its rhythmic complexity. As he listened to a recording on his return from the Far East, the combination of Bartók's unusual instrumentation and the harsh sounds he had heard in ritual oriental dance-theatre suggested a strange new ballet.

He had come back to face yet more problems from the Board, now chaired by Sir Claus Moser. Moser had inherited Drogheda's appointed committee of influential, music-loving friends, some of whom had served on the Board for many years; Moser had selected others for their intellectual and social clout and some for their financial expertise. Predominantly male, they were Establishment heavyweights – literally so, in the case of the outsize Lord Goodman, former Chairman of the Arts Council. Most had little knowledge or experience of the inner workings of ballet and opera companies in Britain or elsewhere: they were amateurs of the arts, not professionals. Their primary concern was safeguarding the reputation of the Royal Opera House for excellence (which meant they preferred guaranteed success to the risk of failure), as well as keeping an eye on the companies' budgets. The Board relied on the Sub-Committees to provide them with relevant information. According to Moser, 'We were careful not to intervene in artistic matters but we did monitor standards.' Board members were expected to inform themselves by attending performances as often as they could. The companies, however, suspected them of giving undue significance to opinions voiced in the Opera House Crush Bar during intervals, and to press reviews.

In the past, Board members had regarded themselves as privileged to sit around the same table as Georg Solti and Frederick Ashton. They did not feel the same about Colin Davis and Kenneth MacMillan. 'We respected them as artists but they were not great figures,' said Moser, who had been on the Board since 1965 before taking over from Drogheda. An era had changed by the 1970s: instead of being regarded as equals or artistic superiors, the Directors of the opera and ballet companies were perceived as staff, ill-equipped by nature or training (of which there was none) to take part in strategic decisions about their companies' futures. In Moser's opinion, MacMillan was not the man to take along to the Arts Council to fight the ballet's corner in funding negotiations.

MacMillan's unease in asserting himself in public had never inspired confidence among Board and Ballet Sub-Committee members. He confessed to Lynn Barber in an interview for the *Sunday Express* magazine of 7 November 1982 that he felt out place in an old-boy network: 'I was confronted by all these [class] barriers and I had to sit on committees with people who'd all been to the same universities, belonged to the same clubs . . . I always did the wrong thing, put my foot in it.' He clammed up, on the defensive, his own worst enemy.

At a time of increasing financial stringency, in one of the most inflationary periods Britain has ever experienced, ballet had lost its post-war prestige. Opera might have cost more, thanks to the high fees singers and conductors could command, but opera patrons (and corporate sponsors) were prepared to pay more for their tickets in order to experience world-class performances. Seat prices went up dramatically in the mid-1970s. Loyal ballet-goers, who had once dug deep to afford the higher prices for Fonteyn and Nureyev performances, now chose to cut back. The anti-MacMillan camp blamed him for damaging the Royal Ballet's once proud popularity at home and abroad.

This view was endorsed by what became an annual ritual in which Clive Barnes's summer visit to Britain resulted in his ever-more-disparaging assessments of the state of the Royal Ballet for the *New York Times*. His articles would be quoted in *The Times* and other British papers, whose arts correspondents added their own comments about whether the Arts Council subsidy was being well spent. The Board then became exercised about how to react to an apparent campaign of criticism. Barnes scoffed at accusations that he came all the way to London in order to make a personal attack on MacMillan or his ballets. He reported what he saw: standards, in his opinion, were no longer as high as they had been under Ashton.

In June 1975, Barnes went to see one of the company's performances in the Big Top in Battersea Park. Stage hands at the London Coliseum had gone on strike, so the Royal Ballet's planned summer season there had been hastily relocated to a converted circus tent. (The Big Top had been acquired in 1974 for the touring company to perform in towns without a suitable theatre for ballet.) The tent's makeshift stage and lack of soundproofing were far from ideal, but audiences enjoyed the informality of the setting as well as the lower seat prices. Barnes, however, was underwhelmed and said so in the *New York Times*. In a follow-up article he commented in some surprise,

I used this one performance as an excuse to voice a few discontents about the course the Royal Ballet was taking in recent years. The article was widely reprinted in excerpts in England, and soon photostated copies of the complete article were being handed around in London dance circles. The tights had hit the fan.

The theatrical hysteria provoked by Barnes's comments was an indication both of hypersensitivity within the Royal Ballet and of the influence Barnes – thanks to the mighty *New York Times* – had on opinion-formers. John Tooley would later spend the good part of an alcohol-fuelled night in New York trying to persuade Barnes to lay off. 'Little impression seemed to be made on Barnes, but I felt better for having attempted to fight MacMillan's case,' Tooley wrote in his account of his years at the Royal Opera House. Four years earlier, Drogheda had set out to put similar pressure on Percival, to equally little effect. Even if MacMillan had known that senior members of the administration had taken such unprecedented steps to protect him and the ballet company, his own paranoia would probably not have diminished. He felt he was always being tested, never accepted and backed. 'They don't want me and they don't know how to get rid of me,' he said to Deborah. He was not yet, however, prepared to give in and resign.

36

Towards the end of 1975, MacMillan's self-esteem was boosted by an academic honour. The University of Edinburgh decided to award him a doctorate, *honoris causa*. According to the citation, this amounted to a double first, since MacMillan had no other degree and the university had never before recognised what it called 'the science and art of choreography'.

The citation was read on 22 November by Professor Iain MacGibbon, Dean of the Faculty of Law at the University and father of Ross MacGibbon, then a young dancer with the Royal Ballet.* MacMillan was acclaimed as a Scotsman, a performer and,

---

* Ross MacGibbon was later to become a member of the ROH Board, from 1999 to 2002, and then executive producer of BBC TV's dance coverage, from 2002 to 2007. He then joined ScreenStage, a TV production company.

above all, as a choreographer: 'a man of his time, carrying conviction in all that he does: a romantic choreographer, but one with a cutting edge – a classicist of the age of anxiety'. Professor MacGibbon concluded his oratory by noting that although the theme of the Outsider was a recurrent one in his subject's ballets, that was not a role in which he was now being cast: on the contrary, MacMillan was to be made 'one of us' by receiving the highest honour the University of Edinburgh could bestow.

Dressed in academic robes, MacMillan took his place with the University's dignitaries. His award was not the result of special pleading by his supporters in London but of Edinburgh University's desire to acclaim a Scottish cultural icon. (The Scots actor Alastair Sim had been elected rector of the University thirty years previously, the first time the 'cap and bells of the theatre' had been honoured by a Scottish seat of learning.) Conscious that he had left school at fifteen without matriculating, MacMillan was proud to be acknowledged by academia.

He was meanwhile preparing his new ballet, *Rituals*, for the Christmas 1975 season. By adapting Japanese martial arts and traditional theatre conventions to his own ends, he could portray extreme states – violence, death, copulation, birth – while keeping emotions at a distance. Like Nō or Kabuki, the ballet would be coded, seemingly remote and exotic to Western eyes. His use of Bartók's Sonata indicated that *Rituals* was not meant to be authentically Oriental. He had asked Yolanda Sonnabend to design ornamental costumes that could both conceal and reveal the dancers' bodies; mask-like make-up would keep their faces unreadable. Sonnabend came up with a suspended set of pleated parchment screens marked with bold black brushstrokes, like ink-spattered rice paper. Their delicate structure offset the sometimes brutal activity going on in the foreground.

In the first movement, *Preparation for Combat and Self-Defence*, a grand master of kung fu puts two male neophytes to the test, watched by their fellow martial-arts students. The two contenders are like the rival brothers in *Cain and Abel* or *Triad*: the younger one, the pretender, keeps getting in the way, upsetting the older one's attempts at self-control. Though the grand master intervenes as umpire, the stylised battle is a vicious one. The young pretender might well be dead at the end.

The second movement is based on Bunraku puppets, with a male and a female dancer manipulated in a nuptial rite by two groups of puppeteers. Dressed in white instead of discreet black, the attendants are highly visible as they ensure that the hapless couple scarcely touch the ground. The pair, exposed as bald dolls with stitching around their joints, are manoeuvred into grotesque couplings, at the mercy of society's requirements for mating and marriage. Once adorned in their elaborate wedding robes, they collapse eerily onto the floor, unsupported.

The final part, called *Celebration and Prayer*, is a birth scene, Kabuki-style. A midwife attends a mother-to-be in the throes of labour, while fluttering female celebrants look on in consternation. Two men bustle about among them like the court officials in Puccini's *Turandot*. The women's nodding heads, fans and gliding walks were influenced by Monica Mason's Nō demonstrations to MacMillan back in Japan: 'We have to begin with your little walk, don't we, Miss Mason?' he said to her. She was cast as the midwife, wrestling with Lynn Seymour as the mother. The mother's solo, tearing her hair – a Kabuki wig like the one in *Images of Love* – is almost obscene in its defiance of the restraint observed by the other women. MacMillan was recalling the birth of his daughter, during which he marvelled at the way hospital staff went routinely about their tasks, chatting about their days off, as his wife was going through labour.

The final scene ends abruptly, as if with a shrug, wondering what the fuss was all about. Society, it seems, carries on with its preoccupations, sweeping aside the individuals who suffer within it. During the birth, the attendant women have scurried through interlocking patterns that challenge dancers and spectators alike (as well as the notator, Jacquie Hollander, who had to struggle to record them, a challenge that amused MacMillan). 'Anything further from the rituals of Japanese theatre than this snarl of bodies, colour, fabric and music would be hard to imagine,' wrote the baffled Deborah Jowitt in the *Village Voice*.

While some reviewers welcomed MacMillan's return to the experimentation with ballet of his earlier work, others could not relate the three parts of *Rituals* to each other, except as pseudo-Oriental sketches. Although MacMillan never again used overt Orientalisms, he recycled some of the moves from *Rituals* in other ballets: the puppet manipulations in *La Fin du jour*, the martial-arts kicks in *The Prince of the Pagodas*.

Seymour's appearance in *Rituals* was her first significant role in a new MacMillan ballet since *Anastasia*. Fearing that her career with the Royal Ballet was in decline, she had contemplated retiring in 1974 at the age of thirty-six, after the birth of her third son, Demian, in July. She was persuaded to change her mind by the prospect of revivals of *Anastasia, Romeo and Juliet* and *Symphony* in 1975. MacMillan would offer her *Manon* at the start of 1976. She had worked assiduously to regain her technical strength, returning after her pregnancy slim and in better form than she had been for years. As well as reassuming her previous roles, she was soon taking on new ones with the resident company and the touring group. Once more in the ascendant, Seymour had, at last, gained the status of a senior ballerina. She would alternate with Makarova in leading roles with the Royal Ballet and be in demand as a guest artist. Most gratifying of all was the opportunity to work with Ashton again: he had chosen her for his latest creations, one of which was to be his first major work for the company since MacMillan had taken charge.

Ashton's retirement deal with the Royal Opera House had included a retaining fee for a further five years in return for at least one ballet a year. By the end of 1975, he had not delivered anything other than gala pas de deux, although he had talked of making a ballet based on Turgenev's *A Month in the Country*. Back in 1971, Tooley had written to Drogheda warning him that Ashton would take his time: 'We have no hold over him to make him meet deadlines. He will, eventually, do *Month in the Country* for us and no one else.'

Before committing himself to the long-promised ballet, Ashton had choreographed a solo for Seymour to perform at a gala in Hamburg on 22 June 1975. She embodied his early memories of Isadora Duncan dancing to classical music – in this case, a Brahms waltz from Op. 39. The barefoot solo, a seemingly spontaneous response to the piano music, was not an attempt to re-create an actual Duncan dance but an evocation of her rapturous abandon. Seymour was so enchanting that Ashton later added further dances: the sequence, *Five Brahms Waltzes in the Manner of Isadora Duncan*, became closely identified with Lynn. With his agreement, and following his death, she has since passed it on to other dancers.

Ashton now declared himself ready to start work on *A Month in the Country*, to be given its premiere in February 1976. Seymour was to be Natalia Petrovna, the beautiful, bored, married woman at the core of Turgenev's play. Ashton took her and the rest of the cast to see Dorothy Tutin play the role in a London production as he began his preparations. The lure of a new Ashton ballet had aroused the interest of Board members, grateful that he was now back on course. Isaiah Berlin, the philosopher and essayist, advised him what music to choose: early Chopin rather than Tchaikovsky, Ashton's initial idea. Julia Trevelyan Oman, the designer married to Roy Strong, Director of the Victoria and Albert Museum and another member of the Royal Opera House Board, was eager to collaborate on a ballet with him once again. She had designed his *Enigma Variations* in 1968, as well as working with opera producers on *Eugene Onegin* and *La Bohème*. *A Month in the Country* was to be a ballet very much to the taste of the Opera House establishment, unlike MacMillan's recent creations.

On 1 January 1976, a month before the premiere of *A Month in the Country*, Seymour made her debut as Manon, with David Wall as Des Grieux and Dowell as Lescaut. She told MacMillan that she intended to develop her own interpretation of the role, and he gave her the freedom to do so. She built up a semi-incestuous relationship with Lescaut, her debauched brother, implying that they were cut from the same cloth, both out for what they could get from their corrupt society. Her Manon was no innocent but a sensually ripe girl fully capable of selling herself for a price negotiated by her brother. Des Grieux was her victim, capriciously though she loved him. MacMillan's ballet gained in dramatic tension, thanks to Seymour's different perspective.

Ashton was meanwhile fretting that *A Month in the Country* might seem old-fashioned to a public attuned to sex and death on a lavish scale. The summer storm-in-a-teacup experienced by Turgenev's characters could appear anticlimactic, however heartfelt their emotions. MacMillan reassured him with a grateful first-night telegram: 'Your ballet is exquisite. Thank you for doing it.' Ovations greeted the Royal Opera House premiere on 12 February 1976, to be followed by yet more when *A Month in the Country* was performed in New

York in April, during the Royal Ballet's next American tour. Clive Barnes's ecstatic review in the *New York Times* was headed: 'Ashton could be our greatest choreographer.'

The United States tour, which included Washington and Philadelphia as well as a month in New York, would, it turned out, be the company's last visit under MacMillan's directorship. Transatlantic touring had become increasingly expensive and, after Sol Hurok's death in 1974, impresarios were reluctant to undertake the financial risk unless star names could attract full houses. Fonteyn no longer toured with the Royal Ballet. Instead, the tour's publicity featured Natalia Makarova as guest artist, making her New York debuts in *Romeo and Juliet*, *Manon* and *Song of the Earth*. MacMillan travelled with the company, while Deborah, with Charlotte, joined her brother Simon in France for a holiday.

Kenneth had already decided to leave the tour to return home sooner than he had intended when he received news that Deborah, Charlotte and Simon had been involved in a bad car accident in France. They had met up with Deborah's former boyfriend, David Williams, in Paris and were on their way to the Loire valley in a Mini driven by Williams. A larger car crashed into them at a cross-roads, sending Deborah and three-year-old Charlotte through the windscreen. They were taken to different hospitals on opposite sides of Paris, Deborah with concussion and Charlotte with facial injuries that were treated in a children's hospital. Simon, seated in the back of the car, escaped with cuts and bruises.

Kenneth caught a direct flight from New York to Paris, deeply alarmed by what might have happened. He had reason to dread car crashes. His sister Jean had been killed in an accident, as had the composer Mátyás Seiber and the Swedish Intendant, Göran Gentele; his own experience of overturning in 1952 with John Cranko at the wheel had deterred him from ever learning to drive. He arrived in Paris to find Deborah in a state of panic about Charlotte. Coming round after her concussion, Deborah had been told, 'Your little boy is all right'; unable to speak French clearly because of a cut lip, Deborah was unable to establish whether her daughter was indeed all right, and if so, where she was.

They were reunited when Kenneth fetched Charlotte, head swathed in bandages, from the children's hospital and brought her to Deborah's side in St Cloud. They were assured that the child's injuries were superficial, but when the dressings were removed back in London, she was found to have a hole in her forehead through which the bone was showing. Carl Lambert recommended a plastic surgeon, who operated at once so that Charlotte would not be scarred for life.

To recuperate as a family after the accident, the MacMillans spent several weeks in the West Country. The Royal Ballet, after its return from the American tour, had finished the summer season in the Big Top in Plymouth and the MacMillans had stayed on in the area. Kenneth was planning his next work and the repertoire for the company's autumn–winter season. It would include another Van Manen piece, *Adagio Hammerklavier*, made for the Dutch National Ballet, and Glen Tetley's *Voluntaries*, created for the Stuttgart Ballet as a memorial to Cranko. *Onegin*, Cranko's 1965 three-act ballet, had been scheduled for February 1977 and its casts allocated, including Seymour and Park in the leading role of Tatiana. But the demands made by its German designer, Jürgen Rose, were causing such problems for the Royal Opera House that the ballet might have to be cancelled (as indeed it was). Rose was insisting that the sets be painted to his precise specifications at considerable expense, even though they were unlikely to meet British fire-proofing requirements. MacMillan would have to be prepared to substitute an alternative ballet.

Tooley was still urging him to make a commitment to re-creating *The Prince of the Pagodas*. Benjamin Britten, unwell and nearing the end of his life, had expressed his frustration over the years that the score was lying dormant. He had become even more exercised about it when he was writing music for dancers in his *Death in Venice* opera, premiered in 1973. Cranko's 1957 ballet to the *Pagodas* score had not been performed by the Royal Ballet since 1960, apart from excerpts given in galas. Both Britten and Cranko had known that the production needed rethinking but relations between them had deteriorated to a point where no further collaboration had been possible. De Valois had continued to agitate for another, preferably British, choreographer to take on *The Prince of the Pagodas*, which she considered an important work in the history of British ballet as 'the first full-length ballet score by such a distinguished composer . . . a work commissioned for an English choreographer'. (Cranko was South African but had taken British nationality.)

'It is all there to be rechoreographed', she wrote in her book of essays, *Step by Step*, adding, 'and this is of greater urgency than half-a-dozen more versions of *The Sleeping Beauty*, or *The Sleep-Walking Prince*, as it shows signs of becoming.' The dig at MacMillan was evident. He had in fact been thinking about making his own version of *The Prince of the Pagodas*, mentioning it in an interview with the *Evening Standard* in January 1976 as a project for Natalia Makarova. A letter to him from Britten, dated 21 January 1976, indicates that the composer had been told of his interest and wanted 'to know how your mind is working'. However, after MacMillan had consulted Georgiadis, his preferred designer, they both concluded that Cranko's invented legend, a combination of *Beauty and the Beast*, *Cinderella*, *The Sleeping Beauty* and *King Lear*, was unmanageable. The scenario would have to rewritten.

MacMillan approached the music critic and author Ronald Crichton (who had drawn up the scenario for Andrée Howard's *La Fête étrange*) for his help in drafting a simplified *Pagodas* scenario. To streamline the ballet, the score would need to be cut, provided the composer agreed. Tooley, determined to have the music back in the repertoire, set up a meeting with Britten at his house in Aldeburgh.

Tooley drove MacMillan to the Suffolk coast, just as de Valois had driven Cranko to see Britten twenty years earlier. On both occasions, the visit turned out to be a strained one: Britten was protective of his music and wary of choreographers' whims. According to Tooley, the encounter with MacMillan was excruciating:

Kenneth was being particularly monosyllabic. He got off on the wrong foot with Ben from the start. The very first cut he proposed, Ben said, 'Oh, Mr MacMillan, that's my favourite section of the score.' And so it went on with every cut Kenneth suggested. Then, when he wanted to move the Prince's variation in the last-act divertissement so that the dancer would have time to recover his breath after the pas de deux, Ben put Kenneth in his place by saying, 'Well, I modelled it exactly on what Petipa and Tchaikovsky did in *The Sleeping Beauty*.'

Horribly ill at ease, MacMillan and Tooley stayed for a brief, awkward lunch with Britten, who was in poor health. He had relented sufficiently as they left to ask MacMillan for a letter setting down his requirements in detail. When no such letter was forthcoming, Britten withdrew his tentative offer of co-operation. He had admitted to Tooley that he knew the score needed cutting, but he would have to be convinced of the reason for each sacrifice of his music. After his death a few months later at the end of 1976, the Executors of his Estate refused to condone any cuts. Tooley continued to press MacMillan for a *Pagodas* ballet, insisting that the commission be written into the terms of his contract renewal with the Royal Opera House.

Negotiations over his salary and royalties for his next three-year period, up to 1978–79, had stalled. MacMillan had been advised for tax reasons to set up a business partnership with Deborah, leasing Kenneth's services as a freelance to the Royal Opera House. It was the kind of agreement to which many self-employed people (including artists and writers) had resorted under Labour-government legislation. Denis Van Thal, Kenneth's agent, was trying to secure higher fees for him: he had been paid £14,000 per annum from September 1975, which Van Thal insisted should be increased by £1,000 each succeeding year. MacMillan's annual salary as the Royal Ballet's Artistic Director would still be a third less than Colin Davis received as Music Director. Van Thal proposed that MacMillan should receive royalties of £15 per performance for a one-act ballet and £45 for each performance of a three-act ballet. The Royal Opera House had delayed agreeing the contract because the government, under Harold Wilson's leadership until Jim Callaghan succeeded him as prime minister in 1976, had imposed a national pay freeze. Disputes about whom the pay freeze affected would precipitate a crisis for MacMillan in the year to come.

In place of the postponed *Prince of the Pagodas* (which would take another thirteen years to come to fruition), MacMillan told the Ballet Sub-Committee that he intended to choreograph a one-act ballet to Gabriel Fauré's *Requiem*. He was ready to create a memorial to John Cranko, three years after his death, and he had long been attracted to Fauré's music. He had used Fauré for short works (*Pavane* and *Ballade*), and the choral *Requiem* suited his purpose as a larger-scale tribute to Cranko's memory. The Committee referred the matter to the Board, which erupted in heated argument. John Pope-Hennessy (Director of the British Museum) declared that in his view, as a Catholic, setting a ballet to sacred music would offend religious members of the audience. Pope-Hennessy's view was strongly backed by another member of the Board, Burnet Pavitt, who associated the *Requiem* with memorial services for friends. (Pavitt, like Pope-Hennessy, was a Drogheda appointee.) They were not prepared to condone such a sacrilegious undertaking.

They were apparently unaware that in 1972–73 the Royal Ballet had performed Robbins's choreography to Stravinsky's *Requiem Canticles*; the music had been played at Stravinsky's own funeral in 1971 and Robbins had choreographed a ballet to it for New York City Ballet's Stravinsky Festival in 1972. Stravinsky, like Fauré, had chosen not to follow the standard liturgical text for a requiem Mass to be performed in a church: their Requiems can be performed as concert oratorios. Fauré left out the *Dies irae*, for example, and added two prayers from the funeral service, the Order of Burial. His 'Requiem without the Last Judgment' was a musical meditation on death and the afterlife, inspired by the recent death of his father.

The two Catholic objectors on the Board won the day after hours of fervent, often nasty, debate. The Chairman, Claus Moser, later regretted his decision not to overrule the consensus view: 'a real failure on my part' is how he came to view the Board's refusal to allow MacMillan to go ahead. Moser was following Drogheda's 1959 decision that great music addressing elevated subjects, such as Mahler's *Song of the Earth*, was unsuitable for ballet. At the time of the Mahler ban, however, MacMillan had been a relatively inexperienced choreographer. He had proved Drogheda wrong by creating a much admired work, obliging the Board, then, to admit its mistake. He was now Director of the Royal Ballet as well as its principal choreographer. His artistic judgement was being questioned by the Board, which should either have trusted him or replaced him.

Aggrieved, MacMillan sought the Archbishop of Canterbury's opinion as head of the Church of England. He wrote to the Archbishop in March 1976 explaining that several members of the Board 'had expressed the feeling that I might offend the religious beliefs of the public at large . . . My intentions are very serious and I have no intention of doing anything other than add dance to a beautiful piece of music akin to the composer's intentions.' He pointed out that although similar doubts had been raised over his use of Mahler's *Song of the Earth*, 'This piece has a permanent place in our repertoire, as well as being considered my best ballet.'

The letter was answered by the Organist at Canterbury Cathedral, Allan Wicks, to whom the Archbishop had entrusted the response in his absence. Wicks, who knew MacMillan's work well, conveyed the Archbishop's view and his own that 'God's work is manifest in everything that we do and to create a ballet to Fauré's *Requiem* is in no way offensive to people with real religious beliefs. Of course, you will certainly offend some people, but I have come to believe that only something very pale and innocuous offends nobody.'

The Board, however, refused to relent. MacMillan telephoned Marcia Haydée, who had recently been appointed Artistic Director of the Stuttgart Ballet. She had already asked Kenneth for a ballet, hoping to renew his relationship with the company. When he proposed the Fauré *Requiem* as a memorial to Cranko, she responded with enthusiasm. The opera company that shared the Württemberg State Theatre with the ballet would, she was confident, provide the chorus and soloists the *Requiem* required. As soon as the Royal Ballet's autumn season was under way, MacMillan flew to Stuttgart with Deborah and Charlotte.

As always in his collaborations with the Stuttgart company, inspiration flowed readily. 'It came so quickly,' he said in an interview with John Higgins in *The Times* in May 1978. 'I had lived with the music for ten years or so and the choreography fell easily into place.' According to the Stuttgart dancers, the ballet was very much a portrait of the company coming to terms with Cranko's death. Haydée, still dancing as well as directing, was the central, consoling figure, 'the glue holding the company together when the light left'. She had been the one to whom the dancers turned for comfort at Cranko's funeral in 1973, embracing them all, a mother with her extended family. Although she had initially resisted replacing him as director (Glen Tetley took over for two years), the responsibility had been an inevitable one.

The other soloists MacMillan chose, Birgit Keil, Richard Cragun, Reid Anderson and Egon Madsen, had also been Cranko's favourite dancers. Their entry with the corps at the start of the ballet to the *Introitus* had all thirty-one dancers shuffling *en masse*, hammering their fists at heaven in anger at the loss of their beloved leader, mouths open in silent howls of grief. They huddled into a circle, raising Haydée aloft like an offering – an echo of the Chosen Maiden in *The Rite of Spring*, and of his early *Journey* for Nora Kaye. Haydée was suspended on a sea of hands, rolling in distress above the 'unfathomed abyss' into which departed souls risked falling for ever. In later sections of the ballet, she seemed transfigured into an angel of mercy, bringing comfort to the mourners.

The principal male soloist was Cragun, who led the *Offertorium*. He was joined by Haydée for a pas de deux framed by a discreet chorus of three couples at the rear of the stage. Cragun was then left alone for an anguished solo in which he repeatedly coiled himself into a knot, supported on the ground by his hands. Haydée was borne on at the end to touch his shoulder in a benison of hope.

For the *Sanctus*, she was paired with Anderson in a duet of acrobatic lifts conveying the exultation of the music. As always, the key pas de deux had been MacMillan's choreographic starting point. 'We were used to high lifts and flips from John's choreography,' says Anderson.

But this was something else. We began in silence, running in from either side of the stage. Then Marcia had to throw herself into a double flip, parallel to the ground, and as I caught her, the music would start. But for a whole day, we never even heard the music – we worked on how to do the flip until my arms gave out. Kenneth knew the effect he wanted. It was up to us to make it happen.

The *Sanctus* ended in Hosannas with Anderson lying on his back, supporting Haydée on his knees as she appeared to float horizontally.

For the *Pie Jesu*, a prayer for eternal peace, she danced a poignant solo. MacMillan's inspiration was Charlotte, just turned four, inventing her own dance to music by Bach. Egon Madsen had invited the MacMillans to lunch at his place and Charlotte had danced on her own to Bach records 'for about two hours [doing] the most extraordinary things', according to her father in interviews. 'I looked at her and thought, "I wish I could do that kind of choreography". The next morning I went into the studio and tried.' Haydée understood that he wanted her, a mature woman, to move with the simplicity of a child in a shaft of sunlight.

She played with her hands and wrists and bent to touch the ground as though exploring the light falling upon it. One reviewer saw her as an angel contemplating the earth far below; another thought she was cradling an imaginary baby. Her maternal role was evident in the *Agnus Dei*, when she returned towards the end to comfort the second woman, Birgit Keil; Haydée was held inverted like a flying angel above the kneeling Keil by a group of men in a frozen tableau.

In the final section, *In Paradisum*, the company assembled around a pool of light in the centre of the stage as if witnessing a funeral and the departure of a soul to heaven. Here, as for much of the ballet, the corps remained anonymous, backs to the audience as they exited in a procession, mourners and blessed spirits, leaving the empty stage bathed in white light.

Although MacMillan did not inform the dancers at the time, he was basing many of the choreographic images on William Blake's drawings and paintings, including his illustrations for Milton's *Paradise Lost*, Dante's *Inferno* and the Old Testament Book of Job. Knowing that de Valois had been inspired by Blake's drawings for her ballet *Job* (1931), he had deliberately chosen different images. (He might also have been influenced by Ashton's studies of illustrations by Gustave Doré and John Flaxman for Dante's *Divine Comedy* when Ashton choreographed his *Dante Sonata* in 1940.) 'The shapes were in his head,' says Haydée. 'He didn't sit with a book in his hand – we never saw the drawings.' The first the company notator, Georgette Tsinguirides, knew of the source was when MacMillan gave her a book of Blake's illustrations as a first-night present. 'He pointed out which ones he had used in which section of the music. Then I saw how the painting was in the choreography.'

Requiem was given its premiere in Stuttgart on 28 November 1976, with designs by Yolanda Sonnabend. The set consisted of six square fibreglass columns rising into the flies as an image of eternity, lit to appear translucent, with a white backcloth and wings. The costumes (apart from those for Haydée and Richard Cragun) were all-over tights, the torsos painted with striations resembling veins and muscles. Sonnabend based them on Vesalius' anatomical studies from the sixteenth century, though there were also echoes of Blake's drawings of bodies in extremis. Haydée was dressed in a semi-transparent white chiffon shift to distinguish her from the other women; Cragun wore only a loin cloth, making him a John the Baptist or Christ figure.

Sonnabend remembers having to alter the costume designs overnight because MacMillan had changed his mind about the effect he wanted. He was seeking the same sort of simplicity that he and Georgiadis had eventually achieved for *Das Lied von der Erde* – the work *Requiem* most closely resembled.

Stuttgart audiences and critics acclaimed *Requiem*, as did the two London critics who went to the premiere, Clement Crisp for the *Financial Times* and John Percival for *The Times*. Percival called it MacMillan's best ballet to date, in 'the vein of *Song of the Earth*, developing it more richly, with more consistent flair'. MacMillan commented in a later interview with John Higgins for *The Times* in May 1978, 'I thought it was a rather good ballet, and when I feel that I rarely expect people to agree with me. But on this occasion they did.'

When the Stuttgart Ballet took *Requiem* to the United States six months later, it was so admired in Washington DC that an extra performance was added 'by popular demand' at the Kennedy Center, in place of Tetley's *Voluntaries*. The company's ballet master, Alan Beale, wrote to MacMillan on 1 June 1977, 'You can draw your conclusions from the fact that [the impresario] is not only prepared but positively raring to fork out the extra 3,000 dollars for the soloists and choir.' The *Washington Post* critic, Alan Kriegsman, had given it a rave review, claiming that it was a milestone 'not only in MacMillan's career but in the evolution of ballet during our century's latter half'.

Although there were some dissenting views in New York when the double bill of *Requiem* and *Voluntaries* was given at the Met, Clive Barnes hailed *Requiem* as a major work. He noted how the serenity of Fauré's music, 'with its suppressed emotions, is very well captured in the slowly shifting prism of Mr MacMillan's choreography, which is deliberately organic rather than symphonic, growing with the music rather than kinetically illustrating its structure'.

Both Barnes and Percival in their reviews reproached the Royal Ballet for missing an important work by its own choreographer. When Tooley reported *Requiem*'s success to the Board, he justified its initial rejection by saying that the Stuttgart ambience brought out the best in MacMillan, enabling him to produce finer ballets than he would have at home. Marcia Haydée was of the same opinion. She was convinced that Kenneth's emotional investment in *Requiem* and in Cranko's company was such that the ballet, like *Das Lied von der Erde*, was special to Stuttgart: 'They cannot carry the same charge as when they were created. Even a video of the original cast cannot capture that emotion. It's gone. What's left is the steps.'

MacMillan agreed that the Stuttgart company should have exclusive rights to *Requiem* for six years. He, too, felt that the ballet was special to them and he did not want to make it available to other companies, as Tetley had done with *Voluntaries*. When Beryl Grey, then Artistic Director of Festival Ballet, wrote to him asking whether her company could perform it, he replied that he was holding it in reserve for the Royal Ballet. (*Requiem* entered the Royal Ballet repertoire in 1983.)

In thanks for *Requiem*, and as a replacement for the cancelled production of Cranko's *Onegin*, Dieter Graefe, the Administrative Director of the Stuttgart Ballet and Cranko's heir, offered *The Taming of the Shrew*. Cranko had created it in Stuttgart in 1969, with Haydée and Cragun as Kate and Petruchio. They came to London as guest stars when the Royal Ballet first performed it in February 1977, and also appeared in their original roles in *The Song of the Earth*. Although the leads in *The Taming of the Shrew* were then taken by Royal Ballet principals, the ballet proved better suited to the touring company, where it found its place in 1981. *Onegin* finally entered the Royal Ballet repertoire in 2001, after that company's long period of neglect of Cranko's work.

37

MacMillan's next assignment had nothing to do with the Royal Ballet. He had been asked to create a solo for John Curry, the great British figure-skater who had revolutionised competitive ice-skating. Curry, who had won European, World and Olympic gold medals in 1976, was determined to show that ice-skating could be an art form as well as a sport. His medal-winning performances had been as elegantly choreographed and executed as any classical ballet solo. When he turned professional after his Olympic win, retiring from competition, Curry set about establishing his own company of dance-skaters, the Theatre of Skating. They would break the *Holiday-on-Ice* mould of entertainment by performing on specially constructed ice-stages in theatres and concert halls instead of sports arenas. He sought the advice of Peter Darrell, Director of Scottish Ballet for the previous seven years, about choreographers who would be interested in exploring what dance-trained skaters could do.

Darrell offered to create two pieces for the company and suggested MacMillan, as well as choreographers who worked for television and the commercial theatre. MacMillan knew nothing about skating (and had never even attempted it) but had loved watching Curry in competition on television. He told the BBC programme *Outlook*, 'Whenever I saw him dance, I always felt if he weren't in ice-skating boots, he'd be a perfect classical dancer, so I wanted to do a classical piece for him. He had to tell me what I can and can't do. I hope I pushed him in certain directions and he's shown me a few things I might be able to use in ballet.' The solo's title, *Feux Follets* ('Will o' the Wisps') came from the music, Liszt's Transcendental Study No. 5, a brilliant piece full of trills. MacMillan exploited Curry's poise and line as well as his speed on the ice. 'There is a manège of turns that, except for the extraordinary stamina it would take to get through it on dry land, might have been choreographed for Anthony Dowell,' wrote Arlene Croce in the *New Yorker* of 18 December, when Curry's company appeared in New York. The US version of the show, called *IceDancing*, was performed at the Felt Forum, Madison Square Garden, with additional pieces by American choreographers, including Twyla Tharp and Peter Martins.

Darrell was artistic co-ordinator of the show, whose London premiere was at the Cambridge Theatre in Covent Garden on Boxing Day 1976. It was the first time since 1961, when MacMillan did *The Seven Deadly Sins* for Western Theatre Ballet at the Edinburgh Festival, that he and Darrell had worked on a joint project. (Darrell had been commissioned, at MacMillan's suggestion, to choreograph dances for the Deutsche Oper's production of Carl Orff's *Carmina Burana/Catulli Carmina* in May 1968. MacMillan, who was not in Berlin at the time, had no wish to undertake the choreography himself.) They had remained friends over the years, sending each other telegrams for important first nights and meeting up occasionally, usually at performances by each other's companies. Darrell, encountering MacMillan in the Royal Opera House Crush Bar, would curtsey low as Queen of Scotland to Kenneth's Queen of England, murmuring, 'You realise, of course, we never met.'

Darrell must have been tantalised by MacMillan's choice of subject matter for his next three-act ballet, *Mayerling*, since Darrell had choreographed his own *Mayerling* back in 1963. He, like MacMillan, had first learned of the story through romanticised film accounts* of the double suicide in 1898 of Crown Prince Rudolf of Austro-Hungary and his teenage mistress, Mary Vetsera, at the Mayerling hunting lodge outside Vienna. In his ballet, Darrell had aimed for greater realism, setting the tragedy in its political context. The over-ambitious result was not a success: the Royal Winnipeg Ballet, which had commissioned the work, gave it only a few performances. MacMillan could not have seen Darrell's *Mayerling* (to music by Fauré), though it is conceivable that they discussed the problems inherent in staging the complex story as a ballet.

MacMillan had already decided on his own approach. He wanted to examine the forces, historical and personal, that had brought about Rudolf's downfall. His interest had been sparked two years previously by a recently published book, *The Eagles Die* by George Marek, which he had given Deborah for her birthday in July 1974. The book described the Viennese court of Emperor Franz Joseph and Empress Elisabeth and chronicled the events leading up to the collapse of the Austro-Hungarian Empire. The Crown Prince's suicide in 1898 and the subsequent cover-up of the circumstances in which he died with his young mistress were part of a much wider picture.

As he had done in the three-act *Anastasia*, MacMillan intended to show the society in which his characters moved before narrowing his focus to the individual's plight. The ballet would need to include political machinations and corruption within the court; the Habsburg family's strained relations with each other; the drugs and disease that undermined Rudolf's unstable personality. Whether Darrell had warned of the pitfalls – 'too many historical figures and lots of papers being passed round' – or whether criticism of the scenario for Manon had made him apprehensive, MacMillan decided to seek the help of a professional writer.

---

* Feature films had been released in 1936, 1949 and 1968, starring pairings of Charles Boyer and Danielle Darrieux, Jean Marais and Sylvia Montfort, and Omar Sharif and Catherine Deneuve, respectively.

His first approach was to John Osborne, whose 1966 play, *A Patriot for Me*, was set in the same decadent Austro-Hungarian period as *Mayerling*. Osborne had originally invited him to choreograph the ball scenes in the play, after seeing the premiere of *Romeo and Juliet*, but MacMillan was working in Berlin by the time *A Patriot for Me* was produced. Osborne failed to reply to MacMillan's request for a scenario, so he turned instead to Gillian Freeman, wife of the *Evening Standard* critic, Edward Thorpe, and an old friend. She was an experienced writer for films, television and radio, as well as being a novelist. For one of her books, *The Alabaster Egg*, she had drawn on the life and times of King Ludwig of Bavaria, cousin and close friend of Empress Elisabeth of Austro-Hungary, so she was already familiar with the period. Over dinner at the MacMillans' house in September 1976, Freeman agreed to prepare a *Mayerling* scenario after she had researched the documents and first-hand accounts of life in the Habsburg court.

Preparations for *Mayerling* were likely to be time-consuming. The premiere, first scheduled for autumn 1977, was soon postponed until early 1978. A new *Sleeping Beauty* would meanwhile be the company's next major undertaking. Tooley and the Ballet Sub-Committee members had been pressing for a return to Oliver Messel's designs for the company's much acclaimed post-war production by de Valois. MacMillan objected, pointing out to the Committee in November 1976 that Messel's designs, re-created for American Ballet Theatre's recent production of *The Sleeping Beauty*, had been dismal. David Walker was chosen as designer instead, and the production was scheduled to open the season in October 1977. To judge from the November minutes, MacMillan does not seem to have been aware that de Valois, nearing eighty, was to be in charge of mounting the ballet. He had evidently assumed that he, as Artistic Director, would be responsible.

As MacMillan knew (and resented), Tooley regularly visited de Valois at her home in Barnes, keeping her in touch with what was going on at the Royal Ballet. Tooley denies that he would have gone behind MacMillan's back and asked her to produce *The Sleeping Beauty* without first informing him. None the less, Deborah remembers Kenneth returning home early in 1977 in a state of great distress, telling her that he had been insulted: he had just learned that all decisions about the new production had been taken out of his hands. He had been passed over in favour of the two previous Artistic Directors, for Ashton would also be involved, restoring his choreography in collaboration with de Valois. MacMillan's own artistic judgement was being questioned, as it had been over his choice of the Fauré *Requiem*. 'How can I be Director of the Royal Ballet if they treat me like this?' he asked Deborah.

As he agonised over what to do next, he accompanied the ballet company on tour to Bristol. He sat through consecutive performances of *Romeo and Juliet*, lamenting that his energies were not being better spent on creating his next three-act ballet, *Mayerling*. He had meanwhile been required to prepare a short new piece for a Royal Opera House gala in May 1977 celebrating the Queen's Silver Jubilee. Tooley had asked him to use Benjamin Britten's Choral Dances from *Gloriana*, the opera Britten had composed for the Coronation of the young Queen Elizabeth in 1953. Ashton, who had supplied the choreography for the opera then, was now in charge of the Jubilee gala. In his retirement, he had become accepted as a member of the Queen Mother's innermost group of friends, a trusted courtier in royal circles. Later in the year, he would receive the Order of Merit, an honour limited to only twenty-five holders and awarded by the sovereign herself. He took his duties as gala organiser very seriously, conscious that he would present the participants to the Royal Family at the end of the evening; if their majesties were not amused, he would be held responsible.

Ashton arrived to watch a dress rehearsal of MacMillan's *Gloriana Dances* and was appalled at what he saw. Lynn Seymour had been cast as Elizabeth I, attended by three ardent suitors and four foppish courtiers. The Virgin Queen, scantily dressed in all-over bodytights, wig, ruffle and farthingale frame, was manhandled by her gallant escorts, who turned her upside-down. As Rodney Milnes was to comment in *Harpers and Queen* magazine, the indecorous activities 'were rather unlike the home life of our own dear Queens'. Ashton, realising that he was too late to insist on alterations, put it about that MacMillan was being deliberately provocative. According to Seymour, Kenneth was absorbed in experimenting with partnering ideas that he intended to use in *Mayerling*: 'He was working out new ways of manipulating the body, a different kind of physicality.'

The result did not go down well with the gala patrons. At the post-performance party in the Crush Bar, after the presentations, MacMillan was snubbed by Royal guests and hangers-on, Board members and VIPs. The exception, Deborah remembers, was Denis Healey, Chancellor of the Exchequer, who made a point of talking to the pariah. Healey, who admired MacMillan's work, considered that a pompous fuss was being stirred up over nothing. Intentionally or otherwise, however, MacMillan had succeeded in further isolating himself from the Royal Opera House establishment.

His simmering rage with the way he was being treated was fuelled by the long-running financial dispute about the renewal of his contract as Artistic Director. The increased salary and royalty fees negotiated by his agent had not been paid by March 1977, so the MacMillans' lawyer, Michael Oliver, raised the issue with Tooley and the Board. Their response was that the contract with MacMillan was invalid under the Labour government's Pay Code introduced in August 1975, freezing wages because of Britain's economic recession. The Royal Opera House, as a state-subsidised institution, was prevented by government policy from awarding any pay increases to its staff.

Oliver responded that MacMillan was not, for tax reasons, on the staff of the Opera House. His three-year contract had been drawn up retrospectively, backdated to September 1975, between the MacMillan Partnership (Kenneth and Deborah) and the ROH, thereby establishing Kenneth as an independent artist offering his services to the Royal Ballet. He was therefore, Oliver argued, technically freelance and not subject to salary restrictions.

Tooley consulted the Royal Opera House lawyers, Rubinsteins, who gave their opinion that the contract was nonetheless invalid because it had been signed after the Pay Code came into effect. In any case, they declared, MacMillan was an employee of the Opera House, as evidenced by his inclusion in the staff pension scheme (albeit for only one year). No exception could be made for him without flouting the government's guidelines. The only way round the impasse would be to draw up a new contract observing Phase Two of the Pay Code, under which MacMillan accepted a frozen salary as Director but received higher royalties for his ballets as an independent choreographer.

The lawyers for both sides were still negotiating the details when MacMillan decided that he preferred to resign. He was fed up with haggling over money with an institution that he felt did not value him. The ballets he had created during his time as Director had not been appreciated, he believed, from *Anastasia* to *Gloriana Dances*. His choice of Fauré's music for *Requiem* had been turned down by the Board. The final straw had been the allocation of *The Sleeping Beauty* to de Valois over his head. He wanted to be shot of responsibilities over which he had little control and reserve his energy for choreographing ballets. To do this, however, he still needed the Royal Ballet's dancers, most immediately for *Mayerling*. He could not afford to alienate the Opera House management by speaking out about his grievances to the press. He would have to go quietly.

He discussed his terms with Tooley, who reported his resignation and his requirements to the Board on 9 June. (MacMillan did not attend the meeting.) According to the minutes, the Artistic Director had come to the conclusion that 'he would welcome a change in his role to free him of the pressures of the directorship and enable him to concentrate on choreography'. He would not be leaving the company, although he would need a new job description and a retainer fee to compensate for his former salary.

There was no suggestion that the Board considered asking him to change his mind. Instead, they merely asked that his proposed new title of Director of Choreography be changed to Principal Choreographer of the Royal Ballet. They gave formal assent to a three-year retainer of £22,500 a year, rising each year until September 1980, with an option to extend the contract for another two years. In return, MacMillan would provide one three-act ballet a year or two 'substantial' one-act ballets (with a duration of not less than fifty minutes). His royalties for existing and new works would rise to £20 per performance of each one-act ballet and £60 for a three-act ballet. The Royal Ballet would guarantee a minimum of forty performances a year of his works. MacMillan was to retain casting rights over his own ballets and would supervise revivals; he could have leave of absence for three months a year. The Board, after congratulating Tooley on his conduct of the negotiations with MacMillan, urged that the resignation announcement be made before the Royal Ballet's annual press conference in a month's time, on 13 July.

The hunt was meanwhile on for a director to replace MacMillan. The Board decided that Peter Wright should remain in charge of the touring company, to which he had given a new sense of confidence and purpose. It was once again based at Sadler's Wells Theatre, whose name was included in the company's latest title, the Sadler's Wells Royal Ballet. Wright was not invited to apply for MacMillan's job, nor consulted about his successor. Instead, members of the Board proposed looking outside the two companies for someone whose appointment would mark a fresh start and give the Royal Ballet a strong contemporary image. This was known internally as the 'Rambert solution', after Ballet Rambert's radical – and successful – change of direction in the mid-1960s, when it relaunched itself as a modern-dance company.

The man Tooley was charged with approaching was Norman Morrice, who had overseen Ballet Rambert's transformation and co-directed the company, with Marie Rambert nominally still in charge, until 1974. He had resigned in order to work as an independent choreographer, most frequently with the Batsheva Dance Company in Israel. That company had just suggested that he should take over as its director as well as chief choreographer, an offer he was seriously considering, when Tooley telephoned with the Royal Ballet's rival invitation.

Morrice was living at the time in a basement flat in Rambert's large house on Campden Hill in West London. He and Rambert went for a long walk in nearby Holland Park to discuss which offer he should accept. Rambert told him emphatically it was his duty, as an Englishman, to take charge of the Royal Ballet. He then consulted MacMillan, de Valois and Ashton about whether he was the right man for the job; all three encouraged him to accept, while warning him of the challenges he would face.

He and MacMillan had known each other since the mid-1950s, when Morrice, as a young dancer, had been in the cast of Ballet Rambert's production of *Laiderette*. 'Rambert was such an enthusiast for Kenneth's work that she told us to go and see everything he did. He had quite an influence on me and my generation of choreographers. He was an inspiration to break all the rules and see what happens.' Morrice, two years younger than MacMillan, had started choreographing for Ballet Rambert in 1958, choosing contemporary themes with dramatic outcomes. He had been invited to make a ballet, *The Tribute*, a modern-day account of a fertility rite, for the Royal Ballet touring company in 1965. Over the years, his style and subject matter had become more diffuse as he worked with different companies. Mulling over the Royal Ballet's offer, he decided that he had reached the point where he was prepared to abandon his ambitions as a choreographer in favour of directing Britain's flagship ballet company.

There would therefore be no conflict of interest between his new job and MacMillan's proposed title as Principal Choreographer. As soon as Morrice made his acceptance known, a press release was issued announcing his appointment and MacMillan's change of role. The word 'resignation' was carefully avoided. The press conference that followed was stage-managed, with Tooley making the announcement that MacMillan was not so much leaving the Royal Ballet as concentrating on choreography 'at his own request'. The press was asked to welcome Morrice as the new Director: Morrice spoke and answered questions while MacMillan said barely a word. Many of those present were unconvinced by the diplomatic description of MacMillan's departure. Some had already heard his side of the story; others smelled a rat without the benefit of inside information.

Rodney Milnes, attending as ballet critic of *Harpers and Queen* magazine, 'longed for someone with the guts to stand up and say, "Stop these mealy-mouthed clichés and tell us what is really going on." No one did, and no one would if we had; so we are left to speculate, which is what I am going to do.' He and others, including Edward Thorpe for the *Evening Standard* and Nicholas Dromgoole of the *Sunday Telegraph*, blamed the Board for failing to back MacMillan. Milnes wrote, 'It is one of the tasks of management to devise working conditions for great creative artists – and I must emphasise here that we are dealing with the balletic equivalent of a Tippett or a Britten – and it is sad, to put it mildly, that this has proved impossible.' Dromgoole wondered what the burdens of directorship were that so hindered creative work. He asked, 'Can it be that neither MacMillan nor John Hart, brought back as Ballet Administrator [in 1975], received the support from the Opera House administration and the Board they were entitled to expect?'

Several of the critics raised 'the scandalous fiasco' over MacMillan's *Requiem*, rejected by the Board and performed in Stuttgart instead.

Thorpe declared, 'One can only conclude that this be(k)nighted Board has as much understanding of the Royal Ballet and the public it serves as could be written on the head of a pin by a dyslexic angel.' Milnes's concluding comment was that MacMillan could have 'cleared the air at that dismal, mystifying press conference by saying he was resigning because at this stage of his career he could no longer be bothered to deal with small-minded, narrow-visioned bureaucrats; but the fact that he held his peace shows that he is a gentleman as well as a great choreographer'.

Milnes was of course right about MacMillan's motivation. He had quit as Director of the Royal Ballet for many of the same reasons as he had left the Berlin company. He was not prepared to compromise in order to accommodate those in authority over him; he found administrative duties onerous and was ill-equipped, temperamentally, to manage them; he was not cut out to be a public figure, able to account for himself to the press or to disgruntled dancers. He was also unlucky. Where Ashton had taken over a smooth-running institution from de Valois, MacMillan had inherited a company plunged into crisis by inept management decisions. The Arts Council was as much to blame for the mishandling as David Webster and the Board of Governors.

A whole new administrative structure should have been put in place to handle the merger between the two companies. There was no manager in sole charge of administrative duties for the ballet, as there has been (in the person of Anthony Russell Roberts) since the 1980s. Instead, the new Artistic Director and his assistant, Peter Wright, had been landed with an unwieldy resident company and a touring offshoot without an identity. Many of MacMillan's and Wright's agonies would have been avoided if the Arts Council had appreciated earlier on that the merger experiment was doomed to fail. De Valois had tried it in the 1950s until the inevitable happened: the touring wing, after an unhappy initial period, grew into a largely autonomous company with its own repertoire and audiences.

A lot of time and energy had been expended on sorting out the New Group from its shaky start in 1970. Ideally, it should have served MacMillan as a testing ground for his own work, as well as developing choreographers from within the company. Thanks to the protracted delay in redefining its role and identity, its record in discovering promising home-grown dance-makers had not been impressive. Wright eventually succeeded in getting it back on course, but MacMillan could take no credit for nurturing young talent in the way that his own choreographic career had been launched at Sadler's Wells.

His achievements purely as an Artistic Director, however, were considerable. He had modernised the Royal Ballet's repertoire during an era when contemporary dance was making great strides in Britain – a shift in aesthetic taste that Ashton had largely ignored. Fifteen works new to the company had been introduced by choreographers as diverse as Balanchine, Robbins, Tetley, Van Manen and Neumeier. Almost all the choreographers he invited to work with either company had done so for the Royal Ballet for the first time. He had continued to programme Ashton's ballets (and de Valois's), while creating two three-act ballets and five short works of his own for the main company, and three for the touring group. He had kept a large roster of principal dancers supplied with roles over the years: Beriosova, MacLeary, Sibley, Dowell, Seymour, Eagling, Park, Penney, Wells, Wall, in addition to guest appearances by Fonteyn and Nureyev, Makarova and Baryshnikov. The corps de ballet had won the *Evening Standard* Award for excellence during his period as Director.

By the time he resigned, however, the main company was short of star dancers to replace those who had left or retired. Beriosova, MacLeary and Wells had stopped dancing; Sibley's career was cut short by injury, though she would make a comeback in the 1980s; Fonteyn, in her late fifties, was reducing her performances. The log-jam of ballerinas held back by her long career had stunted the chances of a number of dancers, as had the top-heavy merger of the two companies. There were too many soloists for the number of performances available, so talent went to waste. MacMillan had brought on some dancers at the expense of others, as director–choreographers tend to do. He favoured the kind of performers he liked for his ballets; he had a remarkable eye for spotting potential in young dancers whom the company's coaches and teachers had overlooked.

He had never, however, been intimately involved in the workings of the Royal Ballet School, beyond selecting the graduating students he wanted to take into the company. He created no ballets for the

School during his directorship, though he enabled the students to perform extracts from existing ones.* Neither he nor Ashton played any direct part in the technical training of dancers, taking classes in the way that de Valois had (and Balanchine did with New York City Ballet, while maintaining close contact with the School of American Ballet). The School's teaching was still largely based on the Cecchetti method that MacMillan had learned as a young dancer. It informed his style and vocabulary, and since the School's graduates had much the same training, modified by de Valois, he saw no reason to intervene.

The pool of talent available to the two Royal Ballet companies had been diminished by recent changes in immigration regulations. Dancers from the Commonwealth were no longer automatically eligible for employment, so the once regular intake of Canadians, Australians, New Zealanders and South Africans had come to an end. Other foreigners, such as the many Europeans and South Americans who have since contributed so much to the Royal Ballet, also faced obstacles in securing work permits. Norman Morrice would therefore have to make do with mainly British recruits. However, since the young generation of graduates from the school by the time he took over in 1977 included Bryony Brind, Fiona Chadwick, Genesia Rosato, Ashley Page and Derek Deane, his situation was far from dire.

None the less, once journalists began to write about Morrice's directorship of the company, MacMillan was accused of having handed over a company that was weaker than the one Ashton had left him. Controversy was stirred by an article Linda Christmas wrote for the *Guardian* in March 1979, asking, 'How is the tarnished fame of the Royal Ballet shining up again under the new Director?' Christmas, a journalist who had recently married John Higgins, Arts Editor of *The Times*, claimed that 'after seven years under the direction of the choreographer Kenneth MacMillan, the company seemed tired – with a shortage of new works, a failure to create new stars, and a haemorrhage of existing talent'. (By 1979,

* MacMillan's only ballets made specially for the RBS were *Dance Suite* in 1962 and *Soirées musicales* in 1988. In 1990, he presented an annual prize for promising would-be choreographers at White Lodge to see other art forms in order to widen their experience.

eighteen months after Morrice took over, yet more dancers had left the company.) She quoted Clive Barnes as saying that the Royal Ballet was no longer welcome in New York.

MacMillan fired off a letter to the *Guardian*, taking exception to Christmas's disparaging comments. He had worked out that during his time as Director he had introduced an average of 3.4 new works a year, designed to give most of the dancers a chance to be seen and to develop. Barnes stirred further controversy by replying to MacMillan in the *Guardian*, dismissing many of the ballets as 'window-dressing [rather] than repertory building': the proportion of Ashton ballets had diminished, 'with considerable weight being given to Mr MacMillan's own operatically styled spectaculars . . . Many people, particularly in the United States, would regard this as unwise stewardship.'

Other responses followed, in defence of MacMillan's record: 'Robbins's *Dances at a Gathering*, Balanchine's *Agon*, Tetley's *Voluntaries*, Ashton's *A Month in the Country* – merely window-dressing?' queried Edward Thorpe, in an angry letter. MacMillan, thin-skinned, was convinced that most critics had damned his directorship and his ballets over the past seven years. This was far from true: as the press response to his resignation had indicated, there had been sympathy for the difficulties he faced and admiration, albeit with reservations, for the ballets he had created. Norman Morrice was to endure an even more problematic period as his successor. MacMillan was meanwhile free, at last, to concentrate on *Mayerling*, the ballet he was longing to create.

5

New Departures

1978–1992

38

Liberated from the demands of the directorship, MacMillan was able to spend more time at home, surrounded by the family life he had always wanted. He was no longer obliged to attend every performance by the Royal Ballet. The Director was (and is) expected to be present whenever the company performs in the Opera House or on tour. 'We'd got used to not eating dinner together or not going out except on non-performance nights. I'd always have to consult the ballet schedules before accepting a dinner invitation,' says Deborah.

Usually Kenneth would come home for 'children's tea' at 6 o'clock with Charlotte and then leave for the theatre. The next day, he'd be back in the office by the time morning class had finished at 10.30. Once he'd stopped being Director, he didn't need to go in except for rehearsals of his own ballets. So we saw more of him, at least until *Mayerling* took over.

Although the worst of the external pressures on him had been lifted, he was incapable of cutting down on the prescription drugs for his chronic depression. He continued to see Carl Lambert on a regular basis. According to Deborah,

Kenneth was unable to be at ease with life. He was always dreading the next horrible thing that might happen. He couldn't tell me what he was frightened of; it was this anticipation of distress that dragged him down, waiting to overwhelm him. I took advice about how to deal with him from Carl, as a friend, because I felt superfluous, and Kenneth made me nervously apprehensive too. But Carl told me I was reacting typically to living with a depressive who's always anxious and disturbed about unknown things.

Deborah had recorded a tape of Charlotte chattering when she was about three and a half, to send to the Williams family in Australia. When Charlotte was asked, 'Where's Daddy?', she replied, 'He's with Carl. He's sick but Carl makes it better.' Kenneth would sometimes take Charlotte with him to Lambert's consulting rooms, where she would play with toys while she waited for the session to be over. She remembers him having injections there.

Deborah tried to keep Kenneth on an even keel by remaining down to earth, calming his fears and enveloping him in domestic life. She also refused to indulge him in the way that the Royal Ballet staff was accustomed to doing: 'They were so concerned to nurture his creative gift, which is what they all wanted a share in, that they'd get him anything he needed, from endless cups of tea to whatever he asked for. It was in nobody's interest to say "No" or "Get it yourself"; everything revolved around him as the creator.'

In her view, Kenneth had become accustomed to living in a cocooned world:

When I first met him, I was amazed how people in the company would put up with him being gloomy and not saying anything, like a sulky child. In a real family, you'd be told to stop it. In a ballet family, power is invested in this person on whom the future of the company depends. All relationships are complicated by the fact that careers depend on this genius, on whether he creates roles or takes them away from dancers who disappoint him. It's a blinkered society with insane expectations. Kenneth was spoilt in a way most people would never get away with, at work – but not at home. Actually, it was good for him to be around with an egomaniac toddler, so he wasn't the centre of attention: she was.

He adored Charlotte and was warmly affectionate with her. 'I could tell he'd been loved as a small child because he related to her so easily,' Deborah says. 'His mother must have been very loving and tactile with him because he was able to show his emotions physically with those he was fond of.' He never resented the demands Charlotte made on Deborah's attention or his own patience:

He'd sit with his arm round Charlotte on the sofa, watching children's TV. Or a video of *The Wizard of Oz*. She loved it and they'd watch it over and over. He didn't necessarily engage with her games because he was so zonked by barbiturates. But he was very involved with her, always observing what she did, how she and her friends behaved. I think it fed into a lot of his ballets, along with memories of his own childhood.

As a distraction from his anxieties, he liked to knit. He launched on a series of garments for Charlotte and was very proud when she chose to wear them. He had less success with his concoctions for Deborah:

He'd say, 'You'll like it when I've finished.' And I'd look at it and say, 'I won't.' 'Yes, you will.' Then he'd start work on something at the Royal

35 Rehearsing Rudolf Nureyev and Margot Fonteyn in *Romeo and Juliet*
36 Full cast curtain call after the premiere of *Romeo and Juliet*, 9 February 1965
37 MacMillan and Cranko in the Stuttgart Ballet canteen

38 Frank Frey
39 Frey with Daniel Job in *Cain and Abel*, Berlin, 1968
40 Kenneth outside Gerd Reinholm's holiday chalet
41 With Gerd Reinholm on holiday in West Germany
42 With Lynn Seymour in Berlin

43 Svetlana Beriosova and Donald MacLeary in *Checkpoint*, 1970
44 Georgina Parkinson holding her son, Tobias Round
45 Kenneth and spaniel in the house he bought as Artistic Director of the Royal Ballet
46 Rehearsing *Manon*, 1974

47 Kenneth and Deborah in the first house they chose together
48 A family at last: Kenneth and Deborah with Charlotte, 1973

49 With Charlotte in Stuttgart during rehearsals for *Requiem*, 1976
50 With Charlotte, the inspiration for the Pie Jesu choreography in *Requiem*
51 Running away on holiday
52 Lifeboat practice on a Mediterranean cruise, August 1984
53 In Venice, on tour with the Royal Ballet
54 Sharing a meal at home with Charlotte, now an art student

55 With Viviana Durante
56 *The Judas Tree*: Durante being walked over Irek Mukhamedov
57 With Natalia Makarova and Mikhail Baryshnikov, preparing *Wild Boy* for American Ballet Theatre
58 Rehearsing Jonathan Cope and Darcey Bussell in *The Prince of the Pagodas*
59 Alessandra Ferri and Wayne Eagling in *Different Drummer*

60 Doctors of Arts: MacMillan with Vivienne Westwood and David Hockney outside the Royal College of Art, July 1992
61 Being introduced to the young Princess Diana backstage at the Royal Opera House
62 Sixtieth birthday ceremony in the Royal Opera House Crush Bar: MacMillan watched by Lord Sainsbury, Sir Anthony Dowell, Dame Ninette de Valois, Sir Peter Wright

63 Last portrait during rehearsals for the National Theatre production of *Carousel*, 1992, a few weeks before he died

Ballet and the tension in the stitches would get tighter and tighter. These strange garments would end up smaller and pointier at the top. At least we had something to laugh about.

He worked out his knitting patterns and stitch counts on scraps of paper, often using the same bits and pieces on which he jotted down schemes for choreography – the orders of sequences or names of dancers he intended to cast in roles. 'He was always pulling backs of envelopes out of his pockets or any old bits of paper and scribbling down lists of numbers,' recalls Monica Mason. 'That was the way he knitted his ballets together.'

The MacMillans entertained more often than before on free evenings, usually inviting old friends and colleagues: Vergie Derman and her husband lived near by, as did Georgina Parkinson and Roy Round. Clement Crisp, Peter Hollamby and Lis Dalton would come round, as would Monica Mason and Nico Georgiadis, Barry Kay and his partner, Michael Werner. Once Charlotte started school, they came to know the parents of her friends, among them Virginia and Simon Fraser and Jocelyn and David Dimbleby (whom they had met through the Panufniks). Kenneth was reluctant to go out to dinner parties. 'As we left, he'd always say, "We're not going to stay late . . ." and he meant it,' says Deborah.

He preferred eating in a small restaurant, usually the same favourite one, or going with Charlotte to Pizza Express. He wasn't social, but he could be very entertaining. He was good at getting people to talk to him, really open up to him. And he liked to get friends to repeat the same, often told stories to him, encouraging them to amuse him.

During the company's summer break, he prepared his plans for *Mayerling*: 'He would sit in the kitchen in an appalling cacophony of noise – Charlotte playing, the dogs barking and the television on and he'd pay no attention at all, lost in his own world.' He had started work on the ballet before he resigned, though rehearsals had been disrupted by the other demands on his time. Dancers he wanted had not always been available. Anthony Dowell, his initial choice as Rudolf, had been injured during early rehearsals for *Mayerling*. After recovering, he had taken stock of his career and requested leave of absence in order to dance elsewhere. He joined American Ballet Theatre as principal guest artist during 1978–80, returning to dance with the Royal Ballet in between. He spent the rest of his career with the Royal Ballet (eventually as Artistic Director) but never danced the role of Rudolf. David Wall replaced him in the preparatory rehearsals in April 1977, so most of the ballet was created with Wall as the central character.

Gillian Freeman had provided a scenario very like a film treatment. She had researched Rudolf's background thoroughly, preparing pen portraits for Kenneth of the historical figures who most affected the Crown Prince's life. She had selected events likely to make dramatic sense, suggesting where they belonged in the ballet's structure: where the pas de deux might come, how the private and public scenes would flow into each other. Somewhat to her surprise, for she was anticipating the many rewrites to which a film scenario is subjected, MacMillan accepted her outline without reservation. He wanted to set to work within a given framework, freeing himself to develop the characters' expressive dance language. He worked out his own analysis of the unhappy Prince's psyche, identifying in Rudolf elements of himself, taken to extremes. The ballet was to be a chronicle of destruction – the breakdown of a man who could not meet the expectations of those around him, and who was undermined by disease, drugs and the flaws of his own personality.

MacMillan was, in effect, the Crown Prince of the Royal Ballet, heir to the institution de Valois had built up. His preparation for the role of its Director had been a kind of exile, as he saw it, in Berlin. There he had felt himself isolated and misunderstood, out of his depth in the politics of the Deutsche Oper and Cold War Berlin. He had become profoundly depressed and alcoholic, his health further damaged by a stroke. On his return to assume his Royal Ballet kingdom, he had been intrigued against, mistrusted by members of the Establishment who thought he was out to destroy everything de Valois and Ashton had stood for. He had no such intention, but neither of them had given him the unconditional loyalty or affection for which he had hoped. He couldn't but be aware that he was his own worst enemy, unable to play the diplomatic games that might have made his life easier. In the end, he had chosen to abdicate from the responsibilities he had once ambitiously wanted to inherit. There were plenty of parallels between him and the anti-hero of his ballet.

Crown Prince Rudolf, heir to the throne of Austria-Hungary, was a misfit on a grand scale. He had endured a harsh and lonely childhood, scarcely seeing his mother, Empress Elisabeth, whom he adored; he had nothing in common with his father, Emperor Franz Josef, who despised him. He was subjected to the stifling etiquette of the Habsburg court and easily manipulated by the corrupt Viennese demi-monde that depended on it. Attracted by the separatist cause of Hungarian Nationalists, Rudolf was unsuited to be the leader for which they hoped. Spies watched his every move, reporting on his political and sexual liaisons.

He had probably already contracted syphilis by the time he was married off to Princess Stéphanie of Belgium. The marriage was an unhappy one, with no male heir, but the ill-matched couple were denied a legal separation. Damaged by disease and drugs, Rudolf became increasingly unstable. He met in Mary Vetsera a young girl all too eager to share his obsessions with sex and death. Not long after their affair started, he persuaded her into a suicide pact. The scandal of their joint deaths in the Mayerling hunting lodge outside Vienna was hushed up. Mary's body was removed and buried in secret, while Rudolf lay in state. His shattered skull was skilfully concealed by the embalmers and the cause of his death given as a heart attack.

Freeman's scenario started with a prologue showing the clandestine burial at the Heiligenkreuz monastery, sixteen miles from Mayerling. Mary's uncles had taken her there by coach, propping her dead body, dressed in coat and hat, between them as if she were still alive. From their arrival and her hasty interment in a coffin, the ballet would unravel like a cinematic flashback, coming full circle to an epilogue back at the cemetery. MacMillan kept the prologue brief, a glimpse of an anonymous coffin being lowered in the rain. Not until the epilogue would the audience see the rigid body being dragged from the coach to the graveside, and realise it was Mary's. They would finally understand why the funeral was so perfunctory and why only one mourner, the coachman, showed any emotion.

After the dark, mysterious prologue, the first act opens with the pomp of a state ball celebrating the marriage of the Crown Prince and his Belgian bride. Among the throng of aristocratic guests, political dignitaries, courtiers and hangers-on, significant figures come to the fore as the drama unfolds. Hints are dropped that Emperor Franz Josef's court is seething with intrigue, personal and political. Four Hungarian officers keep pressing their Nationalist demands on Rudolf, to the concern of his father and the government's ever-present spies. Rudolf offends his bride by paying conspicuous attention to her prettier sister. He then fends off his former mistress, Countess Marie Larisch, who is still making claims on him. After the ball is over and before he joins Princess Stéphanie in their bedchamber, he visits his mother. Their encounter exposes his craving for her love and Elisabeth's inability to give it. He takes out his pain on his bewildered bride, terrifying her with a skull and revolver and raping her on her wedding night.

Poor Princess Stéphanie has evidently had no warning of the psycho-sexual morass in which her arranged marriage has landed her. She is further humiliated in Act II by being obliged to accompany her husband to a brothel. This low-life activity is in pointed contrast to the formal ceremony that opened the previous act. Among the ensemble dances for whores and their clients, Rudolf's current mistress, Mitzi Caspar, is the centre of attention. In a private scene, she dismisses Rudolf's crazed proposal of a joint suicide pact and then conspires with the government spies who watch him.

After leaving the brothel, he is presented with Mary Vetsera, the girl who will fulfil his every fantasy. Larisch sets her up, most probably as a means of retaining power over Rudolf. Freeman, who had read that the real Vetsera consulted a soothsayer before starting her affair with Rudolf, suggested that Larisch should arrange to predict Mary's royal liaison with a pack of cards. MacMillan agreed, recalling how his mother told fortunes by pretending she could read tea leaves. (In Puccini's *La Fanciulla del West*, given in a new production in 1977 at the Royal Opera House, the heroine cheats at cards, letting the audience see that she saves the ones she might need, as Larisch does in the second act of *Mayerling*.)

He drew on his observations of revealing body language for Vetsera's behaviour. At first, she copies Larisch's moves, imitating her steps as if watching herself in a mirror. When Larisch leads her to Rudolf's bedchamber, Vetsera has only a nightdress under her outdoor coat. Although the flimsy garment makes the erotic pas de deux possible in dance terms, the contrast between the girl's demure exterior and her blatant sexual intent was based on an episode at a friend's house. The MacMillans, invited to dinner, became aware that the au pair must be having an affair with the husband: 'Every time the wife left the room, the girl would switch from shy and quiet into this brazen hussy the husband was obviously electrified by. The wife was completely unaware of what was going on, but Kenneth picked it up at once – and that's how he wanted Vetsera to be.'

Mary's sexual appetite distracts Rudolf from his unendurable situation. Before their dangerous relationship can follow its course, however, two scenes involving the court show that Rudolf is near the end of his tether. Emperor Franz Josef's birthday celebration alienates his son: the father's mistress, Katerina Schratt, entertains the assembled courtiers with a sentimental song; Empress Elisabeth dances with her lover, Colonel 'Bay' Middleton. (Schratt was in fact an actress, not a singer. Middleton, an English cavalry officer, whose main relationship with the Empress occurred on her visits to Britain, also had an affair with a married woman, Lady Blanche Ogilvy; he was presumed to be the father of her daughter, Clementine, who married Winston Churchill.) Rudolf is sickened by his parents' hypocrisy and by the hopelessness of his own future.

During the royal shooting party that opens Act III, he fires a shotgun wildly, killing a bystander and narrowly missing his father. In disgrace, he seeks temporary oblivion through morphine and proposes a suicide pact with Vetsera. She agrees: death seems to her a supremely romantic option. She is taken to the hunting lodge at Mayerling by Rudolf's private cabdriver, Bratfisch. An entertainer in nightclubs, he tries to divert the couple by dancing and juggling with his hat but is soon dismissed. (The hat trick evolved by chance. The real Bratfisch was known as a cheerful whistler, and Freeman had suggested an acrobatic solo as a dance equivalent. The dancer who took the role, Graham Fletcher, dropped the hat in rehearsal and caught it in mid-air. When MacMillan commented, 'That looks good', Fletcher asked a juggler friend to teach him how to manipulate the top hat.)

Tension mounts as Rudolf, drugged with morphine, manipulates Vetsera, high on sex and adrenalin, in a frenzied pas de deux. Rudolf shoots her and then himself. The ballet ends with the epilogue at the Heiligenkreuz cemetery.

This would be the first time a male dancer, in the role of Rudolf, was required to carry a full-length British ballet as the central character. Confident that the ability of the men in the company had greatly improved under his directorship, MacMillan was ready to match Soviet choreographers who had created vehicles for compelling male dancers in ballets such as *Spartacus, Ivan the Terrible, Hamlet* and *Othello*.

Rudolf is rarely offstage throughout the ballet, dancing seven major pas de deux with five different women. MacMillan told an interviewer that he had chosen Wall for the role because 'Rudolf was a great womaniser and I think that David has great sex appeal. You believe women would be fascinated by him.' He pushed Wall beyond what he thought he could do, to the point that Wall reckons *Mayerling* took five years off his performing life. The partnering in *Mayerling* was demanding even by MacMillan's standards: each pas de deux reveals more about Rudolf's relationships with the women in his life, as well as charting his deteriorating mental state. The dancer's reactions to each partner have to be re-attuned every time he launches into another duet.

The most extreme of these are with Mary Vetsera. MacMillan had entrusted the role of the teenage temptress to Lynn Seymour, nearly forty and the mother of three children. His choice of her rather than an up-and-coming youngster was a revealing indication of how much he valued her creative understanding, in spite of their often strained relations over the years. For *Mayerling*, his most challenging ballet yet, he relied on her to supply the qualities he needed in Mary Vetsera without his having to spell out what he wanted: Mary was to articulate Rudolf's inchoate desires and amplify his character as well as her own: 'Our working relationship was unchanged. We were always on the same wavelength,' Seymour affirms.

Whenever she was unavailable, rehearsing or performing else-where as a guest artist, MacMillan asked Wall's wife, Alfreda Thorogood, a soloist with the company, to stand in for her. 'Kenneth would never have allowed us to perform it together,' Wall says. 'He didn't like married couples dancing with each other. Too many arguments.' Thorogood (like Penney in *Manon*) would have to cede priority on the opening night to the originator of the role.* Seymour was not going to be usurped in the last part that MacMillan would ever create for her.

Seymour counts Mary Vetsera as one of her trickiest assignments: 'You don't get going until halfway through. You're a mere pawn, a nothing until the first pas de deux in the nightdress.' She underrates

---

* Thorogood was cast as Vetsera later in the run; she also danced the role of Larisch.

the indelible impression she made in Vetsera's first scene with Larisch, and her initial encounter with Rudolf in the street outside the brothel. Her obsession with him was evident from the outset: she was no passive puppet. Seymour's ripe body, pliable and curvaceous, served as a metaphor for Mary's moral malleability. She was able to trust Wall completely as a partner, winding herself around him like the tourniquet Rudolf uses for his morphine injection. Together, they experimented with hazardous lifts until they found what MacMillan had in his mind's eye. Although later generations of dancers have been even more acrobatically extreme, only Seymour captured the imagery of a Minoan bull-dancer provoking a dangerous animal in Vetsera's pas de deux with Rudolf.

While MacMillan knew he could rely on Seymour's ability to find the core of a character, he brought out hitherto unsuspected qualities in Merle Park as Marie Larisch. The role is a complex one, for Larisch reveals different facets of herself in each scene. Park made her a worldly creature, calculating but also compassionate, a mother substitute, mistress and procuress for Rudolf. Georgina Parkinson was cast as beautiful, neurotic Empress Elisabeth, incapable of maternal warmth – the last role MacMillan would create for Parkinson before she retired from dancing. Wendy Ellis as Princess Stéphanie was required to be primly suburban, a sacrificial victim whose traumatic wedding night was horrific but who generated little sympathy once her ordeal was over and she became yet another disapproving member of the oppressive court.

MacMillan turned to Nicholas Georgiadis, once again, as his designer for a ballet set in a specific historical era. He could rely on Georgiadis's encyclopaedic knowledge of period costumes, although when he had first mentioned *Mayerling*, the designer responded in alarm, 'Oh no, Kenneth, you realise there are *bustles*.' He set to work with the Opera House wardrobe staff, experimenting with plain toiles to find ways that the padded skirts could open to accommodate the dancers' movements. It was Georgiadis's idea to convert tailor's dummies into models of guardsmen lining the palace set: they reinforced the claustrophobia of the court and Rudolf's sense that he was always under surveillance.

As with *Manon*, MacMillan opted to have a score arranged from existing music rather than risk a new commission. He sought the advice of John Lanchbery, who immediately thought of Liszt. Not only was Franz Liszt historically and geographically appropriate for a ballet about the waning years of the Austro-Hungarian Empire, but his music was also capable of spanning the extremes of emotion the choreography would encompass. Lanchbery found all sorts of felicities: extracts from Liszt's *Faust Symphony* could serve to set up the opening marriage party from hell, as well as providing the motif for Rudolf's obsession with guns and death; Liszt's transcription of Schubert waltzes would be ideal for the ballroom dances in Act I; a piano piece used for the 'closet scene' between Rudolf and his mother had been actually written by Liszt expressly for Empress Elisabeth.

The knowledge that Liszt was one of Ashton's favourite composers might have been a reason for MacMillan dedicating *Mayerling* to the Royal Ballet's founder-choreographer.* On the face of it, the choice of a ballet devoted to madness, perverse sex and death might seem an unlikely gesture of respect to an elderly choreographer renowned for his treatment of romantic love. But now that MacMillan was no longer Director of the Royal Ballet, he could afford to pay tribute to his predecessor by dedicating a major work to him, with Liszt's music as a pretext. Within the ballet, there was discreet choreographic homage to Ashton, as in the twinkling steps Princess Stéphanie's maids dance as they bring her wedding nightdress into her chamber.

As ever, the Ballet Sub-Committee worried that the production threatened to go way over budget. MacMillan fought for the opulence of Georgiadis's costumes: if no expense was spared on operas, why should a full-length ballet be penalised? *Mayerling* was, after all, a prestigious project for the Royal Opera House. *The South Bank Show*, London Weekend Television's cultural flagship, had already committed funds to recording a documentary of the work in progress. Derek Bailey, the director, filmed *Mayerling* rehearsals for nine months. For the two-hour documentary, he intercut studio

---

* Ashton had used Liszt for his *Mephisto Waltz* (1934), *Apparitions* (1936), *Dante Sonata* (1940) and *Marguerite and Armand* (1963). As well as a pas de deux for Fonteyn and Desmond Kelly to Liszt's setting of a song by Victor Hugo, 'Oh, quand je dors' (1971), he had recently done a gala pas de deux for Fonteyn and Nureyev (1977) to Liszt's symphonic poem *Hamlet*.

sessions showing the choreography in creation with highlights from the ballet in performance; background information included film footage of the Mayerling hunting lodge, historical film and photographs of the Imperial household, and interviews with the ballet's collaborative team. *MacMillan's Mayerling*, which won a Prix Italia in 1978, had one of the largest audiences ever for ballet on British TV: 4.7 million viewers.

In the documentary, although MacMillan's eyes, as he watches dancers in the rehearsal room, are piercingly alert, his voice is slurred in a drawl. The cocktail of barbiturates he regularly took had further slowed his always languid speech. When he saw the documentary again, years later, he was shocked at the way he sounded: 'I had no idea I was in such a bad way,' he told Deborah. At the time of filming, he was wearing his habitual dark glasses, which Bailey persuaded him to remove for the cameras. The glasses and thick moustache covering his upper lip were protective devices: behind them, he felt safe to create the dark, tortured ballet he was about to expose to the public – and the critics.

Mayerling received its premiere, somewhat inappropriately, on Valentine's Day, 14 February 1978, at a royal gala attended by the Queen Mother for the company's Benevolent Fund. MacMillan had protested that *Mayerling* was not gala material, and certainly not the kind of ballet the Queen Mother would appreciate. He was overruled, although his request for the press night to be deferred to the second performance was observed. The critics were sent synopses of the plot in advance to help them follow the action. What the Queen Mother made of the family life of the Habsburgs is not recorded. To MacMillan's surprise, the gala audience gave the ballet and its creator a standing ovation. Ashton had meanwhile graciously accepted the dedication to him, sending MacMillan a letter of thanks and a fine antique Austrian waistcoat as an opening-night present.

In spite of MacMillan's expectation of a hostile reaction from reviewers who had damned *Anastasia, Mayerling* was generally well received – with reservations. The boldness of his approach was applauded, as was the way he placed the tragic events in their social and political context. Some reviewers protested that the historical details were hard to absorb, even after reading the scenario; the large numbers of characters and their relationships with each other were tricky to identify, and he was accused of attempting the impossible in ballet by involving four Hungarian conspirators and their political tracts. There was nothing but praise, however, for David Wall's performance as Rudolf and for his achievement in making a depraved, selfish and unlovable hero sympathetic. Seymour, too, was acknowledged as bringing a depth of understanding to Vetsera's mixed motives in sacrificing herself in the suicide pact.

Clement Crisp in the *Financial Times* found MacMillan 'at his most persuasive as an erotic poet, exploring passion with images of extreme beauty – the final coupling at Mayerling marvellously combining lust and despair'. John Percival in *The Times* was prepared to concede, 'In spite of its faults, I think *Mayerling* is MacMillan's best three-act ballet . . . he has always been addicted to innovative, sometimes hazardous lifts and manoeuvres. This time, even the most far-fetched inventions are worth the fetching.'

Most reviewers found the ballet too long and recommended trimming the three acts and playing down the less important characters. Mary Clarke in the *Guardian*, however, defended its length: 'Easy, after one or two viewings, to say this or that scene must go. But patience and understanding bring rewards; every scene tells something about Rudolf and the Court of Vienna in his time.' None the less, cuts were made, some after the first performances at the Opera House, some in later seasons; a few edited sections were restored, including the song during the Emperor's birthday celebration. The song, 'Ich Scheide' ('I am leaving'), marks Rudolf's turning point as he takes the downward path towards suicide. The song was cut to speed the action and save the expense of a singer but its absence unbalanced the ballet, so it was restored. Rudolf stands still, to one side, throughout the singing, giving the audience time to register his alienation from the court, including his now pregnant wife. Other scenes, mostly involving the corps de ballet, were shortened. As with *Manon*, *Mayerling* found its final form long after its initial season.

During the first run, *Mayerling* had been cast from strength. Each Rudolf, David Wall, Wayne Eagling and Stephen Jefferies, had a different set of women to partner. There was enough leeway in the roles for dancers to interpret the characters in their own ways; some of the women would switch between Vetsera, Larisch and Mitzi Caspar. The ballet proved a great showcase for the Royal Ballet's dance-actors, from its veterans, such as Michael Somes, Leslie Edwards and Gerd Larsen, to the youngsters who had matured during MacMillan's tenure as Artistic Director. He was giving the company a form of dance theatre that stretched the conventional classical vocabulary to extremes, taking the dancers and their audiences into a realm of psychosis where ballet had never ventured before. It was an area he found himself exploring in his next work, on a tauter scale and to a scenario of his own devising.

39

Soon after *Mayerling*'s premiere, MacMillan left for Stuttgart, taking Deborah and Charlotte with him for a three-week stay. Marcia Haydée had asked him to create another ballet for the company, and he had a half-formed idea in mind. He had recently been reading *The Brontë Story*, Margaret Lane's detailed study of the Brontë family. He had read Mrs Gaskell's unreliable *Life of Charlotte Brontë* years before, and was intrigued by the mass of additional, well-sourced material that Lane had unearthed. He found her account of the Brontë siblings' lives more interesting than any of her subjects' novels. The fact that their mother had died early had great resonance for him. Isolated in Haworth vicarage with their difficult father (as Kenneth had been with his widowed father in Great Yarmouth), the three surviving sisters and their brother had resorted to their imaginations for stimulus and consolation. He wanted to use their inner lives as the basis for a one-act ballet, set to a combination of music by Schoenberg and Webern that he had been waiting to use for some four years.

Though the Brontës might seem an odd choice for a German ballet company and its audience, MacMillan did not intend to reveal the starting point for his inspiration. There would be no mention of the Brontë family in publicity material or in the programme notes. 'Kenneth had an open door here, as he always used to have with John [Cranko]', Haydée says.

I didn't ask why he chose a subject – that would imply a lack of respect. I said, 'OK, let's do it', and gave him the time and the dancers he needed. When he made something in Stuttgart, it came from his guts and everybody here accepted what he did. We didn't worry about what the public would say.

The ballet that resulted, *My Brother, My Sisters*, would be one of the strangest, most disturbing works of his choreographic career. He was plumbing intensely personal themes, putting them on stage in the guise of an Expressionist nightmare. The Brontës' highly charged isolation represented his own apprehensions about an intimate group of people on the verge of going out of control. The group might be a family or an assortment of individuals obliged by circumstances to stick together: the sisters in *Las Hermanas*, the refugees in hiding in *The Burrow*, the strolling players in *Laiderette* and *The Poltroon*. These claustrophobic societies provided ample scope for envy, betrayal, collusion; their members succumbed all too easily to violence, twisted sexuality, psychosis.

MacMillan had found his preoccupations mirrored in the pages of *The Rack*, A. E. Ellis's semi-autobiographical novel about a tuberculosis sufferer's experience in a sanatorium in the Swiss Alps soon after the end of World War II. Gillian Freeman had recommended the book, knowing how much it would appeal to him. She had developed a screenplay from *The Rack*, at the request of an American actor Patrick O'Neal, who held the rights; he had never managed, however, to raise the money for a film production. MacMillan was so taken by *The Rack* that, a decade later, he chose it as the book he would most like to have on his fantasy island for the long-running BBC Radio 4 programme *Desert Island Discs*.

The novel's fevered atmosphere would infuse *My Brother, My Sisters*, although MacMillan made no overt use of its story line and sanatorium setting. *The Rack* is a hauntingly graphic account of an enclosed world in which the patients live within the shadow of death. The young narrator, Paul Davenant, is stretched on the rack of pain inflicted by the primitive treatments for TB in use at the time. He is also the observer and recorder of others' suffering: he is inmate and outsider at the same time. Ellis, who was fortunate to survive the treatment he describes, gives Davenant's observations an hallucinatory clarity. The heightened awareness of detail in the book is intensely realised in MacMillan's choreography. When MacMillan sent tickets for the Stuttgart Ballet's London performance of *My Brother, My*

Sisters to A. E. Ellis, he discovered that the author had once been a regular ballet-goer. 'I have always greatly admired your work,' Ellis wrote in his letter of thanks, after seeing the ballet in London. 'I was deeply moved when at certain moments of your ballet I recognised nuances of the excerpt you had chosen from my book.'

MacMillan did not mention his sources to the Stuttgart cast. All they needed to know was that they were meant to be youngsters – five sisters and a brother. (There were five Brontë girls, before the two eldest died of tuberculosis, along with their mother, leaving the three writers, Emily, Charlotte and Anne, and their brother, Branwell, to be brought up by their father.) The boy, danced by Richard Cragun, was the magnetic centre of attraction, the commander of his sisters in their disturbing games. Although the brother was based on Branwell, he had elements of Kenneth's elder brother, George, and of Kenneth himself as a boy, indulged by his two older sisters. He had been thinking about his own childhood as he watched Charlotte play, reminded of how vivid children's imaginations are and how hurtful their games can be.

He was also reflecting on other families whose interplay had fascinated him, particularly because of the imbalance between the sexes. Deborah had told him about her experience of growing up with her brothers, one of whom had been badly burnt as a youngster. Kenneth had known Phyllis Adams's children, three girls and a boy, with whom he played as a young teenager in Great Yarmouth. He went to their house so regularly for ballet lessons with their mother that he was regarded by them as a kind of older brother. His recollection of being part of their lives while remaining an observer, an outsider who would go his own way, could have been at the root of the character he added to the ballet, called simply He.

Reid Anderson, who took the role, recalls that he was included late on in the creative process: 'Maybe Kenneth didn't know he needed this character at first – he put me in it after some while but he didn't tell me anything about it.' The character might bear some resemblance to *The Rack*'s narrator, but as MacMillan explained later in *Dance and Dancers* in February 1979, 'By his presence alone, He provokes: he makes things come out, good luck, disquiet or anger; sometimes he drives people mad. Of course, this character is myself.' He confirmed this identification towards the end of his life in conversation with Clement Crisp.

He was, to some extent, dramatising the part he played within the extended family of a ballet company, whether in London, Berlin or Stuttgart. His gifts as a choreographer had set him apart from the group to which he needed to feel he belonged. He would observe the games people played, consciously and subconsciously – the rivalries, jealousies and sexual intrigues – and put them in his ballets. He 'made things come out' on stage, using the dancers themselves for his psychological studies, whether or not they were fully aware of what he was drawing from them. They, as much as himself, were his raw material. As Lynn Seymour commented in an article she wrote ten years after MacMillan's death, 'Kenneth was a voyeur, a provocateur luring his dancers into the seamy side of life and proposing dark identities and pathological, neurotic motivation whilst trying not to get his own feet wet.'

The work that would be known in Germany as *Mein Bruder, Meine Schwestern* was as much a portrait of his Stuttgart cast as of the Brontës or the Yarmouth families of his youth. (Coincidentally, the combination of five sisters and a single man paralleled that of *Las Hermanas*, his earlier creation for the same company.) Cranko had instilled in his Stuttgart dancers that they should have no reservations about giving a choreographer everything of themselves, and Haydée continued his precepts. In Richard Cragun as the brother, MacMillan could draw on a charismatic dancer, capable of exploding into virtuoso leaps and turns, almost ripping himself apart like Rumpelstiltskin; Reid Anderson could be his impassive alter ego, named in the German cast sheet as ER (He). Birgit Keil, the malevolent First Sister, had coltishly long legs and huge dark eyes in a face that could seem fey to the point of madness. Hers was to be an exceptional role, compelling the other sisters to go too far in persecuting the family scapegoat – Lucia Montagnon as the vulnerable girl with glasses.

MacMillan told John Higgins in an interview for *The Times*, shortly before *My Brother, My Sisters* was given its British premiere, that he intended the ballet to be a mystery:

Up to now with my story ballets I've been giving the spectators more and more information about the characters. Here, quite deliberately, I'm giving them less . . . I've based the ballet on real people, although fact and fiction are always blurred, and tried to realise their inner lives, not the ones they choose to show to the world.

494

The only assistance he would give audiences in programme notes were two enigmatic statements, neither mentioning the Brontës. One was written for him by Deborah, telling of 'a family set apart by landscape and circumstance, intelligence and passion. Their only playmates were each other and their fantasies became their real world.' The second was a passage from *The Rack*. The extract from which the quotation is taken refers to the narrator's semi-hallucinatory flashback, after witnessing the death of a demented female patient in the tuberculosis sanatorium:

He remembered how once he had watched children playing in a tomb-strewn churchyard during a long afternoon in midsummer, running between the irregular head-stones and over the grave-mounds as unaware of what lay beneath as mice frisking about the lids of coffins in the funeral parlour of an undertaker. Under the short print summer dresses and the daisy chains, locked tightly within the confines of each skull was death, death which would feed and blossom on the tender soil of their flesh, absorbing first beauty, then health, then existence itself. And they would return to their playground at the last, but to lie beneath its surface, and other children would play above their heads, whilst even the last remnant of life, the little flesh still adhering to their bones, would be eaten away.

By now, MacMillan tended to turn to Yolanda Sonnabend as the designer for his shorter, Expressionistic works, while relying on Georgiadis for the three-act ballets with definite period settings. For the set of *My Brother, My Sisters*, Sonnabend came up with a series of suspended gauzes, painted and lit in the dramatic, sombre colours of the Yorkshire moors and their lowering skies, the setting of the Brontës' lives and books. The costumes would be based on the passage from *The Rack*.

The sisters (all on pointe) wear childish dresses with neat belts and short skirts, stamped with floral potato-print designs. White 'Peter Pan' collars were added, at Deborah MacMillan's suggestion, to make the dancers' faces clearly visible. The eldest girl (called the First Sister in the cast list), her hair hanging loose, has a daisy chain around her head; the chaplet of flowers marks her out, an already crazed Ophelia. The scapegoat Second Sister wears black-rimmed glasses – an indication that she is impaired in some way. Her near-blindness without the spectacles could be an equivalent for deafness; and since she appears prone to epilepsy, she seems to bear all the afflictions that young Kenneth found so painfully humiliating in his own family.

The ballet starts to Schoenberg's *Five Pieces for Orchestra*, Op. 16, as the sisters vie for their brother's attention. In the opening tableau, he kneels, while four girls on pointe straddle his outstretched arms and the eldest stands behind him. The character called 'He' is present at one remove, motionless at the rear of the stage. The girls look into the palms of their hands, held up towards their faces: the gesture seems narcissistic, as though their palms were mirrors, but the implicit Brontë reference is to the sisters' diaries (and their other writings).

An incestuous attraction is immediately evident between the eldest sister and her brother. Winsomely provocative, she twines around him; when he puts her down, her leg goes suggestively between his. They play dangerously intimate games of physical exploration, intoxicated by each other's nearness. She flutters her fingers in frantic excitement; he nuzzles her neck. The other four sisters cluster around the second male figure, then separate and move towards the couple as if mesmerised. They witness the sexually explicit conclusion of the pas de deux, the girl splayed over her brother's supine body.

The impassive observer, 'He', walks out, leaving the sisters to be drawn into a knot by the eldest. She leads them in covering each other's eyes in a line, colluding in her secret, nodding as if promising never to tell. The youngest appears to have a fit and falls, sat on by her sisters. They comfort her as the brother erupts in a wild solo, crashing to the ground as though drunk (as Branwell Brontë often was). The bespectacled sister comes to the fore, behaving seductively towards the brother and arousing the jealousy of the eldest, who threatens to strangle her; the others join in, grabbing each others' throats in a line. The girl plays dead, her limp body manipulated by her sisters.

The brother dashes off and returns with a set of masks for all the girls. The china-white half-masks turn them into sinister dolls, making them seem anonymous and allowing their repressed selves to emerge. MacMillan had been intrigued by the information in Margaret Lane's book that the Reverend Brontë had asked each of his children to answer his questions from under the cover of a mask. Hidden behind their disguises in the ballet, the siblings try out different personae in solos. As Webern's music takes over from Schoenberg's, their play-fighting becomes more vicious.

The rivalry between the eldest sister and the one with glasses is expressed in a duet of competitive tussles. The brother intervenes between them when they make up with a kiss; the first sister could be trying to entice her younger sibling into further sex-play. The brother's place is then taken by the other man, 'He', who becomes ensnared in a tortuous trio by the over-familiar pair of girls. The brother returns to chase him away, striking out wildly in a tantrum of rage. The two frightened girls try to support their probably drunken brother as he lurches out of control. The eldest, with an air of complicity, bundles the boy's unconscious body off the stage.

'He' comes back to console the bespectacled sister. Whether he is attracted to her or whether she is compromising him remains ambiguous, but their duet starts to resemble the coupling of brother and sister near the start of the ballet. The eldest girl, now wearing a translucent mask, stalks behind them like a predator. 'He' grows apprehensive, kisses the younger girl and leaves. The jealous older girl rips off her sister's glasses, reducing her to a blind, defenceless state. She stumbles, unseeing, hands stretched out before her. The others enter, now sporting shiny masks, to torment her in a cruel game of blind man's buff. Terrified, she has a fit, possibly a heart attack. The siblings crowd round her, removing their masks. The eldest girl mockingly puts on her sister's glasses. She shakes the inert girl and the realisation dawns that she is well and truly dead. 'He' walks past the family and out, leaving an aghast tableau behind him.

According to the Stuttgart cast, MacMillan himself did not know, when he started making *My Brother, My Sisters*, that the ballet would end with a death. Only when he appreciated how the perverse seductions and violent games he was choreographing could get out of hand did he see where his ideas were leading. He was tapping into his own fantasies and fears of boundaries being violated, with sex, guilt and death inextricably entwined. Though the siblings' complicity in their vulnerable sister's fate makes her death seem inevitable (like the killing of Piggy in *The Lord of the Flies*), the ending takes first-time viewers aback. 'It is hard for an audience to identify with,' MacMillan acknowledged in an interview six years later. 'You think you are going to see a straightforward narrative and you are not at all. [Audiences] have to see it several times before they understand it, but they are gripped by it.'

German audiences at the Stuttgart premiere on 25 May 1978 responded with enthusiasm. They recognised the work's Expressionist context, even though the choreography is based on classical ballet – surprisingly so, for such a savage work. The role of the brother resulted in spectacular solos for Cragun, and Keil's strange, febrile quality as the erotically charged lead sister was greatly admired.

The Stuttgart Ballet was to bring *My Brother, My Sisters* to London in June, for a season at the Coliseum that would include MacMillan's *Requiem* and *The Song of the Earth*, as well as Cranko's *Onegin* and his *Carmen*, along with works by young choreographers in the company, including William Forsythe.

Before MacMillan could learn what British audiences would make of his Stuttgart works, he flew with Deborah and Charlotte to California to join the Royal Ballet near the start of its latest American tour. (The company had just completed a two-week season in Seoul.) *Mayerling*, along with the 'new' de Valois production of *The Sleeping Beauty*, were the novel attractions of the visit to Los Angeles, Houston and Chicago. This was the company's first American tour not to include New York.

The MacMillans stayed in Beverly Hills with Herbert Ross and Nora Kaye. Ross, by now a big-name Hollywood director, was about to start work on a film about Nijinsky and Diaghilev's Ballets Russes. Harry Saltzman, executive director of the James Bond films, had bought the rights to a film based on Romola Nijinsky's biography of her husband, and had been looking for a director since 1969. The commercial success of *The Turning Point* in 1977 had convinced him that Ross should do it, with Nora Kaye as co-producer. Ross discussed his plans with the MacMillans, asking Kenneth if he would be interested in re-creating scenes from Nijinsky's lost ballets. The requirement was for pastiche rather than a work of scholarship, since the choreography would be seen only briefly during a story concentrating on the tangled relationships between Diaghilev, Nijinsky and his future wife, Romola. MacMillan agreed to find time in his schedule at the end of the year to accommodate rehearsals and filming, which would take place in Britain.

Hollywood film stars and movie moguls attended *Mayerling*'s opening night in the huge Shrine Auditorium in downtown Los Angeles. Robert Altman, already a distinguished director, told MacMillan that he had learned a lot from watching *Mayerling*: he was fascinated by the multiple relationships and the way in which the choreographer had integrated the corps' background activity with the principals' concerns in the foreground. Without being able to resort to close-ups, MacMillan knew how to focus an audience's interest on the important characters. The minor ones, true to the Royal Ballet's acting tradition, played out their sub-stories on the periphery.

Reviewers from the *Hollywood Reporter* and the theatrical trade paper, *Variety*, were impressed by the scale of the ballet but found the prolixity of roles bewildering. West Coast critics acclaimed *Mayerling* as a masterpiece: 'provocative and absorbing . . . a bold and grandiose achievement' (*LA Times*); 'My God, that final scene – if there's anything more powerful in ballet, I haven't seen it' (Tom Barley in the *Palo Alto Times*).

The MacMillans had already returned to London when they received a letter from the Rosses, congratulating Kenneth on his 'wonderful reviews' and adding a wise-cracking warning: 'Don't let it go to your head, though . . . remember, they're still the same assholes that write the bad ones.'

New York-based critics waited until the Royal Ballet had reached Chicago before reviewing *Mayerling*. Clive Barnes was the first (and worst) to put the boot into MacMillan in a *New York Post* review: 'This is not an easy notice to write, particularly as the Royal Ballet is probably coming to New York next year with *Mayerling* as its major attraction . . . but frankly, what kind of ballet is this? There is no invention, no imagination and no style. It should close in Chicago.' Whether Barnes in the tabloid *Post* still had the clout to influence the Met's management in New York is open to doubt, but another five years would pass before the Royal Ballet performed *Mayerling* in New York. Even then, the Met was reluctant to accept it, until pressure was brought to bear, not least by MacMillan himself.

Writing about the Chicago performances in the *New York Times*, Anna Kisselgoff had meanwhile given *Mayerling* an equivocal verdict: 'Strong on theatricality, the ballet is weak in its choreography . . . A ballet more about ideas than ideas expressed through dancing.' Arlene Croce in the *New Yorker* placed *Mayerling* higher than *Manon* in her critical canon. She was not to be convinced that ballet could or should attempt to tell a complicated story, but 'MacMillan pushes so insistently against the nature of his art and what it is equipped to express that now and then he achieves break-throughs and returns a kind of strength to it which has long been absent.' In her judgement, the pas de deux in *Mayerling*, unlike those in *Manon*, crystallised different dramatic situations, advancing the plot as well as commenting on 'the theme of venery, which MacMillan places at the heart of poor Rudolf's misery'. The sexual duets she found 'as far beyond the sex scenes in Tudor's ballets as contemporary movies are beyond movies of the 1940s, yet they're never inhuman or exploitative'.

In her lengthy assessment of *Mayerling*'s virtues and defects, Croce commended passages that were self-explanatory in dance and gesture, picking out the Hamlet-and-Gertrude scene between Rudolf and his mother and Larisch's scheming with Mary and her mother, 'one of the most wonderful things MacMillan has done'. Such scenes needed no words, unlike other elements of the ballet (the four Hungarian conspirators, Rudolf's suicide proposal to Mitzi Caspar) that were too reliant on a written synopsis. Rudolf's arduous role amounted, in her opinion, to no more than the Crown Prince appeared to have been in real life: 'A titled creep forever Hamletising around the house with a skull in one hand, a gun in the other'. Croce criticised Gillian Freeman's programme notes for proposing ideas and devices that could never be realised convincingly on stage. Yet in spite of the failings in 'this curious, crippled, provocative work', Croce acknowledged its choreographer's achievement: 'In a single stream of dance metaphor growing ever more narrow and deep MacMillan succeeds in telling a story that may never appear on any printed page.'

Although her endorsement might have seemed contentious to MacMillan and the Royal Ballet, Croce, the most highly respected of American dance critics, was standing up for his ballet. She would continue to defend *Mayerling* in later essays (often to the detriment of other MacMillan ballets), but her initial review reinforced the impression that the Royal Ballet should not take *Mayerling* to New York.

Back in London, MacMillan's morale was boosted by the Stuttgart Ballet's two-week season at the Coliseum in June. The company's enthusiastic reception included cheers for his recent works, *My Brother, My Sisters* and *Requiem*, which were given heart-felt performances. London critics admired *Requiem* but had mixed feelings about *My Brother, My Sisters*. While MacMillan could rely on Clement Crisp to give an appreciative analysis in the *Financial Times*, Kathrine Sorley Walker in the *Daily Telegraph* of 7 June 1978 called it, 'one of the most bizarre ballets to be staged recently by a major choreographer . . . The action has a bitter effectiveness but the characters are so lacking in humanity and so unremittingly abnormal that they forfeit any claim to pity or sympathy.'

Mary Clarke in the *Guardian* warned, 'You can't pretend to "like" a ballet of this nature but goodness how you have to admire it . . . the accumulation of evil and horror is brilliantly achieved.' James Kennedy, writing in *Country Life*, found that his former reservations about MacMillan's 'unevenness and untidiness' no longer applied: 'What a marvel [*My Brother, My Sisters*] is of taut, expressive dance – like those previous successes, *The Invitation* and *Las Hermanas*, in being intensely dramatic but unlike them, and better, in transmuting the whole of its ugly theme into the elusive poetry of neo-classical movement.'

To MacMillan's surprise, Ashton raved about *My Brother, My Sisters*, telling everyone (including the critics) that it rang absolutely true: he recognised, he said, his own siblings' behaviour. The endorsement from such an unexpected source helped convince waverers that MacMillan was not being wilfully perverse. The ballet was taken into the Royal Ballet repertoire two years later, in 1980 (with Jennifer Penney as the first sister, Lesley Collier the bespectacled one and Wayne Eagling as the brother).

The first half of the year since MacMillan had resigned as the Royal Ballet's Artistic Director had passed exceptionally well. His claim that he needed to be free of administrative responsibilities in order to create had been more than justified. He had choreographed two substantial ballets that were likely to endure, whatever the critics' reservations. The second half of the year, however, would prove frustrating as projects went awry or failed to materialise.

Soon after the Stuttgart Ballet's season had ended, the MacMillans set out on a visit to Australia. Kenneth had never been there, and since Charlotte was still young enough to travel at a reduced fare (and with no school commitments), they could afford to take a long round trip, flying via Toronto. By making contact with ballet companies *en route*, Kenneth could set some of the trip's expenses off against tax. Alexander Grant, the ex-Royal Ballet dancer who had become Artistic Director of the National Ballet of Canada, had been pressing for another MacMillan ballet for the company. During a stop-over in Toronto, Kenneth watched the company in class and performance, and agreed that they should do *Elite Syncopations*.

The family then flew in several stages to Sydney where Kenneth met his Australian in-laws on their home territory. The whole Williams family had assembled in Sydney, with Deborah's brothers having returned from jobs overseas. The MacMillans stayed for several weeks in a rented flat on the harbour opposite her parents' house. Her father took them out in his fishing boat, exploring creeks in the Hawkesbury river valley. They made an excursion to Queensland to visit some of Deborah's old friends and see the place where she had grown up. Kenneth loved the countryside and later encouraged Deborah to buy 116 acres near land owned by one of her brothers. He got on well with her family, who approved of Deborah's choice of husband and who doted on Charlotte.

He gave an interview to the *Sydney Morning Herald* from the Williams family house, where he and Deborah were photographed sitting together on a chintz-covered sofa. The interviewer was Jill Neville, the novelist and critic. She was an experienced journalist, so the version he gave her of his 'outsider' fixation is presumably how he chose to account for it:

The only explanation I can give is that it's probably something that happened to me when I was eleven years old. I was left alone to look after my mother because everyone else was working, and she died. I suppose I must have felt, unconsciously, that it was my fault. And of course that would make me feel a permanent outcast.

It was an unusually candid confession to a journalist – he looks happy and relaxed in the accompanying photograph – though it was far from true. He had turned his mother's death – when he was in fact aged twelve and away from home at school – into a story that avoided his having to mention his guilty embarrassment at her fits.

He then flew to Adelaide for two days to have discussions with the Australian Ballet about possible productions of his ballets in 1980. Peggy van Praagh was back in charge of the company after a long period of hospitalisation for hip operations. She was eager to have a MacMillan ballet in the repertoire and he had promised to take a look at her dancers. He agreed to supervise a rehearsal of the pas de deux from the central movement of *Concerto*, which two of the Australian Ballet dancers, Marilyn Rowe and Gary Norman, planned to perform as guest artists in Manila. Coincidentally, Margaret Dale, Kenneth's old acquaintance from the Sadler's Wells touring company days as well as in her role as television director, was present at the two-hour rehearsal. She wrote an account of his concentrated attention on the dancers, who had learned their roles from notation.

He seemed initially passive, she recorded, sitting folded up in a chair in rumpled trousers and a high-necked scarlet sweater. 'But those of us who know him well also know that his large sorrowful eyes miss nothing.' He was soon correcting and adjusting, pushing Rowe's head down and Norman's head back as he supported her in a deep arabesque. 'It was as though he had signed an image; put his personal take on a classical arabesque,' Dale wrote. Even on holiday, MacMillan was most at ease in the familiar confines of a rehearsal room.

His negotiations with the Australian Ballet came to no conclusion for the time being. They could not agree on either *The Rite of Spring* or *The Invitation*; his offer of *Manon* was rejected by the company's administrator, Peter Bahen, on the grounds that the operas bearing the heroine's name were not well known to the Australian public, so the ballet would not attract audiences. To van Praagh's regret, MacMillan's ballets did not enter the Australian repertoire until after she had retired.

On the MacMillans' return to London, Kenneth was asked to choreograph a short piece for the Sadler's Wells Royal Ballet to perform in a gala tribute to de Valois for her eightieth birthday. The gala, on 26 September 1978, was somewhat belated since the actual date of de Valois's birthday was 6 June; MacMillan entitled his ballet simply *6.6.78*. Twelve couples represented the signs of the Zodiac, dancing to Samuel Barber's *Capricorn Concerto*. The principal pas de deux was for Marion Tait and Desmond Kelly, dressed identically as the Gemini twins of de Valois's birth sign. Their acrobatic manoeuvres demanded extreme flexibility from Tait as Kelly twisted her into positions reminiscent of Ashton's serene *Monotones*. The guiding idea was that this versatile pair imposed harmony on the unruly ensemble.

Although the choreography incorporated references to steps and poses from de Valois's own ballets, it was a rather laboured conceit. MacMillan had intended it to be 'just a soufflé, and I hope it will make her laugh', but Barber's music had deadened any lightness of touch. The only memorable elements, apart from the *Gemini* pas de deux, were elaborate zodiac head-dresses designed by Ian Spurling. One of the dancers dismissed the piece succinctly: 'I'd rather be given a pair of socks as a birthday present.'

MacMillan had been looking forward to his next big project with a mixture of pleasure and apprehension. His old friend Violette Verdy had become Artistic Director of the Paris Opéra Ballet after retiring as a dancer (the last fifteen years of her career had been mainly with Balanchine's New York City Ballet). She intended to mount an all-MacMillan programme at the end of November 1978 in order to introduce French audiences to his choreography. She had asked him to choose the programme, which should include a new ballet made for members of the company. The Paris Opéra Ballet dancers had a reputation for being difficult to work with, but MacMillan was gratified by the invitation – the first time the company would honour a British choreographer by performing an entire evening devoted to his work.

He proposed a triple bill of *The Song of the Earth*, to be taught initially by its notator, Faith Worth, and an adapted version of *The Four Seasons*, redesigned by Barry Kay; for the new work, he hoped to use an existing score by Henri Dutilleux, the French composer whose music he had first wanted for *Winter's Eve* in 1957. Dutilleux had written the music for Roland Petit's *Le Loup*, in which Verdy had danced, so he asked her to intercede with the composer to secure his agreement. Since Verdy's charm was hard to resist, Dutilleux gave permission for MacMillan to set the new work, *Métaboles*, to his Concerto for Cello and Orchestra.

No sooner had MacMillan arrived, staying at the Grand Hotel around the corner from the ornate Palais Garnier opera house, than he realised he was in for trouble. The Paris Opéra Ballet dancers had long been accustomed to the privileges of status: leading roles could be cast only from the senior ranks, with *étoiles* entitled to pick and choose what they danced; members of the corps could not even address them, let alone upstage them in performance. (The rigid hierarchical system was not to be abolished until 1980.) Faith

Worth was frantic because few of the dancers were prepared to be in *The Song of the Earth*: they declared that its movements weren't really ballet, and insisted on being cast in *The Four Seasons* instead, with its opportunities for show-off solos and duets. MacMillan then further upset their expectations by giving prominence to Patrick Dupond, a young prodigy who had been taken into the company under special licence before he was sixteen, and was now all of nineteen. He was a *sujet*, a soloist, not yet a *premier danseur*. He would soon go on to become one of the company's best known *étoiles* (and its future Director in the 1990s) but in 1978 he was still regarded as an upstart. MacMillan created a new solo for him in *The Four Seasons* and cast him as the Messenger in *The Song of the Earth*.

Outraged by the breach of protocol in assuming that the company's long-established leading ballerina could be partnered by a junior soloist, Noella Pontois refused to dance the role of the Woman in *The Song of the Earth*. MacMillan was adamant that he wanted Dupond as the Messenger. No other principals would consent to appear in the ballet until two senior dancers, Wilfride Piollet and her husband Jean Guizerix, volunteered to dance the roles of the lovers. They were experienced in performing contemporary choreography that the classical *étoiles* scorned, and they succeeded in convincing other dancers that *The Song of the Earth*, *Le Chant de la terre*, was a modern masterpiece. Verdy felt justified: 'Their eyes were opened, which was what I wanted all along by asking Ken to come.'

Verdy had her own problems. A new Director of the Paris Opera (the equivalent of a German opera-house Intendant) had been appointed immediately after she took up her three-year contract as Ballet Director in 1978. He, Bernard Lefort, had already invited Rosella Hightower to be the next Director of the ballet company, so Verdy – and the dancers – knew that her term was limited. The ballet staff, dancers and unions could and did defy her with impunity. Several senior artists, for example, had accepted to appear in a charity performance on the night of the MacMillan programme dress rehearsal without first informing Verdy. Only when MacMillan threatened legal action did the dancers reluctantly agree to attend the dress rehearsal. 'I had no idea they could be so rude,' says Verdy. 'They were not nice to Ken, except the young ones, who loved him.

Faith would ring me, protesting about the dancers' behaviour, in the middle of the night. Ken was reduced to tears, and there was not much I could do.'

According to Faith Worth, MacMillan was meanwhile upsetting his assistants. Two notators were helping with his ballets, Worth and Monica Parker. Then, in front of them, he asked a German girl on the ballet staff to be his personal assistant, thereby arousing the resentment of his long-term colleagues. 'I think he was punishing me for intervening with Violette on his behalf,' says Worth. 'He could be very manipulative.'

Once the casting of *The Song of the Earth* was resolved, most of the trouble was over Barry Kay's designs for *The Four Seasons*. He had studied art in Paris in the 1950s at the Académie Julien and saw his assignment as an opportunity to top the extravagant Second Empire décor of the Palais Garnier (which Verdi had famously described as La Grande Boutique). 'Barry went a bit mad,' says Verdy, 'and Ken was unable to restrain him.' Kay framed the stage picture with plaster models of black angels among inflatable plastic clouds, which refused to stay blown up. Each of the Seasons was introduced by a mythical figure from classical antiquity, accompanied by a gambolling entourage carrying elaborate props, before the dancing started. Spring, for example, was represented by Venus, in the transvestite form of Deborah's Australian friend, David Williams, who appeared as a guest artist. Autumn was led by Bacchus, dressed as Napoleon seated astride a priapic cannon drawn by eunuchs. Irreverent Kay was setting out to provoke French sensibilities.

He and MacMillan were convinced that the props and decorations had been made deliberately heavy and unwieldy as an act of sabotage, part of a backstage rebellion against the Paris Opéra management. Meanwhile, the dancers' union had objected to what they saw as bad-taste jokes at the expense of the 'cocky French'. They ensured that a claque in the audience booed and hissed *The Four Seasons* from the moment the curtain went up, with special opprobrium for the Bacchus–Napoleon procession for Autumn. 'Poor Ken,' sympathised Verdy. 'All the smart people saw the beauty of the choreography, but the ballet was overdecorated and the taste was dubious.'

His new work, *Métaboles*, fared no better: 'A bit much, even for the French,' was Verdy's judgement. A woman, Dominique Khalfouni, was devoured by her lovers, who included Patrick

Dupond and Patrice Bart. The programme note quoted Oscar Wilde: 'For each man kills the thing he loves.' Khalfouni, who had been one of Roland Petit's favourite dancers before she joined the Paris Opéra Ballet, was a compelling performer. 'Ken was very taken with her,' says Verdy. 'She was strange and beautiful, a wild cat. Men fell at her feet like dead flies.' MacMillan placed her on a table, surrounded by men in evening dress who drummed their fists as they mimed eating – a cannibalistic cross between Kurt Jooss's *The Green Table* and Maurice Béjart's *Boléro*. Unfortunately for MacMillan, French audiences who admired *Boléro*, which was in the Paris Opéra Ballet's repertoire, assumed that he was parodying it. Dutilleux came to see what had become of his music and loathed the ballet.

Métaboles and *The Four Seasons* sank without trace from the Paris Opéra repertoire. (Jerome Robbins's *The Four Seasons*, also to Verdi's music, later replaced it.) *The Song of the Earth* remained. Disillusioned as he was by his Paris experience, MacMillan nevertheless respected those of the dancers who had responded to his choreography. Of the others, he remarked in an interview with Noel Goodwin, 'It seemed their main object was to be impressive in class rather than in the theatre. Others have tried to change their approach and nobody has succeeded. So I would think twice about going back there unless they changed that approach.' Twelve years later, after Patrick Dupond had become Artistic Director in 1990, MacMillan would return to mount *Manon* for the company, casting *étoiles* he had first known as youngsters in 1978.

Once back from Paris, he worked on the choreography that Herbert Ross had commissioned for his Nijinsky film. MacMillan's brief was to re-create the effect of two of Nijinsky's mould-breaking ballets, *Le Sacre du printemps* and *Jeux*. Since the dance footage would be intercut with audience reactions and close-ups of Diaghilev (Alan Bates), Stravinsky (Ronald Pickup) and Nijinsky (George de la Peña), the choreography would not need to be sustained at length. MacMillan based the dancers' steps and poses on sketches, accounts and photographs of the 1913 performances of both ballets. Georgiadis researched the original costumes and set designs, reproducing them as faithfully as he could.

Jeux was the ballet whose choreography MacMillan knew least about, so he drew on idiosyncrasies he had observed in Bronislava Nijinska's ballets in the Royal Ballet repertoire, *Les Noces* and *Les*

Biches. Her brother had tried out many of his movement experiments on her, so their choreography was bound to have had elements in common. MacMillan linked the tableaux depicted in photographs of *Jeux* and in Valentine Gross's sketches of the three tennis-playing dancers with Nijinska-like steps to the ballet's original music by Debussy. Those who saw MacMillan's 're-creation' of *Jeux* in rehearsal were stunned by it and hoped, in vain, that he might eventually stage it. His version of Nijinsky's *Sacre du printemps* was very different from his own 1962 *Rite of Spring*. The costumes, copied from the Diaghilev-era ones held by the Theatre Museum in London, helped dictate the 'primitive' movements described in contemporary accounts. Here again, MacMillan referred to sketches and diagrams of the patterns in the 1913 ballet.

Most of the cast in his Nijinsky reconstructions were members of London Festival Ballet, with Monica Mason among the exceptions. She resumed her role of the Chosen Maiden, but this time she was meant to be the dancer Maria Piltz, frantically following Nijinsky's instructions. The filming of the dance sequences was done over two weeks in Pinewood Studios, twenty miles west of London. 'We rehearsed to a recording of Colin Davis conducting the Royal Ballet version. For the filming, Herbert Ross added a soundtrack of the audience booing and shouting, without warning me first,' Mason recalls. 'I couldn't hear the music, just like the dancers couldn't at the premiere, so I looked genuinely terrified and confused on film.'

The film was released in the United States by Paramount in March 1980 in a storm of publicity. The choreographic credits read, in alphabetical order: Michel Fokine, Kenneth MacMillan, Vaslav Nijinsky. Although George de la Peña, a young dancer with American Ballet Theatre, was considered miscast in the central role, the re-creations of the Nijinsky ballets and of the atmosphere within a touring ballet company were much admired – not least by Clive Barnes, in his reviews of the film for various publications. MacMillan, who had become fascinated by Nijinsky, wanted to make his own, very different account of the schizophrenic dancer's life. He had decided to approach London Weekend Television with his proposal for a television docudrama that would come closer to the truth than a big-budget Hollywood movie.

First, though, he had Royal Ballet commissions to fulfil for 1979 under the terms of his new contract. He planned one to Ravel's

Piano Concerto in G for the Covent Garden company in March; the second would be for the Sadler's Wells touring company, a more substantial piece than the slight *6.6.78* for de Valois's eightieth birthday. He was also committed to create another evening-length ballet within the next three years and he had asked Gillian Freeman to collaborate with him again on a scenario. He intended to do a ballet about Isadora Duncan's extraordinarily colourful life. The idea had lain dormant since his Berlin days, when he had become aware of the time Duncan had spent in the city, during which she had established a school there.

He and Lynn Seymour had talked about an Isadora ballet when they were both in Berlin in the 1960s; he had assured her that when he eventually went ahead, she would of course take the role of his heroine. He had told her during the making of *Mayerling* that Isadora might be his next big ballet, though he thought it would take some time to come to fruition. Then, during the Royal Ballet's American tour with *Mayerling* in May, Seymour had been made a tempting offer: the post of Artistic Director of the Bavarian State Opera Ballet in Munich. Coming up for forty, she needed to plan for the future. She decided to accept an initial contract as Director for two years, and moved to Munich in September 1978. She would return to London to dance roles for which she was already engaged with the Royal Ballet during the autumn season. She assumed MacMillan would alert her when he was ready to create his Isadora ballet; she would find a way to make herself available.

40

Kenneth started 1979 with a New Year's resolution to keep a diary. Deborah had given him a leather-bound 'any year' diary for Christmas to supplement the annual appointments diary she filled with his and their family commitments. Until his death in 1992, he recorded in successive diaries the dates when he began and finished his ballets; he made a brief note of his mental and physical state – usually bad; and he mentioned Charlotte and Deborah in almost every entry. As a record of a creative mind at work, his diaries are unrevealing. There are no clues about his ballets, no mention of what he was reading or the music he was listening to. He had no need to write down what he was thinking and feeling. The daily entries were simply aide-memoires, with exclamation marks to remind himself of anything unusual. Mostly, they read like the ruminations of the gloomy donkey, Eeyore, in A. A. Milne's Christopher Robin stories: 'Depressed, did nothing all day. Another bad rehearsal. I have no talent. Terribly anxious – don't know why.' A pattern emerges of mounting apprehension before the premiere of one of his ballets; ecstatic relief at the first performance; and then an inevitable anti-climax, along with a protest at any unappreciative reviews.

The year 1979 began with two honours. On 3 January, he was presented with the Queen Elizabeth II Coronation Award from the Royal Academy of Dancing for 'services to British ballet'. A week later, he was told that he had won the *Evening Standard* Award for his outstanding contributions to dance during 1978: *Mayerling* for the Royal Ballet and his Stuttgart Ballet works, *Requiem* and *My Brother, My Sisters*. The newspaper's award was also intended as a retrospective tribute to his seven-year directorship of the Royal Ballet. Since Edward Thorpe (the *Standard*'s dance critic) and Clement Crisp, both of them his stalwart supporters, were on the selection committee, his nomination was not altogether surprising. To win the *Evening Standard* award was none the less an accolade from a judging panel that covered all the arts.

MacMillan had meanwhile started work on his Ravel ballet. He intended to call it *L'Heure bleue*, after the 1930s Guerlain scent (which remains in production): the French title refers to the 'cocktail hour', the twilight transition when the sky turns deep blue just before darkness falls. The ballet would evoke the hedonistic mood of the 1930s, before the Bright Young Things who had partied through the Depression years realised another world war was upon them. MacMillan was not setting out to anatomise an era or an elite stratum of society. Instead, he wanted to summon up on stage the impossibly glamorous beau monde of which he and his sisters had dreamed as they watched romantic films in Great Yarmouth. His ideas for an elegant, somewhat acid fantasy ballet, as a change from his recent sombre works, had come from listening to Ravel's Piano Concerto in

G, written between 1929 and 1931, with its sophisticated echoes of the Jazz Age surrounding the sensual, shimmering *adagio* at its heart. He had loved the Concerto in G for years, longing to set a ballet to it, but the executors of Ravel's estate, who had refused to let him use the *Mother Goose Suite* for the Deutsche Oper Ballet in Berlin, had only recently lifted their embargo on Ravel's concert pieces being used for ballet.

Still protective of the composer's reputation, the executors now objected to the proposed title of the new ballet. Ravel's music, they declared, should not be associated with anything so frivolous as a fragrance; the title smacked of advertising. MacMillan noted their objection in his new diary on 4 January, with a flurry of exclamation marks. The now nameless ballet would eventually be given another French title, *La Fin du jour*, which means much the same as the more evocative *L'Heure bleue*.

He chose Ian Spurling once again as his designer. *La Fin du jour* was to be paired at its premiere with *Elite Syncopations*, so Spurling's designs for both would play up the contrast between MacMillan's evocations of two early twentieth-century periods, a decade apart. Together, Spurling and MacMillan pored over fashion plates of the 1930s: stylish sketches of haute-couture creations by Schiaparelli, Chanel and the House of Worth; detailed illustrations of sportswear for men and women of leisure; photographs of record-breaking aviatrixes standing by their planes and dashing racing drivers by their cars. Consumerism already held sway as followers of fashion sought out the latest clothes and machines. MacMillan also had in mind the 1920s pleasure-loving society evoked in chic Diaghilev-era ballets, and the Riviera where Isadora Duncan had died in a sports car, her long scarf caught in its wheel.

La Fin du jour begins with ten couples standing in the artificial poses of shop-window mannequins. They twitch into animated life like puppets manipulated by forces outside themselves: they are playthings of fate and of the choreographer. MacMillan was once again pulling the strings of his characters. (The opening of Ravel's first movement has suggestions of Stravinsky's *Petrushka* score.) The setting is a white-lit box, flanked and overhung with abstracted profiles of watching faces. The men wear pink and apricot satin summerwear: open-necked shirts, Bermuda shorts or plus fours and exaggerated golfing caps; the women are dressed in short, sporty outfits and improbably coloured wigs. A door upstage by the backcloth gives onto a garden in deep greens and blues. There is a suggestion of the mysterious garden in Nijinsky's 'tennis' ballet, *Jeux*, which MacMillan had researched for Ross's film, as well as of his sister Bronislava's 1920s ballets, *Le Train bleu* and *Les Biches*, with their casts of athletes and flappers.

Into the brittle, jerky crowd come two pairs of socialites, the men in golfing gear, the women in bathing-suits and helmet-caps. They dance a double duet, now in canon, now in unison, watched in a *dégagé* manner by the ten subordinate couples. The Concerto's limpid slow movement then becomes a male adoration of the two leading women (Jennifer Penney and Merle Park). They take on the appearance of aviatrixes, their bathing caps transformed into flying helmets complete with goggles. Each dancer has five men attending her, like the Japanese puppet manipulators in *Requiem*; the women are slid along the ground in a sitting position, then lifted into the air as if airborne, diving, twisting and gliding. They float on Ravel's serene, long-spun phrases before drifting around the stage on pointe, galvanising each other by a single touch into renewed movement – a daydream of flying in light aircraft, unaware of the war to come that would fill the sky with fighter planes.

In the finale, the women wear chiffon evening dress, the men fondant-coloured tails – a Hollywood fantasy of Continental elegance. The men show off to each other and the women. There is a reminder of Ashton's *La Valse*, with its hectic couples swirling on the edge of an abyss as the light fades. The marionette image of the opening returns as the women, then the men, fall to the floor. One of the principal women (Merle Park) closes the door on the twilit garden: the bleak future looms outside.

The theme of a bright, doomed generation whose young men would be decimated by war had emerged as the choreography developed: the ominous effect of the closing door was realised only once the set was in place in final rehearsals. With hindsight, however, *La Fin du jour* can be seen as a precursor to MacMillan's wartime ballets in the 1980s, *Gloria* and *Valley of Shadows*. An extract from Vera Brittain's poem in her First World War memoir, *Testament of Youth*, later used as a programme note for *Gloria*, seems to sum up the foreboding at the end of *La Fin du jour*:

Those dreams of happiness we thought secure,
while, imminent and fierce outside the door,
watching a generation grow to flower,
the fate that held our youth within its power
waited for its hour.

The ballet's intermittently elegiac tone puzzled its performers and audiences. MacMillan appeared to lament the passing of a superficial, privileged society that would be obliterated by the Second World War. Could he be endorsing the hedonistic attitude of those who could afford to ignore the Depression and overlook the rise of fascism? Or was the ballet simply a diverting pastiche of a once smart era, a pretext for stylish choreography, along the lines of *Elite Syncopations*, but with an ominous conclusion? Spurling's extravagant costumes tended to divert attention from inventive choreography that was above all a response to the moods and images Ravel's music suggested to MacMillan: he had not set out to draw any moral or political conclusions.

He was evidently equivocal about his creation. After the first dress rehearsal on 9 March, he wrote in his diary, 'Don't know what to think.' After the second, he noted, 'The Dame liked it.' De Valois ('the Dame') had gathered the company together after the rehearsal and told them it was a work of genius. Since she had lived through the 1930s, her opinion was particularly valued by MacMillan. None the less, the day before the premiere (on 15 March), he wrote, 'Dread tomorrow. Feel like dying.'

He recorded that the premiere seemed to be a success. *La Fin du jour* was the opening ballet in an all-MacMillan triple bill that included *Elite Syncopations* and a long-overdue revival of *Diversions*. Because of a union dispute, the stage staff refused to change the sets, so the other two ballets were given against *La Fin du jour*'s creamy-white box, with minimal lighting changes. Royal Ballet regulars who remembered the elaborate original sets for *Diversions* preferred the unintended pared-down staging. *Elite Syncopations*, 'a close cousin of the new work', looked witty and fresh, enlivened with improvisations to suit its novel setting. At the end of the evening, Princess Margaret presented MacMillan, on stage, with his *Evening Standard* Award. Showers of congratulatory daffodils rained down from the boxes closest to the proscenium arch. MacMillan made a brief speech of thanks to the dancers who made his ballets possible and noted in his diary, 'Charlotte kissed HRH PM!'

Once *La Fin du jour* was in performance, MacMillan's overriding concern was his attempt to proceed with his idea of a television ballet-drama about Nijinsky's life. London Weekend Television (responsible for the *South Bank Show*, which had screened the documentary about the making of *Mayerling*) wanted to know more about his proposal. The release in Britain of Ross's Nijinsky film was bound to arouse interest in the subject, and the fiftieth anniversary of Diaghilev's death in August 1979 was to be commemorated by the BBC with a series of television programmes. (There had already been a BBC *Omnibus* about Nijinsky, *God of the Dance*, in 1975.) LWT was considering whether to compete with its own contribution. After several meetings, MacMillan drew up a treatment somewhat along the lines of Dennis Potter's television drama, *Pennies from Heaven*, in which narrative scenes were intercut with fantasy sequences where the characters broke into song. In MacMillan's dance-drama, the characters would express their inner selves in movement instead of words.

He outlined his interest in Nijinsky in terms that could apply to himself:

Failure to communicate is the key . . . I think his life illustrates the many facets of success (and associated stress) – talent, determination, a need to communicate, and exploitation. Dance was his only real means of communication and when he tried to extend the language in his own choreography, he was mostly misunderstood and I think retreated into insanity.

Although dialogue would be necessary to establish characters and relationships, MacMillan did not envisage a playwright's approach to his subject so much as a choreographer's. He would develop a physical language to reveal Nijinsky's descent into madness. The actual ballets that Nijinsky danced and created would barely be glimpsed, since a television budget would not stretch as far as a Hollywood one. For the leading role, he suggested Patrick Dupond from the Paris Opéra Ballet (who would, indeed, go on to act as well as dance in films).

When LWT rejected the project, MacMillan refused to be discouraged. Tanya Bruce-Lockhart, who had worked on the *Mayerling* documentary, had recently moved to Granada Television and suggested he approach Sir Denis Forman, the Chairman of Granada Television. Forman agreed to take the project further and raised the question of a scriptwriter. MacMillan had no faith in his own abilities with words: 'All my inferiorities working full blast,' he wrote in his diary.

Dennis Potter, it seemed, might be interested. MacMillan asked to see a video of his recent television drama, *Blue Remembered Hills*, which had been transmitted in January 1979. In it, adult actors take the parts of children, whose games result in a death. 'Very like *My Brother, My Sisters*,' Kenneth commented in his diary. Tentatively, MacMillan rang Potter – 'very nice but non-committal' – who turned down the proposal three weeks later. MacMillan approached Clive James, who prepared a script later in the year. But in spite of MacMillan's persistence (which included his own attempt at a script), the project never came to fruition. Granada TV was hit by a gruelling period of industrial action, which spelled the end for many projected dramas and documentaries.

Potter's *Blue Remembered Hills*, with its adult children, might have influenced MacMillan's next ballet, *Playground*, for the touring company. The Sadler's Wells Royal Ballet was to present a triple bill of his ballets during the Edinburgh Festival in August. The new work would need to be completed by mid-June, since MacMillan intended to spend July in the United States with the Covent Garden company, who were to perform *La Fin du jour*, *Mayerling* and *Romeo and Juliet* on their next tour of North America.

He had already selected a piece of music called *Play Ground* by Gordon Crosse, a contemporary British composer whose work for the Hallé orchestra he had heard on tape. He started the first creative rehearsal with a half-formed idea based on the Orpheus myth, one of his recurring themes. He complained in his diary entries for May, 'Have never been so empty. Don't know what I am doing. V. tense and anxious.' He abandoned what he had done and started again with a new story of his own devising.

It was not entirely new. The scenario for *Playground* bears a clear relationship to *My Brother, My Sisters*, as well as containing elements of his early ballets, such as *The Burrow* and *La Création du monde*. With the exception of *Mayerling*, the works for which he devised his own scenarios were those that revealed his innermost concerns: the fragile divide between reality and hallucination, sanity and madness; the inevitability with which people under pressure betray themselves and their fellows.

Playground opens with a motley group of young people inside a fenced yard. They appear to be children, some in a semblance of school uniform, others dressed up in their parents' clothes. Doubts soon arise: they might be adults pretending to be children, perhaps inmates of a mental hospital acting out childish games of pretence.

MacMillan cast Marion Tait in the leading role of the girl in yellow, obsessed with a handbag and the cosmetics it contains: she daubs make-up on her face, as if to provide herself with an identity, or a mask to hide behind. She is protected from the others by a taller woman who adopts the role of a comforting mother figure; the girl clings to her needily. A man (Desmond Kelly) who has been watching avidly from outside the enclosure climbs into the yard over the high wire-mesh fence enclosing it – a reference to Orpheus's descent into Hades. He is mobbed by the inmates, the object of their alarm and curiosity. He approaches the girl in yellow, who suddenly kisses him and attaches herself to him with a craving that is both childlike and sexual. Their long, acrobatic pas de deux reveals the heightened tension of their feelings, while the other 'children', disturbed, pretend at first not to witness what is taking place.

The motherly woman moves to split up the pair. The boys in the group set upon the intruder, kneeing him in the groin. The girl dances a solo of distress, stepping out in a way that threatens her balance: like all MacMillan heroines, she has a character-revealing way of walking on pointe. Her flailing, angular movements then disintegrate into an epileptic fit, sending her companions into a turmoil of confusion. The only one who dares touch her is the mother figure, holding her ankle as the girl jerks in spasms.

When the intruder tries to intervene, he is set upon by the others even more viciously than before. White-coated attendants pin him down, forcing his arms into a straitjacket and dragging him away. They appear to be doctors who have been observing the patients' recreation time. Meanwhile, two of the inmates, posing as a vicar and his wife, have conducted a funeral service over the girl's prostrate body. The motherly woman removes the cloth covering her, thereby restoring her to life (as Myrtha does to Giselle in Act II of *Giselle*). The other inmates are led off, after exchanging their dressing-up clothes for drab institutional garments. The girl is the last to go, clutching her handbag and smearing mascara down her tear-stained cheeks. The doctors take her inside as the intruder, left behind in his straitjacket, bangs his head against the wire fence.

The audience is left uncertain who is sane and who certifiably mad: are the men in white coats genuine doctors or role-playing inmates? The intruder, like the character He in *My Brother, My Sisters*, is clearly a MacMillan Outsider. Kelly says that, in rehearsal, MacMillan made him feel apart from the other dancers: 'I kept thinking "Why can't I join in? Why doesn't he give me anything to do – he's just leaving me to my own devices." Then I realised he'd deliberately left me as a separate person because that's what my role was in the ballet. Maybe I was the truly crazy one – I don't know.'

Kelly's character embodied Kenneth's fear of being declared mad – a fear he first confided to Jeffrey Solomons when they were both young men in the 1950s. It may be no coincidence that *Playground*'s plot closely resembles that of Janine Charrat's lunatic-asylum ballet, *Les Algues*, from 1953. Kenneth had seen it in London then and would have remembered that the young man seeking to rescue his girlfriend from an asylum had been forced into a straitjacket as one of the inmates.

Immediately after *Playground*'s opening performance, MacMillan was to tell John Auld, Peter Wright's deputy, 'I laid a lot of ghosts tonight, Johnny.' He had put into the open, via the dancers, his con-flicting, ashamed reactions to his mother's fits and the laying-out of her corpse. In a BBC Radio 3 interview with John Drummond towards the end of his life, he acknowledged that the girl's fit was indeed his memory of his mother's illness, forty years on – 'some-thing I didn't want to see as a child'. In *Playground*, he had con-fronted his dread of being 'sectioned' as a mental patient, and he had turned the tables on psychiatrists who assumed they could distin-guish fantasy from reality: the seemingly rational doctors in the ballet could well be madder than their patients.

As usual, he had told the dancers little about their roles. In Marion Tait, he had the advantage of a twenty-eight-year-old dance-actress whose appearance could be childlike. Tiny in stature, she had expressive, wide-apart eyes in a haunted face and long, absolutely straight hair: her range in his ballets would include Margaret Hill's created role in *Solitaire*, as well as Juliet, and the girl in *The Invitation*. When he re-created *The Burrow* in 1991 for the Birmingham Royal Ballet (as the touring company would eventually become), he cast her as the neurotic woman who cracks under the strain of hiding from the enemy. Tait recognised in retrospect how much *Playground* had in common with *The Burrow*: 'They're both encaged, very claustrophobic. You're shut up with this group of people you didn't choose to be with and you're all tense and unstable.'

Yolanda Sonnabend, designer for *Playground* as for *My Brother, My Sisters*, understood intuitively the effect MacMillan wanted. She went to look at the old Friern Barnet mental institution (since closed) in North London and noticed graffiti on the walls and the way rubbish was caught on the wire fence surrounding the buildings. Her bleak, institutional recreation-ground set incorporated a mural of grotesque, crudely drawn figures. She advised MacMillan that the stage lighting should be top-lit, as if by overhead floodlights, so that the faces beneath were drained of colour: 'They were condemned people who couldn't break out.'

Before *Playground* had taken its final shape, the touring company dispersed for its summer break and MacMillan flew with his family to San Francisco to join the Royal Ballet. He rehearsed the company in preparation for *Mayerling* at the city's Memorial Opera House. 'Disastrous – I went for everybody in sight,' he recorded in his diary, noting that first-night reviews were not good, unlike the favourable accounts *Mayerling* had received in Los Angeles the previous year. The MacMillans left San Francisco ahead of the company to stay once again with Herbert Ross and Nora Kaye in Beverly Hills. There, MacMillan was shown the almost final cuts of the Nijinsky film – 'v. good, *Jeux* looked stunning' – and was taken by the Rosses to parties at John Schlesinger's and George Segal's mansions. Ross put MacMillan in touch with Stephen Sondheim, whose music he hoped to use for a ballet. Although Sondheim readily gave permission for his film score for Alain Resnais's 1974 *Stavisky* to be adapted for a ballet, MacMillan proceeded no further.

Los Angeles audiences raved over *Romeo and Juliet* and were polite about *Mayerling* and *La Fin du jour*. While Kenneth and Deborah were attending *Mayerling*'s first night, Charlotte, left at home with the Rosses, was violently sick. Nora Kaye had panicked and summoned a doctor; it turned out that Charlotte had swallowed Kenneth's calomine lotion, used to calm sunburnt skin after too much poolside exposure to the Californian sun. Deborah and Kenneth returned from the Shrine Auditorium to find the household in dramatic turmoil but with no long-term harm done to six-year-old Charlotte.

They flew back home at the start of August in time for final rehearsals for the Edinburgh Festival premiere of *Playground*. The performances would be in the Big Top: to Edinburgh's shame, it had no lyric theatre suitable for ballet.* The all-MacMillan triple bill, *Playground*, *Concerto* and *Elite Syncopations*, was publicised as a Festival tribute to the Scottish-born choreographer. MacMillan, who (according to his diary) had had mixed feelings about his new ballet before his trip to America, discovered during dress rehearsals that he liked it very much: 'Though I think it will disturb people.' He was right. In spite of appreciative reviews during the Edinburgh Festival and after its London premiere at Sadler's Wells, *Playground* proved unpopular on tour and did not remain for long in the repertoire.

MacMillan was acutely sensitive to what he saw as ill-founded criticism of *Playground*. He replied promptly to a letter of protest from an offended audience member who had claimed, 'It really is not the theatre's job to distress and frighten people still more about something that in their minds already carries a stigma . . . Listening to audience reaction during the interval, I know that my anger is not unique and I hope that others will also object.' MacMillan replied:

I feel that it has always been the theatre's job to present serious subjects as well as entertaining ones. I feel any form of mental disturbance should not be escaped from, and there has always been a tendency within society to disregard or lock away people whose behaviour is not socially acceptable. I am sorry you feel that subjects that carry a stigma should not be tackled.

Once the Royal Ballet's new season was under way at the Opera House in October, Kenneth started work on his next ballet, *Gloria*, scheduled for March the following year. According to Deborah, he was always looking for a way to do a war ballet, and a televised dramatisation of Vera Brittain's *Testament of Youth* had given him the key. Now he believed he could express her generation's rage and

---

* The Playhouse, a huge converted cinema later used for musicals and dance performances, was still under threat of demolition. The Festival Theatre was not rebuilt until 1994.

despair at the waste of young lives in the Great War in an angry requiem: he would juxtapose Poulenc's *Gloria* in G – jubilant choral music in praise of God in the highest – with danced visions of devastation. The ballet was to be an elegy, a ceremony of loss, rather than a eulogy of God. In this, he was following the example of Benjamin Britten in his *War Requiem*, in which Wilfred Owen's First World War poems were set in the context of the Catholic liturgy. MacMillan had asked Norman Morrice and John Tooley to secure agreement, and a large budget, for his choice of Poulenc's *Gloria*. This time, no objections were raised to his use of sacred music.

Kenneth would turn fifty at the end of 1979. He had been looking back over his life, however indirectly, as he created his recent ballets. All, in some way, featured memories of childhood and family connections: *My Brother, My Sisters, La Fin du jour, Playground*. *Gloria* would be 'a contemplation of lost hopes, lost joys, lost selves', according to Clement Crisp's *Financial Times* review in March 1980. It would also be a lament for his own father, whose life had been blighted by being gassed in northern France during the First World War. Although William MacMillan had never spoken directly of his wartime experiences, his silence had made a lasting impression on Kenneth. He came to understand that his dour father was a deeply embittered man, consumed with anger at the way he and his fellow soldiers had been used as cannon fodder; William did not believe that the sacrifices his generation had made resulted in a better society. By dedicating *Gloria* to his father's memory, Kenneth was making belated amends for his youthful turning away from his father.

Shortly after his fiftieth birthday on 11 December, he gave a candid interview to the writer Peter Ackroyd, who was filling in as guest columnist for the *Sunday Times*'s Atticus diary. MacMillan had met him at a dinner party given by Barry Kay and the two men had got on well. He told Ackroyd in the interview that he thought of the first forty years of his life as 'a great wasteland. I often wonder how I got through it.' He had no nostalgia for his past or his lost self: 'I was so depressed, I thought it would never end. I imagined that I would never find myself . . . I was entirely alone. Nobody ostracised me. I ostracised them. Or rather, I ostracised myself. I never liked myself, ever.'

Ackroyd commented, 'And then, like a classical reversal, it all changed. He met his wife, Deborah, and they had a child. "Everything is different now. I feel, in a way, as if I have been reborn." He no longer drinks; the anxieties have lifted.' Ackroyd added, 'He has, I imagine, a will manufactured out of woven steel.' All appeared to be going well for the 'artist reborn', the title given to Ackroyd's article, although the photograph at the head of the page showed MacMillan seated on a sofa, propping up a bandaged foot. He was still recovering from an operation to remove a troublesome bunion. Ackroyd attributed his slightly glazed look as coming from 'early retreat and defence: he has concealed himself behind his face for too long'. Though the observation was acute, MacMillan had been taking painkillers for his foot, in addition to his habitual dose of barbiturates. He was all too aware that his anxieties would never be lifted for long.

Although Poulenc's *Gloria*, like Fauré's *Requiem*, is set to words in Latin from the Catholic Mass, MacMillan was not a devout believer or church-goer. He had been brought up in the Christian faith, sent to Sunday School by his parents and to Church of England services by Great Yarmouth Grammar School. As an evacuee, he had attended choral services of any denomination with his friend Vic Stowers, opting to pass tedious wartime Sundays by joining in the hymn-singing. His headmaster had required the school to learn by heart Anglican choral settings of the Mass, which they sang on special occasions. Religious ceremonies, with readings from the Bible and the Book of Common Prayer, were an integral part of his youthful experience. Christian iconography was embedded in his imagination. As he grew up, he retained his faith in ritual, if not in institutionalised religion. He told an interviewer from *Classical Music* magazine in 1983, 'I guess I believe in something. I think there is an order to life and a destiny. There's something spiritual in life that has nothing to do with the Old Testament, for me.'

Death and the after-life were a persistent theme in his ballets, from the early *Journey* of 1957 onwards. *Gloria* came to be seen in retrospect as one of a trilogy of works contemplating mortality, along with *The Song of the Earth* and *Requiem*, all set to vocal music. They were never, however, performed as a trilogy. (A second *Requiem*, to music by Andrew Lloyd Webber, was to follow in 1986, for American Ballet Theatre.)

Poulenc's *Gloria* had first been suggested to MacMillan by Michael Somes, after Ashton had finally relinquished his intention of creating a ballet to it. Coincidentally, the Poulenc recording MacMillan bought (conducted by Georges Prêtre) had on its other side the Concerto in G minor for organ, strings and timpani that Glen Tetley had used for his 1973 *Voluntaries*, in memory of John Cranko. The Royal Ballet was preparing a revival of *Voluntaries* at the time MacMillan was creating *Gloria*, so he and Tetley used to refer to *Gloria* as 'the flip side', when their rehearsals were scheduled back to back.

MacMillan had selected as his designer a young sculptor, Andy Klunder, whose work he had seen at the Slade School of Art graduate show in the summer. He briefed Klunder to look at images of the First World War: photographs, paintings, memorial sculpture. Although he sent back Klunder's initial set design for a rethink, the costume proposals were exactly what he had in mind. The men were to resemble soldiers *in extremis*, their flesh and uniforms decaying. On their heads are helmets like those worn in the trenches, but whose shape also recalls the hats of medieval pilgrims. The women wear silver-grey bodytights with tattered wisps of chiffon as skirts. Their close-fitting caps with coiled ear-muffs make them, too, seem ghosts of an age-long dance of death. Like the Wilis in *Giselle*, they are the wraiths of young women cheated of their wedding day.

The two principal women (Jennifer Penney and Wendy Ellis) represent aspects of Vera Brittain and all the women who had suffered similar experiences: Ellis was the carefree girl, Penney the woman in mourning. The leading men (Julian Hosking and Wayne Eagling) might be her brother and lover, comrades in arms; faces half hidden by their helmets, anonymous, they are unknown warriors. The two sections for Ellis gave MacMillan no trouble, though the multiple partnering was intricate. To the exuberant music of the *Laudamus*, she was thrown from hand to hand by three young men, to be caught out of sight in the wings at the end. Penney remembers that her duet with Hosking to the soprano solo *Domine Deus* was swiftly done, the choreography flowing from the music. MacMillan displayed her elegant legs and feet as though they were dividers measuring a grave, her torso doubled over the man's supporting arm in an access of grief.

In the *Agnus Dei* she exited pressed between the two leading men, her legs embracing them as they lifted her together. Commentators accustomed to seeing sex as the ruling metaphor in MacMillan's imagery have recoiled at the troilism the position suggests. But the silvery girl can be seen as a spirit – the men's shared memory or prayer, their female anima, their angel. MacMillan was using his dancers' suppleness to imply that they were other than worldly. It becomes evident in the flying lifts towards the close of *Gloria* that the women, like those in his *Requiem*, appear to the men as angels of mercy, not lovers.

MacMillan's greatest difficulty came with the opening section, in which he intended to bring on the entire cast. In February 1980, he wrote in his diary, 'Worst rehearsal of *Gloria* or anything I have ever done. Must scrap all of 1st number. Desperate.' He started over again three times, while a patient crowd of dancers waited to discover which version they needed to remember. Deborah recalls that he said to her, 'I can't find the piece of the puzzle', as if the ballet pre-existed and he had mislaid the missing code. 'Cracked it!' he recorded triumphantly after two weeks. 'V. simple solution – walking!' According to Monica Mason, he redid the whole of the first movement in one afternoon, starting from scratch.

In performance, the corps de ballet of men and women files in over a ramp, like soldiers emerging from the trenches or spectres from their graves – a legion of the dead. In contrast to the jubilant music of the opening *Gloria*, their focus is downwards, one arm shielding their eyes, as they step, step, pause, gradually encircling the central characters. Their pacing appears a formal tribal ritual, different in kind from the agitated emotions expressed by the soloists. Klunder's spare set consists of a framework of uprights that could be the skeletons of trees or the poles of shelters. The men lean against them in silhouette or recline on the slope, sleepers and corpses. When MacMillan saw the dancers resting on the ramp during the first stage rehearsal, he kept and adapted their contemplative poses. They reminded him of the soldiers lying on the ground, foreshortened in perspective, in Uccello's battle paintings.

Before the *Requiem*'s final Amens, the corps circles the stage in an echo of *The Rite of Spring*, making the point that their ritual is cyclical. This is not about one particular Great War but about all 'lost hopes, lost joys, lost selves'. As the five Amens resound, they stand still, leaning to one side then the other, looking upwards as if listening. They file out in the same direction in which they entered, disappearing over the ramp at the rear; as they leave, they turn and look back over their shoulders – an image MacMillan remembered from the film of *All Quiet on the Western Front*. In the last moments of the ballet, a solitary man (the Eagling role) peers down over the ramp, then stands to attention at the brink, facing the audience. He leaps backwards and drops soundlessly into the abyss.

He has been the principal outlet for anger and defiance. In his last, explosive solo, he pauses and points directly at the audience. The gesture, while an echo of the Lord Kitchener poster proclaiming 'Your King and Country Need You', is also one associated with guilt and betrayal in MacMillan's ballets (including his last one, *The Judas Tree*). The soldier in *Gloria* is accusing passive spectators of acquiescing in death and destruction.

MacMillan noted in his diary his nerves leading up to *Gloria*'s premiere on 13 March 1980, remarking that Andy Klunder chewed gum all through the first performance – which MacMillan declared to be 'a triumph'. A programme note had requested no applause during the ballet, so the audience's delayed reaction after the breathtaking ending was all the more tumultuous. *Gloria* was performed in the same programme as a revival of *The Four Seasons*, with new, much simpler designs by Deborah (using her maiden name of Williams) and no set. *The Four Seasons* fell so flat that the Royal Ballet administration decided it was not worth keeping in the repertoire. *Gloria* was acclaimed by critics and Board members alike: its future was assured, in spite of the extra cost its choral score entailed.

An uneasy tension, however, continued to dog MacMillan's relationship with the Opera House. He was convinced that a deliberate policy of non-cooperation was designed to scupper an all-MacMillan season proposed for the next year in Los Angeles. Los Angeles would be celebrating its 200th birthday in the summer of 1981 and Music Center Presentations hoped to bring some forty members of the Royal Ballet to give seven performances of MacMillan ballets. The Royal Opera House had agreed in principle, though MacMillan had not been very optimistic after a non-committal meeting with John Tooley in May.

Nora Kaye, who was backing the proposal, kept MacMillan informed about the state of negotiations from the spring of 1980 onwards. Since she was on the inside track, she could tell him the problems the Californian presenters encountered, while he was left in the dark by the Opera House. Music Center Presentations had emphasised that the budget had to be 'lean'. The costings produced by the Royal Opera House for three MacMillan ballets were far too expensive to make the project viable. Kaye, outraged, urged MacMillan to intervene. Even when he offered compromises to cut freight costs, the Opera House still refused to reduce its estimate. Kaye and MacMillan concluded that Tooley was dragging his feet because he was afraid of Ashton's jealousy. Trouble might be stirred up by the pro-Ashton camp if the Royal Ballet were to be represented at the bicentennial by MacMillan's ballets at the expense of Ashton's. In the end, the Los Angeles celebrations went ahead without the Royal Ballet. Kaye arranged instead for MacMillan to create a one-act work for American Ballet Theatre during the summer of 1981, to be given on tour at the end of the year.

Expecting to be away from the Royal Ballet increasingly often in the future, MacMillan had been thinking of an assistant to put in charge of preparing his ballets for performance. When he learned, by chance, from Monica Mason that she was looking for a second career once her dancing days were over, he offered her the job of his répétiteur. She was both delighted and daunted by the proposal:

Though I'd been in most of his ballets over the years, I'd never watched them from the front. I didn't know what the rest of the cast did, and he rather threw me in at the deep end by asking me to rehearse the corps in *The Four Seasons* while I was still dancing Summer. I suspect my first rehearsal was a disaster, but Kenneth insisted he had faith in me.

She gradually became accustomed to sitting by his side when he was in charge, and she sought the advice of the company's experienced répétiteurs, such as Michael Somes and Christopher Carr, when he was absent.

'Kenneth didn't tell dancers what his ballets were about,' she says.

He trusted them just to do the choreography. But he would tell me what things meant if I was preparing a dancer in a role and they weren't getting the meaning across. He'd create instinctively, like a painter choosing colours or shapes to put on a canvas. He was capable of inspiring dancers to do amazing things with their bodies, getting things out of themselves they wouldn't normally achieve. But he always knew what he wanted. You'd show him something, think up a move for him, and he'd go, 'That's awful, go away.' But you didn't feel rejected – it's a wonderful game, making something together. And I had to pass that sense of achievement on to dancers who inherited the roles.

He would challenge her not to typecast dancers when the time came for her to pick dancers for revivals of his ballets:

If it wasn't working, he'd give me a week to see if I could bring that person up to scratch. Then he'd have a look and say, 'Well done, you've saved them' – or not. He always said what he felt, even if it meant being brutally frank. I know I was hurt when he took me out of the lead harlot in *Romeo and Juliet*. He was probably sick of knowing how I did the role and wanted someone else to have a go. But one of the most helpful things for a dancer is to know exactly where you stand. No illusions. His concern was about the company and it was about his ballets.

41

By 1980, the house in Lyford Road MacMillan had bought after Charlotte was born was now proving too small for the family's needs. They wanted more space, with room for a studio in which Deborah could resume work as an artist. With Charlotte now at school for much of the day, Deborah had time to pursue her own interests: painting, designing, making jewellery. Kenneth, too, required a larger study in which to read, listen to music, plan his ballets and watch videos. He liked living in South-West London, equidistant from the Royal Ballet's rehearsal studios in Baron's Court and the Royal Opera House, so Deborah set about house-hunting in the area.

After months of searching, she found a large, dilapidated Victorian house in Wandsworth, facing a small common. The multi-storey house, its numerous rooms arranged on half-landings, stood on its own, with a garden at the back leading onto a park shared with neighbouring residents. (Spencer Park had once been part of a large estate, divided up to provide private houses with plenty of space in between.) Kenneth took one look and declared they had to live there:

the redbrick house reminded him of Eaglehurst in Great Yarmouth, where Phyllis Adams had moved with her family in the 1950s. He associated his former teacher's solid, welcoming home with a period in his youth when he had been able to escape from his anxieties. Now, in his fifties, he would take possession of his own family version of Eaglehurst.

The only drawback was that the old-fashioned building in Spencer Park, its maintenance neglected, required a great deal of work doing to it. Structural repairs would have to be carried out, central heating put in, plumbing and electrical wiring entirely redone. Although the MacMillans' offer for the property was accepted in April 1980, they could not start the alterations for another four months. By then, Kenneth was having panic-stricken nightmares about what they had let themselves in for: 'Dreamed that a knife went straight through the wall. Rushed around at 9.30 a.m. to find kitchen v. damp. Spent all day worrying about dry rot.' The garden that loomed so damply outside the kitchen was an impenetrable wilderness, which Deborah vowed to bring under control so that children and dogs could play in it. The project was going to be a lengthy one.

In the meantime, Kenneth was preparing *Isadora*, his fifth full-length ballet. Isadora Duncan had the kind of larger-than-life personality that had always fascinated him. At the start of her career, a naive American girl with an extraordinary faith in herself as a free-spirited dancer, she had set out to convince audiences and patrons around the world of her 'genius'. In spite of her triumphs in the early decades of the twentieth century, she had been brought several times to the point of despair by tragic events and by the vagaries of her own character. She had died grotesquely in 1927 at the age of fifty, a travesty of the dancer she once was, when her scarf caught in the wheel of a sports car – a Bugatti, according to legend. Her extravagant life and death have been the subject of many books – including her autobiography – plays and films. Two films, one by Ken Russell for BBC Television and the other by Karel Reisz, with Vanessa Redgrave as Isadora, had come out in the 1960s, when MacMillan was in Berlin: while there, he had read about her performances in the city's opera house and learned of the school she had established in Berlin in 1905. The idea for a ballet about Duncan had been at the back of his mind ever since.

Its resurgence seems to have sprung from the same source as his desire to make a television film about Nijinsky. Both dancers were controversial creators as well as performers, driven to extremes by their talent and by the times in which they lived. The self-referential world of the dance studios in which they started their careers was shattered by events beyond their control. They endured, and were eventually broken by, cataclysmic upheavals – war, revolution, penury, exile. Dance was their instinctive means of expression and because they were rebels by nature – outsiders – they broke existing conventions, inventing their own forms of movement. Both destroyed themselves in the process, paying a high price for their fame.

In Duncan's case, MacMillan was more interested in her passionate, melodramatic life than in her qualities as a dancer. She was the kind of outrageous, untrammelled figure he would never dare to be; she represented the theatrical side of himself that he could project on stage through other people's performances but which he preferred to keep hidden in everyday life, as an observer from the sidelines. He respected Duncan's bravery in exposing herself, over and over again, to a public that was not always prepared to appreciate her innovations. She took risks in her private life, suffering sometimes terrible consequences of her love affairs. Her two beloved children died in a tragic accident in Paris, after which her life and career unravelled. He commented in interviews about her, 'At times she led a shabby, sordid life, partly because there was so little discipline about her life or her art. Absence of technique made her insecure . . . she relied heavily upon improvisation and "inspiration". That brings insecurity, because on one day she might feel superb, and the next absolutely vile.'

MacMillan was not persuaded by contemporary accounts of Isadora's dance recitals that she was a truly great artist, although she undoubtedly had tremendous charisma. She and her disciples had left no lasting legacy in Britain, unlike in the United States where Duncan studies and re-creations of her dances have continued to flourish, thanks to the teachings of her surviving protégées. Interest has grown in her work in Europe and Russia since the Soviet Union was disbanded and evidence of her influence there has resurfaced. (Tatjana Gsovsky had studied at the Isadora Duncan Studio in Petrograd in the early years of the twentieth century.)

MacMillan, however, had never seen a convincing evocation of her 'free' style of dancing, given by dedicated followers of Duncan's disciples such as Julia Levien, Hortense Kooluris or Annabelle Gamson in America.* He could not believe that anyone really knew any more how Isadora had danced. He *had* seen Lynn Seymour in Ashton's *Five Brahms Waltzes in the Manner of Isadora Duncan* (1976), but was aware how artfully Ashton and Seymour had contrived the illusion of a spontaneous Duncanesque response to the music. The effect was filtered through Ashton's youthful memory of Isadora and his considerable expertise in making dances, as well as through Lynn's spirited interpretation.

MacMillan asked Ashton to contribute the choreography of Isadora's concert performances for his new ballet. He intended in his own choreography to concentrate on the events and love affairs that shaped Duncan's life, thereby building up an impressionistic picture of her extravagant career. He was going to draw on many different kinds of dance to illustrate her experiences: social and theatre dances of the early decades of the twentieth century; turbulent crowd scenes for the corps de ballet; intimate pas de deux in his own expressive choreography, ecstatic or anguished. The duets for Isadora would need a different kind of *plastique* since she would be barefoot (or wearing soft sandals). Above all, because he was using a ballet company to tell the story of an anti-ballet pioneer, he could pillory the hidebound world of the Establishment, obliging the Opera House company and its audience to confront their preconceptions. His *Isadora* would be, as Clement Crisp put in the December 1984 issue of *Ballet News*, 'a fist smashed into the mirrors that line the ballet studios of the world in order to break through into the theatrical reality beyond'.

Discussing the scenario with Gillian Freeman, whom he had once again asked to collaborate with him, he envisaged a full-length work in a similar vein to the last act of *Anastasia*: a woman's hallucinatory recollections, moving back and forth in time, rather than a historically accurate account of her life. 'If you read her own book,' he told

---

* Levien and Kooluris started a Duncan Dance company in 1976 and Lori Belilove, one of their students, set up the Isadora Duncan Dance Foundation in New York in 1979, the year before MacMillan's *Isadora*. Duncan's dances continue to be performed by soloists and ensembles in the United States.

Robert Penman, 'it is full of terrible lies. She was at the end of her life and had no money, so she had to spice it up. Some of those lies I incorporated in the ballet because it was all part of Isadora.' Freeman started by selecting from the autobiography, *My Life*, and from the many other books about Duncan a sequence of events that had left the deepest impression on Isadora. Her story was then divided into two cinematic flashbacks: Act I would open and close with the birth of Isadora's first child, Deirdre, by the theatre designer Edward Gordon Craig; Act II would start with the moments before Isadora's death, recapitulate the later part of her life, and end as she was strangled by her scarf.

As Freeman prepared the scenario, she appreciated the problems inherent in MacMillan's concept of a jumbled collage of memories. The audience would become thoroughly bewildered over the course of the evening unless the incidents in each half of the ballet were placed in a 'logical if not strictly chronological order'. She suggested a few voiceovers to keep track of the story and its large cast. Isadora would have at least six duets with different characters, most of them her lovers; since she was always on the move, there would need to be some way of identifying which country she was in, without time-consuming scene changes. MacMillan wanted the action to flow as freely as in a film, cutting swiftly between episodes. In his view, the narrative should be fragmented 'because her life was like that; it went in fits and starts'.

The first draft of the scenario was ready by June 1979. Freeman expected to have discussions with MacMillan leading to several more drafts, but once again she was surprised to learn that he had accepted her preliminary outline without changes. He needed the stimulus of a framework to spark his ideas for the ballet. He had sent her scenario immediately to Richard Rodney Bennett, whom he had commissioned to write the score. Bennett had been suggested to him in the past as a possible composer for *Noctambules* and for *Images of Love*, and MacMillan had followed his career ever since. He is a prolific, versatile composer, writing in contrasting veins: serious concert music, jazz and cabaret numbers and some sixty film scores. He had been approached to provide the music for Karel Reisz's *Isadora* film in 1968, which had stirred his interest in Duncan. (Maurice Jarre had written it instead.) Although Bennett was eager to work with MacMillan on a full-length ballet score, he was about to move from London in the autumn of 1979 to live in New York. Before he left, he had long discussions with Freeman and Kenneth about the *Isadora* scenario. MacMillan had provided him with a minutage, commenting that he wanted the scenes to be brief. He had not, however, been very forthcoming about what he wanted to convey within each scene; he was accustomed to making discoveries once he heard the music and began to choreograph with the dancers.

Bennett remembers starting to compose in an empty apartment in Manhattan: his furniture had been held up *en route* from England, so the notes of his piano echoed through the unfurnished rooms:

I was constantly calling Kenneth in London with questions: 'What is she thinking here?' 'What's going on in the background of this scene?' And he often couldn't tell me. It was the biggest project I'd ever collaborated on. Lots of movie music isn't really meant to be heard – it simply enhances what's going on – but with ballet music, you never know. And I'd never been asked to write so many sex scenes before, based on so little information.

He had been unaware that Duncan usually chose to dance to classical music by composers such as Chopin, Brahms, Liszt, Tchaikovsky, even Beethoven; he assumed she had resorted to slighter works, so he set about composing pleasantly danceable music for her solos. When he learned that she preferred great composers, he decided to stick to pastiches in the style of Chopin and Liszt: 'I wasn't going to lift extracts of well-known classics. The ballet wasn't a documentary about the real-life Isadora, so the music for her dances needed to fit in with the rest of the score.'

He composed leitmotifs for Isadora and the other major characters, transposing their themes through the key events in her life. He was able to draw on his wide range of interests for many of the scenes: Russian avant-garde music for her last visit to Russia; 'early sky-scraper music' for her return to New York with the Russian poet Esenin; period jazz for fashionable parties in France and America; melodic themes for romantic liaisons, dissonant ones for her anguished recollections. He told a *New York Times* interviewer in June 1981, 'I suppose what we ended up with was a kind of hierarchy: the music was my interpretation of Gillian Freeman's interpretation of Isadora's life; and then, once the music was finished, Kenneth interpreted that.'

By March 1980, he had recorded a two-piano version of the score with his regular piano partner, Susan Bradshaw, so that MacMillan would have an idea of how the music would sound. Bennett played the tape in London to the MacMillans and Gillian Freeman and her husband Edward Thorpe, graphically describing the music and the action he envisaged. Kenneth laughed and listened intently.

I think he was pleased – though he completely re-interpreted the score once he started choreographing and he never explained to me what he was doing. I found, for example, he'd used music I'd written for Isadora's birth-giving for a solo for one of her lovers, but I didn't argue with what he did with my music – I had too much respect for him.

Their relationship had remained somewhat remote until the MacMillans visited Bennett in New York at his West 54th Street apartment in the summer of 1980.

Kenneth saw a crochet collage I'd made hanging on the wall. He asked who'd done it and when I said, 'I did', he said very sombrely, 'I'm a very good crocheter too, you know.' That broke the ice because we laughed ourselves silly. Then I took him to a wonderful end-of-stock yarn store downtown and Deborah and I made him go to the counter and order what he wanted. Deborah wasn't to do it for him. It was worse for him than taking a bow on a first night, he was so nervous. He thought the women staff would laugh at him, but they loved him. It was a funny and touching moment. He was an extraordinarily touching person.

In preparing for *Isadora*, MacMillan was to inflict a harsh blow on Lynn Seymour. 'Keep yourself in shape,' he had said to her when she left to run the Bavarian State Opera Ballet in Munich. She had expected that he would let her know when he was ready to start on Isadora, and she would organise her schedule with the Munich company to suit him. In the spring of 1980 she was devastated to learn that he did not intend to cast her as Isadora. He sent a letter to her in Munich, informing her that he had offered the role to Merle Park, who, as a Royal Ballet principal, would be on hand whenever he needed her.

As it happened, Seymour was intending to return to London within a few months instead of renewing her contract with the Bavarian Ballet. She had found the German opera-house system as intractable as MacMillan had in Berlin and she wanted to leave as soon as she could. She would therefore be available for *Isadora* but

MacMillan, already committed to Park, was not prepared to change his plans. An unfortunately timed article in the *Evening Standard* in November 1979 had raised his suspicion that Seymour was trying to put pressure on him. Beneath a photograph of Lynn wearing a bandeau round her hair, the arts correspondent (Michael Owen) noted that she hoped soon to rejoin the Royal Ballet, and, knowing that MacMillan's Duncan ballet was scheduled for 1981, Owen speculated, 'Who better to play the part of the daring scarf-loving Isadora than the dramatic Miss Seymour?' The only quote Owen had been able to elicit from MacMillan about his plans for the ballet was a non-committal one: 'It's just an idea – I haven't really had time to develop anything yet.' In fact, MacMillan was furious, as his diary reveals. He rang Park to assure her that the *Evening Standard* article was ill-informed speculation. The announcement that Park was to take the role of Isadora was made in January 1980, two months after the article had appeared.

His reasons for rejecting Seymour were both practical and complex, mired in their joint past. In Freeman's scenario, Isadora, like Rudolf in *Mayerling*, would be in virtually every scene; the dancer would have to adapt to different partners in a series of demanding duets, as well as performing her own Duncanesque solos. MacMillan needed a leading lady of considerable stamina. He was aware that Seymour, drained by her battles with the Munich opera house, was not in good form, physically or emotionally. He doubted whether she would have the endurance to undertake the demands of the role and the numerous rehearsals the ballet's preparation entailed.

Above all, he was not prepared to risk a principal dancer who might prove, yet again, unreliable. There were too many old wounds in the history he shared with Seymour, too many betrayals for there to be perfect trust between the two of them. Although she had been marvellous as Mary Vetsera in *Mayerling*, she did not have to carry the entire ballet; Wall had done that (and his wife, Alfreda Thorogood, had been willing and able to rehearse in Seymour's absence). For *Isadora*, he would rather start afresh with Merle Park, who had made so much of the role of Marie Larisch in *Mayerling*. Park, who had never had an evening-length work made on her and was nearing the end of her dancing career, was eager to dedicate herself completely to *Isadora*. MacMillan had accordingly adapted his view of his heroine to accommodate light and sinewy Park; his

Isadora would be very different from the lusciously rounded figure Seymour had presented when she danced Ashton's waltzes evoking Duncan.

MacMillan's plan was to split the role and bring in a full-bodied actress to narrate the story in Duncan's own words. The actress could depict Isadora's decline into blowsiness while Park represented the dancer's inner image of herself, forever lithe. Ashton had told him that at her concerts Duncan used to speak as much as she danced; MacMillan seized on the idea that the actress could talk fondly or sardonically about her younger self, thereby distancing the audience from expecting an authentic-seeming re-creation of the dances. He was going to devise them himself, since Ashton had declined to contribute the solos on the grounds that the music was merely pastiche. Ashton evidently did not want to associate himself with an enterprise over which he had no control.

For MacMillan, introducing a speaking role required rethinking the scenario, changing the work into an integrated dance-theatre piece rather than a ballet with a few voiceovers as links. The nearest equivalent he had tried before was *The Seven Deadly Sins*, with its singer and dancer sharing aspects of the leading role between them. He asked Gillian Freeman to find suitable passages of text from Duncan's own writings for the actress to speak, while he concentrated on creating the series of pas de deux that expressed Isadora's deepest emotions. He had already started with the key duet for Isadora and Gordon Craig, the theatre designer who was the great love of her life. David Wall was his first choice as Craig; when he was injured during the course of creative rehearsals, Julian Hosking took over the role, with Wayne Eagling as second cast.

By the time the company took its summer break, MacMillan had completed several more duets for Isadora and her many lovers. Freeman had meanwhile selected excerpts from Duncan's autobiography for the amended scenario, before going on a working holiday to Los Angeles. Though the words were purportedly Duncan's own, they did her no favours. Luridly written (and very probably ghosted), the autobiography inadvertently portrays its subject as a misguided, foolish and pretentious woman. Aesthetic pronouncements that might have seemed impressive when uttered with the force of Duncan's personality behind them make little sense on the page. They were likely to seem even more preposterous in someone else's mouth on stage. MacMillan was dissatisfied with the draft text and its place in the scenario but let the matter rest until he could restart work after the company's return in September.

He took his family on holiday to the Isle of Arran, off the southwest coast of Scotland, at the suggestion of new friends, the Alexanders, who lived there. They had first met through Peter and Sonya Wright, who had enjoyed the Alexanders' company on a cruise holiday. Wright had invited them to the premiere of *Playground* at the Edinburgh Festival, and they had got on well with the MacMillans. Tom Alexander, who ran a store with his brother on Arran, had offered to find them a house to rent for the following summer. When they arrived at his house, to be given the key and instructions on how to find the rented place, they discovered an impressive collection of British art on the walls and shelves. On his return from World War II, Tom Alexander had written to every artist whose work interested him, explaining that, as an ex-serviceman, he had very little money but would like whatever pieces of art they could spare. A generous response had enabled him to amass sketches, prints and pottery, sculpture and signed first editions of books.

His wife, Catherine, who was closely involved with island activities, introduced the MacMillans to the crafts of spinning and weaving. They all took lessons, and Deborah bought a spindle and spinning wheel. Most of their time, though, was taken up with picnics and swimming on days when the sun came out. They dined with the Alexanders and went to see the play by a local author that Catherine, in charge of the island's drama society, had mounted in the village hall at Brodick. The production quickened Kenneth's interest in how actors take direction. Emma, the Alexanders' granddaughter, intended to study drama in London: the MacMillans would later invite her to lodge with them in Spencer Park, in return for occasional babysitting duties. Charlotte enjoyed her seventh birthday on Arran, restored to health after a bout of chickenpox. Her proud father had noted in his diary that, while she was convalescing in London, she had won the 'Name the Foal' competition at the local Putney horse show with 'Isadora'.

After the holiday in Scotland, MacMillan resumed his sessions with Carl Lambert. Diary entries reveal that they were both very concerned about Lynn Seymour, who had checked herself into a psychiatric clinic in London after leaving Germany. Exhausted by her frustrating experience as Artistic Director in Munich, and devastated by the loss of 'her' *Isadora* role, she was in despair about her future. To help her recover, the Royal Ballet offered to have her back in the company when she was well again. MacMillan proposed that she should come to *Isadora* rehearsals and learn the role for possible later performances. She watched a few times in October, then preferred to stay away. She decided by the end of the year that attempting to make a comeback with the company would be a mistake and resigned, declaring that she had ended her dancing career. She hadn't, but her disappointment over *Isadora* had defeated her hopes of being involved in the creation of a leading role with which to bow out in glory.

The MacMillans had meanwhile moved into their new house. They were surrounded by workmen repairing the roof, installing plumbing, radiators, gas and telephones. They would spend most of the winter of 1980–81 camped downstairs, trying to keep warm near the Aga cooker in the kitchen, while the house was taken apart around them. Deborah would eventually have her studio, Charlotte her own quarters and Kenneth a study with a television set, video and sound system. None the less, after the workmen finally packed up and left, he continued to gravitate towards the kitchen. The cooking and eating area was the natural hub of the house, filled with warmth from the Aga and the activities of people and pet animals. Deborah had retrieved a staircase from a nearby nurses' home, about to be demolished, and installed it as a link between the lower level kitchen and the dining room, making the back of the house open plan. French windows opened onto the garden, with a spectacular magnolia tree just outside the kitchen providing shade on sunny days. It was a true family house, with room to spare for entertaining. Later, they even managed to accommodate the entire Royal Ballet for a summer party, spilling out into the garden. It was to be the first of a series of large-scale parties celebrating special events.

They found a local man prepared to serve as a driver for Kenneth, collecting him every morning to take him to the Baron's Court studios in Hammersmith and bring him back at the end of the day's rehearsals. Progress on *Isadora* was slow, as MacMillan grappled with the complications of introducing a 'talking Isadora'. Thinking of an actress for the role, he had remembered Mary Miller, whom he had known in their schooldays in Yarmouth and in Retford, where they were both evacuees. They had renewed their acquaintance in the mid-1960s, when he was living in Seymour Street and she was making her way as an actress in London. She had performed with the National Theatre company – most recently in the promenade productions of *Lark Rise* and *The Passion* – as well as in the West End.

We used to watch each other's work, and I told Ken I'd always wanted to tread the Royal Opera House boards. Then suddenly he rang me up in September 1980 and invited me to watch a rehearsal of *Isadora*. 'Don't tell anyone,' he said. 'I just want to see you and Merle near each other – I think it's going to work.'

Although MacMillan had considered auditioning other candidates for the role, he felt he had no need to do so.

Mary Miller had taken dancing lessons as an adolescent in Yarmouth with his teacher, Phyllis Adams, and had heard the same stories about the effect Isadora had made on those who saw her. 'Mind you, when I asked Madam and Fred Ashton what they remembered about her, I got diametrically opposed views,' Miller remembered. 'Madam said she was rubbish, "absolute rubbish", and Fred thought she was wonderful.' Miller immersed herself in the ballet's creation, watching every rehearsal and taking part in company class in the mornings, doing what she could to absorb the way skilled dancers moved. She had no reservations about spending so much preparation time on a production that would have only five performances in its initial season at Covent Garden.

She read all the available books on Duncan and suggested different passages for her spoken script from those Freeman had selected. Since Freeman was away in the United States, MacMillan let Miller have her way. (She would be credited in the programme with the choice of 'dialogue', while Freeman was given credit for the scenario.) Miller claims that it was her idea for the speaking Isadora to remain on stage throughout the production, reclining on a chaise longue during many of the danced scenes, ready to leap up and address the audience. Miller wanted to retain a feeling of Duncanesque spontaneity in her speeches and actions, without fully appreciating that, in performance, the dancers, conductor and stage hands would need to know exactly where she was going to be. The production was becoming more complicated with every week that passed.

The ballet now started with the two Isadoras, dressed alike in long classical Greek chitons (draped tunics), standing together and gradually splitting apart from each other. Their symbolic separation pangs over, the stage filled with the bustle of the Duncan family's arrival in England off the boat train, a crowd scene packed with action. Miller, having expounded some of Duncan's theories about love, life and art during the hectic activity, would inform the audience that young Isadora's great desire was to dance in London.

Park then gave Isadora's first, naive recital to an audience of English socialites, who applauded her youthful grace. In need of money, rather than mere appreciation, Isadora tried to find employment on the Continent of Europe. After several adventures, including an episode in Paris with Loie Fuller's troupe of dancers and a love affair with a Hungarian actor, she met up with Edward Gordon Craig. This was a climactic 'meeting of twin souls', according to Miller's narration. The long pas de deux with Craig was the first occasion for MacMillan to develop his own physical idiom for Isadora, in sexual ecstasies that bore no relation to balletic conventions. Up to this point, most of the choreography (like Bennett's music) had been a parody of period dance forms: decadent European ballet and earnest American 'free' dance experiments.

The passionate affair with Craig burned itself out in a clash of competing artistic egos, though Isadora was pregnant with his child. She founded a school for dancing children in Berlin with her sister and brother-in-law, and travelled to St Petersburg to start another. There she witnessed a funeral procession of coffins in the snow. They bore the bodies of massacred workers in the abortive uprising of 1905; the scene also served as a premonition of the deaths of her own children. Act I ended with her giving birth to her daughter Deirdre by the sea in the Netherlands. Then followed an interval.

Act II started with Isadora holding her small daughter's hand. She spoke of her need for a millionaire to rescue her from penury. Paris Singer, the sewing-machine heir, arrived on cue and swept her into a life of luxury. She had a child, Patrick, by him, while driving him to jealous rages by having casual affairs with other men. Declaring that she was clearly unsuited to domestic life, she visited her school in Berlin, only to find her principles betrayed: her sister's Teutonic lover had taken control, imposing rigid discipline.

Isadora had returned to Singer when news was brought that her children had drowned. The car in which they were sitting had rolled into the Seine, a disaster projected on a screen as if in a newsreel. Their small corpses were carried on stage in the arms of servants. Isadora and Singer collapsed in grief, their knees buckling as they tried to support each other, howling silently with numb horror. It was an agonised pas de deux, grotesque in the rawness of its pain. MacMillan based it on Isadora's own words from her autobiography: 'I turned my head. Singer was there, staggering like a drunken man. His knees gave way, he fell before me.'

The funeral procession took place in the rain, the mourners' umbrellas lowered as Isadora walked past ahead of the cortège of her family and pupils. Immediately following the funeral, MacMillan decided to include a solo for Isadora to show how her dancing had been affected by the death of her children. Richard Rodney Bennett hastily wrote additional music – 'quasi-Liszt, sad but noble' – for her dance of maternal mourning. Up until this scene, Isadora's concert performances were not meant to be taken entirely seriously. They were charming enough sketches, loosely based on the so-called 'classical Greek' styles taught in dance academies as a freer style of movement than the ballet syllabus. (Park had learned Classical Greek Dance, the Ruby Ginner method, as a youngster.) In the grieving solo, MacMillan proposed to reveal Isadora as a truly expressive artist capable of pouring out her emotions in dance. He intended to show the tragic heights she might have reached, just as her life and career began to slide inexorably downwards.

The scene then changed to a beach, where Isadora had a vision of her dead children waving to her from their car. She implored a passing stranger, a handsome young man, to make love to her so that she could have another child. When she went into labour, she hallucinated that her past lovers were dancing before her. The baby died soon after birth. In her distress, Isadora could not grasp whether an attendant's remark, 'C'est la guerre', referred to her loss or to events outside her room. It was 1914.

She accepted an invitation to Russia, where she embraced Communist ideals and a revolutionary poet, Sergei Esenin. By now, Isadora the dancer would be a poignant, broken figure pursuing delusions of romantic love and artistic grandeur, while the narrator became a raddled alcoholic. MacMillan required Miller to dance a defiant solo as an ageing Isadora on tour in America with Esenin. She was to rampage to 'La Marseillaise', making an inflammatory speech that concluded with her baring her breast before a scandalised Boston public. (Hecklers and booers would be strategically placed in the Royal Opera House auditorium, mocking Miller's harangue.)

In the final scene, Isadora, deported from America, returned to the Riviera, where she mingled with a louche set of 1920s flappers and gigolos. Her latest partner was a young chauffeur in a leather jacket, helmet and goggles. As they set out together in a smart new sports car, the fringe of her shawl caught in the rear-wheel spokes. Miller would have declared, 'Je vais à la gloire', just before the curtain fell.

Creating the ballet in the Baron's Court rehearsal rooms, MacMillan and the cast could have little idea how the frequent changes of scene were going to be effected on stage. When Barry Kay was first briefed about his designs in 1979, he had started out with ambitious plans for film and even 3-D holograms for Isadora's hallucinations. He went to see American firms who were developing holograms for exhibitions and visited Disneyland in Los Angeles to check out ways of creating convincing illusions. He and MacMillan hoped that Isadora's staging would break new ground in the theatre, in the way that lavishly staged musicals would eventually manage to do years later. They were disappointed to find that experimental laser technology could not yet be adapted reliably for the stage. Even more frustrating, the old-fashioned Royal Opera House, its stage machinery hopelessly out of date, could barely cope with rudimentary film projection.

Kay proposed to get round the problem of the stage's lack of a revolve by suspending a metal ring on which lights and projectors could be placed. The ring would also serve as a curtain rail for an electrically operated gauze curtain to disguise scenery changes as it swept past like a cinematic 'wipe'. His first model surrounded the arena space below the ring with a two-tiered colonnade. MacMillan sketched a simpler plan on the back of an envelope, to which Kay responded in a note, addressing him under the nom de plume MacMillan had adopted for his early attempts at stage design in the 1950s, 'Dear Kenneth Aadams, I think your design is going to be one of my best sets to date!'

The solution was to keep the stage as stark as possible, requiring the performers to bring on their own props, stored alongside the wings. The dancers, instead of stage hands, would shift the scenery flats that established various settings – railway stations, theatres, Isadora's studio, the Riviera. Two pianos remained in place throughout: a concert grand for Isadora's recitals and a battered upright for her rehearsal scenes and her Berlin dance school. A replica of the sports car in which Duncan died (the Bugatti of legend) would roll down a central ramp from the back of the stage for the dramatic ending.

Apart from the reconstructed car, the main expense was the vast number of costumes. Isadora's career spanned three decades, and though she performed in simple tunics and draperies, her socialite admirers affected the latest haute couture. Kay was determined to dress the numerous extras, as well as the many named characters, in authentically detailed outfits, complete with hats, wigs, corsages, gloves and parasols. The Ballet Sub-Committee protested at the budgeted cost, and succeeded in reducing the number of costumes from the projected 600. Costs continued to rise, however, as the production proceeded. New ideas were introduced even as unworkable ones, together with their props and costumes, were dropped.

MacMillan had taken time out from choreographing *Isadora* in November in order to supervise the Royal Swedish Ballet's production of *Manon* in Stockholm. This would be the first time a company other than the Royal Ballet performed his *Manon*. Ever since he enabled the Swedes to perform *Romeo and Juliet* in 1970, the company had been pressing for another of his three-act ballets. Monica Parker had taught *Manon* from the notated score, after MacMillan had cast the principal characters during a visit to Stockholm in April. Monica Mason had then spent a month in Stockholm coaching the dancers in preparation for MacMillan's arrival. Nicholas Georgiadis had meanwhile adapted his original designs to suit the Royal Swedish Opera House stage. He and MacMillan had their ritual rows over Georgiadis's costumes swamping the ballet, both men obstinate in defending their interests: Opera House staff back in London were used to their arguments every time a production was revived but the Swedes were taken aback by their vehemence.

MacMillan was particularly tense, probably because *Isadora* was not going well. He noted in his diary that his anxiety attacks kept recurring and that he was very depressed. He decided to fly home for weekends during the run-up to *Manon*'s first night in Stockholm on 24 November 1980 to seek support from his family and from Carl Lambert. Airport delays, combined with the stress of flying, added to his anxieties. The fraught dress rehearsal was attended by Ingmar Bergman, but MacMillan recorded no comments from the director in his diary. He was presented to Prince Bertil and Princess Christina of Sweden on the first night – 'a triumph' – and learned of rave reviews after his return to London.

His next immediate task was to choreograph a pas de deux for Jennifer Penney and Anthony Dowell for a gala at the London Palladium on 30 November. Though the duet to Paul McCartney's *Waterfalls* was serviceable enough to reappear in later galas, it attracted less attention than two more newsworthy contributions. One was Ashton's *Soupirs* for Antoinette Sibley and Anthony Dowell, the occasion for Sibley's return to the stage after her premature retirement. The sweetly sentimental duet was rapturously acclaimed. A more contentious novelty was *The Famous Mothers' Club* solo, created for Lynn Seymour by William Forsythe. The gala was for Anya Sainsbury's charity in support of single-parent families, so Seymour and Forsythe had decided on a savage parody of the stereotyped single mother – an angry, strung-out housewife in raincoat and dark glasses, waving a bottle and an aerosol can. The solo was not appreciated by the gala organisers, who interpreted it as a calculated affront. 'Very sad,' MacMillan noted in his diary, adding later, 'Terrible row with Carl [Lambert] over Lynn.'

Progress on *Isadora* into the new year was delayed by injury and illness: Merle Park needed time to recover from two operations during the lengthy creative period. Then MacMillan learned in February that his sister Betty was in Great Yarmouth hospital with cancer of the throat and lungs. He and Deborah went to see her, and learned of the pessimistic prognosis from her consultant. They stayed in Yarmouth for two days with George MacMillan, which proved a further strain. Kenneth, unable to communicate with his brother, remained silent most of the time; the bad news about Betty enveloped them all in unrelieved gloom. In between visits over the following weeks, Kenneth found it difficult to concentrate on *Isadora* rehearsals. Betty died in her sleep two months after her cancer was diagnosed. Attending her funeral on 15 April, Kenneth was taken to see the graves of his parents and elder sister Jean, whose funeral he had missed while he was directing the ballet company in Berlin.

Once Jean had died in 1969, he had seen little of his relatives. After he married, Betty would ring him on Sunday nights, when rates were cheaper than weekdays, and tell him about her depression and poor health. As a distraction, he had invited her to stay in Spencer Park for a few days, but her only visit had been an awkward one for them all and was not repeated. George kept in regular touch with Betty and the rest of the MacMillan and Shreeve clans, but Kenneth's concern was with his own immediate family in London. He felt no nostalgia for his boyhood in Yarmouth, other than fond memories of his ballet teacher, Phyllis Adams. She had sometimes brought her pupils (including Mary Miller) to see his ballets in London but, by now in her eighties, had handed over the teaching at her school to her middle daughter, Wendy Roche.

He was going to dedicate *Isadora* to 'Miss Phyllis Adams, who taught me to love all kinds of dancing'. He invited her and Wendy to attend the opening night gala on 30 April as his guests. The premiere would be just two weeks after Betty's funeral. In an unexpected fashion, the threads of his Yarmouth past were crocheted into the creation of *Isadora*.

The Royal Ballet's press department went into overdrive publicising the forthcoming premiere of *Isadora* and the gala celebrating the company's fiftieth anniversary. Articles about Duncan and MacMillan's view of her life and career appeared in a host of publications, providing background information for a public to whom Isadora was no more than a legendary name. David Dimbleby, better known as a broadcaster than a print journalist, wrote a preview in *The Times* of 30 April 1981 about his friend's ballet, quoting MacMillan as saying, 'I can understand how she [Isadora] behaved quite easily. It's the danger of dancing. It's there for anyone who dances.' Dimbleby also obtained a perceptive tribute to MacMillan as a choreographer from de Valois: 'He has marvellous guts and is not influenced by anybody. He may be hurt by criticism but it does not stop him from going on and doing what he feels he ought to do. Of course, like everyone he comes an awful cropper now and then but he never does anything just for effect. He is doing it because he must.' MacMillan concurred in a later interview for *Dance Theatre*

Journal in 1985 about the creation of *Isadora*: 'If I have an idea, I have to do it, whether people are going to hate it or not. I never sit down and think, "Are people going to hate this?" I hope people will like it, but I have to get it out of my system.'

All kinds of last-minute complications were meanwhile besetting the production, whose rehearsal time on stage at the Opera House proved woefully inadequate. Ideally, the ambitious staging should have been run in with previews, an impossible requirement in a theatre shared with the opera; or the house should have remained dark during the preparation time, as exigent directors were able to demand in some Continental European opera houses. MacMillan and Kay were allowed no such luxury. The first stage rehearsal, with just a week to go before the opening night, was a disaster. The film projection of Isadora's children drowning in the car did not work; the electric motor that drew the revolving curtain for scene changes made an intrusive noise; Bill Besant, the House's experienced lighting designer, had just had a heart attack and his assistant, John B. Read, who replaced him, had to replot the lighting effects from the beginning. MacMillan insisted on an extra day's technical rehearsal.

John Tooley took the decision to cancel a performance of *Swan Lake* four days before *Isadora*'s premiere to accommodate the additional rehearsal. Read and MacMillan worked flat out to plot the lighting with as many props and costumes as were ready; Barry Kay would still be adding finishing touches as the first-night curtain went up. Since the most rudimentary technology continued to fail in technical rehearsals, the production needed to be even more drastically simplified. Dancers were required to draw the scene-change curtain around its ring by hand; the number of props was reduced and the film replaced by slides. Nobody had the time to insist that Mary Miller must be visible and audible in most parts of the auditorium when she delivered Isadora's speeches. She wasn't.

'Sure it will be a colossal flop,' MacMillan wrote gloomily in his diary. After three dress rehearsals he was more optimistic. He rang Phyllis Adams in Great Yarmouth to confirm that she should indeed come to the gala: he invited her and Wendy to have dinner with him afterwards. Because the gala was in recognition of the Royal Ballet's first fifty years, many well-known figures from the company's past would attend the performance, along with sponsors and their guests. Edward Gordon Craig, son of the designer depicted in the ballet, had been invited. Among the first-night good-luck telegrams was a particularly fulsome one from Ashton: 'Isadorable Kenneth my very best loves and wishes for a very great success love Fredora.'

'Wonderful first night,' noted MacMillan in his diary. 'Some booing.' He and Gillian Freeman had been booed by a cluster of audience members as they took their curtain calls but the sound was soon drowned by applause. The reception was mixed, not least because the production appeared to mock the very form of dance the gala was supposed to be celebrating. The only ballet on stage was a deliberate parody of a Parisian company dancing the kind of fin-de-siècle French ballet Duncan despised. Meanwhile, those who believed they knew how the dance pioneers of the early twentieth century performed – Loie Fuller with her swathes of billowing fabric and dramatic lighting effects, Isadora and her barefoot disciples in their Greek tunics – found MacMillan's versions so inauthentic that they assumed he was sending them up, along with the camp Parisian ballet troupe.

Others appreciated MacMillan's theatrical daring, even though, at this early stage, the production's timing was uncertain. Originally intended as two forty-minute acts, the performance came in at nearly twice the length. The critics, as usual, were divided, though many acknowledged tremendous performances by Park and Miller. Some, such as John Percival in *The Times* and Fernau Hall in the *Daily Telegraph*, objected to a ballet about a famous dancer that failed to deliver any real sense of how she danced. Others – Mary Clarke in the *Guardian*, Nicholas Dromgoole in the *Sunday Telegraph* – accepted that MacMillan intended to give only an impression of her art, while concentrating on her turbulent life and loves. Clement Crisp in the *Financial Times* described its structure as a 'profusion of scenes – not a comic strip, but, perhaps a tragic-strip . . . the rapture, the tears and the unquestioned bravery of the woman are marvellously there'. Although a number of reviewers had reservations about the splitting of the role and the fractured scenes, most found high points to admire. Dromgoole thought the experience exhilarating and called MacMillan 'a sure master of theatre'; David Dougill in *The Sunday Times* found the ballet audacious but exhausting; for Alexander Bland in the *Observer*, 'The evening drags depressingly . . . every time our spirits begin to take wing, the action stops, Mary Miller steps forward with her text and the dramatic tension sags. We are left with a series of lurid snap-shots which never builds up into a dramatic or narrative climax.'

A newer generation of reviewers for publications other than the national daily papers (such as the *New Statesman*, *The Times Literary Supplement*, *Ritz*) found too many contradictions in MacMillan's treatment of Duncan. 'Park's portrayal is regal, deli-cate, foot-perfect and faultless, except that it opposes all that we know of Isadora,' wrote Stephanie Jordan in the *New Statesman*. I questioned in the *Listener* why MacMillan had chosen to make a work about an artist he seemed to despise: 'It's the equivalent of an opera about the life and loves of Mario Lanza.' I summed up the production as 'a lecture–demonstration by a foolish woman, with so many episodes that we begin to look forward to her spectacular death'.

Edward Thorpe, whose account of how the ballet came into being, *Creating a Ballet: MacMillan's Isadora*, was published as a book soon after the premiere, concluded his chronicle by juxtaposing extracts from the reviews to show how diametrically opposed the critics' opinions were about every aspect of the production. In spite of the variety of views, MacMillan was upset by what he perceived as a generally hostile reaction from the press: 'Feel vile. Terrible reviews, especially John Percival.' He protested about the *Times* review to John Tooley, who sympathised but wrote explaining there was little he could do. MacMillan was particularly angry that not enough credit had been given for the sheer scale of what he and the company had set out to achieve. He wanted *Isadora* to be experi-enced as a theatrical spectacle, not reviewed in specialist ballet terms. The press office agreed that drama critics should be invited to review the production when it returned the following season.

Their notices proved to be as mixed as the dance critics' had been. The *Guardian*'s theatre critic, Michael Billington, was admiring: 'Nothing I had heard or read about the work had prepared me for its exciting theatricality or for the fact that it opened up whole new possibilities for dance. Its great breakthrough is to integrate speech and ballet . . . Scene after scene bristles with MacMillanesque thea-trical invention.' He concluded, 'What we need is not simply a new theatre: we also desperately need a new audience.' The *Times* thea-tre critic, Irving Wardle, found few virtues in the production, reproaching MacMillan for the lack of clarity in his attitude to Isadora: was she a great dancer or teacher? Was her tragedy one of character or simply bad luck? In Wardle's opinion, a playwright would never be able to get away with such confusion.

Isadora was to remain controversial, with the most enthusiastic reactions coming from audiences for a series of promenade performances, sponsored annually by the Midland Bank. Stalls seats were removed from the Opera House auditorium, allowing many more spectators, at a reduced price, to sit jam-packed on the floor. Three hundred students had been bused in from Manchester and Liverpool. Such informal audiences, many of them first-timers, tended not to have preconceptions about ballet, and were ready to applaud the performers whole-heartedly rather than politely. 'Thrilling, wonderful,' MacMillan recorded in his diary on 9 May 1981.

He had little time to fret over *Isadora* because of his immediate involvement in a television project with Granada in Manchester. After his Nijinsky proposal had fallen through, Granada had agreed that the film and television director, Jack Gold, should make a documentary with him about the process of choreography. The idea was to reveal, step by step, how a dance came into being – a mystery for uninitiated audiences. A camera team would follow MacMillan and his chosen dancers for five days, as they worked in a rehearsal studio at the Northern Ballet School in Manchester. The final performance at the end of the week's preparation would be recorded in Granada's studios and transmitted later in the year, on 15 December 1981.

Denis Forman, Granada's Chairman, had also succeeded in securing the Royal Opera House's agreement to make a television version of *Isadora* in October. Recording Royal Ballet performances was becoming tricky for independent television companies because the BBC had formed a collaboration with Covent Garden Video Productions, set up to market Royal Opera House productions on video cassettes after they had been transmitted on television. The BBC's Music and Arts Department, under Humphrey Burton, was vying to take over the televising of MacMillan's ballets in performance. Forman was meanwhile hanging on to him by recording *Isadora* and proposing the documentary with Jack Gold.

MacMillan was fascinated by the medium and longed to direct his work himself, something that union regulations prevented.

Devising choreography for the cameras and collaborating in the editing afterwards was the best possible alternative. Gold's plan was to follow the creation of two duets from the germ of the very first ideas. He had asked MacMillan to leave his selection of music until the day filming began, so that his initial responses with the dancers would be spontaneous. MacMillan had secured himself a safety net by inviting two of his favourite young dancers with the Stuttgart Ballet, Birgit Keil and her partner, Vladimir Klos, to work with him. He trusted that, as in the past, they would soon be on the same wavelength as him, able to intuit what he wanted and ready to provide their own suggestions.

By choosing two Stuttgart dancers, he was echoing the television pas de deux, *Dark Descent,* he had done for ABC Television eighteen years earlier with Ray Barra and Marcia Haydée. He was even going to use the same subject, Orpheus' descent into Hades to retrieve Eurydice. The Orpheus theme, which had been covert in *Playground,* was always one dear to him: psychiatrists had told him of Jung's theories about myths and archetypes, as well as reminding him that he was bound to be in search of the beloved woman, his mother, who had died and left him bereft. He also had a practical end in mind. The centenary of Stravinsky's birth was coming up in a year's time: MacMillan planned to create a ballet to the *Orpheus* score Stravinsky had composed for Balanchine in 1947. Working out an Orpheus pas de deux in advance (albeit to different music) would help him find the key to the complete ballet. The only problem in creating before the cameras would be having to account for what he was thinking and doing, in answer to Gold's questions. MacMillan was not accustomed to explaining himself.

He selected the first movement of Chopin's Third Piano Sonata and started work with Klos as Orpheus. Keil, his Eurydice, was to materialise on camera like a phantom, vanishing once he sensed her presence. When they eventually danced together, their pas de deux was made convoluted by Orpheus' vow not to look at her – a vow he was fated to break. At one point Keil and Klos became so entangled that MacMillan's physical intervention led to their collapse in a laughing heap. The dancers eventually found their own solution to the knotty problem. Gold asked the kind of questions dancers never posed, either because they would never dare interrupt or because they already understood: 'Why are you doing that?' 'What does that step mean?' MacMillan came up with two memorable statements. One, in answer to a question, was: 'There isn't anything I wouldn't try'; the other was his instruction to the dancers to show 'a lot of happiness', which gave the programme its title.

The instruction applied not to the Orpheus and Eurydice pas de deux but to a second, light-hearted duet, choreographed for a change of mood to Gershwin's Three Preludes. Philip Gammon was the pianist for the televised rehearsals and performance; Deborah designed the simple costumes. In spite of MacMillan's efforts at explaining his motives, viewers were still tempted to come away with the impression that the dancers had invented their movements, steered by the occasional comment from the man who took all the credit. The intuitive process by which dancers absorb and translate a choreographer's ideas and images into movement remained a mystery.

Before the Royal Ballet took *Isadora* on tour to the United States and Canada at the end of June, MacMillan had cut twenty minutes from the production. On the defensive about the probable American response, he told the *Radio Times*, 'I'm braced for criticism from all those old ladies who studied at her schools and remain convinced that she actually created a technique. I anticipate dozens of Isadorables shrieking complaints.' He was right, though the protests were not confined to old ladies. Unfortunately for him, there had been a resurgence of interest in America in Duncan's dancing: recent masterclasses and performances by her followers (including her last surviving adopted 'dancing daughter', Maria Theresa Duncan) had been greeted with respect by New York dance writers and scholars. They were affronted by his re-imagining of her art and the principles of her teaching. MacMillan would protest in vain that his ballet was 'not about the mother of modern dance [but] about a self-destructive woman – which is often passed over'. He was damned as an iconoclast, an 'intellectual lightweight', at an American dance scholars' conference.

Isadora was held in reserve until the end of the three-week season at the Metropolitan Opera House in New York, the first time the company had been invited back to the Met since 1976. They opened with *The Sleeping Beauty*, and then went on to present mixed bills, including two MacMillan one-act ballets, *Gloria* and *La Fin du jour*, and five by Ashton. Both choreographers were present to take their bows in front of audiences welcoming the company back with enthusiasm.

Isadora's American premiere followed on 2 July, to be met with a very mixed reception. Burt Supree wrote dismissively in the *Village Voice*, 'Those people who didn't boo or flee clapped a lot. So somebody likes this crap.' Supree was among those who deplored MacMillan's 'almost spiteful condescension towards his subject':

We get, as usual, the story of Isadora the floozie, not Isadora the artist, and dance pioneer . . . conviction is certainly missing here. Authenticity is not necessarily required. But we must believe, and see, that this woman has a special gift and vision, that she's not just an aesthetic loudmouth in imitation Greek outfits.

There were plenty of accusations of bad taste by other reviewers, though Anna Kisselgoff in the influential *New York Times* refused to be provoked into outrage:

Mr MacMillan has merely done a Ken Russell on us . . . The idea that an artist's achievement can be illuminated by his or her private life is Mr Russell's favorite motif. As extreme and absurd as his films may be – one of his most absurd was about Isadora – Mr Russell nonetheless manages to give us his own interestingly twisted interpretation of the figure in question . . . The trouble with *Isadora* is, despite all admirable appearances, its failure of nerve. Unlike Ken Russell, Mr MacMillan never does get around to telling us what Isadora Duncan's private life reveals about her art . . . What the ballet could have been is seen in the duets in which Mr MacMillan makes a successful effort to clarify the different kind of relationship Isadora had with each lover. Each duet has its own signature. Yet none reaches into a real interpretation beyond a storytelling function. There is, alas, no extra dimension.

Clive Barnes in the *New York Post* delivered an equivocal verdict in his opening paragraph: 'Kenneth MacMillan's *Isadora* is extraordinary – it is extremely amibitous, it fails almost totally, yet it is the kind of grand failure one would prefer to have than a cheap success.' He concluded, 'I do believe that MacMillan is now moving into a kind of theatrical situation that could be interesting.' His review was reprinted in *The Times* in London, countering, to some extent, reports that *Isadora* had received a 'universal slating' in New York. A second wave of American reviews, however, appearing in weekly and monthly magazines, was vituperative. 'A tasteless breast-baring melodrama' (*Time* magazine); 'This extravaganza lived up to its London reputation as a colossal disaster' (*New York* magazine); 'What an atrocity this big production number is . . . he destroys his subject, humiliates its dancers and takes three hours out of our lives' (*Dance News*).

Arlene Croce in the *New Yorker* of 13 July 1981 took MacMillan and Freeman to task for producing not a ballet but an illustrated lecture in which the dancing had a subservient role:

MacMillan . . . seems uninvolved and uninterested in any aspect of Isadora save the love scenes. There are so many floor-slamming, whizbang adagios, with so many acrobatic crotch-held lifts, that they cancel each other out; the heaving and flailing limbs, the convolutions that turn Merle Park's body into Silly Putty cease to have impact.

MacMillan's failing, as in his other narrative ballets, Croce decreed, was to try to deal with subjects dance cannot touch upon, such as war, disease, poverty, death, and above all, dance itself as a source of inspiration. She came to his defence, though, as she had done over *Mayerling*, by stating that his talent made his work 'so much stronger than the hackwork it resembles that charges of blind ambition and bad taste are irrelevant'.

After New York, the Royal Ballet travelled on to Canada, where *Isadora* met with approbation from audiences and critics. MacMillan noted with pleasure in his diary that the director Robert Altman, who was at the first-night party at the O'Keeffe Centre in Toronto, had raved about the production. Audiences in Washington DC and Boston, the next leg of the tour, were also appreciative, which lifted MacMillan's spirits for the family holiday that followed in California.

Nora Kaye and Herbert Ross had asked the MacMillans to join them in August at their new beach house at Malibu. 'Sunbathed in the nude for the first time in my life,' wrote Kenneth. 'Charlotte v. shocked!' Her eighth birthday was a very different affair from the previous year's modest celebration on the Isle of Arran. The Rosses invited their movie-star friends and children to a beach barbecue party, complete with a birthday cake made to Charlotte's own design. The guests included Steve Martin and Bernadette Peters, Mikhail Baryshnikov and Walter Matthau, who presented her with a gold pen. Charlotte danced unstoppably by way of thanks. When her proud but somewhat embarrassed parents apologised to Matthau for her performance, he commented drily, 'If I'd known what she was like, I'd have given her a Rolls-Royce.'

42

Thanks to Nora Kaye's influence, American Ballet Theatre was about to have its first new MacMillan work created for the company since *Journey*, twenty-four years earlier. In the interim, ABT had danced *Concerto, Las Hermanas* and various pas de deux first made for the Royal Ballet: Clive Barnes, writing in *The Times*, had described MacMillan, cuttingly, as the company's 'sort of resident choreographer in almost permanent absentia'. Lucia Chase, who had never ceased asking him for another ballet for her company, had finally handed over as Artistic Director to Mikhail Baryshnikov in 1980. During his first year in charge, no new ballets had been commissioned, so the prospect of a MacMillan creation, with Baryshnikov and Makarova in leading roles, was eagerly awaited. The one-act work would be given its premiere on tour in Washington DC in December 1981.

News of the ABT commission had prompted Michael Owen, arts correspondent for the *Evening Standard*, to ask whether MacMillan was abandoning the Royal Ballet, driven away by hostile criticism. 'I'm used to it now,' MacMillan claimed. 'What should I do? Go away? I don't think so. It would be defeatist to run away from a few people and there are only a few. I've been with the Royal Ballet all my life. The dancers believe in me and I enjoy it here. It's my home.'

For his one-act ballet for ABT, MacMillan had decided to use music by Gordon Crosse, the composer for *Playground*. Crosse had proposed another of his existing scores, *Wild Boy* (1978), inspired by François Truffaut's 1970 film, *L'Enfant sauvage*, which he had urged MacMillan to see. The film told the story of a feral child, who had allegedly lived among wolves, being introduced to the rational values of early nineteenth-century France. Dr Jean-Marc Itard had tried to 'civilise' the boy so that he could be integrated into society. The outcome of this experiment is left ambivalent in the film, but in real life it had failed. The legend of a child nurtured by animals (the basis for Kipling's Mowgli story in *The Jungle Book*) is widespread: Crosse had drawn on its powerful appeal for a score opposing primal and sophisticated musical ideas.

MacMillan kept the title *Wild Boy* and invented his own scenario for the ballet. The choreography was to be ballet-based, in spite of the feral element in the story. He explained his reasons for casting Baryshnikov as the central figure to Arlene Croce for her profile of the performer, 'Le Mystère Baryshnikov', in French *Vogue* in December 1986: 'I saw him as a force of nature. I believe there's a primitive side to Misha, an innocence under all the polish. He's often shocked by the way people behave in the West – the things they say, the vulgarity. Misha cannot be vulgar.' MacMillan seems also to have associated Baryshnikov with one of his earlier ABT roles, the Boy with Matted Hair in Antony Tudor's *Shadowplay*. It was originally made for the Royal Ballet, with Dowell in the leading role, so MacMillan knew it well. Tudor had continued to be a pervasive influence in his work, not least in his fascination with the damaged psychology of his characters. In *Wild Boy*, as in Tudor's *Shadowplay*, the youth loses his innocence when he encounters the corrupt society in which he must come to maturity. Once he has been sexually initiated, he cannot return to the simple, natural world of his boyhood.

Two men, loutish representatives of civilisation, are involved with the same woman. One of the men is her husband, the other his best friend – a relationship spelt out in the programme credits but open to other interpretations on stage. All three characters enter a forest, where the men capture the wild boy in a net, beating and humiliating him. When the men leave, the woman stays behind and copulates with the boy, who is overcome by conflicting emotions. His eyes opened to the true nature of sexual passion, he grabs the men's hair when they return and smacks their faces together; the kiss reveals their homosexuality, to their apparent horror. The boy then swigs from a bottle and collapses, debased. His downfall appears to have been caused by sex, as much as by his contact with 'civilisation'. The animals of the forest, once his companions, sniff at him disdainfully. They have watched his seduction from the shadows, witnesses, as in so many of MacMillan's ballets, to an outsider's betrayal and disillusionment. Soon after starting work in New York with Baryshnikov and Makarova in September, MacMillan wrote in his diary, 'Rehearsals appalling. Nearly pulled out of whole project.' He flew back to London by Concorde to rehearse the Royal Ballet in *Isadora* before its October recording by Granada Television. He was present throughout the videotaping, keeping a close eye on the monitor screens. He went back and forth across the Atlantic during the four-month gestation of *Wild Boy*, working to an interrupted schedule that he had never experienced before.

Kevin McKenzie, then twenty-six, who created the role of the husband, had the impression that MacMillan was discovering where the ballet was going as he went along:

He'd sketch things out and ask you to develop them, like an actor. I knew I wasn't supposed to be the kindest person to my wife, Natasha, so the lifts we worked on should be brutal. It wasn't clear how the story would wrap up. One day he asked me, 'Do you have any objection to kissing a man on stage?' I've no idea if he had it in mind all along: it just seemed to come to him.

McKenzie, who made no objection, was not gay, though Robert La Fosse, who took the role of the friend, was. La Fosse, who had recently been made a soloist at the age of nineteen, would later alternate as the Wild Boy when Baryshnikov was (frequently) unavailable.

MacMillan had problems convincing *Wild Boy*'s designers, Oliver Smith for the jungle set and Willa Kim for the costumes, of the simplicity he wanted. He particularly disliked Kim's chiffon draperies, which he found 'fancy dress'. (They were later described in a *Times* review as 'resembling couturier-designed underwear for chic orgies'.) Baryshnikov hated the set and his skimpy costume; he resented appearing almost nude in a role that displayed him as a virtuoso ballet dancer (albeit a wild one) rather than as a contemporary dancer, the genre he now preferred. Nora Kaye came to see a rehearsal in New York and heard all about MacMillan's worries. She took him out to Pearl's Chinese restaurant with Dennis Potter, Steve Martin and Bernadette Peters to distract him. Kaye confirmed his sense that the ballet was too long, so he persuaded Crosse to let him cut the music shortly before the premiere in Washington.

His fifty-second birthday was the day before the first night, 12 December 1981. Deborah, at home with Charlotte, had decided not to fly over and join him in Washington. 'V pleased as she's not going to miss much,' he recorded pessimistically. He wrote, however, that the premiere – 'not bad, Misha v under par' – had been well received and he duly attended the party afterwards in the Watergate complex.

Critics who had expected more from MacMillan's much anticipated ballet for ABT were disappointed: 'So much for hopes,' reported Clive Barnes in the London *Times*. 'They were almost ignominiously dashed to the ground at the Kennedy Center with the world premiere of *Wild Boy*, the whole project appearing not so much wild as crazy.' Deborah Jowitt confirmed Baryshnikov's worst fears about his role when she wrote in the *Village Voice*, 'You'd think by now that Baryshnikov would have developed a sixth sense for avoiding choreographers who think we'll relish seeing one of the world's greatest dancers hurled around, spread-eagled, walked on and humiliated.' (Neither Baryshnikov nor Makarova were willing to put on record their personal recollections of the ballet and its creation.) For Anna Kisselgoff in the *New York Times*, '*Wild Boy* is more a sketch than a finished work, but its very rawness is what makes it stimulating.' She lamented that it was 'a highly provocative ballet that will set tongues wagging for the wrong reason'.

Critics for regional papers when *Wild Boy* was taken on tour were unimpressed. ABT's press releases had led them to believe that the ballet was daringly erotic, and the outspoken reviews of the Washington premiere had raised expectations of controversy. 'Well, despite more coupling permutations than one would find in the *Kama Sutra*, it was sexually bland . . . old hat,' declared the *San Diego Reader*. Makarova and Baryshnikov soon pulled out of performances, to be replaced by Lise Houlton, with Ross Stretton as the husband and La Fosse as the Boy.

MacMillan returned home in time for Christmas, pleased to have re-established his links with Ballet Theatre. In spite of his difficulties with the two Russians, Baryshnikov and Makarova, he had enjoyed working with American dancers. They offered him a new set of challenges and he valued having a transatlantic outlet for his work. His renewed association with Ballet Theatre would be further strengthened within the next three years, as his relationship with the Royal Ballet and its audiences became more and more strained.

*

By the early 1980s, MacMillan's work was being widely seen on television, thanks to the rivalry between the BBC and independent television arts programmes. Granada's account of *Isadora* was shown on 23 February 1982; in March, the BBC transmitted its recording of *Manon* from the Opera House (with Jennifer Penney as Manon, Anthony Dowell as Des Grieux and David Wall as Lescaut). Granada recorded *Gloria* in June, for transmission on Remembrance Sunday in November 1982. Jack Gold's documentary, *A Lot of Happiness*, about MacMillan's creative process, would win a Performing Arts Emmy in New York later in the year. It took the coveted prize ahead of Christopher Nupen's film biography of the Italian composer Ottorino Respighi. Nupen, who had attended the ceremony in the hope of winning, rang MacMillan at home in London to be the first to break the news to his old friend. Bemused by the 4 a.m. call from New York, MacMillan was convinced at first that Nupen had rung to boast about his own success. Choreography was not usually considered a prize-winning category for Emmy awards.

Two commissions awaited MacMillan at the start of 1982, before he could start work on *Orpheus* for the Royal Ballet. Peter Schaufuss, the virtuoso Danish dancer now pursuing an international career, had asked for a showpiece pas de deux for himself and Elisabetta Terabust. MacMillan's choice of music was the first movement from Verdi's String Quartet in E minor, which he had initially considered including in his *Four Seasons* ballet. In Schaufuss, he had a male dancer who could accomplish any step a choreographer could dream up; unbeknown to Schaufuss, he was being tried out for Orpheus.

The pas de deux, called *Verdi Variations*, was rehearsed in London and given in February at the small northern Italian town of Reggio Emilia, as part of a programme by a recently formed company, Aterballetto, which serves theatres in the region of Emilia-Romagna. John Percival went to see the programme for *The Times*, and reported back appreciatively. His article also served as a preview for MacMillan's new work for the Sadler's Wells Royal Ballet, set to music from the same Verdi string quartet.

MacMillan had originally planned to use music he had commissioned from Richard Rodney Bennett, called *Noctuary* (or

Noctuaries): its teasing title meant 'diary of the night'. Bennett had written it as a non-narrative score but MacMillan had meanwhile conceived an idea for a ballet based on a 1980 film, *Playing for Time*, about Fania Fénelon, the Jewish singer and pianist who played in a women's orchestra in Auschwitz concentration camp. He had struggled to develop the difficult subject with the touring company's dancers before realising it was not going to work. He confided to his diary in January, 'Am lost in the ballet. V. tense and depressed. Don't know what to do.' After what he described as an 'appalling night of anxiety', he planned to postpone the first night and abandon *Orpheus* as well – 'which will cause an uproar'. Instead, he renounced the Fania Fénelon idea, abandoned Bennett's music and reverted to the Verdi String Quartet for inspiration.

He chose four dancers from the Sadler's Wells company for a double duet to the second movement, arranged by Barry Wordsworth, SWRB's Principal Conductor, for full string orchestra. Although romantic relationships were implied between the partners, *Quartet* turned out to be MacMillan's first non-narrative work since *The Four Seasons*. He expanded the chamber ballet after the company's brief season at Sadler's Wells in March, adding a revised version of the Schaufuss–Terabust pas de deux (for David Ashmole and Sherilyn Kennedy) and a final section bringing six couples together. The complete ballet to all four movements of the String Quartet was eventually given on tour in Bristol on 7 April 1982.

MacMillan's change of plans meant that Yolanda Sonnabend's commissioned designs for a Fania Fénelon ballet had to be scrapped. He turned to Deborah to design unadorned costumes for *Quartet*: bodytights for the men, leotards with short skirts for the women, painted in marbled patterns like the endpapers of a book. The ballet, made piecemeal, proved to be a minor work, though it served its dancers well. MacMillan invited the touring company's Russian senior ballerina, Galina Samsova (who appeared in the double duet in the second movement) to dance the role of Isadora in May as a guest artist with the resident company. He felt an instant rapport with her, appreciating her courage in undertaking choreography very different from anything she had danced before.

Peter Schaufuss was surprised and delighted to be rung by MacMillan with a request to arrange his schedule to accommodate *Orpheus* in June, as a guest with the Royal Ballet. When MacMillan was still Director of the Royal Ballet, Schaufuss had asked to join the company, only to be rejected with a curt 'No', without explanation. At that stage, MacMillan already had a complement of fine male dancers, Nureyev, Dowell, Wall and Eagling among them. Now, purely as a choreographer, he could indulge his ability to make use of Schaufuss's outstanding technical ability.

While MacMillan was still in the early stages of planning *Orpheus*, he heard from Wendy Roche that her mother had died, less than a year after his dedication of *Isadora* to her. He attended Phyllis Adams's funeral in Great Yarmouth and went back afterwards to her family house, Eaglehurst, for a gathering of her friends and former pupils. He had lunch with his brother George and his wife Frances first, softening the fact that he visited Yarmouth only for funerals and preferred not to stay any longer than he had to.

Another of his early mentors, Marie Rambert, died at the age of ninety-four shortly before the premiere of *Orpheus*. She, like Miss Adams, had always been his staunch supporter, convinced of his talent from the start. Now only de Valois was left of the mother figures who had guided his way, and he had doubts about de Valois's somewhat conditional loyalty – doubts that would trouble him greatly in a few years' time. Orpheus was a myth whose themes of loss, grief and anger over the death of a woman would continue to have particular resonance for him.

He had chosen Nicholas Georgiadis as his designer for the first time since *Mayerling*. Georgiadis, he knew, could come up with something hieratic and grandly austere to match Stravinsky's stark score. The music had been written in close collaboration with Balanchine, with a synopsis that largely dictated the action. (Balanchine's *Orpheus* had returned to New York City Ballet's repertoire in 1979, so MacMillan might have seen it in New York as well as remembering it from 1950, when the company performed it at Covent Garden.) Discussing his ideas with Georgiadis, MacMillan decided to adapt the scenario slightly to suit his own purposes. Georgiadis had been pondering on his designs for *Orpheus* while sitting in a darkened theatre in Canada, waiting for a technical rehearsal of an opera to start, when he noticed an electrician descending a ladder from the flies. 'There he was, going down to Hell. So I told Kenneth, "golden ladders". And Eurydice's tomb to be based on an ancient Greek funerary stele, a figure sitting in a box.'

At the start of the ballet, Eurydice's effigy, surrounded by flickering candles, was lowered in silence on long ropes until it disappeared beneath the stage. As the music began, Orpheus danced a grieving solo of embittered rage. Two male angels, one of light, the other of darkness, wrestled for possession of his soul. In a *coup de théâtre*, Orpheus and the Dark Angel – representing Pluto, ruler of the Underworld – were then revealed high on the tallest golden ladder. Their descent was watched by the Furies on other ladders; down below was a mass of lost souls, preparing to convey Eurydice's body across the Styx. Orpheus played his lyre to comfort the doomed souls and keep the Furies at bay.

Blindfold, Orpheus was led by the Dark Angel to Eurydice. During the pas de deux with his wife, Orpheus made the fatal mistake of tearing off his blindfold so that he could look at her. She slipped back into Hades while he was torn to pieces by the Furies (rather than the Bacchantes of most versions of the myth). As the Dark Angel triumphed over Orpheus' body, the Angel of Light received his soul – his gift of music – in the form of his lyre. In an apotheosis, the god Apollo took the lyre and held it aloft, raising Orpheus' music to the heavens. Unlike Balanchine's version of the ballet, which ended with Orpheus dead and the lyre ascending, MacMillan ensured that the lovers were united: in the final moments, they rose upwards, embracing each other within a gold-mesh cylinder – a version of the baroque-opera *gloire* in which heroic figures ascended into the skies – their joint immortality assured.

The emblematic god resembled a metal robot, with an impassive mask and a gleaming mechanical hand. The dancer moved in a stiff-jointed, gliding walk, prefiguring C-3PO in *Star Wars*. MacMillan wanted the production to look disturbingly strange, both futuristic and classically timeless. All the characters were masked except Orpheus and Eurydice, human lovers trapped in a hostile universe. The costumes were bodytights painted to resemble draperies, with anatomical outlines for the two angels. Female Furies wore headdresses resembling tangled snakes. John B. Read (who had worked as a lighting designer for contemporary dance companies) recalls that it was the first ballet he lit in the Opera House as a modern dance work, with cross-lighting instead of the overhead follow spots in use at the time:

Kenneth was perturbed at first because he worried I might be destroying the overall effect of the choreography. He'd say, 'John, I can't see the ballet', even though there was plenty of light. What he wanted was for the audience to be helped to watch the significant moments. He was wary of lighting that drew attention to itself – though by then contemporary dance had moved far ahead of ballet in using light to model bodies. We changed the way ballets were lit in the 1980s, starting with *Orpheus*.

Orpheus was admired for its spectacle but otherwise coolly received. Georgiadis's designs, not the choreography, won the *Evening Standard* Award for the Outstanding Contribution to Dance in 1982. In spite of MacMillan's fascination with the Orpheus myth, his ballet was short on the emotional impact audiences had come to expect from his work. While Schaufuss's 'impassioned, powerful elastic muscularity' was acclaimed, his death at the talons of the female Furies was condemned as crudely melodramatic. (One critic noted a similarity with the clawing to death of the Bird Woman in MacMillan's early *House of Birds*.) As Eurydice, Jennifer Penney remained a cipher, her supple body entwined around blindfolded Orpheus. She barely touched the ground in acrobatic partnering during the pas de deux: MacMillan was using her as an infinitely malleable fantasy figure. The original *Orpheus and Eurydice* pas de deux for television in which he had tried out his ideas with the Stuttgart couple, Birgit Keil and Vladimir Klos, had been more personal and poignant, their faces clearly visible in close-ups.*

The most challenging choreography was for the men: Schaufuss, and Wayne Eagling and Ashley Page as the rival angels. MacMillan was wrestling with ballet-inspired movement, pushing dancers' bodies beyond anything he had tried before, even in *Mayerling*. The male dancers he had chosen had the strength and virtuosity to test his powers of invention, but in this ballet he was not entirely clear what he wanted them to articulate. The hectic struggles of the two angels, for example, served only to emphasise that Orpheus was essentially a passive hero, his fate determined by others. And although MacMillan could make use of Schaufuss's remarkable technical ability, he, like Baryshnikov, was not instinctively on the

---

* Keil and Klos had performed the pas de deux on stage at a Sadler's Wells Royal Ballet gala in May, shortly before the *Orpheus* premiere on 11 June 1982.

same wavelength as an interpreter. MacMillan had found it easier to choreograph on Eagling as Orpheus when Schaufuss was unavailable, and Eagling subsequently took on the role. *Orpheus*, however, like *Wild Boy* for ABT, did not remain in performance for long, and Georgiadis's spectacular sets were destroyed.

43

In early summer, while Deborah and Charlotte went on holiday to Australia, MacMillan tried his hand as a director of spoken drama. 'It wasn't because I thought in any way that choreography was inadequate to express my ideas', he said in an interview for the *Out of Line* television documentary. 'I just wanted to work with actors who spoke, as opposed to making up my own movements to express something.' His opportunity came through Keith Gray, principal stage manager at the Royal Opera House, who ran a small theatre group. 'With Equity cards, not amateurs,' Gray emphasised. 'We strove to be professional.'

MacMillan had seen one of Gray's productions at the New Inn pub theatre in Ealing. (It consisted of a room above the saloon bar downstairs.) Since the pub, an old coaching inn, was not far from Ealing Broadway tube station in West London, the theatre jokingly styled itself 'off-Broadway'. MacMillan dropped a hint to its director, John Holloway, that he would be interested in doing a play there. When the hint was swiftly taken up, MacMillan proposed two of Ionesco's one-act plays, *The Chairs* and *The Lesson*. The only reason he gave for the choice was that he liked them 'very, very much' and he thought it was time they were seen again.

One theatre critic speculated that there was a similarity between MacMillan's ballets and Ionesco's Theatre of the Absurd in that both dealt with human archetypes. Another reviewer found the plays resembled verbal dances in their mechanical patterns and repetitions. Both plays have attracted choreographers and dancers. *The Lesson* had been effectively translated in ballet terms by Flemming Flindt in 1960, for television and then the stage; *The Chairs* has subsequently been performed by former dancers Marcia Haydée and John Neumeier in Europe, as well as Valda Setterfield and David Gordon in London and New York.

The double bill required a cast of only three: Mary Miller, Harriet Thorpe (actress daughter of Gillian Freeman and Edward Thorpe) and Peter Baldwin, well known from his appearances in the TV soap *Coronation Street*. Yolanda Sonnabend designed the costumes. MacMillan approached rehearsals with trepidation: 'Feel v. inadequate.' Three weeks in, the first preview performance was so fraught that the actors wanted to cancel the opening night. They went ahead, though, on 23 July when MacMillan's diary records, as ever, 'Thrilling first performance.' Deborah had returned from Australia in time to see the second performance and was very impressed. The only drawback was that on hot nights the windows had to be kept open and the noise of the jukebox in the pub below disrupted the carefully built-up atmosphere in the room above.

In spite of the modesty of the fringe venue, MacMillan's reputation attracted reviews in the *Financial Times*, the *Guardian* and the *Evening Standard*. Praise for the performances was tempered by the critics' lack of enthusiasm for Ionesco's then unfashionable plays. John Holloway, the theatre manager, declared it one of the New Inn's most successful productions and invited him back whenever he wanted to direct again. MacMillan had found the experience frustrating but instructive. He was unaccustomed to the way actors would query his instructions and take possession of their roles as *their* interpretations, not his. He had to renounce a lot of the control to which he was accustomed when he dealt with dancers. Although dancers contributed to his creative process, he made all the decisions; he regarded the resulting ballet and the way it was performed as entirely his responsibility.

He commented in an interview with Paul Allen for the *Guardian* in September 1983 on the difference in approach:

A dancer is very, very concerned with his body and in a perfectionist way with how his body looks. Actors are primarily concerned about feelings, about themselves and about each other. With a dancer, if they say they don't feel comfortable doing something, of course you change it. But a play is somebody else's work. I certainly wouldn't change the words.

He was determined to have another go at directing, next time on a more ambitious scale. The actress Jill Bennett, John Osborne's former wife, had asked whether he would be interested in directing her in Strindberg's *The Dance of Death*, a play that had long intrigued him. The 'dance' is that of a couple locked for twenty-five years in a marriage that becomes a mortal combat, finally won by the wife. A savagely pessimistic play, it poses considerable challenges for the two principal actors – and their director. Jill Bennett, a good friend of Donald MacLeary, often attended performances of MacMillan's ballets and thought he would bring an original approach to Strindberg's play.

As soon as the Ionesco plays were up and running, MacMillan joined the Royal Ballet on tour in Italy; Deborah and Charlotte travelled with him. The company performed his *Romeo and Juliet* in the Fenice Opera House in Venice and then in Verona, where Shakespeare had set his play. Charlotte was taken by her parents to see her first opera, Verdi's *Otello*, in Verona's open-air arena. The tour ended in Rome, with outdoor performances in the Baths of Caracalla. The MacMillans finished the summer in Scotland, returning once again to the Isle of Arran and their friends, the Alexanders. Charlotte had her ninth birthday there and Kenneth discussed his experience of directing with Catherine Alexander and her drama-society colleagues, who encouraged him to keep up the momentum and try again soon.

The Royal Ballet's autumn season began in October with a revival of *Mayerling*. MacMillan, who retained control over casting, chose a relatively unknown youngster as Mary Vetsera. Alessandra Ferri, born in Rome, had entered the Royal Ballet Upper School at sixteen. A year later, Julia Farron, who had taught her in the School, had drawn MacMillan's attention to her talented pupil: 'I think I have a ballerina in my class – come and have a look.' He had watched the students' class before selecting those he wanted for the School's end-of-year performance of *Concerto* in 1980. He promptly picked Ferri for the *andante* pas de deux, in the role created by Seymour in Berlin. His next muse was on her way, although Ferri still had to serve time as a junior member of the corps de ballet when she was taken into the Royal Ballet company.

Before long, she was being tried out in solo roles. Her big break as Mary Vetsera came when she was still only nineteen. While she was learning the part, MacMillan surprised her by saying, 'I'd like you to do Manon next.' 'I said, "Why not Juliet? I don't think I understand

Manon." And he said, "That's why."' He had recognised in her the magnetism of a young woman who draws men to her without consciously setting out to do so, delighting in her power over them. He knew the effect she would have on stage as Mary Vetsera and as Manon, girls as instinctive and ruthless as rogue children: he wanted to capture the power of Ferri's innocence before she was fully aware how to exploit her appeal.

Ferri had a sensational success in her *Mayerling* debut in October 1982. Much younger than previous Mary Vetseras, she incarnated the eager near-nymphet who precipitated Crown Prince Rudolf's downfall. Like the young Seymour before her, she was a natural actress who could convey emotions she had still to experience in real life. Not yet moulded into a classical dancer and still technically unpolished, she had no inhibitions about looking ungainly: 'I don't even know what I do when I feel something. Kenneth taught me to stop thinking, just feel. If he saw that I scented the character, he'd let me go, even in roles not created on me.' With her vivid face, large dark eyes and small, slender, hyper-flexible body, Ferri was the new model of a MacMillan heroine. His next ballet would be created around her as its heroine, with a cast of young men in thrall to her charms.

When he went to see Vittorio de Sica's film of *The Garden of the Finzi-Continis* at the National Film Theatre in November, half-formed ideas he had been gestating for some time crystallised into the basis for a ballet. He re-read the book on which the film was based, Giorgio Bassani's novel about a rich, cultured Jewish family, the Finzi-Continis, living in Italy during the time Mussolini came to power. The novel and film end on the realisation that the family will be deported to Hitler's death camps. In his *Valley of Shadows* MacMillan was going to make the family members' eventual fate graphically clear by contrasting idyllic scenes in the garden with the horrors of the camp. Young people would be shown disporting themselves in ignorance of what awaited them, while the audience would be made fully aware of their fate.

He had first considered tackling the difficult subject matter of the concentration camps in his projected work about Fania Fenelon for the Sadler's Wells touring company. That idea had proved unworkable but now, for the Royal Opera House company, he intended to adapt the Finzi-Contini story into a one-act ballet. He selected music by Tchaikovsky, including the plangent second movement from *Souvenir de Florence*, for the garden interludes, and Martinů's Double Concerto for the scenes in the camp – the same combination of composers he had used for the three-act *Anastasia*. As in that ballet, he would show how an apparently happy, privileged family could be overtaken by political events beyond their control, to be treated with appalling inhumanity for being who they were.

He used the dancers for who they were as well, exploiting their personal relationships with each other to generate dramatic tension. 'He was interested in the person, not just the dancer,' says Ferri. 'He really looked at you and what you were about. He wanted to know what was happening in your life, why you behaved in the way you did. Maybe that's why he could construct a character so well. The role gives you so many facets, not just the movements you dance.' She says she was too guileless to realise how knowingly he was casting male dancers who were, or had been, in love with her. Her role was, after all, that of a beautiful, tempting girl who attracted suitors like bees to pollen.

Other members of the company were well aware what he was up to. Monica Mason says that his curiosity about people meant that he could be 'quite naughty' in casting. Keith Gray, the company's then stage manager and MacMillan's friend as well as colleague, was more forthright:

Kenneth was wicked with people. He'd put dancers together to see what would come from the friction. He'd deny it, saying, 'They're the people I need for these roles . . .' But it was game-playing, manipulation. He was using them, as well as drawing on his own experience. He'd use the conflict creatively in the ballet, not to stir things up just for the hell of it. Though you might not appreciate that if you were the person it was happening to.

Ferri was Micol, daughter of affluent Jewish parents. She had a delicate brother, Alberto (played by Derek Deane); in Bassani's book, Alberto was dying of lymphogranuloma, which was impossible to show in ballet terms, so the brother suffered from what appeared to be epileptic fits. Once again, MacMillan was using his mother's seizures as a signifier of serious illness. Alberto's best friend and possibly lover, Malnate (Ashley Page), was also Micol's lover. Into this triangle came a young outsider, Giorgio, the narrator of the novel. Also Jewish, but from a humbler background than his hosts, he was overawed by their sophistication, and soon helplessly infatuated with Micol. MacMillan cast Guy Niblett as Giorgio in his first major role, aware that he was still heartbroken after Ferri had left him for a senior dancer. David Wall was cast as Giorgio's father, also an outsider in the Finzi-Continis' social world, but who was destined to join them in the concentration camp.

The Arcadian garden scenes, with its characters in fashionable clothes or tennis outfits, contained echoes of the bright young things' world in *La Fin du jour*, MacMillan's earlier 1930s ballet; the prison-camp scenes depicted what happened after the doors closed on the darkening garden. Yolanda Sonnabend's grand Italianate designs for the Finzi-Contini estate featured funerary cypresses and marble urns, obelisks and statues. Family guests were elegantly dressed. The young people wore informal sports clothes; their games and pairings off were filled with sexual tensions.

Ferri's Micol, pliant and ingenuous, shared her favours between Malnate and Giorgio, while expressing a near-incestuous tenderness for her stricken brother. Their quartet, lifting and twisting Ferri between them, was convoluted and complicated to work out. Ashley Page remembers an explosive row with MacMillan at a rehearsal in which the four dancers were required to repeat their moves over and again:

Kenneth just sat there with his dark glasses on, saying it wasn't right but not telling us how to fix it. After the nth time, when we were exhausted, I snapped and refused to do it again until he told us why it was wrong. He was furious – and that was the end of the rehearsal. He walked out. Then he rang me up that night to smooth things over.

Deane comments:

Kenneth would give you the shell of a role and expect you to flesh it out out. He wouldn't tell you what it was about and if he wasn't happy with what you did, he could get very frustrated. He'd be entirely negative and he resented your questions. Then, the next day, everything might be sorted out and all would be well. It was a very topsy-turvy experience, but we all wanted to be part of the creative process.

The ballet showed Micol's increasing isolation as family and friends no longer appeared in the garden, intimidated by Fascist measures against Italian Jews. It had opened with a flash-forward prelude of Giorgio saying farewell to her, throwing down his Star of

David insignia at her feet before he left. In the scene that followed, he was seen being introduced to her family by his father, both of them ill at ease in the grandly appointed grounds, to make up a tennis party. The garden scenes were intended to be seen as a recollected idyll in a privileged world, before the tennis-players fully appreciated what was happening outside their enclave. Lyrical choreography revealed how young hearts were wounded by first love, jealousy and sexual betrayal, as well as by reminders of Alfredo's increasing frailty.

Interspersed with these episodes came contrasting scenes in a concentration camp, showing the humiliation and suffering inflicted on Jews, including characters first seen socialising at the Finzi-Contini estate. In the third and last of the death-camp scenes, Micol had to confront the reality from which she had hidden her eyes in the garden. She joined the rest of her family in time to witness her brother's death and to be lined up with the others in an exit that implied their extinction.

The triple repetition of concentration-camp scenes was intended as a searing reminder of the horror beneath the façade of everyday 'civilised' life. The tennis parties were teetering on the edge of the deepest abyss the Western world had known. MacMillan's choreography for the camp's inmates ranged from ballet-based movements to anguished, contorted Expressionism: he was extending the imagery of physical distress on which he had drawn for Isadora's grief at the death of her children. A large corps de ballet, costumed in drab garments or black-and-white-striped work uniforms, shuddered with anger and despair like a chorus in a Greek tragedy. Huddled into a clump, arms and hands reaching upwards, their actions suggested attempts to survive the gas chambers. Individuals were highlighted in agonised solos against the massed corps before being cowed into submission. As Nicholas Dromgoole pointed out in the *Sunday Telegraph*, 'MacMillan fans will recognise this landscape. This is the world of the madhouse and the tyrannised; and the fact that "they" wear Nazi uniforms makes yet another variation on the white-coated or uniformed symbols of authority in these desolate areas that MacMillan has frightened us with before.'

Nazi camps, however, raised particular problems for Royal Ballet audiences. This was not an area with which ballet was thought equipped to deal. 'I think a lot of people were horrified at seeing that sort of thing at the Opera House – many people told me they were,' MacMillan said in an interview with Robert Penman for *Dance Theatre Journal*. 'I don't think that matters, actually. They [the same people] would go and see the Royal Shakespeare Company do one of the very bloody Shakespeare plays . . . I did not do it for shock. I think I did it because I wanted people to be startled more than shocked – startled is a better word.' Sir Claus Moser, Chairman of the ROH Board, was relieved he was not in a position to pass judgement. Away on business for Rothschilds' Bank, he had not been able to see the ballet and so could not be quoted on whether Jews were offended by the ballet. The redoubtable writer and broadcaster Marghanita Laski certainly was: she berated MacMillan at an Arts Council lunch for what she perceived as unacceptably poor taste.

Criticism also came from sources other than conservative ballet-goers or predictable reviewers. Admirers of dance-theatre and Expressionist modern dance found his concentration-camp scenes coarse and brutal, with 'visual clichés that might have come from Ken Russell [films] at his most lurid'. 'It requires real insensitivity to make the Holocaust ridiculous, but MacMillan achieved it,' wrote Deirdre McMahon in *Dance Theatre Journal*. Chris Savage-King, a feminist writer on dance in the 1980s, found *Valley of Shadows* 'unbearably tasteless' in the same magazine, objecting to the way MacMillan mixed

Nazism with his voyeuristic and sensational attitudes to sexual relationships . . . Characters and circumstances are simplified, then brutalised by their crude treatment. Like authors of trash fiction, and directors of video nasties, MacMillan highlights these aspects only to sensationalise. The concept underlying this emphasis, even at its most sophisticated, is of the 'dark side of human nature variety'. This is not an enlightened view of humanity, nor one associated with Expressionism.

While MacMillan had affronted many sections of his audience, he had also baffled those who were not familiar with the book or film. The synopsis in the programme, as so often with his ballets, was enigmatic – a series of entries from an anonymous (invented) diary, presumably Micol's, apprehensive about what might be happening. Characters from the garden scenes were often unrecognisable when they reappeared in prison garb, hair shorn under caps or concealed by bald wigs. The three central figures in the camp scenes, Micol's mother and grandmother and Giorgio's father, had barely been established as characters before their incarceration, and their relationships were difficult to figure out. Giorgio's father, who had refused to shake hands with the Finzi-Continis when he met them in the garden, now shared their fate, while Giorgio did not. As narrator of the book, his escape, just in time, from Italy was evident. In the ballet, it was conveyed obliquely by his removal of his Star of David armband in the opening scene and before his final exit.

Apart from the ballet's subject matter, the critics' main objections were to its structure. 'To place six episodes alternately in the garden and prison camp is too regular and too much,' wrote David Dougill in *The Sunday Times*, and Mary Clarke in the *Guardian* thought 'MacMillan falls into the trap, as before, of discounting the law of diminishing returns. Each return to the concentration camp is less horrifying.' Clement Crisp, as ever, came to MacMillan's defence in the *Financial Times*: 'Their triple repetition may diminish any shock value but they are essential to the exploration of Micol's story and to the emotional momentum of the piece.' Other reviewers suggested that MacMillan would benefit from the services of a dramaturge (as in many European opera houses) to advise him on how his ballets played in the theatre, as distinct from the rehearsal room.

Since his departure as Artistic Director, he had been tackling ever more challenging themes and experimenting with unconventional forms. He was pioneering new ground, taking ballet closer to the fragmented 'montages' of Expressionist plays and films. For him, his works were like dreams issuing from his subconscious with their own logic. He saw no reason why a ballet had to begin conventionally at the beginning of a simple story and continue in chronological order. Film-makers had accustomed viewers to flashbacks, disjointed sequences and complex plots. But Opera House audiences, resistant to non-linear narratives, found his scenarios hard to follow. Intercut like film scripts, they could be cumbersome to realise on stage, their climaxes (usually pas de deux) bogged down by lengthy ensemble scenes. He seemed unwilling or unable to stand back from his creations and assess their structure with a dispassionate eye: his judgement might have been affected by the tranquillisers and anti-depressant drugs he took. There was no one in the theatre who could serve as a sounding board for his ideas, and little opportunity for revision before a first night or even subsequent revivals. He was out on a limb within the Royal Opera House system, which found his work in the 1980s difficult to programme and to sell at the box office. Yet those of his ballets that have endured in the repertoire of the Royal Ballet and other companies have won audiences round; spectators learn to accept their structure and put up with longueurs for the sake of emotional experiences that no other choreographer can deliver.

Valley of Shadows had been part of an all-MacMillan triple bill on 3 March 1983, along with *Orpheus* and the Royal Ballet's first performance of *Requiem*, six years after the Stuttgart Ballet premiere. In the Olivier Awards for 1983, one went to *Requiem* for Best New (i.e. to London) Ballet Production and another to Ferri for her performance in *Valley of Shadows*. In return for releasing *Requiem* to the Royal Ballet, the Stuttgart company was to take *Gloria* into its repertoire. Though the ballet's anger at World War I carnage might have seemed a contentious choice for a German audience, MacMillan was gratified that it met with an excellent reception. He went to Stuttgart to supervise the final rehearsals and first performances and felt that his ballet had been appreciated as a universal lament over the waste of young lives in any war. Gert Reinholm, now Director of the Deutsche Oper Ballet, had come from Berlin to see *Gloria*, and Kenneth, in Stuttgart. He had kept in touch with Kenneth, who invited him to stay at the Spencer Park house whenever he visited London.

After the always pleasurable experience of mounting a ballet in Stuttgart, MacMillan braced himself for a potentially difficult time in New York. The Royal Ballet had been invited to take part in a Britain Salutes New York festival in April 1983, celebrating the bicentennial of the peace treaty between Britain and its former colony. A new ballet by Ashton, *Varii Capricii*, with designs by David Hockney, had been commissioned for the festival. MacMillan's *Valley of Shadows* was not included in the Metropolitan Opera House season. To add insult to injury, Jane Hermann, in charge of programming for the Met, had initially refused to accept *Mayerling* as part of the package. MacMillan told John Tooley and Norman Morrice that if the Royal Ballet gave in, he would end his choreographer's contract with the company and withdraw all his ballets. Ms Hermann was brought round to the view that New York needed to see the Royal Ballet's new young star, Alessandra Ferri, in a full-length ballet the Met's audience had not yet had the chance to experience. *Mayerling* was duly included at the end of the week-long season, with Ferri as Mary Vetsera, on the last Saturday night.

What nobody had appreciated was that the 1978 *South Bank Show* documentary about the making of *Mayerling* was being shown on television in the spring of 1983 across the Eastern Seaboard at all hours of the day and night. Metromedia Television had recently bought the right to distribute it for three months and was using the ninety-minute documentary to fill air time. A surge of interest had built up as East Coast ballet-lovers, intrigued by the documentary, booked seats by the coachload as soon as the Met box office opened. It was their first opportunity to see *Mayerling* live, while West Coast audiences had last been able to see it four years previously.

The Royal Ballet's first programme on 20 April featured ballets by Ashton: the new *Varii Capricii*, *Enigma Variations* and his *Voices of Spring* pas de deux, along with Glen Tetley's *Dances of Albion*. Ashton was given a standing ovation after *Varii Capricii*, prompting Dale Harris, the dance critic of the *Wall Street Journal*, to report in a review for the *Guardian*, 'For American audiences, Ashton continues to be what he was back in 1949 – the most important single artistic force in the entire company. Britain could have chosen no finer way of saluting New York in the performing arts.' Arlene Croce commented in the *New Yorker*, 'The ardour he commanded from his subjects – stepping up the applause with bow after bow, silencing it with a wave of his hand – was like that for a deposed king. It almost seemed as if the audience hoped to vote him back in power and have the dear old Royal we used to know restored.'

Two days later came the first night of *Mayerling*, and (to the surprise of the Met's management) a standing ovation for MacMillan. Three different casts performed in succession, Ferri being saved for the final performance, with Wayne Eagling as Rudolf. The headline for Anna Kisselgoff's review in the *New York Times* read '*Mayerling* a Triumph as Royal Concludes Season'. Kisselgoff commented,

As Mr MacMillan joined his cast on stage at the Metropolitan Opera House for the final curtain calls, he undoubtedly could not help reflecting upon the ironies of the situation. The evening was a personal vindication for the Royal Ballet's resident choreographer and former Director, who has suffered the ordeal of being booed more than once in the past by American audiences. The biggest irony of all is that this vindication should come by way of *Mayerling* . . . whose potential failure has kept it from being seen in New York before. The final paradox is that not only has *Mayerling* looked even more impressive than expected – especially to some who had seen it five years ago in other American cities – but that it is also now a ballet the Royal should bring back to New York whenever it returns. Yes, it was a success.

Kisselgoff's own ambivalent review from Chicago in 1978 had contributed to the Met's boycott of *Mayerling*. Her rationale for her previous lack of appreciation was the revelation in the New York performances of what she called 'unsuspected opportunities for great dancing as well as great acting'. She continued, 'The Royal Ballet is now simply dancing again at a higher and outstanding level. There is also a dramatic tightening in the ballet itself and, more important, an ensemble spirit that no other ballet company in the world can match.' Kisselgoff went on to justify her change of her heart by referring to the view (held by Croce) that ballet could not and should not take on subjects with which it was ill-equipped to deal: 'If it is still possible to consider costume dramas like *Mayerling* as less than a model for all ballet, it now has to be said that as a model of its own genre, it works completely on a level of sophistication and richness of detail.'

Mayerling, it seems, was now considered acceptable for New York audiences. Some members of the original cast were unchanged – David Wall as Rudolf and Merle Park as Larisch, for example, had danced in the earlier West Coast performances – but there were previously unseen dancers in the three casts. Kisselgoff and other critics enthused over Ferri's performance as Mary Vetsera, which the Met audience greeted with the acclaim due to a new star, in Kisselgoff's words, 'shooting up into the sky'.

Sir Claus Moser, who had been in New York for the first night of the Royal Ballet's season but had missed *Mayerling* at the end, wrote MacMillan a letter of congratulation on 'the fantastic reception you and *Mayerling* had at the Met. I can't tell you how thrilled all of us on the Board of Directors are that you've had this well-deserved triumph in New York. It is wonderful for all of us at Covent Garden, for the Company and for the ballet world.'

MacMillan learned a week later that he was being considered for a knighthood. A letter arrived from the Prime Minister's office informing him 'in the strictest confidence' that she – Margaret Thatcher – intended submitting his name for the Queen's Birthday Honours list. The proposed honour was greeted with seven exclamation marks in his diary. 'Can't believe it. Bemused at thought of me being a "Sir". How will it affect Charlotte? If Deborah is a Lady, hope Charlotte won't feel left out.' He sent off the enclosed form to confirm that he was indeed prepared to accept a knighthood; he still could not quite believe, however, that it would happen. He heard nothing more until his name was published in the Birthday Honours list in the newspapers on 10 June 1983, announcing that he had received a knighthood for services to British ballet. The telephone never stopped ringing: Royal Ballet members on tour in China booked a call from Shanghai to congratulate him; friends in America and Australia rang as soon as they saw his name in the papers; telegrams, cards and letters arrived from friends, colleagues and admirers who knew of him only through his ballets.

His relatives in Great Yarmouth and Scotland were hugely proud to have a knight in the family. Deborah's parents, who had not been told in advance about the honour until it was published, celebrated with a family party in Sydney. Margot Fonteyn, herself a Dame, wrote from her home in Panama to tell Kenneth, 'I am a constant and devoted admirer of what you do for British ballet and the wonderful roles you create for dancers.' Dame Mary Bridges, whom he had known in his youth as Mary Fawkes, a fellow pupil of Joan Thomas in Retford, wrote to say, 'Little did we think forty years ago that we would become Knights . . .'

He had indeed come a long way from dancing for pennies as an urchin in Yarmouth, and then performing in concert parties and competitions with Mary Fawkes in Miss Thomas's troupe. His achievements had finally been formally recognised, both as a choreographer and former Director of the Royal Ballet. Although, at fifty-three, he was younger than Ashton had been when he was knighted in 1962, he had received no previous honours (such as the OBE or CBE, which are currently awarded more liberally to figures in the arts).

His investiture by the Queen took place four months later, on 20 October 1983, when he went to Buckingham Palace in top hat and tails, accompanied by Deborah and Charlotte. While the nervous recipients of honours waited to be received, Kenneth gave practical advice to the new dames on how to curtsey securely. He admired the formal choreography of the ceremony, in which the Queen tapped each knight or dame on the shoulder with a sword. After being ushered out of the palace, he posed for photographs with Deborah and Charlotte, who proudly displayed the medal commemorating his knighthood. They finished the day by going out for a celebratory dinner with some of his closest colleagues: Monica Parker, Monica Mason, Norman Morrice and the designers Barry Kay, Ian Spurling and Yolanda Sonnabend. (Nicholas Georgiadis, his oldest friend and collaborator, was away on a design assignment.) 'The first time I really feel a Sir,' MacMillan recorded in his diary.

44

MacMillan had been shocked to find himself embroiled as the target of a vociferous human-rights political campaign in the first half of 1983. The Chile Committee for Human Rights, set up after the murder of President Allende ten years previously, had urged all its supporters in Britain to write letters of protest to the principal choreographer at the Royal Opera House. Committee members had been (wrongly) informed that MacMillan was going to visit Chile to 'present one of his most famous pieces', *Las Hermanas*, in Santiago, during a season organised by the city's cultural corporation. Two British singers were also castigated for agreeing to appear in the opera season.

In fact, MacMillan had never had any intention of going to Santiago. The Artistic Director of the Chilean National Ballet, Ivan Nagy (a friend since Nagy's days as a dancer with London Festival Ballet) had asked him, by telephone, whether the company could perform *Las Hermanas* and *Concerto*. MacMillan, about to go on holiday to Los Angeles, had told Nagy to contact his agent and the Royal Ballet. Before any negotiations could begin, Nagy announced that the Chilean company was about to acquire MacMillan's ballets, and he hoped that the choreographer might come to mount them. The Chile Committee for Human Rights immediately launched its protest campaign, declaring:

It is clear that the current National Ballet in Chile hopes to build up its image as the 'Ballet Company of the future' by inviting such a prestigious guest from abroad, when in the aftermath of the military coup in 1973 the Chilean National Ballet of the time was seriously broken up in the repression which followed and many of the then leading Chilean artists were forced out of the country and obliged to live in exile.

MacMillan had returned from the United States to find the British campaign in full swing, backed by Equity. A long, accusatory article appeared in the pro-Communist daily, the *Morning Star*, written by its veteran dance critic, Jane King. Her comments were designed to sting MacMillan's conscience as well as provoke her readers into writing protest letters. She pointed out that he had created *The Burrow*, inspired by Anne Frank's diary, and the recent *Valley of Shadows*, based on an anti-Fascist Italian novel. 'Is he aware', she asked,

that there exists in Chile today a political system capable of the same obscene brutality as in Germany, Italy and Nazi-occupied Europe more than forty years ago? Does he now fear to offend those who perpetrate it? Or is the Royal Opera House really such an ivory tower that not even the most agonised cry from today's world ever pierces the hearts within?

MacMillan was appalled to receive a deluge of hate mail as well as a formal letter from the Labour MP Phillip Whitehead, Joint Secretary of the Parliamentary Human Rights Group, asking him to consider how his 'enthusiastic welcome from the Chilean Junta' would be exploited politically. MacMillan informed Nagy and the National Ballet that his ballets could not enter its repertoire. Since he had always identified with the oppressed not the oppressor, he felt he had no option. The Chile Committee for Human Rights duly called off its campaign. Only after the Junta had been deposed and democracy restored to Chile did MacMillan's *Manon* eventually enter the National Ballet's repertoire.

By mid-July 1983, MacMillan had two projects on the go: Granada Television had commissioned him to create a new version of *The Seven Deadly Sins* specifically for the cameras; and the Royal Exchange Theatre in Manchester had agreed that he should direct his next production, Strindberg's *The Dance of Death*, for the start of the theatre's autumn season. Both would take place in Manchester, so he could go from Granada's studios to the play's read-through rehearsals without returning to London.

Derek Bailey was to direct the cameras for *The Seven Deadly Sins of the Bourgeoisie* (as the television production was called, following Brecht's original 1933 German title). MacMillan intended to be in overall charge, since it was his vision of how the satirical drama should appear on the small screen. Yolanda Sonnabend designed the costumes, while Roy Stonehouse, an experienced television designer, was responsible for the sets. The conductor David Atherton, in charge of the music, had selected the singers: Marie Angel, then a young Australian soprano, and well-known British singers Robert Tear, John Tomlinson, Robin Leggate and Stephen Roberts. MacMillan chose the rest of the cast, who included his old friends Mary Miller and April Olrich, as well as the contemporary dancers Christopher Bruce and Robert North in bit parts. He had invited his two favourite Stuttgart dancers, Birgit Keil and Vladimir Klos, to appear in a prologue of his own devising, which would make the work long enough to fill an hour-long slot on commercial television.

The additional fourteen-minute opening scene, to music from Weill's *The Threepenny Opera*, showed refugees from Europe arriving on Ellis Island in 1933, two of whom (Keil and Klos) were refused entry to the New World. Their pas de deux of longing and despair in a holding cell was watched from beyond the bars by the queue of would-be immigrants. The two Annas, lucky enough to be accepted, were met by the rest of their family already settled in Louisiana. Their rural poverty, and the plight of the rejected refugees, served to account for the two Annas' ruthless pursuit of riches during the American Depression as they worked their way through each sin in turn.

For the dual role of the heroine, MacMillan had asked Leslie Browne to be the dancing one, alongside Marie Angel. Leslie was the daughter of Isabel and Kelly Brown, former American Ballet Theatre dancers whom he had known since the 1940s. Nora Kaye was her godmother. Leslie, a dancer in ABT like her brother, had been the young star of Herbert Ross's 1977 ballet film, *The Turning Point*, in which she had danced MacMillan's *Romeo and Juliet* balcony pas de deux. She had also taken the featured role of Romola Pulsky in Ross's *Nijinsky*. Thanks to her screen credits, MacMillan had managed to secure a special Equity permit for her to appear in his *Seven Deadly Sins*, on the grounds that no British-based performer was sufficiently experienced for the television role.

However, by the time he was ready to start work on the production, he was so entranced by Alessandra Ferri's talents that he wanted her as Anna. Browne arrived, jetlagged from New York, to find herself out of her depth. When MacMillan asked her to improvise, which she was unused to doing, she was unable to come up with anything that inspired him. Aware that he found her inadequate, she became increasingly listless and withdrawn – so much so that she was sent off for medical tests to check whether she was on drugs, as a number of American dancers were at the time, or to find out if there was anything physically wrong with her. With precious time being wasted, MacMillan negotiated frantically with the Royal Ballet to have Ferri released from the company's tour in Hamburg. Once he knew Ferri would be available for the role, Browne was released from her contract. A recurring injury was given as the official explanation for her withdrawal. Choreography that had been created on Browne was swiftly adapted for Ferri; Robert North remembers being summoned back from holiday in order to rework a duet with Ferri (in the sin of Lust) in time for the start of recording on 18 July.

Tension mounted even further as filming started in Manchester. The cast had rehearsed in London, so were well prepared, but twelve outsize extras, recruited from an advertisement in the *Stage*, had been brought in at the last minute to embody Pride and Gluttony. The studio schedule was very tight: each sin had to be recorded within its allotted slot, so that the set could be changed while the performers made ready for the next one. The obese, inexperienced extras caused delays, as did Ferri's changes of costume for each scene. According to Bailey,

There was no time for retakes or for Kenneth to change his mind. I had to override him, insisting we kept to the schedule. He resented feeling rushed. I think Herbert Ross was his role model, but television studios aren't Hollywood. You have to accept what you've managed to record, even if it isn't perfect, and he didn't appreciate that. The atmosphere got very frayed. It led to a break in our artistic friendship for a number of years, though we did work together in television again.

The production was transmitted eight months later, on 22 April 1984. Granada publicised it as 'not really an arts programme but an entertainment, sometimes serious, often shocking, often bitterly funny, but never solemn'. To simulate a likeness between the two Annas, Ferri and blond Marie Angel had both worn black, bobbed wigs like Liza Minnelli's in the film of *Cabaret*. Ferri looked delectable in close-up, acting convincingly and adapting swiftly to the different styles of dancing, including tap routines, which she confessed to bluffing her way through. MacMillan was quoted in *People* magazine as saying, 'She is a natural for the cameras. In the old days, she'd have gone straight to Hollywood. She has a very beautiful body, perfect proportions for dancing.' *The Seven Deadly Sins* went out the night after Ferri's debut as Juliet at the Royal Opera House: it was reviewed at the same time, adding to her reputation as a dance-actress in MacMillan's ballets.

Just before recording *The Seven Deadly Sins* in Manchester, MacMillan had conducted the first read-through of *The Dance of Death*. The small cast was a high-profile one: Jill Bennett was the embittered wife, Alice; Edward Fox the Captain, Edgar; Peter Baldwin (who had been in the Ionesco plays) was the wife's cousin, Kurt; the youngest, least experienced performer was Sue Burton as the maid. MacMillan, who had worried that the more he read and analysed Strindberg's play, the less he understood it, was unusually optimistic after the initial read-through. He commented in his diary, 'My performance as director not bad!' While Deborah and Charlotte went on holiday in August to Inverness and then Devon, staying with the Dimblebys, he remained in Manchester to work with the actors on *The Dance of Death*.

The actors' co-operation in rehearsals deteriorated as the first performances neared. The production was complicated by the fact that the Royal Exchange Theatre was constructed in the round, the stage and auditorium suspended within an old circular building. (It has since been rebuilt, still in the round.) The actors would be seen from all directions and the timing of entrances and exits needed to be particularly well prepared. The maid entering to announce that dinner was served, for example, had to set out well in advance of delivering her simple declaration – a time lag that the actors could exploit for devious purposes, as MacMillan was to discover.

He appears to have lost the confidence of the principal pair early on. Jill Bennett took to telephoning her friend Lindsay Anderson, the theatre and film director, for advice on how to approach her role, thereby undermining MacMillan's authority. She threatened to walk out a fortnight before the opening on 15 September. Edward Fox was unhappy with MacMillan's instructions, and reblocked his moves as he saw fit. 'Ghastly atmosphere in rehearsals,' MacMillan wrote in his diary. 'Feel paranoid – I can't go on.' He returned to London to see his psychiatrist, and to give an interview to the *Guardian* as publicity for the production. 'We have all become very affected by the play,' he told Paul Allen. 'We're all in deep gloom, though that may be because we are working long hours. But within the pessimism there's a great deal of life in the play, a kicking and struggling to be alive. And in the kicking and struggling there's an enjoyment. And this is how life is; it isn't all a bed of roses.'

He went back to Manchester to do battle once again with his cast. 'Disastrous run-through with audience,' he noted in his diary after the first preview performance. 'They thought it was a comedy.' The leading actors had resorted to playing *The Dance of Death* for laughs. Jill Bennett was particularly cruel to Sue Burton as the maid, scoring easy sniggers by dismissing her abruptly before she could say her few lines in full view of the audience. The weekend before the premiere, Bennett asked Burton to arrange a car to take all four members of the cast back to London for a break; when the car arrived outside their hotel, Bennett and Fox got in and told the chauffeur to drive them away. Burton and Peter Baldwin were left stranded in Manchester, having let their hotel rooms go.

The press night went with few mishaps, but at the celebratory dinner afterwards Bennett became drunk and abusive. Unhappy with her performance, she had evidently been topping up her alcohol intake throughout the play. She was so foul-mouthed about Kenneth that Deborah threatened to break her jaw; the party ended in disarray as Bennett was forcibly escorted back to her hotel room. *The Dance of Death* marked the disastrous end of her working relationship with MacMillan. She had originally intended him to collaborate with her on a second play, Tennessee Williams's *Kingdom of Earth*, for which he had bought the rights. He decided to do it without her – if he could bring himself to direct a play again.

Reviews for *The Dance of Death* were wan. Critics found the claustrophobic play resistant to staging in the round: the set by Laurie Dennett (costumes were by Barry Kay) obscured vital parts of the action and prevented the actors from making contact with each other and the audience. Performances received more condemnation than praise. 'Miss Bennett and Mr Fox circle each other warily, landing a few jabs here and there, but hardly the body punches required to influence the outcome of a heavyweight contest. Mr Fox fails to unleash the Captain's virulent, tortured anguish and even, surprisingly in these circumstances, makes a hash of the Hungarian dance,' wrote Michael Coveney in the *Financial Times*, while Robert Hewison in *The Sunday Times* commented, 'Jill Bennett does command attention, but she too is unable to create the emotional tension with her partners which would be physically present were this truly a ballet. And that shows where the fault lies. MacMillan has not used the experience gained in one sphere to compensate for his inexperience in another. The dance never truly begins.' Reporting on the production as a coda to a dance review in the *Observer*, I noted that the play was essentially a protracted pas de deux for husband and wife, with an outsider (Kurt) who is reluctantly caught up in the action. Since the leading pair's unease was palpable, I concluded, 'MacMillan's dancers would surely show more physical commitment than his actors do.'

Although *The Dance of Death* had been a painful experience, directing Strindberg's play had reawakened MacMillan's interest in Expressionist theatre. He bought a copy of Georg Büchner's *Woyceck*, a precursor of the Expressionist movement and often described as the first modern play. He had initially known of the play through Alban Berg's use of it for the libretto of his opera, *Wozzeck*. Berg's opera had caused a tremendous stir at the Royal Opera House when it was first performed there in 1952, a period when MacMillan, in his early twenties, had attended every performance he could in the theatre. The designer was Brecht's frequent collaborator, Caspar Neher. British opera-goers' reactions to their first exposure to *Wozzeck* had been wildly diverse: in letters to the press, some described it as the greatest theatrical experience of their lives; others dismissed it as meaningless twaddle. The Royal Opera House revelled in the controversy and continued to perform the same production over the years, including three seasons during MacMillan's directorship of the Royal Ballet. *Wozzeck* was due to return in the Caspar Neher designs in January 1984.

MacMillan might also have seen Büchner's play in performance. A Berlin production first came to London in 1957, and there was a spate of experimental productions during the 1970s, including a much publicised one by Charles Marowitz at the Open Space. After reading different versions of the text, unfinished when Büchner died at the age of twenty-three, MacMillan decided that instead of trying to direct the play, he would use it as the subject of his next ballet. The eventual title would be *Different Drummer*.

Büchner had based the plot on a real-life murder case: a low-ranking German soldier, Johann Christian Woyceck, had been executed in Leipzig in 1824 for killing his mistress in a jealous frenzy. Woyceck had made legal history by being subjected to a lengthy medical examination to establish whether he was fit to stand trial. The doctor's findings about his unstable state of mind and his miserable life had been published in a pompously worded report from which Büchner drew much of his material. As a result, the play was part documentary realism, part poetic licence, its structure fragmented into short scenes held together by themes that obsessed Büchner. These had great resonance for MacMillan: Woyceck, the vulnerable underdog, is pitted against the system, in this case the army; pushed over the edge into insanity, he is at the mercy of pseudo-scientists in white coats; betrayed by the woman he loves, he kills her while suffering the torments of the damned. Events in Büchner's nightmarish drama are seen through Woyceck's eyes, a device MacMillan could use to good effect through visual imagery in a ballet, as he had in the one-act version of *Anastasia*.

Indeed, his worry, expressed in his diary, was that he might be seen to be 'ploughing the same furrow'. But as he had said before, once an idea for a ballet had taken hold of him, he had to do it. He was acutely aware of the pro- and anti-militarism aroused by the 1982 Falklands War, and the resulting surge of popular sentiment that had returned Mrs Thatcher to power for a second term in 1983. Through Woyceck's suffering, he could give vent to his father's resentment of the army in the First World War, which reduced its lowest ranks to military pawns. William MacMillan, poison-gassed, had also deeply distrusted the army doctors who determined which men were fit to serve in the trenches. And William's rage at his daughter Jean's activities with off-duty soldiers in wartime Yarmouth had parallels with Woyceck's uncontrollable jealousy over his mistress Marie's affair with a Drum Major. In Büchner's play, Woyceck sees his fellow soldiers carousing with camp followers and howls, 'Flesh, filth, man, woman – they're all at it out in the open, on the back of the hand like flies.'

Woyceck, beside himself, kills the person he loves – a recurring theme in MacMillan's ballets. His own sense of guilt at the impulse to hurt and betray is evident in such works as *Cain and Abel, My Brother, My Sisters, Mayerling* and his last ballet, *The Judas Tree*. As Woyceck says to Marie in Büchner's play, 'Every man is an abyss. You get dizzy when you look down.' In adapting the play for his own purposes, MacMillan was once again splitting himself in two: he could identify both with instinctive, faithless Marie and angst-ridden, out-of-step Woyceck, who suffers panic fears, sees visions and hears voices from under the ground.

The ballet's title, *Different Drummer*, came from a Thoreau quotation suggested by Deborah: 'If a man does not keep pace with his companions, perhaps it is because he hears a different drummer. Let him step to the music he hears, however measured or far away.' The quote, which was used as a programme note for the ballet, was a clue that MacMillan intended his version of Woyceck's story as a plea for compassion for the misunderstood individual. By choosing Schoenberg's *Verklärte Nacht (Transfigured Night)* as his music, with its theme of forgiveness and lush romantic conclusion, he was evidently considering the promise of redemption for Woyceck and Marie after their wasted lives were over.

After stabbing Marie to death, Woyceck commits suicide by drowning himself. In the 1984 ballet, both their corpses were wheeled across the stage on mortuary trolleys, prepared for autopsy: the programme synopsis stated, 'Even in death, the victims' bodies will be in the service of their inhumane masters.' The two dancers, however, reappeared together in the final moments, freed of their body-double corpses, and the music's ending implied their souls were united after death. Since neither the play nor the opera ends with the unhappy lovers' reconciliation in eternity, MacMillan's introduction of a reassuring apotheosis was an unexpected choice. He had done the same in *Orpheus*, whose scenario, written by Stravinsky for his ballet score, ends without the lovers' reunion. MacMillan, castigated by his critics as a purveyor of doom and gloom, was consoling himself and his audiences with an affirmation of belief in the power of a work of art to outlast death.*

He had planned initially to use the Schoenberg on its own for a chamber ballet in a claustrophobic setting. The action would be centred on the medical officer's clinic in the barracks where Woyceck was experimented upon. The clinic would also serve as an ablution block where Woyceck shaved his commander with a cut-throat razor. MacMillan discussed his ideas with Yolanda Sonnabend, who prepared set designs for a white-tiled laboratory with a bath, and walls through which blood would seep down in rivulets. Behind the walls was a devastated landscape, in which soldiers could be seen on military tasks.

Two months after starting to choreograph the ballet (on 23 November 1983), MacMillan changed his intentions. He wanted to open out the setting and include far more activity within the encampment, so that Woyceck's increasing isolation could be contrasted with busy crowd scenes. He needed extra music, so he added Webern's brief *Passacaglia*, Op. 1, for the start of the ballet: the combination of composers, Webern and Schoenberg, was the same as for *My Brother, My Sisters*. In *Different Drummer*, Webern's opening music was to represent reality, exposing Woyceck's humiliations in front of the other soldiers. Schoenberg's *Verklärte Nacht* then expresses Woyceck's inner life as he withdraws from his inhumane treatment at the hands of the army and his betrayal by his common-law wife, Marie. He experiences hallucinations, is tempted to kill and eventually does so in a demented attempt to end his suffering.

Wayne Eagling had been cast as Woyceck, Stephen Jefferies as the Drum Major and Alessandra Ferri as Marie. Still only twenty, she was required to take on the multiple attributes of virgin and whore, mother and adulteress, betrayer and victim. Marie,

---

* In his 1992 revival of *Different Drummer* for the Berlin Ballet, MacMillan changed the ending: the alterations were subsequently incorporated into the Royal Ballet's revivals in 1993 and 2007. Only one body is wheeled across the stage, with the doctor on top, cutting it open; Woyceck's troubled ghost walks precariously along a railway line at the rear of the set. There is no longer a *Swan Lake* apotheosis for the doomed pair of lovers.

the mother of an illegitimate child, has no hope of a settled future with Woyceck. At first she rejects the lustful Drum Major, then lets herself be seduced by him because she cannot see why not: as far as she is concerned, she has little to lose. In a brief scene in the play (and opera), she turns to the Bible and worries over the woman taken in adultery, reading the passage about Mary Magdalene anointing the feet of Jesus, and longing for her own redemption. It is no coincidence that Marie's name is that of the Virgin and the Magdalene.

MacMillan made visual use of the biblical references by having Woyceck 'see' Marie drying a soldier's feet with her hair as though in an hallucination. The semi-naked man, who makes several brief appearances, wears a crown of thorns and twice holds Marie in a crucified position. The religious imagery extends to Woyceck, who is supported at the start of the *Verklärte Nacht* music by his friend Andres (Guy Niblett in the original cast) as if in a pietà. Other visual reminders of the play appear – a severed head, Woyceck placing his ear to the ground as though listening to sounds beneath the earth. Such allusions would be lost on anyone who did not know Büchner's text, but MacMillan was assuming that audiences would supply their own interpretations of Woyceck's surreal visions. Ballet was better than dialogue, he believed, at conveying dreams and delusions that had nothing to do with reason.

Different Drummer's premiere was due on 24 February 1984. At the start of the year, MacMillan agonised in his diary, 'Petrified of my ballet. Can't do it. Feel helpless.' As usual, he had started with the key pas de deux, first between Woyceck and Marie, then Marie and the Drum Major. When he expanded the corps to include large numbers of soldiers and camp followers, Sonnabend's designs, commissioned four months earlier, were no longer suitable. During the first stage rehearsal with the sets and some of the costumes, he turned to Monica Mason, who sitting next to him in the stalls, and confided, 'I'm going to have to do something terrible. I'll have to tell Yolanda that I don't want the set, not any of it. My ballet has changed so completely.'

He explained his change of mind about the set to Sonnabend, in the presence of Mason and Norman Morrice. 'Kenneth would never have left it to anyone else to tell her,' says Mason, refuting stories that she had been the one deputed to break the news to Sonnabend. Later in the day, MacMillan told Sonnabend that he wanted to get rid of the uniforms she had designed for the soldiers. Grey tracksuits replaced them. 'Yolanda was so upset that she said she'd have to leave the building,' remembers Mason. 'Kenneth said, "Yes, I completely understand. I'm really sorry." He was straightfoward – it was the only way to say it.' John B. Read, who was required to relight the production at short notice, comments,

He could be absolutely ruthless about his ballets. He had an inner vision of what he wanted but he couldn't articulate it until almost the last minute. You had to have an intuitive feel for the look he was after. He'd agree with what you'd done, and then the next day he'd come and say, 'I hate it, I want it all changed.' Yolanda had got out of touch with his idea of the piece and he couldn't tell her why it was all wrong.

Sonnabend felt humiliated. The last-minute cancellation of her designs implied that she was at fault, in spite of a Royal Ballet press release explaining that MacMillan's concept of the ballet had changed during its creation. She kept silent, refusing to speak to journalists who tried to whip up a story about the cost of the cancelled set and costumes, thereby accusing the Opera House of inefficiency and extravagance.* She accepted that their ideas had diverged, 'as happens in the theatre' (and had happened to her before when MacMillan changed his plans for the Fania Fénelon ballet) but she still prefers not to discuss what passed between her and MacMillan when she protested to him about the damage to her reputation.

On the opening night, *Different Drummer* was performed on a virtually bare stage. MacMillan had resorted to the solution he had found for *Anastasia* in Berlin: propping up flats from an opera currently in the repertoire against the bare back wall of the stage, kept in place with sandbags. Coincidentally, rows of arches for the set of *Andréa Chenier* suggested a barracks as well as the 'no place' of Woyceck's inner world. Characters moving around the periphery before making their formal entrances added to the feeling

---

* The Royal Opera House programme credits would include an acknowledgement of thanks from MacMillan for Sonnabend's 'contribution to the creation of this ballet'.

of oppression. Ferri remarked that the absence of a set enabled the principal dancers to concentrate on their 'interior path – the action in our minds'.

An incongruous relic of Sonnabend's original set was the cast-iron bathtub in which Woyceck drowned himself, washing his hands of blood and pulling down its lid after he got in. Its all-too-solid presence was not the stuff of which transfiguring tragedy could be made, unlike Caspar Neher's sombre lakeside setting and blood-red moon for Berg's opera. The banality of Woyceck's death in the ballet led critics to describe the bath-tub suicide as 'plain silly'. The apotheosis that followed, Woyceck and Marie watching their shrouded corpses being wheeled away, was further criticised for its Hollywood-like sentimentality, implausibly capping scenes of unremitting horror.

MacMillan's fears that he was ploughing the same furrow were fulfilled by comments such as 'the sex 'n' violence formula' (*New Statesman*). Even though reviewers found plenty of fault with *Different Drummer*, several recommended it should be seen 'by people who think ballet is just *Swan Lake*' (in repertoire at the same time) as a brave Expressionist study. His choreography for Woyceck and Marie (and the performances by Eagling and Ferri) drew appreciative accounts. 'The breath-taking acrobatic lifts do not here, as perhaps elsewhere in MacMillan's work, appear gratuitous. They are dictated by the music and the risk involved is a translation of Marie's domestic dependence on Woyceck. Her estrangement from him and her wantonness is also conveyed through nuances of movement: Ferri's arching away and the steely splitting of her beautiful legs' – like 'twin compasses' – 'seem to image her inclination to roam', as Julie Kavanagh put it in the *Spectator*.

For Nicholas Dromgoole in the *Sunday Telegraph*,

The power and force of the ballet – and power and force welled up from its murky depths in frightening consistency – lay in the stream of dance images that MacMillan created for each situation. Compelling in themselves, they gave us fresh insight as each incident added to our understanding . . . It is a frightening statement about the human condition that haunts the mind long after the curtain has fallen.

Clement Crisp found parallels with the darkest choreography in MacMillan's previous ballets – the last act of *Anastasia*, the grieving duet for Isadora Duncan and Paris Singer, the concentration-camp scenes in *Valley of Shadows* – as 'indications of his ability to find movement that becomes the physical essence of suffering'.

Unusually, instead of commenting on the critics' responses in his diary, MacMillan drew a line after *Different Drummer*'s first night. 'Now to the play!' he wrote. Michael Attenborough, who had just been appointed Artistic Director of the Hampstead Theatre in North London, had agreed that MacMillan should produce Tennessee Williams's *Kingdom of Earth* in April 1984. The 1967 play, originally called *The Seven Descents of Myrtle*, had never been professionally performed in Britain. MacMillan had secured the rights two years previously, when Jill Bennett had first proposed he should direct it, with herself in the leading role of Myrtle. Once *Different Drummer* had had its premiere, he started auditions to find another actress for the part.

Williams's late play has only three characters, two brothers and a woman. The melodramatic plot involves a struggle to the death between the men for possession of a farmhouse in the Mississippi Delta. The rundown 'estate' is in an area about to be engulfed by the overflowing river. Lot, the sensitive brother who is dying of tuberculosis, returns home to ensure that his low-life half-brother, Chicken, cannot claim his inheritance. Lot has just married Myrtle, a former showgirl, whom he barely knows. He requires her to seduce Chicken in order to get hold of a document giving him ownership. As the Mississippi rises inexorably, the audience waits to discover whether Myrtle will be drowned, raped or make her escape to the roof of the doomed farmhouse.

She is the most positive element in the play, courageous and optimistic. Otherwise, *Kingdom of Earth* parades a catalogue of characteristics common to Williams and MacMillan: humiliation and corruption, men's brutality towards women as well as each other, guilt, sexual betrayal. In the end, Lot expires in a final paroxysm, dressed in his dead mother's clothes; Chicken, the coarse, macho man, inherits the land; Myrtle, who is both Eve and Lilith, survives alongside him. Williams declared that in the play he was eliminating the 'wispy, willowy women' of his earlier writing – Laura from *The Glass Menagerie*, Blanche from *A Streetcar Named Desire*. *Kingdom of Earth* was intended to be a black comedy as well as a Gothic tragedy of the decaying South.

MacMillan had cast David Taylor (who had appeared in *The Seven Deadly Sins*) as Lot; from auditions, he chose the Irish actor Stephen Rea as Chicken; Nicola McAuliffe was surprised to be offered the part of Myrtle after her first reading:

Kenneth saw in me something I wasn't aware of – a pulling power that has nothing to do with looks, though I didn't know that then. I'd thought of myself as a bit of a lump but he sensed a delicacy that he managed to bring out. He gave me this wonderful image of how he wanted Myrtle's hands to be, like a tiny lizard's claws which you hardly feel when it touches you. So I had my battered nails extended and painted – it was a physical approach that really worked for me.

She was fascinated by the way MacMillan sat during rehearsals:

All folded up, like a stick insect, his legs crossed with the calves absolutely parallel. He wore the most terrible trousers and inelegant shoes with crêpe soles. He didn't care what he looked like – he certainly wasn't radiating sexuality like Myrtle.

McAuliffe was aware of his insecurity as a director:

He was an open wound, waiting to be hurt, which can bring out the worst in an actor who's also feeling insecure. When he was challenged by anyone, he'd withdraw and clam up instead of confronting the problem. He almost asked to be bullied – and one of the actors did – but if you helped him, he'd blossom. He could be very funny, in an elliptical, round-the-corner sort of way.

MacMillan was under pressure to deliver a success for the start of Michael Attenborough's regime at Hampstead. The theatre's reputation far exceeded its small size; its plays were regularly reviewed in national newspapers and magazines. Because *Kingdom of Earth* was new to Britain, there was particular interest in the production: the cast and management team were understandably nervous. MacMillan went through his usual agonies, convinced there would be harsh reproaches if his production flopped. It did not, though the critical consensus was that the play was late rather than great Tennessee Williams. The emphasis in most reviews was on the play itself and the persistence of Williams's themes rather than on MacMillan's direction. Little or no mention was made of his career in ballet – probably the greatest compliment he could be paid as a drama director. Milton Shulman in the *Evening Standard* was so unaware of MacMillan's fame as a choreographer that he mis-named him at the end of an appreciative review: 'The spiritual stench of these decaying souls is evident in Terence MacMillan's brooding production.'

The three actors received their share of plaudits, as did Laurie Dennett's ingenious designs for the cramped stage. MacMillan was again disconcerted by the actors' assumption that once the play was launched, they were in charge of the production. He was accus-tomed to dancers being far more obedient to his wishes, especially if he were out front, watching every performance. He kept the stage manager's show reports during the run, which included such com-ments as: 'Miss McAuliffe and Mr Rea corpsed as a member of the audience kept saying, "Tch, tch, tch, this is disgusting!" Otherwise, very jolly audience, though I think they were quite shocked at the blowjob as they went awfully quiet.' MacMillan had staged the sex scene between Myrtle and Chicken more discreetly than in some of his ballets: 'Stephen was sitting on a table with his hands over his crotch, and I had to lean over him as the lights went down,' McAuliffe recalls. 'That's all, though sometimes he held a chocolate biscuit or a baby carrot there to make me laugh.' Some nights a handful of people walked out; on other nights the cast had to cope with gigglers in the audience as well as their own corpsing. The run ended a week earlier than scheduled.

MacMillan had meanwhile turned his attention to the Royal Ballet's latest revival of his *Romeo and Juliet*. After working with actors and absorbing how they achieved their effects, he had grown concerned that *Romeo and Juliet* had become stale, performed by dancers he considered past their best. He had told several principals (David Wall, Merle Park, Derek Rencher, Michael Coleman) that they were no longer to dance their habitual roles in the ballet: 'An unpleasant task,' he noted in his diary – for him but even more so for the often fragile egos of the performers. Ruthless, as always, about his ballets, he did not break the news in the most diplomatic of ways. On 2 May 1984, after Wendy Ellis had just finished a per-formance as Juliet, he went to her dressing-room and informed her that she was never to dance the role again.

Ellis was the girlfriend (later wife) of Michael Somes, whose mar-riage to Antoinette Sibley had ended in divorce in 1973. Somes, who had a notoriously hot temper, was so infuriated by MacMillan's insensitivity that he hit out at him, pushing him out of the dressing-room. News of the hitting and shoving reverberated through the Royal Ballet's ranks and reached the gossip columns of the press: 'It's Battle Royal at the Ballet,' reported the *Daily Star* on 22 June 1964. 'Fists flew as two of the biggest names in ballet fought a backstage battle at Covent Garden.' The story, picked up by other newspapers, coincided with the Royal Ballet's annual press conference. Questions about a punch-up and Somes's subsequent sacking were side-stepped by Norman Morrice. He announced that Somes, by now past retirement age at sixty-six, had left the company after being associated with it for fifty years: 'The manner of his departure is just life in the theatre. We're going to miss him because of his great gifts but companies do go on – things do change.' John Tooley concurred: 'In any institution of this kind there comes a moment when collaboration with one particular individual or several individuals becomes difficult or even impossible.'

MacMillan made no comment to the press, confiding to his diary that he was still shaken several days after the 'assault'. Somes contacted Robin Stringer at the *Daily Telegraph*, insisting that the confrontation had been blown up out of all proportion: 'It was a heated artistic argument during which no blows had been struck. I did push Sir Kenneth but I did want him to hear me out.' Somes claimed that the real reason for his dismissal was his disagreement with the direction the company had been taking for the previous two years under Norman Morrice's direction; the confrontation with MacMillan was simply 'the final shove'. Somes's rupture with the Royal Ballet lasted for two years, until Anthony Dowell, newly appointed as Artistic Director, invited him back as guest répétiteur for a revival of Ashton's *Symphonic Variations* in September 1986.

Ferri, very much MacMillan's favourite dancer, was to be Juliet when the revival was recorded for the BBC (and Covent Garden Video) in August, with Eagling as her Romeo. Before then, MacMillan created a pas de deux for her and David Wall to perform at a gala tribute on 24 June 1984 to Anton Dolin, who had died the previous year. The romantic duet, to music from the second movement of Poulenc's Piano Concerto, had simple designs by Deborah: painted bodytights and a skirt for Ferri, who was manipulated by Wall so that she resembled a Bendy Toy (a children's craze at the time) rather than a woman in love. Since her feet scarcely touched the ground, the duet seemed more of an acrobatic *adagio* act than a pas de deux. MacMillan was exploiting Ferri's extreme suppleness in a way that worried de Valois, by now in her mid-eighties. She would soon voice her objections to what she saw as undesirable tendencies in ballet – objections that MacMillan would take personally.

45

Charlotte was coming up to the age of eleven, when decisions would need to be made about her secondary education. She had been attending the French Lycée in South-West London but did not want to continue studying in French. Her parents had considered the French school system suitable in case Kenneth's career took the family abroad for a lengthy time; she could then transfer to another lycée without losing ground. But she had found herself at a disadvantage alongside pupils who spoke French at home as well as at school. The question was whether she should prepare for entrance exams to a fee-paying secondary school (rather than go to a local state school) or whether she might enter the Royal Ballet School instead.

She was physically gifted as a dancer, with long, supple limbs and high-arched feet like her father's. She had always enjoyed moving to music, inventing her own dances. Once, when her mother came to pick her up from a children's basic ballet class, she saw Charlotte improvising in a corner, ignoring the teacher and the rest of the obedient pupils. 'I hope they weren't thinking, "What a terrible spoilt brat", but I bet they were,' says Charlotte in hindsight. 'Members of the company would indulge me when I showed off because they wanted to please my father, but I wasn't aware of that till later.'

Her father wanted her properly taught, in case, like him, she decided to become a dancer. She went to twice-weekly ballet classes at a school run by a former Royal Ballet dancer, Diana Vere, but didn't take any examinations until near the time for her to try for the Royal Ballet Lower School at eleven. She passed the Royal Academy of Dancing Grade One with Honours, as her father had in Retford, and was sent to Merle Park's ballet school in Knightsbridge to prepare for the audition for White Lodge (the Lower School's premises in Richmond Park). At the same time, she left the French Lycée and went to a 'crammer', a tutorial course to bring her academic subjects up to the standard required for entrance to London secondary schools with good academic records. Her parents were covering all eventualities, aware that Charlotte's life was about to alter course.

So was her father's. Even as Kenneth worried about the probable cost of his daughter's future education, he was approached with a money-earning offer. Mikhail Baryshnikov, in London making the film *White Nights* at Elstree studios in the spring of 1984, telephoned him with a proposition. American Ballet Theatre wanted MacMillan on board in an advisory capacity; the fee and the nature of the post (and its title) were to be negotiated over the coming months. Baryshnikov and his assistant at ABT, Charles France, came to talk terms over dinner at Spencer Park Road.

There had been huge upheavals at ABT during Baryshnikov's first period as Artistic Director, resulting in what France called a 'traumatic catharsis' at the end of 1983. The Board of Trustees, of whom Nora Kaye was one, were unhappy with the way their Russian appointee had been running the company – or not running it, in their view, because Baryshnikov was so often absent, involved with other commitments. France was left in charge; he was an immensely large, abrasive presence, whose autocratic manner and power by proxy were resented. 'Charles was the one who always broke the bad news – he was the bad cop to Misha's good cop,' said Susan Jones, one of the ballet mistresses. Baryshnikov was meanwhile unhappy with what he saw as the Board's failure to understand how he was trying to modernise the company and its repertoire. He had promoted young dancers from the corps in preference to ABT's usual star system; he was introducing work by contemporary choreographers such as Merce Cunningham, Paul Taylor, David Gordon and Karole Armitage, who were considered off-puttingly avant-garde by traditionalists.

By the end of the company's 1983 season at the Met in New York, with the house at only 60 per cent capacity, ABT faced a $1.8 million deficit. The Chairman of the Board of Trustees, Herman Krawitz, resigned, followed by the company's Executive

Director. Their successors, Melville (Micky) Straus as Chairman, financially responsible for the company's funding, and Charles Dillingham as its overseer, feared ABT was going down a perilous route. They decreed that a corporate management ethos should replace the company's old theatrical tradition of keeping the show going on a wing and a prayer. Swingeing economic cutbacks were introduced: ABT's training school was closed in 1982 and its junior company, ABT II, was due to follow. New business sponsors needed to be found and once loyal subscribers wooed back with narrative ballets based on classical technique. Instead of experimental modern works using a small number of dancers, the full company should be presented in spectacular productions of MacMillan's three-act ballets: above all, the Board wanted his *Romeo and Juliet*. As well as acquiring a licence to mount *Romeo and Juliet*, Nora Kaye and Oliver Smith (who had been Co-Director with Lucia Chase before Baryshnikov's appointment) were pushing for MacMillan himself to be closely involved with the company.

Baryshnikov had grown so frustrated with trying to run the company along the lines he wanted that he had offered to resign. He had agreed to stay on, at a token salary of $1 a year, provided he had additional artistic and managerial help. First of all, John Taras was wooed away from New York City Ballet, where he had spent the last eleven years as joint ballet master (with Balanchine and Robbins), to become ABT's Associate Director alongside Baryshnikov. Taras was put in charge of managing the company's day-to-day affairs, while MacMillan was offered the non-specific role of Adviser. The job could be tailored to whatever MacMillan determined, provided he brought his expertise and his ballets to ABT. His knighthood and artistic reputation would impress Board members and potential donors; the dancers and coaches would benefit from his knowledge and experience, as well as having access to his choreography. It was intended that he should make new ballets for the company, in addition to mounting more of his existing works – especially the three-act ones. ABT had already danced his *Pavane* and pas de deux from *Solitaire*, *Romeo and Juliet*, *Anastasia* (Act II) and *Manon*, as well as its own productions of *Concerto* and *Las Hermanas*.

The advantage for MacMillan would be a higher profile in the United States as his major ballets entered ABT's repertoire and were widely seen on tour. He would have the international status of being closely involved with a great American company, which was more than his Royal Ballet predecessors had. He could enjoy the creative stimulus of a different troupe of well-trained dancers, and present his work to audiences with less jaundiced eyes than those at home. Since his recent ballets had met with markedly little enthusiasm at the Royal Opera House, ABT's proposal represented an opportunity to start afresh. A substantial financial inducement was involved. MacMillan, according to his diary entry, was startled by the amount his lawyer, Michael Oliver, who dealt with his contracts, was demanding on his behalf: $100,000 plus first-class air fare every time he crossed the Atlantic. (When ABT's management drew the line at supersonic travel by Concorde because of the expense, MacMillan paid the extra himself. For him, Concorde seemed a necessity, not a luxury. The three-and-a-half hour flight spared him jetlag and limited the duration of the anxiety he endured in the air.)

While the clauses of his contract with ABT were still being negotiated, MacMillan flew (by Concorde) to New York. He was going to mount *Triad* for the company and acquaint himself with the dancers by watching class and performances of other ballets in the repertoire. He had intended Natalia Makarova to take on the role of the *Triad* girl, since she wanted to expand her repertoire with ABT. When she decided it was not for her, he cast the very young Amanda McKerrow instead, with Robert La Fosse and Johan Renvall as the two brothers. During the rehearsal period, although he dined out most nights with old friends and ABT staff members, he felt lonely and uneasy. 'Dreaming of Berlin the whole time,' he confided in his diary. He fretted over whether he was once again letting himself in for a trying experience, thrown back on his own resources, far from home.

Back in London, he talked over his worries with Deborah. On the one hand, he did not look forward to being frequently away from her and Charlotte; on the other, the money would give them the economic freedom to choose whatever form of education might suit their daughter best. Neither had any political objections about choosing the private rather than the state sector. Kenneth, who now voted Conservative, had benefited as a boy from the selective grammar-school system that scarcely existed any longer. He wanted the best available schooling for his only child. His future arrangements with the Royal Ballet could not be guaranteed, so it would be useful to strengthen his association with ABT. He and Deborah, as the MacMillan Partnership, decided he should commit to the contract with ABT. Kenneth went to see John Tooley on 23 June: 'Told Tooley of my new title of Associate Adviser with ABT. He didn't bat an eyelid!'

As far as the Royal Ballet was concerned, MacMillan's transatlantic post appeared to make little difference. His contract as principal choreographer had always stipulated that he could work elsewhere. When the question was asked (by John Percival) at the Royal Ballet's press conference in June, whether MacMillan was about to 'defect' to ABT, Tooley replied, 'Defection is absolutely wrong. What Kenneth is actually talking about is a few weeks per year, and literally weeks rather than months.' The Royal Opera House had raised no objection: there would be difficulties in planning future tours of the United States only if many of MacMillan's ballets were in the repertoire of an American company, and according to Tooley, so far only one full-length ballet, *Romeo and Juliet*, had been agreed. Percival then queried why MacMillan appeared to be making no new works for the Royal Ballet in the 1984–85 season. Norman Morrice replied, 'Sir Kenneth did not want to do a ballet this year, because he wants a year to prepare *The Prince of the Pagodas*, which he will be mounting for us the following season.'

(Morrice was over-optimistic. There were continuing problems over who should provide a new *Pagodas* scenario. MacMillan's latest candidate, the children's writer Roald Dahl, had declined the offer. The hunt went on, while *Pagodas* was postponed, yet again, to the 1986–87 season – possibly for October 1986. The Royal Opera House Board was meanwhile wondering whether the ballet should be offered to another choreographer to prevent further delays.)

During the summer of 1984, the ABT mafia, as MacMillan called them in his diary, came over to London, full of enthusiasm for his new role with them. It had been decided that he was to be called Artistic Associate. There were frequent dinners, at home and in favourite restaurants, with Nora Kaye and Herbert Ross, Charles France and Charles Dillingham, Susan Jones, the ballet mistress, and Baryshnikov. 'When I was dancing in London for first few years, I wondered always why Kenneth didn't want to speak with me,' says Baryshnikov. 'We didn't even have cup of tea or coffee together when he was Director. He just gave me corrections in rehearsal. We only got to talk in more relaxed way afterwards, when he agreed to come to ABT.' Although their working relationship at the time of *Wild Boy* had been fraught, they got on well during the summer in London, which convinced MacMillan that he had made the right decision. Baryshnikov appeared to welcome the prospect of sharing some of his artistic responsibilities. He said he hoped MacMillan would sit in on auditions and advise on programme choices and choreographic workshops as well as supervising rehearsals and performances of his own ballets. Rather less to MacMillan's taste, he could assist the management by attending Board meetings and galas as a senior figurehead when Baryshnikov was absent.

Agreement had been reached that ABT would mount its own production of *Romeo and Juliet* at the start of 1985, with as many different casts as the company could field. The production would be essentially the same as the Royal Ballet's, taught by MacMillan's regular notator, Monica Parker. Georgina Parkinson, who had had her own experience of dancing in it from the mid-1960s, would coach the leading roles. Although adapting Georgiadis's sumptuous designs, which had not originally been intended for touring, was bound to be costly, the Board was confident that the ballet's box-office appeal would recoup the expense.

The ABT mafia watched the Royal Ballet's performances of *Romeo and Juliet* in Covent Garden and talked to backstage staff, apprising themselves of what their production would involve. They were present when the BBC recorded Alessandra Ferri as Juliet, with Wayne Eagling as her Romeo, for transmission at the end of the year. The performance, a special one for the television cameras set up in numerous places in the Royal Opera House, allowed for retakes when necessary which could be edited into the final version. The programme was released on video cassette and is currently available on DVD. MacMillan, as always, concerned himself closely with how his ballet was being filmed, sitting in with the BBC's experienced director, Colin Nears.

By now, Ferri had grown restless at the Royal Ballet, convinced that she was so identified with MacMillan's ballets that she was unlikely to be cast in other roles. Ashton no longer chose her for his ballets and the management evidently did not consider her a pure enough classical dancer for the nineteenth-century ballets in the repertoire. Hungry for experience, she was wondering whether she should follow MacMillan to ABT. Her mind not yet made up, she was considering rival offers, including one from Peter Schaufuss at London Festival Ballet, while giving guest performances in Franco Zeffirelli's *Swan Lake* for La Scala, Milan.

Shortly after the *Romeo and Juliet* recording in August, the MacMillans celebrated Charlotte's eleventh birthday by taking her to a musical, *42nd Street*, at the Theatre Royal Drury Lane, followed by a *thé dansant* the next afternoon at the Waldorf Hotel. The hotel, on the edge of Covent Garden, had reopened its palm-court dance floor, complete with small orchestra, during Saturday afternoon teatimes. Deborah's brother, Simon, and his wife had come over from Australia for a holiday and were staying at the Spencer Park house. They joined in the Waldorf Hotel birthday party, coaxing Charlotte on to the circular dance floor and taking turns partnering her in grown-up social dances to the band's nostalgic tunes.

The three MacMillans then went on a cruise of the Aegean, sailing on the SS *Orpheus* from Venice. Peter Wright and his wife Sonya had been on a similar cruise and recommended it for a summer break. The plan was to give Kenneth a rest and change of scene before he took up his ABT appointment in September. Although he enjoyed the trip, he noted his longing to return home in his diary, alongside an amused comment that Charlotte had danced with boys for the first time in the ship's ballroom.

They flew back from Naples in time for Kenneth to start work on dances for the Royal Opera's new production of Wagner's *Tannhäuser*. The producer, Elijah Moshinsky, had decided that he wanted MacMillan to choreograph the *Venusberg* revels in the way Baudelaire had interpreted the opening scene of the opera. The medieval knight, Tannhäuser, is held captive inside the magic mountain by the charms of Venus and her followers, until he summons the strength of will to tear himself away. Later tempted to return, he is finally saved by the love of a good woman. Wagner had intended his *Venusberg* music to summon up 'a wild yet seductive chaos of movements and groupings, of soft delight, of yearning and burning, carried to the most delirious pitch of frenzied riot'. Baudelaire, in his account of the opera, declared that Venus was ensconced in an underground cavern near to hell, where she ruled over all the she-devils, 'indestructible, irresistible, diabolically sensual', as they paid homage to the Archdemon, 'prince of the flesh and lord of sin'.

When MacMillan had first choreographed the *Venusberg* bacchanale for the Sadler's Wells Opera company back in 1956, he had caused a stir (and a banner headline in the *Daily Mirror*, demanding, 'Has the Lord Chamberlain Seen This?') with an abandoned orgy for nymphs and satyrs, performed by ballet dancers. Now he seized the opportunity to work with members of London Contemporary Dance Theatre, trained in Graham-based technique. Negotiations to release dancers from the LCDT company were protracted, but MacMillan eventually managed to secure Chris Bannerman, Linda Gibbs, Ross McKim and Kate Harrison.

He knew the effect he wanted to achieve, completing the choreography swiftly: 'He told us what we should do, rather than asking us to show him something of the sort we did in class,' remembers Gibbs. He intended them to resemble aliens, costumed in pale bodytights with a dark streak down their spines. Picked out of the surrounding gloom in spotlights, they went through the motions of copulating without passion, contorting themselves into fiendish, almost abstract shapes. The scene evoked Baudelaire's vision of hellish delights, in contrast to the sweetness and purity of the world above ground in the scene that followed. MacMillan's contribution was not appreciated by Wagner fans expecting something easier on the eye. 'Small wonder that Tannhäuser, voyeur rather than participant, wants to leave. But what tempts him back, if this cold carnality is all Venus has to offer?' I asked in the *Observer* of 7 October 1984.

MacMillan had so enjoyed working with the LCDT dancers that he offered to choreograph solos for them to perform in a fundraising gala at the Royal Opera House the following year. He devised the solos in between rehearsals for the opera, relying on the dancers to remember them. To his indignation, his *Venusberg* choreography was dropped from Moshinsky's production when it was revived three years later.

Immediately after *Tannhäuser*'s premiere, MacMillan flew to New York by Concorde on 27 September, and was hard at work rehearsing *Romeo and Juliet* throughout the next day. Inevitably, the choreography already taught to the dancers by Monica Parker and Georgina Parkinson differed slightly, so MacMillan's presence was essential to resolve arguments and make changes to suit the principal dancers. He decided that the Mercutio dancer should also perform the leading jester's role in the Act II mandolin dance, instead of giving it to another virtuoso soloist. Although the rehearsal period was intensive, Susan Jones remembers that he was excited about working with dancers who brought a fresh approach to the ballet: 'It was his best period with the company. We had a wonderful time and he seemed fulfilled, being able to mould dancers to find their own ways of interpreting the roles.'

Before he arrived, four couples had learned the lovers' roles, waiting for him to decide who would be first cast. He evidently had Leslie Browne in mind as Juliet, for Charles France had alerted her, in confidence, to get back into shape during the summer break. Not long after her unhappy experience with MacMillan's *Seven Deadly Sins* in London, she had taken leave of absence from the company, and from dancing, during 1983. She had returned to ABT with renewed determination and MacMillan, who had always appreciated her acting abilities, hoped she could be entrusted with the big opportunity of the opening night. She and Robert La Fosse gave up their summer holidays in order to work hard on the various *Romeo and Juliet* pas de deux, with Parkinson as their coach; they were overjoyed when their names went up on the board as the first cast. La Fosse, at twenty-four, had little experience of leading roles but MacMillan wanted a young Romeo, as Christopher Gable had been. This meant that senior ABT stars were bound to be disgruntled. 'Intrigue everywhere,' MacMillan wrote in his diary.

Kevin McKenzie confirms that there were injured feelings among the principals, although he, at least, was treated honourably. When he had previously approached MacMillan with a request to dance as a guest artist in the Royal Ballet's production of *Romeo and Juliet*, he had been told to wait until ABT acquired the ballet. He took this as an assurance that he would be in ABT's first cast. Instead: 'Kenneth took care to let me know in advance that my turn would come later. He told me about Lynn and Christopher feeling betrayed, and said that this time there were to be no bad surprises. All the same, some people were hurt and angry.'

MacMillan remained in New York until 18 October, staying at the Gramercy Park Hotel near ABT's headquarters. (April Olrich, visiting from London, was amused to find that the hotel receptionist, unused to British titles, had him listed as 'Sirk MacMillan'.) He dined most nights with friends, usually from the company: John Taras, Charles France, Georgina Parkinson and her husband, Susan Jones and the ballet master David Richardson. Jones remembers how a group of them, including La Fosse, would go round to Kenneth's room at the hotel to watch TV soaps with him, laughing themselves silly over each episode of *Dynasty*. 'We made sure to keep him company so that he wouldn't feel lonely,' Jones says. 'We knew how much he missed his family in London.' He and France discovered a shared passion for costume jewellery: France, an avid collector, took MacMillan to Sunday-morning street markets where the best finds were likely to be made. In the mid-1980s, prices were still reasonable for what later became highly prized collectors' items by designers such as Kenneth Lane and Miriam Haskell. Kenneth bought jewellery and beads that he intended to take home for Deborah.

He attended ABT Board and Sub-Committee meetings, giving his views without feeling as intimidated as he had at the Royal Opera House. According to France, the staff and Board members appreciated MacMillan's understanding of the workings of a ballet company, and how dancers needed to be challenged by new opportunities. The arrangement seemed to be working out well for everyone concerned. MacMillan went home for a month, due to return by Thanksgiving in November to supervise preparations for the production of *Romeo and Juliet* in the New Year.

He was back at the Royal Opera House in time for David Wall's farewell performance in *Mayerling* – an emotional occasion for the company as well as for Wall's loyal fans in the audience. Wall had chosen to retire at thirty-eight, while he was still in fine form for a role as demanding as Crown Prince Rudolf. MacMillan joined in the many repeated curtain calls, suffering an unexpected anxiety attack as he did so. He had started to associate curtain calls on the Covent Garden stage with muted or even hostile receptions for his ballets. The huge waves of applause at the end of *Mayerling*, for the ballet as well as for Wall, had caught him off guard. To calm himself in the days that followed, he made beads out of resin and strung them into necklaces with Deborah. She had taken a course in jewellery-making, and was experimenting with the shapes and colours of beads she could combine into necklaces and bracelets. Kenneth contributed his own choices until they had made so many that Deborah decided to see whether she could sell them. Kenneth would take a suitcaseful to New York and ask Charles France's advice about where to place them.

They had seized the opportunity of Charlotte's half-term break from her 'crammer' to take her on a quick trip to Paris before Kenneth was due to return to New York. They visited art exhibitions, went sightseeing and attended a performance by the Paris Opéra Ballet. Nureyev, who had become the company's Artistic Director the year before, was keen to broaden its repertoire. He invited MacMillan to watch the dancers in class as well as in performance, hoping he might consider working with them again.

Talking to Charles France by telephone before leaving for New York, MacMillan gleaned some information that the Royal Ballet had not yet announced: Anthony Dowell was being groomed as its next Artistic Director, deputising for Norman Morrice while continuing to dance with the company. Morrice had been debilitated by a viral disease he had contracted on the Royal Ballet's last tour of the Far East and was unable to work full time. In addition, it was common knowledge within the company and among critics and audience regulars that technical standards of dancing had fallen to an all-time low (Kisselgoff's praise in 1983 for the New York season notwithstanding). Revivals of Ashton's ballets in celebration of his eightieth birthday in September 1984 had exposed how poorly prepared the dancers were. Worse was to come in the New Year, when a misbegotten production of Balanchine's *Ballet Imperial* would provoke a spate of protest in the press. In the meantime, MacMillan noted in his diary the still-confidential news about Dowell as Morrice's replacement, adding many exclamation marks but making no comment.

MacMillan arrived in New York in mid-November to oversee *Romeo and Juliet* before its first night on tour at the Kennedy Center in Washington DC in January. Deborah and Charlotte joined him the day after his fifty-fifth birthday on 11 December. A further cause for celebration was Deborah's deal with Bendels, the up-market department store in New York, who had agreed to sell her hand-made necklaces in their fashion-jewellery section. The MacMillans then flew to Washington in time for Christmas and

New Year, with Kenneth growing increasingly anxious during the final rehearsals for *Romeo and Juliet*.

Although the ballet was well received on the first night, 3 January 1985, La Fosse as Romeo came in for harsh criticism. Anna Kisselgoff in the *New York Times* was not alone in finding that he and Browne were not strong enough to carry ABT's production, which reduced the story to 'duels and duets'. In her view, 'Mr La Fosse's soft limpness – he has possibly been told to be romantic – acts against the firebrand image he needs to establish at the outset.' La Fosse wrote in his autobiography, 'I had often wondered how performers dealt with devastating reviews. Now I knew . . . MacMillan reassured me, telling me to pay no attention.' MacMillan knew very well how hurtful such reviews could be and how hard it was to ignore them. He was convinced, as were most of the ABT staff, that the reason behind the criticism of La Fosse was an attack on Baryshnikov for performing only rarely himself. ABT was expected, by critics and public alike, to deliver star performers on opening nights – and Browne and La Fosse were hardly the American equivalent of Fonteyn and Nureyev twenty years earlier.

46

The year 1985 was to be one of commuting back and forth across the Atlantic as MacMillan fulfilled his ABT commitments. It was vital for the company's future that *Romeo and Juliet* should attract full houses on tour, and that the all-important New York season at the Met in April–May should be a success. Seven different pairings would dance the roles of Romeo and Juliet, displaying the strength and versatility of the company. ABT would also do the one-act version of *Anastasia* (the Berlin asylum act MacMillan had first mounted for the Deutsche Oper) for the first time. MacMillan had promised to start a new work for the following season, before the Royal Ballet claimed him back.

The constant travelling was stressful for him and for his family. His diaries reveal how he dreaded leaving home, working himself into a state of anxiety for many days beforehand. The household was caught up in his panicky preparations, as he insisted on rechecking his supplies of teabags (he couldn't bear American tea) as well as the prescription drugs on which he depended. Charlotte remembers his pockets clinking with pill bottles; Deborah mistrusted the number of prescriptions he convinced doctors he needed. 'He was trying to control his fear of depression, of being on his own in New York. He was always apprehensive. He couldn't live in the moment,' says Deborah. She had no success in her attempts to wean him off the sedatives he took. There was always the excuse of another trip or another ballet to prepare. 'And the doctors would intervene, saying, "Don't you see he *needs* the pills. You can't take them away from him."'

He had to return to ABT, on tour with *Romeo and Juliet* on the West Coast of the United States, when Charlotte did her two-day audition for the Royal Ballet Lower School. Competition for places is fierce, as ballet teachers and parents from all over the country send young hopefuls for appraisal. For Charlotte, the experience was traumatic:

Dad insisted I did the audition, so I couldn't ever say later I didn't have the chance. But I hated every minute of it. I felt like an alien, surrounded by all these obsessive girls desperate to get in. They were ballet mad, mispronouncing the names of dancers I already knew. I suddenly realised I wasn't in love with ballet. The examiners were all people I knew and I felt humiliated. If I was accepted, it could be because of Dad. I just thought, 'Sorry, this isn't for me.' Also, I was aware of the other side of ballet – the injuries, the short careers, the politics that upset Dad. For me, it wasn't a fantasy, like it was for other girls.

She abandoned ballet from that moment on. Her father came back to console her and to congratulate her on being accepted instead by More House, a Catholic single-sex school in South-West London, where she would stay until she was sixteen. He had no regrets about her decision not to become a dancer. Charlotte says that she was never aware in him of a passion for dancing or performing:

He didn't love moving. I think he loved the art of dance. His passion was this form of expression that went beyond words. For some people it's music or painting. He found it in dance – that pleasure of losing yourself, which is different from projecting yourself to an audience. He understood that I didn't want to do it.

For her, he had never been a particularly active figure:

He wasn't a throwing-ball kind of dad. He didn't suggest games to play. I was perfectly happy to lie on the sofa next to him watching television, or go to the cinema with him. Most of my activities, and my arguments when I was little, were with my mother. I remember overhearing somebody from of a family down the road saying, 'Her father knits and her mother does the gardening.' Obviously they thought it was extraordinary.

Kenneth's health was meanwhile giving cause for concern. He had been losing his voice – never loud – in rehearsals, and he had a worryingly persistent cough. His GP referred him to a consultant who arranged for a biopsy on his vocal cords. Terrified of cancer, Kenneth was greatly relieved when the biopsy revealed nothing malignant. His vocal cords were scraped clear and he was advised to have check-ups every three months to monitor his throat condition.

In April, he flew by Concorde to New York in advance of ABT's season at the Met. He was asked to give an interview to Anna Kisselgoff for a long article in the Sunday edition of the *New York Times*. The piece, which appeared on 21 April 1985, introduced him to New York readers as ABT's new Associate, while previewing its spring season with *Romeo and Juliet* as the main attraction. Kisselgoff started her article by declaring that MacMillan's 'potential impact on the American company as its de-facto resident choreographer' could be of crucial importance. She noted that although he was internationally renowned for his dramatic ballets, his recent works for the Royal Ballet had not been seen in the United States because they were shunned by American impresarios. *Different Drummer*, for example, had 'caused some balletomanes to use words like "revolting" ', thereby deterring presenters from taking the risk of taking it on tour. Americans had not been exposed to the full range of his work.

He said he regretted that 'a lot of critics think of me in terms of sexuality on stage'. His narrative ballets had often been misinterpreted, he claimed, since their main concern was not with sex but with 'the person destroyed by the social milieu'. Some (such as *Triad* and *The Invitation*) were about personal trauma; others (*Gloria* and *Valley of Shadows*) reflected the consequences of war. In his ballets about larger-than-life historical figures such as Isadora

Duncan and Crown Prince Rudolf, he protested, 'I don't go out of my way to show the sexual side [but] this side is important to their lives, and this is also 1985.'

He denied any suggestion that he had been recruited by ABT to counter the plotless ballets introduced under Baryshnikov's regime:

I haven't been brought in to do just dramatic ballets. I will do dramatic ballets and I will do so-called abstract ballets as well . . . I think I'm about to change. And this is because of the impetus of this company. It is not that the dancers are not good dramatically. They're excellent. But I detect a sort of energy I haven't found in Europe. There is a concentration on dance technique and the technique is astounding. It's brought back to me the original impetus I had about dance, as a dancer and in my early works – when I could feel the movement in my body.

He insisted that he was a classicist at heart, having grown up within a great classical company. He paid tribute to de Valois as a powerful mother figure during his formative years, commenting that, by the mid-1980s, most major ballet companies were run by male (ex-)dancers, all of them facing great difficulties as they tried to bring repertoires up to date. He must have been thinking of himself as well as Baryshnikov – and probably Anthony Dowell, the Royal Ballet director-in-waiting. His acknowledgement of de Valois's influence was all the more poignant as, within a month, he was to believe that she had publicly rejected him.

ABT's *Romeo and Juliet* was far better received at its New York premiere at the Met than it had been in Washington. Kisselgoff pronounced that it was now 'a complete success. Ballet Theatre has needed six months of rehearsal and performance to reach this point . . . practice has obviously made perfect.' The first cast was once again Browne and La Fosse. This time they were both acclaimed as convincingly ardent young lovers. Clive Barnes found that Browne's 'unexpectedly lyrical dancing carried all before it'. Later in the New York opening run Makarova was praised for her youthful Juliet, nine years after she had last danced MacMillan's ballet at the Met with the Royal Ballet. Baryshnikov gave a few performances as Romeo, the first time he had appeared on stage with the company since filming *White Nights* the year before.

While New York reviewers declared *Romeo and Juliet* a worthy addition to ABT's repertoire, MacMillan's one-act *Anastasia* met with critical derision. Cynthia Gregory danced the first performance at the Met to celebrate her twentieth anniversary with the company: 'Less an anniversary present than a booby prize,' declared Bill Zakariasen in the *New York Daily News*. In the *New York Post* Barnes agreed: 'Personally, I think a firing squad would be the kindest thing for this new *Anastasia*. Which, unlike the ballet, could be brief, humane and conclusive.' Deborah Jowitt, in the *Village Voice*, found 'some stunning ideas' but concluded, 'MacMillan cannot quite find a way to state in ballet terms the complex idea of Anastasia's desire to be recognized and reinstated; he can only show us a sensitive, troubled, perhaps insane woman.'

Kenneth had been joined by Deborah and Charlotte for a week over Easter, but he had to remain in New York to discuss his and ABT's future projects with the Board. By now, the company was deeper in debt, partly due to the expense of touring *Romeo and Juliet*, which had yet to recoup its cost. Board members were getting cold feet about ABT's bold plans to spend its way out of financial trouble. The budget for the following year was limited to $600,000, which meant that MacMillan's hopes of mounting a new production of *The Sleeping Beauty* would have to be postponed. He was given the go-ahead, though, for a new one-act work scheduled for early 1986. This, he assured the Board, would be a box-office winner, generating plenty of publicity wherever it toured.

He intended to use Andrew Lloyd Webber's *Requiem*, which he had heard on a recording at the composer's request in March. (The work's first concert performance had been in New York in February 1985 at St Thomas's Church, Manhattan, sung by Placido Domingo and Sarah Brightman, then Lloyd Webber's wife.) Cameron Mackintosh, who presented Lloyd Webber's musicals, had proposed MacMillan as the right choreographer to turn the *Requiem* into a ballet. Negotiations over the music would continue during the months to come, until agreement was reached in time for MacMillan to start work in October.

In May, reports had reached him in New York of an apparent attack on his work by de Valois at a meeting of the London Ballet Circle. Set up by a group of balletomanes after the war, the circle's soirées were usually members-only affairs. De Valois had, however, asked that dance critics be invited on a confidential basis to listen to her views on the state of ballet. She was deeply concerned about the

Royal Ballet's reputation, unhappy that its fall in standards was regularly deplored in reviews. She had taken to giving what she called 'survival classes' to young dancers to correct faults before they became habitual. A low point had been reached with a production of Balanchine's *Ballet Imperial* in February 1985, on the same programme as a revival of *Different Drummer*. The *Ballet Imperial* production had been condemned as a travesty both of Balanchine's intentions and of the once proud Royal Ballet, now accused of being in 'Imperial decline'. Norman Morrice, interviewed by Michael Owen in the London *Evening Standard* of 25 April, had shouldered the blame for 'lacklustre performances, a loss of the pure classical technique which had been the ensemble's hallmark, inadequately rehearsed ballets and a ragged and uneven corps de ballet'. He denied, however, that he intended to resign: Dowell's interim appointment as his successor (which MacMillan had learned about) was still being kept from the press, to be announced three months later. De Valois, to take the heat off Morrice, who, she knew, had been ill, wanted it known that she believed the accusing finger for the company's decline should be pointed primarily at modern-day choreographers. 'The ballet world and the contemporary dance world are getting too mixed up,' she declared in her opening statement.

Careful not to name names, she deplored the introduction of acrobatic 'contemporary' moves, especially ones that were likely to injure bodies trained for classical ballet. 'I am sick of people rolling round the floor in all-over tights, for this has led to an awful muddle going on, not just with the Royal, but throughout the whole world of ballet . . . I do not believe that when you mix the actual forms choreographically you get the best out of either.' She also made a point of criticising choreographers who, instead of commissioning scores, used existing music by different composers within the same ballet. Although her remarks about music could have applied to a number of choreographers (Maurice Béjart and Jiří Kylián among them), they were taken by many in her audience as being aimed directly at MacMillan – particularly since the recently revived *Different Drummer* was to music by Berg and Schoenberg.

Ann Nugent made the connection in her account of the meeting for the *Stage*, the weekly paper for the theatrical profession. Headed 'Founder Slams Royal Ballet's "Low Standards" ', Nugent's article, published on 2 May 1985, twice mentioned MacMillan, the company's official principal choreographer, as 'a notable offender'. The editor of the *Stage* had decided to blow up the story into a sensational article, to Nugent's surprise, giving her report of an insiders' meeting prominent coverage. Although the paper did not have an extensive general readership, word soon circulated that Madam had lambasted Kenneth in his absence. De Valois was mortified. She prided herself on her diplomacy, guarding her sharp tongue in public. She had regarded the Ballet Circle meeting as a privileged occasion, even though she had asked for critics to be included. Somewhat naively, given her long experience of the press, she had not expected her provocative remarks to be published.

Telephone calls from friends to MacMillan in New York gave him ample cause to fume over the perceived insult to his work. In his eyes, de Valois, once his staunch supporter, had publicly rejected him in front of the very critics who damned his recent ballets. She should have respected him enough to keep her views a private matter between the two of them. He was hurt that she (and the Royal Ballet in general, he believed) did not value his achievements. He asked Deborah to inform de Valois that he expected her to retract her remarks in a letter to the *Stage*. This de Valois refused to do, on the grounds that her policy was never to engage in a dispute with the press.

She wrote to him in New York instead, addressing him as 'Kenneth dear' and underlining her protest that she had never mentioned his name in her talk to the Ballet Circle. She insisted that she had been referring to aspiring choreographers whose work was not yet ready for the Royal Opera House and 'who were living in a world of confusion between contemporary and classical – and no one could accuse *you* of that'. (From this it can be inferred that she was intending to refer to the 1984–85 season, during which Morrice had introduced six short works, most by young members of the company. Although 'rolling round the floor in all-over tights' did not occur in any of them, it could have applied to Kylián's *Return to the Strange Land*, performed by the Royal Ballet in April 1984, shortly after MacMillan's *Different Drummer*.) She accused Ann Nugent of distorting her comments by assuming that MacMillan was the only choreographer in her thoughts: he *had* been at one time, de Valois said in her letter to him, but only 'because I wanted to see you get where you have got to'. Now, she pleaded, 'Come back and put on *Pagodas*. I feel that you are drifting away from us and that would be dreadful.' She ended without quite apologising in so many words, saying, 'All my love and misery for what I have done to the Ballet, love, Madam'.

He replied by return of post:

> I believe that you never mentioned my name and I have had a letter of apology from Ms Nugent. Nevertheless, the article is still in the *Stage* for critics to refer to in the future. I know that you meant me no harm, but some of the things that were said in the paper you have already said to me privately, so you see it was very easy for me to identify with what was said! I don't mean to 'drift away' but at this time, with this regime and policy, I feel I am stagnating and must keep busy. Norman has always been supportive, but his illness has kept him away. My opinion is never sought about anything and it is difficult for me to feel that I am really needed. I know that you have been distressed over the whole business, and I am sorry . . . Much love, Kenneth.

Although he was prepared to mend fences with de Valois, he had kept his distance from the Royal Ballet while it was undergoing its gradual change of regime from Morrice to Dowell. Morrice had already asked him to revive his 1960 *Le Baiser de la fée* for the following year, before the official hand-over to Dowell, but MacMillan was far from optimistic that his more recent work would find a place in future schedules. Meanwhile, his first season with ABT, about to celebrate its forty-eighth anniversary with *Romeo and Juliet* as the main attraction, had indeed kept him busy. He wrote in his diary, however, 'Hate *Romeo* – sick of rehearsing it. Can't wait to get home.' He was suffering from a painful left foot, which had now been operated on twice to remove a bone spur. The foot gave him such trouble during rehearsals in New York that he went to see his doctor as soon as he got back to London. He had yet another operation on it in July, shortly before his throat check-up (which gave him the all-clear for another three months).

Still hobbling, he rehearsed the London Contemporary Dance Theatre members in the solos he had created back in October for their fund-raising gala at the Royal Opera House on 13 July. LCDT's founder, Robin Howard, implored him to choreograph a work for the company: he agreed, but never found time to do so.

Alessandra Ferri announced that she was to leave the Royal Ballet at the end of the season to join American Ballet Theatre. The assumption was that she was following MacMillan, 'her' choreographer, to ABT but she says she was looking for new challenges and new partners – including Baryshnikov, who had invited her to dance with him in his company. She gave her last Juliet in July as a member of the Royal Ballet. Although the Royal Ballet management claimed to the press that she would be gone for only a year and would be welcomed back, she did not return. She would remain with ABT for the next twenty-two years, appearing with the Royal Ballet as a guest Juliet only once, near the end of her dancing career. MacMillan was present in New York to oversee her first Juliet with ABT, with Kevin McKenzie as Romeo. Their performance on 4 September 1985 was declared the official twentieth anniversary of his ballet's American premiere, when it had been danced at the Met by Fonteyn and Nureyev with the Royal Ballet.

He started work on *Requiem* in October, during his fifth visit to New York in 1985. Before leaving London, he had attended a concert performance of the music at the Royal Festival Hall. Andrew Lloyd Webber, after a series of hit musicals, had written the devotional piece of music in homage to his composer father. (William Lloyd Webber's last work had been a Mass, *Missa Sanctae Magdalenae*, shortly before his death in 1982.) Andrew Lloyd Webber's inspiration for the *Requiem* had been an article in the *New York Times* in 1984 about a Cambodian boy forced to kill his sister to save her from rape and torture by the Khmer Rouge. The story, almost subliminal in the music, is conveyed through the voices of a boy alto and a high female soprano (Sarah Brightman's role), singing the Latin text from the Catholic Mass for the Dead.

MacMillan intended to make the brother–sister sacrifice the basis of his ballet for ABT, ensuring that it would be very different in feeling from the Fauré *Requiem* he had choreographed in memory of John Cranko. Instead of spiritual beings, the dancers would be earthbound, finally overcoming their pain to Lloyd Webber's rousing *Hosanna* (which a music writer described as having 'a whiff of the West End about it'). With Baryshnikov and Ferri as the leading couple, the box office should be well satisfied.

Creating the ballet, however, proved trickier than MacMillan had foreseen. He had set out to use a large cast in a range of dance styles, including jazz, break-dance and the 'moon walk' made fashionable by Michael Jackson's music videos. He even incorporated a brief sequence from *Different Drummer*, using it as a device to free himself from a choreographic *impasse*. But he was frustrated that dancers he wanted for rehearsals were often unavailable. He found Baryshnikov (who was nursing an injured knee) difficult to work with and La Fosse (who was making up his mind to leave the company) uncooperative. By the time La Fosse had gone and Ferri was temporarily out of action with flu, MacMillan was worn out, depressed and suffering anxiety attacks about his ballet: 'Feel there are too many styles. Think I've done a dud.'

He consoled himself by going on buying sprees for costume jewellery, justifying his purchases as a means of making contacts through whom Deborah might be able to sell the necklaces she designed. He was horrifed to discover later, when his bank statement spelled out the amount he had spent in dollars during his American visits, just how much his latest obsession was costing him. He had always been a compulsive collector, hoarding things all his life, from wartime souvenirs as a youngster to skeins of wool and necklace beads as an adult. The ABT staff members, Charles France and Susan Jones, who accompanied him on the hunts for his latest craze, described him as 'hyper-focused'. Over the next few years, he would gain a reputation among fellow collectors as a costume-jewellery connoisseur. An article about his interest appeared in *Vogue*, written by Vivienne Becker, who subsequently included items from his collection in a book about costume jewellery. His collection grew so large that in 1992 he was invited to have his own showcase in a 'Jewels of Fantasy' exhibition at the Victoria and Albert Museum in South Kensington.

Over Christmas 1985 and New Year, he flew from New York to join Deborah and Charlotte in Australia, his worries about *Requiem* marring the holiday celebrations with Deborah's family. Back in New York early in January, he learned that Lucia Chase had died. She had been responsible for his first commission for Ballet Theatre in 1957 and had been an enthusiastic supporter of his work ever since. She had performed the role of the Mother in ABT's production of *Las Hermanas* back in the late 1960s and had never ceased requesting more of his ballets for the company. She and Oliver Smith had been joint Directors of ABT for forty-five years, until they handed over to Baryshnikov in 1980. The company was downcast by the news of her death, and MacMillan was so depressed about the state of his new ballet that he considered walking out and going home.

He struggled on, even though Baryshnikov declared a few days before *Requiem*'s opening night in Chicago on 7 February that he was not going to perform the role created for him. His right knee, on which he had had key-hole surgery in the summer, was playing up and his doctors had advised him not to dance, to the great disappointment of ABT's audiences. He was replaced in *Requiem* by a youngster, Gil Boggs, in the role of the brother, with Ferri as the girl: there was, however, no explicit reference in a programme note to the Cambodian tragedy that had initially inspired Lloyd Webber's *Requiem*. The rest of the cast – four other principals and an ensemble of twenty in silver-grey unitards – served as a chorus of mourners. 'Kenneth never let on what it was about,' says Kevin McKenzie. 'We never knew who the *Requiem* was supposed to be for, or how the different sections related to each other.'

The premiere was a much publicised event. Sarah Brightman had been engaged to sing the soprano role, as she had at the music's premiere; the boy alto was a young African American, Joseph Ravenau. Andrew Lloyd Webber came to the opening performance, which was enthusiastically reviewed by Chicago critics. Ann Barzel in *Dance* magazine called it 'a stunning theatre piece', though she was somewhat taken aback by the eclectic choreography: 'Angular limbs, a moon walk, jazz moves . . . and an ensemble that ranged from long stretches of lying on the floor to phases of fleet backward runs'. When *Requiem* was included in ABT's New York spring season, it was dismissed by dance and music critics alike as not worth taking seriously. Dale Harris, critic for the *Wall Street Journal* and no MacMillan fan, used to refer to it in conversation as the 'Chernobyl of dance'. ABT's Board members were embarrassed by accusations that the company was dumbing down, and Baryshnikov, who did eventually perform the leading role, disliked the ballet. It was soon dropped from the repertoire.

In between his trips to New York, MacMillan started making preparations for the Royal Ballet's revival of *Le Baiser de la fée*, which had now been scheduled for May 1986. As he had told Anna Kisselgoff for the *New York Times*, he wanted to return to the classically based impetus of his early years as a choreographer. *Le Baiser de la fée* had been his youthful tribute to Petipa and Ashton:

he intended to revisit his choreography, making changes to suit a new generation of dancers. Since Kenneth Rowell's 1960 designs had been destroyed, he commissioned a fresh set from Martin Sutherland, a Slade graduate who had been recommended by Georgiadis.

Somewhat to his annoyance, MacMillan learned that David Bintley was choreographing a ballet, *The Snow Queen*, for the touring company, using what Kenneth assumed, erroneously, was the same Hans Christian Andersen story as that of *Le Baiser de la fée* (though with different music – Bintley's music was by Bramwell Tovey). Stravinsky's scenario for *Le Baiser de la fée* is in fact adapted from a different Andersen story, *The Ice Maiden*. Bintley had previously trodden on MacMillan's toes by setting his first Royal Ballet commission, *Consort Lessons*, to a Stravinsky concerto that MacMillan considered his preserve. Then Bintley had turned to Gordon Crosse for extra music for his *Young Apollo* in 1984, based on Benjamin Britten's piece for piano, string quartet and string orchestra with the same title. MacMillan was very conscious that Bintley, still in his twenties, was considered by many (including de Valois) as his heir apparent. The pattern of the older, established choreographer being apprehensive of younger talent coming up behind was being repeated.

None the less, MacMillan was confident that his *Baiser de la fée*, last given in 1966, would stand the test of time. Although the choreography could be largely reconstructed from notation, the ballet had never been seen by the dancers he had chosen: delicate Maria Almeida for Seymour's role as the Bride-to-be; tall Jonathan Cope as her Fiancé; Fiona Chadwick as the Fairy. Most of the changes he made were to the Fairy's variations, to suit Chadwick's speed and suppleness. She would be a wilder, spikier ice fairy than beautiful Beriosova had been. Even though all three youngsters were talented, technically secure dancers, they would find the ballet hard to get through: he discovered they had less stamina than their predecessors. Almeida was unaccustomed to the fleet, Ashtonian footwork MacMillan had originally devised for Lynn Seymour.

Rehearsals for *Baiser* were under way when he and Deborah asked for a meeting with the management to discuss his next three-year contract with the Royal Ballet. Anthony Dowell was now officially confirmed as the company's Artistic Director, while continuing to perform as a principal dancer. To date, he had been overseeing Morrice's choice of programming, which included an all-MacMillan triple bill (with *Le Baiser de la fée*) in May, and *Mayerling* in the autumn. For the following season, Dowell's priority as Director in his own right was a new production of *Swan Lake* that he intended to mount himself, with designs by Yolanda Sonnabend. Otherwise, he was interested mainly in scheduling ballets he knew well as a performer: as far as the MacMillan repertoire was concerned, this meant *Manon* and *Romeo and Juliet*, rather than the one-act works Kenneth would like to see revived. Angry and distressed, Kenneth insisted at the meeting with Dowell, Tooley and Anthony Russell-Roberts, the Administrative Director, that his *Rite of Spring* be brought back the following season. Before signing his next contract, he secured a commitment to a revival of the *Rite* in May 1984.

While MacMillan brooded over his future relationship with the Royal Ballet, he supervised rehearsals for *Romeo and Juliet*, yet again. Gelsey Kirkland was to appear as a guest with the Royal Ballet as Juliet in April, just after the ballet's twenty-first anniversary at the Royal Opera House. She had first danced the role with the Royal Ballet in 1980, in memorable performances with Anthony Dowell as Romeo. During the six years since, she had been obliged to leave ABT because of her drug addiction. Her self-destructive history, recounted in her candid autobiography, *Dancing on My Grave*, had been a near-tragic waste of her gifts as a dancer. She had battled to remake her life and career over the past two years and was returning to the stage for the first time, at Dowell's invitation. Together with her (then) husband, Greg Lawrence, she intended to write another book, this time about the comeback experience.

The Shape of Love describes how minutely she reconsidered every detail in her interpretation of Juliet, and how she demanded that her Royal Ballet colleagues think through their every response to her, instead of going through habitual routines. Rehearsals with Kirkland required a great deal of patience but the results were worth it – or so she believed, and the critics reviewing her Juliet, with Dowell as Romeo, agreed with her. MacMillan did not. He confided to his diary that he found her performance tiresomely mannered. He did, however, take a curtain call with her and Dowell, acknowledging the ballet's twenty-first anniversary (three months earlier) and appearing to give Kirkland his blessing.

His lack of appreciation for her intense, Method-acting approach to Juliet might have been because of his recent over-exposure to his ballet in America. He had rehearsed seven different Juliets (and understudies) for ABT's production and here he was, back with the Royal Ballet, confronted by yet another, very exigent American. 'His face hinted he had seen all the *Romeo and Juliet* rehearsals he really needed in this lifetime,' Kirkland wrote in her book. She recorded that he mocked her query about why she, as Juliet, was doing a certain step by asking, 'Why are you dancing?', mimicking her frantic tone. (Since the quote is an echo of the remark made by Lermontov to Moira Shearer as Vicky Page in the film *The Red Shoes*, Kirkland and Lawrence might have re-imagined MacMillan's response.) He was never good at explaining the motives behind his choreography. In any case, he had choreographed Juliet's role so long ago, relying on Lynn Seymour's intuitive understanding of what he wanted, that Kirkland's persistent questioning about her motivation exasperated rather than stimulated him. Monica Mason remembers that he left the rehearsal, so that she finished it with Kirkland. 'Kenneth loved performances to be "real" and finding "real" is difficult, especially for a guest artist who hasn't grown up performing his ballets,' Mason explains. MacMillan considered that Kirkland was making herself and her interpretation more important than the ballet as a whole.

His mind was on finishing *Le Baiser de la fée*, as he reworked the cornucopia of classical steps he had poured into it. When Seymour had first danced the betrayed bride, with Donald MacLeary as the young man, the ballet's story had seemed the girl's tragedy. The revised version put the focus on the Fairy's pursuit of the entranced hero. This returned the ballet to the allegory Stravinsky had in mind: the young man was supposed to be an artist – a poet or musician – in thrall to his implacable muse. The shift of emphasis on MacMillan's part might have been a subconscious one. Without a Seymour or a Ferri to inspire him, his interest reverted to the male protagonist, the man marked out from other mortals by his creative talent – a burdensome gift, as he knew. Jonathan Cope, however, was not experienced enough at twenty-two to make much impact as the hero. Tall and handsome, a fine danseur noble, he had as yet little theatrical presence. That would come with experience much later in his career. Maria Almeida was similarly reticent as a personality on stage. Fiona Chadwick as the Fairy was the one who stamped her role with coldly glittering authority, making the most of the bravura steps MacMillan had given her.

The gala programme on 8 May included *Concerto* and the one-act version of *Anastasia* (set and costumes on loan from ABT), which the Royal Ballet had never given on its own before. The evening was dedicated to the memory of Barry Kay, designer of *Anastasia* and seven other MacMillan ballets. Kay had died of complications caused by Aids the previous year and this was MacMillan's first opportunity to pay tribute to him. The triple bill was also haunted by the memory of Seymour's interpretations of the roles created on her in all three ballets. Lesley Collier, who had the unenviable task of assuming Seymour's roles in *Anastasia* and *Concerto* on the press night, received warm praise in the reviews. Most attention, however, was paid to *Le Baiser de la fée*. David Dougill in *The Sunday Times* welcomed 'the sheer delight of its purely classical dancing – a quality which we have missed in MacMillan's recent output'. As I wrote in the *Observer*, 'It is good to be reminded how brilliantly inventive he can be at making steps as well as expressing moods and emotions.'

Although the solos and pas de deux for the principal characters were widely admired, MacMillan's folk-dance scenes of village revelry met with less enthusiasm. Martin Sutherland's Alpine designs had a mixed reception: some reviewers liked them, while others found them prosaic. As before, Stravinsky's scenario was found to be intractable, his music tantalisingly unrewarding. The ballet never hit a popular chord and once again disappeared from the repertoire.

47
———

On his return to New York in June 1985, MacMillan talked to Jennifer Dunning for an article in the *New York Times*, published on 12 June, about how the ABT 'troika' – Mikhail Baryshnikov, John Taras and himself – worked in practice. According to Dunning's account:

While Mr Baryshnikov makes the final decisions, the three plan new productions together and consult on most matters of daily administration. Their meetings tend to be informal – a matter of 'rushing into corners' as

Sir Kenneth puts it, and exchanging looks of delight or concern in the viewing room at the rear of the [Met] Opera House as they watch the company's New York performances.

Dunning reported that while Taras's role was clear – he delivered artistic reports to the ABT Board when Baryshnikov was absent and was 'a valuable asset at fund-raising events' – MacMillan's relationship with the Artistic Director was more opaque:

The curiously ebullient and intense meshing of their [MacMillan's and Baryshnikov's] personalities has intrigued observers. 'We're both rather shy men,' Sir Kenneth, who usually provides a laconic complement to the hyper-fluent Mr Baryshnikov, said with a smile. 'We have a similar sense of humour,' Mr Baryshnikov said. 'Without a sense of humour around, any directing is just hopeless. We cheer each other up.'

This was not how MacMillan, privately, perceived the relationship. He wrote in his diary of feeling tense and depressed after rows with Baryshnikov and Charles France, who had assumed an outsize role as the Director's assistant. France regarded himself as Baryshnikov's shield against unwelcome intrusion, taking on the role of conduit between the often absent Director and the rest of the company. Staff who resented France's interventions called him 'the house Rasputin' behind his expansive back. MacMillan, no easy communicator himself, found Baryshnikov maddeningly elusive. He was resentfully aware that Baryshnikov disliked the ballets he had created for the company, and they were about to clash over ABT's next project: MacMillan's production of *The Sleeping Beauty*.

Unlike the Royal Ballet, ABT had no great tradition of performing the complete, three-act version (with prologue) of *The Sleeping Beauty*. ABT's earlier production, mounted by Mary Skeaping in Oliver Messel's designs ten years previously, had been its first full-length account of Petipa's 1890 ballet. Baryshnikov, who had danced the ABT premiere with Natalia Makarova as Aurora, was not particularly enamoured of Skeaping's production. The Board was confident that audiences on tour would welcome a new staging, particularly one by Sir Kenneth MacMillan: ABT would be perceived as being back on course as a classically based company. For MacMillan, *The Sleeping Beauty* represented his heritage, the fount of his own choreography. By revisiting the ballet, he would be touching base once again, while revealing to a young generation of American-trained dancers how vital the classics were to their performing lives.

But although Baryshnikov shared his view that *The Sleeping Beauty* was an essential part of the repertoire, its choreographic 'text' was not loaded with iconic significance for him. The Soviet tradition from which he had come did not revere Petipa's choreography in the respectful way the Royal Ballet claimed to have done. Changes had been made to the Kirov and Bolshoi productions over the years by ballet masters such as Alexander Gorsky and Konstantin Sergeyev, changes regarded in Russia as for the better. (The Kirov Ballet did not attempt to return to its original Mariinsky production of *The Sleeping Beauty* until 1999, in a reconstruction very similar choreographically to de Valois's staging for the Royal Ballet. De Valois had, however, made changes to the choreography over the years: the Royal Ballet's 'text' was by no means authentic.) Whenever Baryshnikov had danced excerpts from *The Sleeping Beauty* in ABT galas, he had reverted to the Soviet version he first knew. MacMillan intended to base his production on the Royal Ballet's version, regarded as more-or-less sacred, complete with the mime scenes the Soviets omitted. He would make his own contributions where he saw fit. Baryshnikov's ambivalent attitude to what he came to regard as an 'English' *Sleeping Beauty* was to cause MacMillan considerable difficulty in the months to come.

The ABT Board eventually agreed a budget in June 1986 with an opening night scheduled for February 1987, when the company would be on tour in Chicago. Since Nicholas Georgiadis was to do the designs, the production was going to be opulent – and expensive. The company, having borrowed extensively to pay off its $1.6 million debt, would end up spending $1 million on *The Sleeping Beauty*, hoping, as with *Romeo and Juliet*, to buy its way out of trouble. To save money, the sets and costumes were to be made in London, where specialist workshops charged less than those in New York. A further advantage would be that Georgiadis could supervise every detail from his London base.

He and MacMillan had decided to set the ballet's hundred-year span between the early to mid-seventeenth and eighteenth centuries: the original 1890 scenario had specified that the last act took place in the era of Louis XIV's Palace of Versailles, with fountains flowing in the background. Georgiadis researched the period in depth, as he always did, seeking inspiration from historically accurate sources. Although MacMillan wanted a sumptuous setting to match the splendour of Tchaikovsky's music, the architectural elements would need to be less substantial than the heavy Renaissance sets for *Romeo and Juliet*, which were very expensive to tour. Georgiadis opted for painted 'drops', slender pillars and suspended swags of fabric, supported by cherubs. He said he wanted the result to look 'as if we're in a palace looking at murals representing architecture – not actual *trompe l'oeil* architectural effects'. His palette was going to be lighter than before: 'Cream and more cream, and black for the hunt scene, and apricot. As I'm getting older, I'm getting dis-coloured,' he told the ABT Friends' magazine, *On Point*.

Constructing the set and making 254 costumes would continue in London through the latter half of 1986, before everything was shipped to the United States by the start of the new year. MacMillan had cast the ballet, in consultation with Baryshnikov, as soon as he was given the go-ahead. He left the basic teaching of the choreography to his regular notator, Monica Parker, and the company staff, until he returned to New York in September to choreograph his own contributions to the production. These were to be less radical than the changes he had made in his previous productions for the Deutsche Oper and the Royal Ballet. He intended to redo the Garland Waltz in Act I; create new variations for the Prince and for Aurora in Act II; and add a male role in the 'Jewels' divertissement in Act III. The staging would reflect his vision of the ballet as a majestic display of civilised behaviour and sophisticated dancing, triumphing over the disruptive power of evil.

Before rehearsals for ABT's *Sleeping Beauty* were under way, he accompanied the Royal Ballet to Vancouver, where the company was to represent Britain at the Expo '86 World Festival. The opening night of *Romeo and Juliet* on 13 July was attended by Princess Margaret and the Prime Minister, Margaret Thatcher, and her husband Denis, as well as the Canadian Prime Minister, Brian Mulroney. Anthony Dowell gave his last performance as Romeo, with Lesley Collier as Juliet: Dowell had been the only Romeo left from the original 1965 casts. Later in the week, *Le Baiser de la fée* was part of a triple bill with Ashton's *A Month in the Country* and the premiere of David Bintley's *Galanteries*. Bintley, at twenty-eight, had just been appointed resident choreographer with the Royal Ballet, ten years after joining the touring company as a dancer. MacMillan, who had held the same post in his youth, retained his senior title as the company's principal choreographer.

From Canada, he flew to Los Angeles, where he, Deborah and Charlotte spent the summer holidays once again with the Rosses. They met up with the Cazenove family from London: Christopher and his (then) wife, Angharad Rees, who were both actors, and their children who were friends of Charlotte. Christopher Cazenove, thanks to his English accent, had been cast as a villain in *Dynasty*, the extravagant American television serial. Cazenove invited the MacMillans, to Charlotte's delight, to see *Dynasty* being recorded in Los Angeles. Kenneth, underwhelmed, would have preferred to sunbathe by the Rosses' pool. He enjoyed the absurdity of *Dynasty* on television for reasons other than admiration at its production values.

On his return to London, he inspected Georgiadis's designs for *The Sleeping Beauty*. Although he very much liked the costumes, he and Georgiadis had their inevitable disagreements. MacMillan demanded stronger colours to identify the characters, especially Aurora's fairy godmothers: Georgiadis wanted to stick to his palette of cream and gold. They argued over the set, each refusing to give way. Deborah is convinced that the conflict between the two of them was always productive: 'Out of their clashes something new happened that wasn't there before. But they could both be incredibly stubborn. And with *The Sleeping Beauty*, Nico was designing for the Met in New York, where the production would get most attention – and Kenneth knew it had to be able to tour.'

Once back with ABT in September, MacMillan attended the first of the new series of choreographic workshops in which company members tried out their ideas with fellow dancers. Kenneth himself had profited from Ballet Theatre's workshop scheme back in 1957, when he had made *Journey* for Nora Kaye. The workshops had been only sporadic since then: the company found them an added expense and hard to accommodate in a touring schedule. MacMillan had insisted when he accepted his post as Artistic Associate that the project be revived. He was pleasantly surprised at the work in progress he saw at a showing at the Joyce Theater. He noted in his diary, 'Remarkable talent emerging, especially Clark Tippett and Lisa

Rinehart.' This was praise indeed from a man who rarely enjoyed other choreographers' work. (He was scathing in his diary comments about the Royal Ballet's attempts to find new talent from among its ranks.) Tippett's promise, eagerly encouraged by ABT, was cut short by his premature death from Aids. Rinehart interrupted her ballet career to be the mother of three of Baryshnikov's children; she remains his offstage partner. The choreographic workshops for company members were phased out after MacMillan left. Instead, under a later policy, choreographers were commissioned to try out their ideas on ABT's Studio Company of youngsters about to start their professional careers.

As autumn drew on, preparations for *The Sleeping Beauty* became increasingly fraught. Many members of the company, including Baryshnikov, had been away in Italy for six weeks during the summer, taking part in Herbert Ross's latest film, *Dancers*, a modern-day version of *Giselle*. Ross had wrapped the old ballet within a contemporary parallel story of a young girl's love for her company's leading man, played by Baryshnikov. The filming took place in and around Bari, on the southern Adriatic coast; a privately owned opera house was the setting for the *Giselle* performances. *Dancers* was to be the last project Ross would undertake with his wife, for Nora Kaye had been diagnosed with a malignant tumour of the brain. (*Dancers* turned out to be an artistic disaster and a commercial flop.) The cast was excited by the prospect of appearing in a Hollywood movie. Those left behind were envious, complaining about being stuck with onerous corps-de-ballet rehearsals for *The Sleeping Beauty*. MacMillan, aware of how much work had to be done before the year ended, was convinced that his endeavours were being undermined by the staff Baryshnikov had left behind.

He was especially wary of Elena Tchernichova, the Russian ballet mistress who had taken charge of the classical repertoire since 1977. MacMillan had caught her altering the choreography he had set and had been told she was complaining about him behind his back. 'Hate her for making me feel so vile. Rang Misha in Bari to tell him about rows with her. He non-committal.' In Baryshnikov's absence, Charles France was acting as a busy go-between among the various factions, leaving ill-feeling in his substantial wake. His was a power-broking role in which he was increasingly distrusted by MacMillan. The staff had split into two camps: those who reported to Baryshnikov via Charles France and those who supported MacMillan, including loyal Georgina Parkinson.

The dancers, aware of the dissension, spread rumours about who was in and who out of favour. Since jealousy was already rife among those who had not been selected for the film, there was fertile ground for trouble. The atmosphere was further poisoned on Baryshnikov's return from Italy when he dismissed the work MacMillan had done so far as 'this English shit'. MacMillan's relationship with the dancers deteriorated as a result. Usually deceptively quiet in rehearsals of his own work, when he allowed dancers some leeway in finding their interpretations, he now became imperious in his demands that the ABT casts should execute *The Sleeping Beauty*'s choreography in the style he decreed. Consciously or otherwise, he seemed to have adopted the dictatorial approach Michael Somes used during Royal Ballet rehearsals. According to the Canadian journalist John Fraser, chronicling events during the 1986–87 season in his book about Baryshnikov, *Private View*, 'Accustomed to American egalitarianism and the familiar manifestations of Russian moodiness from Baryshnikov, the dancers were unprepared for the formal hauteur and withering sarcasm of a high British cultural magnate.'

Fraser must have been overstating the dancers' sensitivity. Company members who had been with ABT for some time had been subjected to far more hurtful remarks from Antony Tudor and Jerome Robbins, notorious for their harshness. Both were more than capable of reducing dancers to tears of humiliation. ABT was proud of its theatrical gypsy tradition, its youngsters exposed to unpredictable artistic temperaments and constant crises on tour. It had never been a company accustomed to being coddled. Dancers had, however, picked up on Tchernichova's dislike of MacMillan's version of *The Sleeping Beauty* and shared her hostility to him, challenging the company's loyalties. Leslie Browne, who was coached by Tchernichova, knew all about the ill-feeling. Looking back, she believes that MacMillan was taking out his frustration on the dancers. 'He'd once had great power and respect, but now none of his ballets [created for the company] were sticking. He was restaging *Beauty* in his decline. He could hardly speak. By the time it was on, he was a shell of his former self.'

MacMillan was losing his voice, struggling to make himself heard in crowded rehearsal rooms. He worried about the possibly ominous state of his vocal cords and was distressed that Baryshnikov showed no sign of sympathy. The atmosphere in the company had become so unpleasant by November that Kenneth decided to cut his scheduled stay short and go home at the start of December: 'Can't wait. Felt tearful all day – combination of missing all at home, depression over Nora, feel nobody in company cares about *S. Beauty*. Ballet in a dreadful state.' He knew that he was compounding his problems by leaving: reports reaching him in London over what was happening to the production in his absence would fuel his anxieties at being undermined, but by now he was beyond caring.

His relief at being home was soon dissipated by his throat specialist's insistence that he should have a biopsy before Christmas. The results confirmed his worst fears: the biopsy showed that cells from nodes on his vocal cords had started to change from a pre-cancerous state to a malignant one. To avoid surgery, he would need six weeks of radiotherapy, starting in January. 'I am taking the news quite well, surprisingly,' he confided to his diary, 'though my inevitable suspicion – is the doctor telling the whole truth?' His fear of cancer was to some extent allayed by Dr Frank Tait, who had recently been diagnosed with the same throat cancer and who told Kenneth about the successful outcome of his treatment. Tait was the same psychiatrist who had tried to help Kenneth through his stage fright in the 1950s by standing reassuringly in the wings. Thirty years on, he made himself available once again to calm Kenneth down: 'I'd visit him and whisper about the radiotherapy, telling him that it could be endured and that it would work.'

Before starting his course of radiotherapy, MacMillan steeled himself to return to ABT for a week to finish as much as he could of *The Sleeping Beauty*. Once he left New York, Baryshnikov, with the assistance of Tchernichova, would be in charge of rehearsals leading up to the premiere in Chicago on 10 February 1987. Their relationship was so strained that, as MacMillan noted on the day he flew back to London, 'Misha didn't even say goodbye.'

Then, while he attended Westminster Hospital for daily sessions of radiotherapy, Deborah flew to Chicago in his place to find out what was happening to the production. 'Horrible being left,' he wrote. 'Now I know how she really feels when I go away.' He was in charge of Charlotte, now fourteen, keeping an eye on her after she returned from school in the afternoons and preparing their meals together. She had been shocked to learn he had cancer, realising for the first time that her father was not immortal. Their relationship mellowed as a result. 'He couldn't speak, so we didn't have any arguments,' she says. 'I felt I was looking after him, not the other way round.' Although he fretted over *The Sleeping Beauty*'s progress (reported in regular phone calls from Deborah), the enforced break, together with Charlotte's company, kept him sane – until he returned to ABT in March.

Deborah had acted as his eyes while she was in Chicago, staying in the same hotel as Georgiadis, John Taras and Ashley Lawrence, the conductor. Her role was to liaise with Georgiadis, help sort out design hitches and take responsibility for minor adaptations to the staging as the premiere drew near. John Fraser commented in his book, 'She proved a model of diplomacy, talking only when asked her opinion and reliably supporting Baryshnikov on all public occasions.' She stayed until the first night was over, by which time it was evident that the production was far too long and complicated: cuts would have to be made before the tour continued to Los Angeles and San Diego, and then to New York in April, when it would have its all-important exposure at the Met. By then, the staging problems should have been resolved and the performers be more assured in their roles.

'We got it on stage in Chicago thanks to the usual Ballet Theatre miracle,' remembers Kevin McKenzie, who would become Artistic Director of ABT in 1992.

Let's not build it up in retrospect into a huge drama. It was no worse than the stress of putting on any huge production on tour. That's what Ballet Theatre does. Yes, there were rows between Georgiadis and the costume department; yes, there were problems for the stage crew – but no worse than usual. It wasn't a dreadful experience.

By the start of March, MacMillan had recovered sufficiently from his radiotherapy to undertake the long flight to Los Angeles, where ABT was to perform the Californian premiere of *The Sleeping Beauty* at the Shrine Auditorium. Deborah went with him, leaving Charlotte in the care of Emma Dingwall. The granddaughter of the MacMillan's Scottish friends from the Isle of Arran, the Alexanders, she was staying in the Spencer Park house while taking a drama course at the London Academy of Music and Drama.

MacMillan was determined to reassert his authority over his production. His fears that his rulings had been undermined had been stoked by those he had left in charge: claims and counter-claims of who had changed what had been highly dramatised in reports back to him. By the time of the Los Angeles opening, casts other than those MacMillan had personally rehearsed were performing the ballet, and he found cause to erupt with rage. He objected to Baryshnikov's choice of dancers for certain roles and he disliked Tchernichova's Russian style of coaching. He found the big ensemble scenes far too cluttered, the sets poorly organised and the lighting dismal. He felt that his vision of *The Sleeping Beauty* had been sabotaged by management ineptitude – or malice. He was particularly incensed with Charles France for altering production details, threatening him with legal action for interfering in artistic matters where he had no right to meddle.

Although MacMillan was barely able to speak, he made his dissatisfaction abundantly clear. According to John Fraser's highly coloured account of the production, 'There were ballerinas who could barely mention his name later without virtually spitting it out. Extremely articulate members of staff were momentarily left speechless . . . Some dancers were threatening open revolt and the static between the green room and the stage was heavy.' Fraser, who championed Baryshnikov, nevertheless noted a telling example of what MacMillan was up against. When a corps member, dressed in one of Georgiadis's elaborate costumes, was reproved by a more senior dancer for flopping down to rest on the dusty stage floor, the contemptuous reply came: 'I don't give a fuck about this costume and I don't give one fuck about this fucking production.' According to Fraser, the young dancer then proceeded to yawn his way through every performance, apparently unchallenged.

Once again, *The Sleeping Beauty* had turned out to be an albatross around MacMillan's neck. His vision of the ballet had yet to be satisfied, whether for the Deutsche Oper in Berlin, the Royal Ballet or now in America. His hopes of a productive working relationship with ABT had been confounded; he believed that his efforts to help American dancers appreciate their classical heritage had been spoilt by the Russians within the company who despised his Royal Ballet background. Although he felt embittered at the time, the bad feeling within the company dissipated as the production settled in and the dancers came to respect his insistence on the ballet's values. They learned to accept its conventions, finding a way to bring it to life with an American spirit that did not betray the courtly etiquette on which MacMillan had insisted. 'He could be very wicked and unpleasant at times,' acknowledged Baryshnikov. 'But *The Sleeping Beauty* was good. We didn't have fabulous character actors for mime roles, like European theatres and the Royal Ballet, but I think the company learned a lot from him.' The MacMillan–Georgiadis *Sleeping Beauty* was to remain in ABT's repertoire for the next eighteen years, before it crossed the Atlantic into the repertoire of English National Ballet in 2005, still with the Georgiadis costumes from ABT but now with new sets by Peter Farmer.

The New York premiere on 20 April 1987 took place in the shadow of two recent deaths. Nora Kaye had succumbed to her brain tumour, and Antony Tudor had died of heart failure the day before *The Sleeping Beauty* opened at the Met. ABT's New York season was dedicated to both great figures who had contributed so much to the company. Much now depended on the critical reception the new production received in New York. The press office had been working to build up a head of steam, ensuring that favourable reviews from the tour had been circulated to journalists. The *New York Times* ran previews in two successive Sunday editions, with quotes from MacMillan and Georgiadis, neither of whom would be present at the New York season. MacMillan had spoken by phone in a hoarse whisper, emphasising how much he had learned over the years from Petipa's choreography. Georgiadis explained that although the production was faithful to the original period settings of the seventeenth and eighteenth centuries, 'The greatest effort for me is to find the right proportion of saccharine, because as a twentieth-century person, I like saccharine in my coffee but not in life – or art.'

His sumptuously detailed costumes were based on paintings by Van Dyck and Tiepolo, a hundred years apart. Such historical references were largely lost on spectators, including critics. Anna Kisselgoff, in her review for the *New York Times*, found the designs 'less than specific about period . . . [They] did not square with the sweet lyricism that Sir Kenneth has established as the dancing style.' Marcia Siegel in the *Christian Science Monitor* failed to discern a consistent concept in the production and was unimpressed by

MacMillan's ensemble dances: 'They seldom fit the stage or give a sense of harmonious unfolding that can be the choreographic metaphor for social order. When he sticks to Petipa . . . we get the virtuoso masterpiece everyone recognizes.' Dale Harris in the *Wall Street Journal* and Clive Barnes in the *New York Post* accused MacMillan of not being entirely original in his contributions, which, according to Barnes, 'were scattered through the production like cornflakes in a snowstorm'.

MacMillan had in fact been scrupulous in avoiding any borrowings from Ashton's or de Valois's choreography for the Royal Ballet's various productions. For example, his variation for Aurora in the Act II Vision scene resembled Ashton's only because both were based on descriptions of Petipa's original choreography, set to music Petipa had appropriated from the Gold Fairy's variation in Act III. Indignant at implications of plagiarism, MacMillan insisted, in vain, that the accusations should be retracted in the newspapers that had made them.

Though the critics found fault with aspects of MacMillan's production, most agreed that it was well danced by a company on good form, already growing into their roles. Susan Jaffe and Ross Stretton danced the leading roles on opening night in New York, as they had in Chicago, though Jaffe was nursing an injury that meant she could no longer do the rest of her scheduled performances. An array of different casts followed. Credit was given to Baryshnikov as well as MacMillan for producing such consistency of style: 'This is a British production of a nineteenth-century Russian ballet danced in twentieth-century American style . . . long-lined, clean-limbed, technically meticulous,' wrote David Vaughan in *Ballet Review*.

MacMillan was not present to take any bows at the New York premiere because he had flown to Sydney, where the Australian Ballet was performing his *Song of the Earth* for the first time. Maina Gielgud, its Director, had secured his permission to mount the ballet when he visited Australia over the Christmas period and had seen the dancers in class and performance. His presence for *The Song of the Earth* was useful publicity for the company, reticent and hoarse though he was in interviews. Neil Jillett commented in the *Age*, with typical Australian frankness, that 'the Scottish choreographer's voice and manner are so dour that talking to him soon turns out to be like conducting an interview with a saucepan of porridge that has gone off the simmer'.

Jillett did, however, manage to secure some revealing comments about the impulse behind the creation of *The Song of the Earth* in 1965:

It's a very adult ballet in all its emotions, not just love and death, but all the subtleties in between. I know death well. I was brought up during the war. I saw a lot of people killed. My mother and father died about that time. One of the emotions you feel about death very often is anger, anger that you're left alone, for instance. Yes, this ballet is an elegy – for my childhood, because I was brought up in the war and I saw a lot of awful things. I carry that with me even now.

Kenneth remained in Australia for six weeks, joined for part of his stay by Deborah and Charlotte, during her Easter holiday break from school. Relieved to be away from ABT and *The Sleeping Beauty*, he was considering resigning his post with the company as Artistic Associate: Jillett had reported in the *Age* that he had said 'the constant Atlantic-hopping tires him and disrupts his family life'.

However, a month after his return home, he set out once again for New York in May to negotiate his next three-year contract with ABT. He was anxious and aggrieved when he came away from a discussion with Charles Dillingham, the Executive Director, with the impression that he would be offered a renewal for only one year. Before confirming that his contract would indeed continue until 1990, the Board made full use of his services: he was required to attend a dinner given by the New York State Council on the Arts. He was placed between social figures likely to donate generous sums of money to the arts, and to ABT in particular: Countess Chandon (of Moët et Chandon champagne) and Mrs Harry Traub of Bloomingdale's. It was not the kind of occasion he enjoyed, though he did his best to be socially agreeable. He was then asked to make a presentation to the NYSCA in support of its grant to ABT. 'I was terrible,' he confessed to his diary.

He was so dispirited by the time he returned home for the summer of 1987 that he chose not to accompany the Royal Ballet on its tour to Russia in July, its first visit for twenty-five years. MacMillan had never been to Russia, but he felt too exhausted with travelling to make the trip to Moscow or Leningrad. *Manon* was included in the tour: the Kirov, later renamed the Mariinsky Ballet after the end of the Soviet Union, would be the first Russian company to perform *Manon*, in 1999.

For a holiday break in August, the MacMillans travelled to Scotland, renting a small house outside Edinburgh on the Firth of Forth. They went to see plays and a performance by Circus Oz in the Edinburgh Festival and paid a visit to Kenneth's aunt Jean Watt at her home in Rosyth – the first time Charlotte had met her Scottish great-aunt. To Kenneth's surprise, his older brother George was also there. His wife, Frances, had died of cancer in June; their two grown-up children had left home, so he was now on his own. (Kenneth and Deborah had attended Frances's funeral in Great Yarmouth.) While they were all having tea at Aunt Jean's, George suddenly produced a letter he had concealed behind a clock on the mantelpiece. 'This belongs to you,' he said to Kenneth. It was the last letter their mother had written to twelve-year-old Kenneth, while he was away at school in Retford. George had found the letter while going through family belongings, which included a handbag that had been owned by their eldest sister Jean. In it, as well as the letter, were photographs Jean had kept of Kenneth as a boy and as a young dancer. Kenneth, who had left the precious letter in Jean's care when he went to Berlin, was deeply distressed. On the verge of tears and unable to speak to George, he broke up the tea party by leaving as soon as he could. 'He was distraught for days,' remembers Charlotte. 'It really got to him.' Among his tumult of emotions was rage and resentment at his brother for his insensitivity – or so it seemed to Kenneth – in brandishing the letter as though it were a trophy. He never saw George again.

The Royal Ballet had returned from Russia for the start of the new season at the Opera House with a number of ill and injured dancers. This affected the casting of his *Rite of Spring*, whose revival he had insisted upon when he renegotiated his principal choreographer's contract. It had not been seen since Monica Mason gave up the role of the Chosen Maiden in 1982. The opportunity for a revival came when the Royal Opera's newly appointed Music Director, Bernard Haitink, agreed to conduct an all-Stravinsky programme by the Royal Ballet in October 1987. *The Rite* would conclude a triple bill with Fokine's *Firebird* and Ashton's *Scènes de ballet*. Since Haitink had not conducted for ballet before, an unusually long stage rehearsal period had been allocated with the orchestra, to everyone's relief.

Orchestral standards for ballet had been in serious decline for a number of years and the Royal Opera House was now attempting to raise them again. Haitink's 'guest' appearances as a ballet conductor gave a great boost to the company, infrequent though they proved to be. Unfortunately, the choice of Isaiah Jackson, an American conductor then without great ballet experience, as the Royal Ballet's latest Music Director was to prove a less fortunate appointment than Haitink's for the opera company. Once Jackson took over conducting the Stravinsky programme later in the season, *The Rite of Spring* was less exhilarating for performers and audiences alike.

MacMillan made a radical adaptation to his ballet: the Chosen Maiden was to become the Chosen One at some performances, danced by a young man, Simon Rice. In an interview for the *Observer*, MacMillan said that he had had the idea from the ballet's inception in 1962: 'I wasn't bold enough then to go against the Stravinsky scenario. But I realised the steps I'd worked out on Monica [Mason] were just as suited for a man. In fact, I'd picked Monica out of the "tribe" of the corps because she was so much more athletic than the others, with real energy and attack.'

Rice, small and compact with a powerful jump, found the role even more exhausting than did the later female casts, Fiona Chadwick and Deborah Bull: male solos are rarely so protracted, so he had to learn to build his stamina. The change of sex met with a mixed reception from the critics: some found that although Rice brought more physical weight to the part, he lacked emotional impact; others, such as Clement Crisp in the *Financial Times*, thought him as compelling as Mason had been:

As the rite takes hold of him . . . we see how the possessed being incarnates the tribe's hopes and is touched with a supernatural dignity, driven by the forces outside himself. The dance inhabits him, and it is a measure of Mr Rice's artistry that we should understand so grandly the course of this gripping physical drama. It is a very fine achievement indeed.

The Royal Ballet then took the Stravinsky triple bill to Berlin, as part of the still-divided city's 750th anniversary celebrations. The Prince and Princess of Wales were there for the first night on 1 November 1987, at the start of an official visit to the Federal Republic of Germany. The company was given the full red-carpet treatment at the Deutsche Oper, its performances regarded as 'a birthday present from Great Britain'. It was the royal couple's first joint public appearance for two months, so most of the press coverage involved speculation about the state of their marriage, already evidently under strain. What Princess Diana was wearing, and how aloof she seemed from her husband, warranted far more column inches in British papers than the ballet company's performances.

MacMillan had very mixed feelings about going back to Berlin for the first time in seventeen years. He and Deborah stayed in the same hotel as the dancers, and had dinner with Gert Reinholm, catching up with news of former colleagues and dancers. Kenneth took Deborah round the Western sector of the city, pointing out the buildings in which he had lived; they crossed to the Eastern sector on a guided tour, seeing the museums and opera houses on the other side of the dividing wall. Armed sentries still surveyed the wall and lengthily inspected the visas of every traveller. Not much appeared to have changed since Kenneth had left, although the turbulent student protests of the 1960s seemed far in the past. He was apprehensive about how Deutsche Oper audiences would receive his 1962 ballet: Berliners had already seen various accounts of *Le Sacre du printemps*, ranging from Mary Wigman's to Maurice Béjart's and Glen Tetley's. They greeted MacMillan's *Rite* and his curtain call with roars of approval, although Isaiah Jackson had received boos during his bows as conductor. 'Same old Berlin,' Kenneth recorded in his diary.

He had returned to Germany two years earlier to visit Munich for the first time since he had suffered his stroke there. His old friends, Ronald Hynd and his wife Annette Page, were Artistic Directors of the Bavarian State Ballet company in Munich. They had secured *Elite Syncopations* for the company, which was to prove a popular success. He spent an enjoyable few days with them, rehearsing the dancers and musicians on stage before the premiere. He was outraged when a row broke out after the Hynds had left as Directors. The Munich opera-house orchestra suddenly refused to play Scott Joplin's music for the ballet. A story appeared in the *Guardian*, ascribing the musicians' action to Nazi legislation banning 'degenerate' music by black or Jewish composers. When MacMillan demanded to know what was going on, the theatre's Intendant, Wolfgang Sawallisch, wrote explaining that the orchestra's union was using labour laws that protected classical musicians from playing on stage during a performance – unless they received extra payment. To save money, two pianists accompanied the production in place of the orchestra. The press lost interest in the non-scandal.

Towards the end of 1987, when MacMillan returned to ABT in New York to supervise *The Sleeping Beauty* for its next tour, he took the opportunity to visit other companies across the Atlantic who were doing his ballets. He flew to Toronto, where he insisted on changes in casting for the National Ballet of Canada's account of *Concerto*. Then he went on to Houston, where his old friend Ben Stevenson was hoping to mount *The Song of the Earth*, after trying for years to interest MacMillan in the Texan company. He liked the dancers and gave Stevenson the go-ahead. Before returning to London in December, he rejoined ABT in Miami for performances there of *The Sleeping Beauty*. The flight to Miami had terrified him. The plane had to turn back after the landing gear failed to retract; after a four-hour delay, he eventually reached Miami at two thirty in the morning with terrible backache.

He had treatment for his worsening back pain in America and in London, only to discover after an MRI scan that eight of his ribs had been cracked near the sternum. He had been over-energetically manipulated by physiotherapists accustomed to working with dancers in peak condition. Although he was in considerable discomfort by the time of his fifty-eighth birthday, he was relieved that the pain (and the hot spots on the MRI scan) had not been caused by the spread of cancer from his throat – his great dread. Though he was admittedly something of a hypochondriac, he had cause to be apprehensive. He ended the year's entries in his diary by hoping that 1988 would be better than 1987, during which he had endured radiotherapy to his throat and come through the travails of mounting *The Sleeping Beauty* for ABT. Still to come was *The Prince of the Pagodas* for the Royal Ballet, and a setback to his health from which he would never fully recover.

48

The pressure on MacMillan to create a new version of *The Prince of the Pagodas* to Britten's only full-length ballet score had finally succeeded. De Valois and John Tooley had been nagging him to do it for years. It had even been written into his 1983 choreographer's contract with the Royal Ballet. But whenever he mentioned *The Prince of the Pagodas* as his next project, he referred to it somewhat disparagingly as a children's ballet. While he had failed to find a suitable collaborator for a new scenario, he had nonetheless come to think of the score possessively as 'his' music whenever there was mention of commissioning someone else to have a go. He was more and more attracted to choreographing in the classical idiom he had employed in *Le Baiser de la fée* and in his contributions to *The Sleeping Beauty* for ABT. And as he was to comment in his eventual programme note for *The Prince of the Pagodas*, he and Cranko, as young hopefuls in 1946, had stood side by side, watching the Sadler's Wells Ballet reopen the Royal Opera House with de Valois's production of *The Sleeping Beauty*. 'We were immensely impressed,' Kenneth recalled, 'and I knew that I had not seen anything so magical in my young life. John was equally moved, and it was from *Beauty* that the idea for *The Prince of the Pagodas* was born.'

By the beginning of 1986, MacMillan had at last found a writer willing to provide him with a version of the scenario that would start his creative juices flowing. Monica Mason had suggested the travel writer and novelist Colin Thubron. He was a long-term friend of hers who admired MacMillan's ballets and who knew the Royal Ballet and its workings well. He had written the text for a 1982 publication, filled with photographs, about the Royal Opera House and its backstage life. Since his travel books included accounts of his journeys through China and other regions of Asia, he seemed ideally placed to collaborate with Kenneth on a *Pagodas* rewrite. He came to dinner at Spencer Park and the two men quickly established a rapport.

Thubron agreed to take on the task, which meant familiarising himself with the score and Cranko's use of it. Dr Donald Mitchell, one of the Executors of the Britten Estate and Chairman of Faber Music, would have right of approval over the new scenario. Mitchell was still insisting there should be no cuts, even though Britten himself had shortened the score for the only recording in 1957, in which the composer had conducted the Royal Opera House Orchestra. MacMillan initially relied on that recording to give him a sound-picture for his eventual ballet while he waited for Thubron (who had never written a scenario before) to come up with an initial outline. (Three years later, MacMillan could work with the new recording conducted by Oliver Knussen, with the missing music restored.)

The background to the score's commission was Britten's enthusiasm for composing for ballet. Cranko had met Britten through their mutual friendship with John Piper and asked his advice on a suitable composer for the three-act ballet he had planned. To his surprise, Britten requested a detailed scenario, complete with timings, and started on the score for *The Prince of the Pagodas* in 1954. Britten then put it aside to set out on a round-the-world recital tour with Peter Pears that involved a trip to Bali. There he was entranced by the melodiously percussive gamelan music that would play an important part in his *Pagodas* and in other later works.

The long tour meant that the ballet score was not completed until some two years after it was commissioned. Britten had seized the opportunity the scenario offered to contrast and combine Eastern and Western influences in his music – a cultural commingling that Cranko was not inspired to explore. He had selected elements from familiar Western fables: the Sleeping Beauty, Beauty and the Beast, Cinderella and *King Lear*, linking them by 'a thread of a plot which was as important or unimportant as the audience chose to make it. These images would provide the different divertissements I wished to make,' Cranko told *The Sunday Times* in an interview published on 13 January 1957. Although the synthetic story provided plenty of pretexts for dancing, it lacked emotional coherence. Narrative impetus flagged, sidetracked by too many divertissements. Audiences found it difficult to care what happened to the central characters.

The Prince of the Pagodas, first staged at Covent Garden in 1957, was dropped from the Royal Ballet repertoire within three years. (Excerpts appeared occasionally in galas.) Although Cranko then mounted it for the Stuttgart and La Scala ballet companies, he abandoned plans to revive *Pagodas* later in the 1960s.* He could not obtain Britten's agreement to cut or rearrange the music – the same problem that bedevilled MacMillan.

---

* Other choreographers used the score: Alan Carter in Munich in 1958, Vaslav Orlikovsky in Basle in 1961, and Richard Alston in 1982, in a one-act version for the Royal Danish Ballet, *Dance from the Kingdom of the Prince of the Pagodas*, to a suite.

As Thubron studied the score and Cranko's scenario, he realised how tightly knit they were. His approach was to delve beneath what he called the 'goulash' of fairy-tale fantasies and weave a stronger thread of a plot that would inspire MacMillan. 'Provided you feel that every moment has some emotional/psychological meaning, then we'll be OK,' Thubron wrote in his covering letter for the draft scenario. He had determined that the main theme of the ballet should be an adolescent girl's search for her identity. This would involve examining 'the inner complexities of love' – a concern that Thubron believed he shared with MacMillan.

In Cranko's original scenario, the heroine, Belle Rose, is the younger daughter of an aged emperor. He has invited four kings from the corners of the earth to court his elder daughter, Belle Épine. When they prefer sweet-natured Rose, malicious Épine seizes control of the kingdom. Evicted from the court, Rose is taken on a magical journey to the land of the pagodas, where a prince appears to her in the guise of a salamander. She flees, returning home to find her father and the court abused and manipulated by Épine. Rose is rescued by the salamander, who turns back into human form when she agrees to marry him.

In Thubron's version, which had to fit the structure of Britten's score, Princess Rose's journey to the land of the pagodas was to be a symbolic one into her subconscious. The four suitor-kings would appear to her in nightmare guises, confronting her with difficult choices. She would have to face up to her fears and hopes about growing into womanhood and resolve them through meeting the mysterious salamander prince. In him, she would project a vision of her future mate: alarming and desirable, he would combine aspects of the four kings who had courted her, as well as being the idealised Prince Charming of a young girl's imagination.

There were plenty of Freudian possibilities in Thubron's scenario, including his suggestion of parallels between the salamander prince and Rose's father, the emperor. Both need her love and pity: they are vulnerable, disfigured, the emperor by old age, the prince by his scaly skin. Rose has to overcome her repugnance in order to rescue both of them through a redemptive act of compassion. Having reached maturity, she can leave her father and marry her prince. Intimations of incest in the emperor's preference for Rose would help account for the elder daughter's jealous rage. Here was another theme likely to appeal to MacMillan: sibling rivalry, with the motherless youngest child in a position of impotence.

MacMillan wrote to Thubron on 4 July 1988 to warn him that what happened in the studio was bound to alter the carefully plotted draft:

I appreciate you trying to fill every section of the music with an idea, but it leaves me no room to manoeuvre . . . It is extremely difficult to translate the written word into a visual image and sometimes I have to go in a roundabout sort of way to get things across – not always the direct way! My response to the music in the studio will of course be triggered off by your outline, but not dictated by it.

The projected date for the premiere was not until May 1989, but Nico Georgiadis needed enough information to start work as soon as possible on the designs, based on his discussions with MacMillan and Thubron.

MacMillan meanwhile had two other projects on the go, with much earlier deadlines. The first was a ballet for the Royal Ballet Upper School, whose end-of-year performance in July would celebrate de Valois's ninetieth birthday. Although he regularly gave permission for the students to perform his work, he had not choreographed anything specially for them since *Dance Suite*, back in 1962. Once again, an exceptionally talented set of students in the Upper School offered a challenge to his imagination. He intended to prove to de Valois that he, and the youngsters, could match her memories of the intricate 'English' footwork of which she had been so proud in the past.

Britten's *Soirées musicales* (1936), a brief, bright orchestral suite, was an arrangement of Rossini tunes from the period when Britten was writing music for films and plays; it has its origins in incidental music for a 1935 film made by the GPO Film Unit. MacMillan found a suitable choreographic style for the students by putting his own twist on the academic steps in their syllabus; he included snappy salutes so that the cast could acknowledge de Valois when she attended their matinee performance in the Royal Opera House – as she always did, even in extreme old age.

Soirées musicales, as the ballet too was to be called, was completed by the beginning of February, allowing the students and their teachers plenty of time to prepare for the Opera House matinee in

July. MacMillan would be away by then, on tour with the Royal Ballet in Australia. He had commissioned designs from Ian Spurling, who came to see *Soirées musicales* in rehearsal at the school. Influenced by the salutes, he gave the costumes a quasi-military flavour, complete with quirky hats. The bandbox-smart ballet used a large cast, with a corps of twelve and nine soloists. Dana Fouras, leggy and lyrical, was the leading lady, with Tetsuya Kumakawa, already a virtuoso at fifteen, outstanding among the young men. He would be taken into the Royal Ballet company at sixteen, in time to dance his first created role as the Fool in *The Prince of the Pagodas*.

MacMillan's second project was a commission from Dance Advance, a small company recently formed by six ex-Royal Ballet dancers. Susan Crow, one of the group's four Artistic Directors, had approached him for a work for their inaugural season in March 1988. They offered him carte blanche, within the constraints of a limited budget and a touring schedule to small-scale theatres. For him, it was a chance to experiment out of the mainstream once again, as he had done for choreographic workshops at the start of his career.

As a break from the neo-classical choreography to which he was committed for *The Prince of the Pagodas*, he turned to the Expressionist mode of his most personal works. He adapted the story of *Hamlet*, distilling the play into a phantasmagoric chamber ballet, using all six dancers in interchangeable roles. MacMillan took it for granted that audiences would be familiar with Shakespeare's best-known tragedy. His starting point was the death of Hamlet's father. Incidents from the play, highly compressed, would provide clues to Hamlet's hallucinations, as he confronts and confuses Gertrude and Ophelia, Claudius, Polonius and his father.

In collaboration with the dancers and with Deborah as his designer, MacMillan worked out how to designate the characters through simple props: a wreath of daisies for Ophelia, crowns for Gertrude and Claudius, a transparent shroud for the Ghost of Hamlet's father. Appropriating these symbolic bits and pieces in turn, the performers put on aspects of the people haunting Hamlet.

MacMillan invented his own expressive language, drawing on the dancers' ballet training but keeping their movements earthbound. He was deliberately avoiding comparisons with other ballet

*Hamlet*s, such as Robert Helpmann's (which he knew well) and John Neumeier's *Hamlet Connotations* (danced by the Stuttgart Ballet and ABT). He sought the dancers' contributions, involving them closely in the creative process. The choreography was swiftly done, completed within a fortnight. Unusually for him, his diary comments about the work were always enthusiastic, though he felt 'knackered – palpitations from working too hard'.

He chose music by two modern composers he had used before, Webern and Martinů, defying de Valois's condemnation of choreographers who resorted to combining different composers. Webern's brief pieces for violin and piano were used to establish key fragments of narrative information; then Martinů's studies for piano and cello took over as exchanges between the swiftly alternating characters became more complex. The result was a combination of an Elizabethan masque and an Expressionist film, its multiple characters a precursor of a device that would later be used by contemporary-dance choreographers in Britain, such as Ian Spink and Matthew Bourne.

Sea of Troubles (its title taken from an image in Hamlet's 'To be or not to be' soliloquy) was a tightly wrought piece that contained, in précis form, MacMillan's perennial concerns. It dealt with mother–son–father relationships and their Freudian implications. Hamlet is haunted by guilt. In trying to exorcise his father's ghost, he becomes responsible for the deaths of Ophelia and her father, Polonius, and then of his mother and Claudius, his uncle and resented step-father. All the pre-doomed characters in *Sea of Troubles* are already phantoms, troubling the audience's imagination. MacMillan was free-associating with Shakespeare's play and coming up with his own concerns about betrayal, guilt and death. Jennifer Jackson, a Dance Advance Director (along with Susan Crow, Michael Batchelor and Sheila Styles) considered *Sea of Troubles* a breakthrough for MacMillan's creativity, which had been constrained in his relationships with the Royal Ballet and American Ballet Theatre. He had been able to focus his energies on an intimate psychological study in dance, without the need to accommodate a large company's corps de ballet. *Sea of Troubles* remains a minor work, however, made for a small group in a studio-theatre space; it has rarely been revived. Although MacMillan admired Dance Advance's enterprise, he was never seriously tempted to break away from well-established ballet institutions, which provided the high quality of dancers and the production values he required. He had no desire to set up his own independent company, or to become a freelance choreographer working with dancers he did not already know.

He accompanied the Dance Advance group to Brighton for their inaugural performances, taking them out for a celebratory dinner at Wheeler's fish restaurant. The premiere of *Sea of Troubles* was at the Gardiner Arts Centre in nearby Falmer, on the campus of the University of Sussex. The mainly young audience enjoyed it, and reviews of the inaugural programme, though mixed, were encouraging.*

Before starting on *The Prince of the Pagodas*, MacMillan went to see Anthony Dowell in his Director's office with an ultimatum. The young dancer he wanted for the leading role of Princess Rose must be made available to him as soon as possible. He had spotted Darcey Bussell while she was still in the Upper School, casting her for one of the soloist roles in his *Concerto* for the annual School matinee in 1986. He responded to her physical boldness and freshness, keeping his eye on her for the future. She had been snapped up by Peter Wright for the Sadler's Wells Royal Ballet as soon as she graduated. Dowell had let her go because she was too tall and striking to join the resident company as a corps-de-ballet dancer and too immature, he felt, to start at soloist level. She would have more opportunities to develop within the touring company. Since she joined, Wright had been bringing her on in carefully judged roles, building her confidence. But now MacMillan was insisting on her for a principal role in his new ballet. Arrangements for her transfer to the Royal Opera House company by the next season were put in train and announced at a press conference in June, shortly before the Royal Ballet set out on tour in Australia.

---

* Dance Advance was to survive as a company until 1991; *Sea of Troubles* was revived by Scottish Ballet in May 1992, and, to mark the tenth anniversary of MacMillan's death, by a group headed by Adam Cooper and by English National Ballet in 2002.

49

The MacMillans flew with the company to Australia. Kenneth, as always, was apprehensive about the long flight to Sydney. He asked his GP for a prescription for tranquillisers to calm his nerves and his 'wonky heartbeat'. He kept experiencing palpitations that he put down to overwork and anxiety. He, Deborah and Charlotte intended to take a holiday in Australia once the opening performances of the tour were out of the way. He had not been feeling well at home and seemed to have developed a chest infection by the time they arrived in Sydney. He assumed that his exhaustion was due to jetlag and kept to his schedule of rehearsals for *Manon* and *The Rite of Spring*.

On free days, he joined Deborah and Charlotte on visits to Deborah's family and friends. After a fortnight in Sydney, the MacMillans travelled to Brisbane, where the Royal Ballet was representing Britain at the Expo World Festival '88. Michael Edgeley, the Australian promoter of the tour, entertained the company lavishly, inviting them all to spend the day at his Gold Coast house with its pool and private beach. Kenneth was feeling so breathless the next day that Deborah asked her Australian anaesthetist friend Dan Hogg to arrange for antibiotics to clear his chest.

Dr Hogg referred Kenneth to a young GP whose surgery was near their hotel. A routine check, followed by an electrocardiogram in the surgery, so worried the GP that he rushed Kenneth straight to hospital, where he was immediately taken into intensive care. His lungs had filled with fluid and he was in danger of dying. The initial diagnosis was that a virus had attacked the pericardium, the membranous sac enclosing the heart. Subsequent tests, including two biopsies of heart tissue, showed no sign of a viral infection. The left side of his heart, however, was badly damaged: Kenneth had evidently suffered a 'silent' heart attack some weeks previously and had been going into massive heart failure in the GP's surgery. Although his life had been saved by prompt intervention, the prognosis was not reassuring. Almost all his main arteries were clogged (only one was clear) and his impaired heart would not be able to withstand surgery. He was stabilised, to be released from hospital after two weeks in order to rest and recuperate before returning home for specialist advice.

Deborah tried not to show how shocked and worried she was. She and Charlotte had been in limbo while the tests were done, visiting Kenneth every day and trying to keep his spirits up. He had been petrified by the biopsies and appalled to learn that he had actually had a heart attack – the very thing he had feared since his stage-fright palpitations as a youngster. As soon as he was able to write, he recorded his anxieties tersely in his diary – 'What is going to happen to me?' – writing how sorry he felt for Deborah and Charlotte, whose fifteenth birthday was spent by his bedside. Visiting him the first time in intensive care, they had passed a dead patient being laid out in the ward. Charlotte, horrified, was further upset to see her helpless father hooked up to drips and machines. 'Mum was amazing. She was protecting him from our fear. "Let's not talk about what might happen. Let's get him the best medical advice." Mum went into automatic mode, taking all the practical decisions.'

Kenneth had no need to discuss his deepest fears with Deborah. They both knew that the worst had almost happened, but now that he had to face the reality of the threat he had anticipated for most of his life, he was able to surmount it. 'I think he was much bigger and stronger than he had let himself believe,' says Deborah. 'He could deal with a crisis – it was always dreading the unknown that wore him down. He was determined to survive. And like he'd had to give up alcohol completely after his stroke in Germany, he was going to have to come off the drugs to which he was addicted.'

The barbiturates and sedatives he had taken ever since the 1970s might have contributed to his coronary disease by weakening his heart muscle. He had in any case so abused his health until his forties by drinking and smoking to excess that the consequences were taking their toll. He had put on weight in recent years after finally giving up smoking; from now on he would have to monitor his weight carefully to ensure that he was not retaining fluid and further damaging his heart.

His and Deborah's immediate concern, however, was to get him well enough to return home to London. On his release from hospital, they first flew back to Sydney. He and Deborah stayed quietly with her parents at their house in the Blue Mountains to the west of the city. Charlotte spent her time with Deborah's brother Roger and his family on their nearby farm, within easy reach. Deborah remembers driving back with Kenneth to her parents' house after a day at Roger's farm, stopping the car on the way back to watch a huge herd of kangaroos and their joeys gathering in the dusk. She and Kenneth felt very much at peace with each other and the natural world: an oasis of calm before the return to London.

Deborah's doctor father, who knew the full extent of Kenneth's heart disease, warned her that he might have to remain inactive for the foreseeable future – a depressing prospect for a choreographer. Kenneth saw a heart specialist in Sydney before taking the flight back to London and was prescribed beta blockers, which made him feel low and exhausted. He was further reduced in spirit by having to rely on a wheelchair during the long journey, which involved a stopover in Hong Kong for two days. While there, he went to see the Hong Kong Ballet (where a friend and former colleague, Gary Trinder, was Artistic Director), which restored a feeling of familiarity with the ballet world he would need to re-enter. Kenneth had no intention of retiring: his heart attack was not going to interrupt his work for longer than was absolutely necessary.

On the MacMillans' return to London, Kenneth was referred to a leading cardiologist, Paul Oldershaw, at the Royal Brompton Hospital. He confirmed the Australian doctors' diagnosis of Kenneth's inoperable heart condition but reassured him that it was manageable. With careful monitoring, he would regain the strength to work, though his hours in the rehearsal room would have to be restricted. Dr Oldershaw was calmly optimistic, understanding how vital it was for MacMillan to continue thinking of himself as a choreographer, not as an invalid. Kenneth knew that he would be living on borrowed time, so he needed to keep creating ballets for as long as he was able. He still had plenty of ideas he wanted to communicate in *The Prince of the Pagodas* and in works to come.

In addition, he had been acutely aware ever since his throat-cancer scare that he had to provide for his family in the event of his death. His pension from the Royal Opera House would not be a large one, since he had been entitled to join the scheme only briefly when he first became Artistic Director in his forties. He and Deborah had taken advice on investing the fees and royalties he earned from his ballets on the stock market but the returns were not proving very productive. To maximise the use of the money, the MacMillans' accountant had recommended they became a Name at Lloyds.

The Lloyds insurance market had long been a haven for the moneyed classes, especially for those with inherited wealth and property. In an era of high taxation, it seemed a safe way of using capital twice to guarantee an income. In the Thatcherite 1980s, financial advisers sought the same advantage for 'new' money, suggesting to people like the MacMillans, looking to maximise their income, that they, too, should join the insurance market. More and more Names were recruited, among them people working in the arts and media with unpredictable incomes, while the potential drawback was played down: in underwriting insurance risks, Names were accepting unlimited liability if their syndicates at Lloyds were to be hit by a series of disasters.

The MacMillans were introduced to a Members' Agent, who put Deborah into Lloyds, committing herself as half the MacMillan Partnership and half-owner of their house. She joined in 1988 for a minimum of three years just as the market started to go sour. Apart from various internal Lloyds scandals (such as the LMX spiral), underwriters had to face a growing mountain of claims for damage to health caused by asbestos. Then, exactly at the time of Kenneth's heart attack, came the disaster of the Piper Alpha oil platform, which exploded in the North Sea at a cost of hundreds of millions of pounds to insurers.

Although the MacMillans were told not to panic, Kenneth's anxiety levels were soaring. He insisted that Deborah abandon being a Lloyds Name as soon as possible. She remained liable, however, for the risks she had already underwritten. The MacMillans would have to pay out lump sums (amounting to £70,000) over the next few years, but at least by pulling out of Lloyds as soon as they could they had avoided possible bankruptcy and the loss of the house. Others in their syndicate were less fortunate. Kenneth, like Deborah, dreaded being in debt. He remembered the secret shame of his father's moonlight flit from Scotland and was convinced that his own family should depend on the income he earned from his ballets, not unreliable market investments.

In order to discuss his future prospects with the Royal Ballet, he and Deborah asked to see Jeremy Isaacs, newly installed as General

Manager of the Royal Opera House. Sir John Tooley had retired in July, at the end of the 1987–88 season, and Isaacs had yet to encounter the MacMillans. He had had a distinguished career in television: one of the founders of Channel 4, he had been closely involved in its (then considerable) arts programming. First and foremost an opera man, like his predecessors, he had been well briefed on the Royal Ballet's history and present situation. He had little experience, however, of either of the two ballet companies' repertoires: he was prepared to leave future planning decisions in the hands of their Artistic Directors, Anthony Dowell and Peter Wright. The MacMillan Partnership arrived in his office to insist that, as General Director, Isaacs should take an overview of the contribution Kenneth had made, and should continue to make, to the Royal Ballet's reputation as a world-class ballet company.

He was now Britain's greatest surviving choreographer, since Ashton had died in his sleep of a heart attack in August. What room in the schedules for both Royal Ballet companies was there likely to be for MacMillan's extensive range of work as he approached his sixtieth birthday in 1989, in damaged health? *The Prince of the Pagodas* would have to be postponed until he was fit enough to finish it. He had hoped in vain for revivals of his more recent ballets, such as *Valley of Shadows* and *Different Drummer*, instead of just the usual box-office staples, *Romeo and Juliet* and *Manon*. None of his one-act works had been included in the schedule for 1988–89. Under the terms of his contract, the Royal Ballet owed him money for works they had failed to commission, as well as anticipated royalties for existing ballets that they apparently had no interest in performing.

Isaacs, taken aback, recorded his impression of meeting the MacMillans in his memoirs of his time in the Royal Opera House, *Never Mind the Moon*: 'They sat together on the sofa, Kenneth scarcely saying a word while she let me have it. In the past, Kenneth's work had been scorned by the Board and neglected by the House. I must ensure that he was properly treated, see to it that more of his ballets were given.' Deborah recalls the meeting as forthright, even rude. She was infuriated by Isaacs advising Kenneth not to stress himself. 'Have you any idea of the stress – the soul-destroying effect – of his one-act ballets being dropped as if they were worthless?' she said in Kenneth's defence, while he sat in silence. Isaacs's response was to dismiss her by saying that her job was to get Kenneth well.

Far from reassured, MacMillan was still brooding over his treatment by the Royal Ballet when he bumped into a journalist, Jeffery Taylor, in the Royal Opera House. Taylor, a former dancer with Peter Darrell's Western Theatre Ballet, was now a freelance writer. He had been interviewing a dancer for an article when he came across MacMillan, who was in the building to inspect Georgiadis's model set for *The Prince of the Pagodas*. 'Kenneth looked absolutely dreadful,' Taylor says. 'Tired and drained and depressed about his future. He wanted to talk, so we went for a coffee and he poured out his troubles. I said, "Why don't we do a proper interview, and I'll place it with a newspaper. We'll agree on exactly what you want to say before it's published, so there won't be any nasty surprises."'

Kenneth consulted Deborah, and Taylor was invited to the Spencer Park house to talk to them both on 5 October. The resulting article eventually appeared in the *Evening Standard* magazine on 2 December 1988. It was given a big spread, with colour photographs of Kenneth in the garden with the family dogs and seated indoors on an oriental opium bed. He was cross-legged on the wooden bed, as was an oriental puppet Deborah had picked up in Bangkok, lolling crazily on a cushion matching his. The message, for anyone used to reading visual clues, was that MacMillan was the Royal Ballet's discarded puppet-master and plaything.

The article was headed with rhetorical questions: 'Who put the knife in Mac? Why does the label "black sheep of the Royal Ballet" still stick to Kenneth MacMillan?' Taylor, concerned that the interview might damage MacMillan's relationship with the Royal Ballet, had double-checked that he did not want, after all, to back down. Though anxiety continued to gnaw at MacMillan during the weeks preceding publication, he did not retract his remarks. The article quoted him as saying, 'I have a feeling someone along the line has decided that I have taken a wrong turning, that my works do not fit the current vision of the Royal Ballet.' Taylor added his own comment: 'But then, they rarely have.'

After wondering whether 'some of the mud slung by a hostile press over the years has stuck' to the choreographer's reputation within the Royal Opera House, Taylor ran through controversies over MacMillan's work from the 1950s on, claiming that the seven years of his directorship of the Royal Ballet had 'witnessed one of the most bitter and sustained attacks on an individual by the critical fraternity that have ever been seen in this country'. Deborah was quoted as saying, 'The paranoia is almost tangible in this house.' She pointed out that there were more performances of her husband's work overseas in any one week than in a whole year in his own country. Kenneth's sense of grievance rang out from his statement at the conclusion of the article: 'I have to say I feel I have been treated very strangely by the Royal Ballet. There is no reassurance they will reinstate my works. I am entering only my sixtieth year and I have a lot left to say, balletically. But I genuinely wonder where I am going to say it.'

As MacMillan had anticipated, the *Evening Standard* article was a cause of concern for the company and the Board. It is evident from the handwritten draft of a letter to the Board he had prepared as self-justification that he believed de Valois was the 'someone' who thought his work no longer fitted her vision of the Royal Ballet. He was convinced that her influence had led the Board and Anthony Dowell to lose confidence in him, at a point when the direction his work was taking found little favour with the public or the critics. He felt that he was forever on trial, in spite of all the years his ballets had formed an essential part of the Royal Ballet's repertoire.

Whether or not as a result of the publicity the article had engendered, plans were put in train to mark his sixtieth birthday the following year with revivals of *My Brother, My Sisters* and *Requiem*, as well as the premiere of *The Prince of the Pagodas*. This had been postponed for six months; its opening gala was now scheduled to take place just four days before he turned sixty on 11 December 1989. The Royal Ballet would be seen to be honouring him, some forty years after he first joined the company as a young dancer.

He had meanwhile entered into negotiations with other ballet companies to ensure further outlets for his work. English National Ballet (the new name of London Festival Ballet, directed by Peter Schaufuss) staged the one-act *Anastasia* in June 1989, with Lynn Seymour as a guest in the role she had created in Berlin. Scottish Ballet, still recovering from the death of Peter Darrell at the end of 1987, was planning to mount MacMillan's *Sea of Troubles*, while hoping to afford several of his larger ballets. The Paris Opéra Ballet had finally agreed to take *Manon* into its repertoire. MacMillan was determined to make the most of the time left to him, and to earn as much money as he could for Deborah and Charlotte.

At home, he had accepted a regime of watching his weight and his diet. If his weight fluctuated, it meant he was retaining fluid, and his medication had to be altered. Interviewed in January 1990 for a weekly feature page in the *Sunday Times* magazine, 'A Life in the Day of . . .', he was quoted as saying:

I'm on a very strict diet, so for breakfast I'm restricted to raw oats, skimmed milk, a banana and a cup of tea. Occasionally I long for eggs and sausages and steamed English pud with cream [for lunch]. But that's fantasy! I'm not allowed them and have to eat boring things like salads, fish and fruit. We don't socialise much. Deborah is a wonderful cook, so we often have people round, generally people outside ballet. Sometimes I cook, but usually muck up the kitchen and leave masses of washing up, so I don't often do it.

The domestic routine he described for the feature was one of contentment: his daughter kissing him before going off to school, Deborah painting in her studio, evenings spent watching television together (plays, documentaries, popular soaps such as *EastEnders* and *Dynasty*, and *Top of the Pops* 'to keep up with Charlotte'). People who had lost contact with him over the years were surprised and touched by the article, having never expected him to settle into family life. Though the magazine feature, which always had to be approved by its subject, gave little away, it was nonetheless revealing about the happiness he had allowed himself to acknowledge since his heart attack.

Deborah's recollection is that Kenneth was

a lighter person after the heart attack, able to enjoy things more – when he wasn't enraged by the Royal Ballet. You can't live in constant awareness of mortality. You split yourself off, go into denial, make the most of what time you have left. And because he had to come off all the pills he'd been taking for years, he wasn't so blanked off. I'd begun to see the side of him that people had described when he was young: he could be funny, very affectionate, very endearing.

His doctors had declared him fit enough to return to work on *The Prince of the Pagodas* in November 1988, provided he did not overexert himself: he was advised to work no more than an hour and a half a day. Monica Mason, seated by his side in the rehearsal room, worried about him. Deborah advised her to let him make his own decisions about when he needed to stop, and reassured her stoically, 'If the worst happens, it happens – there's nothing we can do about it.'

He had done some preliminary choreography before his heart attack, beginning with the wicked sister, Épine, and the four Kings. (Lesley Collier, cast as Épine, had to be replaced when she became pregnant; Fiona Chadwick was to be the first Épine.) He had been waiting for Darcey Bussell to join the resident company, before starting on the triumphant wedding pas de deux for Princess Rose and the Prince in the last act, so that he would know where the ballet was leading. Jonathan Cope as the Prince was now an experienced partner who would be able to guide Bussell through the collaborative process. 'What I did was lousy,' MacMillan commented in his diary, 'but good to be back at work.' Within a week, he was pleased with the pas de deux he was creating, noting that it was 'very Petipa Grand Pas' – a conscious echo of *The Sleeping Beauty*'s final pas de deux. He tired easily, sometimes having to skip rehearsals. Catching sight of himself in the studio's mirrored wall, he realised how hot and red he became by the end of a session. He still had the nervous energy, however, to have his habitual rows with Georgiadis over the preliminary costume designs, though he confided to his diary that the scenery would be beautiful.

He and Georgiadis had settled on a kingdom in crisis, with its subjects reverting to savagery. The court was to be dressed in Elizabethan costume, assuming ape-like masks (and behaviour) when evil Épine seized power. The Emperor's domain was represented by miniature castles, the Salamander-Prince's by pagodas and long oriental banners. Georgiadis's maquette of the set looked like an illuminated manuscript translated into three dimensions.

By MacMillan's fifty-ninth birthday on 11 December 1988, he felt back on course as a creator, though he still had a long haul ahead of him to complete *The Prince of the Pagodas*. The day after his birthday, the sound of emergency vehicles and helicopters filled the area around Spencer Park. A commuter train had been derailed just outside Clapham Junction, the nearest station to the house. Thirty-five people were killed in an accident that shocked the nation. The MacMillans followed the news coverage with appalled fascination, aware of how abruptly disaster had struck so many unsuspecting passengers close by.

648

50

As MacMillan started to ease himself back into his former work routine in 1989, he reconsidered his priorities. He had to complete *The Prince of the Pagodas*, which was likely to be the last three-act ballet he would undertake. He wanted his work to be widely seen but he saw little point in continuing his transatlantic association with American Ballet Theatre. While he was recuperating from his heart attack, Baryshnikov had appointed a second Artistic Associate, the American choreographer Twyla Tharp, so MacMillan's role with the company was further diminished. Since it had caused him more anguish than pleasure over the past two years, he decided to resign before his second three-year contract was up. He flew by Concorde to New York in May to see Baryshnikov and the company for the last time, and handed in his resignation. One month later, Baryshnikov quit, after a dispute with ABT's new Executive Director, Jane Hermann, who had sacked Charles France. She was left to pick up the pieces and take charge of the demoralised company.

ABT's Board of Trustees had meanwhile not paid MacMillan royalties for the use of his ballets. Concerned about the company's deficit, the Board was avoiding paying its debts by asking its members to convert their loans into gifts. The Trustees hoped that MacMillan would similarly forgo the money he was owed, but, stung by Lloyds' demands on Deborah, the couple could not afford to do so.

Kenneth turned to Ben Stevenson in Texas, who confirmed that Houston Ballet would welcome him as its Artistic Associate. Stevenson was delighted to consolidate the connection with his old friend. After years of pleading with MacMillan to create a ballet for Houston, Stevenson had secured the promise of a new work involving a well-known Houston jazz singer, Kelly Gray, only to have it fall through because of MacMillan's illness. Instead, Houston now had the right to mount *The Song of the Earth* and *Gloria*. By appointing him as Artistic Associate, Stevenson hoped for many more ballets, including *Manon*, which was finally to enter the Houston Ballet repertoire in 1993, after MacMillan's death.

Houston Ballet, unlike American Ballet Theatre, had been well funded, with the largest endowment of any ballet company in the

United States. During the years of Stevenson's tenure as Artistic Director, it had never exceeded its budgets. Now, in its twentieth year, intensive fund-raising had expanded the 1989–90 budget to $9.1 million. The company had just taken on Christopher Bruce, the British choreographer and former Director of Ballet Rambert/Rambert Dance Company, as its resident choreographer, not long before MacMillan approached Stevenson. Its Executive Director, Gary Dunning, agreed that the company could also afford to employ MacMillan in an advisory capacity for an annual fee of $25,000, plus licence fees and royalties for his ballets. Dunning, who had been General Manager of ABT in the mid-1980s, knew MacMillan well and appreciated the kudos his name would bring the Texan company, even if he could not be present in person very often. Since MacMillan wanted to cut down on long-distance travel, his contract did not specify a minimum amount of time he would have to spend in Houston: consultations could be done by letter, fax or telephone.

MacMillan's new post would come into effect when Houston Ballet, in celebration of its twentieth anniversary, was to appear at the Edinburgh Festival for the first time in August 1989.* The association with MacMillan ensured added publicity for the visit, but since none of his ballets was scheduled for the Festival, he was free to concentrate on finishing *The Prince of the Pagodas* for the Royal Ballet.

As he worked on *Pagodas*, MacMillan was making Darcey Bussell into the ballerina he needed for the leading role. His relationship with her was quasi-paternal: at nineteen, she was only a few years older than Charlotte. Yet because he had no time or energy to spare, he was exigent with Bussell, expecting her to keep up with his changes of mind from day to day. He was experimenting with whatever he could make her do, and she was too inexperienced to protest. Overawed, she could barely bring herself to speak to him. He took Monica Mason aside after one rehearsal and asked her to tell Darcey please to use his name when she addressed him. Mason realised that Darcey didn't dare call him Kenneth, and therefore sounded rudely abrupt when she asked, 'Do you want me to

---

* The Houston company staged Stevenson's *Swan Lake* at the Festival, alongside a mixed bill including two ballets by Christopher Bruce.

stand over here?' Still shy, she was persuaded to be more familiar with him.

According to MacMillan's diary, he found Bussell frustratingly laid back and slow at responding to what he wanted. He had become accustomed to working with dancers who could second guess where he might be going, as well as remembering what he had tried out before. In fact, Bussell's laid-back air was an attempt to disguise the fact that she was overwhelmed, tired and confused. She was coming to his rehearsals in between learning other roles in the repertoire to gain experience before tackling her first three-act ballet.

Bussell was quoted as saying,

I remember Kenneth saying to me, 'Stop, Darcey, you're always running off.' I said, 'Well, I've got another rehearsal to get to.' 'Well, sometimes you've got to stay in my rehearsal a little bit longer and talk about the work we've just done.' I suppose it was a protective thing, but also I had to zoom off for a *Swan Lake* rehearsal.

Instead of being nurtured as a newcomer, as she had been in Peter Wright's company, Bussell was now thrown in at the deep end and expected to justify her sudden prominence. She was over-burdened with all the information she needed to retain, and she was acutely aware of other dancers' envy at the opportunities she was being given. After she had burst into tears one day, MacMillan noted, 'I now know what throws her – when I change things she cannot remember any steps at all!' He realised that he needed to make allowances for her youth and build her fragile confidence instead of undermining it.

He was using Bussell's physical attributes to define Princess Rose's character. She was broad-shouldered, strong and flexible, much taller than the dancers he usually preferred. Thubron described her particular appeal in the *Weekend Telegraph* of 2 December 1989 as 'like the plushness of a grape with the bloom still on it . . . On stage she projects a God-given blend of softness and athleticism.' Like all MacMillan's favourite dancers, she had highly arched feet: her very long legs, extended high in arabesque or second position, could appear phallic; her wide-eyed girlish face, with its tip-tilted nose, proclaimed her innocence. MacMillan's choreography would display her as unknowingly erotic but also bold and powerful, far removed from the waif-like girls of his earliest ballets. Her forthright frankness would make her Princess Rose very different from the flawed heroines in *Manon* and *Mayerling*. He hoped that she would succeed in asserting Rose's independence and sense of identity, coming triumphantly through her rite of passage.

For the start of the last-act pas de deux, in which Rose and the Prince formally declare their commitment to each other, he placed the couple in a strange, suggestive variation on the opening position in *The Sleeping Beauty*'s grand adagio. In that, Aurora turns her back to the audience to address the Prince, holding his hand and extending a leg towards him, before turning round in his embrace. In MacMillan's version, the pair face forward, side by side as equal partners. She extends one leg high to the side as she balances on point, holding the Prince's hand beneath her upraised leg. The eye is inexorably drawn to the clasped hands at the woman's groin, her leg trapped close by her ear. Bussell's natural air of candour, and her athletic ease, made the indecorous position startling but acceptable. On any other dancer, it risks looking grotesque.

The pas de deux is a technically difficult one. Its structure might echo that of *The Sleeping Beauty* grand adagio, but the flying lifts are more daring, the arm's-length promenades at an acute angle more like those in ice-skating than classical ballet. Bussell was still unaccustomed to being partnered, so she had to put complete faith in Jonathan Cope's ability to manoeuvre her into the shapes MacMillan required. As the creation of the ballet progressed, she would have to deal with yet more partners in the four Kings who woo Princess Rose. Bussell had a great deal to learn, since the heroine is on stage for most of the ballet.

MacMillan established Rose at the start as an eager, almost boisterous girl playing with her mercurial companion, the Fool. He is the court jester, wiser than his title implies; he is to be Rose's guide on her journey to maturity. The role was created on the phenomenal abilities of Tetsuya Kumakawa, still only seventeen and not long out of the Royal Ballet School. His leaps were so high and light that some spectators would actually wonder whether he was assisted by wires. Bussell, too, had an impressive jump: *Pagodas* publicity photographs that caught her in mid-flight show her soaring upwards like a jet plane. Both roles, as well as that of the Prince, require tremendous stamina. MacMillan, grounded by his heart condition, was making taxing demands of his young dancers.

He developed a movement motif for Rose to match the wistful oboe theme Britten had given her. By drawing attention to her eyes, MacMillan predicted the insight she would eventually acquire. She is twice blindfolded by the Fool, first for a game in the palace, then again when he has led her through the maze of pagodas to find the enchanted Prince. In a key solo before meeting the Prince, she points her fingers towards her temple, as if seeking clearer sight. Once she learns to see truly during her Act II pas de deux with the Salamander-Prince, her blindfold and his scales fall away; her newly discovered compassion breaks the spell that binds him as she blossoms into a maternal woman, cradling him in her arms.

En route to the kingdom of the pagodas, she has re-encountered the four Kings who courted her in her father's kingdom. The King of the North is coarse and heavy; the King of the East vain; the King of the West is an effete fop with a handkerchief into which he sneezes; the King of the South is both voluptuous and threatening, accompanied by the sound of brass and drums. (The music for the Four Kings' nightmare pas de deux with Rose was appropriated from the 'elements' music originally intended for a corps of clouds, flames and water creatures.) Rose is particularly attracted and repelled by the King of the South, the most brutal and overtly sexual of her suitors. He threatens to overcome her resistance: she fights him off, kicking him between the legs. He has aroused in her feelings that she refuses to acknowledge but which will be transmuted into her love for the Prince.

The Prince is a typically dual MacMillan character. As the Salamander, he writhes in agony, gripping his head like Rudolf in *Mayerling*; he wears a reptilian half-mask, reminiscent of the sinister masks in *My Brother, My Sisters* and *The Song of the Earth*. As the Prince, he is transformed into a reliable, fairy-tale consort for the ballet's happy ending. The scenario does not allow for him to retain aspects of his once beastly nature, though MacMillan managed to slip in a few hints in his pas de deux with Rose. For her, the transition from innocence to experience has been a triumph of love conquering all.

She has overcome her evil 'twin', the bad sister whose sexuality is unchecked: Épine is the whore to Rose's madonna, the two characters kept distinct. MacMillan had a struggle to create a balance between them, since his instinct was to give the most interesting choreography to the unabashedly sensual woman. Both have solo variations, thanks to the music Britten provided. In other ballets, MacMillan's central characters rarely describe or examine themselves in danced monologues. They react instead to the social pressures on them, finding their self-expression in pas de deux rather than solos.

Many of the solo roles in *The Prince of the Pagodas* were, to some extent, portraits or caricatures of the dancers on whom they were created. Cast members recall that MacMillan tended to be terse with them as he was creating *The Prince of the Pagodas*: if he did not get the inspiration he needed from the dancers he had chosen, he took their roles away and gave them to others. (He used the words 'threw' or 'kicked them out' of his ballet repeatedly in his diary.) Stephen Jefferies, for example, who had been cast as King of the South, was abruptly replaced after months of work with MacMillan. Ashley Page, who took over the role, believes he contributed most of the remaining choreography for the character by offering his own ideas. MacMillan, who set the King of the South's sinister solo in slow motion, acclaimed it as his personal breakthrough in his diary, his difficulties solved by the change of dancer.

He put a savage parody of himself into the ballet. The role of the Emperor was an exaggerated account of the man he had become since his heart attack. The infirm ruler, in the person of Anthony Dowell, was surrounded by doctors vying to take charge of him. He was stricken not only by old age but by what looked very like a heart condition. He frequently clutched his chest in distress; when his wicked daughter Épine seized his crown, he suffered a seizure. By the start of the last act he was confined to a wheelchair, as MacMillan had been during his return from Australia. The court, now in the guise of baboons, torments the helpless Emperor, unable to stand up for himself: MacMillan, through Dowell, was showing how ghastly the job of artistic director could be. In the ballet, the ageing Emperor had lost control over his kingdom by rashly giving it away, his trust betrayed: MacMillan feared that the Royal Opera House placed no value on his legacy of ballets.

In July 1989, in the midst of creating *The Prince of the Pagodas*, MacMillan confided to his diary that he felt 'extremely old and lonely – utterly dejected'. Deborah and Charlotte had gone on holiday to Portugal, while he concentrated on the last work he could do on *Pagodas* before the Royal Ballet took its summer break. He was cheered, however, by an end-of-season run-through of the choreography he had so far completed: 'V. nervous. Liked what I have done – 1 hr 10 mins!' He was nearly halfway through.

He set out for the United States shortly afterwards, his visit to New York coinciding with English National Ballet's July season at the Met. They were performing his one-act *Anastasia*, with Lynn Seymour in the title role, in a triple bill that alternated with Ashton's *Romeo and Juliet* (a reworking, commissioned by Peter Schaufuss, of Ashton's 1955 production for the Royal Danish Ballet). MacMillan then flew to Houston to sign his contract as Artistic Associate with the company and choose the cast for *Gloria*, the next of his ballets to enter Houston's repertoire.

While he was in Houston, he visited Margot Fonteyn in the specialist hospital where she was being treated for cancer. News of her illness had been kept from the outside world at her request, but she was pleased to see old friends and colleagues. MacMillan told her he intended to dedicate *The Prince of the Pagodas* to her, in memory of *The Sleeping Beauty* in which she had so impressed him when he was a young dancer. Throughout his career as a choreographer, he kept the good-luck telegrams and cards of congratulation she sent him. Her last letter to him, just before the premiere of *The Prince of the Pagodas*, was a note of thanks for the dedication, saying that she was thinking of him and of the ballet 'which I hear is full of beautiful dancing'. She died on 21 February 1991.

When the Royal Ballet returned after the summer break, rehearsals started for *My Brother, My Sisters* and *Requiem*, for the programme to mark MacMillan's forthcoming sixtieth birthday. Neither ballet had been done for some years and *Requiem* would need extra rehearsal time with the singers from the opera company. MacMillan was meanwhile finishing the choreography for the last act of *Pagodas*, adding to the wedding pas de deux a section of music that he had only just heard in the new recording conducted by Oliver Knussen of the uncut score. Cope protested that his solo variation was too demanding, coming as it did after he had danced flamboyant fights with all four Kings, defiant suitors for Princess Rose. MacMillan insisted that he acquired the stamina to execute the virtuoso steps. Cope was in an unhappy state of mind: disillusioned with his career as a principal dancer, he was intending to retire at the end of the season, along with his ballerina wife, Maria Almeida.* Though they were still in their twenties, she wanted to change their lives and leave ballet behind them: the stress was making her ill. Difficulties and tensions during the creative period of *The Prince of the Pagodas* reinforced their view that an alternative way of living would suit them better.

MacMillan was too preoccupied with *Pagodas* to travel to Houston in September to supervise the staging of *Gloria*. Deborah went in his place, staying for the week leading up to the first night. Kenneth missed her dreadfully while she was away, ringing her six times a day. She came back bearing enthusiastic reviews for Houston Ballet's production of *Gloria*, while he fretted about the Royal Ballet's lack of rehearsal time for the revival of his other choral work, *Requiem*.

The Prince of the Pagodas was nearing its final phase. MacMillan, over-tired ('Feel whole ballet stinks'), had even worse rows than usual with Georgiadis over his costume designs, including those for Rose and the corps de ballet of courtiers. He had to commit his thoughts about the ballet to paper, which he hated doing, for the *Pagodas* programme book. He and Thubron hammered out a concise synopsis of the action, and were required to write their own accounts of how the new version of *The Prince of the Pagodas* had come about. MacMillan asked Thubron to check his contribution for grammatical inelegancies, a task he had often confided to Clement Crisp. He also had to have an up-to-date portrait photograph for the programme (and his sixtieth birthday) taken by his old friend Anthony Crickmay. Kenneth had only recently shaved off the moustache he had worn for most of his adult life and felt vulnerable without it. He half hid his face with the upturned collar of his greatcoat, resulting in a series of theatrically dramatic photographs. (Those were the ones selected for publicity purposes: in others, Kenneth was laughing as he posed for Crickmay, refusing to take himself nearly as seriously as the solemn

---

* They left the company in July 1990 and started a family. Predictions that Cope would return before long were fulfilled within two years, when he resumed his career and developed into one of the Royal Ballet's most admired leading dancers. He retired from dancing in 2006 and became a répétiteur with the company.

photographs implied.) The moustache had come off as a kind of tease for Charlotte, to see if she would notice its absence. She didn't until he pointed it out, even though she had protested for years that it made him look old-fashioned.

He celebrated having finished *The Prince of the Pagodas* on 11 November, a month before his sixtieth birthday, by inviting Anthony Dowell, Jay Jolley and Monica Mason to dinner at home, together with Ben Stevenson, who was visiting from Houston. They were all at ease with each other, optimistic about the new ballet after its long gestation. MacMillan's relief, after nearly two years' work on the choreography, was short-lived. In an interview with the *Evening Standard* to publicise *The Prince of the Pagodas*, which appeared on 30 November, he admitted to Robin Stringer that he felt 'a bit exhausted because the pressure is mounting. I don't think I get quite as hysterical . . . I mean I get hysterical but not quite as often.' Once the run-throughs and full-length rehearsals were under way, however, he agonised over whether Bussell might lose her nerve.

Also at the end of November, Princess Margaret, the Royal Ballet's patron, came to see a rehearsal of Act I in the studio, which went very well. But as soon as rehearsals moved to the Opera House stage, with extras and students from the School, and the orchestra for the first time in the pit, chaos prevailed. The first dress rehearsal on 4 December was so disastrous that MacMillan wondered whether he should cancel the ballet entirely.

There were problems with the costumes, sending the wardrobe department into flurries of alterations. The musicians struggled to familiarise themselves with Britten's music and the tempi the dancers required. The dancers found the orchestrated score impossible to follow, as they failed to recognise phrases and melodies that had been broken down into a series of counts for them in piano rehearsals. Much of the choreography for the corps was so intricately structured that if one person went wrong, whole sequences unravelled. '*Pagodas* was a ballet in which everyone in the house had a hard time,' said an experienced member of the corps. 'I've never known such a fraught run-up to a first night. Nothing and nobody was ready.'

The opening gala on 7 December was in any case imperilled. The dancers were refusing to work overtime, threatening to go on strike under the leadership of their Equity representative, Wayne Eagling. The opera chorus had received a pay increase for the 1989–90 season, while the dancers had not. (The members of the opera chorus were paid a flat-rate salary, which had just been increased, whereas the dancers' pay was on different levels, according to status and experience.) The dancers were further aggrieved by being asked to perform the Polovtsian dances in Borodin's opera *Prince Igor*, for no extra fee. From the start of his tenure as General Manager, Isaacs had decreed that the Royal Opera House was a single institution, not two rival companies requiring to be paid extra to participate in each other's productions. This assertion came as an unwelcome surprise to the dancers. They claimed they were being treated as underpaid fodder for a grandiose opera production. Isaacs suspected their grievances were being stirred by a few militants, led by Eagling, who were trying to test his mettle. They expected him to concede their wage increase since the fundraising gala of *The Prince of the Pagodas* would otherwise have to be cancelled.

Isaacs refused. In order to save the gala, whose date could not be postponed, he cancelled instead two performances of the triple bill that included *My Brother, My Sisters, Requiem* and, ironically, Eagling's own ballet as a tyro choreographer, *Frankenstein, a Modern Prometheus*. The dancers would therefore not go into overtime during the crucial dress and technical rehearsals for *Pagodas*, provided they were prepared to co-operate. If they refused or procrastinated, the tight schedule of preparations would be compromised. MacMillan, already frantic with anxiety over his ballet, feared the worst.

Deborah took matters into her hands. Encountering Eagling as she walked through the staff car park, she informed him with the vehemence of Australian frankness at its most forceful that he was endangering her husband's life by persisting in 'industrial action'. He knew that Kenneth was ill, she said, and that he had given all the strength he had to creating *Pagodas* (in which Eagling had no role). The company depended on Kenneth for its creative life and reputation – and here was Eagling devaluing all that Kenneth had done, simply in order to score points against the management. He should be mature enough to see the bigger picture, she said, instead of misleading youngsters in the corps into a dispute that could be settled by other means. Shaken, Eagling reported her distress to the dancers, who agreed to co-operate for Kenneth's sake. Eagling was convinced at the time that the dancers' militant action was justified. He claimed that he was championing the cause of underpaid youngsters by taking a tough line. Only later, once he was himself Artistic Director of the Dutch National Ballet and then English National Ballet, did he fully appreciate the distress his stance had caused in the preparations for an important new work.

The gala premiere went ahead as scheduled, the dancers giving of their best. The performance was warmly applauded for the quality of the dancing in a cornucopia of neo-classical choreography, though there were many reservations about whether the new scenario sustained sufficient interest over three acts. When MacMillan stepped forward to take his bow at the end, he made a short declaration to the effect that 'classical ballet was alive and well and living in London'. 'It was so unlike him to speak from the stage,' says Deborah. 'He had to shout because he didn't have a microphone, but it was obviously something he wanted to say.' It was his defiant response to an article by John Drummond opining that the art form was in terminal decline. John Drummond, who was knighted in 1995, was a Governor of the Royal Ballet from 1986 to 1997. He had been Director of the Edinburgh Festival between 1978 and 1983, and Controller of Radio 3, as well as a writer and producer of radio and TV programmes. Drummond, who had first been entranced as a young man by the Ballets Russes, had reached the conclusion that classical ballet now faced an uncertain future. MacMillan and the Royal Ballet disagreed. To add to the euphoria at the end of the premiere, Darcey Bussell was promoted to principal, aged twenty – the youngest in the company's recent history.

Kenneth's first ballet teacher from Retford, Joan Thomas, and her daughter stayed overnight with the MacMillans so that they could attend the next performance on 8 December. Miss Thomas, as Kenneth still thought of her, had been in contact, thanks to the publicity *The Prince of the Pagodas* and his imminent sixtieth birthday had received. He had invited her to London to see his ballet, arranging tickets for her, as he had done when she came to see *Romeo and Juliet* nearly twenty-five years earlier. Joan Thomas wanted to re-establish that *she* had been the teacher who set his future career on course, despite the attention Phyllis Adams had received when

Isadora was dedicated to her eight years previously. Satisfied that her own role had been acknowledged, Miss Thomas and her daughter returned to the dance school they ran together in Newark, not far from Retford.

On 11 December, the day of MacMillan's sixtieth birthday, the audience at *The Prince of the Pagodas* gave him a standing ovation. He came on stage wearing a pink-grey cord jacket and bow-tie, an outfit he had chosen himself in place of the dinner jacket he had donned for the gala premiere, or the informal clothes in which he usually took curtain calls. After the performance, he attended a dinner in his honour in the de Valois Studio at the back of the Opera House. Birmingham Royal Ballet also fêted him with a party at Sadler's Wells, where the company's London season included a triple bill of his ballets in the repertoire: *Danses concertantes*, *Solitaire* and *Las Hermanas*. He was, at last, being publicly acknowledged as the Royal Ballet's greatest living choreographer. (A list of his ballets, over seventy so far, was included as a birthday tribute in *The Prince of the Pagodas* programme.) Now that Ashton was no longer around, loyal colleagues and Board members who had been apprehensive about upsetting him felt able to give due praise to MacMillan's achievements. Deborah remarked how greatly the atmosphere at the Royal Opera House had changed over the past year: 'People had exaggerated Fred's sensitivity in his old age. He was perfectly friendly to Kenneth and came round quite often for meals at our house. He and Kenneth got on together. But I noticed that we received invitations to certain people's houses only after Fred had died.'

For Kenneth, one of the most touching tributes he received was from the pupils at the Royal Ballet's Junior School at White Lodge in Richmond Park. They sang 'Happy Birthday' to him when he arrived on 15 December to award the prize for student choreography he had instituted the previous year. He had stipulated that the sum of money the winner received was to be spent on seeing arts other than ballet. He was concerned that ballet-mad youngsters no longer had the stimulus or opportunity he had enjoyed, growing up in post-war London, to experience what was taking place outside the narrow, obsessive world of technical training.

Deborah gave a birthday party for him at home two days later, with ninety friends and colleagues. 'Great success,' he enthused in his diary. 'Deb. a wonder!' For once, he thoroughly enjoyed a big party and was unembarrassed about making a short speech. His wife remarked that he was becoming quite good at public speaking. His diary entry was full of praise for her: she was his lioness, defending him against attack and celebrating his achievements. He in turn was always pleased when her artistic skills were recognised, and encouraged her to display her work in galleries and exhibitions. 'He'd spin a fantasy about the future, when he would become a mere footnote to my career as an artist: "Ah, Deborah Williams," he'd muse. "Wasn't that man called Kenneth or Keith something . . . ah yes, Kenneth MacMillan, wasn't he somehow involved with her?"'

By the end of the year, *The Prince of the Pagodas* and his sixtieth birthday had prompted considerable media coverage. BBC Television (via Derek Bailey's production company, Landseer) was preparing a documentary profile of him for the New Year. Bailey was also to record *Pagodas* in performance: the two videos would later be sold together in a cassette or DVD format. Feature articles assessing MacMillan's career appeared in the national press and in dance magazines in Britain, Germany and the United States. Some were by his loyal supporters (Clement Crisp and Edward Thorpe), others by critics who had often been hostile to those of his works they took against (John Percival, Horst Koegler, Deirdre McMahon) but who acknowledged his refusal to be limited by convention.

Percival's appraisal in *The Times* of 2 December, headed 'Opportunities Lost and Taken' concluded by speculating that MacMillan's considerable talent had been stifled by the artistic conservatism of the Royal Opera House. He might have fared better, Percival suggested, if he had been given a hand-picked company, like those of Pina Bausch, Jiří Kylián and William Forsythe, and 'the opportunity obsessively to pursue his own purposes'. Horst Koegler compared his Royal Ballet circumstances unfavourably with those in which John Cranko had flourished in Stuttgart. McMahon in *Dance Theatre Journal* considered him very much a product of the Royal Ballet's tradition of dramatic choreography, but found that his work had followed an increasingly 'sterile course' after *Mayerling*. In the *Royal Academy of Dancing Magazine* Thorpe acknowledged that:

These last five years have been, for many of us, a dispiriting hiatus in MacMillan's choreographic career. Now, at the comparatively young age of sixty, restored to health and imbued with that same imaginative ferment that has produced such a large canon of great works, we may look forward to many more years of his creative genius.

MacMillan had less than three years to live.

51

Eighteen months after MacMillan's heart attack in Australia, his health appeared to be relatively stable, although he complained of always feeling tired and breathless. Then a new scare presented itself. The left side of his body had been weaker than the right since his stroke in Munich in 1969. The movement in his left arm had become so restricted in the mid-1980s that he was unable to demonstrate properly in rehearsals. A six-month course of exercises with Dreas Reyneke, a Pilates instructor much trusted by dancers, had alleviated the problem, but now his left leg had to started to wither alarmingly. His GP referred him to a neurologist, who took one look at him and declared, 'I can see you have Parkinson's Disease from the way you're holding your left hand.' Always prone to hypochondria, MacMillan spent the next few days dreading either the onset of Parkinson's or a brain tumour. An MRI scan of his brain showed no sign of disease, though the scan revealed scar tissue confirming that he had indeed suffered a stroke in Germany twenty years earlier. It turned out that the problem of his weakened left leg was caused not by incipient Parkinson's Disease but by a pinched nerve in his back, which was eased by manipulation and physiotherapy.

Scares about her father's health disturbed Charlotte, who was studying for her O-level exams at More House School. She would turn seventeen in August and a family decision had been taken that she should change schools for her A levels. She had applied to Bedales in East Hampshire, a progressive, co-educational boarding school that was particularly strong in the arts. Bedales had accepted her in January for entry in September 1990, provided her O-level grades were good enough. She would know the results towards the end of August, after her birthday. Although she had agreed that she should go to boarding school, Charlotte felt that she was being sent away by her parents so that she would not be troubled by their worries:

I resented being left out of this triangular relationship. I was the child, who wasn't told what was going on when Dad was ill or upset, because they were trying to protect me. But Dad was also the child who had to be looked after. So where was I in this relationship?

She was having frequent arguments with her parents:

I was used to rows with Mum, but now that Dad had come off his medication, he was more emotional, more expressive about his anger, so I bore the brunt. And I suppose I wanted his attention because I was a bit jealous of Darcey. For two years, he'd talked about her constantly at home, like he used to about Alex [Alessandra Ferri]. I wanted him to focus on me.

He did, in his diary entries, though she was not to know of his constant concern.

The Prince of the Pagodas continued to occupy much of MacMillan's time during the first part of 1990. He had new casts to rehearse, including two guests from the Bolshoi, Nina Ananiashvili and Alexei Fadeyechev, both of whom were favourites of his. Sylvie Guillem was next. She had become principal guest artist with the Royal Ballet the previous year, leaving the Paris Opéra Ballet for London. She and MacMillan 'got off on the wrong foot from the start and spent the rest of the time stepping on each other's toes', according to Deborah. Guillem (who had danced in his *Song of the Earth* with the Paris Opéra Ballet) had declared that she did not want to appear in any of his ballets in the English repertoire, even though she had only seen them on video. MacMillan, who thought she had a prodigious talent but an arrogant attitude, was not interested in propitiating her. However, when she asked to dance Princess Rose in his new three-act ballet, he agreed – and then vetoed her first scheduled performances because she wanted to make changes to the choreography. She danced the role in April, with his approval, though they had one of their screaming matches afterwards.

Some time later, the substance of one outburst was broadcast accidentally over the Opera House Tannoy after a dress rehearsal of

Manon. Guillem had, by then, changed her mind about his ballets and had taken on the roles of Juliet and Manon. After yet another clash over alterations she wanted made to costumes and choreography, she had shouted at MacMillan, 'Who do you think you are – a bigger star than me?' His (unrepeatable) response was heard all over the building, to ironic cheers from dancers and backstage staff.

MacMillan had been planning his next ballet while he choreographed *The Prince of the Pagodas*. He intended it to be an antidote to the three-act *Pagodas*, with its intractable scenario and uncuttable score. The new work would spring from his imagination, not someone else's. He decided to risk commissioning a score to inspire him. Instead of preparing a scenario in advance, he hoped to find a composer with whom he could discuss his ideas and who would then come up with music strong enough to stand on its own: he wanted to commission a concert piece, not the equivalent of a film score. Deborah suggested a composer whose music she had enjoyed at a recent Festival Hall concert by the BBC Symphony Orchestra: Brian Elias, whose settings of *Five Songs to Poems by Irina Ratushinskaya* had impressed her as a darkly dramatic work. At the MacMillans' request, Elias sent Kenneth a cassette tape of the music. They invited him to dinner soon afterwards, in June of 1989. Elias, surprised and excited by the idea of writing a ballet, accepted the commission, warning MacMillan that he was a slow worker. Once the collaboration was under way, the score was unlikely to be ready for at least twenty months.

In the meantime, MacMillan had several gala pas de deux to complete. He worried that he no longer had the energy to dash off *pièces d'occasion* with his former facility. As it turned out, one for Darcey Bussell and Stuart Cassidy, for an Aids fundraiser on 25 March, was something of a fiasco. Bussell had had no time to learn it (Dana Fouras had deputised for her while it was being created) and forgot most of the choreography in performance.

Of more moment was the pas de deux MacMillan was planning for a gala on 19 July in honour of the Queen Mother's ninetieth birthday. He intended to create a substantial role for Bussell, matching her with a new, as yet untried partner, Irek Mukhamedov. The former Bolshoi star had joined the Royal Ballet after leaving Russia in a hurry in May. He had no desire to defect politically, as Soviet dancers had in the past, but his career with the Bolshoi was in crisis.

He had fallen out with the autocratic Artistic Director, Yuri Grigorovich, and his future, at the age of thirty, looked bleak. His new wife, Maria Kovbas, a dancer in the Bolshoi company who had been married to a Soviet official, was pregnant and they wanted the baby born in a place of safety, outside Russia. They decided to capitalise on Mukhamedov's international fame and move abroad, where they could bring up a family in economic security.

Mukhamedov had been a favourite of Grigorovich's until their working relationship turned sour. From early on, Grigorovich, the company's principal choreographer as well as its Director, had cast the young Tatar, with his flashing dark eyes and tremendous elevation, in dramatic leading roles in *Spartacus, Ivan the Terrible, The Golden Age*. As Mukhamedov matured, however, he realised that since Grigorovich was no longer creating ballets, the Bolshoi repertoire had ossified. There were no new roles for him to conquer. The company was riven by jealousy and resentment, its internal politics as byzantine as the Politburo's. Mukhamedov calculated that his only option was to leave without warning, taking his new wife with him.

He had sent a letter to Anthony Dowell, asking whether the Royal Ballet would welcome him as a dancer. Dowell consulted MacMillan, among others, who agreed that Mukhamedov was likely to prove a valuable asset for the company. Before the offer of a contract could be made, the Mukhamedovs had left Russia for Austria, where Irek had an invitation to guest with the Vienna Opera Ballet. The Royal Ballet sent tickets for a flight to London, and once Mukhamedov had met up with Dowell and the company's Administrative Director, Anthony Russell Roberts, he signed a five-year contract as a principal with the company: he was to be a member, not a guest artist. Although he knew about the range of the Royal Ballet's repertoire, he had yet to see a MacMillan ballet in performance. The choreographer was merely a name he had heard about. British dance-lovers who had admired Mukhamedov's performances with the Bolshoi during its London seasons were already envisaging him in *Mayerling* and other ballets with meaty male roles. MacMillan was still reserving judgement, watching the dancer in class before starting work with him.

First, he and MacMillan needed to make each other's acquaintance. Anya and John Sainsbury invited both families for a weekend at their country house in Preston Candover. Kenneth and Irek got on famously, in spite of Irek's lack of English. Soon afterwards, on 12 June, they started on what was to become the 'Farewell' pas de deux with Bussell and finished ten days later: the music was Tchaikovsky's Romance in F major, coupled with an arrangement of the song 'Does the Day Reign?' MacMillan had chosen the Tchaikovsky (the same music Cranko had used for a pas de deux in Onegin) because of Mukhamedov's Russian background: he had no idea, yet, how the dancer would respond to unfamiliar twentieth-century composers. Mukhamedov was out of shape, not having performed for several months, but was eager to try everything MacMillan proposed. They experimented in the studio, and came up with a series of hurtling leaps that looked as though Mukhamedov were tearing himself apart. Bussell was required to match him in passion, responding to his ardour with frantic runs and flying jumps, imploring him not to leave her. MacMillan claimed that only after he had completed the pas de deux did he realise, 'My God, that's from The Three Sisters.' He had just seen and been greatly impressed by the Cusack family of actors in The Three Sisters at the Royal Court Theatre. The production was to serve as a stimulus for a ballet he had been contemplating for a number of years. Although the audience was not to know it at the time, the gala pas de deux turned out to have a context: it would be part of MacMillan's next work, his version of Chekhov's play. The Three Sisters (the one-act ballet's title was eventually Winter Dreams) could be done while he waited for Elias's score to be completed for the project they had discussed.

The 'Farewell' pas de deux was given on its own at the Queen Mother's birthday gala to great acclaim. It came across as an extravagantly romantic parting, with Bussell revealing a newly womanly side of herself. Mukhamedov was applauded for his first British heroic role, dressed (by Peter Farmer) in a military uniform that flattered his bulky figure. At the start of the duet he flung his military cap into the wings and his greatcoat to the back of the stage. At the end, after he had left, broken-hearted Bussell picked up the coat and clutched it to her in distress. But although the two of them seemed ideally suited, their partnership proved more fragile than it first appeared.

In the meantime, MacMillan had set the pas de deux in its context. His intention was to conjure up Chekhov's elegiac atmosphere in *The Three Sisters* but avoid a précis of the play's plot by concentrating on the inner lives of the characters. Instead of retelling the story, as Ashton had done with Turgenev's *A Month in the Country*, he used the events in Chekhov's play as reference points, compressing them into a single evening: 'A bit like *Anastasia* Act III,' he told John Drummond for a BBC radio interview in April 1991. The ballet would occupy the spaces in between Chekhov's dialogue. It was meant to be a meditation more than a drama – very different from his earlier work about a household of discontented sisters, *Las Hermanas*.

Bussell's role was that of the middle, married sister, Masha, with Mukhamedov as Lieutenant Colonel Vershinin, the officer with whom she has fallen in love. Their farewell duet was revealed to be one of frustrated longing, ending with the departure of Vershinin: his regiment had been transferred elsewhere, so Masha would be left with her provincial schoolteacher husband. Her 'tragedy', so graphic when the pas de deux was given on its own, would be just one of the Prozorov household's many unhappinesses.

Before *Winter Dreams* could be included in the Royal Ballet schedule the following season, in February 1991, Mukhamedov was to learn the two leading male roles in *Manon*, Des Grieux and Lescaut. Bussell was scheduled to make her debut as Manon with him as Des Grieux. He would also dance Romeo in MacMillan's ballet to the Prokofiev score, very different from the one by Yuri Grigorovich he had known with the Bolshoi. Although MacMillan's choreography in both ballets had been created on Royal Ballet-trained dancers, Mukhamedov was able to adapt his broad Russian style of dancing and acting to suit his new roles. MacMillan was beginning to believe that he had found, as with Frank Frey in Berlin, another male muse in a heroic mould to inspire him.

During the August break, Kenneth and Deborah went to see the Mukhamedovs' new baby, Alexandra, and entertained the proud parents to dinner at Spencer Park. Charlotte's seventeenth-birthday treat was to be taken to Le Caprice, the sophisticated restaurant near the Ritz. Kenneth, Deborah and Charlotte had gone shopping together to buy her a present ('rowed all the time', he recorded in his diary) and ended up kitting out Kenneth with smart new clothes from Joseph in the King's Road. Having not updated his wardrobe for a long time, he was shocked at how much his suit and extra jacket cost.

Charlotte's GCSE O-level results arrived, to great rejoicing: her provisional place in Bedales' sixth form was secure. To celebrate, the family went on a week's holiday to the West Country. 'Looking forward to going home even though we have had a wonderful time,' Kenneth wrote in his diary. 'Can't bear the thought of Charlotte going away to school. Great separation angst!'

Although he and Deborah were in tears after Charlotte had left for Bedales, she seemed happy enough when she telephoned. They brought her home at the end of September for her first weekend outing – an emotional whirlwind, according to Kenneth – and sent her back to school by train. Bedales prided itself on being a friendly, liberal-minded institution, but Charlotte was finding it hard to adjust to boarding at a school with boys as well as girls and a sixth form in which most of the pupils already knew each other. Her parents were meanwhile having difficulty in adapting to life at home without her.

Kenneth's next work commitment was with the Paris Opéra Ballet, which was due to mount *Manon* in November. Patrick Dupond, who had become the youngest-ever Director of the company earlier in the year, was determined to have a three-act MacMillan ballet in the repertoire, and *Manon*, with its origin in a famous French novel and music by a renowned French composer, was the ideal one. The MacMillans had visited Paris earlier in the year for Kenneth to choose the casts and discuss changes to Georgiadis's designs to suit the Palais Garnier's large stage. An unexpected problem over copyright had come up. The heir to Massenet's estate was objecting to possible confusion between the ballet and Massenet's opera *Manon*. After protracted legal wrangling, it had been decided that MacMillan's ballet should henceforth be known in Europe (with the exception of the United Kingdom) as *L'Histoire de Manon*. The United States, along with Britain, could retain the original title.

MacMillan went to Paris in October to coach the principals and supervise final rehearsals. (*Manon* had been mounted from the 1974 notation by Monica Parker and Gary Harris, with further assistance from John Auld and Patricia Ruanne.) Jean-Yves Lormeau, the first-cast Des Grieux, missed a rehearsal, thereby enraging MacMillan, who promptly replaced him with Manuel Legris: as always, MacMillan was prepared to be ruthless in the service of his ballets. Monique Loudières was the first-cast Manon; Sylvie Guillem appeared later as a guest artist in the role with her original company. The Parisian audience and critics acclaimed *L'Histoire de Manon* as a ballet that had, at last, found its rightful place in the French repertoire. The Paris Opéra production, like ABT's account of MacMillan's *Romeo and Juliet*, soon acquired its own national sensibility, distinct from the Royal Ballet version, although the choreography remained the same.

When *Manon* was revived by the Royal Ballet at the start of the New Year, it became evident in rehearsal that Mukhamedov was having difficulty partnering Bussell in the ballet's acrobatic lifts. His back was prone to injury and Bussell was taller than the ballerinas with whom he had been used to dancing in the Bolshoi Ballet. Although he could cope with Bussell easily enough in the 'Farewell' pas de deux created for the two of them, the series of duets in *Manon* were a different matter. Shortly before the final dress rehearsal, MacMillan took the decision that Bussell's debut as Manon would have to be postponed and performed with a different Des Grieux; small, light Viviana Durante would dance with Mukhamedov instead.

Bussell's rapid promotion to leading roles had been much publicised, with interviews and feature articles in national newspapers and magazines about the new young star. Because the change of cast for *Manon* was announced at short notice, the *Evening Standard* and the following day's papers splashed the story that Bussell had lost the leading role: the implication was that she had been sacrificed in favour of Mukhamedov, the Russian superstar. Bussell was immensely popular, considered the company's most promising English ballerina since Antoinette Sibley. Now MacMillan and the Royal Ballet had publicly humiliated her by taking away her first night as Manon. Though this was a blow from which she would recover, it was a harsh way to learn that MacMillan was never prepared to put a dancer's hurt feelings ahead of what he wanted for his ballets.

Manon duly went ahead in January 1991, with Durante taking over Bussell's scheduled performances with Mukhamedov, as well as her own with Bruce Sansom as Des Grieux. The premiere of *Winter Dreams* followed shortly after, bringing Bussell and Mukhamedov together again as the adulterous lovers. The ballet's title was a reworking of the nickname for Tchaikovsky's First Symphony (which MacMillan had used for Act I of *Anastasia*), *Winter Daydreams*. The music for the new ballet came from a selection of Tchaikovsky's piano studies, with the addition of traditional Russian tunes, arranged for guitars to sound like balalaikas. The musicians, in costume, were placed behind a scrim at the rear of the stage with the cast, as though the Prozorov family were holding a dinner party, the sound of laughter or chatter occasionally audible. Characters then came forward for danced reveries, chance encounters or secret assignations.

There were cameo parts for veteran colleagues, such as Gerd Larsen (the old nurse) and Derek Rencher (drunken Doctor Chebutikyn). Anthony Dowell was Masha's schoolmaster husband, Kulygin, the most complex character in the ballet. Ineffectual Kulygin was trapped in a wretched situation, aware that his beautiful wife found him inadequate, and incapable of articulating his need for her. His solo was full of half-completed gestures, abandoned in hopelessness, his body seeming old before its time. His attempt to console Masha in her unhappiness was achingly pathetic: he put on a clown's nose, making himself the inept jester of earlier MacMillan ballets. Now, in their maturity, choreographer and performer imbued the role with deeply felt compassion. It was to be the last role MacMillan created for Dowell, with whom he had worked for twenty-six years.

Mukhamedov's Lieutenant Colonel Vershinin was the handsome, virile figure that Kulygin would have wished to be. Vershinin, the outsider in this claustrophobic society, is able to walk away, as the enigmatic 'He' does at the end of *My Brother, My Sisters*. The Prozorov family is left locked in grief, the three sisters holding each other in a linked embrace. The youngest's admirer has been killed by his rival in a clumsy duel. Deborah remembers watching 'some dreadful B-movie with Kenneth, in which a character was shot holding an umbrella. "Oh, I know exactly how to end *Winter Dreams*," Kenneth said.'

MacMillan defied criticism of the ballet's structure – described by Judith Mackrell in the *Independent* as 'each episode jolting almost abrasively against the next with the climactic pas de deux occurring two-thirds of the way through' – by saying, 'It's not badly constructed. It's a different way of construction, that's all.' Reviews were otherwise full of praise for MacMillan's richness of invention, his skill in finding dance language to express the characters' predicaments. 'Best of all, perhaps, *Winter Dreams* shows MacMillan at sixty, not sitting back comfortably for his anniversary, but still tussling with intractable issues of narrative and form,' wrote Mackrell. Clement Crisp noted in the *Financial Times* the recurring theme in his work from *The Burrow* onwards: 'The erosion of every kind of joy and of social order . . . characters facing the destruction of their lives and of their dearest hopes. Their winter dreams are no bulwark against the disillusion that gradually erodes every relationship . . . It is a superb achievement.'

The ballet was recorded in a studio in January 1992 by the BBC and transmitted on 29 December 1992 in a version adapted for the small screen. Peter Farmer's spare, impressionist setting for the stage had been redesigned by Eric Walmsley, so that the action took place in and around a realistic Russian dacha, sheltered by transplanted trees, with a birch gazebo sheltering the 'balalaika' band. Mukhamedov's Vershinin, circling the dacha before he entered it, looked like a wolf lurking in the undergrowth. Indoors, the Prozorovs' dinner party, complete with close-ups of the guests, was typical of BBC period-costume dramas, apart from pointe shoes under the elaborately dressed table. The cameras panned from face to face, while MacMillan directed the dancers as he would actors, telling them what thoughts and feelings they should be conveying. The TV version, which was directed by Derek Bailey, in collaboration with MacMillan, and produced by Bob Lockyer, is one of the most successful translations of MacMillan's work to video or DVD.

The Royal Ballet presented *Winter Dreams* on its next visit to New York in the summer of 1991, when MacMillan's ballet shared a triple bill with Ashton's *Scènes de ballet* and Bintley's *Still Life at the Penguin Café*. *The Prince of the Pagodas*, however, was not included in the Met season. It had been given during the company's visit to the Kennedy Center in Washington DC earlier in the year. Fonteyn, to whom the ballet was dedicated, had just died, so it provided a timely tribute to her. None the less, its critical reception had been unfavourable, deterring promoters from taking it to New York. (It was finally to reach New York in July 1997.)

MacMillan had meanwhile suffered a scare about his state of health in the spring, when he fainted in Copenhagen in the big department store Le Magasin du Nord. He had gone to Denmark with Deborah in May to cast *Concerto* for the Royal Danish Ballet. He was rushed by ambulance from the store to hospital, where he was kept in overnight. He was discharged the next day when nothing was found to be wrong. His blood pressure had fallen, causing him to faint, because he had been taking anti-depressants that he had been advised to come off after his heart attack. He confessed to Deborah that he had secretly hoarded the pills and promised not to take any more, no matter how anxious he felt.

He reproved himself in his diary on 29 May: 'I wish I believed in myself more. I get so stupidly nervous.' His next assignment, at Peter Wright's request, was a revival of *The Burrow* for Birmingham Royal Ballet. The touring company had been transplanted to Birmingham in 1990, under Wright's continued leadership, along with its orchestra. The renamed company was fast becoming the pride of the city, after the already well-established City of Birmingham Symphony Orchestra. MacMillan had agreed the year before that the company should mount its own production of his *Romeo and Juliet*, but had not found time in his schedule for the supervision it would need. The new production had been postponed: in the meantime, *The Burrow* was to be added to the repertoire of seminal modern works Wright had acquired for the company, with ballets by Kurt Jooss, Leonide Massine, Agnes de Mille, Ashton and de Valois.

MacMillan was apprehensive about how his 1958 ballet would work in the 1990s, especially for younger generations that had not experienced the Second World War. He wanted *The Burrow*'s context to be interpreted as widely as possible. When he went to Birmingham to meet the company, he told the dancers to put any thought of Anne Frank's *Diary* out of their minds. 'There's no specific story at all,' Marion Tait remembers him saying. 'Just people reacting to having to hide from persecution.'

He intended to rethink the original choreography, which had been notated in the 1960s, coming to it afresh as he had with the revival of *Le Baiser de la fée*. He disliked tinkering with his choreography for a ballet once it was established in performance, though he would make small changes to suit dancers. He explained the process to me in an interview for the *Observer* in March 1992: 'By altering one section, you affect all the other strands of thought. It's like a fabric, you have to go back and change the whole thing, and by the time it's revived, I've forgotten the initial impulse.' Because *The Burrow* had been created so long ago, he was prepared to start again, though not from scratch: he kept the same basic structure and many of the same characters, expanding the cast to fit the large stage of the Birmingham Hippodrome.

He played down the parts of the young lovers and gave greater prominence to the role of the neurotic woman, once Anne Heaton's part, which he now gave to Marion Tait. The woman was made into a crazed Norma Desmond figure, an ex-actress dependent on an over-loyal companion, her former dresser. MacMillan introduced the role of the dresser for the company's ballet mistress and character dance-actress, Anita Landa, who was married to his old colleague Michael Hogan. She was a foil for Tait as the raddled star, whose face was caked in white make-up, her hair caught up in a 1940s turban. 'She's a woman on the edge, who probably hadn't slept for three months. She's hysterical by the end, and the Jester has to put his hand over her mouth to stop her scream giving them all away,' says Tait.

Although *The Burrow* was well received in Birmingham and on tour (including a London season in March 1992 at Sadler's Wells) it remained in the company's repertoire for only one season. In reviving it MacMillan had revisited his youth and still-fresh memories of the war. Spurred on by his recollections, he had started writing his attempt at a memoir while on holiday in the summer.

He, Deborah and Charlotte had been invited to spend twelve days in July at the Sainsburys' house on Corfu. They were flown there by private jet, a journey that would take three hours. Kenneth had worried himself into a lather of anxiety in advance, only to find that the trip was smooth and uneventful. Other house guests included friends who were also ballet-lovers, some on the Royal Opera House Board: Bamber Gascoigne and his wife Christina; Colette Clark, daughter of the art historian Lord (Kenneth) Clark, as well as a gaggle of young people invited by the Sainsburys' children. Kenneth, who had been apprehensive about sharing the holiday with Kelly, as Colette Clark is known to her friends, because of her long friendship with Ashton, discovered the joy of gossiping with her over breakfast, a meal that went on long into the morning. Kenneth held court as other guests came and went from the table in the courtyard, attracted by gales of laughter. At ease among people he knew, he was no longer silent and reclusive in company, provided he could escape when he wanted to. He withdrew to write down, in longhand, what he could recall of his childhood. According to Charlotte, he never talked about his youth. 'Whenever I asked, he'd just say, "Can't remember", and that was it.'

He continued reworking his account when he and his family returned to London, going over and over the same ground, scoring out what he had written, then repeating it with minor variations: 'Find it v. hard to express myself,' he confessed to his diary, eventually abandoning his attempt at an autobiography. He turned instead to making papier-mâché bowls as an outlet for his frustration, filling the house with semi-congealed containers of soaked paper. Once he had mastered the consistency he wanted, his creations made admirable presents for his family and friends.

At the same time as Birmingham Royal Ballet mounted *The Burrow*, Peter Schaufuss had requested *Different Drummer* for the Deutsche Oper Ballet in Berlin, where he had been Artistic Director since leaving English National Ballet in 1990. Schaufuss had taken a number of ENB dancers with him to Berlin, including Martin James and Leanne Benjamin, whom MacMillan chose for the leading roles of Woyceck and Marie. MacMillan went to supervise the final phase of the Berlin production in September 1991. Although he had revisited Berlin, briefly, with the Royal Ballet in 1987, this was the first time he had worked with the Deutsche Oper company since his resignation in 1969. Berlin was now a very different city, no longer divided by the Wall and by different systems of government. The politics of its cultural institutions, however, were more byzantine than ever, as rival opera houses and theatres from the former East and West sectors struggled to keep their companies and orchestras going. MacMillan had to be diplomatic when German arts journalists asked for his views on how many ballet companies a city like Berlin could support, and what sort of works they should offer. (The three subsidised ballet companies belonging to the Deutsche Oper (formerly West Berlin) and the Staatsoper and the Komische Oper (both formerly East Berlin) eventually merged in January 2004 as the Staatsballett Berlin. Vladimir Malakhov was appointed as Artistic Director.)

He told the *Neue Berlinische Musikzeitung* in March that although ballet classics, such as *The Sleeping Beauty* and *Swan*

Lake, needed to be done, they should not be the principal fare on offer. Contemporary works were vital. He claimed that the main difference between Berlin and London was that German audiences had more respect for serious theatre. British ballet-goers, especially Royal Opera House patrons, had become very conservative, expecting ballet to serve as light entertainment. They had found *Different Drummer* unacceptable, whereas he did not expect the same negative reaction from Deutsche Oper audiences.

German critics certainly appreciated the ballet's Expressionist genre, reviewing it more favourably than most British critics had. The disparate elements of the original production had come together, helped by the elements of a set MacMillan had selected from the opera house's store. Its spare design of receding telegraph poles worked so well as a background for the ballet that he intended to adopt it for all future productions.

He hoped to persuade the Royal Ballet to revive *Different Drummer*, with Mukhamedov as Woyceck and Leanne Benjamin as Marie. (This was not to come to fruition until October 1993, after MacMillan's death.) He had taken an immediate interest in Benjamin, an Australian who had started her career with the (then) Sadler's Wells Royal Ballet before moving to English National Ballet. He reworked the role of Marie around her, instructing other dancers to watch and absorb how she interpreted his choreography. Benjamin, who had been overawed by him when he first arrived in Berlin, came to realise how much he appreciated warmth and companionship in a city he no longer knew.

He proposed that she should return to Britain and dance his ballets, either with the Birmingham-based company or the Covent Garden one. She was reluctant to uproot herself again, but he persuaded her to come to London in December to perform one of his pas de deux for an Aids fundraising gala at Her Majesty's Theatre. He adapted the Poulenc pas de deux he had created for a previous gala, pairing Benjamin with Stephen Jefferies from the Royal Ballet. Anthony Dowell would attend the gala and see why MacMillan was so keen on her joining the Royal Ballet. However, when Dowell offered Benjamin a contract as a soloist, she hesitated for six months about accepting the lower status, since she was already an established principal with Schaufuss's company. MacMillan telephoned her in Berlin at frequent intervals, insisting that she came and assuring her that she would soon be promoted to principal. He told her he wanted to develop the Poulenc pas de deux into a complete ballet, with her in the lead, as one of his future projects. Benjamin could no longer resist, and joined the Royal Ballet as a first soloist. She was a principal by the time he died, before he could fulfil his plans for her.

When MacMillan came back from Berlin, he faced the realisation that Charlotte had developed an eating disorder. He had commented in his diary for some months that she was looking slim and beautiful. Now he recognised, as Deborah had before him, that Charlotte was starving herself: she eventually confessed to being both anorexic and bulimic. She says that both conditions were not uncommon among girls at her school; unhappy and insecure, she had resorted to an eating disorder as a way of gaining attention. She had been surrounded all her life by dancers obsessed with their shape and weight. She wanted to look like them to ensure her father's approval, and to resemble her slender mother. Unfulfilled at school, she resented being 'kept out of the picture' of what was happening at home.

Her parents went into a tailspin of anxiety about her, pleading and arguing with her and each other over what to do. She was sent to a psychiatrist who specialised in eating disorders at the Priory Hospital in South-West London. He wanted her taken out of school at once, to be treated on an anorexic ward at the Priory. 'Dad was brilliant,' says Charlotte.

He told the psychiatrist, 'I will not have my daughter treated like a small child, taking away any kind of responsibility for herself.' So I went back to Bedales, promising to eat sensibly, and he wrote me a letter. It was very sweet and tender, acknowledging that I must be very unhappy. He said he'd seen anorexia in dancers and he was worried about the repercussions for my health. He wasn't threatening – just 'I really want you to get over this.'

When MacMillan mentioned the letter in his diary, he wrote merely, 'Inadequate I'm sure.' He continued to worry about Charlotte, sending her postcards three times a week, and noting in his diary what mood she seemed to be in every time she rang from school. They managed to have long talks together when she came back for the Christmas break, though there were inevitable tensions in the household. His concerns about his vulnerable daughter would be reflected in his next – and what was to be his last – ballet.

52

Brian Elias had finished a preliminary version of the score MacMillan had commissioned for his new ballet by the autumn of 1990. They had discussed ideas for the work over the past year and Elias had kept MacMillan in touch with his progress. However, when the composer had tried to give him an impression of how the music would sound by playing it to him on the piano, MacMillan was baffled. He insisted on hearing the fully orchestrated score before he could start to choreograph the ballet.

Elias had warned him, and the ROH orchestra director, that he intended to use lots of unconventional percussion: steel pans, gongs, woodblocks, cowbell, vibraphone and glockenspiel, as well as a range of other instruments. The sounds could not be simulated on a synthesiser, so a way had to be found to record a performance of the completed score, played by the Royal Opera House orchestra. The Friends of Covent Garden raised £14,000 to pay for orchestra rehearsals and a tape recording, with Barry Wordsworth as conductor, which he would be for the first performances. MacMillan declared himself delighted with the result. By July 1991, he could start familiarising himself with the recorded music, although Musicians' Union regulations still meant that the ballet's creation in the rehearsal room would have to be to piano.

He and Elias had agreed that the ballet was to be about betrayal. This had been a recurring theme in MacMillan's work, even though he claimed in an *ROH News* preview for *The Judas Tree* that he was not conscious that betrayal had featured in any of his previous ballets. 'This is new to me,' he said, disingenuously. His initial title for the work when he first referred to it in his diary was 'The Last Supper'. When he mentioned it to Elias, the composer's half-joking response was: 'You can't ask a good Jewish boy to work with anything overtly Christian!' They discussed other infamous instances of betrayal, including the massacre in Tiananmen Square in June of 1989: protesting students demanding democratic reforms had been mown down by the Chinese military, in spite of politicians' assurances that there would be no violence. Deborah remembers how Kenneth had watched the television coverage of the seven-week-long occupation of Tiananmen Square with appalled apprehension: 'They're going to be betrayed,' he kept saying. 'They're all going to be betrayed.'

But in his discussions with Elias, MacMillan kept coming back to the iconic Christian action of betrayal: the Judas kiss. He intended to create a ballet for Mukhamedov and the young men in the company, who were a particularly talented cohort, under-used in a repertoire that favoured the female corps de ballet. The disciples who followed Jesus would provide the rationale for a largely male ballet, whose themes would span past and present. The setting was to be an urban, modern-day one, which was why Elias had chosen to use metallic percussion. The men would appear to be a gang of construction-site workers; the biblical references that underlay the ballet would not be immediately obvious.

Looking for material to inspire his music, Elias had informed himself of myths and scholarly research relating to the Apostles. As he worked on the score, he supplied MacMillan with photocopies of his findings: entries from religious encyclopedias, extracts from studies of the Gnostic Gospels, accounts from different cultures of the legends surrounding Judas Iscariot and Satan. He prepared a detailed chart of the Apostles' alternative names and of their attributes and symbols in art. He invented his own scenario to shape the forty-minute score and drew on his mine of information for the nine short variations for male dancers that MacMillan had asked him to write in the middle section.

Underlinings and scribbled words in MacMillan's hand on the photocopies indicate that he took the Apostles' attributes as inspiration for his choreography, although he did not follow Elias's scheme precisely. Names and associations appear in MacMillan's jottings for solos and duets: James and John, for example, were known as the Boanerges, the Sons of Thunder; James the Great was associated with horses; Matthew's symbol was wings. The disciples would not be identified by name in cast lists, though traces of their iconography would appear in their movement motifs. Such arcane information could not possibly be evident to the public, but this was to be MacMillan's Gnostic ballet.

It is worth examining in some detail the influences that determined the ballet's eventual shape, since they help explain its strange context. MacMillan and Elias were fascinated by the Gnostic Gospels, papyrus books (known as codices) discovered in 1945 in Egypt, near the town of Nag Hammadi. They were Coptic translations, made in AD 350–400, of more ancient manuscripts written in Greek. The texts, unauthorised 'secret' gospels, poems, myths and magic spells, had been denounced as heresy by orthodox Christians by the mid-second century AD. The Gnostic writers claimed to reveal stories about Jesus that were hidden from 'the many'. They used terminology that related to Jewish beliefs and possibly to Buddhism from South India: to psychoanalysts like Jung and his followers, the writers appeared to be drawing on universal archetypes.

Among the codices offering rich material for interpretation was *The Exegesis on the Soul,* a text that presupposed that God was a dyad, embracing masculine and feminine elements. The soul was presented as a woman, virginal while she was with her Father in heaven, but a prostitute when she fell into the world and into a female body. She had many lovers who abused her: 'The wanton creatures passed her from one to another . . . some made use of her by force, while others did so by seducing her with a gift.' She remained in psychic and sexual captivity until she repented and called on her Father to restore her to himself. He made her womb turn inwards to purge her and protect her from further sexual contamination. She regained her former purity and was resurrected into heaven.

The codices also included the Gospel of Mary (Magdalene), condemned as heretical because it claimed to come from a direct, erotic communication with the Saviour. In this private dialogue, sexual and mystical experiences were indistinguishable. In yet other Gnostic writings, Mary Magdalene was recognised as a disciple, one of three followers privileged to receive special teaching: there was rivalry between her and jealous male disciples because the Saviour loved her more than the others, rewarding her with special knowledge.

A key to the *Judas Tree* ballet was a discourse by an unnamed woman, transcribed as a poem, 'The Thunder':

> I am the honoured one and the scorned one
> I am the whore and the holy one
> I am the wife and the virgin
> I am the mother and the daughter
> Why, you who hate me, do you love me
> and hate those who love me?

This paradoxical figure became the sole woman in the ballet. She has no name on the cast list, but she is Mary, both the Magdalene and the Virgin. (She is called Mary in MacMillan's notes and Elias's guidelines.) In creating the role, MacMillan was incorporating his own feelings about women, as well as drawing on the Judaeo-Christian tradition in which he had grown up. By keeping the woman's name undisclosed, he was leaving her open to many interpretations, while giving his subconscious free rein. He was seeing a psychiatrist, Dr Goldblatt, on a weekly basis at the time of the ballet's creation: he noted in his diary that sessions about his mother were 'difficult'. (It is a classic of Freudian analysis that a persistent sense of betrayal goes back to losing the beloved – the mother.)

A further strand in the already complex web of myths, archetypes and images affecting the creation of the ballet was, as so often, a film. Kenneth and Deborah had been to see *Last Exit to Brooklyn*, Uli Edel's 1989 film of Hubert Selby Jr's short stories. Kenneth re-read the book, in which each overlapping story about outcasts and low-lifes in New York has a biblical quote as a heading. In the longest story, Harry, a shop steward in a factory, has a wife called Mary, whom he beats up. He goes to a gay/transvestite club called Mary's and ends up crucified on an advertising billboard. In another story, a teenage whore, Tralala, is gang-raped in an abandoned car on an empty lot. In the underworld Selby describes with compassion, violent men cannot come to terms with the feminine side of themselves. They resort to sex with homosexual 'fairies', whom they despise, and abuse the women in their lives. By assimilating *Last Exit to Brooklyn* into his ballet, MacMillan might have been exorcising demons that he recognised in himself and other men.

When, for a preview article about *The Judas Tree* for the *Observer* in March 1992, I asked him how much he knew what he was doing when he created a ballet, he replied,

In the case of *Judas Tree*, it's mostly my subconscious at work. I told Brian and the designer, Jock [McFadyen], 'You'll have to wait and see.' I wasn't being difficult or secretive. I had to wait for it to happen in the room. There are things in me that are untapped and that have come out in this ballet that I find frightening. This is a dark one.

He would not elucidate or give any further clues about the ballet.

What came out in the rehearsal room was rather different from the ideas MacMillan had discussed with Elias (and different again from Elias's own working scenario). *The Judas Tree* is a ballet about guilt as much as betrayal: individual guilt and communal guilt at having colluded, as part of a mob, in an atrocity. The only clue MacMillan would give as a programme note was a quote from the Sufi writer, Khalil Gibran, in his book *The Prophet*: 'As a single leaf turns not yellow but with the silent knowledge of the whole tree, so the wrongdoer cannot do wrong without the hidden will of you all.'

MacMillan had remembered the quote shortly before the ballet's premiere, by which time it already had its horticultural (and symbolic) title. Elias, a keen gardener, had suggested the biblical name given to the tree, *Cercis siliquastrum*, that bears purple-red flowers along its branches in spring before the new leaves come out. The flowers were supposed to be drops of Judas's blood, spilt when he hanged himself from the tree in remorse for having betrayed Jesus. In the set for the ballet, the 'tree' is an East London landmark, the Canary Wharf tower, looming behind a construction site.

MacMillan had chosen the Scottish painter Jock McFadyen as the designer after Deborah had shown him a catalogue of McFadyen's 1991 exhibition at the William Jackson gallery in Cork Street. As Kenneth turned the pages of the catalogue, he said, 'I want that – and that – and that.' He went to the exhibition on his own, asking the gallery how he could contact the artist. At this point in his career, McFadyen was depicting inner-city life in desolate areas of London, Belfast, Berlin. His cityscapes were daubed with graffiti, his working-class subjects dead-eyed, pasty-skinned, without hope. His studio was in East London at the time, close to the derelict areas he was painting. He was incredulous about MacMillan's proposal that he should design a ballet at the Royal Opera House. 'He'd left this message on my answering machine in his fey, posh voice, saying he was Kenneth MacMillan of the Royal Ballet,' says McFadyen. The gallery had told him that *Sir* Kenneth MacMillan had asked for his telephone number.

When I rang him back and he said he was from Dunfermline, and his father had been a chicken farmer, I had to put the phone down while I laughed.

He said he was particularly interested in one painting, *Costa del Dogs*, that has a man with a huge gut, in white shorts, pointing at a big girl dressed like a tart. He wanted that image for the woman in the ballet. Then he said he wanted an object, an icon, in the set, which could be construed as a Judas tree. It crossed my mind it could be Canary Wharf tower, which was under construction outside my studio, so it appeared in a lot of my paintings.

A huge complex of skyscrapers was under way, providing headquarters for financial firms (and newspapers) in the run-down Isle of Dogs area of the city where the London docks had once prospered. For decades, the docklands had remained blighted, a lot of the residents long-term unemployed. Now they were living on the margins of the biggest building site in Europe.

When McFadyen and MacMillan talked about Canary Wharf as the background to the set, they saw the ambitious capitalist development as a betrayal of the East End working class. 'The people of the Isle of Dogs had been totally forgotten for years,' says McFadyen. 'Then out of the ashes comes this skyscraper penis, this monument to Thatcherite capitalism in the boom years of the 1980s.' The set was to be a wasteland, littered with abandoned cars and scarred with scaffolding, the Canary Wharf tower looming like a modern totem pole over the dereliction below. The men in the ballet wore tattered working clothes, the Foreman in jeans and torn white singlet; for the final scene, they put on yellow oilskins, making themselves an anonymous gang. MacMillan took the idea of the bright yellow slickers from one of McFadyen's paintings of workmen, *Reconstruction 1* (1991). The woman in *The Judas Tree* was dressed very like the slag in *Costa del Dogs*, her mini-skirt further abbreviated into a leotard.

Audience members seeing the ballet for the first time would wonder why any woman would wander onto a building site so inappropriately clad. McFadyen and MacMillan supplied a clue that the location, however recognisable as a new London landmark, was surreal. A multiplicity of red suns or moons surrounded the Canary Wharf tower: they had been left in place after a try-out session checking the sightlines in the Royal Opera House. According to MacFadyen, 'I'd intended to have just one or two, because the sun and moon can be visible at the same time, but Kenneth said, "Leave them all there." ' He was alerting audiences to the heightened state of the ballet they were about to see, warning them that this was not a linear narrative.

In outlining what happens in *The Judas Tree*, it is simpler to use the biblical names of the four principal characters, even though they are listed only as the Foreman, his Friends and the Woman. The dancers knew who they were: Mukhamedov was Judas; Michael Nunn, Jesus; Mark Silver, Peter; Viviana Durante was Mary.

All four are conspicuous soon after the start of the ballet. The three men have entered, greeting each other on the opening chords of the music. The Foreman (Judas) summons four bearers whose burden is hidden under a white, silken veil. It is the body of the Woman (Mary), who is dragged out and lifted into the air in a cruciform position by Judas and his two friends, Jesus and Peter. She comes to life like an insect emerging from a cocoon, her feet like pincers in pointe shoes. The ritual has echoes of the birth of the Novice in Robbins's ballet *The Cage*, and Giselle's rebirth as a Wili in Act II.

Mary submits to being handled by the men, though she remains defiantly self-confident. She could be interpreted as the Soul from the Gnostic Gospel taking on female form, passed among the men who have unveiled her. Her behaviour is provocative, arousing Judas to possessive jealousy. He commands the woman to veil herself modestly, while in the background, the shrouded body of a woman is carried across the set by two men in yellow slickers, in a time-warp repetition of Mary's entrance.

Events are not happening sequentially; Mary, wanton and innocent, damaged and intact, is no ordinary being. She removes her veil, trailing it behind her as she flings herself at the workmen, who are now bare-chested. She ends up in the arms of Jesus: their kiss drives Judas to strike her and then studiously ignore her as she continues to dance with the men.

When Judas points threateningly at Jesus, he joins Mary under her veil, hidden from sight with his head in her lap. Jesus seems to be returning to his mother for comfort, or allying himself with the feminine principle. Judas hurls himself into the air in a jealous frenzy as if trying to tear himself apart: MacMillan was making the most of Mukhamedov's extraordinary propulsive power, encouraging him to try leaps neither of them had seen in a ballet before.

Judas rips the covering veil off Mary and Jesus and continues to flail in rage, as she plays the two men off against each other, setting Cain against Abel in a typical MacMillan triad. Peter then comes to the fore in a frenetic solo: to repeated chords in the music, he flaps his arms three times – the cock-crows that signal his denial of Jesus in the Gospels' account. An angry confrontation between Peter and

Judas is echoed in a wrestling bout between two of the workmen. The duet ends with the two men lying on their backs, thrusting their pelvises into the air: Judas forces Mary to watch them, then covers her with the veil as if she should no longer see.

All the men scatter, leaving Mary alone with Judas. Jesus, and then Peter, soon return to watch, hidden on a gantry: there are always witnesses to what happens in the ballet. Mary remains provocative, dismissive, refusing to bend to Judas's will. He cannot come to terms with her, the woman he loves and hates – the feminine side of himself – so he abuses her until she collapses, apparently dead. He grabs a piece of chalk and draws lines around her body, marking out the scene of his crime. Jesus descends from the gantry and restores her to life: in an echo of the opening scene, she is weak and floppy, gradually gaining in strength.

Judas jeers at her and dismisses Jesus; Mary turns to Peter for protection, leaning her head against his chest. Meanwhile, the rest of the workmen have gathered, wearing yellow oilskins. Encouraged by Judas, they set upon Mary, ready to rape her. Jesus tries to rescue her, while Peter stands aside, helplessly. Peter witnesses her violation and her distress afterwards, as she shudders, knees bent, clutching at her womb. As Judas rages in a circle around her, she points accusingly at him as the author of her agony. Incensed, he appears to break her neck, killing her a second time. When Jesus comes forward to mourn over her body, Judas grabs him and kisses him – the signal for the gang to lynch him.

Peter turns away, his hand over his mouth. He shrouds Mary's limp body in her veil and carries her out, taking no part in the gang's murder of Jesus but betraying him by failing to help him, just as he failed Mary. The men descend like a pack of animals on Jesus, eventually holding his lifeless body upside-down, crucified between them. They stuff him into one of the derelict cars on the set as a makeshift sepulchre, setting a dunce's cap mockingly on his head in place of a crown of thorns. Judas, aware of the enormity of what he has done, climbs onto the central gantry with a rope and hangs himself. As his body dangles, Mary walks in, draped in her veil, and stands between him and Jesus, her head bowed. Above them, a warning light flashes at the tip of the Canary Wharf tower.

Judas has not died in isolation, as he did in legend; whether the Jesus figure rises again is unresolved at the end of the ballet, but the light on the tower could be a beacon of hope. The redemptive elements – the return of the woman, the flashing light – occur in the very last moments, while the audience is still aghast at the suicide and the violence that has preceded it. Judas's body swings in silence as the curtain descends. Applause, inevitably, is slow to build. There has been too much to absorb, especially at a first viewing, for any kind of catharsis.

The ballet's evolution was a difficult one. MacMillan recorded more than his usual doubts and anxieties in his diary during the two months of its creation: 'Don't know how to do it. Frightened. Worst rehearsal of my life today. I think my ballet is MAD. Think public will hate it.' Each time he felt pleased or excited with the way things were going, he lost confidence again. His notes, jotted on his habitual scraps of paper, show that he appropriated moves from his earlier ballets: *Rituals* was one source, with its bouts of male sparring dominated by a masterful leader; *Playground* was another, in the way the male characters round on the most vulnerable member of the group. There were similarities (in reverse) with *Las Hermanas*, in which a cast of women is confronted with a single man, and the guilt-ridden youngest sister hangs herself. He gave the eldest sister's signature gesture to Mary: holding her hands clenched together, she swiftly outlines her face, crosses herself over her breasts with a question mark then pushes her fists down over her groin. The gesture is a curious combination of sensuality and repression.

The rape scene had caused problems for MacMillan during the creation of the ballet because his original estimate of its duration, seven minutes, proved too long. He asked Elias to cut the music, in order for the scene to leave more to the imagination. He had warned Viviana Durante that though the rape would be distressing, its full impact would come in the aftermath, when she clutches her womb and accuses Judas of betraying her. 'Kenneth made me feel beautiful and confident,' Durante says, 'so I was prepared to do whatever he needed. I knew he wouldn't humiliate me.'

The violence in the ballet resulted in numerous injuries during rehearsals, the most dangerous of which was to Mukhamedov. In trying out the harness used in Judas's hanging, Mukhamedov had slipped and fallen. 'Absolutely terrifying,' MacMillan recorded in his diary. 'Am in shock.' So was Mukhamedov. As a result of his fall, so many precautions had to be taken in fitting the harness (which supports the performer's upper torso, hidden under his yellow oilskin), that the startling effect of the suicide was somewhat compromised.

Final technical rehearsals on stage were fraught with tension, not least because of Mukhamedov's earlier accident. Jock McFadyen came to watch the lighting of his set – the first time he had seen it in its full theatrical context. Later, he would pay MacMillan the compliment of calling him the Francis Bacon of ballet. But, ill at ease in the unfamiliar surroundings of the Royal Opera House, he took umbrage when MacMillan drawled to him from his seat in the near-empty auditorium, 'Jock, I can see "Fuck" from the stalls – can you change it?' McFadyen was outraged: 'Here was this great rebel going all Establishment on me, protecting the rich patrons in the stalls from seeing a graffitti swear word. I thought, "He's just as bad as the rest of them in this poncy Opera House", so I just left and went off on a bender with friends.' He was arrested at home early the next morning, hung over and truculent, by police who were looking for the previous owner of the house. By the time the mistake had been sorted out, and McFadyen released from a police cell, the Royal Opera House was frantic with worry that *The Judas Tree*'s imminent premiere would have to be cancelled.

With two days to go, McFadyen and MacMillan, both in an advanced state of nerves, made up their differences. 'Thought I would die of fright,' MacMillan confided to his diary before the first night. All went well, including Judas's hanging, though the audience response was muted. The first reviews were baffled, many of them hostile (with the usual exceptions of the *Financial Times* and the *Evening Standard*). 'A muddled, incoherent, nasty little shocker,' wrote John Percival in *The Times*. 'So distasteful is the ballet's material that it is hard to disentangle your own feelings about it, let alone figure out what MacMillan thinks he is doing,' was Judith Mackrell's view in the *Independent*. 'Only briefly, in showing the woman's humiliation after the rape, does the ballet speak to the heart. Otherwise characters and situations are underdeveloped and motivation is often obscure,' wrote Kathrine Sorley Walker in the *Daily Telegraph*.

Although the performers were acclaimed for their commitment, critics' accounts of the plot, filled with question marks as to what it might mean, revealed their bewilderment. By the time the Sunday papers appeared three days later on 22 March, MacMillan was so relieved at the first review that showed some perception of what he was trying to convey that he pinned the article to the company notice board, with a note drawing the dancers' attention to it. The review was mine in the *Observer*, hazarding my understanding of the ballet:

The Judas Tree is far from being a simple story of gang rape, murder and suicide in the shadow of Canary Wharf . . . [It] is a psychological fable. The woman is not a person but a force – the female principle, whom men deny at their peril. Like the Miraculous Mandarin, she keeps coming back to life: like the magdelene, whore and madonna, she mourns the man who hangs from the tree. At least, that's one interpretation of a shattering work that had the Opera House foyers abuzz with indignation.

To my surprise, MacMillan rang me that Sunday to confirm that I was on the right track. He said no more, and I was unaware of the Gnostic Gospels background to the ballet until Brian Elias informed me much later of the research he and MacMillan had undertaken.

In July, four months after the premiere of what was to be his last ballet, MacMillan was presented with an honorary doctorate from the Royal College of Art, the first time the College had honoured the dance profession. Jeremy Isaacs, who was a friend of the RCA's Rector, Jocelyn Stevens, had ensured that MacMillan received the letter offering the doctorate just before the premiere of *The Judas Tree*. Knowing how anxious Kenneth became before a first night, Isaacs had arranged for a courier to deliver the letter to Spencer Park shortly before the MacMillans set out for the Opera House, as a boost to Kenneth's morale.

MacMillan was particularly gratified that the select group of new Doctors of Arts included David Hockney, whose work he admired and enjoyed. Although his own profession was essentially a visual one, he had not expected to be academically acknowledged as a fine artist. The Public Orator who made the presentation at the Royal College of Art, Professor Christopher Frayling, concluded his encomium of MacMillan with the words: 'He is the poet of passion . . . and his means of expression is movement. His classical training has provided him with a built-in formal equipment that shapes, channels and guides his dance imagination.'

Birmingham Royal Ballet had meanwhile mounted its own production of *Romeo and Juliet*, supervised by MacMillan. He had
commissioned new designs from Paul Andrews, a recent graduate of
the Wimbledon School of Art, so that it would look quite different
from the Royal Ballet's veteran version by Georgiadis. After seeing
the initial designs, MacMillan had asked Andrews for a number of
adaptations to the set. Then, once its Early Renaissance columns
and statuary were erected on the Birmingham Hippodrome stage,
he adjusted his choreography to suit the new setting. Nina
Ananiashvili and Alexei Fadeyechev from the Bolshoi had been
invited to dance the Birmingham premiere as guest artists. When
Fadeyechev was injured shortly before the first night, company
member Kevin O'Hare replaced him as Ananiashvili's Romeo.
MacMillan was particularly impressed by Marion Tait as Juliet in
subsequent performances. She had been gratified by the opportunity to dance the role late in her career and was delighted when
Kenneth suggested she should be the first-cast Juliet when the production toured to London.

MacMillan's next assignment meant that he had been unable to
take up John Osborne's invitation to be involved in his latest play,
Déjàvu, choreographing dance routines for the leading actor, a
latter-day Jimmy Porter. The play, after many setbacks, had already
opened on tour in May 1992, with Peter Egan as Jimmy Porter.
Osborne felt that Egan needed help with the brief dance sequences
before *Déjàvu* reached the West End in June (where it soon folded).
Osborne wrote to MacMillan on 18 May, saying, 'I know that
Look Back [*in Anger*] had some influence, or, at least, lasting
impression on you. I assume it must be an abiding one as you have
mentioned it so often.' Kenneth would enjoy *Déjàvu* as a sort of
sequel, Osborne assured him. 'It's full of cheap jokes, including one
of your own.' If Kenneth could find time for a bit of tactful choreography, 'It would be a great gift to me, because I feel it has a certain sense of continuity that you, of all people, should have a part in
this latest (last?) enterprise of mine. It would make me proud to clip
up a final, historic, if fleeting, link.'

Regretfully, MacMillan had to decline, writing to Osborne how
frustrating it was 'to have been in touch with you again – and then
the mistimings and managerial problems that make it all impossible'.
Before explaining why, he commented (in the letter quoted earlier),

'You are quite right. *Look Back in Anger* did have an enormous influence on me, not least because it made everything else in the theatre seem so trivial. Certainly it made me look at what was happening in dance, and your bombshell made me see that everything in my world was merely windowdressing.' Coincidentally, the main reason why he could not assist with *Déjàvu* was because he was engaged on a musical-theatre production – the first musical since he had worked with Osborne on *The World of Paul Slickey* in 1959.

The National Theatre was preparing to mount Rodgers and Hammerstein's 1945 *Carousel* as part of its policy of reviving classic American musicals. Nicholas Hytner, who was to direct it, had approached Richard Eyre, Artistic Director of the National Theatre, with the proposal three years previously. Eyre, whose own production of *Guys and Dolls* in 1982 had launched the NT's policy, had agreed; securing the rights and finding the money for the production, however, had been a long process. *Carousel* was infrequently staged, in spite of its memorable songs – 'You'll Never Walk Alone', 'If I Loved You', 'June Is Bustin' Out All Over' and the long soliloquy, 'My Boy Bill'. Its central character, Billy Bigelow, is an unlikely hero who dies in the second act and goes to purgatory, leaving his pregnant wife to fend for herself and her child. Though the 1956 Hollywood film had sanitised the musical in an attempt to make it as popular as *Oklahoma!*, the story is a dark one – until its sentimental ending.

As in *Oklahoma!*, created two years earlier, the plot is advanced by a dream ballet in which a young girl's fears and desires are revealed. Louise, Billy's teenage daughter, encountering a 'carnival boy' – a fairground barker very like Billy himself – threatens to repeat her parents' doomed affair. (Both *Carousel* and *Oklahoma!* were originally choreographed by Agnes de Mille.) Hytner's choice as choreographer for the duet and the big ensemble numbers was MacMillan:

He was the one classical-ballet choreographer whose work I always sought out because it spoke to me from a theatrical perspective. He made dance out of the most unexpected dark, wicked stuff. I rang to ask him if he'd be interested in *Carousel*, never thinking he'd do it, and he jumped at the opportunity. When we met, he asked me what I thought *Carousel* was about. When I said, 'It's about sex and violence', he drawled in that voice of his, 'Well, that's what I do.'

They discussed their ideas for the production during the year before it was scheduled: it was to open in the National's Lyttelton Theatre in December 1992. 'I knew how serious and meticulous he was about the quality of the dancers he wanted,' says Hytner. They were both so concerned about the casting that the audition process dragged on and on. Hytner was looking for actor-singers, MacMillan for dancers who might be able to sing. He recorded in his diary, 'Auditioned 150 girls, only 3 any good. 100 boys, only 2.' He and Hytner did a deal: out of the twenty-four performers needed for the ensemble, half would be chosen primarily for their dancing skills and half for their singing ability. He would find a way of integrating the singers into his choreography, provided all the cast did basic ballet class together as well as practising singing exercises every day. Those chosen were so eager to work at the National Theatre that they trained together for four months before rehearsals started in mid-October.

For MacMillan, the hardest task had been finding a dancer for the role of Louise. Billy is given a vision of his daughter 'from above', seeing her teased and treated like an outcast by other youngsters. In the ballet sequence, a group of fairground hands arrives, ready to set up a carousel, and Louise is strongly attracted to their raffish leader. MacMillan had his own *Romeo and Juliet* in mind for their pas de deux: an impulsive young girl is swept off her feet by the kind of man she is not supposed to lust after. He needed ballet dancers who were accustomed to dealing with the demanding lifts he intended to use. He persuaded Bonnie Moore to take leave of absence from the Royal Ballet. Moore, whom he had known at American Ballet Theatre, had followed her English husband to Britain but had never felt at home in the Royal Ballet. With her American accent and slight frame, she was perfect for Louise. For the Carnival Boy, MacMillan chose Stanislav Tchassov, a tall, dark, former Bolshoi dancer who was a guest artist with London City Ballet (and who would later direct his own touring company, the European Ballet).

Hytner watched, fascinated, as MacMillan created the pas de deux: 'He started from almost nothing – a couple of shapes and images – and then it evolved quickly into this searing pas de deux. It gave me a real insight into the language of classical dance, and I've been hooked ever since.' Louise's innocent sexuality is awakened by the roustabout, whose rough handling both excites and terrifies her, as she starts to experience the kind of violence her father inflicted on her mother before she was born. Her teenage infatuation for a dangerously attractive man was what MacMillan feared might happen with his own daughter, whose boyfriends he mistrusted. He watched her make her choices as apprehensively as Billy Bigelow watched Louise.

Charlotte, who turned nineteen in August, was talking of leaving home now that she was about to go to Wimbledon School of Art. Her father was so worried about her first 'serious' boyfriend and the risk of her involvement with drugs that he had written her another letter of concern. He found it difficult to talk to her without an argument, and a refusal to back down on both their parts. He and Deborah had been alarmed and angry after finding cigarettes and alcohol in her room. 'They went over the top,' says Charlotte. 'They'd never been involved with a stroppy teenager before and they thought it was the end of the world.' The house was filled with tension, especially if Charlotte stayed out late or refused to say where she was going (she had reached the age of majority, after all).

Deborah proposed taking Charlotte to Australia during August and September, while Kenneth remained at home. Deborah wanted to see her father, who had been ill, and she hoped that the break from London, and the boyfriend, might calm Charlotte's rebellion before she started her art-college course. Kenneth would have time to himself before *Carousel*'s rehearsals began. Deborah flew to Sydney a week ahead of Charlotte. Kenneth confided in his diary, 'How am I going to bear a month without Deborah? I am desperate. I miss and love her so much.' As well as telephoning her frequently, he wrote long, affectionate letters – something he had never done before. She wondered later whether he was putting his feelings on paper because he had a presentiment that she would soon need a record of how much he loved her.

His week alone with Charlotte proved exceptionally trying for both of them. When she stayed out overnight with her boyfriend, Kenneth confronted her with emotional blackmail the next day; 'You worried me so much last night that I packed a bag to check myself into hospital because I thought I was going to have another heart attack.' Charlotte assumed that her father's over-reaction was because he was reverting to his prudish Scottish roots. Indeed, although she had no way of knowing it, he was behaving towards her much as his own father had behaved towards Jean, his eldest daughter. 'He was trying to shame me for having sex,' says Charlotte. 'But his ballets were full of sex – it's what he was famous for.'

He went with her in a minicab to Heathrow airport to see her off on her flight to Sydney:

He was fussing all the way about how somebody was going to steal my wallet out of my bag or nick something out of my backpack. I kept saying, 'Dad, what is wrong with you? Stop fussing.' I gave him a goodbye hug in the airport, and as I walked off, I looked back and he was crying. I'd never seen him cry before. I was in shock that he was so vulnerable.

He found it hard to sleep on his own in the empty house. A six-hour photographic session with Lord Snowdon for a *Vogue* picture spread about *Carousel* so exhausted him that he felt ill the next day. With Deborah and Charlotte away, he was more prone to hypochondria than ever, though he had good cause to be anxious about his health. His chest hurt, so he went to see his GP, Dr Russell, for tests: the results showed nothing alarming. Feeling lonely, he invited himself to Clement Crisp's place in Sussex for several days, touching base with old friends. Crisp found him unusually serene and easily amused. They laughed a lot, sharing jokes about his ballets.

Crisp recalled his memories of the visit for an article published on 26 October in the *Financial Times* after Kenneth's death: 'As we motored through a village, a friend with us [Peter Hollamby] said, "Look, Kenneth! The name of that house!" We were passing a bijou residence named Mayerling. "And just think," MacMillan said, "it's all going on in their front room!" ' He called for suggestions for a dramatic gala in his honour, consisting of scenes from his ballets, as had been organised for Ashton's retirement gala. 'We'll have to have the rape scene from *The Invitation* and the epileptic fit from *Playground*, Manon fellating the gaoler and her death from a double-tour, and the last duet and shooting in *Mayerling*, and the Nazi death-camp scene from *Valley of Shadows* and the gang-rape in *Judas Tree*.'

MacMillan, so sensitive to critics' slights about his ballets, had no qualms about sending them up himself, among friends. He made no mention during his visit of any future ballet he had in mind after *Carousel* was out of the way. Crisp, with hindsight, assumed

MacMillan might have predicted that time was soon to run out. However, Deborah knew, as did Leanne Benjamin, that he was planning a ballet to Poulenc's motets for unaccompanied voices. 'He loved hearing the vocal warm-ups before *Carousel* rehearsals. He was looking for inspiration that wasn't "abstract",' says Deborah. He was also hoping to continue his collaboration with Hytner and the National Theatre on classic American musicals. He had signed another three-year contract with Houston Ballet, which was going to mount *Manon*; he was trying to secure the Britten Estate's approval for cuts to *The Prince of the Pagodas*; and *Mayerling* was imminent at the start of the Royal Ballet's season, after a gap of six years. Mukhamedov would make his debut as Crown Prince Rudolf on the opening night.

While Kenneth waited for his wife and daughter to return from Australia, he added to his already substantial collection of costume jewellery, buying yet more vintage pieces. His best items had already gone on show in the Victoria and Albert Museum, in a 'Jewels of Fantasy' exhibition that ran from April until September 1992. A case displayed examples from his eclectic collection, which ranged from Edwardian paste to present-day pieces. His favourites were the elaborate, mainly American, confections of the kind seen in films of the 1930s and 1940s. For him, they continued his childhood fascination with the fashions his older sisters had pored over in magazines while he was growing up. The 'Jewels of Fantasy' display coincided with the V&A's popular 'Sovereign' exhibition about the Royal family's jewellery, so there were hordes of visitors. According to Deborah, 'Kenneth was gratified that he was recognised as a serious collector, not just an obsessive amateur. And his array was unusual because it reflected his personal taste. He'd persist with whatever a designer he liked had done, whether it was admired or not. He wasn't buying as an investment for re-sale. He just loved collecting.'

After Deborah and Charlotte had returned, MacMillan was busy with intensive rehearsals for both *Mayerling* and *Carousel*, commuting between home, the Royal Ballet studios at Baron's Court and the National Theatre. Exhausted and insomniac, he drove himself hard. Unable to suppress his anxiety attacks, he continued to see his psychiatrist, Dr Goldblatt, fitting in sessions before rehearsals started so that he could make the most of the time available to him.

53

MacMillan reproached himself in his diary with feeling 'stupidly anxious' over *Carousel*. His nerves, however, had not been apparent when rehearsals started on 12 October, with six weeks to go. The performers were too much in awe of him, and too preoccupied with their own concerns, to have been conscious of his anxiety. Richard Eyre was first to address the assembled cast, welcoming them to the rehearsal room in which he had started *Guys and Dolls* exactly ten years ago. 'I envy you all,' he said, and handed over to Hytner. Hytner launched on a pep talk, starting to explain why the production was employing classical dance when MacMillan interrupted him. 'We're doing classical dance because it's the best way to tell a story. And it's more sexy that way.' A watching journalist, David Gritten writing for the *Sunday Telegraph* magazine, commented, 'The exchange illustrated the two men's complementary styles: Hytner's chummy chatter constrasted with MacMillan's laconic contributions.'

In fact, MacMillan was hiding his worry that he did not have enough experience in mounting the big production numbers that are a speciality of skilled Broadway choreographers – from Jack Cole, whom he admired in his youth, to Jerome Robbins and Susan Stroman (who would choreograph *Oklahoma!* for the National Theatre in 1999). He was confident that he could outdo Agnes de Mille's original version of the twelve-minute 'dream ballet' in Act II, which was dance without lyrics. But he would also have to deal with singers and actors for 'June Is Bustin' Out All Over' and 'Blow High, Blow Low'. He could seek advice from the musical director, Justin Brown, and rely on the assistance of Jane Elliott, his notator and right-hand woman, but the actual staging was up to him – and Hytner.

As the production got underway, MacMillan came to enjoy the collaborative process, relieved that he would not have the sole responsibility of delivering the show. According to Hytner, 'He didn't at all mind not having the total control he was used to. We'd worked out in advance what needed to be done in the dance numbers, along with Bob Crowley [the designer]. Certain things needed to happen at

certain times in the music, and in between Kenneth had a free hand.'
A typical example was the opening number, in which Richard
Rodgers's intoxicating Carousel Waltz builds to a climax. The script
simply mentions 'A Prologue, set in an Amusement Park on the New
England coast in May'. In a radical departure for a 1945 musical, no
words were spoken or sung as the hurdy-gurdy waltz lilted and
swirled for eight long minutes. Most revivals followed the original
Broadway staging, in which the curtain rose on the town's inhabitants enjoying themselves at the fairground. The central characters
emerged from the throng, establishing themselves as the carousel
revolved centre stage: Rodgers and Hammerstein had skipped the
usual opening-scene exposition, plunging directly into the story.

MacMillan proposed an alternative option, starting in the work
place, with impatient cotton-mill girls pent up at their looms until
the hands of the clock reached six. Then they burst, dancing, out of
the gates, met up with waiting workmen and hurried to the fair.
Hytner encouraged MacMillan to make full use of the revolving
stage: the cotton-mill looms would be swiftly replaced by side-show
attractions in the fairground. Bob Crowley provided sections of the
carousel for the cast to assemble as the waltz music gathered
momentum; once completed, the gilded horses circled round,
tended by Billy Bigelow. The amusement park represented the magical realm to which hard-working, low-earning people dreamed of
escaping. The National's team aimed to recapture the rapturous
excitement the prologue had generated when it first appeared on
Broadway. They succeeded: the exhilarating opening sequence
guaranteed the production's success and the awards it would garner
– but MacMillan never saw it staged.

He worked with almost manic urgency, waking at four in the
morning as his brain churned with ideas. He needed to inspire the
cast to reach the rampant level of energy the ensemble numbers
required: he and Hytner wanted to show the barely suppressed passions raging beneath the New England community's ordered façade.
Scribbled notes reveal that he was borrowing moves from his own
ballets (as well as paying homage to Agnes de Mille) in his anxiety
to get things done. Hytner became convinced that MacMillan's personal deadline was way ahead of the production schedule.

MacMillan's other concern was the Royal Ballet's revival of
Mayerling, whose first night, on 29 October 1992, was several

weeks before *Carousel*'s previews. He was rehearsing the ballet's various casts in the principal roles, but spent most of his time and energy on working with Mukhamedov. The role of Rudolf is a demanding one for any newcomer because it builds over three acts. The dancer has to learn to pace and vary his performance in the numerous duets with the women in Rudolf's life, even before he meets his nemesis in Mary Vetsera. Viviana Durante, who would be making her debut as Mary, was by now Mukhamedov's regular partner. MacMillan concentrated on rehearsing their two pas de deux, which were challenging for both of them.

They then left for a few days to perform as guest artists at a gala in Rome. MacMillan did not come in for the rehearsals of other casts, which exasperated Lynn Seymour, who was coaching the role of Mary Vetsera. She telephoned Kenneth at home late one night, accusing him of favouring Mukhamedov at the expense of other dancers. He was obsessed with Irek, she said, and was paying no attention to the alternate casts. He put the telephone down on her, refusing to listen any further. She resigned from her coaching job the next day, and never had the opportunity to speak to him again.

During October, MacMillan continued to divide his time between rehearsals for *Mayerling* and *Carousel*. He tired quickly. 'By lunchtime at the National, he was green,' remembers Jane Elliott. 'He'd have a nap, do some more and then I'd drive him home, worn out.' Exhausted though he was by the end of the day, he felt duty bound to accept an invitation to attend an evening of new works by the Royal Ballet Choreographic Group on 8 October. The group, similar in intent to the one for which he had choreographed his first ballets in the 1950s, had been re-established by Leslie Edwards in 1967. Edwards had remained in charge until Norman Morrice took over. 'An Evening for Leslie Edwards' had been organised as part of the Dance Umbrella festival, in celebration of the group's twenty-fifth anniversary and Edwards's retirement, at seventy-six, from the company. MacMillan had known Edwards for over forty years, ever since joining the Sadler's Wells Ballet School. Leslie had been in many of his ballets over the years: the first Prince of Verona in *Romeo and Juliet*, he had continued to perform the role in the ballet's frequent revivals until he had been obliged to retire.

In addition to paying affectionate respects to Edwards at the party afterwards in the Riverside Studios, MacMillan had been interested to see the work of dancers he knew well: they included Ashley Page and Simon Rice, who was now a member of the *Carousel* cast. The young choreographer who caught his eye, however, was still very much a novice. Christopher Wheeldon had recently joined the Royal Ballet company from the School, where he had won the Ursula Moreton Choreographic Award. For the Choreographic Group showing, he had created a piece to Brahms, *Celestial Spaces*. MacMillan went up to him afterwards and told him to seize every chance to develop his great potential. Kenneth, who did not readily praise other choreographers, had unerringly picked out a talent for the future. Wheeldon, who joined New York City Ballet the following year as a dancer, was to be its resident choreographer from 2001 to 2008, resigning to set up his own ensemble, Morphoses. He has continued to be much sought after by other companies, including the Royal Ballet. He has always acknowledged MacMillan's influence: when he was asked to create a work for New York City Ballet to Richard Rodgers's music, in celebration of the composer's centennial in 2002, he choreographed his own version of the Carousel Waltz – *Carousel (A Dance)* – partly as a personal tribute to MacMillan's account ten years earlier.

With *Mayerling*'s premiere less than a fortnight later, MacMillan was particularly anxious about two scenes. One was the very first one, in which Rudolf's outsider position within the Habsburg court is made plain to the audience through his opening solo. Mukhamedov was struggling with the twists and turns of the choreography, which had first been made on Anthony Dowell and adapted for David Wall as his replacement. The steps, designed to show an elegant, princely arabesque line disguising a tortured psyche, were awkward for Mukhamedov's burly physique. For him, the solo was a daunting obstacle at the very start of a marathon course. The other worrying scene was Mary Vetsera's arrival in Rudolf's bedchamber, wearing only a black chiffon nightdress under her coat. Durante, who could be brazen as Mary in *The Judas Tree*, was oddly shy about Vetsera's provocative boldness. MacMillan had tried to break down her resistance by being very direct with her. 'He told me that when I grab the gun and let it off, shooting the gun is like having an orgasm. He actually asked me if I'd had one, if I knew what he meant. I said, "Yeah", ever so casually, because I knew if you showed you were embarrassed, he'd keep at you.'

She was very embarrassed by having the top of the nightgown pulled down by Mukhamedov as Rudolf, exposing her breasts, even though her back would be to the audience. In the rehearsal studio, she dreaded the other dancers glimpsing her semi-naked; in the theatre, stage hands might also see.

Kenneth said I should go through with it, get it out of the way: 'Viv, do it now, in rehearsal, before you go on stage and seize up.' I only sort of let Irek do it in the stage call and Kenneth was upset that it didn't look right. Just before the show on the first night, he asked me, 'Please, tonight, think of what I've said. It's no big deal, just do it.' He was really comforting. So I thought, 'I'll do it for him, the way he wants.' And of course, I never saw him again.

On the day of the first performance, MacMillan attended his weekly session with his psychiatrist and then went home. He had taken two days off from *Carousel*, expecting to return to finish the big 'June' number, which was causing problems. Charlotte was at home earlier than usual in the afternoon. She and her father were now on better terms, having made up their differences after the arguments of previous weeks. She spent several hours with him and sat on his knee affectionately while they had tea. 'I hadn't done that for some time, but we were both in a good mood. He was quite giggly and sweet when he came downstairs with Mum, ready to go off to the Opera House. "How do I look?" he said, showing off his dinner jacket. I gave him a hug and wished him good luck with *Mayerling*.' Her plans for the evening were yet to be decided: she would probably go out with friends to a bar or club.

Deborah drove Kenneth to the Opera House, waving to Edward Thorpe and Gillian Freeman in the line of traffic outside the theatre. They, and other friends and critics who had been at *Mayerling*'s premiere fourteen years before, would be watching an almost entirely new generation of dancers in the demanding roles. Kenneth went backstage to wish the performers well, then visited de Valois (now ninety-four) in her accustomed box near the stage. He took his seat, with Deborah beside him, in the Grand Tier. He was as nervous as ever as the overture started. The curtains parted on the sombre scene of Mary Vetsera's clandestine burial, the witnesses half hidden under black umbrellas, the coachman stifling his sobs. MacMillan was watching his ballet for the last time.

Halfway through the first act, he left his seat because his coughing was uncontrollable. One of the regular ballet-goers in the row in front had swung round in reprimand, but once Richard Hanson recognised the offender as the choreographer of the ballet, he smiled in apology. MacMillan slipped back in before the act ended, whispering to Deborah, 'I'm having the most terrible anxiety attack – I can't stand it.' When the interval started, they went together to the back-stage area, making their way to the canteen. Kenneth, distressed, sat down on the stairs while Deborah went to fetch him a cup of tea. She returned to find him talking to the two Monicas, Mason and Parker, about Viviana Durante's inhibition over allowing her top to be pulled down in the next act. He said to Deborah, 'I can't watch – I'm too anxious. You go and tell me if she does it or not.'

Deborah wanted to stay with him while he rested backstage in the green room. 'But he sent me back – he was adamant. I think he suspected something was happening to him and wanted to be on his own. His psychiatrist told me later that Kenneth had told him his greatest fear was that he would make an undignified spectacle of himself by falling to bits in public. Like his mother when she had fits.' Reluctantly, she returned to her seat for the next act, and hurried to look for him in the next interval, growing increasingly frantic.

When the third act started, the only thing Deborah felt she could do was return to the auditorium. She stood in the aisle behind the staff seats in the Grand Tier, noticing that Kenneth's old friend and colleague, Violette Verdy, was seated in front of her. Desperately, Deborah counted over and over again the number of years since his heart attack, trying to convince herself that his time could not yet have run out. When the St John Ambulance first-aiders rushed past her, she knew something must have happened to Kenneth. While the ballet continued, she was taken by Dowell to the Opera dressing-rooms where Kenneth's body was lying in the corridor. 'He might have become confused or wanted privacy and instead of going to the green room, he went into the Opera section, where nobody thought to look for him.'

One of the stage staff, an electrician at the end of her shift, had found him by chance as she went to the newly built Opera quarters for a shower before going home. During a ballet performance, the Opera dressing-rooms would normally be deserted. She had no idea who the crumpled figure might be. She reported to the stage-door office that an unknown person had collapsed in the maze of corridors. Dowell had overheard the stage-door discussion and made his way urgently to the Opera quarters, a part of the house unfamiliar to him. He found a St John Ambulance nurse kneeling by MacMillan's lifeless form, and hurried back into the auditorium to fetch Deborah.

She cradled Kenneth's body in her arms as Jeremy Isaacs was called from his seat and decisions were taken over her head. *Mayerling* was about to end, and the dancers, assembling in the wings for the curtain calls, were aware that something dreadful had happened. Viviana Durante, on stage with Mukhamedov for the double-suicide scene, saw 'people running about backstage, looking aghast. We stared at each other behind the screen, where Irek was supposed to shoot me, wondering what was going on. Irek was told just before his curtain call. I still had no idea.'

Isaacs had swiftly decided that as many dancers as possible must be told of MacMillan's death before they took their bows in confusion as rumours spread. It was his view that the audience needed to know as well.

They would have sensed something was very wrong. It would have been a dreadful charade if the curtain calls had gone on and on for a first-night triumph. Too much to ask of the performers, and the audience would soon have found out they'd been deceived. Better to honour Kenneth by letting everyone in the theatre know of his death and the end of an era for the Royal Ballet.

Isaacs gave instructions to Keith Gray, the stage manager, that he would come on stage to make the announcement after the first, full-cast curtain call. Gray arranged for the bouquets of flowers, usually presented individually to the soloists on stage, to be placed in front of the massed line-up of dancers before Isaacs stepped forward.

Kenneth's death had been made into a spectacle, devastatingly insensitive for those closest to him, but not, as he had feared, without dignity. He had died on his own, out of sight, but an audience of two thousand people, and the company and theatre staff who had produced his ballet, had been his first mourners.

Aftermath

Kenneth MacMillan's funeral was a private affair at St Paul's Church, Hammersmith, attended by his family, close friends and colleagues. Obituaries had poured out in the media soon after the theatrical announcement of his death. As a public figure, he would be commemorated four months later by a memorial service in Westminster Abbey, an honour accorded only to people of national significance.

The impact of his sudden death had to be quickly absorbed by the two theatres performing his work, the Royal Opera House and the National. *Mayerling* was next due to be given two days after his death, at a Saturday matinee that went ahead; like the rest of *Mayerling*'s scheduled run, it was dedicated to his memory. Deborah and Charlotte attended the performance, painful for them though it was. They were there to support the company: Michael Nunn and Gillian Revie were making their debuts in the leading roles, chosen by Kenneth as youngsters who deserved a chance to prove themselves in a three-act ballet. Their longed-for opportunity was a difficult one. Deborah went backstage before the performance to reassure all the dancers that Kenneth would have wanted them to do their best. De Valois made a point of being present at the matinee, stumping along on her walking stick to her box by the stage: the company and audience regulars, including critics covering the matinee, would know that she was there. As the curtains opened on the scene of Mary Vetsera's burial in the rain, her coffin lowered beneath the stage, tears started to flow.

At the National Theatre, Hytner asked the *Carousel* cast to run through all the dance sequences to show how much MacMillan had achieved in the two-and-a-half weeks he had worked on the show. Heartened in their sorrow, the cast pulled together as a company determined to do him justice. With less than a month to go before the previews, cast members Simon Rice and Michael Keegan-Dolan completed 'Blow High, Blow Low' and Jane Elliott, MacMillan's assistant, filled in missing sections he had already outlined. She was now responsible for staging all the dances once the set was ready for final rehearsals and previews, in collaboration with Hytner. The opening night, dedicated to MacMillan, was a huge hit for the National Theatre. *Carousel* went on to win four Olivier Awards and five Tonys (including a posthumous 'Best Choreography' one for MacMillan) when the production was mounted in New York in March 1994, at the Lincoln Center's Vivian Beaumont Theater.

The publicity surrounding MacMillan's contribution to *Carousel* led his loyal supporters to believe that it acquired a disproportionate importance after his death. 'It was as if the National Theatre had much greater status than the Royal Ballet,' said John Copley, the opera producer who had known MacMillan since the early days of their careers. 'Kenneth was being claimed as a grand old man of British theatre by the Establishment who didn't really rate ballet.' Hytner comments that MacMillan was 'tickled, not awed' by his connection with the National, adding, 'We were the beneficiaries, far more than him.' When the Carousel Waltz was played at the start of MacMillan's memorial service in Westminster Abbey, it was not to underline his association with the National Theatre but to raise the spirits of the congregation before the service proper started. Deborah had chosen it because its hurdy-gurdy irreverence would enliven the Abbey 'as it was the last thing he had been working on, and because it wasn't too turgid'.

During the service, the Royal Ballet Sinfonia (Birmingham Royal Ballet's orchestra), conducted by Barry Wordsworth, played music from MacMillan's ballets, concluding with the *Pie Jesu* from Fauré's *Requiem*, with its ghostly memory of Charlotte dancing as a small child. Ninette de Valois, who could not be present, wrote a tribute to Kenneth that was read by Anthony Dowell. Peter Wright and Nicholas Hytner spoke about the man they had known; Lynn Seymour had chosen verses from C. Day Lewis's poem, 'Pegasus', and Jeremy Isaacs read from St Paul's Second Epistle to the Corinthians. As the congregation filed out, the Abbey's bells pealed in celebration of MacMillan's life.

Epilogue

The Royal Ballet did not mount a memorial gala in MacMillan's honour. There was no immediate need to do so, for *Mayerling* was still in performance and others of his ballets were embedded in the repertoire. Rather fewer were scheduled by the tenth anniversary of his death in 2002, when *Mayerling* was performed in tribute to him by another new generation of dancers. The recently appointed Artistic Director, Ross Stretton, had shown little interest in the one-act ballets, assuming that MacMillan's legacy consisted primarily of the popular blockbusters, *Romeo and Juliet* and *Manon*. He was swiftly disabused of this view, not least by Deborah MacMillan, who is in charge of her late husband's estate. Once Stretton had departed, after just over a year in his post, the Royal Ballet, under Monica Mason's leadership, reclaimed MacMillan as a vital part of its ongoing history.

He is an essential link in the line of choreographers who determined what British ballet was to become. He followed the formative figures of de Valois, Ashton, Tudor and Cranko, while continuing the dramatic narrative vein of the important lesser contributors: Helpmann, Darrell, Walter Gore. He saw ballet above all as theatre, capable of dealing with all society's concerns, as well as exploring the darkest recesses of the human psyche. This he set out to do using the technique of classical dance, however far he pushed it to extremes. His instruments, the dancers, had to be highly skilled in the physical language which he created, capable of helping him find the shapes and images he saw in his mind's eye. Although he could choreograph semi-abstract ballets focusing on the relationship between movement and music – *Danses concertantes, Symphony, Diversions, Concerto* – his instinct was to use dancers as people, not just bodies, aiming to show their inner lives through the way they moved.

He drew up his own scenarios, often adapted from books or films, for his disturbing one-act works – *The Invitation, Anastasia, My Brother, My Sisters, Valley of Shadows, Different Drummer* and the biblical/apocryphal *The Judas Tree*. In these ballets, he expected

703

audiences to make leaps of understanding, instead of relying on programme synopses. Spectators do not need to be familiar with ballet steps or mime gestures to understand what the characters are conveying: their motives and emotions strike chords of recognition that can go deeper than words on a page.

His three-act ballets, however, do require synopses. Based on literature (Shakespeare's play for *Romeo and Juliet*, Prévost's novel for *Manon*), historical characters and events (*Mayerling* and *Isadora*), and a conflation of legends for *The Prince of the Pagodas*, their scenarios are outlined in programmes to assist audiences to follow their plots. Although this seems unexceptional to theatre-goers accustomed to opera, foreign-language dramas and nineteenth-century ballets, some dance critics find synopses, especially lengthy ones, a failing. They share Balanchine's belief that ballet should be self-explanatory, revealing its meaning through movement alone. In their view, expressed most cogently by Arlene Croce, ballet is ill-equipped to cover the subjects MacMillan insisted on tackling, such as war, politics, poverty, psychosis, the physical aspects of sex, disease and death. Croce did, however, applaud his boldness in pushing against its limitations, taking risks that might not always have come off: when they did, he succeeded in imparting a depth of meaning that lesser talents could never achieve – and she acknowledged that he was a master choreographer.

Herein lies a dilemma for MacMillan's successors. He set up expectations of what ballet-theatre could do that have daunted choreographers since. Audiences and impresarios are attracted by evening-length narrative ballets, but there are not many choreographers who can rise to the challenge. Those coming from the Soviet tradition of 'dramballet' (such as Boris Eifman, based in St Petersburg) have pursued their own dramatic vein. On tour in the West, however, such ballets risk being compared with MacMillan's, often to their disadvantage. This canot be said, though, of the work of Alexei Ratmansky, who knew MacMillan's ballets in the repertoire of the Royal Danish Ballet before he returned to the Bolshoi, choreographing for it as well as New York City Ballet. He has proved to be an original talent, combining different traditions of dance.

In Britain, narrative ballets have been the mainstay of Birmingham Royal Ballet and Northern Ballet Theatre; their director–choreographers, David Bintley for BRB and David Nixon for NBT, would, however, claim their own sources of inspiration rather than be considered indebted to MacMillan. So might former Royal Ballet choreographers who nevertheless grew up performing his ballets and could hardly avoid being influenced by him: Michael Corder, Ashley Page, Derek Deane, Will Tuckett. Christopher Wheeldon, who started his career with the Royal Ballet but soon moved to New York City Ballet, has been unusually frank in his acknowledgement of MacMillan's influence, as well as Balanchine's.

MacMillan's most direct heir, as an unorthodox creator of provocative dance works based on literary and film sources, would seem to be Matthew Bourne. His iconoclastic *Swan Lake*, with its male swans and disturbed misfit of a hero, has an encounter between the unhappy prince and his icily regal mother that echoes a scene in *Mayerling*. There are direct references to *Romeo and Juliet* in *Dorian Gray*, Bourne's darkest work to date. In it, as in *The Car Man*, his remake of *Carmen*, he addresses sexual compulsion, the corruption of innocence, violence and death. But Bourne is essentially a maker of wordless musicals, an inventive movement director, rather than a choreographer – and certainly not a ballet-based one.

MacMillan worked, by choice, within the institution of a classical-ballet company: the Royal Ballet, Stuttgart Ballet, Berlin Ballet, American Ballet Theatre. He had no desire to work as a freelance or to set up his own independent company (as Bourne and Wheeldon have done). He needed to be able to take his casts' technique for granted, which is why he valued dancers accustomed to testing themselves in the demanding 'classics', such as *The Sleeping Beauty*. He was defined to a large extent by the Royal Ballet, the company in which he grew up and to which he belonged, however much he rebelled against it.

His relationship with it was a mass of contradictions. He thought of himself as an outsider, not a team player within an institution. He dreaded the claustrophobia of an enclosed society, yet he depended on an intimate group of people to enable him to create. He was prepared to obey the conventions of the opera-house system even while resenting them: he accommodated the Royal Ballet's rehearsal schedules, met its deadlines, provided roles for the corps de ballet and alternative-cast soloists as well as the principal dancers who inspired him. He fulfilled his ambition to become the company's

Artistic Director, though he was not cut out to be an administrator and tactician. He wanted to be acknowledged by the Establishment, of which he never felt part, and was proud to be honoured with a knighthood. Yet he refused to mellow into respectability in his later ballets: *The Prince of the Pagodas*, the 'fairy-tale' commission he was required to fulfil, is not an easily assimilable experience and *The Judas Tree*, his last work, is the most challenging of all.

As well as roughing up expectations of what ballet should be, he was instrumental in changing what it looked like on stage. He had an expert eye for design, collaborating with artists who understood that set designs could be evocative rather than literal. His ballets were always distinctively designed and lit, conceived from the start as an imaginative world of their own. He would fight for a designer's vision to be realised without compromise; he could equally well be ruthless in scrapping designs that did not suit his purpose. He was ahead of his time, too early for technological advances that would have made his creative processes simpler: computer-assisted images, digital film and video, music synthesisers to enable him to hear in advance what an orchestrated score would sound like. He envisaged his story ballets almost as dreams, their images and events changing and dissolving seamlessly: they should have been staged using state-of-the-art equipment instead of manual scene changes. (His death came seven years before the Royal Opera House was modernised in time for the Millennium.)

The leading roles in his ballets have been one of the principal attractions for dancers wanting to join the Royal Ballet. According to Monica Mason, its Director since 2002,

Dancers apply to me from other companies saying they're longing to dance Juliet or Manon, Romeo or Rudolf. But it can be difficult for them to adjust to the kind of acting he required, if they haven't been in his ballets all along, as our dancers have from the time they start. He wanted his characters to be real, not 'acted'. He was wonderful at picking dancers who were naturally right.

Roles he created on particular dancers have proved surprisingly open to different understandings of the characters, performed by dancers with very different physiques and personalities, from Lynn Seymour to Sylvie Guillem, Antoinette Sibley to Tamara Rojo, Anthony Dowell and David Wall to Irek Mukhamedov and Johan

Kobborg. Once hooked by his ballets, dance-goers never tire of seeing them again to find out what a performer makes of them, just as theatre-goers return to productions of classic plays. And for the Royal Ballet, his works have become classics of its repertoire.

Directors of other ballet companies have persisted in acquiring his works to satisfy their dancers and audiences. Since MacMillan's death, his ballets have continued to spread through the world, entering the repertoires of companies in Japan, Russia and South America, as well as the United States, Canada, Australia, Turkey and Europe. At the time of his tenth anniversary celebrations in 2002, some twenty companies in a dozen different countries were performing his work: twelve productions of *Manon*, five of *Romeo and Juliet*, three of *The Song of the Earth*.

His extensive back catalogue of less-popular one-act works, however, lies largely untapped. Which ones will survive remains unpredictable, dependent on the taste of artistic directors and audiences. MacMillan trusted that at least some of his more personal creations would long outlive him, confident that he had created work of lasting significance.

Of the many enduring moments MacMillan left for performers and audiences, perhaps among the most powerful are the surprising number of concluding images of transfiguration: the young man claimed by the Fairy in *Le Baiser de la fée*, Stravinsky's metaphor for the artist and his muse; the three figures stepping sublimely into eternity at the end of *The Song of the Earth*; the mourners/angelic spirits in *Requiem* and *Gloria*; the apotheosis for the ill-fated lovers at the end of *Orpheus*; Anastasia touring triumphantly on her bed, defying oblivion.

Chronology of MacMillan's Choreography

Somnambulism – 1 February 1953
Sadler's Wells Choreographers' Group, Sadler's Wells Theatre
Music Stan Kenton, Peter Rugolo
Cast Maryon Lane, David Poole, Kenneth MacMillan

Fragment – 14 June 1953
Sadler's Wells Choreographic Group, Sadler's Wells Theatre
Music Stan Kenton
Cast Sara Neil, Donald Britton, Annette Page

Laiderette – 24 January 1954
Sadler's Wells Choreographic Group, Sadler's Wells Theatre
Music Frank Martin
Cast Maryon Lane, David Poole
(Ballet Rambert production, with designs by Kenneth Rowell, 4 July 1955)

Steps Into Ballet – 29 November 1954
BBC Television, directed by Naomi Capon
Music Richard Arnell
Design Michael Yates
Cast Peggy Van Praagh, Maureen Bruce, Donald Britton,
Susan Saloman, Kenneth MacMillan

Danses concertantes – 18 January 1955
Sadler's Wells Theatre Ballet, Sadler's Wells Theatre
Music Igor Stravinsky
Design Nicholas Georgiadis
Cast Maryon Lane, David Poole, Donald Britton

House of Birds – 26 May 1955
Sadler's Wells Theatre Ballet, Sadler's Wells Theatre
Music Federico Mompou, *arr.* John Lanchbery
Design Nicholas Georgiadis
Cast Maryon Lane, David Poole, Doreen Tempest

Turned Out Proud – 23 October 1955
BBC Television, directed by Margaret Dale
Cast John Neville, Violette Verdy, Julia Farron, Gilbert Vernon,
Sonya Hana, Sheila O'Neill, John Stevens

Tannhäuser: Venusberg Ballet – 21 November 1955
Royal Opera, Royal Opera House
Music Richard Wagner
Design Ralph Koltai
Cast Julia Farron, Gilbert Vernon

Noctambules – 1 March 1956
Sadler's Wells Ballet, Royal Opera House
Music Humphrey Searle
Design Nicholas Georgiadis
Cast Leslie Edwards, Maryon Lane, Nadia Nerina

Solitaire – 7 June 1956
Sadler's Wells Theatre Ballet, Sadler's Wells Theatre
Music Malcolm Arnold
Design Desmond Heeley
Cast Margaret Hill, Donald MacLeary, Sara Neil

Fireworks pas de deux – August 1956
Music Igor Stravinsky
Cast Nadia Nerina, Alexis Rassine

Valse eccentrique – 10 December 1956
Gala, Sadler's Wells Theatre
Music Jacques Ibert
Cast Alexander Grant, Anya Linden, Brian Shaw

Winter's Eve – 16 January 1957
American Ballet Theatre, Lisbon
Music Benjamin Britten
Design Nicholas Georgiadis
Cast Nora Kaye, John Kriza

Journey – 6 May 1957
American Ballet Theatre Choreographic Group,
New York
Music Béla Bartók
Cast Nora Kaye, John Kriza, Erik Bruhn, Scott Douglas

The Burrow – 2 January 1958
Royal Ballet Touring Company, Royal Opera House
Music Frank Martin
Design Nicholas Georgiadis
Cast Anne Heaton, Donald Britton, Edward Miller, Lynn Seymour,
Donald MacLeary

Agon – 20 August 1958
Royal Ballet, Royal Opera House
Music Igor Stravinsky
Design Nicholas Georgiadis
Cast Anya Linden, David Blair, Deirdre Dixon, Ronald Hynd

The World of Paul Slickey – 14 April 1959
Musical written and directed by John Osborne
Music Christopher Whelen
Set Design Hugh Casson *Costume Design* Jocelyn Rickards
Choreography Kenneth MacMillan

Expresso Bongo – 1959
Musical film, directed by Val Guest
Music Monty Norman

Le Baiser de la fée – 12 April 1960
Royal Ballet, Royal Opera House
Music Igor Stravinsky
Design Kenneth Rowell
Cast Lynn Seymour, Svetlana Beriosova, Donald MacLeary

The Invitation – 10 November 1960
Royal Ballet Touring Company, Oxford
Music Mátyás Seiber
Design Nicholas Georgiadis
Cast Lynn Seymour, Christopher Gable, Anne Heaton,
Desmond Doyle

The Seven Deadly Sins – 1961
Western Theatre Ballet, Edinburgh Festival
Music Kurt Weill
Design Ian Spurling
Cast Anya Linden, Cleo Laine

Diversions – 15 September 1961
Royal Ballet, Royal Opera House
Music Arthur Bliss
Design Philip Prowse
Cast Maryon Lane, Svetlana Beriosova, Donald MacLeary,
Graham Usher

The Rite of Spring – 3 May 1962
Royal Ballet, Royal Opera House
Music Igor Stravinsky

Design Sidney Nolan
Chosen Maiden Monica Mason

Dance Suite – 14 July 1962
Royal Ballet School, Royal Opera House
Music Darius Milhaud
Cast Vergie Derman, Richard Cragun, Kerrison Cooke

Symphony – 15 February 1963
Royal Ballet, Royal Opera House
Music Dmitri Shostakovich
Design Yolanda Sonnabend
Cast Antoinette Sibley, Georgina Parkinson, Donald MacLeary,
Desmond Doyle

Las Hermanas – 13 July 1963
Stuttgart Ballet, Stuttgart
Music Frank Martin
Design Nicholas Georgiadis
Cast Marcia Haydée, Birgit Keil, Ray Barra, Ruth Papendick

Dark Descent – 29 September 1963
ABC Television
Music Darius Milhaud
Design James Goddard
Cast Marcia Haydée, Ray Barra

La Création du monde – 12 February 1964
Royal Ballet Touring Company, Stratford upon Avon
Music Darius Milhaud
Design James Goddard
Cast Doreen Wells, Richard Farley, Elisabeth Anderton,
Ronald Emblen, Adrian Grater

Images of Love – 2 April 1964
Royal Ballet, Royal Opera House
Music Peter Tranchell
Design Barry Kay
Cast Svetlana Beriosova, Donald MacLeary, Nadia Nerina,
Alexander Grant, Lynn Seymour, Christopher Gable,
Rudolf Nureyev

Divertimento pas de deux – 9 May 1964
Bath Festival
Music Béla Bartók

Design Barry Kay
Cast Margot Fonteyn, Rudolf Nureyev

Romeo and Juliet – 9 February 1965
Royal Ballet, Royal Opera House
Music Sergey Prokofiev
Design Nicholas Georgiadis
Cast Margot Fonteyn, Rudolf Nureyev, David Blair, Anthony Dowell,
Desmond Doyle

Song of the Earth/Das Lied von der Erde – 7 November 1965
Stuttgart Ballet, Stuttgart
Music Gustav Mahler
Design Nicholas Georgiadis
Cast Egon Madsen, Marcia Haydée, Ray Barra

Albertine, or The Crimson Curtain – 13 May 1966
BBC Television, directed by Peter Wright
Cast Lynn Seymour, Desmond Doyle

Valses nobles et sentimentales – 30 November 1966
Deutsche Oper Ballet, Berlin
Music Maurice Ravel
Design Jürgen Rose
Cast Vergie Derman, Didi Carli, Falco Kapuste

Concerto – 30 November 1966
Deutsche Oper Ballet, Berlin
Music Dmitri Shostakovich
Design Jürgen Rose
Cast Didi Carli, Falco Kapuste, Lynn Seymour, Rudolf Holz,
Rudolf Kesselheim

Anastasia (one-act version) – 25 June 1967
Deutsche Oper Ballet, Berlin
Music Bohuslav Martinů *Electronic Music* Fritz Winckel and
Rüdiger Rufer
Cast Lynn Seymour

The Sleeping Beauty (production) – 8 October 1967
Deutsche Oper Ballet, Berlin
Music Piotr Ilyich Tchaikovsky
Choreography Marius Petipa, Kenneth MacMillan
Design Barry Kay
Cast Lynn Seymour, Rudolf Holz

Olympiade – 11 March 1968
Deutsche Oper Ballet, Berlin
Music Igor Stravinsky
Cast Lynn Seymour, Falco Kapuste, Klaus Beelitz

The Sphinx/Der Sphinx – 1 June 1968
Stuttgart Ballet, Stuttgart
Music Darius Milhaud
Design Elisabeth Dalton
Cast Marcia Haydée, Richard Cragun, Egon Madsen,
Heinz Clauss

Cain and Abel/Kain und Abel – 1 November 1968
Deutsche Oper Ballet, Berlin
Music Andrzej Panufnik
Design Barry Kay
Cast Frank Frey, Daniel Job, Gerhard Bohner

Olympiad (reworking of *Olympiade*) – 21 February 1969
Royal Ballet, Royal Opera House
Music Igor Stravinsky
Cast Deanne Bergsma, Keith Rosson, Robert Mead

Swan Lake (production) – 14 May 1969
Deutsche Oper Ballet, Berlin
Music Piotr Ilyich Tchaikovsky
Design Nicholas Georgiadis
Choreography Marius Petipa, Lev Ivanov, Kenneth MacMillan
Cast Lynn Seymour, Frank Frey

Miss Julie – 8 March 1970
Stuttgart Ballet, Stuttgart
Music Andrzej Panufnik
Design Barry Kay
Cast Marcia Haydée, Frank Frey

Checkpoint – 27 November 1970
Royal Ballet New Group, Manchester
Music Roberto Gerhard
Design Elisabeth Dalton
Cast Svetlana Beriosova, Donald MacLeary

Anastasia (three-act version) – 22 July 1971
Royal Ballet, Royal Opera House
Music Piotr Ilyich Tchaikovsky, Bohuslav Martinů

Design Barry Kay
Cast Lynn Seymour, Svetlana Beriosova, Derek Rencher,
Antoinette Sibley, Anthony Dowell

Pas de sept – 14 December 1971
Royal Ballet, Royal Opera House
Music Piotr Ilyich Tchaikovsky
Choreography adapted from *The Sleeping Beauty* production for
Deutsche Oper Ballet
Design Barry Kay
Cast Deanne Bergsma, Lesley Collier, Vergie Derman, Ann Jenner,
Georgina Parkinson, Jennifer Penney, Diana Vere

Triad – 19 January 1972
Royal Ballet, Royal Opera House
Music Sergey Prokofiev
Design Peter Unsworth
Cast Antoinette Sibley, Anthony Dowell, Wayne Eagling

Ballade – 19 May 1972
Royal Ballet New Group, Lisbon
Music Gabriel Fauré
Cast Vyvyan Lorrayne, Kerrison Cooke, Nicholas Johnson,
Stephen Jefferies

Side Show pas de deux – 24 April 1972
Royal Ballet, Liverpool
Music Igor Stravinsky
Costume Design Thomas O'Neil
Cast Lynn Seymour, Rudolf Nureyev

The Poltroon – 12 October 1972
Royal Ballet New Group, Sadler's Wells Theatre
Music Rudolf Maros
Design Thomas O'Neil
Cast Brenda Last, Donald MacLeary, Stephen Jefferies

Pavane pas de deux – 13 January 1973
Royal Ballet, Royal Opera House
Music Gabriel Fauré
Costume Design Anthony Dowell
Cast Antoinette Sibley, Anthony Dowell

The Sleeping Beauty (production) – 15 March 1973
Royal Ballet, Royal Opera House

Music Piotr Ilyich Tchaikovsky
Choreography Marius Petipa, Kenneth MacMillan
Design Peter Farmer
Cast Antoinette Sibley, Anthony Dowell

The Seven Deadly Sins – 19 July 1973
Royal Ballet, Royal Opera House
Music Kurt Weill
Design Ian Spurling
Cast Jennifer Penney, Georgia Brown

Manon – 7 March 1974
Royal Ballet, Royal Opera House
Music Jules Massenet, *arr.* Leighton Lucas
Design Nicholas Georgiadis
Cast Antoinette Sibley, Anthony Dowell, David Wall

Gala pas de deux – 17 July 1974
Royal Opera House gala
Music Igor Stravinsky
Cast Natalia Makarova, Donald MacLeary

Elite Syncopations – 7 October 1974
Royal Ballet, Royal Opera House
Music Scott Joplin *et al.*
Design Ian Spurling
Cast Merle Park, Donald MacLeary, Monica Mason,
Michael Coleman, Jennifer Penney, David Wall, Vergie Derman,
Wayne Sleep

The Four Seasons – 5 March 1975
Royal Ballet, Royal Opera House
Music Giuseppe Verdi
Design Peter Rice
Cast Vergie Derman, Donald MacLeary, Marguerite Porter,
Lesley Collier, Michael Coleman, David Ashmole, Wayne Eagling,
Monica Mason, David Wall, Anthony Dowell, Jennifer Penney,
Wayne Sleep

Rituals – 11 December 1975
Royal Ballet, Royal Opera House
Music Béla Bartók
Design Yolanda Sonnabend
Cast David Drew, Wayne Eagling, Stephen Beagley,
Vergie Derman, David Wall, Lynn Seymour, Monica Mason

Requiem – 28 November 1976
Stuttgart Ballet, Stuttgart
Music Gabriel Fauré
Design Yolanda Sonnabend
Cast Marcia Haydée, Birgit Keil, Egon Madsen, Richard Cragun,
Reid Anderson

Feux Follets solo – 26 December 1976
Theatre of Skating, Cambridge Theatre, London
Music Franz Liszt
Cast John Curry

Gloriana – 30 May 1977
Royal Ballet, Royal Opera House gala
Music Benjamin Britten
Design Yolanda Sonnabend
Cast Lynn Seymour, Wayne Eagling, Michael Coleman,
Stephen Beagley, Graham Fletcher, Andrew Moore, Ashley Page

Mayerling – 14 February 1978
Royal Ballet, Royal Opera House
Music Franz Liszt, *arr.* John Lanchbery
Design Nicholas Georgiadis
Cast David Wall, Lynn Seymour, Merle Park, Georgina Parkinson,
Wendy Ellis, Michael Somes, Laura Connor, Graham Fletcher

My Brother, My Sisters/Mein Bruder, Meine Schwestern –
21 May 1978
Stuttgart Ballet, Stuttgart
Music Arnold Schoenberg, Anton Webern
Design Yolanda Sonnabend
Cast Birgit Keil, Richard Cragun, Lucia Montagnon,
Reid Anderson

6.6.78 (Homage to Ninette de Valois) – 26 September 1978
Sadler's Wells Royal Ballet, Sadler's Wells Theatre
Music Samuel Barber
Design Ian Spurling
Cast Marion Tait, Desmond Kelly

Métaboles – 23 November 1978
Paris Opéra Ballet, Paris
Music Henri Dutilleux
Design Barry Kay
Cast Dominique Khalfouni, Patrice Bart, Patrick Dupond

La Fin du jour – 15 March 1979
Royal Ballet, Royal Opera House
Music Maurice Ravel
Design Ian Spurling
Cast Merle Park, Jennifer Penney, Wayne Eagling, Julian Hosking

Playground – 24 August 1979
Sadler's Wells Royal Ballet, Edinburgh Festival
Music Gordon Crosse
Design Yolanda Sonnabend
Cast Marion Tait, Desmond Kelly

Gloria – 13 March 1980
Royal Ballet, Royal Opera House
Music Francis Poulenc
Design Andy Klunder
Cast Wayne Eagling, Julian Hosking, Jennifer Penney, Wendy Ellis

Waterfalls pas de deux – 30 November 1980
London Palladium gala
Music Paul McCartney
Cast Jennifer Penney, Anthony Dowell

Isadora – 30 April 1981
Royal Ballet, Royal Opera House
Music Richard Rodney Bennett
Design Barry Kay
Cast Merle Park, Mary Miller, Julian Hosking, Derek Deane, Derek Rencher

Wild Boy – 12 December 1981
American Ballet Theatre, Washington DC
Music Gordon Crosse
Set Design Oliver Smith *Costume Design* Willa Kim
Cast Mikhail Baryshnikov, Natalia Makarova, Kevin McKenzie, Robert La Fosse

A Lot of Happiness – 15 December 1981
Granada Television, directed by Jack Gold
Music Fryderyk Chopin, George Gershwin
Costume Design Deborah MacMillan
Cast Birgit Keil, Vladimir Klos

Verdi Variations pas de deux – 1 March 1982
Aterballetto, Reggio-Emilia

Music Giuseppe Verdi
Cast Peter Schaufuss, Elisabetta Terabust

Quartet – 7 April 1982
Sadler's Wells Royal Ballet, Bristol
Music Giuseppe Verdi
Design Deborah MacMillan
Cast Sherilyn Kennedy, David Ashmole, Galina Samsova, Desmond Kelly,
Marion Tait, Carl Myers, Sandra Madgwick, Roland Price

Orpheus – 11 June 1982
Royal Ballet, Royal Opera House
Music Igor Stravinsky
Design Nicholas Georgiadis
Cast Jennifer Penney, Peter Schaufuss, Wayne Eagling, Ashley Page

Valley of Shadows – 3 March 1983
Royal Ballet, Royal Opera House
Music Bohuslav Martinů, Piotr Ilyich Tchaikovsky
Design Yolanda Sonnabend
Cast Alessandra Ferri, Derek Deane, Ashley Page, Guy Niblett,
David Wall, Sandra Conley, Julie Wood

Different Drummer – 24 February 1984
Royal Ballet, Royal Opera House
Music Anton Webern, Arnold Schoenberg
Costume Design Yolanda Sonnabend
Cast Wayne Eagling, Alessandra Ferri, Stephen Jefferies

The Seven Deadly Sins of the Bourgeoisie – 22 April 1984
Granada Television, directed by Derek Bailey
Music Kurt Weill
Set Design Roy Stonehouse *Costume Design* Yolanda Sonnabend
Cast Alessandra Ferri, Marie Angel, Birgit Keil, Vladimir Klos

Gala pas de deux – 24 June 1984
Royal Ballet, Royal Opera House
Music Francis Poulenc
Costume Design Deborah Williams [MacMillan]
Cast Alessandra Ferri, David Wall

Tannhäuser: Venusberg Ballet – 25 September 1984
Royal Opera, Royal Opera House
Music Richard Wagner
Design Timothy O'Brien, Luciana Arrighi

718

Cast Linda Gibbs, Kate Harrison, Christopher Bannerman,
Ross McKim

Three Solos – 11 July 1985
Contemporary Dance Trust gala, Royal Opera House
Music Johann Sebastian Bach, Sergey Rachmaninov,
Georg Philipp Telemann
Cast Christopher Bannerman, Linda Gibbs, Ross McKim

Requiem – 7 February 1986
American Ballet Theatre, Chicago
Music Andrew Lloyd Webber
Design Yolanda Sonnabend
Cast Alessandra Ferri, Gil Boggs

Le Baiser de la fée – 8 May 1986
Royal Ballet, Royal Opera House
Music Igor Stravinsky
Design Martin Sutherland
Cast Fiona Chadwick, Jonathan Cope, Maria Almeida

The Sleeping Beauty (production) – 11 February 1987
American Ballet Theatre, Chicago
Music Piotr Ilyich Tchaikovsky
Choreography Marius Petipa, Kenneth MacMillan
Design Nicholas Georgiadis
Cast Susan Jaffe, Ross Stretton

Sea of Troubles – 17 March 1988
Dance Advance, Brighton
Music Anton Webern, Bohuslav Martinů
Design Deborah MacMillan
Cast Michael Batchelor, Jennifer Jackson, Susan Crow,
Russell Maliphant, Stephen Sherriff, Sheila Styles

Soirées musicales – 21 July 1988
Royal Ballet School, Royal Opera House
Music Benjamin Britten
Design Ian Spurling
Cast Dana Fouras, Gary Shuker, Tetsuya Kumakawa

The Prince of the Pagodas – 7 December 1989
Royal Ballet, Royal Opera House
Music Benjamin Britten
Design Nicholas Georgiadis

719

Cast Darcey Bussell, Jonathan Cope, Tetsuya Kumakawa, Fiona Chadwick, Anthony Dowell

Farewell pas de deux – 19 July 1990
Royal Ballet, London Palladium
Music Piotr Ilyich Tchaikovsky
Costume Design Peter Farmer
Cast Darcey Bussell, Irek Mukhamedov

Gala pas de deux (reworking of the pas de deux of
24 June 1984) – 1 December 1990
Royal Opera House
Music Francis Poulenc
Cast Darcey Bussell, Stuart Cassidy

Winter Dreams – 7 February 1991
Royal Ballet, Royal Opera House
Music Piotr Ilyich Tchaikovsky, *arr.* Philip Gammon
Design Peter Farmer
Cast Irek Mukhamedov, Darcey Bussell, Viviana Durante,
Nicola Tranah, Anthony Dowell, Derek Rencher

The Burrow – 31 October 1991
Birmingham Royal Ballet, Birmingham
Music Frank Martin
Design Nicholas Georgiadis
Cast Marion Tait, Desmond Kelly, Anita Landa

Gala pas de deux (reworking of the pas de deux of 24 June 1984 and 1
December 1990) – 1 December 1991
Royal Opera House
Music Francis Poulenc
Cast Leanne Benjamin, Stephen Jefferies

The Judas Tree – 19 March 1992
Royal Ballet, Royal Opera House
Music Brian Elias
Design Jock McFadyen
Cast Irek Mukhamedov, Viviana Durante, Michael Nunn, Mark Silver

Carousel (posthumous) – 10 December 1992
National Theatre, directed by Nicholas Hytner
Music Richard Rodgers
Design Bob Crowley
Dream Ballet Cast Bonnie Moore, Stanislav Tchassov

Selected Recordings, Broadcasts and Big-Screen Relays of MacMillan's Choreography

Performances are by the Royal Ballet unless otherwise stated.

The Dreamers (Somnabulism) – 1 April 1954
BBC Television
Cast Maryon Lane, David Poole, Sara Neil

House of Birds – 16 September 1956
BBC Television
Cast Sara Neil, Michael Boulton, Margaret Hill

Dark Descent – 29 September 1963
ABC Television
Cast Marcia Haydée, Ray Barra

Gala Performance – 18 March 1965
BBC Television
Romeo and Juliet, Act I, Balcony Scene
Cast Margot Fonteyn, Rudolf Nureyev

Romeo and Juliet – 1965
Poetic Films Ltd (Rank Film Distributors)
First shown on BBC Television, 10 October 1977
Commercial release DVD, 1999; VHS, 2000
Cast Margot Fonteyn, Rudolf Nureyev

Behind the Scenes – The Royal Ballet – 14 April 1966
BBC Television
Rehearsal of *Romeo and Juliet* and *Monotones*
Cast Frederick Ashton, Margot Fonteyn, Rudolf Nureyev, Lynn Seymour, Christopher Gable, Anthony Dowell

Albertine or The Crimson Curtain – 13 May 1966
BBC Television
Cast Lynn Seymour, Desmond Doyle

Elite Syncopations – 21 September 1975
BBC Television
Cast Monica Mason, Jennifer Penney, David Wall, Merle Park, Vergie Derman, Wayne Sleep, Donald MacLeary, Wayne Eagling

The Queen's Silver Jubilee Gala: Part 2 The Royal Ballet – 30 May 1977
BBC Television/WNET co-production (93 minutes)

Programme included *Pavane*
Cast Lesley Collier, Donald MacLeary
and *Gloriana Choral Dances*
Cast Lynn Seymour, Stephen Beagley, Michael Coleman, Derek Deane,
Graham Fletcher, Andrew Moore, Ashley Page

Pavane – *c.* March 1978
Recording of performance by American Ballet Theatre at the Opera House,
John F. Kennedy Center for the Performing Arts, Washington
Cast Gelsey Kirkland, Ivan Nágy

Mayerling – 17 June 1978
London Weekend Television
Documentary-style presentation on the creation of the ballet. Rehearsal and
performance excerpts are interspersed throughout.
Cast David Wall, Lynn Seymour, Merle Park, Michael Somes, Georgina
Parkinson, Wendy Ellis‚

In Performance: An Evening with The Royal Ballet – 28 October 1978 (UK)
Metromedia co-production (137 minutes)
Recording of the evening performance on 22 July 1978 relayed by satellite for
transmission in USA the same day and recorded for later broadcast in the UK
Programme included *Elite Syncopations*
Cast Vergie Derman, Judith Howe, Jennifer Jackson, Monica Mason,
Jennifer Penney, Alfreda Thorogood, Michael Coleman, Derek Deane, David
Drew, Wayne Eagling, Stephen Jefferies, Robert Jude, Wayne Sleep
and the balcony scene from *Romeo and Juliet*
Cast Lesley Collier, Anthony Dowell

Tonight in Town: La Fin du jour – 09 March 1979
BBC (5 minutes)
Michael Billington attends rehearsals and interviews the choreographer and
four principal dancers
Cast Merle Park, Jennifer Penney, Wayne Eagling, Julian Hosking

Behind the Scenes at Covent Garden – 01 May 1979
BBC (63 minutes)
Programme included excerpts from *Romeo and Juliet*
Cast Anthony Dowell, Merle Park

A Lot of Happiness – 15 December 1981
Granada TV
Cast Birgit Keil, Vladimir Klos

Isadora – 1981
Granada Television
Cast Merle Park, Mary Miller, Derek Deane, Julian Hosking, Derek Rencher,
Ashley Page, David Drew, Ross MacGibbon, Stephen Jefferies, Monica Mason

Omnibus: When the Dancing has to Stop – 27 January 1981
BBC (60 minutes)
Documentary film about Lynn Seymour, featuring excerpts from:

Mayerling, Act II, Bedroom Scene pas de deux
Cast Lynn Seymour, David Wall
Gloriana Choral Dances pas de deux
Cast Lynn Seymour, Wayne Eagling
Romeo and Juliet, Act I, Balcony Scene pas de deux
Cast Lynn Seymour, Rudolf Nureyev
and *Anastasia*, Act III pas de deux
Cast Lynn Seymour

Right Royal Company: Fifty Years of The Royal Ballet – 19 May 1981
Armand Hammer Films co-production (69 minutes)
Features excerpts from *Romeo and Juliet* and *Isadora* (casts not known)

The Royal Ballet in *Manon* – 13 March 1982
BBC/Covent Garden Video production (117 minutes)
Commercial release NVC Arts/Warner Music Vision, DVD, 2000 and 2004
Cast Jennifer Penney, Anthony Dowell, David Wall, Derek Rencher,
Monica Mason, Gerd Larsen, David Drew

Gloria – 1982
Granada Television
Cast Wayne Eagling, Julian Hosking, Jennifer Penney, Wendy Ellis

The Seven Deadly Sins of the Bourgeoisie – 22 April 1984
Granada Television
Cast Marie Angel, Alessandra Ferri

Dancer – 28 October–18 November 1984
A series of four programmes about the male dancer
BBC/Arts International co-production (49 minutes)
Features excerpts from:
Side Show, finale
Cast Elisabetta Terabust, Peter Schaufuss
Romeo and Juliet, Act I, Balcony Scene
Cast Margot Fonteyn, Rudolf Nureyev
Mayerling, Act I, Wedding Night pas de deux
Cast Wendy Ellis, David Wall
and *Orpheus* pas de deux
Cast Jennifer Penney, Peter Schaufuss (first cast); Stephen Jefferies,
Alessandra Ferri (second cast)

Romeo and Juliet – 1984
NVC Arts/Warner Music Vision
Commercial release VHS, 1998; DVD, 2005
Cast Alessandra Ferri, Wayne Eagling, Stephen Jefferies, David Drew,
Mark Freeman, Julian Hosking, Derek Rencher

American Ballet Theatre at the Met – 1984
Mixed bill includes *Triad*
Commercial release DVD
Cast Amanda McKerrow, Robert La Fosse, Johan Renvall

American Ballet Theatre in San Francisco – 1985
Filmed at the War Memorial Opera House in San Francisco
Commercial release DVD, 2005
Programme included the *Romeo and Juliet* Balcony Scene pas de deux
Cast Natalia Makarova, Kevin McKenzie

Omnibus: MacMillan at 60 – 6 December 1989
Filming of the dress rehearsal of *The Prince of the Pagodas*

Out of Line – 1989
BBC Television/Landseer Film and Television Productions
A documentary portrait of MacMillan with extracts from *The Burrow,*
Gloria, Manon and *The Prince of the Pagodas*

The Prince of the Pagodas – 1989
BBC Television
NVC Arts/Warner Music Vision
Commercial release VHS, 1991; DVD, 2005
Cast Darcey Bussell, Jonathan Cope, Fiona Chadwick, Anthony Dowell,
Bruce Sansom, Mark Silver, Ashley Page
(includes *Out of Line*)

Highlights from The Royal Ballet – 1990
NVC Arts (59 minutes)
Commercial release DVD
Features excerpts from *Romeo and Juliet*
Cast Alessandra Ferri, Wayne Eagling
and *Manon*
Cast Jennifer Penney, Anthony Dowell

The Late Show: MacMillan Obituary – 2 November 1992
BBC
Extract from *Elite Syncopations* (cast not known)

Winter Dreams – 1992
BBC/NVCL/Landseer Film and Television Productions Ltd
Cast Irek Mukhamedov, Viviana Durante, Darcey Bussell, Anthony Dowell,
Nicola Tranah

Mayerling – 1994
BBC, Covent Garden Pioneer and FSP Ltd co-production
Commercial release VHS and DVD, 1995 and 2004; DVD (Opus Arte), 2008
Cast Irek Mukhamedov, Viviana Durante, Lesley Collier, Darcey Bussell,
Jane Burn, Derek Rencher, Nicola Tranah, Matthew Hart

Manon – 1995
The Australian Ballet at the Adelaide Festival Centre
Commercial release DVD, 2000 and 2006
Cast Justine Summers, Steven Heathcote, Nigel Burley, Jonathan Kelly

Farewell Gala – 14 July 1997
BBC TV live broadcast and live relay to Big Screen in Covent Garden Piazza

Programme featured *Romeo and Juliet*, Balcony Scene pas de deux
Cast Darcey Bussell, Igor Zelensky
and *Manon*, Act I pas de deux
Cast Sylvie Guillem, Jonathan Cope

The Judas Tree – 1997
BBC TV/NVC Arts
Commercial release DVD, 2006; with David Bintley's *Nutcracker Sweeties*
Cast Irek Mukhamedov, Leanne Benjamin

American Ballet Theatre: Variety and Virtuosity – 1998
Romeo and Juliet pas de deux
Commercial release DVD
Cast Alessandra Ferri, Julio Bocca

Opening Celebration: Gala Performance – 01 December 1999
BBC Television live broadcast
Programme featured *Romeo and Juliet*, Balcony Scene pas de deux
Cast Viviana Durante, Angel Corella
Manon, Act III pas de deux
Cast Sylvie Guillem, Jonathan Cope
Elite Syncopations: Cascades
Cast Belinda Hatley, Gillian Revie, Nicola Tranah
Gloria pas de deux
Cast Leanne Benjamin, Christopher Saunders
and *The Prince of the Pagodas*, Act III pas de deux
Cast Darcey Bussell, Jonathan Cope

Romeo and Juliet – January 2000
La Scala Ballet at the Teatro alla Scala, Milan
Euro Arts (115 minutes)
Commercial release DVD, 2002
Cast Alessandra Ferri, Angel Corella, Michele Villanove, Alessandro Grillo,
Gianni Ghisleni, Bryan Hewison

Romeo and Juliet – 23 May 2002
Big Screen Relay to Covent Garden Piazza and Victoria Park, London
Cast Sylvie Guillem, Jonathan Cope

Golden Jubilee Gala – 23 July 2002
Big Screen Relay to Covent Garden Piazza, Linbury Studio Theatre and Clore
Studio Stairs, Royal Opera House
Programme included *Romeo and Juliet*, Balcony Scene pas de deux
Cast Darcey Bussell, Roberto Bolle

Manon – 26 May 2003
Big Screen Relay to Covent Garden Piazza, Liverpool, Sheffield and Norfolk
Heritage Park
Cast Tamara Rojo, Carlos Acosta

Curtain Up for Aid – 27 March 2005
Performance in aid of relief projects following the tsunami of 26 December 2004

BBC Television; recorded for future broadcast
Programme featured *Elite Syncopations: Bethena Waltz*
Cast Darcey Bussell, Gary Avis
Manon, Act III pas de deux
Cast Jonathan Cope, Sylvie Guillem
and *Requiem: Pie Jesu*
Cast Leanne Benjamin

Song of the Earth – 2007
BBC1 Television, the 'Darcey Farewell Performance', with the second, fifth and sixth songs broadcast live
Cast Darcey Bussell, Carlos Acosta, Gary Avis

Manon – 14 June 2007
American Ballet Theatre, Metropolitan Opera House, New York
Commercial release DVD, 2007
Cast Alessandra Ferri, Roberto Bolle, Herman Cornjeo, Gillian Murphy

Romeo and Juliet – 25 December 2007
BBC Television
Recordings of performances on 12 and 16 November 2007
Cast Carlos Acosta, Tamara Rojo

Romeo and Juliet – 01 June 2008
Relayed to Big Screens in Trafalgar Square, London, and Canada Square Park, Canary Wharf, London

Manon – 2008
Opus Arte
Commercial release DVD
Cast Carlos Acosta, Tamara Rojo

MacMillan Ballet Classics: *Romeo and Juliet, Manon* and *The Prince of the Pagodas* – October 2008
NVC Arts/Warner Music Entertainment
Includes *Out of Line*, a documentary portrait of MacMillan with extracts from *The Burrow, Gloria, Manon* and *The Prince of the Pagodas*
Commercial release DVD, 2008
Romeo and Juliet (1984)
Cast Alessandra Ferri, Wayne Eagling, Stephen Jefferies, David Drew, Mark Freeman, Julian Hosking, Derek Rencher
Manon (1982)
Cast Jennifer Penney, Anthony Dowell, David Wall, Derek Rencher, Monica Mason, David Drew
The Prince of the Pagodas (1990)
Cast Darcey Bussell, Fiona Chadwick, Jonathan Cope, Anthony Dowell, Simon Rice, Antony Dowson, Bruce Sansom

Sources

References for quotations, opinions and information within the text can be found in the Sources (pp. 727–40). This section is divided as follows:

NOTE ON MAIN CRITICS
Many of the dance critics active at the period covered by this biography wrote for a number of different publications – and sometimes under more than one name; their careers are briefly itemised here.

NOTE ON PERIODICALS AND SPECIALIST DANCE
PUBLICATIONS
A list of frequently referenced journals, giving their span and country of origin.

SELECT BIBLIOGRAPHY
Books, press articles and profiles, and broadcast documentaries cited in the text relating to MacMillan's life and work.

REVIEWS AND PRESS COVERAGE OF WORKS BY
MACMILLAN
Media responses to MacMillan's choreography cited in the text are listed under each ballet in chronological sequence.

PERSONAL CONTACT: INTERVIEWS AND
CORRESPONDENCE
Many people involved in MacMillan's life gave generously of their time to Jann Parry during the preparation of this book. They are credited here, gathered geographically, in relation to MacMillan's childhood and family, or, for his adult and creative life, under the heading 'Ballet and Theatre'.

* * *

NOTE ON MAIN CRITICS
Clive Barnes wrote about dance (and theatre) for numerous publications, often concurrently. In addition to contributing to specialist dance magazines, he wrote in Britain for the *New Statesman* and the *Spectator*. He was dance critic for the *Daily Express* 1956–65 and *The Times* 1962–65. He moved to New York in 1965 to become dance critic (and later, theatre critic as well) for the *New York Times* 1965–77, then for the *New York Post* 1977, until his death in 2008.

Alexander Bland was the pen name of Nigel Gosling, when he wrote about dance, with the advice of his wife, Maude Lloyd (a former Ballet Rambert dancer), for the *Dancing Times* and other publications, and as the author of books about ballet and dancers. He was dance critic of the *Observer* 1958–82, while being that paper's art critic 1950–80, and the author of books about art, under his own name.

Clement Crisp succeeded Clive Barnes as dance critic of the *Spectator* 1966–70 while writing for the *Financial Times* as second string to Andrew Porter from 1960. He has been the main dance critic of the *Financial Times* since 1970, while continuing to write for other publications. He has been co-author of many dance books, first with Peter Brinson, then with Mary Clarke.

Mary Clarke was editor of *Dancing Times* 1963–2008 and dance critic of the *Guardian* 1977–94. She was assistant editor of *Ballet Annual* 1952–63, as well as contributing to it. She is the author of numerous books on dance, many with Clement Crisp.

James Kennedy was the pen name of James Monahan. Under his own name he also wrote for the *Dancing Times* and *Country Life* magazine. Monahan worked for the BBC World Service from 1945 until 1971, ending his career there as Controller, World Programmes. He then became Director of the Royal Ballet School 1977–83.

John Percival wrote about dance for numerous publications, succeeding Clive Barnes as dance critic of *The Times* 1965–94. He was editor of *Dance and Dancers* 1981–94 and author of several books, including a biography of John Cranko, *Theatre in My Blood*.

NOTE ON PERIODICALS AND SPECIALIST DANCE PUBLICATIONS

About the House, magazine of the Royal Ballet and Royal Opera 1962–
Ballet, UK magazine edited by Richard Buckle, 1939–52
Ballet, 17 issues published by Covent Garden Opera Trust, promoting productions and performances by the Royal Ballet 1947–64
Ballet Annual, hardback published by A. & C. Black every year between 1947 and 1963
Ballet News, US monthly magazine 1979–86
Ballet Review US quarterly magazine 1964–
Ballet Today, UK magazine 1946–70
Dance Magazine, US monthly magazine 1926–
Dance and Dancers, UK monthly magazine 1950–94
Dance Gazette, international magazine published three times a year by the Royal Academy of Dance
Dance Theatre Journal, UK quarterly magazine published by Laban 1983–
Dancing Times, UK monthly magazine 1910–
On Point, American Ballet Theatre Friends newsletter, published biannually since 1970s
Revealing MacMillan, Royal Academy of Dance souvenir booklet of RAD Conference, 12–13 October 2002

SELECT BIBLIOGRAPHY

Ackroyd, Peter, 'Artist Reborn', *The Sunday Times*, 30 December 1979
Allen, Paul, interview with KM, *Guardian*, 14 September 1983

Austin, Richard, *Lynn Seymour: An Authorised Biography* (Angus & Robertson, 1980)

Balanchine, George, and Francis Mason, *Festival of Ballets* (W. H. Allen, 1978)

Baldick, Robert, *Pages from the Goncourt Journal* (Oxford University Press, 1988)

Barber, Lynn, 'Things I wish I'd known when I was 18', Kenneth MacMillan interview, *Sunday Express* magazine, 7 November 1982

Barnes, Clive, 'The Dancer you will know', *Dance and Dancers*, December 1951

– *Ballet in Britain since the War* (Thrift Books, 1953)

– 'What happened to MacMillan?', *New York Times*, 14 May 1972

– 'For the Royal, a Matter of Morale', New York Times, 30 July 1972

– 'The Royal Ballet Revisited', *New York Times*, 14 September 1975

– *The Decca Book of Ballet* (Frederick Muller, 1978)

Baudelaire, Charles, trans. P. Charvet, *Selected Writings on Art and Artists* (Penguin, 1972)

Berger, Arthur, *Stravinsky in the Theatre* [1949] (Da Capo, 1975)

Billington, Rachel, 'At the feet of the master' (profile of KM), *The Times*, 23 February 1984

Bland, Alexander, profile of KM, *About the House*, Christmas 1970

– *The Royal Ballet: The First Fifty Years* (Threshold Books, 1981)

Box, Charles G., *Great Yarmouth: Front Line Town 1939–1945* (publisher unknown, 1945)

Bradley, Lionel, *Ballet Bulletin* notebooks, held by Theatre Museum

Brahms, Caryl, *A Seat at the Ballet* (Evans, 1951)

Buckle, Richard, *Modern Ballet Design* (A. & C. Black, 1955)

– *Buckle at the Ballet* (Dance Books, 1980)

Christmas, Linda, 'How is the tarnished fame of the Royal Ballet shining up again under the new Director?', *Guardian*, 9 March 1979

Clarke, Mary, *The Sadler's Wells Ballet Book: A History and Appreciation* (A. & C. Black, 1955)

Clarke, Mary, and Clement Crisp, *Making a Ballet* (Macmillan, 1974)

Clarson-Leach, Robert, *Vergie Derman: Dancing with the Royal Ballet* (Artmusique, 1986)

Crickmay, Anthony, and Clement Crisp, *Lynn Seymour: A Photographic Study* (Studio Vista, 1980)

Crisp, Clement, 'Romeo, Juliet and Kenneth MacMillan', *Dancing Times*, February 1965

– 'Kenneth MacMillan, *Romeo and Juliet* and the full-length ballet', *Ballet News*, October 1984

– 'Kenneth MacMillan' (sixtieth birthday tribute), *About the House*, spring 1990

– 'The Man Who Makes His Emotions Dance', *Financial Times*, 20 April 1991

– posthumous memories of KM, *Financial Times*, 26 October 2002

Croce, Arlene, *Afterimages* (Vintage Books, 1977)

– *Going to the Dance* (Knopf, 1982)

– *Sight Lines* (Knopf, 1987)

Crookston, Peter, 'I had to keep my dancing secret', *The Times*, 1991

Crow, Susan, 'Kenneth MacMillan 1945–1955, Emergence of a
Choreographer' (1987; available at the National Centre for Dance Studies,
University of Surrey)

Daneman, Meredith, *Margot Fonteyn* (Viking Penguin, 2004)

Davies, Richard, 'What Drew Kenneth MacMillan's to Fauré's Requiem?',
Classical Music, 19 February 1983

Denby, Edwin, *Dance Writings* (Dance Books, 1986)

Dick, Kay, *Pierrot: An Investigation into Commedia dell'arte* (Hutchinson,
1960)

Dimbleby, David, preview of *Isadora*, *The Times*, 30 April 1981

Donaldson, Frances, *Royal Opera House in the Twentieth Century*
(Weidenfeld & Nicolson, 1988)

Drogheda, Lord, *Double Harness* (Weidenfeld & Nicolson, 1978)

Drummond, John, interview with KM, BBC Radio 3, 2 April 1991

Dunning, Jennifer, interview with KM, *New York Times*, 12 June 1985

Edwards, Leslie, *In Good Company: Sixty Years with the Royal Ballet* (Dance
Books, 2003)

Edwards, Sydney, interview with KM and Lynn Seymour, *Evening Standard*,
28 October 1967

– 'The survivor', *Evening Standard*, 2 January 1976

Ellis, A. E., *The Rack* (Wm Heinemann, 1958)

Fisher, Hugh (ed.), *The Sadler's Wells Theatre Ballet* (A. & C. Black, 1956)

Fonteyn, Margot, *Margot Fonteyn* (W. H. Allen, 1975)

Fosse, Robert La, *Nothing to Hide: A Dancer's Life* (Donald A. Fine, 1987)

Fraser, John, *Private View: Inside Baryshnikov's American Ballet Theatre*,
(Bantam, 1988)

Goodwin, Noel, *The Total Experience: Royal Ballet/Sadler's Wells Royal
Ballet Yearbook 1979–90*

Gruen, John, interview with KM, New York Public Library for the
Performing Arts, 26 July 1972

Haltrecht, Montague, *The Quiet Showman: Sir David Webster and the Royal
Opera House* (Collins, 1975)

Hart, John [photographs], and Margaret Dale [text], *The Royal Ballet in
Performance at Covent Garden* (Faber and Faber, 1958)

Heilpern, John, *John Osborne: A Patriot for Us* (Chatto & Windus, 2006)

Henze, Hans Werner, *Ondine: Diary of a Ballet* (Dance Books, 2003)

Higgins, John, interview with KM, *The Times*, 17 May 1978

Hodgson, Moira, interview with KM, *Dance News* 1978

Huckenpahler, Victoria, *Ballerina: A Biography of Violette Verdy* (Marcel
Dekker, 1978)

Isaacs, Jeremy, *Never Mind the Moon* (Bantam Press, 1999)

Jackson, Jennifer, 'Problems of Perception: A Sea of Troubles', *Revealing
MacMillan* conference, 2002

Jillett, Neil, interview with KM, *Age*, 20 June 1987

Joseph, Charles, *Stravinsky and Balanchine* (Yale University Press, 1972)

Kavanagh, Julie, *Secret Muses: The Life of Sir Frederick Ashton* (Faber and
Faber, 1996)

– *Rudolf Nureyev: The Life* (Figtree, 2007)

Kennedy, James, 'Cosseted Choreographer', *Guardian*, 28 May 1964
– 'The MacMillan hallmark . . . ', Guardian, 6 March 1974
Kennedy, Ludovic, 'With the Sadler's Wells Ballet in America', *Ballet Annual*, no. 6 (1952)
Kersley, Leo, obituary of KM, *Dance and Dancers*, March 1993
Kewley, Vanya, 'A Life in the Day of Sir Kenneth MacMillan', *The Sunday Times* magazine, 21 January 1990
Killar, Ashley, interview with Susan Crow, *Revealing MacMillan* souvenir booklet (RAD, 2002)
Kirkland, Gelsey, *Dancing on My Grave* (Doubleday, 1986)
Kirkland, Gelsey, and Greg Lawrence, *The Shape of Love* (Hamish Hamilton, 1990)
Kisselgoff, Anna, interview with KM, *New York Times*, 21 April 1985
Koegler, Horst, *Ballett International*, December 1989
– profile of KM, *Stuttgarter Zeitung*, December 1989
Lane, Margaret, *The Brontë Story: A Reconsideration of Mrs Gaskell's Life of Charlotte Brontë* (Wm Heinemann, 1953)
Lebrecht, Norman, *Covent Garden: The Untold Story* (Simon & Schuster UK, 2000)
Lee, Gemma, interview with KM, 1969
Leslie, Ann, 'The loner behind Romeo', *Daily Express*, 11 February 1965
McMahon, Deirdre, 'MacMillan at Sixty', *Dance Theatre Journal*, February 1990, vol. 7 no. 4 (December 1989)
MacMillan, Kenneth:
– Memoir, unpublished
– *About the House*, vol. 1 no. 2 (1963)
– *Schwanensee*, programme note for Deutsche Oper Berlin, 14 May 1969
– Programme notes for *The Prince of the Pagodas*
– [article], *Dance Gazette*, June 1990
MacMillan, Kenneth, *interviews with*:
– *Ballet* (Covent Garden Books no. 15)
– *Ballet Today*, no. 5 (1956)
– SWTB no. 1, SW Foundation, 1957
– *The Times*, 29 December 1960
– BBC, 17 April 1964 (British Library Sound Archive)
– *About the House*, vol. 2 no. 2 (June 1966)
– *Der Tagesspiegel*, 1 May 1968
– *Stuttgarter Nachtrichten*, 1970
– *About the House*, summer 1971
– *New Yorker*, 6 May 1974
– *Evening Standard*, 21 January 1976
– *Outlook* (BBC Television), 1976
– *People* magazine, October 1983
– *Dance Theatre Journal*, vol. 3 no. 5, 1985
– *Neue Berlinische Musikzeitung*, March 1991
– *Dance*, September 1991
– *ROH News*, January–February 1992
– (see also entries for individual journalists)

SOURCES

Manchester, P. W., Ballet Workshop programme no. 1
Marek, George R., *The Eagles Die* (Hart-Davis, MacGibbon, 1974)
Meinertz, Alexander, *Vera Volkova: A Biography* (Dance Books, 2007)
Milnes, Rodney, *Harpers and Queen*, January 1970
– 'Queen's Counsel', *Harpers and Queen*, August 1977
Money, Keith, *The Art of the Royal Ballet* (Harrap, 1964)
– *Fonteyn and Nureyev: The Great Years* (Harvill, 1994)
Neville, Jill, 'The Lively Man from the Royal Ballet' (interview with KM),
    Sydney Morning Herald, 2 September 1978
Newman, Barbara, *Striking a Balance* (Elm Tree Books, 1982)
– *Antoinette Sibley: Reflections of a Ballerina* (Century Hutchinson, 1986)
Noble, Peter, *British Ballet* (Skelton Robinson, 1949)
Nugent, Ann, 'Founder Slams Royal Ballet's "Low Standards" ', *Stage*,
    2 May 1985
Osborne, John, *Almost a Gentleman* (Faber and Faber, 1991)
– papers, Harry Ransom Humanities Research Center, Austin, Texas
Owen, Michael, interview with KM, *Evening Standard*, 21 June 1974
– interview with KM, *Evening Standard*, 16 October 1981
– interview with KM, *Evening Standard*, 25 April 1985
Parry, Jann, 'Gang rape explodes from dark corners', *Observer*, 15 March
    1992
Payne, Charles, *American Ballet Theatre* (Knopf, 1978)
Penman, Robert, 'Kenneth MacMillan: Doing It His Way', *Dance Theatre
    Journal*, vol. 3 no. 1, 1985
Percival, John, 'Just the man for Covent Garden', *The Times*, 9 November
    1968
– *Theatre in My Blood* (The Herbert Press, 1983)
– 'Opportunities lost and taken', *The Times*, 2 December 1989
Plisetskaya, Maya, *I Maya Plisetskaya* (Yale University Press, 2001)
Roberts, Glenys, 'Braces, Bombs and Ballet', *Evening Standard*, 1 November
    1985
Robertson, Allen, tape-recorded interview with KM, 9 February 1991
Savage-King, Chris, 'Kenneth MacMillan: Post-Expressionist', *Dance Theatre
    Journal*, vol. 2 no. 2, 1984
Schmidt, Jochen, *Tanztheater in Deutschland* (Propylaen-Verlag, 1992)
Sexton, Christopher, *Peggy van Praagh: A Life in Dance* (Macmillan
    Australia, 1985)
Seymour, Lynn, with Paul Gardner, *Lynn: An Autobiography* (Granada, 1984)
– 'Kenneth MacMillan – the early years', *Dancing Times*, March 2002
Sorley Walker, Kathrine, *Ninette de Valois: Idealist without Illusions* (Hamish
    Hamilton, 1987)
Stringer, Robin, interview with KM, *Evening Standard*, 30 November 1989
– 'Keeping 130 egoes on their toes', *Saturday Telegraph Magazine*, 1974
Taylor, Jeffery, 'Who Put the Knife in Mac?', *Evening Standard* magazine,
    2 December 1988
Thorpe, Edward, *Creating a Ballet: MacMillan's Isadora* (Evans Brothers, 1981)
– *Kenneth MacMillan: The Man and the Ballets* (Hamish Hamilton, 1985)
– profile of KM, *Royal Academy of Dancing Magazine*, December 1989

Tomalin, Nicholas, 'Ballet-struck', *The Sunday Times*, 2 February 1965

Tooke, Colin, *Great Yarmouth and Gorleston, Front Line Towns* (Tookes Books, 1999)

– *Great Yarmouth, the Rows and the Old Town* (Tookes Books, 2000)

Tooke, Colin, and David Scarles, *Great Yarmouth at War* (Poppyland Publishing, 1989)

Tooley, John, *In House: Covent Garden – 50 Years of Opera and Ballet* (Faber and Faber, 2000)

Valois, Ninette de, *Step by Step: The Formation of an Establishment* (W. H. Allen, 1977)

Vaughan, David, *Frederick Ashton and His Ballets* (A. & C. Black, 1987)

White, Peter Franklin, *Sadler's Wells Ballet Goes Abroad* (Faber and Faber, 1951)

Williamson, Audrey, *Contemporary Ballet* (Rockliff, 1946)

Woodcock, Sarah C., *The Sadler's Wells Royal Ballet* (Sinclair-Stevenson, 1991)

Woodward, Ian, 'Boos in Berlin', *Guardian*, 24 March 1969

Wright, Peter, *Revealing MacMillan* conference, 2002

REVIEWS AND PRESS COVERAGE OF WORKS BY MACMILLAN

Somnambulism (1953)
Ballet Annual, no. 8 (1954)
Dance and Dancers, vol. 5 no. 5 (May 1954)
Clive Barnes, *Dance and Dancers*, August 1956

Fragment (1953)
Peter Williams, *Dance and Dancers*, July 1953

Laiderette (1954)
Richard Buckle, *Observer*, 10 July 1955
Clive Barnes, *Dance and Dancers*, September 1955

Danses concertantes (1955)
Clive Barnes, *Dance and Dancers*, February 1955
Ballet Annual, no. 10 (1956)
Mary Clarke, *Dancing Times*
A. V. Coton, *Spectator*
Cormac Rigby, *Royal Repertoire*, BBC Third Programme

House of Birds (1955)
Clive Barnes, *Dance and Dancers*, July 1955
Richard Buckle, *Observer*
Illustrated London News
New Statesman
The Times

Turned Out Proud (1955)
Mary Clarke, *Ballet Annual*, no. 11

Tannhäuser: Venusberg Ballet (1955)
Caryl Brahms, *Dancing Times*

Noctambules (1956)
Scenario, *Ballet Annual*, no. 11
Andrew Porter, *Financial Times*, 2 March 1956
John Martin, *New York Times*, 16 May 1956

Fireworks (1956)
Dance and Dancers, September 1956

Valse eccentrique (1956)
Ballet Annual, no. 12

Winter's Eve (1957)
Ann Barzel, *Ballet Annual*, no. 12
John Martin, *New York Times*, 11 February 1957
Walter Terry, *New York Herald Tribune*, 11 February 1957

Journey (1957)
Arthur Todd, *Dance and Dancers*, August 1957
David Vaughan, *The Times*

The Burrow (1958)
Clive Barnes, *Daily Express*, 3 January 1958
Oleg Kerensky, *Daily Mail*, 3 January 1958
Clive Barnes, *Dance and Dancers*, March 1958

Agon (1958)
Clive Barnes, *Dance and Dancers*, October 1958
Noel Goodwin, *Daily Express*, 31 October 1958
V. Coton, *Daily Telegraph*
Clement Crisp, *Financial Times*
Clive Barnes, *Ballet Annual*, no. 17

The World of Paul Slickey (1959)
Mollie Panter-Downes, *New Yorker*, 20 June 1959

Le Baiser de la fée (1960)
Mary Clarke, *Ballet Annual*, no. 15
Philip Hope-Wallace, *Guardian*
Noel Goodwin, *Scottish Daily Express*, 13 April 1960
David Dougill, *The Sunday Times* 11 May 1986
Jann Parry, *Observer* 11 May 1986

The Invitation (1960)
Peter Brinson, 'A Choreographer's Progress', *The Times*, 11 November 1960
The Times, 31 December 1960
Annabel Farjeon, *New Statesman*, 6 January 1961

The Seven Deadly Sins (1961)
Percy Cater (undated cutting, newspaper unknown)

Diversions (1961)
Alexander Bland, *Observer*, 17 September 1961
Clive Barnes, *Dance and Dancers*, April 1963

SOURCES

The Rite of Spring (1962)
Oleg Kerensky, *Daily Mail*, 4 May 1962
A. V. Coton, *Daily Telegraph* 4 May 1962
Andrew Porter, *Financial Times*, 4 and 9 May 1962
Daily Herald, 4 May 1962
John Percival, *New Daily*, 5 May 1962
Clive Barnes, *Spectator*, 11 May 1962
Deutsche Zeitung, 28 May 1962
Clement Crisp, *Financial Times*, 29 October 1987

Symphony (1963)
Clive Barnes, *The Times*, 16 February 1963
Clive Barnes, *Dance and Dancers* March 1963
The Times, 6 March 1963
Mary Clarke, *Dancing Times*, April 1963
Clive Barnes, *The Times*, 16 December 1963
Clement Crisp, *About the House*, August 1967

La Création du monde (1964)
G. B. L. Wilson, *Dancing Times*, March 1964
Peter Williams, *Dance and Dancers*, June 1964

Images of Love (1964)
Ballet Today, May–June 1964
Noel Goodwin, *Dance and Dancers* June 1964
Peter Williams, *Dance and Dancers*, June 1964

Divertimento (1964)
Alexander Bland, *Observer*, 14 June 1964

Romeo and Juliet (1965)
Nicholas Tomalin, *The Sunday Times*, 7 February 1965
Andrew Porter, *Financial Times*, 10 February 1965
Clive Barnes, *Spectator*, 12 February 1965
James Kennedy, *Guardian*, February 1965
Daily Express, February 1965
Daily Mail, February 1965
Alexander Bland, *Observer*, 14 and 21 February 1965
Edward Mason, *Sunday Telegraph*, 14 February 1965
Clement Crisp, *Dancing Times*, February 1965
James Monahan, *Dancing Times*, April 1965
Allen Hughes, *New York Times*, 22 April 1965
World Telegram and New York Journal, 22 April 1965
Walter Terry, *New York Herald Tribune*, 23 April 1965
Clement Crisp, *Spectator*, 3 December 1965
Peter Williams, *Dance and Dancers*, March 1966
John Chapman, *Daily News*, 22 April 1966
Nigel Gosling, *About the House*, vol. 3 no. 7 (1970)
Anna Kisselgoff, *New York Times*, 24 April 1985

Song of the Earth (1965)
Horst Koegler, *Dance and Dancers*, January 1966
Noel Goodwin, *Dance and Dancers*, January 1966
Alexander Bland, *Observer*, 22 May 1966
Richard Buckle, *The Sunday Times*, 22 May 1966
Clive Barnes, *New York Times*, 30 June 1966
Neil Jillett, *Age*, 20 June 1987

Sleeping Beauty (1967)
Klaus Geitel, *Die Welt*, 9 October 1967
Clement Crisp, *Financial Times*, 19 October 1967
Alexander Bland, *Dancing Times*, December 1967

Anastasia (one-act version; 1967)
Horst Koegler, *Suddeutsche Zeitung*, June 1967
Klaus Geitel, *Die Welt*, 6 June 1967
C. Mueller, *Bergischer Volksbote*, June 1967

The Sphinx (1968)
John Percival, *Dance and Dancers*, August 1968

Cain and Abel (1968)
John Percival, *The Times*, 4 November 1968
Alexander Bland, *Observer*, 10 November 1968
Clement Crisp, *Financial Times*, November 1968
Horst Koegler, *Stuttgarter Zeitung*, (undated cutting)
Alexander Bland, *Dancing Times*, December 1968
John Percival, *Dance and Dancers*, December 1968

Olympiad (1969)
Peter Williams, *Dance and Dancers*, April 1969

Swan Lake (1969)
Die Welt am Sonntag, 20 May 1969
Alexander Bland, *Dancing Times*, July 1969

Anastasia (three-act version; 1971)
Andrew Porter, *Financial Times*, 23 July 1971
John Percival, *The Times*, 23 July 1971
Clive Barnes, *New York Times*, 7 May 1972
Nicholas Dromgoole, *Sunday Telegraph*, 25 July 1984
Bill Zakariasen, *New York Daily News*, 2 May 1985
Clive Barnes, *New York Post*, 2 May 1985
Deborah Jowitt, *Village Voice*, 28 May 1985

Triad (1972)
Annabel Farjeon, *Evening Standard*, 20 January 1972
Richard Buckle, *The Sunday Times*, 28 January 1972
Oleg Kerensky, *New Statesman*, (undated cutting)

The Poltroon (1972)
Philip Hope-Wallace, *Guardian*, 13 October 1972

The Sleeping Beauty (1973)
Richard Buckle, *The Sunday Times*, 18 March 1973
John Higgins, *The Times*, 4 May 1973
Nicholas Dromgoole, *Sunday Telegraph*, 10 April 1974

Manon (1974)
Andrew Porter, *Financial Times*, 8 March 1974
Robin Stringer, *Daily Telegraph*, 8 March 1974
John Percival, *The Times*, 8 and 14 March 1974
Mary Clarke, *Guardian*, 9 March 1974
Alexander Bland, *Observer*, 10 March 1974
Jane King, *Morning Star*, 11 March 1974
Julie Kavanagh, *Women's Wear Daily*, 26 March 1974
Arlene Croce, *New Yorker*, 27 May 1974

The Four Seasons (1975)
John Percival, *The Times*, 4 March 1975
Clement Crisp, *Financial Times*, 6 March 1975
David Gillard, *Daily Mail*, 6 March 1975

Rituals (1975)
Deborah Jowitt, *Village Voice*, 11 May 1982

Requiem (1976)
John Percival, *The Times*, 2 December 1976
Clement Crisp, *Financial Times*, 2 December 1976
Alan Kriegsman, *Washington Post*, 30 May 1977
Clive Barnes, *New York Times*, 18 June 1977
Clement Crisp, *Financial Times*, 5 June 1978
Ann Barzel, *Dance*, May 1986

Feux Follets (1976)
Arlene Croce, *New Yorker*, 18 December 1978

Gloriana (1977)
Rodney Milnes, *Harpers and Queen*, August 1977

Mayerling (1978)
John Percival, *The Times*, 16 February 1974
Mary Clarke, *Guardian*, 16 February 1974
Clement Crisp, *Financial Times*, 17 February 1974
David Wisely, *Hollywood Reporter*, 1 June 1974
Variety, 1 June 1974
Martin Bernheimer, *LA Times*, 1 and 2 June 1974
Gay Morris, *Pal Alto Times*, 3 June 1974
Clive Barnes, *New York Post*, 8 June 1978
Anna Kisselgoff, *New York Times*, 9 June 1978
Arlene Croce, *New Yorker*, 3 July 1978
Anna Kisselgoff, *New York Times*, 8 June 1974 and 25 April 1983

My Brother, My Sisters (1978)
Clement Crisp, *Financial Times*, 7 June 1978

737

Kathrine Sorley Walker, *Daily Telegraph*, 7 June 1978
Mary Clarke, *Guardian*, 7 June 1978
James Monahan, 'The Spirit of Stuttgart', *Country Life*, 6 July 1978

Gloria (1980)
Clement Crisp, *Financial Times*, March 1980
Arlene Croce, *New Yorker*, 13 July 1981

Isadora (1981)
John Percival, *The Times*, 1 May 1981
Fernau Hall, *Daily Telegraph*, 1 May 1981
Mary Clarke, *Guardian*, 1 May 1981
Nicholas Dromgoole, *Sunday Telegraph*, 3 May 1981
David Dougill, *The Sunday Times*, 3 May 1981
Alexander Bland, *Observer*, 3 May 1981
Clement Crisp, *Financial Times*, 5 May 1981
Stephanie Jordan, *New Statesman*, 15 May 1981
Michael Billington, *Guardian*, 17 May 1981
Jann Parry, *Listener*, 21 May 1981
Anna Kisselgoff, *New York Times*, 1 July 1981
Arlene Croce, *New Yorker*, 13 July 1981
Burt Supree, *Village Voice*, 14 July 1981
Clive Barnes, *New York Post*
Irving Wardle, *Dance and Dancers*, November 1981
Clement Crisp, *Ballet News*, December 1984

Wild Boy (1981)
The Times, 21 December 1981

Valley of Shadows (1983)
Mary Clarke, *Guardian*, 4 March 1983
Clement Crisp, *Financial Times*, March 1983
Nicholas Dromgoole, *Sunday Telegraph*, 6 March 1983
David Dougill, *The Sunday Times*, 6 March 1983
Chris Savage-King, *Dance Theatre Journal*, vol. 2 no. 2, 1984
Deirdre McMahon, *Dance Theatre Journal*, vol. 7 no. 4, 1989

Different Drummer (1984)
Nicholas Dromgoole, *Sunday Telegraph*, 26 February 1984
Clement Crisp, *Financial Times*, 27 February 1984
New Statesman, 2 March 1984
Julie Kavanagh, *Spectator*, 3 March 1984

The Sleeping Beauty (1987)
Clive Barnes, *New York Post*, 22 April 1987
Marcia Siegel, *Christian Science Monitor*, 27 April 1987
New York Times, 10 May 1987
Anna Kisselgoff, *New York Times*, 15 May 1987
David Vaughan, *Ballet Review*, summer 1987
Dale Harris, *Wall Street Journal* (date unknown)

Winter Dreams (1991)
Judith Mackrell, *Independent*, 9 February 1991
Deborah Jowitt, 'Fred's Heirs', *Village Voice*, 30 July 1991

The Judas Tree (1992)
Judith Mackrell, *Independent*, 21 March 1992
Kathrine Sorley Walker, *Daily Telegraph*, 21 March 1992
Jann Parry, *Observer*, 22 March 1992
John Percival, *The Times*, 23 March 1992
Brian Elias, *BBC Music Magazine* (ballet special issue), 1997

PERSONAL CONTACT: INTERVIEWS AND
CORRESPONDENCE

Great Yarmouth
Valerie Bowles (Jordan), Frank Drew, Ernest Fulcher, Betty Greenham
(Aldred), George MacMillan, Mary Miller, Percy Read, Wendy Roche,
Graham Swann, Victor Stowers, Joan Tooley (Broad), John Tripp

Retford
Doreen Anthony, Margaret Bacon, Jean Bradley (Raymond), Mary Fawkes
(Dame Mary Bridges), Roger Levick, Joan Thomas

Fife
Jean MacMillan (Watt)

Ballet and Theatre
Graeme Anderson, Reid Anderson, Elizabeth Anderton, Patricia Ashworth,
John Auld, Derek Bailey, Clive Barnes, Ray Barra, Mikhail Baryshnikov,
Geoffrey Baskerville, Leanne Benjamin, Alexander Bennett, Richard Rodney
Bennett, Michael Boulton, Leslie Browne, Yvonne Cartier, Hilary Cartwright,
Robert Cohan, John Copley, Adrienne Corri, Clement Crisp, Margaret Dale,
Elisabeth Dalton, Derek Deane, Zoë Dominic, Viviana Durante, Wayne
Eagling, Brian Elias, Jane Elliott, Ronald Emblen, Meriel Evans (Lady
Asquith), Richard Farley, Julia Farron, Alessandra Ferri, Barbara Fewster,
Charles France, Gillian Freeman, Frank Frey, Philip Gammon, Paul Gardner,
Nicholas Georgiadis, Josephine Gordon, Alexander Grant, Adrian Grater,
Keith Gray, Greta Hamby (Carreras), Sonya Hana (Lady Wright), John Hart,
Marcia Haydée, Anne Heaton (Field), Michael Hogan, Peter Hollamby,
Jaquie Hollander, Michael Holmes, Ronald Hynd, Nicholas Hytner,
Sir Jeremy Isaacs, Colin Jones, Susan Jones, Janet Judd, Desmond Kelly,
Leo Kersley, Anna Kisselgoff, John Lanchbery, Maryon Lane, Gerd Larsen,
Brenda Last, Anya Linden (Lady Sainsbury), Thelma Lister, Maude Lloyd
(Gosling), Nichola McAuliffe, Kevin McKenzie, Donald MacLeary, Deborah,
Lady MacMillan, Charlotte MacMillan, Egon Madsen, Natalia Makarova,
Dame Monica Mason, Mary Miller, Norman Morrice, Claus Moser (Lord
Moser), Irek Mukhamedov, Colin Nears, Sara Neil, Nadia Nerina, Robert
North, Christopher Nupen, April Olrich, Sheila O'Neill, Annette Page,
Ashley Page, Monica Parker, Georgina Parkinson (Round), Jennifer Penney,
Robert Penman, John Percival, John B. Read, Valerie Reece, Gert Reinholm,

Derek Rencher, Jocelyn Rickards, Allen Robertson Alfred Rodrigues, Herbert Ross, Roy Round, Tobias Round, Peter Schaufuss, Dame Margaret Scott, Lynn Seymour, Jane Shore (Nicholas), Dame Antoinette Sibley, Jeffery Solomons, Yolanda Sonnabend, Ben Stevenson, Dr Frank Tait, Marion Tait, Jeffrey Taylor, Valerie Taylor, Doreen Tempest, Glen Tetley, Edward Thorpe, Colin Thubron, Sir John Tooley, Pirmin Trecu, Georgette Tsinguirides, Violette Verdy, Gilbert Vernon, David Wall, Donna-Day Washington, Geoffrey Webb, Christopher Wheeldon, Peter Franklin White, Faith Worth, Sir Peter Wright

Index

Roope, Clover 214–15
Rosato, Genesia 475
Rose, Jürgen 320, 456
Ross, Herbert 191, 231, 336, 414, 498,
    507, 508, 551; *Paen* 191
Round, Roy 298, 322, 332, 354, 364
Rowell, Kenneth 158, 221, 274, 290
Royal Academy of Dancing 510
Royal Academy of Dancing Production
    Club 71
Royal Ballet 8; accused of being in
    decline 607; administrative offices 412;
    American tours 256, 408, 409, 410,
    438–9, 455, 498, 515, 518, 549–50,
    671; appointment of first full-time
    notator 231; appointment of Morrice
    as new Artistic Director 471–2;
    assessment of by Bonham Carter
    (1972) 415–16; Australian tour by
    touring company (1958/59) 206–7;
    Bonham Carter's assessments of
    415–16, 441–2; and Britain States
    New York festival (1983) 570–1;
    commissioning of ballets from KM *see*
    MacMillan, Kenneth: Choreography;
    contracts for choreographers 194–5;
    criticism of by Barnes 449–50; decline
    in popularity 449; diminishing of pool
    of talent available to 474–5; dropping
    of merger with Northern Dance
    Company proposal 443; Italian tour
    563; joining of by Nureyev 241; KM
    as Artistic Director *see* MacMillan,
    Kenneth: Artistic Director; KM's
    relationship with 8, 312–13, 332, 555,
    609, 614, 644–6, 705–6; merger plan
    and problems with (1970) 376–7,
    473–4; name change from Sadler's
    Wells 179; organisational changes and
    failure of merger of two groups (1957)
    193–4; performing in Berlin (1987)
    630–1; resignation of KM as Artistic
    Director 470, 472–3; South American
    tour (1973) 421–3; sub-committee to
    Royal Opera House 217; tour of
    Japan (1975) 447; visit to Russia
    (1987) 628–9; wining of *Evening
    Standard* award by corps de ballet
    445, 474
Royal Ballet Benevolent Fund gala (1971)
    395–6
Royal Ballet Choreographic Group 76
Royal Ballet School 474–5; KM's *Soirées
    musicales* production 636–7, 719
Royal Danish Ballet 181, 241–2, 241–3
Royal Exchange Theatre (Manchester)
    575, 578
Royal Opera House 8, 58, 82–3, 206,

215–17; preference of opera over
    ballet 424
Royal Opera House Board 376, 415,
    448; rejection of KM's *Das Lied* by
    Board 218–19
Royal Opera House (ROH) Trust 216
Royal Swedish Ballet 243, 320; and KM's
    production of *Romeo and Juliet*
    368–70; production of *Manon* 541
Rudolf, Crown Prince 466, 482–3

Sadler's Wells Ballet 58–9; American
    tours 82, 85–9, 95–9; anniversary gala
    performances 164–5, 169; criticism of
    ballets 104–5; performing during war
    51–2; proposed exchange visit to
    Moscow and cancellation 169,
    179–80; residency at Royal Opera
    House 58–9; tours 82, 84, 159, 199
Sadler's Wells Ballet School 45, 57; KM's
    audition for 51–2
Sadler's Wells Choreographic Group 133,
    136
Sadler's Wells Opera Ballet 58, 59–60,
    62, 63–5, 67; auditioning for by KM
    and acceptance into 59–60, 62;
    creation 58–9; expansion of repertoire
    70–1, 72–3; first provincial tour
    (1946) 68, 69; male dancers at 67;
    performances 63–5; *see also* Sadler's
    Wells Theatre Ballet
Sadler's Wells Opera Ballet (new group)
    164, 165
Sadler's Wells Theatre Ballet (was Sadler's
    Wells Opera Ballet) 71–2; changes in
    mid-1950s and emphasis on touring
    159–60, 164; departure of van Praagh
    159–60, 164; Edinburgh Festival
    appearances (1952) 122; repertoire
    and ballets performed 77–8; KM ballet
    commissions for *see* MacMillan,
    Kenneth: Choreography; salaries and
    dancers' pay claims 142–4; takes part
    in national Rhodes centenary
    celebrations (1953) 134; tour of South
    Africa (1954) 140–2; tours 71–2,
    77–8, 79–80, 132; unsuccessful merger
    with Sadler's Wells Ballet 194; van
    Praagh as director 160
Sainsbury, John 258
Saltzman, Harry 498
Samsova, Galina 557
Savage-King, Chris 568
Sayer, Gilbert ('Sammy') 44
Schaufuss, Peter 556, 557–8, 560–1, 674
Schilling, Tom 310
School of American Ballet 87
Scott, Margaret 118, 119, 120, 130